THE PORTABLE GREEK READER

The Viking Portable Library

Each Portable Library volume is made up of representative works of a favorite modern or classic author, or is a comprehensive anthology on a special subject. The format is designed for compactness and for pleasurable reading. The books average about 700 pages in length. Each is intended to fill a need not hitherto met by any single book. Each is newly edited by an authority distinguished in his field, who adds a thoroughgoing introductory essay and other helpful material. The "Portables" are original publications in this form, issued in durable cloth covers. Some of the titles—printed from the same plates—have been brought out also in stiff paper covers.

THE PORTABLE

GREEK

READER

EDITED, AND WITH AN INTRODUCTION, BY

W. H. AUDEN

NEW YORK · THE VIKING PRESS

The editor wishes to thank the following for permission to use excerpts from English translations of Greek texts:

A. & C. Black, Ltd., London, and The Macmillan Company, New York: excerpts from John Burnet's *Early Greek Philosophy: Xenophanes, Heraclitus, Parmenides, Empedocles.*

Cambridge University Press, Cambridge: "The Sorceress" from *The Idylls of Theocritus,* tr. R. C. Trevelyan; Sappho's "To a Bride" from *A Book of Greek Verse* by Walter Headlam; *Agamemnon, Choephoroe, Eumenides,* from Aeschylus' *Oresteia* tr. George Thomson.

The Clarendon Press, Oxford: from *The Works of Aristotle:* extracts, *Nicomachean Ethics, Metaphysics, Politics,* tr. W. D. Ross, *Physics* tr. R. P. Hardie and R. K. Gaye; excerpts from Epictetus' *The Manual,* tr. P. E. Matheson; Anacreon's "To Dionysus" tr. T. F. Higham and Alcaeus' "Immortalia ne Speres" tr. C. M. Bowra, from *The Oxford Book of Greek Verse in Translation.*

Gilbert Highet and Curtis Brown, Ltd., New York: Simonides' "Human Imperfection" tr. Mr. Highet.

George Allen & Unwin, Ltd., London: extract, *The Bacchae* of Euripides, tr. Gilbert Murray.

Harcourt, Brace and Company, Inc., New York: choruses from *The Antigone of Sophocles: An English Version,* by Dudley Fitts and Robert Fitzgerald. Copyright 1939 by Harcourt, Brace.

Harvard University Press, Cambridge: excerpts from volumes in the Loeb Classical Library: *The Characters of Theophrastus,* tr. J. M. Edmonds; Philostratus and Eunapius, *The Lives of the Sophists,* tr. Wilmer Cave Wright; *Hesiod: The Homeric Hymns and Homerica,* tr. H. G. Evelyn-White; *Selections Illustrating the History of Greek Mathematics,* tr. Ivor Thomas, Vol. I-II; *Galen: On the Natural Faculties,* tr. Arthur John Brock.

New Directions, Norfolk, Conn.: "Pythia," *Some Odes of Pindar,* tr. Richmond Lattimore.

Penguin Books Limited, Harmondsworth: "The Book of the Dead" from the *Odyssey,* tr. E. V. Rieu.

Charles Scribner's Sons, New York, and Williams & Norgate, Ltd., London: excerpts from *The Poems of Sappho,* tr. Edward Marion Cox.

University of Chicago Press, Chicago: "Nemea," *Odes of Pindar,* tr. Richmond Lattimore.

CONTENTS

O

v

PART TWO. THE HERO

PART THREE. NATURE

viii CONTENTS

PART FIVE. SOCIETY

EDITOR'S INTRODUCTION

ONCE upon a time there was a little boy. Before he could read, his father told him stories about the War between the Greeks and the Trojans. Hector and Achilles were as familiar to him as his brothers, and when the Olympians quarreled he thought of his uncles and aunts. At seven he went to a boarding school and most of the next seven years were spent in translating Greek and Latin into English and vice versa. Then he went on to another boarding school which had a Classical Side and a Modern Side.

The latter was regarded by boys and masters alike in much the same way as, in a militarist country, civilians are regarded by officers, and with the same kind of degrees of inferiority: history and mathematics were, like professional men, possible; the natural sciences, comprehensively labeled Stinks, like tradesmen were not. The Classical Side, too, had its nice distinctions: Greek, like the Navy, was the senior, the aristocratic service.

It is hard to believe now that this story is not a fairy tale but a historical account of middle-class education in England thirty-five years ago.

For anyone brought up in this way, Greece and Rome are so mixed up with his personal memories of childhood and classroom that it is extremely difficult to look at these civilizations objectively. This is particularly so, perhaps, in the case of Greece. Until near the end of the eighteenth century, Europe thought of itself less as Europe than as Western Christendom, the heir to the Roman Empire, and its educational system was based on the study of Latin. The rise of Hellenic studies to an

1

equal and then a superior position was a nineteenth century phenomenon and coincided with the development of European nations and nationalist feeling.

It is significant, surely, that when, today, an after-dinner speaker refers to the sources of our civilization, he always names Jerusalem and Athens, but rarely Rome, for the last is the symbol of a religious and political unity which has ceased to exist and the revival of which few believe in or desire. The historical discontinuity between Greek culture and our own, the disappearance for so many centuries of any direct influence, made it all the easier, when it was rediscovered, for each nation to fashion a classical Greece in its own image. There is a German Greece, a French Greece, an English Greece—there may even be an American Greece—all quite different. Had Hölderlin met Jowett, for instance, one suspects that neither would have understood a word the other said, and their parting would have been cold.

Even within a single country different Greeces co-exist. For instance here are two English caricatures:

Professor X. Reade Chair of Moral Philosophy. 59. Married. Three daughters. Religion: C of E (Broad). Politics: Conservative. Lives in a small suburban house stuffed with Victorian knickknacks. Does not entertain. Smokes a pipe. Does not notice what he eats. Hobbies: gardening and long solitary walks. Dislikes: foreigners, Roman Catholicism, modern literature, noise. Current worry: his wife's health.

Mr. Y. Classical tutor. 41. Unmarried. Religion: none. Politics: none. Lives in college. Has private means and gives wonderful lunch parties for favorite undergraduates. Hobbies: travel and collecting old glass. Dislikes: Christianity, girls, the poor, English cooking. Current worry: his figure.

To X, the word Greece suggests Reason, the Golden

Mean, emotional control, freedom from superstition; to Y it suggests Gaiety and Beauty, the life of the senses, freedom from inhibitions.

Of course, being good scholars, both know that their respective views are partial; X cannot deny that many Greeks were attracted to mystery cults and addicted to habits upon which "the common moral sense of civilized mankind has pronounced a judgement which requires no justification as it allows of no appeal"; Y is equally aware that the Plato of the *Laws* is as puritanical as any Scotch Presbyter; but the emotional tie to the Greece of their dreams, formed in childhood and strengthened by years of study and affection, is stronger than their knowledge.

There could be no stronger proof of the riches and depth of Greek culture than its powers of appeal to every kind of personality. It has been said that everyone is born either a Platonist or an Aristotelian; but it seems to me that there are more contrasted and significant divisions than this, between, for instance, the lovers of Ionia and the lovers of Sparta, between those who are devoted to both Plato *and* Aristotle and those who prefer Hippocrates and Thucydides to either.

II

The days when classical studies were the core of higher learning have now passed and are not likely, in any future we can envisage, to return. We have to accept as an accomplished fact that the educated man of today and tomorrow can read neither Latin nor Greek. This means, I think, that, if the classics are to continue to exert any educational effect at all, a change must be made in the emphasis and direction of Roman and Hellenic studies.

If Greek literature has to be read in translation, then the approach can no longer be an aesthetic one. The aesthetic loss in translation from one language into another is always immense; in the case of languages and cultures as far apart as Greek and English, it becomes practically fatal; one can almost say that the better a translation is as English poetry, the less like Greek poetry it is (e.g., Pope's *Iliad*) and vice versa.

To begin with there is the prosodic difficulty; quantitative unrhymed verse and qualitative rhymed verse have nothing in common except that they are both rhythmical patterns. An English poet can have much fun attempting, as a technical exercise or an act of piety, to write quantitatively:

With these words Hermes sped away for lofty Olympos:
And Priam all fearlessly from off his chariot alighted,
Ordering Idaeus to remain i' the entry to keep watch
Over the beasts: th'old king meanwhile strode doughtily onward,

(Robert Bridges. *Iliad*, xxiv, 468-471)

But no one can read this except as a qualitative meter of an eccentric kind, and eccentricity is a very unhomeric characteristic.

Then there are the problems of word-order and diction; Greek is an inflected language where the sense does not depend on the position of the words in the sentence as it does in English; Greek is rich in compound epithets, English is not.

Lastly and most important of all, the poetic sensibility of the two literatures is radically different. Compared with English poetry Greek poetry is primitive, i.e. the emotions and subjects it treats are simpler and more direct than ours while, on the other hand, the *manner* of language tends to be more involved and complex.

Primitive poetry says simple things in a roundabout way where modern poetry tries to say complicated things straightforwardly. The continuous efforts of English poets in every generation to rediscover "a language really used by men" would have been incomprehensible to a Greek.

In his introduction to *Greek Plays in Modern Translation,* Dudley Fitts quotes a translation of a bit of stichomythy from *Medea.*

MEDEA: Why didst thou fare to earth's prophetic navel?
AEGEUS: To ask how seed of children might be mine.
MEDEA: 'Fore Heaven!—aye childless is thy life till now?
AEGEUS: Childless I am, by chance of some god's will.
MEDEA: This with a wife, or knowing not the couch?
AEGEUS: Nay, not unyoked to wedlock's bed am I.

This is, as he says, comically absurd, but what is the poor translator to do? If, for instance, he translates the last two lines into modern idiom, he must write:

MEDEA: Are you married or single?
AEGEUS: Married.

This is no longer funny, but it has completely lost an essential element of the original style, the poetic ornamentation of simple questions and answers by casting them in the form of riddles.

It is significant that, in spite of the familiarity with and enormous admiration for Greek poetry of many English poets in the past, very few indeed show any signs of having been influenced by it in their style of writing— Milton and possibly Browning by the tragedians, Hopkins by Pindar, are the only names I can think of.

The attempt to translate the poetry of one language into another is an invaluable training for a poet, and it is to be hoped that new versions of Homer, Aeschylus,

Aristophanes, Sappho, etc., will continue to be made in every generation, but their public importance is likely to be small.

Even when he is reading the epics or the plays, the average modern reader is going to find that a historical and anthropological approach is more fruitful than an aesthetic one.

Instead of asking "How good a tragedy is *Oedipus?*" or "Is such and such an argument of Plato's true or false?" he will try to see all aspects of Greek activity, their drama, their science, their philosophy, their politics as interrelated parts of one complete and unique culture.

Accordingly, in selecting the material for this anthology, I have tried to make it an introduction to Greek culture rather than Greek literature. In a literary anthology it would be absurd to represent Greek tragedy by Aeschylus alone, omitting Sophocles and Euripides, but if one wishes to understand the form and idea of Greek tragedy, it is better to give a trilogy like *The Oresteia* than three separate plays by three authors; so too with all the other poetic selections which have been chosen for their representative character as literary forms rather than for their individual poetic excellences.

Again, in the extracts from the philosophers the intention has been not to give a comprehensive picture of Plato and Aristotle, but to show how Greek thinkers dealt with certain kinds of problems, for instance the problem of cosmology.

Lastly, Greek medicine and Greek mathematics are so essential parts of their culture, that they cannot be ignored even by a beginner.

The exigencies of space in a volume of this size exclude much important material, but I have only consciously excluded one author, for reasons of personal distaste. I believe, however, that I am not alone in finding Lucian, one of the most popular of Greek writers, too "enlightened" for a generation as haunted by devils as our own.

III

There is no single Greek literary work of art as great as *The Divine Comedy;* there is no extant series of works by a single Greek literary artist as impressive as the complete plays of Shakespeare; as a period of sustained creative activity in one medium, the seventy-five-odd years of Athenian drama, between the first tragedies of Aeschylus and the last comedy of Aristophanes, are surpassed by the hundred and twenty-five years, between Gluck's *Orpheus* and Verdi's *Otello,* which comprise the golden age of European opera: nevertheless, the bewildered comment of any fifth century Athenian upon our society from Dante's time till our own, and with increasing sharpness every decade, would surely be: "Yes, I can see all the works of a great civilization; but why cannot I meet any civilized persons? I only encounter specialists, artists who know nothing of science, scientists who know nothing of art, philosophers who have no interest in God, priests who are unconcerned with politics, politicians who only know other politicians."

Civilization is a precarious balance between what Professor Whitehead has called barbaric vagueness and trivial order. Barbarism is unified but undifferentiated; triviality is differentiated but lacking in any central unity; the ideal of civilization is the integration into a complete whole and with the minimum strain of the maximum number of distinct activities.

It is impossible to say, for example, of a harvest dance

of a primitive tribe whether it is aesthetic play, under-
taken for the pleasure it gives the participants in per-
forming it well, or religious ritual, an outward expression of an inward piety towards the powers who control
the harvest, or a scientific technique for securing the
practical effect of a better harvest: it is indeed foolish
to think in such terms at all, since the dancers have not
learned to make such distinctions and cannot understand
what they mean.

In a society like our own, on the other hand, when a
man goes to the ballet, he goes simply to enjoy himself
and all he demands is that choreography and performance shall be aesthetically satisfying; when he goes to
Mass, he knows that it is irrelevant whether the Mass
be well or badly sung, for what matters is the attitude
of his will towards God and his neighbor; when he plows
a field, he knows that whether the tractor be beautiful
or ugly or whether he be a repentant or a defiant sinner
is irrelevant to his success or failure. His problem is
quite different from that of the savage; the danger for
him is that, instead of being a complete person at every
moment, he will be split into three unrelated fragments
which are always competing for dominance: the aesthetic fragment which goes to the ballet, the religious
which goes to Mass, and the practical which earns its
living.

If a civilization be judged by this double standard,
the degree of diversity attained and the degree of unity
retained, then it is hardly too much to say that the
Athenians of the fifth century B.C. were the most civilized people who have so far existed. The fact that
nearly all the words we use to define activities and
branches of knowledge, e.g. chemistry, physics, eco-
nomics, politics, ethics, aesthetics, theology, tragedy,
comedy, etc., are of Greek origin is proof of their pow-

ers of conscious differentiation; their literature and their history are evidence of their ability to maintain a sense of common interrelation, a sense which we have in great measure lost as they themselves lost it in a comparatively short time.

> ". . . as their forefathers were they,
> those old seapirates, who with roving robbery
> built up their island lordships on the ruin of Crete,
> when the unforbearing rivalry of their free cities
> wrec'd their confederacy within the sevenscore years
> 'twixt Marathon and Issus; until from the pride
> of routing Xerxes and his fabulous host, they fell
> to make that most memorable of all invasions
> less memorable in the glory of Alexander,
> under whose alien kingship they conspired to outreach
> their own ambition, winning dominions too wide
> for domination; and were, with their virtue, dispersed
> and molten into the great stiffening alloy of Rome."
> (Robert Bridges. *Testament of Beauty*, I, 758-70)

The geography of Greece, where barren mountains separate small fertile localities from each other, encouraged diversity, migration to new colonies, and an economy of exchange rather than production for use. In consequence, the Greeks, who, when they first invaded the Aegean were not so very different from any other patriarchal military tribe—the kind of life described in the *Iliad* is much the same as that described in *Beowulf*—rapidly developed within a comparatively small area a great variety of forms of social organization, tyrannies and constitutional city-states in Ionia, feudal oligarchy in Boeotia, a militarist police state in Sparta, democracy in Athens, almost every possible kind, in fact, but one, the extended centralized state typical of major river-basin areas like Egypt or Babylonia. The initial stimulus, therefore, to comprehension, inquiry, speculation, and experiment was present; but this explains neither the extraordinary talent the Greeks displayed in these activities nor their capacity to absorb influences and make them their own: unlike the Romans, the Greeks never give the impression of being eclectics; everything they do and say is stamped with their distinctive character.

Greek culture, as a glance at the chronological table at the end of this introduction will show, had successively three centers, the Ionian seaboard, Athens, and Alexandria. Sparta remained outside the general cultural development in a fossilized state of primitivism, exciting in her neighbors a mixture of fear, repulsion, and admiration. Nevertheless, she made, indirectly through Plato, a contribution which for good or ill, has influenced the world as much as any other element in Greek culture, namely, the idea of a consciously planned education of its citizens by the state; indeed the very concept of the state as something distinct from the ruling class, from the individual, and from the community might be said to be derived from Sparta.

At the beginning of Greek literature stands Homer. If the *Iliad* and the *Odyssey* are better than the epics of other nations, this is due not to their content but to their more sophisticated imagination—as if the original material had been worked over into its present form under much more civilized conditions than existed among, say, the Teutonic peoples until their heroic age was too far behind them to seem real. It is difficult, however, to make objective comparisons, since the Teutonic epics had little further history; Homer became, through the Romans, one of the basic inspirations of European literature, without which there would be neither an *Aeneid,* a *Divine Comedy,* a *Paradise Lost,* nor the comic epics of Ariosto or Pope or Byron.

The next development after Homer took place largely in Ionia and for the most part in and around the courts of tyrants who were, of course, more like the Medicis than like a modern dictator.

The Ionian scientist and the Ionian lyric poets had one thing in common, a hostility to polytheistic myth. The former saw Nature in terms of law rather than arbitrary volition; the latter saw their feelings as their own, as belonging to a single personality, rather than as visitations from without.

Thales' guess that all things are made of water was wrong; but the insight behind it, namely, that however many different realms of Nature there may be they must all be related was a basic presupposition without which science as we know it would be impossible. Equally influential was the assertion of Pythagoras, as a result of his work in acoustics, that all things are number, i.e. that the "nature" of things, that by virtue of which they are what they are and behave as they do, is not a question of what they are made of but of their structure, which can be described in mathematical terms.

The great difference between the Greek conception of Nature and later ones is that the Greeks thought of the universe as analogous to a city-state, so that for them natural laws, like human laws, were not laws *of* things, descriptions of how in fact they behave, but laws *for* things. When we speak of a falling body "obeying" the law of gravitation, we are unconsciously echoing Greek thought; for obedience implies the possibility of disobedience. To the Greeks this was no dead metaphor; consequently, their problem was not the relation of Mind to Matter, but of Substance to Form, how matter became "educated" enough, so to speak, to conform to law.

The lyric poets were equally important in their own

sphere; for it was through them that Western civilization has learned to distinguish poetry from history, pedagogy, and religion.

The most famous phase of Greek civilization is, of course, that associated with Athens. If he knows nothing else about them, every man in the street has heard the names of Homer, Aeschylus, Sophocles, Euripides, Aristophanes, Socrates, Plato, Aristotle, and, if he is a little better informed, of Pericles, Demosthenes, and Thucydides. All but Homer are Athenian.

The Athenian period divides into two; the first is preceded by the political and economic establishment of the Athenian state as a mercantile democracy by Solon and Cleisthenes, and the demonstration of its strength through its victory over the Persian Invasion; the second is the product of political defeat, first by Sparta, then by Macedonia. The typical expression of the first period is drama, of the second philosophy.

In comparison with the preceding Ionian culture, Athenian drama is marked by a revulsion from luxury and frivolity towards austerity and simplicity, and by a return to myth. Above all, for the first and last time in history, an art, drama, became the dominant religious expression of a whole people, the dramatist the most important figure in their spiritual life. Compared with the Greek tragedians, Homer and Pindar seem secular writers, of educational value certainly for a ruling minority, but still primarily entertainers, subordinate in importance to the priest and the oracle. Like modern drama, which grew out of religious festivals such as Easter and Corpus Christi, Athenian drama was associated with the festivals of the Wine Press and of the Greater Dionysus. But, whereas modern drama was at first subordinate to the religious rituals and then developed a secular life of its own, leaving the festivals to themselves, Athenian drama, while being definitely works of art, whose value can be judged by vote, became the dominant religious exercise, of greater importance than sacrifices or prayers. In the nineteenth century and in our own the individual artistic genius has sometimes claimed a supreme importance and even persuaded a minority of aesthetes to agree with him; but only in Athens was this a universal social fact, so that the genius was not a lonely figure claiming exceptional rights for himself but the acclaimed spiritual leader of society.

The nearest modern equivalent is not any work of the theater, but a ball game or a bull-fight.

Greek tragedy returned to myth, but it was no longer the Homeric mythology; the Ionian cosmologists had done their work. The gods are no longer essentially strong and accidentally righteous; their strength is now secondary, the means by which they enforce the laws which they themselves keep and represent. In consequence, the mythology is subjected to strain; for, the more monotheistic it becomes, the greater the importance of Zeus, the less individual, the more allegorical, become the other gods. Furthermore, behind Zeus himself appears the quite unmythological concept of Fate. Now either the personal Zeus and the impersonal Fate must coalesce as the Creator God of the Jews, a step which the Greek religious imagination never took, or, in the end, Zeus becomes a Demiurge, an allegorical figure for the order in nature, and Fate becomes the true God, either as Fortune or as an impersonal Idea or First Cause, in which case drama ceases to be the natural vehicle for teaching about the nature of God and is replaced by the science of Theology.

It is partly for such reasons, perhaps, that the development from the piety of Aeschylus to the skepticism of Euripides is so rapid, and the period of Greek tragedy so short. As Werner Jaeger has pointed out, Sophocles stands a little apart from the other two in that, while their interests are basically the same, his concern was more with human character than with religious or social problems. For Greek tragedy to have developed further, it would have had to go on from Sophocles, abandon its relation to myth and festival, and become a frankly secular art; perhaps its very triumphs tied it too firmly to myth and festival to allow it to make the break which the Elizabethan drama, for instance, made. Thus, greatly as the Greek tragedians have been admired by later writers, they cannot be said to have exerted much direct literary influence. The influence of the philosophers is in striking contrast to this, for Plato and Aristotle between them established the basic premises of an intellectual life, the unity and the diversity of truth; moreover, they are responsible for the particular kinds of divisions to which we are accustomed. If, for example, one tries to read Indian philosophy, the great obstacle to understanding what it means is that the joints of man and nature, so to speak, are carved differently. Our cuts, our carving are Greek; and we find it hard for us to believe that there can be any others.

The final period of Greek culture, the Hellenist, or Alexandrian, returns to Ionian hedonism and materialism but without its relation to political and social life. The important achievements are technological. The literature, as typified by the Greek Anthology, is highly polished, pretty, but on the whole boring, at least to the present age, because of its immense influence on minor poetry since the Renaissance. To it we owe all the worst "classical" properties, the little rogue of a Cupid, the catalogue of flowers, Celia's bosom, etc., etc.

Christendom was a product of Jewish historical religious experience and Gentile speculation upon and organization of that experience. The Greek mind is the typically Gentile mind, and it is at odds with the Jewish consciousness. As a Greek the Christian is tempted to a seesaw between worldly frivolity and a falsely spiritual other-worldliness, both of them, *au fond,* pessimistic; as a Jew he is tempted to the wrong kind of seriousness, to an intolerance which persecutes dissenters as wicked rather than stupid. The Inquisition was a product of a Gentile interest in rationality and a Jewish passion for truth.

The clearest historical example is the Crucifixion. In their book *Talking of Dick Whittington* Hesketh Pearson and Hugh Kingsmill report an interview with Hilaire Belloc in which he says of the Jews:

"Poor darlings, it must be terrible to be born with the knowledge that you belong to the enemies of the human race . . . because of the Crucifixion."

I cannot believe that Mr. Belloc is an altogether stupid man. Nevertheless, his statement is on a par with Adam's "The woman beguiled me and I did eat." He can hardly be unaware that the Crucifixion was actually performed by the Romans, or, to make it contemporary, by the French (the English said, "Oh dear!" and consented; the Americans said, "How undemocratic!" and sent photographers) for the frivolous reason that Jesus was a political nuisance. The Jews who demanded it did so for the serious reason that, in their opinion, Jesus was guilty of blasphemy, i.e. of falsely claiming to be the Messiah. Every Christian is, of course, both Pilate and Caiaphas.

IV

If there is any reaction to the Greeks which may be
called typical of our age as compared with preceding
times, it is, I think, a feeling that they were a very odd
people indeed, so much so that when we come across
something they wrote which seems similar to our own
way of thinking, we immediately suspect that we have
misunderstood the passage. It is the unlikeness of the
Greeks to ourselves, the gulf between the kind of assumptions they made, the kind of questions they asked
and our own that strikes us more than anything else.

Take, for instance, the following passage from the
Timaeus:

"Such was the whole plan of the eternal God about the god
that was to be, to whom for this reason he gave a body,
smooth and even, having a surface in every direction equidistant from the centre, a body entire and perfect, and formed
out of perfect bodies. And in the centre he put the soul,
which he diffused throughout the body, making it also to be
the exterior environment of it; and he made the Universe a
circle moving in a circle, one and solitary, yet by reason of
its excellence able to converse with itself, and needing no
other friendship or acquaintance. Having these purposes in
view he created the world a blessed god."

Surely this kind of thinking is as extraordinary to us
as any habits of an African tribe.

Even those of us whose mathematical equipment is
of the most meager, have so imbibed the modern conception of number as an instrument for explaining nature, that we can no more think of ourselves back into
a state of mind where numbers were regarded as physical or metaphysical entities so that one number was
"better" than another than we can return to a belief

in sympathetic magic. Nor is the Platonic assumption about the moral nature of godhead any less peculiar to us than his shape. We may or may not believe that god exists, but the only kind of god in which we can think of believing is a god who suffers, either involuntarily like the Pantheist god because he is emergent, or voluntarily like the Christian god because he loves his creatures and suffers with them; the kind of god who is both self-sufficient and content to remain so could not interest us enough to raise the question of his existence.

It is impudent of me to trespass at all inside a field where so many great and good men have spent their lifetimes. I can only try to limit the offense by confining my remarks to one aspect of Greek thought of which I am less ignorant than I am of others, namely to a comparison of the various Greek conceptions of the hero with our own, as an illustration of the distance between our culture and theirs.

V

The Homeric Hero: The Homeric hero has the military virtues of courage, resourcefulness, magnanimity in victory, and dignity in defeat to an exceptional degree. His heroism is manifested in exceptional deeds which can be judged by others who are forced to admit "He achieved what we could not have achieved." His motive is to win admiration and glory from his equals whether they are on his side or the enemy's. The code by which he lives is a code of honor which is not a universal requirement like law but an individual one, that which I require of myself and that which in view of my achievements I have a right to demand of others.

He is not a tragic figure, i.e. he does not suffer more than others, but his death has exceptional pathos—the great warrior comes to the same end as the lowest churl. He exists only in the present moment when he comes into collision with another heroic individual; his future forms the past traditions of others. The closest modern equivalent to the Homeric hero is the ace fighter pilot. Because he is so often engaged in single combat, he gets to recognize individual pilots on the side of the enemy and war becomes a matter of personal rivalry rather than any political issue; in fact he has a closer relation to the enemy ace than he has to the infantry on his own side. His life is so full of risks and hairbreadth escapes, so almost certain to end in death, and the effects of good luck and bad luck, of a sudden engine failure or an unforeseen change in the weather, are so serious that chance takes on all the aspects of a personal intervening power. The sense of having good days when he is protected and bad days when he is being worked against and the conviction that he will die when Fate decrees but not before become almost necessary attitudes to life.

There is still however an essential difference between the fighter pilot and the Homeric hero; to make the analogy close one would have to imagine that all the countries of the world had been continuously at war for centuries and that being a fighter pilot had become a hereditary profession. For the assumption of the *Iliad,* as of all early epics, which is so strange to us, is that war is the normal condition of mankind and peace an accidental breathing space. In the foreground are men locked in battle, killing or being killed, farther off their wives, children, and servants waiting anxiously for the outcome, overhead, watching the spectacle with interest and at times interfering, the gods who know neither sorrow nor death, and around them all indifferent and unchanging, the natural world of sky and sea and earth.

That is how things are; that is how they always have been and always will be.

Consequently, there can be no moral or historical significance about the result of any conflict; it brings joy to the victor and sorrow to the vanquished but neither could imagine raising the question of justice. If one compares the *Iliad* with, for example, Shakespeare's *Henry IV* or Tolstoy's *War and Peace,* one sees that the modern writers are deeply concerned first with historical questions: "How did Henry IV or Napoleon come to power?" "What were the causes of the civil or international war?" and secondly with general moral questions: "What is the moral effect of war on human beings?" "What virtues and vices does it encourage as contrasted with those encouraged by peace?" "Irrespective of the individuals on both sides, did the defeat of Hotspur and Napoleon promote or retard the establishment of a Just Society?" These are questions which to Homer would seem meaningless. He does, it is true, give a cause for the Trojan war, the Apple of Discord; but this is both a divine cause, i.e. outside human control, and a frivolous cause, i.e. Homer does not take it seriously but uses it as a literary device for beginning his tale.

He does make moral judgments about his heroes. Achilles should not have refused for so long to aid the Greeks because of his quarrel with Agamemnon nor should he have treated the body of Hector as he did, but these are minor blemishes which neither affect the outcome of the war nor the final proof of his heroism, namely that he vanquishes Hector.

The pathos of Hector's death is simple: the nobler character is defeated; the pathos of Hotspur's death is ironic: he is a much more sympathetic individual than Prince Hal, but he dies defending the wrong cause.

Further, in the Homeric world where war is the norm, there can be no criticism of the military hero as such. The wrath of Achilles could never be a tragic flaw in his character in the way that the wrath of Shakespeare's Coriolanus is in his. Homer might well have described Achilles taking a bath but it would have been simply a description of a hero taking a bath not, as in Tolstoy's description of Napoleon being bathed, a revelation that the military hero is an ordinary mortal just as weak as any of the thousands for whose death he is responsible.

Though it would be unfair to describe the Homeric hero as a mere puppet of the gods, his area of free choice and responsibility is pretty circumscribed. In the first place he is born, not made (often he is the son of an immortal father) so that though he does brave deeds, he cannot be called brave in our sense of the word because he never feels fear; in the second the situations in which he displays his heroism are given him; he can, on occasion, choose to fight or not to fight, this or that opponent, but he cannot choose his profession or his side.

The world of Homer is unbearably sad because it never transcends the immediate moment; one is happy, one is unhappy, one wins, one loses, finally one dies. That is all. Joy and suffering are simply what one feels at the moment; they have no meaning beyond that; they pass away as they came; they point in no direction; they change nothing. It is a tragic world but a world without guilt for its tragic flaw is not a flaw in human nature, still less a flaw in an individual character, but a flaw in the nature of existence.

The Tragic Hero: The warrior-hero of the Homeric epics (and his civilian counterpart, the athlete of the Pindaric odes) is an aristocratic ideal. He is what every member of the ruling class should try to imitate, what every member of the subject class should admire without envy and obey without resentment, the closest approximation to a god—the divine being conceived as the ideally strong—possible to man.

The Tragic Hero, on the other hand, is not an ideal but a warning, and the warning is addressed not to an aristocratic audience, i.e. other potentially heroic individuals, but to the *demos,* i.e. the collective chorus. At the beginning of the play he appears in glory and good-fortune, a man of pedigree and achievement who has already demonstrated *arete* in the Homeric sense. By the end he has been plunged into exceptional suffering, i.e. he suffers more than the chorus, who are average citizens who have achieved nothing remarkable. He suffers because he has come into collision, not with other individuals, but with the universal law of righteousness. As a rule, however, the actual violation of which he is guilty is not his own conscious choice in the sense that he could have avoided it. The typical Greek tragic situation is one in which whatever the hero does must be wrong—Agamemnon must either kill his daughter or betray his duty to his army, Orestes must either disobey the orders of Apollo or be guilty of matricide, Oedipus must either persist in asking questions or let Thebes be destroyed by plague, Antigone must violate her duty either to her dead brother or to her city, etc. But the fact that he finds himself in a tragic situation where he has sinned unwittingly or must sin against his will is a sign that he is guilty of another sin for which the gods hold him responsible, namely the sin of hybris, an overweening self-confidence which makes him believe that he, with all his *arete,* is a god who cannot be made to suffer. Sometimes but not always he manifests this hybris in acts—Agamemnon walks on the purple carpet, Darius tries to bridge the Hellespont—but even if he does not, he must be assumed to be guilty of hybris, otherwise he would not be punished by being made guilty of other sins. Through witnessing the fall of the tragic hero from happiness to misery, the chorus learns that the Homeric hero is not the ideal man they should try to imitate or admire. On the contrary, the strong man is tempted by his strength into becoming the impious man whom the gods punish, for the gods are not gods because they are ideally strong but because they are ideally just. Their strength is only the instrument by which they enforce their justice.

The ideal man whom every member of the democracy should try to become is not the aristocratic heroic individual but the moderate law-abiding citizen who does not want to be stronger and more glorious than everybody else.

Here again, as in Homer, we find ourselves in a world which is quite alien to us. We are so habituated to the belief that a man's actions are a mixed product of his own free choices for which he is responsible and circumstances for which he is not that we cannot understand a world in which a situation by itself makes a man guilty. Take the story of Oedipus, for instance. Here is a man who hears a prophecy that he is to kill his father and marry his mother, tries to prevent it coming true, but in vain. How would a modern playwright treat this? He would reason that the only way for Oedipus to make certain of escaping what is foretold is for him never to kill anybody and never to marry anybody. He would therefore begin by showing Oedipus leaving Thebes and making these two resolutions. He would then proceed to involve him in two situations, firstly, one in which he is done a mortal injury by a man, secondly one in which he falls passionately in love with a woman who returns his love, situations, that is, of *temptation,* in which he is torn between doing what he wants and breaking his resolve.

He yields to both temptations, he kills the man and marries the woman, excusing himself as he does so with a lie of self-deception, that is, instead of saying to himself, "There is a possibility, however slight, that they are my father and mother; therefore I must not risk it," he says, "It is quite impossible that they should be my father and mother; therefore I may break my resolve." Unfortunately, of course, the slight possibility turns out to be the actual fact.

In Sophocles nothing like this happens. Oedipus meets an old man on the road, they have a trivial quarrel, and he kills the old man. He comes to Thebes, solves the riddle of the Sphinx, and makes a political match. About these two deeds he feels no guilt nor is he expected to feel guilty. It is only when in fact they turn out to be his father and mother that he becomes guilty. At no time has he been conscious of being tempted to do what he knows he should not do, so that at no time is it possible to say, "That was where he made his fatal mistake."

The original sin of the Greek tragic hero is hybris, believing that one is godlike. Nobody can be tempted into hybris except one who is exceptionally fortunate. Sometimes he can manifest his hybris directly, but it does not change his character in any way, only he is punished for it by being made by the gods to sin unwittingly or involuntarily.

The original sin of the modern tragic hero is pride, the refusal to accept the limitations and weaknesses which he knows he has, the determination to *become* the god he is not. A man, therefore, does not have to be fortunate, to be tempted into pride; a misfortune like

Richard of Gloucester's hunchback will do just as well. Pride can never be manifested directly because it is a purely subjective sin. Self-examination can reveal to me that I am lustful or envious but it can never reveal to me that I am proud because my pride, if it exists, is in the "I" which is doing the examining; I can, however, infer that I am proud because the lust and envy which I can observe in myself are caused by it and it alone.

The secondary sins of which our kind of tragic hero is guilty and which cause his fall are not, therefore, a divine punishment for his initial sin, but its effects and he is as responsible for them as he is for it. He is not an unwitting sinner but a self-deceiving one, who refuses his guilty conscience. When Orestes slays Clytemnestra he does not anticipate the arrival of the Furies; when the Macbeths plan their murders they try to persuade themselves that they will not suffer the torments of guilt which they really know in their hearts they are going to.

In Greek tragedy suffering is a visitation from Heaven, a punishment imposed upon the hero from without. Through enduring it he expiates his sins and ends reconciled to the law, though it is for the gods not him to decide when his expiation is complete. In modern tragedy, on the other hand, this exterior kind of suffering which humbles the great and erring and leads them to repent is not tragic. The truly tragic kind of suffering is the kind produced and defiantly insisted upon by the hero himself so that, instead of making him better, it makes him worse and when he dies he is not reconciled to the law but defiant, that is, damned. Lear is not a tragic hero, Othello is.

These two differences between Greek and modern tragedy in their conceptions, first of the relation of the hero's original subjective sin of hybris or of pride to his secondary sinful acts, and secondly of the nature and function of suffering, produce different attitudes towards time.

Unity of time is not only possible but right and proper in Greek tragedy because the characters do not change, only their situation so that the dramatic time required is simply the time required for the situation to change. In modern tragedy, unity of time is possible as a technical tour-de-force but rarely desirable, since one of the dramatist's principal tasks is to show how his characters not only are changed by changes of situation but also play active parts in creating these situations, and it is almost impossible to show this in a single uninterrupted passage of time.

The Erotic Hero: About three-quarters of modern literature is concerned with one subject, the love between a man and a woman, and assumes that falling in love is the most important and valuable experience that can happen to human beings. We are so conditioned to this attitude that we are inclined to forget that it does not go back beyond the twelfth century. It does not exist, for instance, in Greek literature. There we find two attitudes. There are plenty of lyrics of the serenade type —the "In delay there lies no plenty, then come kiss me sweet-and-twenty" kind of thing, expressing a simple, good-tempered, and unserious sensuality. There are also, as in the poems of Sappho or the story of Jason and Medea, descriptions of serious and violent sexual passion, but this is not regarded as something to be proud of but as a disaster, the work of merciless Aphrodite, a dreadful madness which makes one lose one's dignity and betray one's friends and from which any sane man or woman will pray to be spared. Our romantic conception, that sexual love can transform the lover's character and turn him into a hero, was unknown.

It is not until we come to Plato that we find descriptions of something like what we mean by romantic love spoken of with approval, yet the differences are still greater than the resemblances. In the first place it is assumed that this kind of love is only possible in a homosexual relation; and in the second, it is only approved of as the necessary first stage in the growth of the soul. The ultimate good is the love of the impersonal as universal good; the best thing that could happen to a man would be that he should fall in love with the Good immediately, but owing to the fact that his soul is entangled in matter and time, he can only get there by degrees; first he falls in love with a beautiful individual, then he can progress to love of beauty in general, then to love of justice, and so on. If erotic passion can or ought to be transformed in this way, then it was sound psychological insight on Plato's part and not simply the cultural pattern of erotic life in Greece that made him exclude the heterosexual relation, for the latter leads beyond itself, not to the universal, but to more individuals, namely the love of and responsibility for a family, whereas, in the homosexual case, since the relation of itself leads nowhere, the love which it has aroused is free to develop in any direction the lovers choose, and that direction should be towards wisdom which, once acquired, will enable them to teach human beings procreated in the normal way how to become a good society. For love is to be judged by its social and political value. Marriage provides the raw material, the masculine eros the desire and knowledge to mold that material into its proper form.

The two great modern erotic myths, which have no parallels in Greek literature, are the myth of Tristan and Isolde, or the World Well Lost for Love, and the countermyth of Don Juan, the seducer.

The Tristan-Isolde situation is this: both possess heroic *arete* in the epic sense; he is the bravest warrior, she is the most beautiful woman; both are of noble birth. They cannot marry each other because she is already the wife of his king and friend, nevertheless they fall in love. In some versions they accidentally drink a love potion but the effect of this is not really to make them fall in love but rather to make them realize that they already have and to accept the fact as predestined and irrevocable. Their relation is not "platonic" in the conventional sense, but the barriers of marriage and circumstances give them few opportunities for going to bed together, and on each occasion they can never be certain that it will not be the last. The love they feel for each other is religiously absolute, i.e. each is the other's ultimate good so that not only is sexual infidelity inconceivable, but all other relations to other people and the world cease to have any significance. Yet, though their relation is the only value that exists for them, it is a torment, because their sexual desire is only the symbolic expression of their real passion, which is the yearning of two souls to merge and become one, a consummation which is impossible so long as they have bodies, so that their ultimate goal is to die in each other's arms.

Don Juan, on the other hand, is not an epic hero; ideally, his external appearance is that of the man who nobody notices is there because he is so utterly commonplace, for it is important to the myth that he, the man of heroic will and achievement, should look to the outward eye like a member of the chorus.

If Don Juan is either handsome or ugly, then the woman will have feelings about him before he sets to work, and the seduction will not be absolute, i.e. a pure triumph of his will. For that, it is essential that his victim should have no feelings of her own towards him, until he chooses to arouse them. Vice versa, what is essential for him about her is not her appearance but simply her membership in the class Woman; the ugly and the old are as good as the beautiful and the young. The Tristan-Isolde myth is unGreek because no Greek could conceive of attributing absolute value to another individual, he could only think in comparative terms, this one is more beautiful than that one, this one has done greater deeds than that one, etc. The Don Juan myth is unGreek, as Kierkegaard has pointed out, not because he sleeps with a number of women, but because he keeps a list of them.

A Greek could understand seducing a girl because one found her attractive and then deserting her because one met a more attractive girl and forgot the first one; but he could not have understood doing so for an arithmetical reason, because one had resolved to be the first lover of every woman in the world, and she happened to be the next integer in this infinite series.

Tristan and Isolde are tormented because they are compelled to count up to two when they long to be able only to count up to one; Don Juan is in torment because, however great the number of his seductions, it still remains a finite number and he cannot rest until he has counted up to infinity.

The great enemy of both is time: Tristan and Isolde dread it because it threatens change, and they wish the moment of intense feeling to remain unchanged forever, hence the love potion and the irremovable obstacle in the situation which serve as defense against change; Don Juan dreads it because it threatens repetition and he wishes each moment to be absolutely novel, hence his insistence that for each of his victims it must be her first sexual experience and that he only sleep with her once.

Both myths are dependent upon Christianity, i.e. they could only have been invented by a society which has been taught to believe *a*) that every individual is of unique and eternal value to God irrespective of his or her social importance in the world, *b*) that dedication of the self to God is an act of free-choice, an absolute commitment irrespective of feeling, made with infinite passion, and *c*) that one must neither allow oneself to be ruled by the temporal moment nor attempt to transcend it but make oneself responsible for it, turning time into history.

Both myths are diseases of the Christian imagination and while they have inspired a great body of beautiful literature, their influence upon human conduct, particularly in their frivolous watered-down modern versions, which gloss over the fact that both the romantic couple and the solitary seducer are intensely unhappy, has been almost wholly bad. Whenever a married couple divorce because having ceased to be a divine image to each other, they cannot endure the thought of having to love a real person no better than themselves, they are acting under the spell of the Tristan myth. Whenever a man says to himself "I must be getting old. I haven't had sex for a week. What would my friends say if they knew," he is re-enacting the myth of Don Juan. It is significant also—it might interest Plato though it would probably not surprise him—that the instances in real life which conform most closely to the original pattern of both myths are not, in either case, heterosexual; the Tristan and Isolde one actually meets are a Lesbian couple, the Don Juan a pederast.

The Contemplative Hero: The Ideal Man of Greek Epic is the strong individual; the Ideal Man of Greek Tragedy is the modest citizen with a reverence for the law of justice; the Ideal Man of Greek Philosophy has something in common with both: Like the latter he is one who keeps the Law but, like the former, he is an exceptional individual, not a member of the chorus, for to learn how to keep the Law has become a heroic task which is beyond the power of the average man. To the question "What is the cause of evil and suffering?" Homer can only answer, "I don't know. The caprice of the gods perhaps"; Tragedy answers, "The violation of the laws of righteousness and justice by arrogant strong men"; Philosophy answers, "Ignorance of what the Law is which leaves the minds of men at the mercy of their bodily passions."

The Homeric hero hopes by brave deeds to win glory before he dies; the tragic chorus hopes by living modestly to escape misfortune as long as they live; the contemplative hero hopes for ultimate happiness of soul when he has succeeded in learning to know the true and eternal good, and so delivering his soul from the entanglements of his body and the temporal flux; and beyond this he must teach society how to attain the same freedom from injustice.

In theory, the possibility of doing this should be open to all alike but in practice it is limited to those souls whom the heavenly eros has inspired with a passion for knowledge, and whom temporal circumstances allow them to devote their lifetime to the search for wisdom; the stupid who cannot, the frivolous who will not, and the poor who have no time to understand are debarred. They may have valuable social functions to perform but it is not for them to say what the laws of society should be. That is the duty of the philosopher.

This ideal is stranger to us than it looks at first sight. We are familiar with two kinds of contemplative men:

First, with the religious contemplative as represented by the various orders of monks and nuns or by the individual mystic. His aim is to know the hidden God, the reality behind all phenomena, but he thinks of this God as a person, i.e. what he means by knowledge is not objective knowledge *about* something which is the same for all minds and once perceived can be passed on to others by teaching, like the truths of mathematics, but a subjective relationship which is unique for every individual. A relationship can never be taught, it has to be voluntarily entered into, and the only possible method of persuading another to do it is personal example. If B is a friend of A and C is not, B cannot make C a friend of A by describing A, but if B, as the result of his friendship with A has become the kind of person C would like to be and is not, C may decide to try and make A's acquaintance, too.

Objective knowledge is the field of another kind of contemplative, the intellectual, the scientist, the artist, etc., and the knowledge he seeks is not about any transcendent reality but about phenomena. The intellectual, like the religious contemplative, requires individual passion but in his case it is confined to the search for knowledge; towards the object of his search, the facts, he must be passionless.

What is puzzling to us about the Greek conception of the contemplative hero is that these two kinds of activity are inextricably mixed, sometimes he seems to talk of a transcendent God as if He were a passive object, at other times of observable phenomena, like the movements of the planets, as if they were persons for which one could feel personal passion. Nothing is more bewildering to us about Plato, for instance, than the way in which, in the middle of a piece of dialectic, he will introduce what he himself admits to be a myth but without any feeling on his part that it is a peculiar thing to do.

It is hard to say whether one should call the Greeks more anthropomorphic in their thinking than we or less. On the one hand, in Greek cosmology everything in nature is thought of as being alive; the laws of nature are not descriptions of how things actually behave, laws *of*, but, like human laws, laws *for*, laws which they ought to obey and can fail to obey properly. On the other, in Greek political theory, human beings are thought of as if they were merely the matter out of which through his *techne* the craftsman-politician fashions the good society as a potter makes a vase out of clay.

To the Greeks the essential difference between man and nature was that the former can reason if he wants to, whereas for us the essential difference is that man has a self, i.e. that he and, so far as we know, apart from God, he alone is conscious of existing, and this consciousness is his whether he wants it or not, whether he is intelligent or not. The Greeks therefore had no real conception of the will as distinct from desire, so that, though they had, of course, observed the psychological fact of temptation, that one can desire what one knows is wrong, they were at a loss as to how to explain it. The weakest point in Greek Ethics is its analysis of Choice. This is all the more serious because politics is not peripheral but central to Greek Philosophy; the formation of the Good Society comes first, the quest for personal salvation or for scientific truths about matter or imaginative truths about the human heart, second. Through identifying the active source of the Good with Reason not with Will, they doomed themselves to the hopeless task of finding the ideal form of society which, like the truths of reason, would be valid everywhere and for everyone, irrespective of their individual character or their historical circumstances.

A concept is either true or false. A mind which entertains a false concept may be brought through steps of argument to entertain the true one, but this does not mean that a false concept has grown into the true; there is always a point in the dialectic, like the moment of recognition in tragedy, when the revolutionary change happens and the false concept is abandoned with the realization that it always was false. The dialectic process may take time, but the truth it discovers has no history.[1]

To think of the political problem as a problem of finding the true form of organization leads either to political despair, if one knows one has failed to find it, or, if one thinks one has been successful, to a defense of tyranny for, if it is presupposed that people living in the wrong kind of order cannot have a good will and people living

---

[1] I do not know whether there is any historical relation but when I read the Platonic Dialogues I am constantly reminded of the stichomythy of tragedy. There also seems a parallel between the role of the Socratic dialectic in the education of the intellect and the role of free-association in the psychoanalytic education of the emotions. Both are developed from the observation that virtue cannot be taught, i.e. the truth cannot simply be stated by the teacher and learned by rote by the pupil because the results of learning cannot be separated from the process of inquiry which each individual must live through for himself at first-hand.

Both the Socratic and psychoanalytic techniques, too, are open to the same objections. They require individual supervision and take a very long time which makes them too expensive for the majority, and they presuppose on the part of the pupil or patient a genuine passion for truth or health. When the passion for truth is lacking, dialectic becomes a technique for avoiding coming to any conclusion just as, when the passion for health is lacking, self-examination is used to justify neurosis.

Isocrates was unfair to the Academy and overestimated the value of his own brand of education but he was not altogether wrong, perhaps, in believing that his method was better adapted to the needs of the average student and the talents of the average teacher. At any rate it was his method rather than Plato's which was adopted by the Romans and inherited by the West.

in the right kind cannot have a bad one, then not only will coercion be necessary to establish that order but also its application will be the ruler's moral duty.

The *Republic*, the *Laws*, even the *Politics*, should be read in conjunction with Thucydides; only a political situation as desperate as that which the historian describes could have produced in the philosophers who were looking for cure at once a radicalism which would break completely with the past to build up society again *ab initio* and a pathological horror of disunity and change. Living as we do in an age of similar stasis on a world-wide scale, we have witnessed a recurrence on both the Right and the Left, at both the economic and the psychiatric epicenters, of similar symptoms.

Further, we have seen with our own eyes the theory of creative politics put into practice, and the spectacle is anything but Utopian. This experience by forcing us to take Plato's political dialogues seriously not as playful exercises in logic, has altered our attitude, I think, to the other dialogues. If there is an essential not an accidental relation between his metaphysics and his politics, and the latter seem to us disastrously mistaken, then there must be a crucial error in the former as well, which it is of the utmost importance that we detect, if we are to offer a positive substitute for the Platonic kind of solution to the political crisis.

The Comic Hero: "Comedy," Aristotle says, "is an imitation of men worse than the average; worse, however, not as regards any and every kind of fault, but only as regards one particular kind, the Ridiculous, which is a species of the Ugly. The Ridiculous may be defined as a mistake or deformity not productive of pain or harm to others."

The most primitive form of comedy seems to have

been tales in which, firstly, Gods, and, secondly, heroes and rulers behave in an undignified and ridiculous manner, that is to say, no better than the average man who lacks their *arete,* but, indeed, rather worse. Such primitive comedy is associated with holidays of license, during which the resentments of the small and the weak against the great and the strong may be freely expressed, in order that on the morrow when the habits of respect are re-established, the air shall be clear.

When, as in Athens, a growing rationalism comes to think of the Gods as keeping their own laws, and political power comes to be concentrated in the hands of a few, comedy finds new victims and new themes.

It is no longer the rulers as a class, but particular public figures who are made butts of; it is not authority as such that is the subject but topical political issues. The laughter of the audience is not the compensatory outburst of the weak against those who are above the law, but the confident laughter of people who know their strength, that is, either the scorn of the normal majority for the eccentric or arrogant individual whose behavior is not so much above the law as outside it, or the polemical passion of one political party directed against its rival. The target of such comedy is the man who violates the ethical norm because he does not believe it is binding; he has, that is, no social conscience. As a result he comes into collision, not with the law itself—it would be beneath the dignity of the law to concern itself with those who do not recognize it—but with others as outside the law as himself. He suffers, but the audience do not because they do not identify themselves with him. His suffering, too, is educational; through it he is cured of his individualistic mania and learns to conform to the law, out of prudence, if not from conscience.

This second type of comedy was invented by the Greeks and developed in Europe into the comedy of humor, as in the plays of Ben Jonson, and the comedy of manners and problem plays. If one disregards their lack of genuine poetry, the Gilbert and Sullivan operas are the closest approximation in English to the Aristophanic type of comedy.

There is, however, a third type which the Greeks did not possess—the greatest example is Don Quixote—in which the comic figure is at the same time the hero; the audience admire the very man they laugh at. Such a kind of comedy is based on a sense that the relations of the individual and society to each other and of both to the true good contain insoluble contradictions which are not so much comic as ironic. The comic hero is comic because he is different from his neighbors; either, like Don Quixote, because he refuses to accept their values, or, like Falstaff, because he refuses to pretend, as they do, to one set of values while really living by another: at the same time he is a hero because he is an individual, and not to be an individual, to think and behave in a certain way simply because everyone else does, is equally a comic madness.

The tragic hero suffers, and the audience, because they identify themselves with him through admiration, suffers too; the comic butt suffers but the audience, since they feel superior, do not. The relations of the comic hero and the audience to suffering, on the other hand, are ironic; the audience see the hero thwarted and defeated, experiences which they would regard as suffering, but the whole point is that to the hero himself these experiences are nothing of the sort; on the contrary, he glories in them, either because he has no shame or because he regards them as proof of his being right.

The nearest approach to such a figure among the

Greeks is, of course, Socrates. In his person he exhibits the contradiction, so disliked by Nietzsche, between his subjective *arete* of soul, and his manifest lack of objective *arete;* he, the best man, is the ugliest man. Further, he suffers death at the hands of society and does not regard his fate as a tragic one. To the Greeks, however, he is either, as he is to Aristophanes, a comic butt who is justly punished, or as he is to Plato, a tragic martyr who suffers because the wrong party was in power, the individual who represents the Right Society. The notion that any individual claim to be the exception is guilty of pride and that all societies and parties, good and bad, are in the wrong simply because they are collectives would have been incomprehensible to them, as would have been the Christian insistence that Jesus was either the Incarnate God or not a good man and that his condemnation was by due process of Roman law.

VI

I have stressed the differences between Greek civilization and our own, firstly, because it seems to me one possible approach to an inexhaustible subject and one cannot take them all, and, secondly, because I can think of no better way of indicating what we owe to Greece than drawing distinctions, for, of all intellectual acts, that is, perhaps, the most characteristically Greek.

It is they who have taught us, not to think—that all human beings have always done—but to think about our thinking, to ask such questions as "What do I think?" "What do this and that other person or people think?" "On what do we agree and disagree. Why?" And not only did they learn to ask questions about thinking, but they also discovered how, instead of giving immediate answers, to suppose something to be the case and then see what would follow if it were.

To be able to perform either of these mental operations, a human being must first be capable of a tremendous feat of moral courage and discipline for he must have learned how to resist the immediate demands of feeling and bodily needs, and to disregard his natural anxiety about his future so that he can look at his self and his world as if they were not his but a stranger's.

If some of the Greek questions turned out to have been incorrectly put, if some of their answers have proved wrong, that is a trivial matter. Had Greek civilization never existed, we might fear God and deal justly with our neighbors, we might practice arts and even have learned how to devise fairly simple machines, but we would never have become fully conscious, which is to say that we would never have become, for better or worse, fully human.

W. H. AUDEN

O

CHRONOLOGICAL OUTLINE OF CLASSICAL GREEK CIVILIZATION

DATES	BIRTHS and DEATHS	EVENTS
1300 B.C.		Sack of Cnossos
1300-900 (Homeric Age)		1193-1184 Trojan War 1104? Dorian migration to Peloponnesus 1000 Beginning of geometric art
900-800		Epic poetry
800-700		776 First Olympiad 750 Dipylon vases at Athens. Hesiod 734 Foundation of Syracuse 720 Sparta conquers Messenia
700-650		700 End of geometric art 670 Archilochus fl. 669 Argives defeat Sparta at Hysiae
	665 Periander b.	
650-600		650 Callinus of Ephesus, Terpander of Lesbos fl. Alcman at Sparta
	640 Thales b. 638 Solon b.	
		630 Tyrtaeus fl. Messenian revolt against Sparta 625 Accession of Periander at Corinth 621 Laws of Draco Lycurgus' Eunomia
	620? Aesop b. 611 Anaximander b.	

DATES	BIRTHS and DEATHS	EVENTS
600-590		600 Alcaeus Mimnermus fl. Foundation of Massilia. Rise of: free statuary, Doric and Ionic temple architecture, Attic black-figured pottery, Orphism
		594 Archonate of Solon
590-580		590 Sappho Stesichorus fl.
	585 Periander d.	585 Accession of Pittacus at Mitylene. Thales makes the first prediction of a solar eclipse
580-570		580 Susarion's "Megarian farces"
		575 End of Pittacus's rule at Mitylene
	572 Anacreon b.	
570-560	570 Pythagoras b.	561 Peisistratus's first tyranny
560-550	560 Xenophanes b. 560? Aesop d. 558 Solon d. 556 Simonides b.	
550-540		550 Rise of Attic red-figured pottery. Beginnings of Peloponnesian League Theognis Hipponax fl.
	547 Anaximander d. 546 Thales d. 544 Heraclitus b.	
		541 Beginning of Peisistratus's last and longest tyranny
540-530	540 Epicharmus b.	540 Polycrates fl.

DATES	BIRTHS and DEATHS	EVENTS
	540 Parmenides b.	
		534 Thespis's dramatic performances at Athens Ibycus fl.
530-520	530 Aristeides b. 527 Peisistratus d. 525 Aeschylus b. 522 Polycrates d.	
520-510	518 Pindar b. 514 Themistocles b.	514 Harmodius and Aristogeiton assassinate Hipparchus
510-500	510 Bacchylides b. 507 Cimon b.	510 Expulsion of Hippias. End of the Peisistratid tyranny in Athens 508 Dithyrambic contests in Athens 507 Reforms of Cleisthenes
500-490	500 Pheidias b. 500 Anazagoras b. 500 Zeno of Elea b. 499 Pericles b. 497 Pythagoras d. 496 Sophocles b. 496 Empedocles b.	500 Heraclitus's book. Hecataeus of Miletus fl. 499 Beginning of Persian War: Ionian revolt 493 Destruction of the Persian fleet off Mount Athos
490-480	 487 Anacreon d. 484 Herodotus b. 484 Euripides b.	490 Battle of Marathon 485 Gelon becomes tyrant of Gela

DATES	BIRTHS and DEATHS	EVENTS
	484 Heraclitus d.	
	483 Gorgias b.	483 Ostracism of Aristeides
	481 Protagoras b.	
480-470	480 Antiphon b.	480 Thermopylae. Salamis. Sicilians defeat Carthage (Himera). Aeschylus's *The Suppliants*
		479 Greeks defeat Persia at Plataea and in Asia Minor (Mycale)
		477 Hegemony transferred from Sparta to Athens. Foundation of Delian League
		476 *First Olympian* of Pindar
	475 Xenophanes d.	475 Temple of Aphaea at Aegina
		472 Aeschylus's *Persae*
		471 Ostracism of Themistocles
470-460	470 Parmenides d.	
	469 Socrates b.	
	468 Aristeides d.	
	466 Simonides d.	
		461 Ostracism of Cimon
460-450	460 Hippocrates b.	
	460 Democritus b.	
	460 Thucydides b.	
	459 Lysias b.	
		458 Aeschylus's *Oresteia*
		457 Completion of the Temple of Zeus. Outbreak of the Boeotian War. Archonship thrown open to Zeugitæ
	456 Aeschylus d.	

DATES	BIRTHS and DEATHS	EVENTS
		455 Polygnotus fl.
		454 Removal of the treasury of the Delian League from Delos to Athens
		451 Payment of jurors in Athens. Pericles' law of citizenship
450-440	450 Aristophanes b.	450 Prosecution of Anaxagoras for impiety.
	450 Alcibiades b.	Myron Sophron fl.
	450 Epicharmus d.	
	450 Themistocles d.	
	449 Cimon d.	449 End of Persian Wars
		446 Pindar's latest epinician *Pythian VIII*
	445 Pindar d.	445 End of the Boeotian War. Leucippus (?) fl.
	445 Bacchylides d.	
		444 Beginning of Pericles' government
		443 Sophocles' *Antigone*
	441 Antisthenes b.	441 Samos revolts against Athens
440-430		440 Pericles' first funeral oration
		439 Crushing of Samian revolt
		438 Dedication of Pheidias's Athena. Euripides' *Alcestis*
	436 Isocrates b.	
	435 Empedocles d.	
	432 Dionysius I of Syracuse b.	432 Completion of the Parthenon
		431 Euripides' *Medea*. Outbreak of the Peloponnesian War. Pericles' second funeral oration
430-420	430 Xenophon b.	430 Plague at Athens

DATES	BIRTHS and DEATHS	EVENTS
		430-424 Euripides' *Andromache* and *Hecuba*
	429 Pericles d.	429 Sophocles' *Oedipus Tyrannus*
	428 Plato b.	428 Euripides' *Hippolytus*. Property tax imposed at Athens
		427 Embassy of Gorgias of Leontini to Athens
		427-426 Great Plague at Athens
		425 Aristophanes' *Acharnians*. Athenian jurymen's pay raised to 3 obols by Cleon
		424 The Spartan Brasidas captures Amphipolis. Thucydides exiled. Aristophanes' *Knights*
		423 Aristophanes' *Clouds*
		421 Peace of Nicias. Aristophanes' *Peace*
420-410	420 Isaeus b.	420 Polycleitus's *Hera* at Argos
	418 Epaminondas b.	
		415 Euripides' *Troades*. Mutilation of the Hermae. Flight of Alcibiades. Law against using real people's names in comedy
		414 Aristophanes' *Birds*
		413 Euripides' *Electra*. Renewal of war between Sparta and Athens. Failure of Athens' expedition against Syracuse

DATES	BIRTHS and DEATHS	EVENTS
	411 Protagoras d.	411 Aristophanes' *Lysistrata*
		411-410 The Four Hundred
410-400	409 Antiphon d.	409 Sophocles' *Philoctetes*
		409-406 Completion of the Erechtheum
	408 Eudoxus of Cnidus b.	
	406 Euripides d.	
	405 Sophocles d.	405 Zeuxis fl. Rise of Dionysius I of Syracuse. Aristophanes' *Frogs*
	404 Alcibiades d.	404 End of Peloponnesian War (Aegispotami). The Thirty Tyrants
		403 Lysias's *Against Eratosthenes*
		401 Production of Sophocles' *Oedipus Coloneus*
400-390	400 Thucydides d.	400 *The Sacred Disease*
	399 Socrates d.	399 Execution of Socrates. Andocides' *De Mysteriis.*
		395 Corinthian War breaks out between Sparta and an Athenian-Corinthian coalition
		392 Aristophanes' *Ecclesiazusae.* Gorgias' *Olympiacus*
390-380	390 Hypereides b.	
		388 Aristophanes' *Plutus.* Lysias' *Olympiacus*
		386 The King's Peace:

DATES	BIRTHS and DEATHS	EVENTS
		indecisive end of the Corinthian War
	385 Aristophanes d.	385? Symposia
	384 Aristotle b.	
	384 Demosthenes b.	
	382 Philip of Macedon b.	
380-370	380 Lysias d.	380 Isocrates' *Panegyricus*
	376 Antisthenes d.	
	375 Georgias d.	375 Xenophon's *Anabasis*
	372 Theophrastus b.	
		371 Theban defeat of Sparta (Leuctra)
370-360	370 Democritus d.	
		368 Plato's *Theaetetus*
	367 Dionysius I of Syracuse d.	
		366-365 Plato's visit to Syracuse
	362 Epaminondas d.	362 Theban defeat of Sparta (Mantineia)
360-350		359 Accession of Philip of Macedon
	356 Alexander the Great b.	
	355 Hippocrates d.	355 Outbreak of the Sacred War between Philip and a Greek coalition. Xenophon's last extant work
	355 Eudoxus of Cnidus d.	
		354 Isocrates' *Areopagiticus*
		353 Beginning of work on the Mausoleum
		351 Demosthenes' *First Philippic*
350-340	350 Isaeus d.	

DATES	BIRTHS and DEATHS	EVENTS
		349 Demosthenes' *Olynthiacs*
	347 Plato d.	
		346 End of the Sacred War. Isocrates' *Philippus*. Philip presides at the Pythian games.
		344 Demosthenes' *Second Philippic*. Aristotle Alexander's tutor
		343 Demosthenes vs. Aeschines' *On the Embassy*
	342 Menander b.	
	341 Epicurus b.	341 Demosthenes' *On the Chersonese* and *Third Philippic*
340-330		340 Demosthenes' *Fourth Philippic*. Athens declares war on Macedon
		339 Isocrates' *Panathenaicus*
	338 Isocrates d.	338 Macedonian defeat of Thebes (Chaeronea)
	336 Philip of Macedon d.	
		335 Destruction of Thebes. Aristotle settles at Athens
		334 Beginning of Alexander's invasion of Persia
		331 Foundation of Alexandria
330-320		330 Lycurgus's *Against Leocrates*. Aeschines' *Against*

DATES	BIRTHS and DEATHS	EVENTS
		Ctesiphon. Demosthenes' *On the Crown.* Apelles Lysippus fl.
		326 Alexander crosses the Indus
		324 Exile of Demosthenes
	323 Alexander the Great d.	
	322 Aristotle d.	
	322 Demosthenes d.	
	322 Hypereides d.	
320-310		314 Zeno the Stoic comes to Athens
	312 Theocritus b.	
310-300	310 Callimachus b.	310 Murder of Alexander IV of Macedon. Rise of the Succession States: the Seleucids in Asia, the Antigonids in Greece, the Ptolemies in Egypt
		306 Epicurus opens a a school in Athens
300-290		300 Euclid Euhemerus fl. Foundation of Antioch
290-280	290 Menander d.	290 Probable foundation of the Library and Museum at Alexandria
	287 Archimedes b.	
	287 Theophrastus d.	
		285 Herophilus Erasistratus anatomists fl.
280-270		280 Final reorganization of the Achaean

DATES	BIRTHS and DEATHS	EVENTS
		League. Aristarchus of Samos fl.
	276 Eratosthenes b.	
		275 Final defeat of Pyrrhus in Italy
270-260	270 Epicurus d.	270 Herodas' Mimiambi
	262 Apollonius of Perga b.	
260-250	260 Theocritus d.	
250-225		250 Hegesias of Magnesis fl.
	240 Callimachus d.	
225-200	212 Archimedes d.	
	201 Polybius b.	
200-150	200 Apollonius of Perga d.	200 Apollonius Rhodius fl.
	194 Eratosthenes d.	
		180 Altar of Zeus at Pergamum
150-100		150 Bion fl.
		146 Rome defeats and dissolves the Achaean League
		136 Hipparchus fl.
	120 Polybius d.	
100-1		100 Milesian Tales of Aristeides. Moschus fl.
		60 Meleager's *Anthologia* End of Roman Republic and establishment of the Principate by Augustus
1-100 A.D.		?4 B.C.-29 A.D. Birth, life, and death of Jesus Christ
		40 *On the Sublime* (Longinus)

DATES	BIRTHS and DEATHS	EVENTS
	46 Plutarch b.	
		49? St. Paul preaches in Athens
	60 Epictetus b.	
100-200	120 Plutarch d.	
	121 Marcus Aurelius b.	
	125 Lucian b.	
	130 Galen b.	
		135 Ptolemy fl.
		165 Pausanias fl.
		178 Celsus's *The True Word*
	180 Marcus Aurelius d.	
	190 Lucian d.	
200-300	200 Galen d.	
	204 Plotinus b.	
	233 Porphyry b.	
	270 Plotinus d.	
300-500		300 *Daphnis and Chloë* (Longus)
	304 Porphyry d.	305 Dissolution of the Sacred College
		312 Constantine becomes Emperor
		313 Edict of Milan
	331 Julian b.	
		361-363 Attempt by Julian to replace Christianity by Philosophy
	363 Julian d.	
		529 Justinian closes the schools at Athens

PART ONE

COSMOGONIES
AND
COSMOLOGIES

○

THE CREATION

HESIOD

VERILY at the first Chaos came to be, but next wide-bosomed Earth, the ever-sure foundation of all the deathless ones who hold the peaks of snowy Olympus, and dim Tartarus in the depth of the wide-pathed Earth, and Eros (Love), fairest among the deathless gods, who unnerves the limbs and overcomes the mind and wise counsels of all gods and all men within them. From Chaos came forth Erebus and black Night; but of Night were born Aether and Day, whom she conceived and bare from union in love with Erebus. And Earth first bare starry Heaven, equal to herself, to cover her on every side, and to be an ever-sure abiding-place for the blessed gods. And she brought forth long Hills, graceful haunts of the goddess-Nymphs who dwell amongst the glens of the hills. She bare also the fruitless deep with his raging swell, Pontus, without sweet union of love. But afterwards she lay with Heaven and bare deep-swirling Oceanus, Coeus and Crius and Hyperion and Iapetus, Theia and Rhea, Themis and Mnemosyne and gold-crowned Phoebe and lovely Tethys. After them was born Cronos the wily, youngest and most terrible of her children, and he hated his lusty sire.

And again, she bare the Cyclopes, overbearing in spirit, Brontes, and Steropes and stubborn-hearted Arges, who gave Zeus the thunder and made the thunderbolt: in all else they were like the gods, but one eye only was set in the midst of their foreheads. And they were surnamed Cyclopes (Orb-eyed) because one orbed eye was set in their foreheads. Strength and might and craft were in their works.

And again, three other sons were born of Earth and Heaven, great and doughty beyond telling, Cottus and Briareos and Gyes, presumptuous children. From their shoulders sprang an hundred arms, not to be approached, and each had fifty heads upon his shoulders on their strong limbs, and irresistible was the stubborn strength that was in their great forms. For of all the children that were born of Earth and Heaven, these were the most terrible, and they were hated by their own father from the first. And he used to hide them all away in a secret place of Earth so soon as each was born, and would not suffer them to come up into the light: and Heaven rejoiced in his evil doing. But vast Earth groaned within, being straitened, and she thought a crafty and an evil wile. Forthwith she made the element of grey flint and shaped a great sickle, and told her plan to her dear sons. And she spoke, cheering them, while she was vexed in her dear heart:

"My children, gotten of a sinful father, if you will obey me, we should punish the vile outrage of your father; for he first thought of doing shameful things."

So she said; but fear seized them all, and none of them uttered a word. But great Cronos the wily took courage and answered his dear mother:

"Mother, I will undertake to do this deed, for I reverence not our father of evil name, for he first thought of doing shameful things."

So he said: and vast Earth rejoiced greatly in spirit, and set and hid him in an ambush, and put in his hands a jagged sickle, and revealed to him the whole plot.

And Heaven came, bringing on night and longing for love, and he lay about Earth spreading himself full upon her. Then the son from his ambush stretched forth his left hand and in his right took the great long sickle with jagged teeth, and swiftly lopped off his own father's members and cast them away to fall behind him. And not vainly did they fall from his hand; for all the bloody drops that gushed forth Earth received, and as the seasons moved round she bare the strong Erinyes and the great Giants with gleaming armour, holding long spears in their hands, and the Nymphs whom they call Meliae all over the boundless earth. And so soon as he had cut off the members with flint and cast them from the land into the surging sea, they were swept away over the main a long time: and a white foam spread around them from the immortal flesh, and in it there grew a maiden. First she drew near holy Cythera, and from there, afterwards, she came to sea-girt Cyprus, and came forth an awful and lovely goddess, and grass grew up about her beneath her shapely feet. Her gods and men call Aphrodite, and the foam-born goddess and rich-crowned Cytherea, because she grew amid the foam, and Cytherea because she reached Cythera, and Cyprogenes because she was born in billowy Cyprus, and Philommedes because she sprang from the members. And with her went Eros, and comely Desire followed her at her birth at the first and as she went into the assembly of the gods. This honour she has from the beginning, and this is the portion allotted to her amongst men and undying gods— the whisperings of maidens and smiles and deceits with sweet delight and love and graciousness.

But these sons whom he begot himself great Heaven used to call Titans (Strainers) in reproach, for he said that they strained and did presumptuously a fearful deed, and that vengeance for it would come afterwards.

And Night bare hateful Doom and black Fate and Death, and she bare Sleep and the tribe of Dreams. And again the goddess murky Night, though she lay with none, bare Blame and painful Woe, and the Hesperides who guard the rich, golden apples and the trees bearing fruit beyond glorious Ocean. Also she bare the Destinies and ruthless avenging Fates, Clotho and Lachesis and Atropos, who give men at their birth both evil and good to have, and they pursue the transgressions of men and of gods: and these goddesses never cease from their dread anger until they punish the sinner with a sore penalty. Also deadly Night bare Nemesis (Indignation) to afflict mortal men, and after her, Deceit and Friendship and hateful Age and hard-hearted Strife.

From *Theogony*. Translated 1914 by H. G. Evelyn-White.

O

THE FIVE AGES

HESIOD

I WILL sum you up another tale well and skilfully —and do you lay it up in your heart—how the gods and mortal men sprang from one source.

First of all the deathless gods who dwell on Olympus made a golden race of mortal men who lived in the time of Cronos when he was reigning in heaven. And they lived like gods without sorrow of heart, remote and free from toil and grief: miserable age rested not on them; but with legs and arms never failing they made merry with feasting beyond the reach of all evils. When they died, it was as though they were overcome with sleep, and they had all good things; for the fruitful earth unforced bare them fruit abundantly and without stint. They dwelt in ease and peace upon their lands with many good things, rich in flocks and loved by the blessed gods.

But after the earth had covered this generation—they are called pure spirits dwelling on the earth, and are kindly delivering from harm, and guardians of mortal men; for they roam everywhere over the earth, clothed in mist and keep watch on judgements and cruel deeds, givers of wealth; for this royal right also they received —then they who dwell on Olympus made a second generation which was of silver and less noble by far. It was like the golden race neither in body nor in spirit. A child was brought up at his good mother's side an hundred years, an utter simpleton, playing childishly in his own home. But when they were full grown and were come to the full measure of their prime, they lived only a little time and that in sorrow because of their foolishness, for they could not keep from sinning and from wronging one another, nor would they serve the immortals, nor sacrifice on the holy altars of the blessed ones as it is right for men to do wherever they dwell. Then Zeus the son of Cronos was angry and put them away, because they would not give honour to the blessed gods who live on Olympus.

But when earth had covered this generation also— they are called blessed spirits of the underworld by men, and, though they are of second order, yet honour attends them also—Zeus the Father made a third generation of mortal men, a brazen race, sprung from ash-trees; and it was in no way equal to the silver age, but was terrible and strong. They loved the lamentable works of Ares and deeds of violence; they ate no bread, but were hard of heart like adamant, fearful men. Great was their strength and unconquerable the arms which grew from their shoulders on their strong limbs. Their armour was of bronze, and their houses of bronze, and of bronze were their implements: there was no black iron. These were destroyed by their own hands and passed to the dank house of chill Hades, and left no name: terrible though they were, black Death seized them, and they left the bright light of the sun.

But when earth had covered this generation also, Zeus the son of Cronos made yet another, the fourth, upon the fruitful earth, which was nobler and more righteous, a god-like race of hero-men who are called demi-gods, the race before our own, throughout the boundless earth. Grim war and dread battle destroyed a part of them, some in the land of Cadmus at seven-gated Thebe when they fought for the flocks of Oedipus, and some, when it had brought them in ships over the great sea gulf to Troy for rich-haired Helen's sake: there death's end enshrouded a part of them. But to the others father Zeus the son of Cronos gave a living and an abode apart from men, and made them dwell at the ends of earth. And they live untouched by sorrow in the islands of the blessed along the shore of deep swirling Ocean, happy heroes for whom the grain-giving earth bears honey-sweet fruit flourishing thrice a year, far from the deathless gods, and Cronos rules over them; for the father of men and gods released him from his bonds. And these last equally have honour and glory.

And again far-seeing Zeus made yet another generation, the fifth, of men who are upon the bounteous earth.

Thereafter, would that I were not among the men of the fifth generation, but either had died before or been born afterwards. For now truly is a race of iron, and men never rest from labour and sorrow by day, and from perishing by night; and the gods shall lay sore trouble upon them. But, notwithstanding, even these shall have some good mingled with their evils. And Zeus will destroy this race of mortal men also when they come to have grey hair on the temples at their birth. The father will not agree with his children, nor the children with their father, nor guest with his host, nor comrade with comrade; nor will brother be dear to brother as aforetime. Men will dishonour their parents as they grow quickly old, and will carp at them, chiding them with bitter words, hard-hearted they, not knowing the fear of the gods. They will not repay their aged parents the cost of their nurture, for might shall be their right: and one man will sack another's city. There will be no favour for the man who keeps his oath or for the just or for the good; but rather men will praise the evil-doer and his violent dealing. Strength will be right and reverence will cease to be; and the wicked will hurt the worthy man, speaking false words against him, and will swear an oath upon them. Envy, foul-mouthed, delighting in evil, with scowling face, will go along with wretched men one and all. And then Aidôs and Nemesis, with their sweet forms wrapped in white robes, will go from the wide-pathed earth and forsake mankind to join the company of the deathless gods: and bitter sorrows will be left for mortal men, and there will be no help against evil.

From *Works and Days*. Translated 1914 by H. G. Evelyn-White.

O

PROMETHEUS

HESIOD

NOW Iapetus took to wife the neat-ankled maid Clymene, daughter of Ocean, and went up with her into one bed. And she bare him a stout-hearted son,

Atlas: also she bare very glorious Menoetius and clever Prometheus, full of various wiles, and scatter-brained Epimetheus who from the first was a mischief to men who eat bread; for it was he who first took of Zeus the woman, the maiden whom he had formed. But Menoetius was outrageous, and far-seeing Zeus struck him with a lurid thunderbolt and sent him down to Erebus because of his mad presumption and exceeding pride. And Atlas through hard constraint upholds the wide heaven with unwearying head and arms, standing at the borders of the earth before the clear-voiced Hesperides; for this lot wise Zeus assigned to him. And ready-witted Prometheus he bound with inextricable bonds, cruel chains, and drove a shaft through his middle, and set on him a long-winged eagle, which used to eat his immortal liver; but by night the liver grew as much again everyway as the long-winged bird devoured in the whole day. That bird Heracles, the valiant son of shapely-ankled Alcmene, slew; and delivered the son of Iapetus from the cruel plague, and released him from affliction—not without the will of Olympian Zeus who reigns on high, that the glory of Heracles the Theban-born might be yet greater than it was before over the plenteous earth. This, then, he regarded, and honoured his famous son; though he was angry, he ceased from the wrath which he had before because Prometheus matched himself in wit with the almighty son of Cronos. For when the gods and mortal men were divided at Mecone, even then Prometheus was forward to cut up a great ox and set portions before them, trying to befool the mind of Zeus. Before the rest he set flesh and inner parts thick with fat upon the hide, covering them with an ox paunch; but for Zeus he put the white bones dressed up with cunning art and covered with shining fat. Then the father of men and of gods said to him:

"Son of Iapetus, most glorious of all lords, good sir, how unfairly you have divided the portions!"

So said Zeus whose wisdom is everlasting, rebuking him. But wily Prometheus answered him, smiling softly and not forgetting his cunning trick:

"Zeus, most glorious and greatest of the eternal gods, take which ever of these portions your heart within you bids." So he said, thinking trickery. But Zeus, whose wisdom is everlasting, saw and failed not to perceive the trick, and in his heart he thought mischief against mortal men which also was to be fulfilled. With both hands he took up the white fat and was angry at heart, and wrath came to his spirit when he saw the white ox-bones craftily tricked out: and because of this the tribes of men upon earth burn white bones to the deathless gods upon fragrant altars. But Zeus who drives the clouds was greatly vexed and said to him:

"Son of Iapetus, clever above all. So, sir, you have not yet forgotten your cunning arts!"

So spake Zeus in anger, whose wisdom is everlasting; and from that time he was always mindful of the trick, and would not give the power of unwearying fire to the Melian race of mortal men who live on the earth. But the noble son of Iapetus outwitted him and stole the far-seen gleam of unwearying fire in a hollow fennel stalk. And Zeus who thunders on high was stung in spirit, and his dear heart was angered when he saw amongst men the far-seen ray of fire. Forthwith he made an evil thing for men as the price of fire; for the very famous Limping God formed of earth the likeness of a shy maiden as the son of Cronos willed. And the goddess bright-eyed Athene girded and clothed her with silvery raiment, and down from her head she spread with her hands a broidered veil, a wonder to see; and she, Pallas Athene, put about her head lovely garlands, flowers of new-grown herbs. Also she put upon her head a crown of gold which the very famous Limping God made himself and worked with his own hands as a favour to Zeus his father. On it was much curious work, wonderful to see; for of the many creatures which the land and sea rear up, he put most upon it, wonderful things, like living beings with voices: and great beauty shone out from it.

But when he had made the beautiful evil to be the price for the blessing, he brought her out, delighting in the finery which the bright-eyed daughter of a mighty father had given her, to the place where the other gods and men were. And wonder took hold of the deathless gods and mortal men when they saw that which was sheer guile, not to be withstood by men.

For from her is the race of women and female kind: of her is the deadly race and tribe of women who live amongst mortal men to their great trouble, no helpmeets in hateful poverty, but only in wealth. And as in thatched hives bees feed the drones whose nature is to do mischief—by day and throughout the day until the sun goes down the bees are busy and lay the white combs, while the drones stay at home in the covered skeps and reap the toil of others into their own bellies— even so Zeus who thunders on high made women to be an evil to mortal men, with a nature to do evil. And he gave them a second evil to be the price for the good they had: whoever avoids marriage and the sorrows that women cause, and will not wed, reaches deadly old age without anyone to tend his years, and though he at least has no lack of livelihood while he lives, yet, when he is dead, his kinsfolk divide his possessions amongst them. And as for the man who chooses the lot of marriage and takes a good wife suited to his mind, evil continually contends with good; for whoever happens to have mischievous children, lives always with unceasing grief in his spirit and heart within him; and this evil cannot be healed.

So it is not possible to deceive or go beyond the will of Zeus; for not even the son of Iapetus, kindly Prometheus, escaped his heavy anger, but of necessity strong bands confined him, although he knew many a wile.

From *Theogony.* Translated 1914 by H. G. Evelyn-White.

O

ZEUS

SOPHOCLES

CHORUS: O may my constant feet not fail,
Walking in paths of righteousness,
Sinless in word and deed—
True to those eternal laws
That scale for ever the high steep
Of heaven's pure ether, whence they sprang:
For only in Olympus is their home,
Nor mortal wisdom gave them birth,
And howsoe'er men may forget,
They will not sleep;
For the might of the god within them grows not old.

Rooted in pride, the tyrant grows;
But pride that with its own too-much
Is rashly surfeited,
Heeding not the prudent mean,
Down the inevitable gulf
From its high pinnacle is hurled,
Where use of foothold there is none.
But, O kind gods, the noble strength,
That struggles for the city's good,

Unbend not yet:
In the gods have I put my trust—I will not fear.

But whoso walks disdainfully,
In act or word,
And fears not justice, nor reveres
The thronèd gods,
Him let misfortune slay
For his ill-starred wantoning,
Should he heap unrighteous gains,
Nor from unhallowed paths withhold his feet,
Or reach rash hands to pluck forbidden fruit.
Who shall do this, and boast
That yet his soul is proof
Against the arrows of offended Heaven?
If honour crowns such deeds as those,
No song, but silence, then for me!

To Earth's dread centre, unprofaned
By mortal touch,
No more with awe will I repair,
Nor Abæ's shrine,
Nor the Olympian plain,
If the truth stands not confessed,
Pointed at by all the world.
O Zeus supreme, if rightly thou art called—
Lord over all—let not these things escape
Thee and thy timeless sway!
For now men set at nought
Apollo's word, and cry "Behold, it fails!"
His praise is darkened with a doubt;
And faith is sapped, and Heaven defied.

From *Oedipus Tyrannus*.
Translated by Robert M. Whitelaw.

○

DIONYSUS

EURIPIDES

SOME MAIDENS: Thou Immaculate on high;
Thou Recording Purity;
Thou that stoopest, Golden Wing,
Earthward, manward, pitying,
Hearest thou this angry King?
Hearest thou the rage and scorn
  'Gainst the Lord of Many Voices,
Him of mortal mother born,
  Him in whom man's heart rejoices,
Girt with garlands and with glee,
First in Heaven's sovranty?
  For his kingdom, it is there,
  In the dancing and the prayer,
In the music and the laughter,
  In the vanishing of care,
And of all before and after;
In the God's high banquet, when
  Gleams the grape-blood, flashed to heaven:
Yea, and in the feasts of men
Comes his crownèd slumber; then
  Pain is dead and hate forgiven!

OTHERS: Loose thy lips from out the rein;
Lift thy wisdom to disdain;
Whatso law thou canst not see,
Scorning; so the end shall be
Uttermost calamity!
'Tis the life of quiet breath,
  'Tis the simple and the true,

Storm nor earthquake shattereth,
    Nor shall aught the house undo
Where they dwell. For, far away,
Hidden from the eyes of day,
    Watchers are there in the skies,
    That can see man's life, and prize
Deeds well done by things of clay.
    But the world's Wise are not wise,
Claiming more than mortal may.
Life is such a little thing;
    Lo, their present is departed,
And the dreams to which they cling
Come not. Mad imagining
    Theirs, I ween, and empty-hearted!

DIVERS MAIDENS: Where is the Home for me?
    O Cyprus, set in the sea,
Aphrodite's home in the soft sea-foam,
    Would I could wend to thee;
Where the wings of the Loves are furled,
And faint the heart of the world.

    Aye, unto Paphos' isle,
    Where the rainless meadows smile
With riches rolled from the hundred-fold
    Mouths of the far-off Nile,
Streaming beneath the waves
To the roots of the seaward caves.

    But a better land is there
    Where Olympus cleaves the air,
The high still dell where the Muses dwell,
    Fairest of all things fair!
O there is Grace, and there is the Heart's Desire,
And peace to adore thee, thou Spirit of Guiding]

A God of Heaven is he,
And born in majesty;
Yet hath he mirth in the joy of the Earth,
And he loveth constantly
Her who brings increase,
The Feeder of Children, Peace.
No grudge hath he of the great;
No scorn of the mean estate;
But to all that liveth His wine he giveth,
Grieflless, immaculate;
Only on them that spurn
Joy, may his anger burn.

Love thou the Day and the Night;
Be glad of the Dark and the Light;
And avert thine eyes from the lore of the wise,
That have honour in proud men's sight.
The simple nameless herd of Humanity
Hath deeds and faith that art truth enough for me

From *The Bacchae*. Translated by Gilbert Murray.

O

THE EARTH MOTHER

A HOMERIC HYMN

O UNIVERSAL Mother, who dost keep
From everlasting thy foundations deep,
Eldest of things, Great Earth, I sing of thee!
All shapes that have their dwelling in the sea,
All things that fly, or on the ground divine
Live, move, and there are nourished—these are thine;
These from thy wealth thou dost sustain; from thee

Fair babes are born, and fruits on every tree
Hang ripe and large, revered Divinity!

The life of mortal men beneath thy sway
Is held; thy power both gives and takes away!
Happy are they whom thy mild favours nourish;
All things unstinted round them grow and flourish.
For them, endures the life-sustaining field
Its load of harvest, and their cattle yield
Large increase, and their house with wealth is filled.
Such honoured dwell in cities fair and free,
The homes of lovely women, prosperously;
Their sons exult in youth's new budding gladness,
And their fresh daughters free from care or sadness,
With bloom-inwoven dance and happy song,
On the soft flowers the meadow-grass among,
Leap round them sporting—such delights by thee
Are given, rich Power, revered Divinity.

Mother of gods, thou Wife of starry Heaven,
Farewell! be thou propitious, and be given
A happy life for this brief melody,
Nor thou nor other songs shall unremembered be.

Translated by P. B. Shelley.

O

MINOR DEITIES

I

ARCHIAS

Small to see, I, Priapus, inhabit this spit of shore, not
much bigger than a sea-gull, sharp-headed, footless, such

an one as upon lonely beaches might be carved by the sons of toiling fishermen. But if any basket-fisher or angler call me to succour, I rush fleeter than the blast: likewise I see the creatures that run under water; and truly the form of godhead is known from deeds, not from shape.

II

ANYTE

To Pan the bristly-haired, and the Nymphs of the farm-yard, Theodotus the shepherd laid this gift under the crag, because they stayed him when very weary under the parching summer, stretching out to him honey-sweet water in their hands.

Translated by J. W. Mackail.

O

THE TRUE GOD

XENOPHANES

Homer and Hesiod have ascribed to the gods all things that are a shame and a disgrace among mortals, stealings and adulteries and deceivings of one another.

Since they have uttered many lawless deeds of the gods, stealings and adulteries and deceivings of one another.

But mortals deem that the gods are begotten as they are, and have clothes like theirs, and voice and form.

Yes, and if oxen and horses or lions had hands, and could paint with their hands, and produce works of art as men do, horses would paint the forms of the gods like horses, and oxen like oxen, and make their bodies in the image of their several kinds.

The Ethiopians make their gods black and snub-nosed; the Thracians say theirs have blue eyes and red hair.

The gods have not revealed all things to men from the beginning, but by seeking they find in time what is better.

One god, the greatest among gods and men, neither in form like unto mortals nor in thought. . . .

He sees all over, thinks all over, and hears all over.

But without toil he swayeth all things by the thought of his mind.

And he abideth ever in the selfsame place, moving not at all; nor doth it befit him to go about now hither now thither.

Translated 1892 by John Burnet.

O

THE WORD

HERACLITUS

(1) It is wise to hearken, not to me but to my word, and to confess that all things are one.

(2) Though this Word is true evermore, yet men are as unable to understand it when they hear it for the first

time as before they have heard it at all. For, though all things come to pass in accordance with this Word, men seem as if they had no experience of them, when they make trial of words and deeds such as I set forth, dividing each thing according to its kind and showing how it truly is. But other men know not what they are doing when awake, even as they forget what they do in sleep.

(3) Fools when they do hear are like the deaf: of them does the saying bear witness that they are absent when present.

(4) Eyes and ears are bad witnesses to men if they have souls that understand not their language.

(5) The many do not take heed of such things as those they meet with, nor do they mark them when they are taught, though they think they do.

(6) Knowing not how to listen nor how to speak.

(7) If you do not expect the unexpected, you will not find it; for it is hard to be sought out and difficult.

(8) Those who seek for gold dig up much earth and find a little.

(10) Nature loves to hide.

(11) The lord whose is the oracle at Delphoi neither utters nor hides his meaning, but shows it by a sign.

(12) And the Sibyl, with raving lips uttering things mirthless, unbedizened, and unperfumed, reaches over a thousand years with her voice, thanks to the god in her.

(13) The things that can be seen, heard, and learned are what I prize the most.

(14) . . . bringing untrustworthy witnesses in support of disputed points.

(15) The eyes are more exact witnesses than the ears.

(16) The learning of many things teacheth not understanding, else would it have taught Hesiod and Pythagoras, and again Xenophanes and Hekataios.

(17) Pythagoras, son of Mnesarchos, practised scien-

tific inquiry beyond all other men, and making a selection of these writings, claimed for his own wisdom what was but a knowledge of many things and an imposture.

(18) Of all whose discourses I have heard, there is not one who attains to understanding that wisdom is apart from all.

(19) Wisdom is one thing. It is to know the thought by which all things are steered through all things.

(20) This world, which is the same for all, no one of gods or men has made; but it was ever, is now, and ever shall be an ever-living Fire, with measures of it kindling, and measures going out.

(21) The transformations of Fire are, first of all, sea; and half of the sea is earth, half whirlwind. . . .

(22) All things are an exchange for Fire, and Fire for all things, even as wares for gold and gold for wares.

(23) It becomes liquid sea, and is measured by the same tale as before it became earth.

(24) Fire is want and surfeit.

(25) Fire lives the death of air, and air lives the death of fire; water lives the death of earth, earth that of water.

(26) Fire in its advance will judge and convict all things.

(27) How can one hide from that which never sets?

(28) It is the thunderbolt that steers the course of all things.

(29) The sun will not overstep his measures; if he does, the Erinyes, the handmaids of Justice, will find him out.

(30) The limit of dawn and evening is the Bear; and opposite the Bear is the boundary of bright Zeus.

(31) If there were no sun it would be night, for all the other stars could do.

(32) The sun is new every day.

(33) (Thales foretold an eclipse.)

(34) . . . the seasons that bring all things.

(35) Hesiod is most men's teacher. Men are sure he knew very many things, a man who did not know day or night! They are one.

(36) God is day and night, winter and summer, war and peace, surfeit and hunger; but he takes various shapes, just as oil, when it is mingled with spices, is named according to the savour of each.

(37) If all things were turned to smoke, the nostrils would distinguish them.

(38) Souls smell in Hades.

(39) Cold things become warm, and what is warm cools; what is wet dries, and the parched is moistened.

(40) It scatters and it gathers; it advances and retires.

(41, 42) You cannot step twice into the same rivers; for fresh waters are ever flowing in upon you.

(43) Homer was wrong in saying: "Would that strife might perish from among gods and men!" He did not see that he was praying for the destruction of the universe; for, if his prayer were heard, all things would pass away. . . .

(44) War is the father of all and the king of all; and some he has made gods and some men, some bond and some free.

(45) Men do not know how what is at variance agrees with itself. It is an attunement of opposite tensions, like that of the bow and the lyre.

(46) It is the opposite which is good for us.

(47) The hidden attunement is better than the open.

(48) Let us not conjecture at random about the greatest things.

(49) Men that love wisdom must be acquainted with very many things indeed.

(50) The straight and the crooked path of the fuller's comb is one and the same.

(51) Asses would rather have straw than gold.

(51a) Oxen are happy when they find bitter vetches to eat.

(52) The sea is the purest and the impurest water. Fish can drink it, and it is good for them; to men it is undrinkable and destructive.

(53) Swine wash in the mire, and barnyard fowls in dust.

(54) . . . to delight in the mire.

(55) Every beast is driven to pasture with blows.

(56) Same as 45.

(57) Good and ill are one.

(58) Physicians who cut, burn, stab, and rack the sick, demand a fee for it which they do not deserve to get.

(59) Couples are things whole and things not whole, what is drawn together and what is drawn asunder, the harmonious and the discordant. The one is made up of all things, and all things issue from the one.

(60) Men would not have known the name of justice if these things were not.

(61) To God all things are fair and good and right, but men hold some things wrong and some right.

(62) We must know that war is common to all and strife is justice, and that all things come into being and pass away (?) through strife.

(64) All the things we see when awake are death, even as all we see in slumber are sleep.

(65) The wise is one only. It is unwilling and willing to be called by the name of Zeus.

(66) The bow ($\beta\iota\acute{o}s$) is called life ($\beta\acute{\iota}os$), but its work is death.

(67) Mortals are immortals and immortals are mor-

tals, the one living the others' death and dying the others' life.

(68) For it is death to souls to become water, and death to water to become earth. But water comes from earth; and from water, soul.

(69) The way up and the way down is one and the same.

(70) In the circumference of a circle the beginning and end are common.

(71) You will not find the boundaries of soul by travelling in any direction, so deep is the measure of it.

(72) It is pleasure to souls to become moist.

(73) A man, when he gets drunk, is led by a beard-less lad, tripping, knowing not where he steps, having his soul moist.

(74-76) The dry soul is the wisest and best.

(77) Man kindles a light for himself in the night-time, when he has died but is alive. The sleeper, whose vision has been put out, lights up from the dead; he that is awake lights up from the sleeping.

(78) And it is the same thing in us that is quick and dead, awake and asleep, young and old; the former are shifted and become the latter, and the latter in turn are shifted and become the former.

(79) Time is a child playing draughts, the kingly power is a child's.

(80) I have sought for myself.

(81) We step and do not step into the same rivers; we are and are not.

(82) It is a weariness to labour for the same masters and be ruled by them.

(83) It rests by changing.

(84) Even the posset separates if it is not stirred.

(85) Corpses are more fit to be cast out than dung.

(86) When they are born, they wish to live and to meet with their dooms—or rather to rest—and they leave children behind them to meet with their dooms in turn.

(87-89) A man may be a grandfather in thirty years.

(90) Those who are asleep are fellow-workers (in what goes on in the world).

(91a) Thought is common to all.

(91b) Those who speak with understanding must hold fast to what is common to all as a city holds fast to its law, and even more strongly. For all human laws are fed by the one divine law. It prevails as much as it will, and suffices for all things with something to spare.

(92) So we must follow the common, yet though my Word is common, the many live as if they had a wisdom of their own.

(93) They are estranged from that with which they have most constant intercourse.

(94) It is not meet to act and speak like men asleep.

(95) The waking have one common world, but the sleeping turn aside each into a world of his own.

(96) The way of man has no wisdom, but that of God has.

(97) Man is called a baby by God, even as a child by a man.

(98, 99) The wisest man is an ape compared to God, just as the most beautiful ape is ugly compared to man.

(100) The people must fight for its law as for its walls.

(101) Greater deaths win greater portions.

(102) Gods and men honour those who are slain in battle.

(103) Wantonness needs putting out, even more than a house on fire.

(104) It is not good for men to get all they wish to get. It is sickness that makes health pleasant; evil, good; hunger, plenty; weariness, rest.

(105-107) It is hard to fight with one's heart's desire. Whatever it wishes to get, it purchases at the cost of soul.

(108, 109) It is best to hide folly; but it is hard in times of relaxation, over our cups.

(110) And it is law, too, to obey the counsel of one.

(111) For what thought or wisdom have they? They follow the poets and take the crowd as their teacher, knowing not that there are many bad and few good. For even the best of them choose one thing above all others, immortal glory among mortals, while most of them are glutted like beasts.

(112) In Priene lived Bias, son of Teutamas, who is of more account than the rest. (He said, "Most men are bad.")

(113) One is ten thousand to me, if he be the best.

(114) The Ephesians would do well to hang themselves, every grown man of them, and leave the city to beardless lads; for they have cast out Hermodoros, the best man among them, saying, "We will have none who is best among us; if there be any such, let him be so elsewhere and among others."

(115) Dogs bark at every one they do not know.

(116) . . . (The wise man) is not known because of men's want of belief.

(117) The fool is fluttered at every word.

(118) The most esteemed of them knows but fancies, and holds fast to them, yet of a truth justice shall overtake the artificers of lies and the false witnesses.

(119) Homer should be turned out of the lists and whipped, and Archilochos likewise.

(120) One day is like any other.

(121) Man's character is his fate.

(122) There awaits men when they die such things as they look not for nor dream of.

(123) . . . that they rise up and become the wakeful guardians of the quick and dead.

(124) Night-walkers, Magians, Bakchoi, Lenai, and the initiated . . .

(125) The mysteries practised among men are unholy mysteries.

(126) And they pray to these images, as if one were to talk with a man's house, knowing not what gods or heroes are.

(127) For if it were not to Dionysos that they made a procession and sang the shameful phallic hymn, they would be acting most shamelessly. But Hades is the same as Dionysos in whose honour they go mad and rave.

(129, 130) They vainly purify themselves by defiling themselves with blood, just as if one who had stepped into the mud were to wash his feet in mud. Any man who marked him doing thus, would deem him mad.

Translated 1892 by John Burnet.

O

THE REAL

PARMENIDES

COME now, I will tell thee—and do thou hearken to my saying and carry it away—the only two ways of search that can be thought of. The first, namely, that *It is,* and that it is impossible for it not to be, is the way of belief, for truth is its companion. The other, namely, that *It is not,* and that it must needs not be—that, I tell thee, is a path that none can learn of at all. For thou canst not know what is not—that is impossible—nor utter it; for it is the same thing that can be thought and that can be.

(2) It needs must be that what can be spoken and thought *is;* for it is possible for it to be, and it is not possible for what is nothing to be. This is what I bid thee ponder. I hold thee back from this first way of inquiry, and from this other also, upon which mortals knowing naught wander two-faced; for helplessness guides the wandering thought in their breasts, so that they are borne along stupefied like men deaf and blind. Undiscerning crowds, who hold that it is and is not the same and not the same, and all things travel in opposite directions!

(3) For this shall never be proved, that the things that are not are; and do thou restrain thy thought from this way of inquiry.

(4) One path only is left for us to speak of, namely, that *It is.* In this path are very many tokens that what is is uncreated and indestructible; for it is complete, immovable, and without end. Nor was it ever, nor will it be; for now *it is,* all at once, a continuous one. For what kind of origin for it wilt thou look for? In what way and from what source could it have drawn its increase? . . . I shall not let thee say nor think that it came from what is not; for it can neither be thought nor uttered that anything is not. And, if it came from nothing, what need could have made it arise later rather than sooner? Therefore must it either be altogether or be not at all. Nor will the force of truth suffer aught to arise besides itself from that which is not. Wherefore, Justice doth not loose her fetters and let anything come into being or pass away, but holds it fast. Our judgment thereon depends on this: *"Is it* or *is it not?"* Surely it is adjudged, as it needs must be, that we are to set aside the one way as unthinkable

and nameless (for it is no true way), and that the other
path is real and true. How, then, can what *is* be going
to be in the future? Or how could it come into being?
If it came into being, it is not; nor is it if it is going to be
in the future. Thus is becoming extinguished and passing
away not to be heard of.

Nor is it divisible, since it is all alike, and there is no
more of it in one place than in another, to hinder it from
holding together, nor less of it, but everything is full of
what is. Wherefore it is wholly continuous; for what is,
is in contact with what is.

Moreover, it is immovable in the bonds of mighty
chains, without beginning and without end; since coming into being and passing away have been driven afar,
and true belief has cast them away. It is the same, and
it rests in the self-same place, abiding in itself. And thus
it remaineth constant in its place; for hard necessity
keeps it in the bonds of the limit that holds it fast on
every side. Wherefore it is not permitted to what is to
be infinite; for it is in need of nothing; while, if it were
infinite, it would stand in need of everything.

The thing that can be thought and that for the sake
of which the thought exists is the same; for you cannot
find thought without something that is, as to which it is
uttered. And there is not, and never shall be, anything
besides what is, since fate has chained it so as to be
whole and immovable. Wherefore all these things are
but names which mortals have given, believing them to
be true—coming into being and passing away, being and
not being, change of place and alteration of bright
colour.

Since, then, it has a furthest limit, it is complete on
every side, like the mass of a rounded sphere, equally
poised from the centre in every direction; for it cannot
be greater or smaller in one place than in another. For

there is no nothing that could keep it from reaching out equally, nor can aught that is be more here and less there than what is, since it is all inviolable. For the point from which it is equal in every direction tends equally to the limits.

Translated 1892 by John Burnet.

O

LOVE AND STRIFE

EMPEDOCLES

I SHALL tell thee a twofold tale. At one time it grew to be one only out of many; at another, it divided up to be many instead of one. There is a double becoming of perishable things and a double passing away. The coming together of all things brings one generation into being and destroys it; the other grows up and is scattered as things become divided. And these things never cease continually changing places, at one time all uniting in one through Love, at another each borne in different directions by the repulsion of Strife. Thus, as far as it is their nature to grow into one out of many, and to become many once more when the one is parted asunder, so far they come into being and their life abides not. But, inasmuch as they never cease changing their places continually, so far they are ever immovable as they go round the circle of existence.

. . . .

But come, hearken to my words, for it is learning that increaseth wisdom. As I said before, when I declared the heads of my discourse, I shall tell thee a twofold tale. At one time it grew together to be one only out of many, at another it parted asunder so as to be many instead of one;—Fire and Water and Earth and the mighty height of Air; dread Strife, too, apart from these, of equal weight to each, and Love in their midst, equal in length and breadth. Her do thou contemplate with thy mind, nor sit with dazed eyes. It is she that is known as being implanted in the frame of mortals. It is she that makes them have thoughts of love and work the works of peace. They call her by the names of Joy and Aphrodite. Her has no mortal yet marked moving round among them, but do thou attend to the undeceitful ordering of my discourse.

For all these are equal and alike in age, yet each has a different prerogative and its own peculiar nature, but they gain the upper hand in turn when the time comes round. And nothing comes into being besides these, nor do they pass away; for, if they had been passing away continually, they would not be now, and what could increase this All and whence could it come? How, too, could it perish, since no place is empty of these things? There are these alone; but, running through one another, they become now this, now that, and like things evermore.

This (the contest of Love and Strife) is manifest in the mass of mortal limbs. At one time all the limbs that are the body's portion are brought together by Love in blooming life's high season; at another, severed by cruel Strife, they wander each alone by the breakers of life's sea. It is the same with plants and the fish that make their homes in the waters, with the beasts that have their lairs on the hills and the seabirds that sail on wings.

Come now, look at the things that bear witness to my earlier discourse, if so be that there was any shortcoming as to their form in the earlier list. Behold the sun, everywhere bright and warm, and all the immortal things that are bathed in heat and bright radiance. Behold the rain, everywhere dark and cold; and from the earth issue forth things close-pressed and solid. When they are in strife all these are different in form and separated; but they come together in love, and are desired by one another.

For out of these have sprung all things that were and are and shall be—trees and men and women, beasts and birds and the fishes that dwell in the waters, yea, and the gods that live long lives and are exalted in honour.

For there are these alone; but, running through one another, they take different shapes—so much does mixture change them.

For all of these—sun, earth, sky, and sea—are at one with all their parts that are cast far and wide from them in mortal things. And even so all things that are more adapted for mixture are like to one another and united in love by Aphrodite. Those things, again, that differ most in origin, mixture and the forms imprinted on each, are most hostile, being altogether unaccustomed to unite and very sorry by the bidding of Strife, since it hath wrought their birth.

Just as when painters are elaborating temple-offerings, men whom wisdom hath well taught their art—they, when they have taken pigments of many colours with their hands, mix them in due proportion, more of some and less of others, and from them produce shapes like unto all things, making trees and men and women, beasts and birds and fishes that dwell in the waters, yea, and gods, that live long lives, and are exalted in honour—so let not the error prevail over thy mind, that there is any other source of all the perishable creatures that appear in countless numbers. Know this for sure, for thou hast heard the tale from a goddess.

Translated 1892 by John Burnet.

○

GOD AND THE WORLD

○

TIMAEUS

PLATO

Persons of the Dialogue

SOCRATES   CRITIAS
TIMAEUS   HERMOCRATES

SOCRATES. One, two, three; but where, my dear Timaeus, is the fourth of those who were yesterday my guests and are to be my entertainers today?

TIMAEUS. He has been taken ill, Socrates; for he would not willingly have been absent from this gathering.

Soc. Then, if he is not coming, you and the two others must supply his place.

TIM. Certainly, and we will do all that we can; having been handsomely entertained by you yesterday, those of us who remain should be only too glad to return your hospitality.

Soc. Do you remember what were the points of which I required you to speak?

TIM. We remember some of them, and you will be here to remind us of anything which we have forgotten: or

rather, if we are not troubling you, will you briefly reca-
pitulate the whole, and then the particulars will be more
firmly fixed in our memories?

Soc. To be sure I will: the chief theme of my yesterday's discourse was the State—how constituted and of
what citizens composed it would seem likely to be most
perfect.

Tim. Yes, Socrates; and what you said of it was very
much to our mind.

Soc. Did we not begin by separating the husbandmen
and the artisans from the class of defenders of the State?

Tim. Yes.

Soc. And when we had given to each one that single
employment and particular art which was suited to his
nature, we spoke of those who were intended to be our
warriors, and said that they were to be guardians of the
city against attacks from within as well as from without,
and to have no other employment; they were to be merciful in judging their subjects, of whom they were by
nature friends, but fierce to their enemies, when they
came across them in battle.

Tim. Exactly.

Soc. We said, if I am not mistaken, that the guardians
should be gifted with a temperament in a high degree
both passionate and philosophical; and that then they
would be as they ought to be, gentle to their friends and
fierce with their enemies.

Tim. Certainly.

Soc. And what did we say of their education? Were they
not to be trained in gymnastic, and music, and all other
sorts of knowledge which were proper for them?

Tim. Very true.

Soc. And being thus trained they were not to consider
gold or silver or anything else to be their own private
property; they were to be like hired troops, receiving pay

for keeping guard from those who were protected by them—the pay was to be no more than would suffice for men of simple life; and they were to spend in common, and to live together in the continual practice of virtue, which was to be their sole pursuit.

TIM. That was also said.

SOC. Neither did we forget the women; of whom we declared, that their natures should be assimilated and brought into harmony with those of the men, and that common pursuits should be assigned to them both in time of war and in their ordinary life.

TIM. That, again, was as you say.

SOC. And what about the procreation of children? Or rather was not the proposal too singular to be forgotten? for all wives and children were to be in common, to the intent that no one should ever know his own child, but they were to imagine that they were all one family; those who were within a suitable limit of age were to be brothers and sisters, those who were of an elder generation, parents and grandparents, and those of a younger, children and grandchildren.

TIM. Yes, and the proposal is easy to remember, as you say.

SOC. And do you also remember how, with a view of securing as far as we could the best breed, we said that the chief magistrates, male and female, should contrive secretly, by the use of certain lots, so to arrange the nuptial meeting, that the bad of either sex and the good of either sex might pair with their like; and there was to be no quarrelling on this account, for they would imagine that the union was a mere accident, and was to be attributed to the lot?

TIM. I remember.

SOC. And you remember how we said that the children of the good parents were to be educated, and the chil-

dren of the bad secretly dispersed among the inferior
citizens; and while they were all growing up the rulers
were to be on the look-out, and to bring up from below
in their turn those who were worthy, and those among
themselves who were unworthy were to take the places
of those who came up?

TIM. True.

SOC. Then have I now given you all the heads of our
yesterday's discussion? Or is there anything more, my
dear Timaeus, which has been omitted?

TIM. Nothing, Socrates; it was just as you have said.

SOC. I should like, before proceeding further, to tell you
how I feel about the State which we have described. I
might compare myself to a person who, on beholding
beautiful animals either created by the painter's art, or,
better still, alive but at rest, is seized with a desire of
seeing them in motion or engaged in some struggle or
conflict to which their forms appear suited; this is my
feeling about the State which we have been describing.
There are conflicts which all cities undergo, and I should
like to hear some one tell of our own city carrying on a
struggle against her neighbours, and how she went out
to war in a becoming manner, and when at war showed
by the greatness of her actions and the magnanimity of
her words in dealing with other cities a result worthy of
her training and education. Now I, Critias and Hermocrates, am conscious that I myself should never be able
to celebrate the city and her citizens in a befitting manner, and I am not surprised at my own incapacity; to me
the wonder is rather that the poets present as well as
past are no better—not that I mean to depreciate them;
but every one can see that they are a tribe of imitators,
and will imitate best and most easily the life in which
they have been brought up; while that which is beyond
the range of a man's education he finds hard to carry out

in action, and still harder adequately to represent in language. I am aware that the Sophists have plenty of brave words and fair conceits, but I am afraid that being only wanderers from one city to another, and having never had habitations of their own, they may fail in their conception of philosophers and statesmen, and may not know what they do and say in time of war, when they are fighting or holding parley with their enemies. And thus people of your class are the only ones remaining who are fitted by nature and education to take part at once both in politics and philosophy. Here is Timaeus, of Locris in Italy, a city which has admirable laws, and who is himself in wealth and rank the equal of any of his fellow-citizens; he has held the most important and honourable offices in his own state, and, as I believe, has scaled the heights of all philosophy; and here is Critias, whom every Athenian knows to be no novice in the matters of which we are speaking; and as to Hermocrates, I am assured by many witnesses that his genius and education qualify him to take part in any speculation of the kind. And therefore yesterday when I saw that you wanted me to describe the formation of the State, I readily assented, being very well aware, that, if you only would, none were better qualified to carry the discussion further, and that when you had engaged our city in a suitable war, you of all men living could best exhibit her playing a fitting part. When I had completed my task, I in return imposed this other task upon you. You conferred together and agreed to entertain me today, as I had entertained you, with a feast of discourse. Here am I in festive array, and no man can be more ready for the promised banquet.

HER. And we too, Socrates, as Timaeus says, will not be wanting in enthusiasm; and there is no excuse for not complying with your request. As soon as we arrived yesterday at the guest-chamber of Critias, with whom we are staying, or rather on our way thither, we talked the matter over, and he told us an ancient tradition, which I wish, Critias, that you would repeat to Socrates, so that he may help us to judge whether it will satisfy his requirements or not.

CRIT. I will, if Timaeus, who is our other partner, approves.

TIM. I quite approve.

CRIT. Then listen, Socrates, to a tale which, though strange, is certainly true, having been attested by Solon, who was the wisest of the seven sages. He was a relative and a dear friend of my great-grandfather, Dropides, as he himself says in many passages of his poems; and he told the story to Critias, my grandfather, who remembered and repeated it to us. There were of old, he said, great and marvellous actions of the Athenian city, which have passed into oblivion through lapse of time and the destruction of mankind, and one in particular, greater than all the rest. This we will now rehearse. It will be a fitting monument of our gratitude to you, and a hymn of praise true and worthy of the goddess, on this her day of festival.

SOC. Very good. And what is this ancient famous action of the Athenians, which Critias declared, on the authority of Solon, to be not a mere legend, but an actual fact?

CRIT. I will tell an old-world story which I heard from an aged man; for Critias, at the time of telling it, was as he said, nearly ninety years of age, and I was about ten. Now the day was that day of the Apaturia which is called the Registration of Youth, at which, according to custom, our parents gave prizes for recitations, and the poems of several poets were recited by us boys, and many of us sang the poems of Solon, which at that time had not gone out of fashion. One of our tribe, either be-

cause he thought so or to please Critias, said that in his
judgment Solon was not only the wisest of men, but also
the noblest of poets. The old man, as I very well remember, brightened up at hearing this and said, smiling: Yes,
Amynander, if Solon had only, like other poets, made
poetry the business of his life, and had completed the
tale which he brought with him from Egypt, and had not
been compelled, by reason of the factions and troubles
which he found stirring in his own country when he
came home, to attend to other matters, in my opinion he
would have been as famous as Homer or Hesiod, or any
poet.

And what was the tale about, Critias? said Amynander.

About the greatest action which the Athenians ever
did, and which ought to have been the most famous, but,
through the lapse of time and the destruction of the actors, it has not come down to us.

Tell us, said the other, the whole story, and how and
from whom Solon heard this veritable tradition.

He replied:—In the Egyptian Delta, at the head of
which the river Nile divides, there is a certain district
which is called the district of Sais, and the great city of
the district is also called Sais, and is the city from which
King Amasis came. The citizens have a deity for their
foundress; she is called in the Egyptian tongue Neith,
and is asserted by them to be the same whom the Hellenes call Athene; they are great lovers of the Athenians,
and say that they are in some way related to them. To
this city came Solon, and was received there with great
honour; he asked the priests who were most skilful in
such matters, about antiquity, and made the dis-
covery that neither he nor any other Hellene knew anything worth mentioning about the times of old. On one
occasion, wishing to draw them on to speak of antiquity,

he began to tell about the most ancient things in our part
of the world—about Phoroneus, who is called "the first
man," and about Niobe; and after the Deluge, of the
survival of Deucalion and Pyrrha; and he traced the genealogy of their descendants, and reckoning up the dates,
tried to compute how many years ago the events of
which he was speaking happened. Thereupon one of
the priests, who was of a very great age, said: O Solon,
Solon, you Hellenes are never anything but children, and
there is not an old man among you. Solon in return asked
him what he meant. I mean to say, he replied, that in
mind you are all young; there is no old opinion handed
down among you by ancient tradition, nor any science
which is hoary with age. And I will tell you why. There
have been, and will be again, many destructions of mankind arising out of many causes; the greatest have been
brought about by the agencies of fire and water, and
other lesser ones by innumerable other causes. There is
a story, which even you have preserved, that once upon
a time Phaëthon, the son of Helios, having yoked the
steeds in his father's chariot, because he was not able to
drive them in the path of his father, burnt up all that
was upon the earth, and was himself destroyed by a
thunderbolt. Now this has the form of a myth, but really
signifies a declination of the bodies moving in the
heavens around the earth, and a great conflagration of
things upon the earth, which recurs after long intervals;
at such times those who live upon the mountains and in
dry and lofty places are more liable to destruction than
those who dwell by rivers or on the seashore. And from
this calamity the Nile, who is our never-failing saviour,
delivers and preserves us. When, on the other hand, the
gods purge the earth with a deluge of water, the survivors in your country are herdsmen and shepherds who
dwell on the mountains, but those who, like you, live

in cities are carried by the rivers into the sea. Whereas
in this land, neither then nor at any other time, does the
water come down from above on the fields, having always a tendency to come up from below; for which reason the traditions preserved here are the most ancient.
The fact is, that wherever the extremity of winter frost
or of summer sun does not prevent, mankind exist, sometimes in greater, sometimes in lesser numbers. And whatever happened either in your country or in ours, or in any
other region of which we are informed—if there were
any actions noble or great or in any other way remarkable, they have all been written down by us of old, and
are preserved in our temples. Whereas just when you
and other nations are beginning to be provided with
letters and the other requisites of civilized life, after the
usual interval, the stream from heaven, like a pestilence,
comes pouring down, and leaves only those of you who
are destitute of letters and education; and so you have
to begin all over again like children, and know nothing
of what happened in ancient times, either among us or
among yourselves. As for those genealogies of yours
which you just now recounted to us, Solon, they are no
better than the tales of children. In the first place you remember a single deluge only, but there were many previous ones; in the next place, you do not know that there
formerly dwelt in your land the fairest and noblest race
of men which ever lived, and that you and your whole
city are descended from a small seed or remnant of them
which survived. And this was unknown to you, because,
for many generations, the survivors of that destruction
died, leaving no written word. For there was a time,
Solon, before the great deluge of all, when the city
which now is Athens was first in war and in every way
the best governed of all cities, and is said to have performed the noblest deeds and to have had the fairest

constitution of any of which tradition tells, under the face of heaven. Solon marvelled at his words, and earnestly requested the priests to inform him exactly and in order about these former citizens. You are welcome to hear about them, Solon, said the priest, both for your own sake and for that of your city, and above all, for the sake of the goddess who is the common patron and parent and educator of both our cities. She founded your city a thousand years before ours, receiving from the Earth and Hephaestus the seed of your race, and afterwards she founded ours, of which the constitution is recorded in our sacred registers to be 8000 years old. As touching your citizens of 9000 years ago, I will briefly inform you of their laws and of their most famous action; the exact particulars of the whole we will hereafter go through at our leisure in the sacred registers themselves. If you compare these very laws with ours you will find that many of ours are the counterpart of yours as they were in the olden time. In the first place, there is the caste of priests, which is separated from all the others; next, there are the artificers, who ply their several crafts by themselves and do not intermix; and also there is the class of shepherds and of hunters, as well as that of husbandmen; and you will observe, too, that the warriors in Egypt are distinct from all the other classes, and are commanded by the law to devote themselves solely to military pursuits; moreover, the weapons which they carry are shields and spears, a style of equipment which the goddess taught of Asiatics first to us, as in your part of the world first to you. Then as to wisdom, do you observe how our law from the very first made a study of the whole order of things, extending even to prophecy and medicine which gives health, out of these divine elements deriving what was needful for human life, and adding every sort of knowledge which was akin to them.

All this order and arrangement the goddess first imparted to you when establishing your city; and she chose the spot of earth in which you were born, because she saw that the happy temperament of the seasons in that land would produce the wisest of men. Wherefore the goddess, who was a lover both of war and of wisdom, selected and first of all settled that spot which was the most likely to produce men likest herself. And there you dwelt, having such laws as these and still better ones, and excelled all mankind in all virtue, as became the children and disciples of the gods.

Many great and wonderful deeds are recorded of your state in our histories. But one of them exceeds all the rest in greatness and valour. For these histories tell of a mighty power which unprovoked made an expedition against the whole of Europe and Asia, and to which your city put an end. This power came forth out of the Atlantic Ocean, for in those days the Atlantic was navigable; and there was an island situated in front of the straits which are by you called the pillars of Heracles; the island was larger than Libya and Asia put together, and was the way to other islands, and from these you might pass to the whole of the opposite continent which surrounded the true ocean; for this sea which is within the Straits of Heracles is only a harbour, having a narrow entrance, but that other is a real sea, and the surrounding land may be most truly called a boundless continent. Now in this island of Atlantis there was a great and wonderful empire which had rule over the whole island and several others, and over parts of the continent, and, furthermore, the men of Atlantis had subjected the parts of Libya within the columns of Heracles as far as Egypt, and of Europe as far as Tyrrhenia. This vast power, gathered into one, endeavoured to subdue at a blow our country and yours and the whole of the region within the straits; and then, Solon, your country shone forth, in the excellence of her virtue and strength, among all mankind. She was pre-eminent in courage and military skill, and was the leader of the Hellenes. And when the rest fell off from her, being compelled to stand alone, after having undergone the very extremity of danger, she defeated and triumphed over the invaders, and preserved from slavery those who were not yet subjugated, and generously liberated all the rest of us who dwell within the pillars. But afterwards there occurred violent earthquakes and floods; and in a single day and night of misfortune all your warlike men in a body sank into the earth, and the island of Atlantis in like manner disappeared in the depths of the sea. For which reason the sea in those parts is impassable and impenetrable, because there is a shoal of mud in the way; and this was caused by the subsidence of the island.

I have told you briefly, Socrates, what the aged Critias heard from Solon and related to us. And when you were speaking yesterday about your city and citizens, the tale which I have just been repeating to you came into my mind, and I remarked with astonishment how, by some mysterious coincidence, you agreed in almost every particular with the narrative of Solon; but I did not like to speak at the moment. For a long time had elapsed, and I had forgotten too much; I thought that I must first of all run over the narrative in my own mind, and then I would speak. And so I readily assented to your request yesterday, considering that in all such cases the chief difficulty is to find a tale suitable to our purpose, and that with such a tale we should be fairly well provided.

And therefore, as Hermocrates has told you, on my way home yesterday I at once communicated the tale to my companions as I remembered it; and after I left them, during the night by thinking I recovered nearly the whole of it. Truly, as is often said, the lessons of our childhood make a wonderful impression on our memories; for I am not sure that I could remember all the discourse of yesterday, but I should be much surprised if I forgot any of these things which I have heard very long ago. I listened at the time with childlike interest to the old man's narrative; he was very ready to teach me, and I asked him again and again to repeat his words, so that like an indelible picture they were branded into my mind. As soon as the day broke, I rehearsed them as he spoke them to my companions, that they, as well as myself, might have something to say. And now, Socrates, to make an end of my preface, I am ready to tell you the whole tale. I will give you not only the general heads, but the particulars, as they were told to me. The city and citizens, which you yesterday described to us in fiction, we will now transfer to the world of reality. It shall be the ancient city of Athens, and we will suppose that the citizens whom you imagined, were our veritable ancestors, of whom the priest spoke; they will perfectly harmonize, and there will be no inconsistency in saying that the citizens of your republic are these ancient Athenians. Let us divide the subject among us, and all endeavour according to our ability gracefully to execute the task which you have imposed upon us. Consider then, Socrates, if this narrative is suited to the purpose, or whether we should seek for some other instead.

Soc. And what other, Critias, can we find that will be better than this, which is natural and suitable to the festival of the goddess, and has the very great advantage of being a fact and not a fiction? How or where shall we find another if we abandon this? We cannot, and therefore you must tell the tale, and good luck to you; and I in return for my yesterday's discourse will now rest and be a listener.

CRIT. Let me proceed to explain to you, Socrates, the order in which we have arranged our entertainment. Our intention is, that Timaeus, who is the most of an astronomer amongst us, and has made the nature of the universe his special study, should speak first, beginning with the generation of the world and going down to the creation of man; next, I am to receive the men whom he has created of whom some will have profited by the excellent education which you have given them; and then, in accordance with the tale of Solon, and equally with his law, we will bring them into court and make them citizens, as if they were those very Athenians whom the sacred Egyptian record has recovered from oblivion, and thenceforward we will speak of them as Athenians and fellow-citizens.

SOC. I see that I shall receive in my turn a perfect and splendid feast of reason. And now, Timaeus, you, I suppose, should speak next, after duly calling upon the Gods.

TIM. All men, Socrates, who have any degree of right feeling, at the beginning of every enterprise, whether small or great, always call upon God. And we, too, who are going to discourse of the nature of the universe, how created or how existing without creation, if we be not altogether out of our wits, must invoke the aid of Gods and Goddesses and pray that our words may be acceptable to them and consistent with themselves. Let this, then, be our invocation of the Gods, to which I add an exhortation of myself to speak in such manner as will be most intelligible to you, and will most accord with my own intent.

First then, in my judgment, we must make a distinction and ask, What is that which always is and has no becoming; and what is that which is always becoming and never is? That which is apprehended by intelligence and reason is always in the same state; but that which is conceived by opinion with the help of sensation and without reason, is always in a process of becoming and perishing and never really is. Now everything that becomes or is created must of necessity be created by some cause, for without a cause nothing can be created. The work of the creator, whenever he looks to the unchangeable and fashions the form and nature of his work after an unchangeable pattern, must necessarily be made fair and perfect; but when he looks to the created only, and uses a created pattern, it is not fair or perfect. Was the heaven then or the world, whether called by this or by any other more appropriate name—assuming the name, I am asking a question which has to be asked at the beginning of an enquiry about anything—was the world, I say, always in existence and without beginning? or created, and had it a beginning? Created, I reply, being visible and tangible and having a body, and therefore sensible; and all sensible things are apprehended by opinion and sense and are in a process of creation and created. Now that which is created must, as we affirm, of necessity be created by a cause. But the father and maker of all this universe is past finding out; and even if we found him, to tell of him to all men would be impossible. And there is still a question to be asked about him: Which of the patterns had the artificer in view when he made the world—the pattern of the unchangeable, or of that which is created? If the world be indeed fair and the artificer good, it is manifest that he must have looked to that which is eternal; but if what cannot be said without blasphemy is true, then to the created pattern. Every one will see that he must have looked to the eternal; for the world is the fairest of creations and he is the best of causes. And having been created in this way, the world has been framed in the likeness of that which is apprehended by reason and mind and is unchangeable, and must therefore of necessity, if this is admitted, be a copy of something. Now it is all-important that the beginning of everything should be according to nature. And in speaking of the copy and the original we may assume that words are akin to the matter which they describe; when they relate to the lasting and permanent and intelligible, they ought to be lasting and unalterable, and, as far as their nature allows, irrefutable and immovable—nothing less. But when they express only the copy or likeness and not the eternal things themselves, they need only be likely and analogous to the real words. As being is to becoming, so is truth to belief. If then, Socrates, amid the many opinions about the gods and the generation of the universe, we are not able to give notions which are altogether and in every respect exact and consistent with one another, do not be surprised. Enough, if we adduce probabilities as likely as any others; for we must remember that I who am the speaker, and you who are the judges, are only mortal men, and we ought to accept the tale which is probable and enquire no further.

Soc. Excellent, Timaeus; and we will do precisely as you bid us. The prelude is charming, and is already accepted by us—may we beg of you to proceed to the strain?

Tim. Let me tell you then why the creator made this world of generation. He was good, and the good can never have any jealousy of anything. And being free from jealousy, he desired that all things should be as like himself as they could be. This is in the truest sense the origin of creation and of the world, as we shall do well in believing on the testimony of wise men: God desired that all things should be good and nothing bad, so far as this was attainable. Wherefore also finding the whole visible sphere not at rest, but moving in an irregular and disorderly fashion, out of disorder he brought order, considering that this was in every way better than the other. Now the deeds of the best could never be or have been other than the fairest; and the creator, reflecting on the things which are by nature visible, found that no unintelligent creature taken as a whole was fairer than the intelligent taken as a whole; and that intelligence could not be present in anything which was devoid of soul. For which reason, when he was framing the universe, he put intelligence in soul, and soul in body, that he might be the creator of a work which was by nature fairest and best. Wherefore, using the language of probability, we may say that the world became a living creature truly endowed with soul and intelligence by the providence of God.

This being supposed, let us proceed to the next stage: In the likeness of what animal did the Creator make the world? It would be an unworthy thing to liken it to any nature which exists as a part only; for nothing can be beautiful which is like any imperfect thing; but let us suppose the world to be the very image of that whole of which all other animals both individually and in their tribes are portions. For the original of the universe contains in itself all intelligible beings, just as this world comprehends us and all other visible creatures. For the Deity, intending to make this world like the fairest and most perfect of intelligible beings, framed one visible animal comprehending within itself all other animals of a kindred nature. Are we right in saying that there is one world, or that they are many and infinite? There must be one only, if the created copy is to accord with the original. For that which includes all other intelligible creatures cannot have a second or companion; in that case there would be need of another living being which would include both, and of which they would be parts, and the likeness would be more truly said to resemble not them, but that other which included them. In order then that the world might be solitary, like the perfect animal, the creator made not two worlds or an infinite number of them; but there is and ever will be one only-begotten and created heaven.

Now that which is created is of necessity corporeal, and also visible and tangible. And nothing is visible where there is no fire, or tangible which has no solidity, and nothing is solid without earth. Wherefore also God in the beginning of creation made the body of the universe to consist of fire and earth. But two things cannot be rightly put together without a third; there must be some bond of union between them. And the fairest bond is that which makes the most complete fusion of itself and the things which it combines; and proportion is best adapted to effect such a union. For whenever in any three numbers, whether cube or square, there is a mean, which is to the last term what the first term is to it; and again, when the mean is to the first term as the last term is to the mean—then the mean becoming first and last, and the first and last both becoming means, they will all of them of necessity come to be the same, and having become the same with one another will be all one. If the universal frame had been created a surface only and having no depth, a single mean would have sufficed to bind together itself and the other terms; but now, as the world must be solid, and solid bodies are always compacted not by one mean but by two, God placed water and air in the mean between fire and earth, and made them to have the same proportion so far as was possible (as fire is to air so is air to water, and as air is to water so is water to earth); and thus he bound and put together a visible and tangible heaven. And for these reasons, and out of such elements which are in number four, the body of the world was created, and it was harmonized by proportion, and therefore has the spirit of friendship; and having been reconciled to itself, it was indissoluble by the hand of any other than the framer.

Now the creation took up the whole of each of the four elements; for the Creator compounded the world out of all the fire and all the water and all the air and all the earth, leaving no part of any of them nor any power of them outside. His intention was, in the first place, that the animal should be as far as possible a perfect whole and of perfect parts: secondly, that it should be one, leaving no remnants out of which another such world might be created: and also that it should be free from old age and unaffected by disease. Considering that if heat and cold and other powerful forces which unite bodies surround and attack them from without when they are unprepared, they decompose them, and by bringing diseases and old age upon them, make them waste away—for this cause and on these grounds he made the world one whole, having every part entire, and being therefore perfect and not liable to old age and disease. And he gave to the world the figure which was suitable and also natural. Now to the animal which was to comprehend all animals, that figure was suitable which comprehends within itself all other figures. Wherefore he made the world in the form of a globe, round as from a lathe, having its extremes in every direction equidistant from the centre, the most perfect and the most like itself of all figures; for he considered that the like is infinitely fairer than the unlike. This he finished off, making the surface smooth all around for many reasons; in the first place, because the living being had no need of eyes when there was nothing remaining outside him to be seen; nor of ears when there was nothing to be heard; and there was no surrounding atmosphere to be breathed; nor would there have been any use of organs by the help of which he might receive his food or get rid of what he had already digested, since there was nothing which went from him or came into him: for there was nothing beside him. Of design he was created thus, his own waste providing his own food, and all that he did or suffered taking place in and by himself. For the Creator conceived that a being which was self-sufficient would be far more excellent than one which lacked anything; and, as he had no need to take anything or defend himself against any one, the Creator did not think it necessary to bestow upon him hands: nor had he any need of feet, nor of the whole apparatus of walking; but the movement suited to his spherical form was assigned to him, being of all the seven that which is most appropriate to mind and intelligence; and he was made to move in the same manner and on the same spot, within his own limits revolving in a circle. All the other six motions were taken away from him, and he was made not to partake of their deviations. And as this circular movement required no feet, the universe was created without legs and without feet.

Such was the whole plan of the eternal God about the god that was to be, to whom for this reason he gave a body, smooth and even, having a surface in every direction equidistant from the centre, a body entire and perfect, and formed out of perfect bodies. And in the centre he put the soul, which he diffused throughout the body, making it also to be the exterior environment of it; and he made the universe a circle moving in a circle, one and solitary, yet by reason of its excellence able to converse with itself, and needing no other friendship or acquaintance. Having these purposes in view he created the world a blessed god.

Now God did not make the soul after the body, al-

though we are speaking of them in this order; for having
brought them together he would never have allowed that
the elder should be ruled by the younger; but this is a
random manner of speaking which we have, because
somehow we ourselves too are very much under the
dominion of chance. Whereas he made the soul in origin
and excellence prior to and older than the body, to be
the ruler and mistress, of whom the body was to be the
subject. And he made her out of the following elements
and on this wise: Out of the indivisible and unchangeable, and also out of that which is divisible and has to
do with material bodies, he compounded a third and intermediate kind of essence, partaking of the nature of
the same and of the other, and this compound he placed
accordingly in a mean between the indivisible, and the
divisible and material. He took the three elements of the
same, the other, and the essence, and mingled them into
one form, compressing by force the reluctant and unsociable nature of the other into the same. When he had
mingled them with the essence and out of three made
one, he again divided this whole into as many portions
as was fitting, each portion being a compound of the
same, the other, and the essence. And he proceeded to
divide after this manner:—First of all, he took away one
part of the whole [1], and then he separated a second
part which was double the first [2], and then he took
away a third part which was half as much again as the
second and three times as much as the first [3], and then
he took a fourth part which was twice as much as the
second [4], and a fifth part which was three times the
third [9], and a sixth part which was eight times the first
[8], and a seventh part which was twenty-seven times
the first [27]. After this he filled up the double intervals [i. e. between 1, 2, 4, 8] and the triple [i. e. between
1, 3, 9, 27], cutting off yet other portions from the mix-

ture and placing them in the intervals, so that in each
interval there were two kinds of means, the one exceeding and exceeded by equal parts of its extremes [as for
example 1, $\frac{4}{3}$, 2, in which the mean $\frac{4}{3}$ is one-third of 1
more than 1, and one-third of 2 less than 2], the other
being that kind of mean which exceeds and is exceeded
by an equal number. Where there were intervals of $\frac{3}{2}$ and
of $\frac{4}{3}$ and of $\frac{9}{8}$, made by the connecting terms in the former
intervals, he filled up all the intervals of $\frac{4}{3}$ with the interval of $\frac{9}{8}$, leaving a fraction over; and the interval which
this fraction expressed was in the ratio of 256 to 243.
And thus the whole mixture out of which he cut these
portions was all exhausted by him. This entire compound
he divided lengthways into two parts, which he joined
to one another at the centre like the letter X, and bent
them into a circular form, connecting them with themselves and each other at the point opposite to their original meeting-point; and, comprehending them in a uniform revolution upon the same axis, he made the one
the outer and the other the inner circle. Now the motion
of the outer circle he called the motion of the same, and
the motion of the inner circle the motion of the other or
diverse. The motion of the same he carried round by the
side to the right, and the motion of the diverse di-
agonally to the left. And he gave dominion to the motion of the same and like, for that he left single and undivided; but the inner motion he divided in six places
and made seven unequal circles having their intervals
in ratios of two and three, three of each, and bade the
orbits proceed in a direction opposite to one another; and
three [Sun, Mercury, Venus] he made to move with
equal swiftness, and the remaining four [Moon, Saturn,
Mars, Jupiter] to move with unequal swiftness to the
three and to one another, but in due proportion.

Now when the Creator had framed the soul according to his will, he formed within her the corporeal universe, and brought the two together, and united them centre to centre. The soul, interfused everywhere from the centre to the circumference of heaven, of which also she is the external envelopment, herself turning in herself, began a divine beginning of never-ceasing and rational life enduring throughout all time. The body of heaven is visible, but the soul is invisible, and partakes of reason and harmony, and being made by the best of intellectual and everlasting natures, is the best of things created. And because she is composed of the same and of the other and of the essence, these three, and is divided and united in due proportion, and in her revolutions returns upon herself, the soul, when touching anything which has essence, whether dispersed in parts or undivided, is stirred through all her powers, to declare the sameness or difference of that thing and some other; and to what individuals are related, and by what affected, and in what way and how and when, both in the world of generation and in the world of immutable being. And when reason, which works with equal truth, whether she be in the circle of the diverse or of the same—in voiceless silence holding her onward course in the sphere of the self-moved —when reason, I say, is hovering around the sensible world and when the circle of the diverse also moving truly imparts the intimations of sense to the whole soul, then arise opinions and beliefs sure and certain. But when reason is concerned with the rational, and the circle of the same moving smoothly declares it, then intelligence and knowledge are necessarily perfected. And if any one affirms that in which these two are found to be other than the soul, he will say the very opposite of the truth.

When the father and creator saw the creature which he had made moving and living, the created image of the eternal gods, he rejoiced, and in his joy determined to make the copy still more like the original; and as this was eternal, he sought to make the universe eternal, so far as might be. Now the nature of the ideal being was everlasting, but to bestow this attribute in its fulness upon a creature was impossible. Wherefore he resolved to have a moving image of eternity, and when he set in order the heaven, he made this image eternal but moving according to number, while eternity itself rests in unity; and this image we call time. For there were no days and nights and months and years before the heaven was created, but when he constructed the heaven he created them also. They are all parts of time, and the past and future are created species of time, which we unconsciously but wrongly transfer to the eternal essence; for we say that he "was," he "is," he "will be," but the truth is that "is" alone is properly attributed to him, and that "was" and "will be" are only to be spoken of becoming in time, for they are motions, but that which is immovably the same cannot become older or younger by time, nor ever did or has become, or hereafter will be, older or younger, nor is subject at all to any of those states which affect moving and sensible things and of which generation is the cause. These are the forms of time, which imitates eternity and revolves according to a law of number. Moreover, when we say that what has become *is* become and what becomes *is* becoming, and that what will become *is* about to become and that the non-existent *is* non-existent—all these are inaccurate modes of expression. But perhaps this whole subject will be more suitably discussed on some other occasion.

Time, then, and the heaven came into being at the same instant in order that, having been created together, if ever there was to be a dissolution of them, they might be dissolved together. It was framed after the pattern of the eternal nature, that it might resemble this as far as was possible; for the pattern exists from eternity, and the created heaven has been, and is, and will be, in all time. Such was the mind and thought of God in the creation of time. The sun and moon and five other stars, which are called the planets, were created by him in order to distinguish and preserve the numbers of time; and when he had made their several bodies, he placed them in the orbits in which the circle of the other was revolving—in seven orbits seven stars. First, there was the moon in the orbit nearest the earth, and next the sun, in the second orbit above the earth; then came the morning star and the star sacred to Hermes, moving in orbits which have an equal swiftness with the sun, but in an opposite direction; and this is the reason why the sun and Hermes and Lucifer overtake and are overtaken by each other. To enumerate the places which he assigned to the other stars, and to give all the reasons why he assigned them, although a secondary matter, would give more trouble than the primary. These things at some future time, when we are at leisure, may have the consideration which they deserve, but not at present.

Now, when all the stars which were necessary to the creation of time had attained a motion suitable to them, and had become living creatures having bodies fastened by vital chains, and learnt their appointed task, moving in the motion of the diverse, which is diagonal, and passes through and is governed by the motion of the same, they revolved, some in a larger and some in a lesser orbit—those which had the lesser orbit revolving faster, and those which had the larger more slowly. Now by reason of the motion of the same, those which revolved fastest appeared to be overtaken by those which moved slower although they really overtook them; for the motion of the same made them all turn in a spiral,

and, because some went one way and some another, that
which receded most slowly from the sphere of the same,
which was the swiftest, appeared to follow it most
nearly. That there might be some visible measure of their
relative swiftness and slowness as they proceeded in
their eight courses, God lighted a fire, which we now call
the sun, in the second from the earth of these orbits, that
it might give light to the whole of heaven, and that the
animals, as many as nature intended, might participate
in number, learning arithmetic from the revolution of the
same and the like. Thus, then, and for this reason the
night and the day were created, being the period of
the one most intelligent revolution. And the month is accomplished when the moon has completed her orbit and
overtaken the sun, and the year when the sun has completed his own orbit. Mankind, with hardly an exception,
have not remarked the periods of the other stars, and
they have no name for them, and do not measure them
against one another by the help of number, and hence
they can scarcely be said to know that their wanderings,
being infinite in number and admirable for their variety,
make up time. And yet there is no difficulty in seeing
that the perfect number of time fufils the perfect year
when all the eight revolutions, having their relative degrees of swiftness, are accomplished together and attain
their completion at the same time, measured by the rotation of the same and equally moving. After this manner,
and for these reasons, came into being such of the stars
as in their heavenly progress received reversals of motion, to the end that the created heaven might imitate the
eternal nature, and be as like as possible to the perfect
and intelligible animals.

Thus far and until the birth of time the created universe was made in the likeness of the original, but inasmuch as all animals were not yet comprehended therein,

it was still unlike. What remained, the creator then proceeded to fashion after the nature of the pattern. Now as in the ideal animal the mind perceives ideas or species of a certain nature and number, he thought that this created animal ought to have species of a like nature and number. There are four such; one of them is the heavenly race of the gods; another, the race of birds whose way is in the air; the third, the watery species; and the fourth, the pedestrian and land creatures. Of the heavenly and divine, he created the greater part out of fire, that they might be the brightest of all things and fairest to behold, and he fashioned them after the likeness of the universe in the figure of a circle, and made them follow the intelligent motion of the supreme, distributing them over the whole circumference of heaven, which was to be a true cosmos or glorious world spangled with them all over. And he gave to each of them two movements: the first, a movement on the same spot after the same manner, whereby they ever continue to think consistently the same thoughts about the same things; the second, a forward movement, in which they are controlled by the revolution of the same and the like; but by the other five motions they were unaffected, in order that each of them might attain the highest perfection. And for this reason the fixed stars were created, to be divine and eternal animals, ever-abiding and revolving after the same manner and on the same spot; and the other stars which reverse their motion and are subject to deviations of this kind, were created in the manner already described. The earth, which is our nurse, clinging around the pole which is extended through the universe, he framed to be the guardian and artificer of night and day, first and eldest of gods that are in the interior of heaven. Vain would be the attempt to tell all the figures of them circling as in dance, and their juxtapositions, and the return of them in their revolutions upon themselves, and their approximations, and to say which of these deities in their conjunctions meet, and which of them are in opposition, and in what order they get behind and before one another, and when they are severally eclipsed to our sight and again reappear, sending terrors and intimations of the future to those who cannot calculate their movements—to attempt to tell of all this without a visible representation of the heavenly system would be labour in vain. Enough on this head; and now let what we have said about the nature of the created and visible gods have an end.

To know or tell the origin of the other divinities is beyond us, and we must accept the traditions of the men of old time who affirm themselves to be the offspring of the gods—that is what they say—and they must surely have known their own ancestors. How can we doubt the word of the children of the gods? Although they give no probable or certain proofs, still, as they declare that they are speaking of what took place in their own family, we must conform to custom and believe them. In this manner, then, according to them, the genealogy of these gods is to be received and set forth.

Oceanus and Tethys were the children of Earth and Heaven, and from these sprang Phorcys and Cronos and Rhea, and all that generation; and from Cronos and Rhea sprang Zeus and Herè, and all those who are said to be their brethren, and others who were the children of these.

Now, when all of them, both those who visibly appear in their revolutions as well as those other gods who are of a more retiring nature, had come into being, the creator of the universe addressed them in these words: "Gods, children of gods, who are my works, and of whom I am the artificer and father, my creations are indissoluble, if so I will. All that is bound may be undone, but only an evil being would wish to undo that which is harmonious and happy. Wherefore, since ye are but creatures, ye are not altogether immortal and indissoluble, but ye shall certainly not be dissolved, nor be liable to the fate of death, having in my will a greater and mightier bond than those with which ye were bound at the time of your birth. And now listen to my instructions: —Three tribes of mortal beings remain to be created— without them the universe will be incomplete, for it will not contain every kind of animal which it ought to contain, if it is to be perfect. On the other hand, if they were created by me and received life at my hands, they would be on an equality with the gods. In order then that they may be mortal, and that this universe may be truly universal, do ye, according to your natures, betake yourselves to the formation of animals, imitating the power which was shown by me in creating you. The part of them worthy of the name immortal, which is called divine and is the guiding principle of those who are willing to follow justice and you—of that divine part I will myself sow the seed, and having made a beginning, I will hand the work over to you. And do ye then interweave the mortal with the immortal, and make and beget living creatures, and give them food, and make them to grow, and receive them again in death."

Thus he spake, and once more into the cup in which he had previously mingled the soul of the universe he poured the remains of the elements, and mingled them in much the same manner; they were not, however, pure as before, but diluted to the second and third degree. And having made it he divided the whole mixture into souls equal in number to the stars, and assigned each soul to a star; and having there placed them as in a chariot, he showed them the nature of the universe, and declared to them the laws of destiny, according to which their first birth would be one and the same for all—no one should suffer a disadvantage at his hands; they were to be sown in the instruments of time severally adapted to them, and to come forth the most religious of animals; and as human nature was of two kinds, the superior race would hereafter be called man. Now, when they should be implanted in bodies by necessity, and be always gaining or losing some part of their bodily substance, then in the first place it would be necessary that they should all have in them one and the same faculty of sensation, arising out of irresistible impressions; in the second place, they must have love, in which pleasure and pain mingle; also fear and anger, and the feelings which are akin or opposite to them; if they conquered these they would live righteously, and if they were conquered by them, unrighteously. He who lived well during his appointed time was to return and dwell in his native star, and there he would have a blessed and congenial existence. But if he failed in attaining this, at the second birth he would pass into a woman, and if, when in that state of being, he did not desist from evil, he would continually be changed into some brute who resembled him in the evil nature which he had acquired, and would not cease from his toils and transformations until he followed the revolution of the same and the like within him, and overcame by the help of reason the turbulent and irrational mob of later accretions, made up of fire and air and water and earth, and returned to the form of his first and better state. Having given all these laws to his creatures, that he might be guiltless of future evil in any of them, the creator sowed some of them in the earth, and some in the moon, and some in the other instruments of time; and when he had sown them he committed to the younger gods the fashioning of their mortal bodies, and desired them to furnish what was still lacking to the human soul, and having made all the suitable additions, to rule over them, and to pilot the mortal animal in the best and wisest manner which they could, and avert from him all but self-inflicted evils.

When the creator had made all these ordinances he remained in his own accustomed nature, and his children heard and were obedient to their father's word, and receiving from him the immortal principle of a mortal creature, in imitation of their own creator they borrowed portions of fire, and earth, and water, and air from the world, which were hereafter to be restored—these they took and welded them together, not with the indissoluble chains by which they were themselves bound, but with little pegs too small to be visible, making up out of all the four elements each separate body, and fastening the courses of the immortal soul in a body which was in a state of perpetual influx and efflux. Now these courses, detained as in a vast river, neither overcame nor were overcome; but were hurrying and hurried to and fro, so that the whole animal was moved and progressed, irregularly however and irrationally and anyhow, in all the six directions of motion, wandering backwards and forwards, and right and left, and up and down, and in all the six directions. For great as was the advancing and retiring flood which provided nourishment, the affections produced by external contact caused still greater tumult—when the body of any one met and came into collision with some external fire, or with the solid earth or the gliding waters, or was caught in the tempest borne on the air, and the motions produced by any of these impulses were carried through the body to the soul. All such motions have consequently received the general name of 'sensations,' which they still retain. And they did in fact at that time create a very great and mighty movement; uniting with the everflowing stream in stirring up and violently shaking the courses of the soul, they completely stopped the revolution of the same by their opposing current, and hindered it from predominating and advancing; and they so disturbed the nature of the other or diverse, that the three double intervals [i. e. between 1, 2, 4, 8], and the three triple intervals [i. e. between 1, 3, 9, 27], together with the mean terms and connecting links which are expressed by the ratios of 3 : 2, and 4 : 3, and of 9 : 8—these, although they cannot be wholly undone except by him who united them, were twisted by them in all sorts of ways, and the circles were broken and disordered in every possible manner, so that when they moved they were tumbling to pieces, and moved irrationally, at one time in a reverse direction, and then again obliquely, and then upside down, as you might imagine a person who is upside down and has his head leaning upon the ground and his feet up against something in the air; and when he is in such a position, both he and the spectator fancy that the right of either is his left, and left right. If, when powerfully experiencing these and similar effects, the revolutions of the soul come in contact with some external thing, either of the class of the same or of the other, they speak of the same or of the other in a manner the very opposite of the truth; and they become false and foolish, and there is no course or revolution in them which has a guiding or directing power; and if again any sensations enter in violently from without and drag after them the whole vessel of the soul, then the courses of the soul, though they seem to conquer, are really conquered.

And by reason of all these affections, the soul, when encased in a mortal body, now, as in the beginning, is at first without intelligence; but when the flood of growth and nutriment abates, and the courses of the soul, calming down, go their own way and become steadier as time goes on, then the several circles return to their natural form, and their revolutions are corrected, and they call the same and the other by their right names, and make the possessor of them to become a rational being. And if these combine in him with any true nurture or education, he attains the fulness and health of the perfect man, and escapes the worst disease of all; but if he neglects education he walks lame to the end of his life, and returns imperfect and good for nothing to the world below. This, however, is a later stage; at present we must treat more exactly the subject before us, which involves a preliminary enquiry into the generation of the body and its members, and as to how the soul was created—for what reason and by what providence of the gods; and holding fast to probability, we must pursue our way.

First, then, the gods, imitating the spherical shape of the universe, enclosed the two divine courses in a spherical body, that, namely, which we now term the head, being the most divine part of us and the lord of all that is in us: to this the gods, when they put together the body, gave all the other members to be servants, considering that it partook of every sort of motion. In order then that it might not tumble about among the high and deep places of the earth, but might be able to get over the one and out of the other, they provided the body to be its vehicle and means of locomotion; which consequently had length and was furnished with four limbs extended and flexible; these God contrived to be instruments of locomotion with which it might take hold and find support, and so be able to pass through all places, carrying on high the dwelling-place of the most sacred and divine part of us. Such was the origin of legs and hands, which for this reason were attached to every man; and the gods, deeming the front part of man to be more honourable and more fit to command than the hinder part, made us to move mostly in a forward direction. Wherefore man must needs have his front part unlike and distinguished from the rest of his body. And so in the vessel of the head, they first of all put a face in which they inserted organs to minister in all things to the providence of the soul, and they appointed this part, which has authority, to be by nature the part which is in front. And of the organs they first contrived the eyes to give light, and the principle according to which they were inserted was as follows: So much of fire as would not burn, but gave a gentle light, they formed into a substance akin to the light of every-day life; and the pure fire which is within us and related thereto they made to flow through the eyes in a stream smooth and dense, compressing the whole eye, and especially the centre part, so that it kept out everything of a coarser nature, and allowed to pass only this pure element. When the light of day surrounds the stream of vision, then like falls upon like, and they coalesce, and one body is formed by natural affinity in the line of vision, wherever the light that falls from within meets with an external object. And the whole stream of vision, being similarly affected in virtue of similarity, diffuses the motions of what it touches or what touches it over the whole body, until they reach the soul, causing that perception which we call sight. But when night comes on and the external and kindred fire departs, then the stream of vision is cut off; for going forth to an unlike element it is changed and extinguished, being no longer of one nature with the surrounding atmosphere which is now deprived of fire: and so the eye no longer sees, and we feel disposed to sleep. For when the eyelids,

which the gods invented for the preservation of sight,
are closed, they keep in the internal fire; and the power
of the fire diffuses and equalizes the inward motions;
when they are equalized, there is rest, and when the rest
is profound, sleep comes over us scarce disturbed by
dreams; but where the greater motions still remain, of
whatever nature and in whatever locality, they engender
corresponding visions in dreams, which are remembered
by us when we are awake and in the external world. And
now there is no longer any difficulty in understanding
the creation of images in mirrors and all smooth and
bright surfaces. For from the communion of the internal
and external fires, and again from the union of them and
their numerous transformations when they meet in the
mirror, all these appearances of necessity arise, when
the fire from the face coalesces with the fire from the
eye on the bright and smooth surface. And right appears left and left right, because the visual rays come
into contact with the rays emitted by the object in a
manner contrary to the usual mode of meeting; but the
right appears right, and the left left, when the position
of one of the two concurring lights is reversed; and this
happens when the mirror is concave and its smooth surface repels the right stream of vision to the left side,
and the left to the right.[1] Or if the mirror be turned
vertically, then the concavity makes the countenance appear to be all upside down, and the lower rays are driven
upwards and the upper downwards.

All these are to be reckoned among the second and
co-operative causes which God, carrying into execution
the idea of the best as far as possible, uses as his ministers. They are thought by most men not to be the sec-

---

[1] *He is speaking of two kinds of mirrors, first the plane, secondly
the concave; and the latter is supposed to be placed, first horizontally,
and then vertically.*

ond, but the prime causes of all things, because they freeze and heat, and contract and dilate, and the like. But they are not so, for they are incapable of reason or intellect; the only being which can properly have mind is the invisible soul, whereas fire and water, and earth and air, are all of them visible bodies. The lover of intellect and knowledge ought to explore causes of intelligent nature first of all, and, secondly, of those things which, being moved by others, are compelled to move others. And this is what we too must do. Both kinds of causes should be acknowledged by us, but a distinction should be made between those which are endowed with mind and are the workers of things fair and good, and those which are deprived of intelligence and always produce chance effects without order or design. Of the second or co-operative causes of sight, which help to give to the eyes the power which they now possess, enough has been said. I will therefore now proceed to speak of the higher use and purpose for which God has given them to us. The sight in my opinion is the source of the greatest benefit to us, for had we never seen the stars, and the sun, and the heaven, none of the words which we have spoken about the universe would ever have been uttered. But now the sight of day and night, and the months and the revolutions of the years, have created number, and have given us a conception of time, and the power of enquiring about the nature of the universe; and from this source we have derived philosophy, than which no greater good ever was or will be given by the gods to mortal man. This is the greatest boon of sight: and of the lesser benefits why should I speak? even the ordinary man if he were deprived of them would bewail his loss, but in vain. Thus much let me say however: God invented and gave us sight to the end that we might behold the courses of intelligence in the heaven, and apply them to the courses of our own intelligence which are akin to them, the unperturbed to the perturbed; and that we, learning them and partaking of the natural truth of reason, might imitate the absolutely unerring courses of God and regulate our own vagaries. The same may be affirmed of speech and hearing: they have been given by the gods to the same end and for a like reason. For this is the principal end of speech, whereto it most contributes. Moreover, so much of music as is adapted to the sound of the voice and to the sense of hearing is granted to us for the sake of harmony; and harmony, which has motions akin to the revolutions of our souls, is not regarded by the intelligent votary of the Muses as given by them with a view to irrational pleasure, which is deemed to be the purpose of it in our day, but as meant to correct any discord which may have arisen in the courses of the soul, and to be our ally in bringing her into harmony and agreement with herself; and rhythm too was given by them for the same reason, on account of the irregular and graceless ways which prevail among mankind generally, and to help us against them.

Thus far in what we have been saying, with small exception, the works of intelligence have been set forth; and now we must place by the side of them in our discourse the things which come into being through necessity—for the creation is mixed, being made up of necessity and mind. Mind, the ruling power, persuaded necessity to bring the greater part of created things to perfection, and thus and after this manner in the beginning, when the influence of reason got the better of necessity, the universe was created. But if a person will truly tell of the way in which the work was accomplished, he must include the other influence of the variable cause as well. Wherefore, we must return again and find another suitable beginning, as about the former matters, so also about these. To which end we must consider the nature of fire, and water, and air, and earth, such as they were prior to the creation of the heaven, and what was happening to them in this previous state; for no one has as yet explained the manner of their generation, but we speak of fire and the rest of them, whatever they mean, as though men knew their natures, and we maintain them to be the first principles and letters or elements of the whole, when they cannot reasonably be compared by a man of any sense even to syllables or first compounds. And let me say thus much: I will not now speak of the first principle or principles of all things, or by whatever name they are to be called, for this reason—because it is difficult to set forth my opinion according to the method of discussion which we are at present employing. Do not imagine, any more than I can bring myself to imagine, that I should be right in undertaking so great and difficult a task. Remembering what I said at first about probability, I will do my best to give as probable an explanation as any other—or rather, more probable; and I will first go back to the beginning and try to speak of each thing and of all. Once more, then, at the commencement of my discourse, I call upon God, and beg him to be our saviour out of a strange and unwonted enquiry, and to bring us to the haven of probability. So now let us begin again.

This new beginning of our discussion of the universe requires a fuller division than the former; for then we made two classes, now a third must be revealed. The two sufficed for the former discussion: one, which we assumed, was a pattern intelligible and always the same; and the second was only the imitation of the pattern, generated and visible. There is also a third kind which we did not distinguish at the time, conceiving that the two would be enough. But now the argument seems to require that we should set forth in words another kind, which is difficult of explanation and dimly seen. What nature are we to attribute to this new kind of being? We reply, that it is the receptacle, and in a manner the nurse, of all generation. I have spoken the truth; but I must express myself in clearer language, and this will be an arduous task for many reasons, and in particular because I must first raise questions concerning fire and the other elements, and determine what each of them is; for to say, with any probability or certitude, which of them should be called water rather than fire, and which should be called any of them rather than all or some one of them, is a difficult matter. How, then, shall we settle this point, and what questions about the elements may be fairly raised?

In the first place, we see that what we just now called water, by condensation, I suppose, becomes stone and earth; and this same element, when melted and dispersed, passes into vapour and air. Air, again, when inflamed, becomes fire; and again fire, when condensed and extinguished, passes once more into the form of air; and once more, air, when collected and condensed, produces cloud and mist; and from these, when still more compressed, comes flowing water, and from water comes earth and stones once more; and thus generation appears to be transmitted from one to the other in a circle. Thus, then, as the several elements never present themselves in the same form, how can any one have the assurance to assert positively that any of them, whatever it may be, is one thing rather than another? No one can. But much the safest plan is to speak of them as follows:—Anything which we see to be continually changing, as, for example, fire, we must not call "this" or "that," but rather say that it is "of such a nature"; nor let us speak of water as "this," but always as "such"; nor must we imply that there is any stability in any of those things which we indicate by the use of the words "this" and "that," supposing ourselves to signify something thereby; for they are too volatile to be detained in any such expressions as "this," or "that," or "relative to this," or any other mode of speaking which represents them as permanent. We ought not to apply "this" to any of them, but rather the word "such"; which expresses the similar principle circulating in each and all of them; for example, that should be called "fire" which is of such a nature always, and so of everything that has generation. That in which the elements severally grow up, and appear, and decay, is alone to be called by the name "this" or "that"; but that which is of a certain nature, hot or white, or anything which admits of opposite qualities, and all things that are compounded of them, ought not to be so denominated. Let me make another attempt to explain my meaning more clearly. Suppose a person to make all kinds of figures of gold and to be always transmuting one form into all the rest—somebody points to one of them and asks what it is. By far the safest and truest answer is, That is gold; and not to call the triangle or any other figures which are formed in the gold "these," as thought they had existence, since they are in process of change while he is making the assertion; but if the questioner be willing to take the safe and indefinite expression, "such," we should be satisfied. And the same argument applies to the universal nature which receives all bodies—that must be always called the same; for, while receiving all things, she never departs at all from her own nature, and never in any way, or at any time, assumes a form like that of any of the things which enter into her; she is the natural recipient of all impressions, and is stirred and informed by them, and appears different from time to time by reason of them. But the forms which enter into and go out of her are the likenesses of real existences modelled after their patterns in a wonderful and inexplicable manner, which we will hereafter investigate. For the present we have only to conceive of three natures: first, that which is in process of generation; secondly, that in which the generation takes place; and thirdly, that of which the thing generated is a resemblance. And we may liken the receiving principle to a mother, and the source or spring to a father, and the intermediate nature to a child; and may remark further, that if the model is to take every variety of form, then the matter in which the model is fashioned will not be duly prepared, unless it is formless, and free from the impress of any of those shapes which it is hereafter to receive from without. For if the matter were like any of the supervening forms, then whenever any opposite or entirely different nature was stamped upon its surface, it would take the impression badly, because it would intrude its own shape. Wherefore, that which is to receive all forms should have no form; as in making perfumes they first contrive that the liquid substance which is to receive the scent shall be as inodorous as possible; or as those who wish to impress figures on soft substances do not allow any previous impression to remain, but begin by making the surface as even and smooth as possible. In the same way that which is to receive perpetually and through its whole extent the resemblances of all eternal beings ought to be devoid of any particular form. Wherefore, the mother and receptacle of all created and visible and in any way sensible things, is not to be termed earth, or air, or fire, or water, or any of their compounds or any of the elements from which these are derived, but is an invisible and formless being which receives all things and in some mysterious

way partakes of the intelligible, and is most incomprehensible. In saying this we shall not be far wrong; as far,
however, as we can attain to a knowledge of her from
the previous considerations, we may truly say that fire
is that part of her nature which from time to time is inflamed, and water that which is moistened, and that the
mother substance becomes earth and air, in so far as she
receives the impressions of them.

Let us consider this question more precisely. Is there
any self-existent fire? and do all those things which we
call self-existent exist? or are only those things which we
see, or in some way perceive through the bodily organs,
truly existent, and nothing whatever besides them? And
is all that which we call an intelligible essence nothing at
all, and only a name? Here is a question which we must
not leave unexamined or undetermined, nor must we
affirm too confidently that there can be no decision; neither must we interpolate in our present long discourse a
digression equally long, but if it is possible to set forth a
great principle in a few words, that is just what we want.

Thus I state my view:—If mind and true opinion are
two distinct classes, then I say that there certainly are
these self-existent ideas unperceived by sense, and apprehended only by the mind; if, however, as some say,
true opinion differs in no respect from mind, then everything that we perceive through the body is to be regarded as most real and certain. But we must affirm them
to be distinct, for they have a distinct origin and are of
a different nature; the one is implanted in us by instruction, the other by persuasion; the one is always accompanied by true reason, the other is without reason; the
one cannot be overcome by persuasion, but the other
can: and lastly, every man may be said to share in true
opinion, but mind is the attribute of the gods and of
very few men. Wherefore also we must acknowledge

that there is one kind of being which is always the same, uncreated and indestructible, never receiving anything into itself from without, nor itself going out to any other, but invisible and imperceptible by any sense, and of which the contemplation is granted to intelligence only. And there is another nature of the same name with it, and like to it, perceived by sense, created, always in motion, becoming in place and again vanishing out of place, which is apprehended by opinion and sense. And there is a third nature, which is space, and is eternal, and admits not of destruction and provides a home for all created things, and is apprehended without the help of sense, by a kind of spurious reason, and is hardly real; which we beholding as in a dream, say of all existence that it must of necessity be in some place and occupy a space, but that what is neither in heaven nor in earth has no existence. Of these and other things of the same kind, relating to the true and waking reality of nature, we have only this dreamlike sense, and we are unable to cast off sleep and determine the truth about them. For an image, since the reality, after which it is modelled, does not belong to it, and it exists ever as the fleeting shadow of some other, must be inferred to be in another [i. e. in space], grasping existence in some way or other, or it could not be at all. But true and exact reason, vindicating the nature of true being, maintains that while two things [i. e. the image and space] are different they cannot exist one of them in the other and so be one and also two at the same time.

Thus have I concisely given the result of my thoughts; and my verdict is that being and space and generation, these three, existed in their three ways before the heaven; and that the nurse of generation, moistened by water and inflamed by fire, and receiving the forms of earth and air, and experiencing all the affections which accompany these, presented a strange variety of appearances; and being full of powers which were neither similar nor equally balanced, was never in any part in a state of equipoise, but swaying unevenly hither and thither, was shaken by them, and by its motion again shook them; and the elements when moved were separated and carried continually, some one way, some another; as, when grain is shaken and winnowed by fans and other instruments used in the threshing of corn, the close and heavy particles are borne away and settle in one direction, and the loose and light particles in another. In this manner, the four kinds or elements were then shaken by the receiving vessel, which, moving like a winnowing machine, scattered far away from one another the elements most unlike, and forced the most similar elements into close contact. Wherefore also the various elements had different places before they were arranged so as to form the universe. At first, they were all without reason and measure. But when the world began to get into order, fire and water and earth and air had only certain faint traces of themselves, and were altogether such as everything might be expected to be in the absence of God; this, I say, was their nature at that time, and God fashioned them by form and number. Let it be consistently maintained by us in all that we say that God made them as far as possible the fairest and best, out of things which were not fair and good. And now I will endeavour to show you the disposition and generation of them by an unaccustomed argument, which I am compelled to use; but I believe that you will be able to follow me, for your education has made you familiar with the methods of science.

In the first place, then, as is evident to all, fire and earth and water and air are bodies. And every sort of body possesses solidity, and every solid must necessarily be contained in planes; and every plane rectilinear figure is composed of triangles; and all triangles are originally of two kinds, both of which are made up of one right and two acute angles; one of them has at either end of the base the half of a divided right angle, having equal sides, while in the other the right angle is divided into unequal parts, having unequal sides. These, then, proceeding by a combination of probability with demonstration, we assume to be the original elements of fire and the other bodies; but the principles which are prior to these God only knows, and he of men who is the friend of God. And next we have to determine what are the four most beautiful bodies which are unlike one another, and of which some are capable of resolution into one another; for having discovered thus much, we shall know the true origin of earth and fire and of the proportionate and intermediate elements. And then we shall not be willing to allow that there are any distinct kinds of visible bodies fairer than these. Wherefore we must endeavour to construct the four forms of bodies which excel in beauty, and then we shall be able to say that we have sufficiently apprehended their nature. Now of the two triangles, the isosceles has one form only; the scalene or unequal-sided has an infinite number. Of the infinite forms we must select the most beautiful, if we are to proceed in due order, and any one who can point out a more beautiful form than ours for the construction of these bodies, shall carry off the palm, not as an enemy, but as a friend. Now, the one which we maintain to be the most beautiful of all the many triangles (and we need not speak of the others) is that of which the double forms a third triangle which is equilateral; the reason of this would be long to tell; he who disproves what we are saying, and shows that we are mistaken, may claim a friendly victory. Then let us choose two triangles, out of which fire and the other elements have been constructed, one isosceles, the other having the square of the longer side equal to three times the square of the lesser side.

Now is the time to explain what was before obscurely said: there was an error in imagining that all the four elements might be generated by and into one another; this, I say, was an erroneous supposition, for there are generated from the triangles which we have selected four kinds—three from the one which has the sides unequal; the fourth alone is framed out of the isosceles triangle. Hence they cannot all be resolved into one another, a great number of small bodies being combined into a few large ones, or the converse. But three of them can be thus resolved and compounded, for they all spring from one, and when the greater bodies are broken up, many small bodies will spring up out of them and take their own proper figures; or, again, when many small bodies are dissolved into their triangles, if they become one, they will form one large mass of another kind. So much for their passage into one another. I have now to speak of their several kinds, and show out of what combinations of numbers each of them was formed. The first will be the simplest and smallest construction, and its element is that triangle which has its hypothenuse twice the lesser side. When two such triangles are joined at the diagonal, and this is repeated three times, and the triangles rest their diagonals and shorter sides on the same point as a centre, a single equilateral triangle is formed out of six triangles; and four equilateral triangles, if put together, make out of every three plane angles one solid angle, being that which is nearest to the most obtuse of plane angles; and out of the combination of these four angles arises the first solid form which distributes into equal and similar

parts the whole circle in which it is inscribed. The
second species of solid is formed out of the same triangles, which unite as eight equilateral triangles and
form one solid angle out of four plane angles, and out
of six such angles the second body is completed. And
the third body is made up of 120 triangular elements,
forming twelve solid angles, each of them included in
five plane equilateral triangles, having altogether twenty
bases, each of which is an equilateral triangle. The one
element [that is, the triangle which has its hypothenuse
twice the lesser side] having generated these figures,
generated no more; but the isosceles triangle produced
the fourth elementary figure, which is compounded of
four such triangles, joining their right angles in a centre,
and forming one equilateral quadrangle. Six of these
united form eight solid angles, each of which is made by
the combination of three plane right angles; the figure
of the body thus composed is a cube, having six plane
quadrangular equilateral bases. There was yet a fifth
combination which God used in the delineation of the
universe.

Now, he who, duly reflecting on all this, enquires
whether the worlds are to be regarded as indefinite or
definite in number, will be of opinion that the notion of
their indefiniteness is characteristic of a sadly indefinite
and ignorant mind. He, however, who raises the question whether they are to be truly regarded as one or five,
takes up a more reasonable position. Arguing from probabilities, I am of opinion that they are one; another, regarding the question from another point of view, will
be of another mind. But, leaving this enquiry, let us
proceed to distribute the elementary forms, which have
now been created in idea, among the four elements.

To earth, then, let us assign the cubical form; for
earth is the most immoveable of the four and the most

plastic of all bodies, and that which has the most stable bases must of necessity be of such a nature. Now, of the triangles which we assumed at first, that which has two equal sides is by nature more firmly based than that which has unequal sides; and of the compound figures which are formed out of either, the plane equilateral quadrangle has necessarily a more stable basis than the equilateral triangle, both in the whole and in the parts. Wherefore, in assigning this figure to earth, we adhere to probability; and to water we assign that one of the remaining forms which is the least moveable; and the most moveable of them to fire; and to air that which is intermediate. Also we assign the smallest body to fire, and the greatest to water, and the intermediate in size to air; and, again, the acutest body to fire, and the next in acuteness to air, and the third to water. Of all these elements, that which has the fewest bases must necessarily be the most moveable, for it must be the acutest and most penetrating in every way, and also the lightest as being composed of the smallest number of similar particles: and the second body has similar properties in a second degree, and the third body in the third degree. Let it be agreed, then, both according to strict reason and according to probability, that the pyramid is the solid which is the original element and seed of fire; and let us assign the element which was next in the order of generation to air, and the third to water. We must imagine all these to be so small that no single particle of any of the four kinds is seen by us on account of their smallness: but when many of them are collected together their aggregates are seen. And the ratios of their numbers, motions, and other properties, everywhere God, as far as necessity allowed or gave consent, has exactly perfected, and harmonized in due proportion.

From all that we have just been saying about the ele-

ments or kinds, the most probable conclusion is as follows:—earth, when meeting with fire and dissolved by
its sharpness, whether the dissolution take place in the
fire itself or perhaps in some mass of air or water, is
borne hither and thither, until its parts, meeting together
and mutually harmonizing, again become earth; for they
can never take any other form. But water, when divided
by fire or by air, on re-forming, may become one part
fire and two parts air; and a single volume of air divided becomes two of fire. Again, when a small body
of fire is contained in a larger body of air or water or
earth, and both are moving, and the fire struggling is
overcome and broken up, then two volumes of fire form
one volume of air; and when air is overcome and cut up
into small pieces, two and a half parts of air are condensed into one part of water. Let us consider the matter in another way. When one of the other elements is
fastened upon by fire, and is cut by the sharpness of its
angles and sides, it coalesces with the fire, and then
ceases to be cut by them any longer. For no element
which is one and the same with itself can be changed
by or change another of the same kind and in the same
state. But so long as in the process of transition the
weaker is fighting against the stronger, the dissolution
continues. Again, when a few small particles, enclosed
in many larger ones, are in process of decomposition
and extinction, they only cease from their tendency to
extinction when they consent to pass into the conquering
nature, and fire becomes air and air water. But if bodies
of another kind go and attack them [i. e. the small par-
ticles], the latter continue to be dissolved until, being
completely forced back and dispersed, they make their
escape to their own kindred, or else, being overcome and
assimilated to the conquering power, they remain where
they are and dwell with their victors, and from being

many become one. And owing to these affections, all things are changing their place, for by the motion of the receiving vessel the bulk of each class is distributed into its proper place; but those things which become unlike themselves and like other things, are hurried by the shaking into the place of the things to which they grow like.

Now all unmixed and primary bodies are produced by such causes as these. As to the subordinate species which are included in the greater kinds, they are to be attributed to the varieties in the structure of the two original triangles. For either structure did not originally produce the triangle of one size only, but some larger and some smaller, and there are as many sizes as there are species of the four elements. Hence when they are mingled with themselves and with one another there is an endless variety of them, which those who would arrive at the probable truth of nature ought duly to consider.

Unless a person comes to an understanding about the nature and conditions of rest and motion, he will meet with many difficulties in the discussion which follows. Something has been said of this matter already, and something more remains to be said, which is, that motion never exists in what is uniform. For to conceive that any thing can be moved without a mover is hard or indeed impossible, and equally impossible to conceive that there can be a mover unless there be something which can be moved—motion cannot exist where either of these are wanting, and for these to be uniform is impossible; wherefore we must assign rest to uniformity and motion to the want of uniformity. Now inequality is the cause of the nature which is wanting in uniformity; and of this we have already described the origin. But there still remains the further point—why things when divided after their kinds do not cease to

pass through one another and to change their place—
which we will now proceed to explain. In the revolution
of the universe are comprehended all the four elements,
and this being circular and having a tendency to come
together, compresses everything and will not allow any
place to be left void. Wherefore, also, fire above all
things penetrates everywhere, and air next, as being next
in rarity of the elements; and the two other elements in
like manner penetrate according to their degrees of
rarity. For those things which are composed of the largest particles have the largest void left in their compositions, and those which are composed of the smallest
particles have the least. And the contraction caused by
the compression thrusts the smaller particles into the interstices of the larger. And thus, when the small parts
are placed side by side with the larger, and the lesser
divide the greater and the greater unite the lesser, all
the elements are borne up and down and hither and
thither towards their own places; for the change in the
size of each changes its position in space. And these
causes generate an inequality which is always maintained, and is continually creating a perpetual motion
of the elements in all time.

In the next place we have to consider that there are
divers kinds of fire. There are, for example, first, flame;
and secondly, those emanations of flame which do not
burn but only give light to the eyes; thirdly, the remains
of fire, which are seen in red-hot embers after the flame
has been extinguished. There are similar differences in
the air; of which the brightest part is called the aether,
and the most turbid sort mist and darkness; and there
are various other nameless kinds which arise from the
inequality of the triangles. Water, again, admits in the
first place of a division into two kinds; the one liquid
and the other fusile. The liquid kind is composed of

the small and unequal particles of water; and moves itself and is moved by other bodies owing to the want of uniformity and the shape of its particles; whereas the fusile kind, being formed of large and uniform particles, is more stable than the other, and is heavy and compact by reason of its uniformity. But when fire gets in and dissolves the particles and destroys the uniformity, it has greater mobility, and becoming fluid is thrust forth by the neighbouring air and spreads upon the earth; and this dissolution of the solid masses is called melting, and their spreading out upon the earth flowing. Again, when the fire goes out of the fusile substance, it does not pass into a vacuum, but into the neighbouring air; and the air which is displaced forces together the liquid and still moveable mass into the place which was occupied by the fire, and unites it with itself. Thus compressed the mass resumes its equability, and is again at unity with itself, because the fire which was the author of the inequality has retreated; and this departure of the fire is called cooling, and the coming together which follows upon it is termed congealment. Of all the kinds termed fusile, that which is the densest and is formed out of the finest and most uniform parts is that most precious possession called gold, which is hardened by filtration through rock; this is unique in kind, and has both a glittering and a yellow colour. A shoot of gold, which is so dense as to be very hard, and takes a black colour, is termed adamant. There is also another kind which has parts nearly like gold, and of which there are several species; it is denser than gold, and it contains a small and fine portion of earth, and is therefore harder, yet also lighter because of the great interstices which it has within itself; and this substance, which is one of the bright and denser kinds of water, when solidified is called copper. There is an alloy of earth mingled with

it, which, when the two parts grow old and are dis-
united, shows itself separately and is called rust. The
remaining phenomena of the same kind there will be no
difficulty in reasoning out by the method of probabilities.
A man may sometimes set aside meditations about eternal things, and for recreation turn to consider the truths
of generation which are probable only; he will thus gain
a pleasure not to be repented of, and secure for himself
while he lives a wise and moderate pastime. Let us grant
ourselves this indulgence, and go through the probabilities relating to the same subjects which follow next in
order.

Water which is mingled with fire, so much as is fine
and liquid (being so called by reason of its motion and
the way in which it rolls along the ground), and soft,
because its bases give way and are less stable than those
of earth, when separated from fire and air and isolated,
becomes more uniform, and by their retirement is compressed into itself; and if the condensation be very great,
the water above the earth becomes hail, but on the
earth, ice; and that which is congealed in a less degree
and is only half solid, when above the earth is called
snow, and when upon the earth, and condensed from
dew, hoar-frost. Then, again, there are the numerous
kinds of water which have been mingled with one another, and are distilled through plants which grow in
the earth; and this whole class is called by the name of
juices or saps. The unequal admixture of these fluids
creates a variety of species; most of them are nameless,
but four which are of a fiery nature are clearly distinguished and have names. First, there is wine, which
warms the soul as well as the body: secondly, there is
the oily nature, which is smooth and divides the visual
ray, and for this reason is bright and shining and of a
glistening appearance, including pitch, the juice of the

castor berry, oil itself, and other things of a like kind: thirdly, there is the class of substances which expand the contracted parts of the mouth, until they return to their natural state, and by reason of this property create sweetness—these are included under the general name of honey: and, lastly, there is a frothy nature, which differs from all juices, having a burning quality which dissolves the flesh; it is called *opos* (a vegetable acid).

As to the kinds of earth, that which is filtered through water passes into stone in the following manner:—The water which mixes with the earth and is broken up in the process changes into air, and taking this form mounts into its own place. But as there is no surrounding vacuum it thrusts away the neighbouring air, and this being rendered heavy, and, when it is displaced, having been poured around the mass of earth, forcibly compresses it and drives it into the vacant space whence the new air had come up; and the earth when compressed by the air into an indissoluble union with water becomes rock. The fairer sort is that which is made up of equal and similar parts and is transparent; that which has the opposite qualities is inferior. But when all the watery part is suddenly drawn out by fire, a more brittle substance is formed, to which we give the name of pottery. Sometimes also moisture may remain, and the earth which has been fused by fire becomes, when cool, a certain stone of a black colour. A like separation of the water which had been copiously mingled with them may occur in two substances composed of finer particles of earth and of a briny nature; out of either of them a half-solid body is then formed, soluble in water—the one, soda, which is used for purging away oil and earth, the other, salt, which harmonizes so well in combinations pleasing to the palate, and is, as the law testifies, a substance dear to the gods. The compounds of earth and water are not soluble by water, but by fire only, and for this reason:—Neither fire nor air melt masses of earth; for their particles, being smaller than the interstices in its structure, have plenty of room to move without forcing their way, and so they leave the earth unmelted and undissolved; but particles of water, which are larger, force a passage, and dissolve and melt the earth. Wherefore earth when not consolidated by force is dissolved by water only; when consolidated, by nothing but fire; for this is the only body which can find an entrance. The cohesion of water again, when very strong, is dissolved by fire only—when weaker, then either by air or fire—the former entering the interstices, and the latter penetrating even the triangles. But nothing can dissolve air, when strongly condensed, which does not reach the elements or triangles; or if not strongly condensed, then only fire can dissolve it. As to bodies composed of earth and water, while the water occupies the vacant interstices of the earth in them which are compressed by force, the particles of water which approach them from without, finding no entrance, flow around the entire mass and leave it undissolved; but the particles of fire, entering into the interstices of the water, do to the water what water does to earth and fire to air, and are the sole causes of the compound body of earth and water liquefying and becoming fluid. Now these bodies are of two kinds; some of them, such as glass and the fusible sort of stones, have less water than they have earth; on the other hand, substances of the nature of wax and incense have more of water entering into their composition.

I have thus shown the various classes of bodies as they are diversified by their forms and combinations and changes into one another, and now I must endeavour to set forth their affections and the causes of them. In the first place, the bodies which I have been describing are necessarily objects of sense. But we have not yet considered the origin of flesh, or what belongs to flesh, or of that part of the soul which is mortal. And these things cannot be adequately explained without also explaining the affections which are concerned with sensation, nor the latter without the former: and yet to explain them together is hardly possible; for which reason we must assume first one or the other and afterwards examine the nature of our hypothesis. In order, then, that the affections may follow regularly after the elements, let us presuppose the existence of body and soul.

First, let us enquire what we mean by saying that fire is hot; and about this we may reason from the dividing or cutting power which it exercises on our bodies. We all of us feel that fire is sharp; and we may further consider the fineness of the sides, and the sharpness of the angles, and the smallness of the particles, and the swiftness of the motion—all this makes the action of fire violent and sharp, so that it cuts whatever it meets. And we must not forget that the original figure of fire [i. e. the pyramid], more than any other form, has a dividing power which cuts our bodies into small pieces ($\chi\epsilon\rho\mu\alpha\tau\iota\zeta\epsilon\iota$), and thus naturally produces that affection which we call heat; and hence the origin of the name ($\Theta\epsilon\rho\mu\dot{o}s$, $\chi\dot{\epsilon}\rho\mu\alpha$). Now, the opposite of this is sufficiently manifest; nevertheless we will not fail to describe it. For the larger particles of moisture which surround the body, entering in and driving out the lesser, but not being able to take their places, compress the moist principle in us; and this from being unequal and disturbed, is forced by them into a state of rest, which is due to equability and compression. But things which are contracted contrary to nature are by nature at war, and force themselves apart; and to this war and convulsion the name of shivering and trembling is given; and the whole affection and the cause of the affection are both termed cold. That is called hard to which our flesh yields, and soft which yields to our flesh; and things are also termed hard and soft relatively to one another. That which yields has a small base; but that which rests on quadrangular bases is firmly posed and belongs to the class which offers the greatest resistance; so too does that which is the most compact and therefore most repellent. The nature of the light and the heavy will be best understood when examined in connexion with our notions of above and below; for it is quite a mistake to suppose that the universe is parted into two regions, separate from and opposite to each other, the one a lower to which all things tend which have any bulk, and an upper to which things only ascend against their will. For as the universe is in the form of a sphere, all the extremities, being equidistant from the centre, are equally extremities, and the centre, which is equidistant from them, is equally to be regarded as the opposite of them all. Such being the nature of the world, when a person says that any of these points is above or below, may he not be justly charged with using an improper expression? For the centre of the world cannot be rightly called either above or below, but is the centre and nothing else; and the circumference is not the centre, and has in no one part of itself a different relation to the centre from what it has in any of the opposite parts. Indeed, when it is in every direction similar, how can one rightly give to it names which imply opposition? For if there were any solid body in equipoise at the centre of the universe, there would be nothing to draw it to this extreme rather than to that, for they are all perfectly similar; and if a person were to go round the world in a circle, he would often, when standing at the antipodes of his former position, speak of the same point as above and below; for, as I was saying just now, to speak of the whole which is in the form of a globe as having one part above and another below is not like a sensible man. The reason why these names are used, and the circumstances under which they are ordinarily applied by us to the division of the heavens, may be elucidated by the following supposition:—If a person were to stand in that part of the universe which is the appointed place of fire, and where there is the great mass of fire to which fiery bodies gather—if, I say, he were to ascend thither, and, having the power to do this, were to abstract particles of fire and put them in scales and weigh them, and then, raising the balance, were to draw the fire by force towards the uncongenial element of the air, it would be very evident that he could compel the smaller mass more readily than the larger; for when two things are simultaneously raised by one and the same power, the smaller body must necessarily yield to the superior power with less reluctance than the larger; and the larger body is called heavy and said to tend downwards, and the smaller body is called light and said to tend upwards. And we may detect ourselves who are upon the earth doing precisely the same thing. For we often separate earthy natures, and sometimes earth itself, and draw them into the uncongenial element of air by force and contrary to nature, both clinging to their kindred elements. But that which is smaller yields to the impulse given by us towards the dissimilar element more easily than the larger; and so we call the former light, and the place towards which it is impelled we call above, and the contrary state and place we call heavy and below respectively. Now the relations of these must necessarily vary, because the principal masses of the different elements hold opposite positions; for that which is light,

heavy, below or above in one place will be found to be
and become contrary and transverse and every way diverse in relation to that which is light, heavy, below or
above in an opposite place. And about all of them this
has to be considered:—that the tendency of each towards its kindred element makes the body which is
moved heavy, and the place towards which the motion
tends below, but things which have an opposite tendency we call by an opposite name. Such are the causes
which we assign to these phenomena. As to the smooth
and the rough, any one who sees them can explain the
reason of them to another. For roughness is hardness
mingled with irregularity, and smoothness is produced
by the joint effect of uniformity and density.

The most important of the affections which concern
the whole body remains to be considered—that is, the
cause of pleasure and pain in the perceptions of which
I have been speaking, and in all other things which are
perceived by sense through the parts of the body, and
have both pains and pleasures attendant on them. Let
us imagine the causes of every affection, whether of
sense or not, to be of the following nature, remembering that we have already distinguished between the nature which is easy and which is hard to move; for this
is the direction in which we must hunt the prey which
we mean to take. A body which is of a nature to be
easily moved, on receiving an impression however slight,
spreads abroad the motion in a circle, the parts communicating with each other, until at last, reaching the
principle of mind, they announce the quality of the
agent. But a body of the opposite kind, being immobile,
and not extending to the surrounding region, merely receives the impression, and does not stir any of the
neighbouring parts; and since the parts do not distribute
the original impression to other parts, it has no effect

of motion on the whole animal, and therefore produces
no effect on the patient. This is true of the bones and
hair and other more earthy parts of the human body;
whereas what was said above relates mainly to sight
and hearing, because they have in them the greatest
amount of fire and air. Now we must conceive of pleasure and pain in this way. An impression produced in
us contrary to nature and violent, if sudden, is painful;
and, again, the sudden return to nature is pleasant; but a
gentle and gradual return is imperceptible and *vice
versa*. On the other hand the impression of sense which
is most easily produced is most readily felt, but is not
accompanied by pleasure or pain; such, for example, are
the affections of the sight, which, as we said above, is
a body naturally uniting with our body in the day-time
(45); for cuttings and burnings and other affections
which happen to the sight do not give pain, nor is there
pleasure when the sight returns to its natural state; but
the sensations are clearest and strongest according to
the manner in which the eye is affected by the object,
and itself strikes and touches it; there is no violence
either in the contraction or dilation of the eye. But
bodies formed of larger particles yield to the agent only
with a struggle; and then they impart their motions to
the whole and cause pleasure and pain—pain when
alienated from their natural conditions, and pleasure
when restored to them. Things which experience gradual
withdrawings and emptyings of their nature, and great
and sudden replenishments, fail to perceive the empty-
ing, but are sensible of the replenishment; and so they
occasion no pain, but the greatest pleasure, to the mortal
part of the soul, as is manifest in the case of perfumes.
But things which are changed all of a sudden, and only
gradually and with difficulty return to their own nature,
have effects in every way opposite to the former, as is

evident in the case of burnings and cuttings of the body.

Thus have we discussed the general affections of the whole body, and the names of the agents which produce them. And now I will endeavour to speak of the affections of particular parts, and the causes and agents of them, as far as I am able. In the first place let us set forth what was omitted when we were speaking of juices, concerning the affections peculiar to the tongue. These too, like most of the other affections, appear to be caused by certain contractions and dilations, but they have besides more of roughness and smoothness than is found in other affections; for whenever earthy particles enter into the small veins which are the testing instruments of the tongue, reaching to the heart, and fall upon the moist, delicate portions of flesh—when, as they are dissolved, they contract and dry up the little veins, they are astringent if they are rougher, but if not so rough, then only harsh. Those of them which are of an abstergent nature, and purge the whole surface of the tongue, if they do it in excess, and so encroach as to consume some part of the flesh itself, like potash and soda, are all termed bitter. But the particles which are deficient in the alkaline quality, and which cleanse only moderately, are called salt, and having no bitterness or roughness, are regarded as rather agreeable than otherwise. Bodies which share in and are made smooth by the heat of the mouth, and which are inflamed, and again in turn inflame that which heats them, and which are so light that they are carried upwards to the sensations of the head, and cut all that comes in their way, by reason of these qualities in them, are all termed pungent. But when these same particles, refined by putrefaction, enter into the narrow veins, and are duly proportioned to the particles of earth and air which are there, they set them whirling about one another, and while they are in a whirl cause them to dash against and enter into one another, and so form hollows surrounding the particles that enter—which watery vessels of air (for a film of moisture, sometimes earthy, sometimes pure, is spread around the air) are hollow spheres of water; and those of them which are pure, are transparent, and are called bubbles, while those composed of the earthy liquid, which is in a state of general agitation and effervescence, are said to boil or ferment—of all these affections the cause is termed acid. And there is the opposite affection arising from an opposite cause, when the mass of entering particles, immersed in the moisture of the mouth, is congenial to the tongue, and smooths and oils over the roughness, and relaxes the parts which are unnaturally contracted, and contracts the parts which are relaxed, and disposes them all according to their nature— that sort of remedy of violent affections is pleasant and agreeable to every man, and has the name sweet. But enough of this.

The faculty of smell does not admit of differences of kind; for all smells are of a half-formed nature, and no element is so proportioned as to have any smell. The veins about the nose are too narrow to admit earth and water, and too wide to detain fire and air; and for this reason no one ever perceives the smell of any of them; but smells always proceed from bodies that are damp, or putrefying, or liquefying, or evaporating, and are perceptible only in the intermediate state, when water is changing into air and air into water; and all of them are either vapor or mist. That which is passing out of air into water is mist, and that which is passing from water into air is vapour; and hence all smells are thinner than water and thicker than air. The proof of this is, that when there is any obstruction to the respiration, and a man draws in his breath by force, then no smell

filters through, but the air without the smell alone penetrates. Wherefore the varieties of smell have no name,
and they have not many, or definite and simple kinds;
but they are distinguished only as painful and pleasant,
the one sort irritating and disturbing the whole cavity
which is situated between the head and the navel, the
other having a soothing influence, and restoring this
same region to an agreeable and natural condition.

In considering the third kind of sense, hearing, we
must speak of the causes in which it originates. We may
in general assume sound to be a blow which passes
through the ears, and is transmitted by means of the air,
the brain, and the blood, to the soul, and that hearing
is the vibration of this blow, which begins in the head
and ends in the region of the liver. The sound which
moves swiftly is acute, and the sound which moves
slowly is grave, and that which is regular is equable
and smooth, and the reverse is harsh. A great body of
sound is loud, and a small body of sound the reverse.
Respecting the harmonies of sound I must hereafter
speak.

There is a fourth class of sensible things, having many
intricate varieties, which must now be distinguished.
They are called by the general name of colours, and are
a flame which emanates from every sort of body, and
has particles corresponding to the sense of sight. I have
spoken already, in what has preceded, of the causes
which generate sight, and in this place it will be natural
and suitable to give a rational theory of colours.

Of the particles coming from other bodies which fall
upon the sight, some are smaller and some are larger,
and some are equal to the parts of the sight itself. Those
which are equal are imperceptible, and we call them
transparent. The larger produce contraction, the smaller
dilation, in the sight, exercising a power akin to that of

hot and cold bodies on the flesh, or of astringent bodies
on the tongue, or of those heating bodies which we
termed pungent. White and black are similar effects of
contraction and dilation in another sphere, and for this
reason have a different appearance. Wherefore, we ought
to term white that which dilates the visual ray, and the
opposite of this is black. There is also a swifter motion
of a different sort of fire which strikes and dilates the
ray of sight until it reaches the eyes, forcing a way
through their passages and melting them, and eliciting
from them a union of fire and water which we call tears,
being itself an opposite fire which comes to them from
an opposite direction—the inner fire flashes forth like
lightning, and the outer finds a way in and is extinguished in the moisture, and all sorts of colours are
generated by the mixture. This affection is termed dazzling, and the object which produces it is called bright
and flashing. There is another sort of fire which is intermediate, and which reaches and mingles with the moisture of the eye without flashing; and in this, the fire
mingling with the ray of the moisture, produces a colour
like blood, to which we give the name of red. A bright
hue mingled with red and white gives the colour called
auburn (ξανθόν). The law of proportion, however, according to which the several colours are formed, even
if a man knew he would be foolish in telling, for he
could not give any necessary reason, nor indeed any
tolerable or probable explanation of them. Again, red,
when mingled with black and white, becomes purple,
but it becomes umber (ὄρφνινον) when the colours are
burnt as well as mingled and the black is more thoroughly mixed with them. Flame-colour (πυρρὸν) is produced by a union of auburn and dun (φαιδν), and dun
by an admixture of black and white; pale yellow
(ὠχρὸν), by an admixture of white and auburn. White

and bright meeting, and falling upon a full black, become dark blue ($\chi\nu\alpha\nu o\tilde{\nu}\nu$), and when dark blue mingles with white, a light blue ($\gamma\lambda\alpha\nu\chi\dot{o}\nu$) colour is formed, as flame-colour with black makes leek green ($\pi\rho\acute{a}\sigma\iota o\nu$). There will be no difficulty in seeing how and by what mixtures the colours derived from these are made according to the rules of probability. He, however, who should attempt to verify all this by experiment, would forget the difference of the human and divine nature. For God only has the knowledge and also the power which are able to combine many things into one and again resolve the one into many. But no man either is or ever will be able to accomplish either the one or the other operation.

These are the elements, thus of necessity then subsisting, which the creator of the fairest and best of created things associated with himself, when he made the self-sufficing and most perfect God, using the necessary causes as his ministers in the accomplishment of his work, but himself contriving the good in all his creations. Wherefore we may distinguish two sorts of causes, the one divine and the other necessary, and may seek for the divine in all things, as far as our nature admits, with a view to the blessed life; but the necessary kind only for the sake of the divine, considering that without them and when isolated from them, these higher things for which we look cannot be apprehended or received or in any way shared by us.

Seeing, then, that we have now prepared for our use the various classes of causes which are the material out of which the remainder of our discourse must be woven, just as wood is the material of the carpenter, let us revert in a few words to the point at which we began, and then endeavour to add on a suitable ending to the beginning of our tale.

As I said at first, when all things were in disorder God created in each thing in relation to itself, and in all things in relation to each other, all the measures and harmonies which they could possibly receive. For in those days nothing had any proportion except by accident; nor did any of the things which now have names deserve to be named at all—as, for example, fire, water, and the rest of the elements. All these the creator first set in order, and out of them he constructed the universe, which was a single animal comprehending in itself all other animals, mortal and immortal. Now of the divine, he himself was the creator, but the creation of the mortal he committed to his offspring. And they, imitating him, received from him the immortal principle of the soul; and around this they proceeded to fashion a mortal body, and made it to be the vehicle of the soul, and constructed within the body a soul of another nature which was mortal, subject to terrible and irresistible affections —first of all, pleasure, the greatest incitement to evil; then, pain, which deters from good; also rashness and fear, two foolish counsellors, anger hard to be appeased, and hope easily led astray—these they mingled with irrational sense and with all-daring love according to necessary laws, and so framed man. Wherefore, fearing to pollute the divine any more than was absolutely unavoidable, they gave to the mortal nature a separate habitation in another part of the body, placing the neck between them to be the isthmus and boundary, which they constructed between the head and breast, to keep them apart. And in the breast, and in what is termed the thorax, they encased the mortal soul; and as the one part of this was superior and the other inferior they divided the cavity of the thorax into two parts, as the women's and men's apartments are divided in houses, and placed the midriff to be a wall of partition between them. That part of the inferior soul which is endowed with courage and passion and loves contention they settled nearer the head, midway between the midriff and the neck, in order that it might be under the rule of reason and might join with it in controlling and restraining the desires when they are no longer willing of their own accord to obey the word of command issuing from the citadel.

The heart, the knot of the veins and the fountain of the blood which races through all the limbs, was set in the place of guard, that when the might of passion was roused by reason making proclamation of any wrong assailing them from without or being perpetrated by the desires within, quickly the whole power of feeling in the body, perceiving these commands and threats, might obey and follow through every turn and alley, and thus allow the principle of the best to have the command in all of them. But the gods, foreknowing that the palpitation of the heart in the expectation of danger and the swelling and excitement of passion was caused by fire, formed and implanted as a supporter to the heart the lung, which was, in the first place, soft and bloodless, and also had within hollows like the pores of a sponge, in order that by receiving the breath and the drink, it might give coolness and the power of respiration and alleviate the heat. Wherefore they cut the air-channels leading to the lung, and placed the lung about the heart as a soft spring, that, when passion was rife within, the heart, beating against a yielding body, might be cooled and suffer less, and might thus become more ready to join with passion in the service of reason.

The part of the soul which desires meats and drinks and the other things of which it has need by reason of the bodily nature, they placed between the midriff and the boundary of the navel, contriving in all this region a sort of manger for the food of the body; and there they bound it down like a wild animal which was chained up with man, and must be nourished if man was to exist. They appointed this lower creation his place here in order that he might be always feeding at the manger, and have his dwelling as far as might be from the council-chamber, making as little noise and disturbance as possible, and permitting the best part to advise quietly for the good of the whole. And knowing that this lower principle in man would not comprehend reason, and even if attaining to some degree of perception would never naturally care for rational notions, but that it would be led away by phantoms and visions night and day—to be a remedy for this, God combined with it the liver, and placed it in the house of the lower nature, contriving that it should be solid and smooth, and bright and sweet, and should also have a bitter quality, in order that the power of thought, which proceeds from the mind, might be reflected as in a mirror which receives likenesses of objects and gives back images of them to the sight; and so might strike terror into the desires, when, making use of the bitter part of the liver, to which it is akin, it comes threatening and invading, and diffusing this bitter element swiftly through the whole liver produces colours like bile, and contracting every part makes it wrinkled and rough; and twisting out of its right place and contorting the lobe and closing and shutting up the vessels and gates, causes pain and loathing. And the converse happens when some gentle inspiration of the understanding pictures images of an opposite character, and allays the bile and bitterness by refusing to stir or touch the nature opposed to itself, but by making use of the natural sweetness of the liver, corrects all things and makes them to be right and smooth and free, and renders the portion of the soul which resides about the liver happy and joyful, enabling it to pass the night in peace, and to practise divination in sleep, inasmuch as it has no share in mind and reason. For the authors of our being, remembering the command of their father when he bade them create the human race as good as they could, that they might correct our inferior parts and make them to attain a measure of truth, placed in the liver the seat of divination. And herein is a proof that God has given the art of divination not to the wisdom, but to the foolishness of man. No man, when in his wits, attains prophetic truth and inspiration; but when he receives the inspired word, either his intelligence is enthralled in sleep, or he is demented by some distemper or possession. And he who would understand what he remembers to have been said, whether in a dream or when he was awake, by the prophetic and inspired nature, or would determine by reason the meaning of the apparitions which he has seen, and what indications they afford to this man or that, of past, present or future good and evil, must first recover his wits. But, while he continues demented, he cannot judge of the visions which he sees or the words which he utters; the ancient saying is very true, that "only a man who has his wits can act or judge about himself and his own affairs." And for this reason it is customary to appoint interpreters to be judges of the true inspiration. Some persons call them prophets; they are quite unaware that they are only the expositors of dark sayings and visions, and are not to be called prophets at all, but only interpreters of prophecy.

Such is the nature of the liver, which is placed as we have described in order that it may give prophetic intimations. During the life of each individual these intimations are plainer, but after his death the liver becomes blind, and delivers oracles too obscure to be intelligible. The neighbouring organ [the spleen] is situated on the left-hand side, and is constructed with a view of keeping the liver bright and pure—like a napkin, always ready prepared and at hand to clean the mirror. And hence, when any impurities arise in the region of the liver by reason of disorders of the body, the loose nature of the spleen, which is composed of a hollow and bloodless tissue, receives them all and clears them away, and when filled with the unclean matter, swells and festers, but, again, when the body is purged, settles down into the same place as before, and is humbled.

Concerning the soul, as to which part is mortal and which divine, and how and why they are separated, and where located, if God acknowledges that we have spoken the truth, then, and then only, can we be confident; still, we may venture to assert that what has been said by us is probable, and will be rendered more probable by investigation. Let us assume thus much.

The creation of the rest of the body follows next in order, and this we may investigate in a similar manner. And it appears to be very meet that the body should be framed on the following principles:—

The authors of our race were aware that we should be intemperate in eating and drinking, and take a good deal more than was necessary or proper, by reason of gluttony. In order then that disease might not quickly destroy us, and lest our mortal race should perish without fulfilling its end—intending to provide against this, the gods made what is called the lower belly, to be a receptacle for the superfluous meat and drink, and formed the convolution of the bowels, so that the food might be prevented from passing quickly through and compelling the body to require more food, thus producing insatiable gluttony, and making the whole race an enemy to philosophy and music, and rebellious against the divinest element within us.

The bones and flesh, and other similar parts of us, were made as follows. The first principle of all of them was the generation of the marrow. For the bonds of life which unite the soul with the body are made fast there, and they are the root and foundation of the human race. The marrow itself is created out of other materials: God took such of the primary triangles as were straight and smooth, and were adapted by their perfection to produce fire and water, and air and earth—these, I say, he separated from their kinds, and mingling them in due proportions with one another, made the marrow out of them to be a universal seed of the whole race of mankind; and in this seed he then planted and enclosed the souls, and in the original distribution gave to the marrow as many and various forms as the different kinds of souls were hereafter to receive. That which, like a field, was to receive the divine seed, he made round every way, and called that portion of the marrow, brain, intending that, when an animal was perfected, the vessel containing this substance should be the head; but that which was intended to contain the remaining and mortal part of the soul he distributed into figures at once round and elongated, and he called them all by the name "marrow"; and to these, as to anchors, fastening the bonds of the whole soul, he proceeded to fashion around them the entire framework of our body, constructing for the marrow, first of all, a complete covering of bone.

Bone was composed by him in the following manner. Having sifted pure and smooth earth he kneaded it and wetted it with marrow, and after that he put it into fire and then into water, and once more into fire and again into water—in this way by frequent transfers from one to the other he made it insoluble by either. Out of this he fashioned, as in a lathe, a globe made of bone, which he placed around the brain, and in this he left a narrow

opening; and around the marrow of the neck and back
he formed vertebrae which he placed under one another
like pivots, beginning at the head and extending through
the whole of the trunk. Thus wishing to preserve the
entire seed, he enclosed it in a stone-like casing, inserting
joints, and using in the formation of them the power of
the other or diverse as an intermediate nature, that they
might have motion and flexure. Then again, considering
that the bone would be too brittle and inflexible, and
when heated and again cooled would soon mortify and
destroy the seed within—having this in view, he contrived the sinews and the flesh, that so binding all the
members together by the sinews, which admitted of
being stretched and relaxed about the vertebrae, he
might thus make the body capable of flexion and extension, while the flesh would serve as a protection against
the summer heat and against the winter cold, and also
against falls, softly and easily yielding to external bodies,
like articles made of felt; and containing in itself a warm
moisture which in summer exudes and makes the surface
damp, would impart a natural coolness to the whole
body; and again in winter by the help of this internal
warmth would form a very tolerable defence against the
frost which surrounds it and attacks it from without. He
who modelled us, considering these things, mixed earth
with fire and water and blended them; and making a
ferment of acid and salt, he mingled it with them and
formed soft and succulent flesh. As for the sinews, he
made them of a mixture of bone and unfermented flesh,
attempered so as to be in a mean, and gave them a yellow
colour; wherefore the sinews have a firmer and more
glutinous nature than flesh, but a softer and moister
nature than the bones. With these God covered the
bones and marrow, binding them together by sinews,
and then enshrouded them all in an upper covering of

flesh. The more living and sensitive of the bones he enclosed in the thinnest film of flesh, and those which had
the least life within them in the thickest and most solid
flesh. So again on the joints of the bones, where reason
indicated that no more was required, he placed only a
thin covering of flesh, that it might not interfere with the
flexion of our bodies and make them unwieldy because
difficult to move; and also that it might not, by being
crowded and pressed and matted together, destroy sensation by reason of its hardness, and impair the memory
and dull the edge of intelligence. Wherefore also the
thighs and the shanks and the hips, and the bones of
the arms and the forearms, and other parts which have
no joints, and the inner bones, which on account of the
rarity of the soul in the marrow are destitute of reason
—all these are abundantly provided with flesh; but such
as have mind in them are in general less fleshy, except
where the creator has made some part solely of flesh in
order to give sensation—as, for example, the tongue.
But commonly this is not the case. For the nature which
comes into being and grows up in us by a law of necessity, does not admit of the combination of solid bone and
much flesh with acute perceptions. More than any other
part the framework of the head would have had them,
if they could have co-existed, and the human race, having a strong and fleshy and sinewy head, would have had
a life twice or many times as long as it now has, and also
more healthy and free from pain. But our creators, considering whether they should make a longer-lived race
which was worse, or a shorter-lived race which was better, came to the conclusion that every one ought to prefer a shorter span of life, which was better, to a longer
one, which was worse; and therefore they covered the
head with thin bone, but not with flesh and sinews, since
it had no joints; and thus the head was added, having

more wisdom and sensation than the rest of the body, but also being in every man far weaker. For these reasons and after this manner God placed the sinews at the extremity of the head, in a circle round the neck, and glued them together by the principle of likeness and fastened the extremities of the jawbones to them below the face, and the other sinews he dispersed throughout the body, fastening limb to limb. The framers of us framed the mouth, as now arranged, having teeth and tongue and lips, with a view to the necessary and the good, contriving the way in for necessary purposes, the way out for the best purposes; for that is necessary which enters in and gives food to the body; but the river of speech, which flows out of a man and ministers to the intelligence, is the fairest and noblest of all streams. Still the head could neither be left a bare frame of bones, on account of the extremes of heat and cold in the different seasons, nor yet be allowed to be wholly covered, and so become dull and senseless by reason of an overgrowth of flesh. The fleshy nature was not therefore wholly dried up, but a large sort of peel was parted off and remained over, which is now called the skin. This met and grew by the help of the cerebral moisture, and became the circular envelopment of the head. And the moisture, rising up under the sutures, watered and closed in the skin upon the crown, forming a sort of knot. The diversity of the sutures was caused by the power of the courses of the soul and of the food, and the more these struggled against one another the more numerous they became, and fewer if the struggle were less violent. This skin the divine power pierced all round with fire, and out of the punctures which were thus made the moisture issued forth, and the liquid and heat which was pure came away, and a mixed part which was composed of the same material as the skin, and had a fineness equal to the punctures, was borne up by its own impulse and extended far outside the head, but being too slow to escape, was thrust back by the external air, and rolled up underneath the skin, where it took root. Thus the hair sprang up in the skin, being akin to it because it is like threads of leather, but rendered harder and closer through the pressure of the cold, by which each hair, while in process of separation from the skin, is compressed and cooled. Wherefore the creator formed the head hairy, making use of the causes which I have mentioned, and reflecting also that instead of flesh the brain needed the hair to be a light covering or guard, which would give shade in summer and shelter in winter, and at the same time would not impede our quickness of perception. From the combination of sinew, skin, and bone, in the structure of the finger, there arises a triple compound, which, when dried up, takes the form of one hard skin partaking of all three natures, and was fabricated by these second causes, but designed by mind which is the principal cause with an eye to the future. For our creators well knew that women and other animals would some day be framed out of men, and they further knew that many animals would require the use of nails for many purposes; wherefore they fashioned in men at their first creation the rudiments of nails. For this purpose and for these reasons they caused skin, hair, and nails to grow at the extremities of the limbs. And now that all the parts and members of the mortal animal had come together, since its life of necessity consisted of fire and breath, and it therefore wasted away by dissolution and depletion, the gods contrived the following remedy: They mingled a nature akin to that of man with other forms and perceptions, and thus created another kind of animal. These are the trees and plants and seeds which have been improved by cultivation and are now domesticated among us; anciently there were only the wild kinds, which are older than the cultivated. For everything that partakes of life may be truly called a living being, and the animal of which we are now speaking partakes of the third kind of soul, which is said to be seated between the midriff and the navel, having no part in opinion or reason or mind, but only in feelings of pleasure and pain and the desires which accompany them. For this nature is always in a passive state, revolving in and about itself, repelling the motion from without and using its own, and accordingly is not endowed by nature with the power of observing or reflecting on its own concerns. Wherefore it lives and does not differ from a living being, but is fixed and rooted in the same spot, having no power of self-motion.

Now after the superior powers had created all these natures to be food for us who are of the inferior nature, they cut various channels through the body as through a garden, that it might be watered as from a running stream. In the first place, they cut two hidden channels or veins down the back where the skin and the flesh join, which answered severally to the right and left side of the body. These they let down along the backbone, so as to have the marrow of generation between them, where it was most likely to flourish, and in order that the stream coming down from above might flow freely to the other parts, and equalize the irrigation. In the next place, they divided the veins about the head, and interlacing them, they sent them in opposite directions; those coming from the right side they sent to the left of the body, and those from the left they diverted towards the right, so that they and the skin might together form a bond which should fasten the head to the body, since the crown of the head was not encircled by sinews; and also in order that the sensations from both sides might be distributed over the whole body. And next, they ordered the water-courses of the body in a manner which I will describe, and which will be more easily understood if we begin by admitting that all things which have lesser parts retain the greater, but the greater cannot retain the lesser. Now of all natures fire has the smallest parts, and therefore penetrates through earth and water and air and their compounds, nor can anything hold it. And a similar principle applies to the human belly; for when meats and drinks enter it, it holds them, but it cannot hold air and fire, because the particles of which they consist are smaller than its own structure.

These elements, therefore, God employed for the sake of distributing moisture from the belly into the veins, weaving together a network of fire and air like a weel, having at the entrance two lesser weels; further he constructed one of these with two openings, and from the lesser weels he extended cords reaching all round to the extremities of the network. All the interior of the net he made of fire, but the lesser weels and their cavity, of air. The network he took and spread over the newly-formed animal in the following manner:—He let the lesser weels pass into the mouth; there were two of them, and one he let down by the air-pipes into the lungs, the other by the side of the air-pipes into the belly. The former he divided into two branches, both of which he made to meet at the channels of the nose, so that when the way through the mouth did not act, the streams of the mouth as well were replenished through the nose. With the other cavity (i. e. of the greater weel) he enveloped the hollow parts of the body, and at one time he made all this to flow into the lesser weels, quite gently, for they are composed of air, and at another time he caused the lesser weels to flow back again; and the net he made to find a way in and out through the pores of the body, and the rays of fire which are bound fast within followed the passage of the air either way, never at any time ceasing so long as the mortal being holds together. This process, as we affirm, the name-giver named inspiration and expiration. And all this movement, active as well as passive, takes place in order that the body, being watered and cooled, may receive nourishment and life; for when the respiration is going in and out, and the fire, which is fast bound within, follows it, and ever and anon moving to and fro, enters through the belly and reaches the meat and drink, it dissolves them, and dividing them into small portions and guiding them through the passages where it goes, pumps them as from a fountain into the channels of the veins, and makes the stream of the veins flow through the body as through a conduit.

Let us once more consider the phenomena of respiration, and enquire into the causes which have made it what it is. They are as follows:—Seeing that there is no such thing as a vacuum into which any of those things which are moved can enter, and the breath is carried from us into the external air, the next point is, as will be clear to every one, that it does not go into a vacant space, but pushes its neighbour out of its place, and that which is thrust out in turn drives out its neighbour; and in this way everything of necessity at last comes round to that place from whence the breath came forth, and enters in there, and following the breath, fills up the vacant space; and this goes on like the rotation of a wheel, because there can be no such thing as a vacuum. Wherefore also the breast and the lungs, when they emit the breath, are replenished by the air which surrounds the body and which enters in through the pores of the flesh and is driven round in a circle; and again, the air which is sent away and passes out through the body forces the breath inwards through the passage of the mouth and the nostrils. Now the origin of this movement may be supposed to be as follows. In the interior of every animal the hottest part is that which is around the blood and veins; it is in a manner an internal fountain of fire, which we compare to the network of a creel, being woven all of fire and extended through the centre of the body, while the outer parts are composed of air. Now we must admit that heat naturally proceeds outward to its own place and to its kindred element; and as there are two exits for the heat, the one out through the body, and the other through the mouth and nostrils, when it moves towards the one, it drives round the air at the other, and that which is driven round falls into the fire and becomes warm, and that which goes forth is cooled. But when the heat changes its place, and the particles at the other exit grow warmer, the hotter air inclining in that direction and carried towards its native element, fire, pushes round the air at the other; and this being affected in the same way and communicating the same impulse, a circular motion swaying to and fro is produced by the double process, which we call inspiration and expiration.

The phenomena of medical cupping-glasses and of the swallowing of drink and of the projection of bodies, whether discharged in the air or bowled along the ground, are to be investigated on a similar principle; and swift and slow sounds, which appear to be high and low, and are sometimes discordant on account of their inequality, and then again harmonical on account of the equality of the motion which they excite in us. For when the motions of the antecedent swifter sounds begin to pause and the two are equalized, the slower sounds overtake the swifter and then propel them. When they overtake them they do not intrude a new and discordant motion, but introduce the beginnings of a slower, which answers to the swifter as it dies away, thus producing a

single mixed expression out of high and low, whence
arises a pleasure which even the unwise feel, and which
to the wise becomes a higher sort of delight, being an
imitation of divine harmony in mortal motions. Moreover, as to the flowing of water, the fall of the thunderbolt, and the marvels that are observed about the attraction of amber and the Heraclean stones—in none of
these cases is there any attraction; but he who investigates rightly, will find that such wonderful phenomena
are attributable to the combination of certain conditions
—the non-existence of a vacuum, the fact that objects
push one another round, and that they change places,
passing severally into their proper positions as they are
divided or combined.

Such as we have seen, is the nature and such are the
causes of respiration—the subject in which this discussion originated. For the fire cuts the food and following
the breath surges up within, fire and breath rising together and filling the veins by drawing up out of the
belly and pouring into them the cut portions of the food;
and so the streams of food are kept flowing through the
whole body in all animals. And fresh cuttings from kindred substances, whether the fruits of the earth or herb
of the field, which God planted to be our daily food,
acquire all sorts of colours by their inter-mixture; but red
is the most pervading of them, being created by the cutting action of fire and by the impression which it makes
on a moist substance; and hence the liquid which circu-
lates in the body has a colour such as we have described.
The liquid itself we call blood, which nourishes the flesh
and the whole body, whence all parts are watered and
empty places filled.

Now the process of repletion and evacuation is effected
after the manner of the universal motion by which all
kindred substances are drawn towards one another. For

the external elements which surround us are always
causing us to consume away, and distributing and sending off like to like; the particles of blood, too, which are
divided and contained within the frame of the animal as
in a sort of heaven, are compelled to imitate the motion
of the universe. Each, therefore, of the divided parts
within us, being carried to its kindred nature, replenishes
the void. When more is taken away than flows in, then
we decay, and when less, we grow and increase.

The frame of the entire creature when young has the
triangles of each kind new, and may be compared to the
keel of a vessel which is just off the stocks; they are
locked firmly together and yet the whole mass is soft and
delicate, being freshly formed of marrow and nurtured
on milk. Now when the triangles out of which meats and
drinks are composed come in from without, and are comprehended in the body, being older and weaker than the
triangles already there, the frame of the body gets the
better of them and its newer triangles cut them up, and
so the animal grows great, being nourished by a multitude of similiar particles. But when the roots of the triangles are loosened by having undergone many conflicts
with many things in the course of time, they are no
longer able to cut or assimilate the food which enters,
but are themselves easily divided by the bodies which
come in from without. In this way every animal is overcome and decays, and this affection is called old age.
And at last, when the bonds by which the triangles of the
marrow are united no longer hold, and are parted by
the strain of existence, they in turn loosen the bonds of the
soul, and she, obtaining a natural release, flies away with
joy. For that which takes place according to nature is
pleasant, but that which is contrary to nature is painful.
And thus death, if caused by disease or produced by
wounds, is painful and violent; but that sort of death

which comes with old age and fulfils the debt of nature is the easiest of deaths, and is accompanied with pleasure rather than with pain.

Now every one can see whence diseases arise. There are four natures out of which the body is compacted, earth and fire and water and air, and the unnatural excess or defect of these, or the change of any of them from its own natural place into another, or—since there are more kinds than one of fire and of the other elements— the assumption by any of these of a wrong kind, or any similar irregularity, produces disorders and diseases; for when any of them is produced or changed in a manner contrary to nature, the parts which were previously cool grow warm, and those which were dry become moist, and the light become heavy, and the heavy light; all sorts of changes occur. For, as we affirm, a thing can only remain the same with itself, whole and sound, when the same is added to it, or subtracted from it, in the same respect and in the same manner and in due proportion; and whatever comes or goes away in violation of these laws causes all manner of changes and infinite diseases and corruptions. Now there is a second class of structures which are also natural, and this affords a second opportunity of observing diseases to him who would understand them. For whereas marrow and bone and flesh and sinews are composed of the four elements, and the blood, though after another manner, is likewise formed out of them, most diseases originate in the way which I have described; but the worst of all owe their severity to the fact that the generation of these substances proceeds in a wrong order; they are then destroyed. For the natural order is that the flesh and sinews should be made of blood, the sinews out of the fibres to which they are akin, and the flesh out of the clots which are formed when the fibres are separated. And the glutinous and rich matter which comes away from the sinews and the flesh, not only glues the flesh to the bones, but nourishes and imparts growth to the bone which surrounds the marrow; and by reason of the solidity of the bones, that which filters through consists of the purest and smoothest and oiliest sort of triangles, dropping like dew from the bones and watering the marrow. Now when each process takes place in this order, health commonly results; when in the opposite order, disease. For when the flesh becomes decomposed and sends back the wasting substance into the veins, then an over-supply of blood of diverse kinds, mingling with air in the veins, having variegated colours and bitter properties, as well as acid and saline qualities, contains all sorts of bile and serum and phlegm. For all things go the wrong way, and having become corrupted, first they taint the blood itself, and then ceasing to give nourishment to the body they are carried along the veins in all directions, no longer preserving the order of their natural courses, but at war with themselves, because they receive no good from one another, and are hostile to the abiding constitution of the body, which they corrupt and dissolve. The oldest part of the flesh which is corrupted, being hard to decompose, from long burning grows black, and from being everywhere corroded become bitter, and is injurious to every part of the body which is still uncorrupted. Sometimes, when the bitter element is refined away, the black part assumes an acidity which takes the place of the bitterness; at other times the bitterness being tinged with blood has a redder colour; and this, when mixed with black, takes the hue of grass; and again, an auburn colour mingles with the bitter matter when new flesh is decomposed by the fire which surrounds the internal flame—to all which symptoms some physician perhaps, or rather some philosopher, who had the power of seeing in many dissimilar things one nature deserving of a name, has assigned the common name of bile. But the other kinds of bile are variously distinguished by their colours. As for serum, that sort which is the watery part of blood is innocent, but that which is a secretion of black and acid bile is malignant when mingled by the power of heat with any salt substance, and is then called acid phlegm. Again, the substance which is formed by the liquefaction of new and tender flesh when air is present, if inflated and encased in liquid so as to form bubbles, which separately are invisible owing to their small size, but when collected are of a bulk which is visible, and have a white colour arising out of the generation of foam—all this decomposition of tender flesh when inter-mingled with air is termed by us white phlegm. And the whey or sediment of newly-formed phlegm is sweat and tears, and includes the various daily discharges by which the body is purified. Now all these become causes of disease when the blood is not replenished in a natural manner by food and drink but gains bulk from opposite sources in violation of the laws of nature. When the several parts of the flesh are separated by disease, if the foundation remains, the power of the disorder is only half as great, and there is still a prospect of an easy recovery; but when that which binds the flesh to the bones is diseased, and no longer being separated from the muscles and sinews, ceases to give nourishment to the bone and to unite flesh and bone, and from being oily and smooth and glutinous becomes rough and salt and dry, owing to bad regimen, then all the substance thus corrupted crumbles away under the flesh and the sinews, and separates from the bone, and the fleshy parts fall away from their foundation and leave the sinews bare and full of brine, and the flesh again gets into the circulation of the blood and makes the previously-mentioned disorders still greater.

And if these bodily affections be severe, still worse are the prior disorders; as when the bone itself, by reason of the density of the flesh, does not obtain sufficient air, but becomes mouldy and hot and gangrened and receives no nutriment, and the natural process is inverted, and the bone crumbling passes into the food, and the food into the flesh, and the flesh again falling into the blood makes all maladies that may occur more virulent than those already mentioned. But the worst case of all is when the marrow is diseased, either from excess or defect; and this is the cause of the very greatest and most fatal disorders, in which the whole course of the body is reversed.

There is a third class of diseases which may be conceived of as arising in three ways; for they are produced sometimes by wind, and sometimes by phlegm, and sometimes by bile. When the lung, which is the dispenser of the air to the body, is obstructed by rheums and its passages are not free, some of them not acting, while through others too much air enters, then the parts which are unrefreshed by air corrode, while in other parts the excess of air forcing its way through the veins distorts them and decomposing the body is enclosed in the midst of it and occupies the midriff; thus numberless painful diseases are produced, accompanied by copious sweats. And oftentimes when the flesh is dissolved in the body, wind, generated within and unable to escape, is the source of quite as much pain as the air coming in from without; but the greatest pain is felt when the wind gets about the sinews and the veins of the shoulders, and swells them up, and so twists back the great tendons and the sinews which are connected with them. These disorders are called tetanus and opisthotonus, by reason of the tension which accompanies them. The cure of them is difficult; relief is in most cases given by fever supervening. The white phlegm, though dangerous when detained within by reason of the air-bubbles, yet if it can communicate with the outside air, is less severe, and only discolours the body, generating leprous eruptions and similar diseases. When it is mingled with black bile and dispersed about the courses of the head, which are the divinest part of us, the attack if coming on in sleep, is not so severe; but when assailing those who are awake it is hard to be got rid of, and being an affection of a sacred part, is most justly called sacred. An acid and salt phlegm, again, is the source of all those diseases which take the form of catarrh, but they have many names because the places into which they flow are manifold.

Inflammations of the body come from burnings and inflamings, and all of them originate in bile. When bile finds a means of discharge, it boils up and sends forth all sorts of tumours; but when imprisoned within, it generates many inflammatory diseases, above all when mingled with pure blood; since it then displaces the fibres which are scattered about in the blood and are designed to maintain the balance of rare and dense, in order that the blood may not be so liquefied by heat as to exude from the pores of the body, nor again become too dense and thus find a difficulty in circulating through the veins. The fibres are so constituted as to maintain this balance; and if any one brings them all together when the blood is dead and in process of cooling, then the blood which remains becomes fluid, but if they are left alone, they soon congeal by reason of the surrounding cold. The fibres having this power over the blood, bile, which is only stale blood, and which from being flesh is dissolved again into blood, at the first influx coming in little by little, hot and liquid, is congealed by the power of the fibres; and so congealing and made to cool, it produces internal cold and shuddering. When it enters with more of a flood and overcomes the fibres by its heat, and boiling up throws them into disorder, if it have power enough to maintain its supremacy, it penetrates the marrow and burns up what may be termed the cables of the soul, and sets her free; but when there is not so much of it, and the body though wasted still holds out, the bile is itself mastered, and is either utterly banished, or is thrust through the veins into the lower or upper belly, and is driven out of the body like an exile from a state in which there has been civil war; whence arise diarrhoeas and dysenteries, and all such disorders. When the constitution is disordered by excess of fire, continuous heat and fever are the result; when excess of air is the cause, then the fever is quotidian; when of water, which is a more sluggish element than either fire or air, then the fever is a tertian; when of earth, which is the most sluggish of the four, and is only purged away in a four-fold period, the result is a quartan fever, which can with difficulty be shaken off.

Such is the manner in which diseases of the body arise; the disorders of the soul, which depend upon the body, originate as follows. We must acknowledge disease of the mind to be a want of intelligence; and of this there are two kinds; to wit, madness and ignorance. In whatever state a man experiences either of them, that state may be called disease; and excessive pains and pleasures are justly to be regarded as the greatest diseases to which the soul is liable. For a man who is in great joy or in great pain, in his unseasonable eagerness to attain the one and to avoid the other, is not able to see or to hear anything rightly; but he is mad, and is at the time utterly incapable of any participation in reason. He who has the seed about the spinal marrow too plentiful and overflowing, like a tree overladen with fruit, has many throes, and also obtains many pleasures in his desires and their offspring, and is for the most part of his life deranged, because his pleasures and pains are so very great; his soul is rendered foolish and disordered by his body; yet he is regarded not as one diseased, but as one who is voluntarily bad, which is a mistake. The truth is that the intemperance of love is a disease of the soul due chiefly to the moisture and fluidity which is produced in one of the elements by the loose consistency of the bones. And in general, all that which is termed the incontinence of pleasure and is deemed a reproach under the idea that the wicked voluntarily do wrong is not justly a matter for reproach. For no man is voluntarily bad; but the bad become bad by reason of an ill disposition of the body and bad education, things which are hateful to every man and happen to him against his will. And in the case of pain too in like manner the soul suffers much evil from the body. For where the acid and briny phlegm and other bitter and bilious humours wander about in the body, and find no exit or escape, but are pent up within and mingle their own vapours with the motions of the soul, and are blended, with them, they produce all sorts of diseases, more or fewer, and in every degree of intensity; and being carried to the three places of the soul, whichever they may severally assail, they create infinite varieties of ill-temper and melancholy, of rashness and cowardice, and also of forgetfulness and stupidity. Further, when to this evil constitution of body evil forms of government are added and evil discourses are uttered in private as well as in public, and no sort of instruction is given in youth to cure these evils, then all of us who are bad become bad from two causes which are entirely beyond our control. In such cases the planters are to blame rather than the plants, the educators rather than the educated. But however that may be, we should endeavour as far as we can by education, and studies, and learning, to avoid vice and attain virtue; this, however, is part of another subject.

There is a corresponding enquiry concerning the mode of treatment by which the mind and the body are to be preserved, about which it is meet and right that I should say a word in turn; for it is more our duty to speak of the good than of the evil. Everything that is good is fair, and the fair is not without proportion, and the animal which is to be fair must have due proportion. Now we perceive lesser symmetries or proportions and reason about them, but of the highest and greatest we take no heed; for there is no proportion or disproportion more productive of health and disease, and virtue and vice, than that between soul and body. This however we do not perceive, nor do we reflect that when a weak or small frame is the vehicle of a great and mighty soul, or conversely, when a little soul is encased in a large body, then the whole animal is not fair, for it lacks the most important of all symmetries; but the due proportion of mind and body is the fairest and loveliest of all sights to him who has the seeing eye. Just as a body which has a leg too long, or which is unsymmetrical in some other respect, is an unpleasant sight, and also, when doing its share of work, is much distressed and makes convulsive efforts, and often stumbles through awkwardness, and is the cause of infinite evil to its own self—in like manner we should conceive of the double nature which we call the living being; and when in this compound there is an impassioned soul more powerful than the body, that soul, I say, convulses and fills with disorders the whole inner nature of man; and when eager in the pursuit of some sort of learning or study, causes wasting; or again, when teaching or disputing in private or in public, and strifes and controversies arise, inflames and dissolves the composite frame of man and introduces rheums; and the nature of this phenomenon is not understood by most professors of medicine, who ascribe it to the opposite of the real cause. And once more, when a body large and too strong for the soul is united to a small and weak intelligence, then inasmuch as there are two desires natural to man—one of food for the sake of the body, and one of wisdom for the sake of the diviner part of us—then, I say, the motions of the stronger, getting the better and increasing their own power, but making the soul dull, and stupid, and forgetful, engender ignorance, which is the greatest of diseases. There is one protection against both kinds of disproportion:—that we should not move the body without the soul or the soul without the body, and thus they will be on their guard against each other, and be healthy and well balanced. And therefore the mathematician or any one else whose thoughts are much absorbed in some intellectual pursuit, must allow his body also to have due exercise, and practise gymnastic; and he who is careful to fashion the body, should in turn impart to the soul its proper motions, and should cultivate music and all philosophy, if he would deserve to be called truly fair and truly good. And the separate parts should be treated in the same manner, in imitation of the pattern of the universe; for as the body is heated and also cooled within by the elements which enter into it, and is again dried up and moistened by external things, and experiences these and the like affections from both kinds of motions, the result is that the body if given up to motion when in a state of quiescence is overmastered and perishes; but if any one, in imitation of that which we call the foster-mother and nurse of the universe, will not allow the body ever to be inactive, but is always producing motions and agitations through its whole extent, which form the natural defence against other motions both internal and external, and by moderate exercise reduces to order according to their affinities the particles and affections which are wandering about the body, as we have already said when speaking of the universe, he will not allow enemy placed by the side of enemy to stir up wars and disorders in the body, but he will place friend by the side of friend, so as to create health. Now of all motions that is the best which is produced in a thing by itself, for it is most akin to the motion of thought and of the universe; but that motion which is caused by others is not so good, and worst of all is that which moves the body, when at rest, in parts only and by some external agency. Wherefore of all modes of purifying and re-uniting the body the best is gymnastic; the next best is a surging motion, as in sailing or any other mode of conveyance which is not fatiguing; the third sort of motion may be of use in a case of extreme necessity, but in any other will be adopted by no man of sense: I mean the purgative treatment of physicians; for diseases unless they are very dangerous should not be irritated by medicines, since every form of disease is in a manner akin to the living being, whose complex frame has an appointed term of life. For not the whole race only, but each individual— barring inevitable accidents—comes into the world having a fixed span, and the triangles in us are originally framed with power to last for a certain time, beyond which no man can prolong his life. And this holds also of the constitution of diseases; if any one regardless of the appointed time tries to subdue them by medicine, he only aggravates and multiplies them. Wherefore we ought always to manage them by regimen, as far as a man can spare the time, and not provoke a disagreeable enemy by medicines.

Enough of the composite animal, and of the body

which is a part of him, and of the manner in which a man may train and be trained by himself so as to live most according to reason: and we must above and before all provide that the element which is to train him shall be the fairest and best adapted to that purpose. A minute discussion of this subject would be a serious task; but if, as before, I am to give only an outline, the subject may not unfitly be summed up as follows.

I have often remarked that there are three kinds of soul located within us, having each of them motions, and I must now repeat in the fewest words possible, that one part, if remaining inactive and ceasing from its natural motion, must necessarily become very weak, but that which is trained and exercised, very strong. Wherefore we should take care that the movements of the different parts of the soul should be in due proportion.

And we should consider that God gave the sovereign part of the human soul to be the divinity of each one, being that part which, as we say, dwells at the top of the body, and inasmuch as we are a plant not of an earthly but of a heavenly growth, raises us from earth to our kindred who are in heaven. And in this we say truly; for the divine power suspended the head and root of us from that place where the generation of the soul first began, and thus made the whole body upright. When a man is always occupied with the cravings of desire and ambition, and is eagerly striving to satisfy them, all his thoughts must be mortal, and, as far as it is possible altogether to become such, he must be mortal every whit, because he has cherished his mortal part. But he who has been earnest in the love of knowledge and of true wisdom, and has exercised his intellect more than any other part of him, must have thoughts immortal and divine, if he attain truth, and in so far as human nature is capable of sharing in immortality, he must altogether be immortal; and since he is ever cherishing the divine power, and has the divinity within him in perfect order, he will be perfectly happy. Now there is only one way of taking care of things, and this is to give to each the food and motion which are natural to it. And the motions which are naturally akin to the divine principle within us are the thoughts and revolutions of the universe. These each man should follow, and correct the courses of the head which were corrupted at our birth, and by learning the harmonies and revolutions of the universe, should assimilate the thinking being to the thought renewing his original nature, and having assimilated them should attain to that perfect life which the gods have set before mankind, both for the present and the future.

Thus our original design of discoursing about the universe down to the creation of man is nearly completed. A brief mention may be made of the generation of other animals, so far as the subject admits of brevity; in this manner our argument will best attain a due proportion. On the subject of animals, then, the following remarks may be offered. Of the men who came into the world, those who were cowards or led unrighteous lives may with reason be supposed to have changed into the nature of women in the second generation. And this was the reason why at that time the gods created in us the desire of sexual intercourse, contriving in man one animated substance, and in woman another, which they formed respectively in the following manner. The outlet for drink by which liquids pass through the lung under the kidneys and into the bladder, which receives and then by the pressure of the air emits them, was so fashioned by them as to penetrate also into the body of the marrow, which passes from the head along the neck and through the back, and which in the preceding discourse we have named the seed. And the seed having life, and becoming endowed with respiration, produces in that part in which it respires a lively desire of emission, and thus creates in us the love of procreation. Wherefore also in men the organ of generation becoming rebellious and masterful, like an animal disobedient to reason, and maddened with the sting of lust, seeks to gain absolute sway; and the same is the case with the so-called womb or matrix of women; the animal within them is desirous of procreating children, and when remaining unfruitful long beyond its proper time, gets discontented and angry, and wandering in every direction through the body, closes up the passages of the breath, and, by obstructing respiration, drives them to extremity, causing all varieties of disease, until at length the desire and love of the man and the woman, bringing them together and as it were plucking the fruit from the tree, sow in the womb, as in a field, animals unseen by reason of their smallness and without form; these again are separated and matured within; they are then finally brought out into the light, and thus the generation of animals is completed.

Thus were created women and the female sex in general. But the race of birds was created out of innocent light-minded men, who, although their minds were directed toward heaven, imagined, in their simplicity, that the clearest demonstration of the things above was to be obtained by sight; these were remodelled and transformed into birds, and they grew feathers instead of hair. The race of wild pedestrian animals, again, came from those who had no philosophy in any of their thoughts, and never considered at all about the nature of the heavens, because they had ceased to use the courses of the head, but followed the guidance of those parts of the soul which are in the breast. In consequence of these habits of theirs they had their front-legs and their heads resting upon the earth to which they were drawn by natural affinity; and the crowns of their heads were elongated and of all sorts of shapes, into which the courses of the soul were crushed by reason of disuse. And this was the reason why they were created quadrupeds and polypods: God gave the more senseless of them the more support that they might be more attracted to the earth. And the most foolish of them, who trail their bodies entirely upon the ground and have no longer any need of feet, he made without feet to crawl upon the earth. The fourth class were the inhabitants of the water: these were made out of the most entirely senseless and ignorant of all, whom the transformers did not think any longer worthy of pure respiration, because they possessed a soul which was made impure by all sorts of transgression; and instead of the subtle and pure medium of air, they gave them the deep and muddy sea to be their element of respiration; and hence arose the race of fishes and oysters, and other aquatic animals, which have received the most remote habitations as a punishment of their outlandish ignorance. These are the laws by which animals pass into one another, now, as ever, changing as they lose or gain wisdom and folly.

We may now say that our discourse about the nature of the universe has an end. The world has received animals, mortal and immortal, and is fulfilled with them, and has become a visible animal containing the visible— the sensible God who is the image of the intellectual, the greatest, best, fairest, most perfect—the one only-begotten heaven.

Translated by Benjamin Jowett.

O

THE FIRST CAUSE

ARISTOTLE

1. The subject of our inquiry is substance; for the principles and the causes we are seeking are those of substances. For if the universe is of the nature of a whole, substance is its first part; and if it coheres merely by virtue of serial succession, on this view also substance is first, and is succeeded by quality, and then by quantity. At the same time these latter are not even being in the full sense, but are qualities and movements of it—or else even the not-white and the not-straight would be being; at least we say even these *are,* e. g. "there is a not-white." Further, none of the categories other than substance can exist apart. And the early philosophers also in practice testify to the primacy of substance; for it was of substance that they sought the principles and elements and causes. The thinkers of the present day tend to rank universals as substances (for genera are universals, and these they tend to describe as principles and substances, owing to the abstract nature of their inquiry); but the thinkers of old ranked particular things as substances, e. g. fire and earth, not what is common to both, body.

There are three kinds of substance—one that is sensible (of which one subdivision is eternal and another is perishable; the latter is recognized by all men, and includes, e. g., plants and animals), of which we must grasp the elements, whether one or many; and another that is immovable, and this certain thinkers assert to be capable of existing apart, some dividing it into two, others identifying the Forms and the objects of mathematics, and others positing, of these two, only the objects of mathematics. The former two kinds of substance are the subject of physics (for they imply movement); but the third kind belongs to another science, if there is no principle common to it and to the other kinds.

2. Sensible substance is changeable. Now if change proceeds from opposites or from intermediates, and not from all opposites (for the voice is not-white [but it does not therefore change to white]), but from the contrary, there must be something underlying which changes into the contrary state; for the *contraries* do not change. Further, something persists, but the contrary does not persist; there is, then, some third thing besides the contraries, viz. the matter. Now since changes are of four kinds—either in respect of the "what" or of the quality or of the quantity or of the place, and change in respect of "thisness" is simple generation and destruction, and change in quantity is increase and diminution, and change in respect of an affection is alteration, and change of place is motion, changes will be from given states into those contrary to them in these several respects. The matter, then, which changes must be capable of both states. And since that which "is" has two senses, we must say that everything changes from that which is potentially to that which is actually, e. g. from potentially white to actually white, and similarly in the case of increase and diminution. Therefore not only can a thing come to be, incidentally, out of that which is not, but also all things come to be out of that which is, but is potentially, and is not actually. And this is the "One" of Anaxagoras; for instead of "all things were together"—and the "Mixture" of Empedocles and Anaximander and the account given by Democritus—it is better to say "all things were together potentially but not actually." Therefore these thinkers seem to have had some notion

of matter. Now all things that change have matter, but different matter; and of eternal things those which are not generable but are movable in space have matter—not matter for generation, however, but for motion from one place to another.

One might raise the question from what sort of non-being generation proceeds; for "non-being" has three senses. If, then, one form of non-being exists potentially, still it is not by virtue of a potentiality for any and every thing, but different things come from different things; nor is it satisfactory to say that "all things were to-gether"; for they differ in their matter, since otherwise why did an infinity of things come to be, and not one thing? For "reason" is one, so that if matter also were one, that must have come to be in actuality which the matter was in potency. The causes and the principles, then, are three, two being the pair of contraries of which one is definition and form and the other is privation, and the third being the matter.

3. Note, next, that neither the matter nor the form comes to be—and I mean the last matter and form. For everything that changes is something and is changed by something and into something. That by which it is changed is the immediate mover; that which is changed, the matter; that into which it is changed, the form. The process, then, will go on to infinity, if not only the bronze comes to be round but also the round or the bronze comes to be; therefore there must be a stop.

Note, next, that each substance comes into being out of something that shares its name. (Natural objects and other things both rank as substances.) For things come into being either by art or by nature or by luck or by spontaneity. Now art is a principle of movement in something other than the thing moved, nature is a principle in the thing itself (for man begets man), and the other causes are privations of these two.

There are three kinds of substance—the matter, which is a "this" in appearance (for all things that are characterized by contact and not by organic unity are matter and substratum, e. g. fire, flesh, head; for these are all matter, and the last matter is the matter of that which is in the full sense substance); the nature, which is a "this" or positive state towards which movement takes place; and again, thirdly, the particular substance which is composed of these two, e. g. Socrates or Callias. Now in some cases the "this" does not exist apart from the composite substance, e. g. the form of house does not so exist, unless the art of building exists apart (nor is there generation and destruction of these forms, but it is in another way that the house apart from its matter, and health, and all ideals of art, exist and do not exist); but if the "this" exists apart from the concrete thing, it is only in the case of natural objects. And so Plato was not far wrong when he said that there are as many Forms as there are kinds of natural object (if there *are* Forms distinct from the things of this earth). The moving causes exist as things preceding the effects, but causes in the sense of definitions are simultaneous with their effects. For when a man is healthy, then health also exists; and the shape of a bronze sphere exists at the same time as the bronze sphere. (But we must examine whether any form also survives afterwards. For in some cases there is nothing to prevent this; e. g. the soul may be of this sort—not all soul but the reason; for presumably it is impossible that *all* soul should survive.) Evidently then there is no necessity, on this ground at least, for the existence of the Ideas. For man is begotten by man, a given man by an individual father; and similarly in the arts; for the medical art is the formal cause of health.

4. The causes and the principles of different things are in a sense different, but in a sense, if one speaks universally and analogically, they are the same for all. For one might raise the question whether the principles and elements are different or the same for substances and for relative terms, and similarly in the case of each of the categories. But it would be paradoxical if they were the same for all. For then from the same elements will proceed relative terms and substances. What then will this common element be? For (1) (*a*) there is nothing common to and distinct from substance and the other categories, viz. those which are predicated; but an element is prior to the things of which it is an element. But again (*b*) substance is not an element in relative terms, nor is any of these an element in substance. Further, (2) how can all things have the same elements? For none of the elements can be the same as that which is composed of elements, e. g. *b* or *a* cannot be the same as *ba*. (None, therefore, of the intelligibles, e. g. being or unity, is an element; for these are predicable of each of the compounds as well.) None of the elements, then, will be either a substance or a relative term; but it must be one or other. All things, then, have not the same elements.

Or, as we are wont to put it, in a sense they have and in a sense they have not; e. g. perhaps the elements of perceptible bodies are, as *form*, the hot, and in another sense the cold, which is the *privation;* and, as *matter*, that which directly and of itself potentially has these attributes; and substances comprise both these and the things composed of these, of which these are the principles, or any unity which is produced out of the hot and the cold, e. g. flesh or bone; for the product must be different from the elements. These things then have the same elements and principles (though specifically different things have specifically different elements); but *all* things have not the same elements in this sense, but only analogically; i. e. one might say that there are three principles—the form, the privation, and the matter. But each of these is different for each class; e. g. in colour they are white, black, and surface, and in day and night they are light, darkness, and air.

Since not only the elements present in a thing are causes, but also something external, i. e. the moving cause, clearly while "principle" and "element" are different both are causes, and "principle" is divided into these two kinds and that which acts as producing movement or rest is a principle and a substance. Therefore analogically there are three elements, and four causes and principles; but the elements are different in different things, and the proximate moving cause is different for different things. Health, disease, body; the moving cause is the medical art. Form, disorder of a particular kind, bricks; the moving cause is the building art. And since the moving cause in the case of natural things is—for man, for instance, man, and in the products of thought the form or its contrary, there will be in a sense three causes, while in a sense there are four. For the medical art is in some sense health, and the building art is the form of the house, and man begets man; further, besides these there is that which as first of all things moves all things.

5. Some things can exist apart and some cannot, and it is the former that are substances. And therefore all things have the same causes, because, without substances, modifications and movements do not exist. Further, these causes will probably be soul and body, or reason and desire and body.

And in yet another way, analogically identical things

are principles, i. e. actuality and potency; but these also are not only different for different things but also apply in different ways to them. For in some cases the same thing exists at one time actually and at another potentially, e. g. wine or flesh or man does so. (And these two fall under the above-named causes. For the form exists actually, if it can exist apart, and so does the complex of form and matter, and the privation, e. g. darkness or disease; but the matter exists potentially; for this is that which can become qualified either by the form or by the privation.) But the distinction of actuality and potentiality applies in another way to cases where the matter of cause and of effect is not the same, in some of which cases the form is not the same but different; e. g. the cause of man is (1) the elements in man (viz. fire and earth as matter, and the peculiar form), and further (2) something else outside, i. e. the father, and (3) besides these the sun and its oblique course, which are neither matter nor form nor privation of man nor of the same species with him, but moving causes.

Further, one must observe that some causes can be expressed in universal terms, and some cannot. The proximate principles of all things are the "this" which is proximate in actuality, and another which is proximate in potentiality. The universal causes, then, of which we spoke do not *exist*. For it is the individual that is the originative principle of the individuals. For while man is the originative principle of man universally, there *is* no unversal man, but Peleus is the originative principle of Achilles, and your father of you, and this particular *b* of this particular *ba,* though *b* in general is the originative principle of *ba* taken without qualification.

Further, if the causes of substances are the causes of all things, yet different things have different causes and elements, as was said; the causes of things that are not in the same class, e. g. of colours and sounds, of substances and quantities, are different except in an analogical sense; and those of things in the same species are different, not in species, but in the sense that the causes of different individuals are different, your matter and form and moving cause being different from mine, while in their universal definition they are the same. And if we inquire what are the principles or elements of substances and relations and qualities—whether they are the same or different—clearly when the names of the causes are used in several senses the causes of each are the same, but when the senses are distinguished the causes are not the same but different, except that in the following senses the causes of all are the same. They are (1) the same or analogous in this sense, that matter, form, privation, and the moving cause are common to all things; and (2) the causes of substances may be treated as causes of all things in this sense, that when substances are removed all things are removed; further, (3) that which is first in respect of complete reality is the cause of all things. But in another sense there are different first causes, viz. all the contraries which are neither generic nor ambiguous terms; and, further, the matters of different things are different. We have stated, then, what are the principles of sensible things and how many they are, and in what sense they are the same and in what sense different.

6. Since there were three kinds of substance, two of them physical and one unmovable, regarding the latter we must assert that it is necessary that there should be an eternal unmovable substance. For substances are the first of existing things, and if they are all destructible, all things are destructible. But it is impossible that movement should either have come into being or cease to be

(for it must always have existed), or that time should. For there could not be a before and an after if time did not exist. Movement also is continuous, then, in the sense in which time is; for time is either the same thing as movement or an attribute of movement. And there is no continuous movement except movement in place, and of this only that which is circular is continuous.

But if there is something which is capable of moving things or acting on them, but is not actually doing so, there will not necessarily be movement; for that which has a potency need not exercise it. Nothing, then, is gained even if we suppose eternal substances, as the believers in the Forms do, unless there is to be in them some principle which can cause change; nay, even this is not enough, nor is another substance besides the Forms enough; for if it is not to *act*, there will be no movement. Further, even if it acts, this will not be enough, if its essence is potency; for there will not be *eternal* movement, since that which is potentially may possibly not be. There must, then, be such a principle, whose very essence is actuality. Further, then, these substances must be without matter; for they must be eternal, if *anything* is eternal. Therefore they must be actuality.

Yet there is a difficulty; for it is thought that everything that acts is able to act, but that not everything that is able to act acts, so that the potency is prior. But if this is so, nothing that is need be; for it is possible for all things to be capable of existing but not yet to exist.

Yet if we follow the theologians who generate the world from night, or the natural philosophers who say that "all things were together," the same impossible result ensues. For how will there be movement, if there is no actually existing cause? Wood will surely not move itself—the carpenter's art must act on it; nor will the menstrual blood nor the earth set themselves in motion, but the seeds must act on the earth and the *semen* on the menstrual blood.

This is why some suppose eternal actuality—e. g. Leucippus and Plato; for they say there is always movement. But why and what this movement is they do not say, nor, if the world moves in this way or that, do they tell us the cause of its doing so. Now nothing is moved at random, but there must always be something present to move it; e. g. as a matter of fact a thing moves in one way by nature, and in another by force or through the influence of reason or something else. (Further, what sort of movement is primary? This makes a vast difference.) But again for Plato, at least, it is not permissible to name here that which he sometimes supposes to be the source of movement—that which moves itself; for the soul is later, and coeval with the heavens, according to his account. To suppose potency prior to actuality, then, is in a sense right, and in a sense not; and we have specified these senses. That actuality is prior is testified by Anaxagoras (for his "reason" is actuality) and by Empedocles in his doctrine of love and strife, and by those who say that there is always movement, e. g. Leucippus. Therefore chaos or night did not exist for an infinite time, but the same things have always existed (either passing through a cycle of changes or obeying some other law), since actuality is prior to potency. If, then, there is a constant cycle, something must always remain, acting in the same way. And if there is to be generation and destruction, there must be something else which is always acting in different ways. This must, then, act in one way in virtue of itself, and in another in virtue of something else—either of a third agent, therefore, or of the first. Now it must be in virtue of the first. For otherwise this again causes the motion both of the second agent and of the third. Therefore it is better to say "the first." For it was the cause of eternal uniformity; and something else is the cause of variety, and evidently both together are the cause of eternal variety. This, accordingly, is the character which the motions actually exhibit. What need then is there to seek for other principles?

7. Since (1) this is a possible account of the matter, and (2) if it were not true, the world would have proceeded out of night and "all things together" and out of non-being, these difficulties may be taken as solved. There is, then, something which is always moved with an unceasing motion, which is motion in a circle; and this is plain not in theory only but in fact. Therefore the first heaven must be eternal. There is therefore also something which moves it. And since that which is moved and moves is intermediate, there is something which moves without being moved, being eternal, substance, and actuality. And the object of desire and the object of thought move in this way; they move without being moved. The primary objects of desire and of thought are the same. For the apparent good is the object of appetite, and the real good is the primary object of rational wish. But desire is consequent on opinion rather than opinion on desire; for the thinking is the starting-point. And thought is moved by the object of thought, and one of the two columns of opposites is in itself the object of thought; and in this, substance is first, and in substance, that which is simple and exists actually. (The one and the simple are not the same; for "one" means a measure, but "simple" means that the thing itself has a certain nature.) But the beautiful, also, and that which is in itself desirable are in the same column; and the first in any class is always best, or analogous to the best.

That a final cause may exist among unchangeable

entities is shown by the distinction of its meanings. For the final cause is (*a*) some being for whose good an action is done, and (*b*) something at which the action aims; and of these the latter exists among unchangeable entities though the former does not. The final cause, then, produces motion as being loved, but all other things move by being moved.

Now if something is moved it is capable of being otherwise than as it is. Therefore if its actuality is the primary form of spatial motion, then in so far as it is subject to change, in *this* respect it is capable of being otherwise—in place, even if not in substance. But since there is something which moves while itself unmoved, existing actually, this can in no way be otherwise than as it is. For motion in space is the first of the kinds of change, and motion in a circle the first kind of spatial motion; and this the first mover *produces*. The first mover, then, exists of necessity; and in so far as it exists by necessity, its mode of being is good, and it is in this sense a first principle. For the necessary has all these senses—that which is necessary perforce because it is contrary to the natural impulse, that without which the good is impossible, and that which cannot be otherwise but can exist only in a single way.

On such a principle, then, depend the heavens and the world of nature. And it is a life such as the best which we enjoy, and enjoy for but a short time (for it is ever in this state, which we cannot be), since its actuality is also pleasure. (And for this reason are waking, perception, and thinking most pleasant, and hopes and memories are so on account of these.) And thinking in itself deals with that which is best in itself, and that which is thinking in the fullest sense with that which is best in the fullest sense. And thought thinks on itself because it shares the nature of the object of thought; for it becomes an object of thought in coming into contact with and thinking its objects, so that thought and object of thought are the same. For that which is *capable* of receiving the object of thought, i. e. the essence, is thought. But it is *active* when it *possesses* this object. Therefore the possession rather than the receptivity is the divine element which thought seems to contain, and the act of contemplation is what is most pleasant and best. If, then, God is always in that good state in which we sometimes are, this compels our wonder; and if in a better this compels it yet more. And God *is* in a better state. And life also belongs to God; for the actuality of thought is life, and God is that actuality; and God's self-dependent actuality is life most good and eternal. We say therefore that God is a living being, eternal, most good, so that life and duration continuous and eternal belong to God; for this *is* God.

Those who suppose, as the Pythagoreans and Speusippus do, that supreme beauty and goodness are not present in the beginning, because the beginnings both of plants and of animals are *causes,* but beauty and completeness are in the *effects* of these, are wrong in their opinion. For the seed comes from other individuals which are prior and complete, and the first thing is not seed but the complete being; e. g. we must say that before the seed there is a man—not the man produced from the seed, but another from whom the seed comes.

It is clear then from what has been said that there is a substance which is eternal and unmovable and separate from sensible things. It has been shown also that this substance cannot have any magnitude, but is without parts and indivisible (for it produces movement through infinite time, but nothing finite has infinite power; and, while every magnitude is either infinite or finite, it cannot, for the above reason, have finite magnitude, and it cannot have infinite magnitude because there is no infinite magnitude at all). But it has also been shown that it is impassive and unalterable; for all the other changes are posterior to change of place.

8. It is clear, then, why these things are as they are. But we must not ignore the question whether we have to suppose one such substance or more than one, and if the latter, how many; we must also mention, regarding the opinions expressed by others, that they have said nothing about the number of the substances that can even be clearly stated. For the theory of Ideas has no special discussion of the subject; for those who speak of Ideas say the Ideas are numbers, and they speak of numbers now as unlimited, now as limited by the number 10; but as for the reason why there should be just so many numbers, nothing is said with any demonstrative exactness. We however must discuss the subject, starting from the presuppositions and distinctions we have mentioned. The first principle or primary being is not movable either in itself or accidentally, but produces the primary eternal and single movement. But since that which is moved must be moved by something, and the first mover must be in itself unmovable, and eternal movement must be produced by something eternal and a single movement by a single thing, and since we see that besides the simple spatial movement of the universe, which we say the first and unmovable substance produces, there are other spatial movements—those of the planets—which are eternal (for a body which moves in a circle is eternal and unresting; we have proved these points in the physical treatises), each of *these* movements also must be caused by a substance both unmovable in itself and eternal. For the nature of the stars is eternal just because it is a certain kind of sub-

stance, and the mover is eternal and prior to the moved, and that which is prior to a substance must be a substance. Evidently, then, there must be substances which are of the same number as the movements of the stars, and in their nature eternal, and in themselves unmovable, and without magnitude, for the reason before mentioned.

That the movers are substances, then, and that one of these is first and another second according to the same order as the movements of the stars, is evident. But in the number of the movements we reach a problem which must be treated from the standpoint of that one of the mathematical sciences which is most akin to philosophy —viz. of astronomy; for this science speculates about substance which is perceptible but eternal, but the other mathematical sciences, i. e. arithmetic and geometry, treat of no substance. That the movements are more numerous than the bodies that are moved is evident to those who have given even moderate attention to the matter; for each of the planets has more than one movement. But as to the actual number of these movements, we now—to give some notion of the subject—quote what some of the mathematicians say, that our thought may have some definite number to grasp; but, for the rest, we must partly investigate for ourselves, partly learn from other investigators, and if those who study this subject form an opinion contrary to what we have now stated, we must esteem both parties indeed, but follow the more accurate.

Eudoxus supposed that the motion of the sun or of the moon involves, in either case, three spheres, of which the first is the sphere of the fixed stars, and the second moves in the circle which runs along the middle of the zodiac, and the third in the circle which is inclined across the breadth of the zodiac; but the circle in which the moon moves is inclined at a greater angle than that in which the sun moves. And the motion of the planets involves, in each case, four spheres, and of these also the first and second are the same as the first two mentioned above (for the sphere of the fixed stars is that which moves all the other spheres, and that which is placed beneath this and has its movement in the circle which bisects the zodiac is common to all), but the *poles* of the third sphere of each planet are in the circle which bisects the zodiac, and the motion of the fourth sphere is in the circle which is inclined at an angle to the equator of the third sphere; and the poles of the third sphere are different for each of the other planets, but those of Venus and Mercury are the same.

Callippus made the position of the spheres the same as Eudoxus did, but while he assigned the same number as Eudoxus did to Jupiter and to Saturn, he thought two more spheres should be added to the sun and two to the moon, if one is to explain the observed facts; and one more to each of the other planets.

But it is necessary, if all the spheres combined are to explain the observed facts, that for each of the planets there should be other spheres (one fewer than those hitherto assigned) which counteract those already mentioned and bring back to the same position the outermost sphere of the star which in each case is situated below the star in question; for only thus can all the forces at work produce the observed motion of the planets. Since, then, the spheres involved in the movement of the planets themselves are—eight for Saturn and Jupiter and twenty-five for the others, and of these only those involved in the movement of the lowest-situated planet need not be counteracted, the spheres which counteract those of the outermost two planets will be six in number, and the spheres which counteract those of the next four planets will be sixteen; therefore the number of all the spheres—both those which move the planets and those which counteract these—will be fifty-five. And if one were not to add to the moon and to the sun the movements we mentioned, the whole set of spheres will be forty-seven in number.

Let this, then, be taken as the number of the spheres, so that the unmovable substances and principles also may probably be taken as just so many; the assertion of *necessity* must be left to more powerful thinkers. But if there can be no spatial movement which does not conduce to the moving of a star, and if further every being and every substance which is immune from change and in virtue of itself has attained to the best must be considered an end, there can be no other being apart from these we have named, but this must be the number of the substances. For if there are others, they will cause change as being a final cause of movement; but there cannot *be* other movements besides those mentioned. And it is reasonable to infer this from a consideration of the bodies that are moved; for if everything that moves is for the sake of that which is moved, and every movement belongs to something that is moved, no movement can be for the sake of itself or of another movement, but all the movements must be for the sake of the stars. For if there is to be a movement for the sake of a movement, this latter also will have to be for the sake of something else; so that since there cannot be an infinite regress, the end of every movement will be one of the divine bodies which move through the heaven.

(Evidently there is but one heaven. For if there are many heavens as there are many men, the moving principles, of which each heaven will have one, will be one in form but in *number* many. But all things that are

many in number have matter; for one and the same definition, e. g. that of man, applies to many things, while
Socrates is one. But the primary essence has not matter;
for it is complete reality. So the unmovable first mover is
one both in definition and in number; so too, therefore,
is that which is moved always and continuously; therefore there is one heaven alone.)

Our forefathers in the most remote ages have handed
down to their posterity a tradition, in the form of a
myth, that these bodies are gods and that the divine
encloses the whole of nature. The rest of the tradition
has been added later in mythical form with a view to
the persuasion of the multitude and to its legal and
utilitarian expediency; they say these gods are in the
form of men or like some of the other animals, and they
say other things consequent on and similar to these
which we have mentioned. But if one were to separate
the first point from these additions and take it alone—
that they thought the first substances to be gods, one
must regard this as an inspired utterance, and reflect
that, while probably each art and each science has often
been developed as far as possible and has again perished, these opinions, with others, have been preserved
until the present like relics of the ancient treasure. Only
thus far, then, is the opinion of our ancestors and of our
earliest predecessors clear to us.

9. The nature of the divine thought involves certain
problems; for while thought is held to be the most divine of things observed by us, the question how it must
be situated in order to have that character involves
difficulties. For if it thinks of nothing, what is there here
of dignity? It is just like one who sleeps. And if it thinks,
but this depends on something else, then (since that
which is its substance is not the act of thinking, but

a potency) it cannot be the best substance; for it is through thinking that its value belongs to it. Further, whether its substance is the faculty of thought or the act of thinking, what does it think of? Either of itself or of something else; and if of something else, either the same thing always or of something different. Does it matter, then, or not, whether it thinks of the good or of any chance thing? Are there not some things about which it is incredible that it should think? Evidently, then, it thinks of that which is most divine and precious, and it does not change; for change would be change for the worse, and this would be already a movement. First, then, if "thought" is not the act of thinking but a potency, it would be reasonable to suppose that the continuity of its thinking is wearisome to it. Secondly, there would evidently be something else more precious than thought, viz. that which is thought of. For both thinking and the act of thought will belong even to one who thinks of the worst thing in the world, so that if this ought to be avoided (and it ought, for there are even some things which it is better not to see than to see), the act of thinking cannot be the best of things. Therefore it must be of itself that the divine thought thinks (since it is the most excellent of things), and its thinking is a thinking on thinking.

But evidently knowledge and perception and opinion and understanding have always something else as their object, and themselves only by the way. Further, if thinking and being thought of are different, in respect of which does goodness belong to thought? For to *be* an act of thinking and to *be* an object of thought are not the same thing. We answer that in some cases the knowledge is the object. In the productive sciences it is the substance or essence of the object, matter omitted, and in the theoretical sciences the definition or the act of thinking is the object. Since, then, thought and the object of thought are not different in the case of things that have not matter, the divine thought and its object will be the same, i. e. the thinking will be one with the object of its thought.

A further question is left—whether the object of the divine thought is composite; for if it were, thought would change in passing from part to part of the whole. We answer that everything which has not matter is indivisible—as human thought, or rather the thought of composite beings, is in a certain period of time (for it does not possess the good at this moment or at that, but its best, being something *different* from it, is attained only in a whole period of time), so throughout eternity is the thought which has *itself* for its object.

10. We must consider also in which of two ways the nature of the universe contains the good and the highest good, whether as something separate and by itself, or as the order of the parts. Probably in both ways, as an army does; for its good is found both in its order and in its leader, and more in the latter; for he does not depend on the order but it depends on him. And all things are ordered together somehow, but not all alike —both fishes and fowls and plants; and the world is not such that one thing has nothing to do with another, but they are connected. For all are ordered together to one end, but it is as in a house, where the freemen are least at liberty to act at random, but all things or most things are already ordained for them, while the slaves and the animals do little for the common good, and for the most part live at random; for this is the sort of principle that constitutes the nature of each. I mean, for

instance, that all must at least come to be dissolved into their elements, and there are other functions similarly in which all share for the good of the whole.

We must not fail to observe how many impossible or paradoxical results confront those who hold different views from our own, and what are the views of the subtler thinkers, and which views are attended by fewest difficulties. All make all things out of contraries. But neither "all things" nor "out of contraries" is right; nor do these thinkers tell us how all the things in which the contraries are present can be made out of the contraries; for contraries are not affected by one another. Now for us this difficulty is solved naturally by the fact that there is a third element. These thinkers however make one of the two contraries matter; this is done for instance by those who make the unequal matter for the equal, or the many matter for the one. But this also is refuted in the same way; for the one matter which underlies any pair of contraries is contrary to nothing. Further, all things, except the one, will, on the view we are criticizing, partake of evil; for the bad itself is one of the two elements. But the other school does not treat the good and the bad even as principles; yet in all things the good is in the highest degree a principle. The school we first mentioned is right in saying that it is a principle, but *how* the good is a principle they do not say— whether as end or as mover or as form.

Empedocles also has a paradoxical view; for he identifies the good with love, but this is a principle both as mover (for it brings things together) and as matter (for it is part of the mixture). Now even if it happens that the same thing is a principle both as matter and as mover, still the being, at least, of the two is not the same. In which respect then is love a principle? It is paradoxical also that strife should be imperishable; the nature of his "evil" is just strife.

Anaxagoras makes the good a motive principle; for his "reason" moves things. But it moves them for an end, which must be something other than it, except according to *our* way of stating the case; for, on our view, the medical art is in a sense health. It is paradoxical also not to suppose a contrary to the good, i. e. to reason. But all who speak of the contraries make no use of the contraries, unless we bring their views into shape. And why some things are perishable and others imperishable, no one tells us; for they make all existing things out of the same principles. Further, some make existing things out of the non-existent; and others to avoid the necessity of this make all things one.

Further, why should there always be becoming, and what is the cause of becoming?—this no one tells us. And those who suppose two principles must suppose another, a superior principle, and so must those who believe in the Forms; for why did things come to participate, or why do they participate, in the Forms? And all other thinkers are confronted by the necessary consequence that there is something contrary to Wisdom, i. e. to the highest knowledge; but *we* are not. For there is nothing contrary to that which is primary; for all contraries have matter, and things that have matter exist only potentially; and the ignorance which is contrary to any knowledge leads to an object contrary to the object of the knowledge; but what is primary has no contrary.

Again, if besides sensible things no others exist, there will be no first principle, no order, no becoming, no heavenly bodies, but each principle will have a principle before it, as in the accounts of the theologians and all the natural philosophers. But if the Forms or the numbers are to exist, they will be causes of nothing; or if not that, at least not of movement. Further, how is extension, i. e. a *continuum,* to be produced out of un-extended parts? For number will not, either as mover or as form, produce a *continuum.* But again there cannot be any *contrary* that is also essentially a productive or moving principle; or it would be possible not to be. Or at least its action would be posterior to its potency. The world, then, would not be eternal. But it is; one of these premises, then, must be denied. And we have said how this must be done. Further, in virtue of what the numbers, or the soul and the body, or in general the form and the thing, are one—of this no one tells us any-thing; nor can any one tell, unless he says, as we do, that the mover makes them one. And those who say mathematical number is first and go on to generate one kind of substance after another and give different prin-ciples for each, make the substance of the universe a mere series of episodes (for one substance has no in-fluence on another by its existence or non-existence), and they give us many governing principles; but the world refuses to be governed badly.

"The rule of many is not good; one ruler let there be."

From *Metaphysics*, Book XII, Chaps. 1-10.
Translated by W. D. Ross.

PART TWO

THE HERO

o

THE EPIC HERO

o

THE DEATH OF HECTOR

HOMER

THUS to their bulwarks, smit with panic fear,
The herded Ilians rush like driven deer;
There safe they wipe the briny drops away,
And drown in bowls the labour of the day.
Close to the walls advancing o'er the fields
Beneath one roof of well-compacted shields,
March bending on the Greeks' embodied powers,
Far-stretching in the shade of Trojan towers.
Great Hector singly staid; chain'd down by Fate,
There fix'd he stood before the Scæan gate;
Still his bold arms determined to employ,
The guardian still of long-defended Troy.

Apollo now to tired Achilles turns;
(The power confess'd in all his glory burns.)
And what (he cries) has Peleus son in view,
With mortal speed a godhead to pursue?
For not to thee to know the gods is given,
Unskill'd to trace the latent marks of Heaven.
What boots thee now, that Troy forsook the plain?
Vain thy past labour, and thy present vain:
Safe in her walls are now her troops bestow'd,
While here thy frantic rage attacks a god.
The chief incensed—Too partial god of day!
To check my conquest in the middle way;
How few in Ilion else had refuge found!

What gasping numbers now had bit the ground!
Thou robb'st me of a glory justly mine,
Powerful of godhead, and of fraud divine:
Mean fame, alas! for one of heavenly strain,
To cheat a mortal who repines in vain.

    Then to the city, terrible and strong,
With high and haughty steps he tower'd along.
So the proud courser, victor of the prize,
To the near goal with double ardour flies.
Him, as he blazing shot across the field,
The careful eyes of Priam first beheld.
Not half so dreadful rises to the sight,
Through the thick gloom of some tempestuous night,
Orion's dog (the year when autumn weighs,)
And o'er the feeble stars exerts his rays:
Terrific glory! for his burning breath
Taints the red air with fevers, plagues, and death.
So flamed his fiery mail. Then wept the sage;
He strikes his reverend head now white with age:
He lifts his wither'd arms; obtests the skies;
He calls his much-loved son with feeble cries:
The son resolved Achilles force to dare,
Full at the Scæan gate expects the war:
While the sad father on the rampart stands,
And thus adjures him with extended hands:

    Ah stay not, stay not! guardless and alone;
Hector! my loved, my dearest, bravest son!
Methinks already I behold thee slain,
And stretch'd beneath that fury of the plain.
Implacable Achilles! might'st thou be
To all the gods no dearer than to me!
The vultures wild should scatter round the shore
And bloody dogs grow fiercer from thy gore.
How many valiant sons I late enjoy'd,
Valiant in vain! by thy cursed arm destroy'd:

Or worse than slaughter'd, sold in distant isles
To shameful bondage and unworthy toils.
Two while I speak my eyes in vain explore,
Two from one mother sprung, my Polydore,
And loved Lycaon: now perhaps no more!
Oh! if in yonder hostile camp they live,
What heaps of gold, what treasures would I give!
(Their grandsire's wealth by right of birth their own,
Consign'd his daughter with Lelegia's throne:)
But if (which Heaven forbid) already lost,
All pale they wander on the Stygian coast,
What sorrows then must their sad mother know
What anguish I! unutterable woe!
Yet less that anguish, less to her, to me,
Less to all Troy, if not deprived of thee.
Yet shun Achilles! enter yet the wall;
And spare thyself, thy father, spare us all!
Save thy dear life; or if a soul so brave
Neglect that thought, thy dearer glory save.
Pity, while yet I live, these silver hairs!
While yet thy father feels the woes he bears,
Yet cursed with sense! a wretch, whom, in his rage
(All trembling on the verge of helpless age)
Great Jove has placed, sad spectacle of pain!
The bitter dregs of Fortune's cup to drain:
To fill with scenes of death his closing eyes,
And number all his days by miseries;
My heroes slain, my bridal bed o'erturn'd,
My daughters ravish'd, and my city burn'd,
My bleeding infants dash'd against the floor;
These I have yet to see, perhaps yet more!
Perhaps e'en I, reserved by angry Fate
The last sad relic of my ruin'd state,
(Dire pomp of sovereign wretchedness!) must fall
And stain the pavement of my regal hall·

Where famish'd dogs, late guardians of my door,
Shall lick their man, led master's spatter'd gore.
Yet for my sons I thank ye, gods! 'twas well:
Well have they perish'd, for in fight they fell.
Who dies in youth and vigour dies the best,
Struck through with wounds, all honest on the breast
But when the Fates, in fulness of their rage,
Spurn the hoar head of unresisting age,
In dust the reverend lineaments deform,
And pour to dogs the life blood scarcely warm:
This, this is misery! the last, the worst,
That man can feel; man, fated to be cursed!

 He said, and acting what no words could say,
Rent from his head the silver locks away.
With him the mournful mother bears a part;
Yet all their sorrows turn not Hector's heart:
The zone unbraced, her bosom she display'd;
And thus, fast falling the salt tears, she said:

 Have mercy on me, O my son! revere
The words of age; attend a parent's prayer!
If ever thee in these fond arms I press'd,
Or still'd thy infant clamours at this breast;
Ah! do not thus our helpless years forego,
But by our walls secured repel the foe.
Against his rage if singly thou proceed,
Shouldst thou (but Heaven avert it!) shouldst thou
  bleed,
Nor must thy corse lie honour'd on the bier,
Nor spouse nor mother grace thee with a tear;
Far from our pious rites, those dear remains
Must feast the vultures on the naked plains.

 So they, while down their cheeks the torrents roll,
But fix'd remains the purpose of his soul:
Resolved he stands, and with a fiery glance
Expects the hero's terrible advance.

So roll'd up in his den, the swelling snake
Beholds the traveller approach the brake;
When fed with noxious herbs his turgid veins
Have gather'd half the poisons of the plains;
He burns, he stiffens with collected ire,
And his red eye-balls glare with living fire.
Beneath a turret, on his shield reclined,
He stood, and question'd thus his mighty mind:
    Where lies my way? To enter in the wall?
Honour and shame the ungenerous thought recall:
Shall proud Polydamas before the gate
Proclaim his counsels are obey'd too late,
Which timely follow'd but the former night,
What numbers had been saved by Hector's flight?
That wise advice rejected with disdain,
I feel my folly in my people slain.
Methinks my suffering country's voice I hear,
But most her worthless sons insult my ear,
On my rash courage charge the chance of war,
And blame those virtues which they cannot share.
No—If I e'er return, return I must
Glorious, my country's terror laid in dust:
Or if I perish, let her see me fall
In field at least, and fighting for her wall.
And yet suppose these measures I forego,
Approach unarm'd and parley with the foe,
The warrior-shield, the helm, and lance, lay down,
And treat on terms of peace to save the town:
The wife withheld, the treasure ill-detain'd
(Cause of the war, and grievance of the land,)
With honourable justice to restore;
And add half Ilion's yet remaining store,
Which Troy shall sworn produce; that injured Greece
May share our wealth, and leave our walls in peace.
But why this thought? Unarm'd if I should go,

What hope of mercy from this vengeful foe,
But woman-like to fall, and fall without a blow?
We greet not here as man conversing man,
Met at an oak, or journeying o'er a plain;
No season now for calm familiar talk,
Like youths and maidens in an evening walk;
War is our business, but to whom is given
To die or triumph, that determine Heaven!
　　Thus pondering, like a god the Greek drew nigh,
His dreadful plumage nodded from on high;
The Pelian javelin in his better hand
Shot trembling rays that glitter'd o'er the land;
And on his breast the beamy splendours shone,
Like Jove's own lightning or the rising sun.
As Hector sees, unusual terrors rise,
Struck by some god, he fears, recedes, and flies;
He leaves the gates, he leaves the walls behind:
Achilles follows like the winged wind.
Thus at the panting dove a falcon flies
(The swiftest racer of the liquid skies;)
Just when he holds or thinks he holds his prey,
Obliquely wheeling through the aërial way,
With open beak and shrilling cries he springs,
And aims his claws and shoots upon his wings;
No less fore-right the rapid chase they held
One urged by fury, one by fear impell'd;
Now circling round the walls their course maintain,
Where the high watch-tower overlooks the plain:
Now where the fig-trees spread their umbrage broad
(A wider compass,) smoke along the road.
Next by Scamander's double source they bound,
Where two famed fountains burst the parted ground
This hot through scorching clefts is seen to rise,
With exhalations steaming to the skies;
That the green banks in summer's heat o'erflows,

Like crystal clear, and cold as winter snows.
Each gushing fount a marble cistern fills,
Whose polish'd bed receives the falling rills;
Where Trojan dames (ere yet alarm'd by Greece)
Wash'd their fair garments in the days of peace.
By these they pass'd, one chasing, one in flight:
(The mighty fled, pursued by stronger might.)
Swift was the course; no vulgar prize they play,
No vulgar victim must reward the day,
(Such as in races crown the speedy strife,)
The prize contended was great Hector's life.

  As when some hero's funerals are decreed
In grateful honour of the mighty dead;
Where high rewards the vigorous youth inflame
(Some golden tripod, or some lovely dame;)
The panting coursers swiftly turn the goal,
And with them turns the raised spectator's soul:
Thus three times round the Trojan wall they fly:
The gazing gods lean forward from the sky;
To whom, while eager on the chase they look,
The sire of mortals and immortals spoke:

  Unworthy sight! the man beloved of Heaven,
Behold, inglorious round yon city driven!
My heart partakes the generous Hector's pain;
Hector, whose zeal whole hecatombs has slain,
Whose grateful fumes the gods received with joy,
From Ida's summits and the towers of Troy:
Now see him flying! to his fears resign'd,
And Fate and fierce Achilles close behind.
Consult, ye powers! ('tis worthy your debate)
Whether to snatch him from impending Fate,
Or let him bear, by stern Pelides slain,
(Good as he is,) the lot imposed on man?

  Then Pallas thus: Shall he whose vengeance forms
The forky bolt, and blackens heaven with storms,

Shall he prolong one Trojan's forfeit breath?
A man, a mortal, pre-ordain'd to death?
And will no murmurs fill the courts above?
No gods indignant blame their partial Jove?

Go then (return'd the sire) without delay,
Exert thy will: I give the fates their way.
Swift at the mandate pleased Tritonia flies,
And stoops impetuous from the cleaving skies.

As through the forest o'er the vale and lawn,
The well-breathed beagle drives the flying fawn;
In vain he tries the covert of the brakes,
Or deep beneath the trembling thicket shakes;
Sure of the vapour in the tainted dews,
The certain hound his various maze pursues:
Thus step by step, where'er the Trojan wheel'd,
There swift Achilles compass'd round the field.
Oft as to reach the Dardan gates he bends,
And hopes the assistance of his pitying friends
(Whose showering arrows, as he coursed below,
From the high turrets might oppress the foe,)
So oft Achilles turns him to the plain:
He eyes the city, but he eyes in vain.
As men in slumber seem with speedy pace
One to pursue and one to lead the chase,
Their sinking limbs the fancied course forsake,
Nor this can fly, nor that can overtake:
No less the labouring heroes pant and strain,
While that but flies, and this pursues in vain.

What god, O muse! assisted Hector's force,
With Fate itself so long to hold the course?
Phœbus it was; who in its latest hour
Endued his knees with strength, his nerves with power:
And great Achilles, lest some Greek's advance
Should snatch the glory from his lifted lance,
Sign'd to the troops to yield his foe the way,

And leave untouch'd the honours of the day.

    Jove lifts the golden balances that show
The fates of mortal men and things below;
Here each contending hero's lot he tries,
And weighs with equal hand their destinies.
Low sinks the scale surcharged with Hector's fate;
Heavy with death it sinks, and hell receives the weight.

    Then Phœbus left him. Fierce Minerva flies
To stern Pelides, and triumphing cries:
Oh, loved of Jove! this day our labours cease,
And conquest blazes with full beams on Greece.
Great Hector falls: that Hector famed so far,
Drunk with renown, insatiable of war,
Falls by thy hand and mine; nor force nor flight
Shall more avail him, nor his god of light.
See where in vain he supplicates above,
Roll'd at the feet of unrelenting Jove!
Rest here: myself will lead the Trojan on,
And urge to meet the fate he cannot shun.

    Her voice divine the chief with joyful mind
Obey'd; and rested, on his lance reclined.
While like Deïphobus the martial dame
(Her face, her gesture, and her arms the same)
In show and aid, by hapless Hector's side
Approach'd, and greets him thus with voice belied:
Too long, O Hector, have I borne the sight
Of this distress, and sorrow'd in thy flight:
It fits us now a noble stand to make,
And here as brothers equal fates partake.

    Then he: O prince! allied in blood and fame,
Dearer than all that own a brother's name;
Of all that Hecuba to Priam bore,
Long tried, long loved; much loved, but honour'd more,
Since you of all our numerous race alone
Defend my life regardless of your own.

Again the goddess: Much my father's prayer,
And much my mother's press'd me to forbear:
My friends embraced my knees, adjured my stay,
But stronger love impell'd, and I obey.
Come then, the glorious conflict let us try,
Let the steel sparkle and the javelin fly:
Or let us stretch Achilles on the field,
Or to his arm our bloody trophies yield.

Fraudful she said; then swiftly march'd before:
The Dardan hero shuns his foe no more.
Sternly they met. The silence Hector broke;
His dreadful plumage nodded as he spoke:

Enough, O son of Peleus! Troy has view'd
Her walls thrice circled, and her chief pursued:
But now some god within me bids me try
Thine, or my fate: I kill thee, or I die.
Yet on the verge of battle let us stay,
And for a moment's space suspend the day;
Let heaven's high power be call'd to arbitrate
The just conditions of this stern debate
(Eternal witnesses of all below,
And faithful guardians of the treasured vow!)
To them I swear; if, victor in the strife,
Jove by these hands shall shed thy noble life
No vile dishonour shall thy corse pursue;
Stripp'd of its arms alone (the conqueror's due)
The rest to Greece uninjured I'll restore:
Now plight thy mutual oath, I ask no more.

Talk not of oaths (the dreadful chief replies,
While anger flash'd from his disdainful eyes:)
Detested as thou art, and ought to be,
Nor oath nor pact Achilles plights with thee.
Such pacts as lambs and rabid wolves combine,
Such leagues as men and furious lions join,
To such I call the gods! one constant state

Of lasting rancour and eternal hate;
No thought but rage and never-ceasing strife,
Till death extinguish rage, and thought, and life
Rouse then thy forces this important hour,
Collect thy soul, and call forth all thy power.
No farther subterfuge, no farther chance;
'Tis Pallas, Pallas gives thee to my lance.
Each Grecian ghost by thee deprived of breath
Now hovers round, and calls thee to thy death.

He spoke, and launch'd the javelin at the foe:
But Hector shunn'd the meditated blow:
He stoop'd, while o'er his head the flying spear
Sung innocent, and spent its force in air.
Minerva watch'd it falling on the land,
Then drew and gave to great Achilles' hand,
Unseen of Hector, who, elate with joy,
Now shakes his lance, and braves the dread of Troy

The life you boasted to that javelin given,
Prince! you have miss'd. My fate depends on Heaven.
To thee presumptuous as thou art, unknown
Or what must prove my fortune or thy own.
Boasting is but an art our fears to blind,
And with false terror sink another's mind.
But know, whatever fate I am to try,
By no dishonest wound shall Hector die;
I shall not fall a fugitive at least,
My soul shall bravely issue from my breast.
But first try thou my arm! and may this dart
End all my country's woes, deep buried in thy heart!

The weapon flew, its course unerring held;
Unerring, but the heavenly shield repell'd
The mortal dart; resulting with a bound
From off the ringing orb, it struck the ground
Hector beheld his javelin fall in vain,
Nor other lance, nor other hope remain;

He calls Deïphobus, demands a spear,
In vain, for no Deïphobus was there.
All comfortless he stands: then, with a sigh,
'Tis so—Heaven wills it, and my hour is nigh!
I deem'd Deïphobus had heard my call,
But he secure lies guarded in the wall.
A god deceived me: Pallas, 'twas thy deed:
Death and black Fate approach! 'tis I must bleed.
No refuge now, no succour from above,
Great Jove deserts me, and the son of Jove,
Propitious once, and kind! then welcome Fate!
'Tis true I perish, yet I perish great:
Yet in a mighty deed I shall expire,
Let future ages hear it and admire!
　　Fierce at the word his weighty sword he drew
And all-collected on Achilles flew
So Jove's bold bird, high balanced in the air,
Stoops from the clouds to truss the quivering hare.
Nor less Achilles his fierce soul prepares;
Before his breast the flaming shield he bears,
Refulgent orb! above his fourfold cone
The gilded horse-hair sparkled in the sun,
Nodding at every step (Vulcanian frame!)
And as he moved his figure seem'd on flame.
As radiant Hesper shines with keener light,
Far beaming o'er the silver host of night,
When all the starry train emblaze the sphere:
So shone the point of great Achilles' spear.
In his right hand he waves the weapon round,
Eyes the whole man, and meditates the wound:
But the rich mail Patroclus lately wore,
Securely ceased the warrior's body o'er!
One place at length he spies to let in Fate,
Where 'twixt the neck and throat the jointed plate
Gave entrance: through that penetrable part

Furious he drove the well-directed dart:
Nor pierced the windpipe yet, nor took the power
Of speech, unhappy! from thy dying hour.
Prone on the field the bleeding warrior lies,
While thus triumphing stern Achilles cries:

  At last is Hector stretch'd upon the plain,
Who fear'd no vengeance for Patroclus slain?
Then, prince, you should have fear'd what now you
    feel;
Achilles absent was Achilles still.
Yet a short space the great avenger stay'd,
Then low in dust thy strength and glory laid.
Peaceful he sleeps with all our rites adorn'd,
For ever honour'd, and for ever mourn'd:
While cast to all the rage of hostile power,
Thee birds shall mangle and the dogs devour.

  Then Hector, fainting at the approach of death:
By thy own soul! by those who gave thee breath!
By all the sacred prevalence of prayer!
Ah, leave me not for Grecian dogs to tear!
The common rites of sepulture bestow,
To soothe a father's and a mother's woe;
Let their large gifts procure an urn at least,
And Hector's ashes in his country rest.

  No, wretch accursed! relentless he replies
(Flames as he spoke shot flashing from his eyes.)
Not those who gave me breath should bid me spare,
Nor all the sacred prevalence of prayer.
Could I myself the bloody banquet join!
No—to the dogs that carcass I resign.
Should Troy to bribe me bring forth all her store,
And giving thousands, offer thousands more;
Should Dardan Priam, and his weeping dame,
Drain the whole realm to buy one funeral flame:
Their Hector on the pile they should not see,

Nor rob the vultures of one limb of thee.

    Then thus the chief his dying accents drew:
Thy rage implacable too well I knew:
The Furies that relentless breast have steel'd,
And cursed thee with a heart that cannot yield.
Yet think, a day will come, when Fate's decree
And angry gods shall wreak this wrong on thee;
Phœbus and Paris shall avenge my fate,
And stretch thee here before this Scæan gate.

    He ceased. The Fates suppress'd his labouring breath,
And his eyes stiffen'd at the hand of death;
To the dark realm the spirit wings its way
(The manly body left a load of clay,)
And plaintive glides along the dreary coast,
A naked, wandering, melancholy ghost!

    Achilles, musing as he roll'd his eyes
O'er the dead hero, thus (unheard) replies;
Die thou the first! When Jove and Heaven ordain,
I follow thee—He said, and stripp'd the slain
Then forcing backward from the gaping wound
The reeking javelin, cast it on the ground.
The thronging Greeks behold with wondering eyes
His manly beauty and superior size:
While some ignobler the great dead deface
With wounds ungenerous, or with taunts disgrace
'How changed that Hector, who like Jove of late
Sent lightning on our fleets, and scatter'd fate!'

    High o'er the slain the great Achilles stands,
Begirt with heroes and surrounding bands;
And thus aloud, while all the host attends:
Princes and leaders! countrymen and friends!
Since now at length the powerful will of Heaven
The dire destroyer to our arm has given,
Is not Troy fall'n already? Haste, ye powers!
See if already their deserted towers

Are left unmann'd; or if they yet retain
The souls of heroes, their great Hector slain.
But what is Troy, or glory what to me?
Or why reflects my mind on aught but thee,
Divine Patroclus! Death has seal'd his eyes;
Unwept, unhonour'd, uninterr'd, he lies!
Can his dear image from my soul depart,
Long as the vital spirit moves my heart?
If in the melancholy shades below,
The flames of friends and lovers cease to glow,
Yet mine shall sacred last; mine undecay'd
Burn on through death, and animate my shade.
Meanwhile, ye sons of Greece, in triumph bring
The corse of Hector, and your Pæans sing.
Be this the song, slow-moving toward the shore,
'Hector is dead, and Ilion is no more.'

　　Then his fell soul a thought of vengeance bred
(Unworthy of himself and of the dead.)
The nervous ancles bored, his feet he bound
With throngs inserted through the double wound.
These fix'd up high behind the rolling wain,
His graceful head was trail'd along the plain.
Proud on his car the insulting victor stood,
And bore aloft his arms distilling blood.
He smites the steeds; the rapid chariot flies;
The sudden clouds of circling dust arise.
Now lost is all that formidable air;
The face divine, and long-descending hair,
Purple the ground, and streak the sable sand;
Deform'd, dishonour'd, in his native land,
Given to the rage of an insulting throng!
And in his parents' sight now dragg'd along!

　　The mother first beheld with sad survey:
She rent her tresses, venerably gray,
And cast far off the regal veils away.

With piercing shrieks his bitter fate she moans,
While the sad father answers groans with groans
Tears after tears his mournful cheeks o'erflow
And the whole city wears one face of woe:
Not less than if the rage of hostile fires,
From her foundations curling to her spires,
O'er the proud citadel at length should rise,
And the last blaze send Ilion to the skies.
The wretched monarch of the falling state
Distracted presses to the Dardan gate
Scarce the whole people stop his desperate course,
While strong affliction gives the feeble force:
Grief tears his heart, and drives him to and fro,
In all the raging impotence of woe.
At length he roll'd in dust, and thus begun,
Imploring all, and naming one by one:
Ah! let me, let me go where sorrow calls;
I, only I, will issue from your walls
(Guide or companion, friends! I ask you none,)
And bow before the murderer of my son:
My grief perhaps his pity may engage;
Perhaps at least he may respect my age.
He has a father too; a man like me;
One not exempt from age and misery:
(Vigorous no more, as when his young embrace
Begot this pest of me and all my race.)
How many valiant sons, in early bloom,
Has that cursed hand sent headlong to the tomb!
Thee, Hector! last: thy loss (divinely brave)
Sinks my sad soul with sorrow to the grave.
Oh had thy gentle spirit pass'd in peace,
The son expiring in the sire's embrace,
While both thy parents wept thy fatal hour,
And bending o'er thee, mix'd the tender shower!
Some comfort that had been, some sad relief,

To melt in full satiety of grief!

Thus wail'd the father, grovelling on the ground,
And all the eyes of Ilion stream'd around.

Amidst her matrons Hecuba appears
(A mourning princess, and a train in tears.)
Ah, why has heaven prolong'd this hated breath,
Patient of horrors, to behold thy death!
O Hector! late thy parents' pride and joy,
The boast of nations! the defence of Troy!
To whom her safety and her fame she owed
Her chief, her hero, and almost her god!
O fatal change! become in one sad day
A senseless corse! inanimated clay!

But not as yet the fatal news had spread
To fair Andromache, of Hector dead;
As yet no messenger had told his fate,
Nor e'en his stay without the Scæan gate.
Far in the close recesses of the dome,
Pensive she plied the melancholy loom;
A growing work employ'd her secret hours,
Confusedly gay with intermingled flowers.
Her fair-hair'd handmaids heat the brazen urn,
The bath preparing for her lord's return:
In vain: alas! her lord returns no more:
Unbathed he lies, and bleeds along the shore!
Now from the walls the clamours reach her ear,
And all her members shake with sudden fear;
Forth from her ivory hand the shuttle falls,
And thus, astonish'd, to her maids she calls:

Ah! follow me! (she cried) what plaintive noise
Invades my ear? 'Tis sure my mother's voice.
My faltering knees their trembling frame desert,
A pulse unusual flutters at my heart;
Some strange disaster, some reverse of fate
(Ye gods, avert it!) threats the Trojan state.

Far be the omen which my thoughts suggest!
But much I fear my Hector's dauntless breast
Confronts Achilles; chased along the plain,
Shut from our walls! I fear, I fear him slain!
Safe in the crowd he ever scorn'd to wait,
And sought for glory in the jaws of fate:
Perhaps that noble heat has cost his breath,
Now quench'd for ever in the arms of death.

    She spoke; and furious with distracted pace,
Fears in her heart, and anguish in her face,
Flies through the dome (the maids her steps pursue)
And mounts the walls, and sends around her view.
Too soon her eyes the killing object found,
The godlike Hector dragg'd along the ground
A sudden darkness shades her swimming eyes,
She faints, she falls; her breath, her colour flies
Her hair's fair ornaments, the braids that bound
The net that held them, and the wreath that crown'd,
The veil and diadem flew far away
(The gift of Venus on her bridal day,)
Around a train of weeping sisters stands,
To raise her sinking with assisting hands.
Scarce from the verge of death recall'd again
She faints, or but recovers to complain.

    O wretched husband of a wretched wife!
Born with one fate to one unhappy life!
For sure one star its baleful beam display'd
On Priam's roof and Hippoplacia's shade.
From different parents, different climes, we came,
At different periods, yet our fate the same!
Why was my birth to great Aëtion owed.
And why was all that tender care bestow'd.
Would I had never been!—O thou, the ghost
Of my dead husband, miserably lost!
Thou to the dismal realms for ever gone!

And I abandon'd, desolate, alone!
An only child, once comfort of my pains,
Sad product now of hapless love remains!
No more to smile upon his sire, no friend
To help him now! no father to defend!
For should he 'scape the sword, the common doom,
What wrongs attend him, and what griefs to come!
E'en from his own paternal roof expell'd,
Some stranger ploughs his patrimonial field.
The day that to the shades the father sends,
Robs the sad orphan of his father's friends:
He, wretched outcast of mankind! appears
For ever sad, for ever bathed in tears!
Among the happy unregarded he
Hangs on the robe or trembles at the knee:
While those his father's former bounty fed,
Nor reach the goblet nor divide the bread!
The kindest but his present wants allay,
To leave him wretched the succeeding day:
Frugal compassion! Heedless they who boast
Both parents still, nor feel what he has lost,
Shall cry, 'Begone! thy father feasts not here':
The wretch obeys, retiring with a tear.
Thus wretched, thus retiring all in tears,
To my sad soul Astyanax appears!
Forced by repeated insults to return,
And to his widow'd mother vainly mourn.
He who, with tender delicacy bred,
With princes sported, and on dainties fed,
And when still evening gave him up to rest
Sunk soft in down upon his nurse's breast,
Must—ah what must be not? Whom Ilion calls
Astyanax, from her well-guarded walls,
Is now that name no more, unhappy boy!
Since now no more thy father guards his Troy

But thou, my Hector! liest exposed in air,
Far from thy parents' and thy consort's care,
Whose hand in vain, directed by her love,
The martial scarf and robe of triumph wove
Now to devouring flames be these a prey,
Useless to thee from this accursed day!
Yet let the sacrifice at least be paid,
An honour to the living, not the dead!
　So spoke the mournful dame: her matrons hear,
Sigh back her sighs, and answer tear with tear.

From *The Iliad*, Book XXII. Translated by Alexander Pope.

○

THE BOOK OF THE DEAD

HOMER

"OUR first task, when we came down to the sea and reached our ship, was to turn her into the good salt water and put the mast and sails on board. We then picked up the sheep we found there, and stowed them in the vessel. After which we ourselves embarked. And a melancholy crew we were. There was not a dry cheek in the company. However, Circe of the lovely tresses, human though she was in speech, proved her powers as a goddess by sending us the friendly escort of a favourable breeze, which sprang up from astern and filled the sail of our blue-prowed ship. All we had to do, after putting the tackle in order fore and aft, was to sit still, while the wind and the helmsman kept her straight. With a taut sail she forged ahead all day, till the sun went down and left her to pick her way through the darkness.

"Thus she brought us to the deep-flowing River of

Ocean and the frontiers of the world, where the fog-bound Cimmerians live in the City of Perpetual Mist. When the bright Sun climbs the sky and puts the stars to flight, no ray from him can penetrate to them, nor can he see them as he drops from heaven and sinks once more to earth. For dreadful Night has spread her mantle over the heads of that unhappy folk.

"Here we beached our boat and after disembarking the sheep made our way along the banks of the River of Ocean till we reached the spot that Circe had described. There, while Perimedes and Eurylochus caught hold of the victims, I drew my sharp sword from my side and dug a trench about a cubit long and a cubit wide. Around this trench I poured libations to all the dead, first with mingled honey and milk, then with sweet wine, and last of all with water. Over all this I sprinkled some white barley, and then began my prayers to the helpless ghosts of the dead, promising them that directly I got back to Ithaca I should sacrifice a barren heifer in my palace, the best I had in my possession, and heap the pyre with treasures, and make Teiresias a separate offering of the finest jet-black sheep to be found in my flocks. When I had finished my prayers and invocations to the communities of the dead, I took the sheep and cut their throats over the trench so that the dark blood poured in. And now the souls of the dead who had gone below came swarming up from Erebus—fresh brides, unmarried youth, old men with life's long suffering behind them, tender young girls still nursing this first anguish in their hearts, and a great throng of warriors killed in battle, their spear-wounds gaping yet and all their armour stained with blood. From this multitude of souls, as they fluttered to and fro by the trench, there came a moaning that was horrible to hear. Panic drained the blood from my cheeks. I turned to my comrades and told them quickly to flay the sheep I had slaughtered with my sword and burn them, while they prayed to the gods, to mighty Hades and august Persephone. But I myself sat on guard, bare sword in hand, and prevented any of the feckless ghosts from approaching the blood before I had speech with Teiresias.

"The first soul that came up was that of my own man Elpenor, for he had not yet had his burial in the wide bosom of Earth. So urgent had we felt our other task to be that we had left his corpse unburied and unwept in Circe's house. Now, when I saw him, tears started to my eyes and I was stirred with pity for him.

"I called across to him at once: 'Elpenor! How did you come here, under the western gloom? You have been quicker on foot than I in my black ship!'

"I heard him sigh, and then his answer came: 'My royal master, Odysseus of the nimble wits, it was the malice of some evil power that was my undoing, and all the wine I swilled before I went to sleep in Circe's palace. For I clean forgot to go to the long ladder and take the right way down, and so fell headlong from the roof. My neck was broken and my soul came down to Hades. And now, since I know that when you leave this kingdom of the dead you will put in with your good ship at the Isle of Aeaea, I beseech you, my prince, by all the absent friends we left behind, by your wife, by the father who supported you as a child, and by Telemachus, your only son, whom you left at home—by all these I beg you to remember me then and not to sail away and forsake me utterly nor leave me there unburied and unwept, or the gods may turn against you when they see my corpse. So burn me there with all my arms, such as they are, and raise a mound for me on the shore of the grey sea, in memory of an unlucky man, to mark the spot for future voyagers. Do this for me, and on my barrow plant the oar I used to pull when I was alive and on the benches with my mates.'

"To which I answered: 'All this, my poor Elpenor, I will do. Nothing shall be forgotten.'

"Thus we two faced each other across the trench in solemn colloquy, I on the one side, with my sword stretched out above the blood, and on the other the ghost of my comrade pouring out his tale.

"Next came the soul of my dead mother, Anticleia, the daughter of the great Autolycus, who had still been alive when I said farewell and sailed for sacred Ilium. My eyes filled with tears when I saw her there, and I was stirred to compassion. Yet, deeply moved though I was, I would not allow her to approach the blood out of turn, before I had had speech with Teiresias. And the soul of the Theban prophet now came up, with a gold rod in his hand, saw who I was, and saluted me.

" 'Royal son of Laertes, Odysseus of the nimble wits, what has brought you, the man of misfortune, to forsake the sunlight and to visit the dead in this mirthless place? Step back now from the trench and hold your sword aside, so that I can drink the blood and prophesy the truth to you.'

"I backed away, driving my sword home in its silver scabbard. And when Teiresias spoke, after drinking the dark blood, it was the voice of the authentic seer that I heard.

" 'My lord Odysseus,' he began, 'you are in search of some easy way to reach your home. But the powers above are going to make your journey hard. For I cannot think that you will slip through the hands of the Earthshaker, who has by no means forgotten his resentment against you for blinding his beloved son. Notwithstanding that, you and your friends may yet reach Ithaca, though not without mishap, if only you deter-

mine to keep a tight hand on yourself and your men
from the moment when your good ship leaves the deep
blue seas and approaches the Isle of Thrinacie, and you
see there at their pasture the cattle and the fat sheep of
the Sun-god, whose eye and ear miss nothing in the
world. If you leave them untouched and fix your mind
on getting home, there is some chance that all of you
may yet reach Ithaca, though not in comfort: But if you
hurt them, then I warrant you that your ship and company will be destroyed, and if you yourself do manage
to escape, you will come home late, in evil plight, upon
a foreign ship, with all your comrades dead. You will
find trouble too in your house—a set of scoundrels eating up your stores, making love to your royal consort
and offering wedding gifts. It is true that you will pay
out these men for their misdeeds when you reach home.
But whichever way you choose to kill them, whether by
stratagem or in a straight fight with the naked sword,
when you have cleared your palace of these Suitors, you
must then set out once more upon your travels. You must
take a well-cut oar and go on till you reach a people
who know nothing of the sea and never use salt with
their food, so that our crimson-painted ships and the
long oars that serve those ships as wings are quite beyond their ken. And this will be your cue—a very clear
one, which you cannot miss. When you fall in with some
other traveller who speaks of the "winnowing-fan" you
are carrying on your shoulder, the time will have come
for you to plant your shapely oar in the earth and offer
Lord Poseidon the rich sacrifice of a ram, a bull, and a
breeding-boar. Then go back home and make ceremonial
offerings to the immortal gods who live in the broad
heavens, to all of them, this time, in due precedence.

" 'As for your own end, Death will come to you out of
the sea, Death in his gentlest guise. When he take you,

you will be worn out after an easy old age and surrounded by a prosperous people. This is the truth that
I have told you.'

" 'Teiresias,' I answered him, 'I cannot doubt that
these are the threads of destiny which the gods themselves have spun. But there is another matter that I wish
you to explain. I see the soul of my dead mother over
there. She sits in silence by the blood and cannot bring
herself to look her own son in the face or say a single
word to him. Tell me, my prince, is there no way to
make her know that I am he?'

" 'There is a simple rule,' said Teiresias, 'which I will
explain. Any ghost to whom you give access to the blood
will hold rational speech with you, while those whom
you reject will leave you and retire.'

"These were the last words I heard from Prince
Teiresias. He had spoken his prophecies and now withdrew into the Halls of Hades. But I kept steady at my
post and waited till my mother came up and took a
draught of the black blood. She recognized me then at
once, and the pitiful words fell fast enough from her lips:

" 'My child, how did you come here under the western gloom, you that are still alive? This is no easy place
for living eyes to find. For between you and us flow the
wide waters of the Rivers of Fear, and the very first
barrier is Ocean, whose stream a man could never cross
on foot, but only in a well-found ship. Have you come
here now from Troy and been wandering over the seas
with your comrades ever since you left? Have you not
been to Ithaca yet, nor seen your wife and home?'

" 'Mother,' I answered her, 'I had no choice but to
come down to Hades and consult the soul of Theban
Teiresias. For I have never yet been near to Achaea, nor
set foot on our own land, but have been a wretched
wanderer from the very day when I sailed with King

Agamemnon for Ilium to fight the Trojan charioteers.
But tell me your own story. What was your fate; what
death overtook you? Had you some lingering disease? Or
did Artemis the Archeress visit and kill you with her
gentle darts? And tell me of my father and the son I
left behind. Is my royal prerogative safe in their hands,
or did it fall to some other man when it was assumed
that I should never return? And what of my good wife?
How does she feel and what does she intend to do? Is
she still living with her son and keeping our estate in-
tact? Or has the likeliest of her countrymen already married her?'

" 'There is no question of her not staying in your
house,' my royal mother replied. 'She has schooled her
heart to patience, though her eyes are never free from
tears as the slow nights and days pass sorrowfully by.
Your princely rights have not yet passed into other
hands, but Telemachus is in peaceful possession of the
royal lands and attends all public banquets such as the
magistrates are expected to give, for every one of them
invites him. But your father has made a recluse of himself in the country and never goes down to the city. He
has given up sleeping in laundered sheets and blankets
on a proper bed. Instead, he lies down in the wintertime
with the labourers at the farm in the dust by the fire,
and goes about in rags. But when the summer and the
mellow autumn days come round, he makes himself
a humble couch of fallen leaves anywhere on the high
ground of his vineyard plot. There he lies in his misery,
nursing his grief and yearning for you to come back,
while to make things worse old age is pressing hard upon
him. That was my undoing too; it was that that brought
me to the grave. It was not that the keen-eyed Archeress
sought me out in our home and killed me with her gentle
darts. Nor was I attacked by any of the malignant dis-

eases that so often make the body waste away and die. No, it was my heartache for you, my glorious Odysseus, and for your wise and gentle ways that brought my life and all its sweetness to an end.'

"As my mother spoke, there came to me out of the confusion in my heart the one desire, to embrace her spirit, dead though she was. Thrice, in my eagerness to clasp her to me, I started forward with my hands outstretched. Thrice, like a shadow or a dream, she slipped through my arms and left me harrowed by an even sharper pain.

" 'Mother,' I cried in my despair, 'why do you avoid me when I try to reach you, so that even in Hell we may throw our loving arms around each other's necks and draw cold comfort from our tears? Or is this a mere phantom that grim Persephone has sent me to accentuate my grief?'

" 'My child, my child!' came her reply. 'What man on earth has more to bear than you? This is no trick played on you by Persephone, Daughter of Zeus. You are only witnessing here the law of our mortal nature, when we come to die. We no longer have sinews keeping the bones and flesh together, but once the life-force has departed from our white bones, all is consumed by the fierce heat of the blazing fire, and the soul slips away like a dream and flutters on the air. But you must hasten back now to the light of day. And bear in mind all you have learnt here, so that one day you can tell your wife.'

"Such was the talk that we two had together. And now, impelled by dread Persephone, there came up all the women who had been the wives or the daughters of princes, and gathered round the black blood in a throng. I cast about me for a way to question each in turn, and in the end I solved the problem by drawing my long sword from my side and preventing them from drinking the dark blood all together. So they came forward and announced their lineage one by one, and thus I was able to question them all.

"The first I saw was highborn Tyro, who told me she was the daughter of the noble Salmoneus and had married Cretheus, Aeolus' son. She fell in love with the god of the River Enipeus, the loveliest river that runs on earth, and often wandered on the banks of his beautiful stream, until one day the Lord of the Earthquake, the Girdler of the World, disguised himself as the river-god and lay with her where the river rushes out to sea. A dark wave gathered mountain-high, curled over them, and hid the woman and the god. He then unclasped her virgin belt and sealed her eyes in sleep. But when his love had had its way, he took her hand in his; and now he spoke. 'Lady,' he said, 'be happy in this love of ours, and as the year completes its course, since a god's embrace is never fruitless, you will give birth to beautiful children, whom you must nurse and rear with care. But now go home, and guard your tongue. Tell no-one; but I wish you to know that I am Poseidon, the Shaker of the Earth.' The god then disappeared under the heaving sea. Tyro conceived, and gave birth to Pelias and Neleus, who both rose to power as servants of almighty Zeus. Pelias lived in the spacious lands of Iolcus, and his wealth lay in his flocks; while Neleus had his home in sandy Pylos. Nor were these the only children of this queen among women. To Cretheus she bore three other sons, Aeson and Pheres and Amythaon, that gallant charioteer.

"The next I saw was Antiope, the daughter of Asopus; and it was in the arms of Zeus that she claimed to have slept. She had two sons, Amphion and Zethus, the founders of Thebes of the Seven Gates, who first fortified its site with towers, since for all their prowess they could not establish themselves in the open lands of Thebes without a wall to their city.

"After Antiope I saw Alcmene, Amphitryon's wife, who lay in the loving arms of almighty Zeus and brought the all-daring lion-hearted Heracles into the world. Megare I also saw, proud Creon's daughter, who married that indomitable son of Amphitryon.

"Then I met Oedipus' mother, the lovely Epicaste. She in her ignorance committed the sin of marrying her son. For Oedipus killed his father and took his mother to wife. But the gods soon let the truth come out. For Oedipus they then conceived a cruel punishment: they left him to suffer the tortures of remorse as king of the Cadmeians in his beloved Thebes. But Epicaste, obsessed by anguish at her deed, hanged herself with a long rope she made fast to the roof-beam overhead, and so came down to the Halls of Hades, the mighty Warden of the Gates, leaving Oedipus to suffer all the horrors that mother's curses can inflict.

"Next, and loveliest of all, came Chloris, the youngest daughter of Amphion son of Iasus, who once lorded it in Orchomenus as King of the Minyae. Neleus married her for her beauty and paid a fortune for her hand. So she was Queen in Pylos, and bore him glorious children, Nestor and Chromius and princely Periclymenus; and besides these the stately Pero, the wonder of her age, whom all their neighbours wished to marry. But Neleus announced that he would give her hand to no-one but the man who should succeed in lifting from Phylace the cattle of the mighty Iphicles. It was a dangerous task to round up these shambling broad-browed cattle. A certain chivalrous seer was the only man who undertook the adventure. And the gods were against him. Misfortune dogged his steps; and he was left a wretched prisoner in the savage herdsmen's hands. The days passed and mounted up into months. But it was not until a year had run its course and the seasons came round once more, that the mighty Iphicles set him free in return for all the oracles he had uttered. Thus the will of Zeus was done.

"Then I saw Lede, wife of Tyndareus, who bore him those stout-hearted twins, Castor the trainer of horses, and Polydeuces the great boxer, both of whom are still alive, though the fruitful earth has received them in her lap. For even in the world below they have been singled out by Zeus; each is a living and a dead man on alternate days, and they are honoured like the gods.

"My eyes fell next on Iphimedeia, the consort of Aloeus, who claimed that she had slept with Poseidon, and was the mother of those short-lived twins, the god-like Otus and Ephialtes famed in story, the tallest men Earth ever nourished on her bread, and finer by far than all but the glorious Orion. In their ninth year they were nine cubits across the shoulders and nine fathoms tall. It was this pair that threatened to confound the very gods on Olympus with the din and turmoil of battle. It was their ambition to pile Mount Ossa on Olympus, and wooded Pelion on Ossa, so as to make a stairway up to heaven. And this they would have accomplished had they reached their full stature. But the son whom Leto of the lovely tresses bore to Zeus destroyed them both before the down came curling on their cheeks and decked their chins with its fleecy mantle.

"Phaedre I also saw, and Procris, and the lovely Ariadne, that daughter of the wizard Minos whom Thesus once attempted to carry off from Crete to the sacred soil of Athens, though he had no joy of her, for before their journey's end Dionysus brought word to Artemis, and she killed her in sea-girt Dia.

"Maera too, and Clymene I saw, and the hateful Eriphyle, who bartered her own husband's life for lucre. Indeed I could not tell you the tales, nor even give you the names, of all the great men's wives and daughters whom I saw, for before I had done the livelong night would have slipped away.

"But now the time has come for me to go and sleep, whether I join my crew on board or remain in your palace. As for my journey, I leave the arrangements in the gods' hands and in yours."

Odysseus came to a stop. And such was the spell he had cast on the entire company that not a sound was heard in the whole length of that shadowy hall, till white-armed Arete broke the silence at last.

"Phaeacians," she said, "what is your verdict, now that you have seen the looks and stature of our guest and have sampled his wisdom? *My* guest, I should have said. But each of you shares in the honour. So do not send him on his way with undue haste, nor stint your generosity to one who stands in such sore need. For heaven has filled your homes with riches."

The venerable lord Echeneus, the oldest man among them, followed this up. "My friends," he said, "our wise queen's advice goes straight to the mark and is just what we might have expected. I think you should follow it. But it rests with Alcinous here to say the word and take the appropriate action."

Alcinous replied without hesitation: "As I live and rule this sailor folk, it shall be so. But our guest must curb his eagerness to get home and make up his mind to stay till tomorrow, so as to give me time and to fulfill my generous plans. Meanwhile his passage home shall be the concern of the whole people, and my own in particular, since I am monarch here."

"Lord Alcinous, my most worshipped prince," Odysseus discreetly put in, "nothing would suit me better than that you should press me to stay among you even for a year, provided you saw me safely back and loaded me with your splendid gifts. It would be a great advantage to me to arrive in my own country with fuller coffers. For thus enriched I should win a kindlier welcome and greater respect from everyone I met after returning to Ithaca."

"Odysseus," said Alcinous, "we are far from regarding you as one of those impostors and humbugs whom this dark world brings forth in such profusion to spin their lying yarns which nobody can test. On the contrary, not only is your speech a delight but you have sound judgment too, and you have told us the stories of your compatriots and your own grievous misadventures with all the artistry that a ballad-singer might display. I beg you now to continue and let us know whether you also saw any of those heroic comrades of yours who joined you on the expedition to Ilium and fell in action there. The night is still long, too long for reckoning; and the time has not yet come for us to seek our sleeping-quarters. Tell me more of your marvellous doings. I could hold out till the blessed dawn, if only you could bring yourself to stay in this hall and continue the tale of your misfortunes."

In response to this the resourceful Odysseus went on with his story.

"Lord Alcinous, my most worshipful prince," he began, "there is a time for long tales, but there is also a time for sleep. However, if you really wish to hear me further, far be it from me to deny you an even more tragic tale than you have heard already. I will tell you the sad fate of my comrades-in-arms, who perished after the sack and escaped from the perils and turmoil of the Trojan war only to lose their lives when homeward bound, all through the whim of one unfaithful wife.

"In the end, holy Persephone drove off the women's ghosts. They scattered in all directions, and I was approached by the soul of Agamemnon son of Atreus. He came in sorrow, and round about him were gathered the souls of all those who had met their doom and died with him in Aegisthus' palace. As soon as he had drunk the dark blood, he recognized me, uttered a loud cry and burst into tears, stretching his arms out in my direction in his eagerness to reach me. But this he could not do, for all the strength and vigour had gone for ever from those once supple limbs. Moved to compassion at the sight, I too gave way to tears and spoke to him from my heart:

" 'Illustrious son of Atreus, Agamemnon, King of men, tell me what mortal stroke of fate it was that laid you low. Did Poseidon rouse the winds to fury and overwhelm your ships? Or did you fall to some hostile tribe on land as you were rounding up their cattle and their flocks or fighting with them for their town and women?'

" 'Royal son of Laertes, Odysseus of the nimble wits,' he answered me at once, 'Poseidon did not wreck my ships; nor did I fall to any hostile tribe on land. It was Aegisthus who plotted my destruction and with my accursed wife put me to death. He invited me to the palace, he feasted me, and he killed me as a man fells an ox at its manger. That was my most miserable end. And all around me my companions were cut down in ruthless succession, like white-tusked swine slaughtered in the mansion of some great and wealthy lord, for a wedding, a club-banquet or a sumptuous public feast. You, Odysseus, have witnessed the deaths of many men in single combat or the thick of battle, but none with such horror as you would have felt had you seen us lying there by the wine-bowl and the laden tables in the hall, while the whole floor swam with our blood. Yet the most pitiable thing of all was the cry I heard from Cassandra, daughter of Priam, whom that foul traitress Clytaemnestra murdered at my side. As I lay on the ground, I raised my hands in a dying effort to grip her sword. But the harlot turned her face aside, and had not even the grace, though I was on my way to Hades, to shut my eyes with her hands or to close my mouth. And so I say that for brutality and infamy there is no-one to equal a woman who can contemplate such deeds. Who else could conceive so hideous a crime as her delicate deliberate butchery of her husband and her lord? Indeed, I had looked forward to a rare welcome from my children and my servants when I reached my home. But now, in the depth of her villainy, she has branded not herself alone but the whole of her sex and every honest woman for all time to come.'

"'Alas!' I exclaimed. 'All-seeing Zeus has indeed proved himself a relentless foe to the House of Atreus, and from the beginning he has worked his will through women's crooked ways. It was for Helen's sake that so many of us met our deaths, and it was Clytaemnestra who hatched the plot against her absent lord.'

"'Let this be a lesson to you also,' replied Agamemnon. 'Never be too gentle even with your wife, nor show her all that is in your mind. Reveal a little of your counsel to her, but keep the rest of it to yourself. Not that *your* wife, Odysseus, will ever murder you. Icarius' daughter is far too sound in heart and brain for that. The wise Penelope! She was a young bride when we said goodbye to her on our way to the war. She had a baby son at her breast. And now, I suppose, he has begun to take his seat among the men. The lucky lad! His loving father will come home and see him, and he will kiss his father. That is how things should be. Whereas that wife of mine refused me even the satisfaction of setting eyes

on my son. She could not wait so long before she killed
his father. And now let me give you a piece of advice
which I hope you will take to heart. Do not sail openly
into port when you reach your home-country. Make a
secret approach. Women, I tell you, are no longer to be
trusted. But to go back to my son, can you give me the
truth about him? Do you and your friends happen to
have heard of him as still alive, in Orchomenus possibly,
or sandy Pylos, or maybe with Menelaus in his spreading
city of Sparta? For I know that my good Orestes has not
yet died and come below.'

"'Son of Atreus,' I answered him, 'why ask me that?
I have no idea whether he is alive or dead. And it would
be wrong of me to give you idle gossip.'

"Such was the solemn colloquy that we two had as we
stood there with our sorrows and the tears rolled down
our cheeks. And now there came the souls of Peleus' son
Achilles, of Patroclus, of the noble Antilochus, and of
Aias, who in stature and in manly grace was second to
none of the Danaans but the flawless son of Peleus. It
was the soul of Achilles, the great runner, who recognized me. In mournful, measured tones he greeted me by
my titles, and went on: 'What next, Odysseus, dauntless
heart? What greater exploit can you plan to cap your
voyage here? How did you dare to come below to Hades'
realm, where the dead live on without their wits as dis-
embodied ghosts?'

"'Achilles,' I answered him, 'son of Peleus and flower
of Achaean chivalry, I came to consult with Teiresias in
the hope of finding out from him how I could reach my
rocky Ithaca. For I have not managed to come near
Achaea yet, nor set foot on my own island, but have
been dogged by misfortune. How different from you,
Achilles, the most fortunate man that ever was or will
be! For in the old days when you were on earth, we

Argives honoured you as though you were a god; and now, down here, you are a mighty prince among the dead. For you, Achilles, Death should have lost his sting.'

" 'My lord Odysseus,' he replied, 'spare me your praise of Death. Put me on earth again, and I would rather be a serf in the house of some landless man, with little enough for himself to live on, than king of all these dead men that have done with life. But enough. Tell me what news there is of that fine son of mine. Did he follow me to the war and play a leading part or not? And tell me anything you have heard of the noble Peleus. Does the Myrmidon nation still do him homage, or do they look down on him in Hellas and Phthie now that old age has made a cripple of him? For I am not up there in the sunlight to protect him with the mighty arms that once did battle for the Argives and laid the champions of the enemy low on the broad plains of Troy. If I could return for a single hour to my father's house with the strength I then enjoyed, I would make those who injure him and rob him of his rights shrink in dismay before my might and my unconquerable hands.'

" 'Of the noble Peleus,' I answered Achilles, 'I have heard nothing. But of your dear son Neoptolemus I will give you all the news you ask for, since it was I who brought him from Scyros in my own fine ship to join the Achaean army. And there in front of the city of Troy, when we used to discuss our plans, he was always the first to speak and no words of his ever missed their mark. King Nestor and I were his only betters in debate. Nor, when we Achaeans gave battle on the Trojan plain, was he ever content to linger in the ranks or with the crowd. That impetuous spirit of his gave place to none, and he would sally out beyond the foremost. Many was the man he brought down in mortal combat. I could not tell you of all the people he killed in battle for the Argives, nor give you their names; but well I remember how the lord Eurypylus son of Telephus fell to his sword, and how many of his Hittite men-at-arms were slaughtered at his side, all on account of a bribe that a woman had taken. He was the handsomest man I ever saw, next to the god-like Memnon. Then again, when we Argive captains took our places in the wooden horse Epeius made, and it rested solely with me to throw our ambush open or to keep it shut, all the other Danaan chieftains and officers were wiping the tears from their eyes and every man's legs were trembling beneath him, but not once did I see your son's fine colour change to pallor nor catch him brushing a tear from his cheek. On the contrary he begged me time and again to let him sally from the Horse and kept fumbling eagerly at his sword-hilt and his heavy spear in his keenness to fall on the Trojans. And when we had brought Priam's city tumbling down in ruins, he took his share of the booty and his special prize, and embarked safe and sound on his ship without a single wound either from a flying dart or from a sword at close quarters. The War-god in his fury is no respecter of persons, but the mischances of battle had touched your son not at all.'

"When I had done, the soul of Achilles, whose feet had been so fleet on earth, passed with great strides down the meadow of asphodel, rejoicing in the news I had given him of his son's renown.

"The mourning ghosts of all the other dead and departed pressed round me now, each with some question for me on matters that were near his heart. The only soul that stood aloof was that of Aias son of Telamon, still embittered by the defeat I had inflicted on him at the ships when defending my claim to the arms of Achilles, whose divine mother had offered them as a prize, with the Trojan captives and Pallas Athene for judges. Would to God I had never won such a prize—the arms that brought Aias to his grave, the heroic Aias, who next to the peerless son of Peleus was the finest Danaan of all in looks and the noblest in action. I called to him now, using his own and his royal father's names, and sought to placate him:

" 'So not even death itself, Aias, could make you forget your anger with me on account of those accursed arms! Yet it was the gods that made them a curse to us Argives, who lost in you so great a tower of strength and have never ceased to mourn your death as truly as we lament Achilles, Peleus' son. No-one else is to blame but Zeus, that bitter foe of the Danaan army, who brought you to your doom. Draw near, my prince, and hear me tell our story. Curb your resentment and conquer your pride.'

"But Aias gave me not a word in answer and went off into Erebus to join the souls of the other dead, where, for all his bitterness, he might yet have spoken to me, or I to him, had not the wish to see the souls of other dead men filled my heart.

"And indeed I there saw Minos, glorious son of Zeus, sitting gold sceptre in hand and delivering judgment to the dead, who sat or stood all round the King, putting their cases to him for decision within the wide portals of the House of Hades.

"My eyes fell next on the giant hunter Orion, who was rounding up game on the meadow of asphodel, the very beasts his living hands had killed among the lonely hills, armed with a club of solid bronze, that could never be broken.

"And I saw Tityos, son of the majestic Earth, prone on the ground and covering nine roods as he lay. A pair of vultures sat by him, one on either side, and plucked at his liver, plunging their beaks into his body; and his hands were powerless to drive them off. This was his punishment for assaulting Leto, the glorious consort of Zeus, as she was travelling to Pytho across the pleasant lawns of Panopeus.

"I also saw the awful agonies that Tantalus has to bear. The old man was standing in a pool of water which nearly reached his chin, and his thirst drove him to unceasing efforts; but he could never get a drop to drink. For whenever he stooped in his eagerness to lap the water, it disappeared. The pool was swallowed up, and all he saw at his feet was the dark earth, which some mysterious power had parched. Trees spread their foliage high over the pool and dangled fruits above his head —pear-trees and pomegranates, apple-trees with their glossy burden, sweet figs and luxuriant olives. But whenever the old man tried to grasp them in his hands, the wind would toss them up towards the shadowy clouds.

"Then I witnessed the tortures of Sisyphus, as he tackled his huge rock with both his hands. Leaning against it with his arms and thrusting with his legs, he would contrive to push the boulder up-hill to the top. But every time, as he was going to send it toppling over the crest, its sheer weight turned it back, and the misbegotten rock came bounding down again to level ground. So once more he had to wrestle with the thing and push it up, while the sweat poured from his limbs and the dust rose high above his head.

"Next after him I observed the mighty Heracles—his wraith, that is to say, since he himself banquets at ease with the immortal gods and has for consort Hebe of the slim ankles, the Daughter of almighty Zeus and golden-sandalled Here. From the dead around him there rose a clamour like the call of wild fowl, as they scattered in their panic. His looks were sombre as the blackest night, and with his naked bow in hand and an arrow on the string he glanced ferociously this way and that as though at any moment he might shoot. Terrible too was the golden strap he wore as a baldric over his breast, depicting with grim artistry the forms of bears, wild boars, and glaring lions, with scenes of conflict and of battle, of bloodshed and the massacre of men. That baldric was a masterpiece that no-one should have made, and I can only hope that the craftsman who conceived the work will rest content.

"One look was enough to tell Heracles who I was, and he greeted me in mournful tones. 'Unhappy man!' he exclaimed, after reciting my titles. 'So you too are working out some such miserable doom as I was a slave to when the sun shone over my head. Son of Zeus though I was, unending troubles came my way. For I was bound in service to a master far beneath my rank, who used to set me the most arduous tasks. Once, being unable to think of anything more difficult for me to do, he sent me down here to bring away the Hound of Hell. And under the guiding hands of Hermes and bright-eyed Athene, I did succeed in capturing him and I dragged him out of Hades' realm.'

"Heracles said no more, but withdrew into the House of Hades, while I stuck to my post, in the hope that I might yet be visited by other men of note who had perished long ago. And now I should have gone still further back in time and seen the heroes whom I wished to meet, Theseus, for instance, and Peirithous, those glorious children of the gods. But before that could happen, the tribes of the dead came up and gathered round me in their tens of thousands, raising their eerie cry. Sheer panic turned me pale, gripped by the sudden fear that dread Persephone might send me up from Hades' Halls some ghastly monster like the Gorgon's head. I made off quickly to my ship and told my men to embark and loose the hawsers. They climbed in at once and took their seats on the benches, and the current carried her down the River of Ocean, helped by our oars at first and later by a friendly breeze."

From *The Odyssey*, Book XI. Translated 1945 by E. V. Rieu.

O

THE PATRIOT

O

TWO EPITAPHS

SIMONIDES

ON THE SPARTANS AT THERMOPYLAE

O passer by, tell the Lacedaemonians that we lie here obeying their orders.

ON THE ATHENIANS AT CHALCIS

We fell under the fold of Dirphys, and a memorial is reared over us by our country near the Euripus, not unjustly; for we lost lovely youth facing the rough cloud of war.

Translated by J. W. Mackail.

o

THE ATHLETE

o

TWO ODES

PINDAR

PYTHIA 10

BLESSED is Lakedaimon,
happy Thessaly. Both have kings of one line
from Herakles, best in battle.
Is this boasting to no point? But Pytho and Pelinna lead
    me
on, and Aleuas' sons, to bring to Hippokleas
ringing praise of a chorus of men.

He has his share of prizes.
In the host of the dwellers-about, the crook of Parnassos
knew him best of boys in the double race.
Apollo, the end is made sweet and the beginning
for men when God drives; by your design he did it,
only he stepped in the tracks of his father,

Olympic winner twice in the warlike
armor of Ares,
and the games in the deep meadow under Kirrha's
rocks saw Phrikias best of sprinters.
May destiny, closing in later days,
make wealth blossom to glory about them.

Out of the joys in Hellas
let them take no small share, never encounter
the gods' thought shifting to evil. To be without grief
of heart is to be god; but blessed, worthy the poet's song,
 is the man
who by excellence of hand and speed in his feet
takes by strength and daring the highest of prizes,

living yet, sees his son
in the turn of his youth reaping Pythian garlands.
He cannot walk in the brazen sky, but among
those goods that we of mortality attain to he goes
the whole way. Never on foot or ship could you find
the marvelous road to the feast of the Hyperboreans.

Perseus came to them once, a leader of men,
entered their houses,
found them making hecatombs of asses
to Apollo, who in their joyance and favorable
speech rejoices, and smiles to see
the rampant lust of the lewd beasts.

Never the Muse is absent
from their ways: lyres clash, and the flutes cry,
and everywhere maiden choruses whirling.
They bind their hair in golden laurel and take their
 holiday.
Neither disease nor bitter old age is mixed
in their sacred blood; far from labor and battle

they live; they escape Nemesis,
the overjust. Danaë's son came that day,
breathing strength in his heart, and Athene led him

to mix with those blessed men. He killed the Gorgon,
    came
bearing the head, intricate with the snake hair,
the stone death to the islanders. It is not mine

to wonder; when the gods appoint it,
nothing is too strange.
Check the oar now, grapple the anchor quick to the
beach at the prow, guard at the rock-reef.
See, the shimmering of the song's praise
skims as a bee does, story to story.

Now as the Ephyraians
shed my sweet song at the Peneios banks, I hope
even more to make with songs for the garlands' sake
Hippokleas honored among the youth and his elders,
and to young maidens a troubled thought, for, as
the age changes, new loves flutter the heart.

That which a man desires,
if he grasp, he must keep it in care beside him.
A year hence nothing is plain to see.
My trust is in the hospitality of Thorax; his favor,
    wafted,
yoked me this chariot of the Pierides,
friend to friend, leader to leader in kindness.

Gold shines gold when you test it
and the right wisdom.
Also I shall praise the noble brothers, because
they carry aloft the Thessalian way
and increase it. In their good hands is rested
the gift of their fathers, excellent government of cities.

                    Translated by Richmond Lattimore.

NEMEA 6

THERE is one
race of men, one race of gods; both have breath
of life from a single mother. But sundered power
holds us divided, so that the one is nothing, while for the
    other the brazen sky is established
their sure citadel forever. Yet we have some likeness in
    great
intelligence, or strength, to the immortals,
though we know not what the day will bring, what
    course
after nightfall
destiny has written that we must run to the end.

For witness
even now, behold how his lineage works in Alkimidas.
It is like cornfields that exchange their estate,
now in their year to yield life to men from their level
    spaces
while again they lie fallow to gather strength. He came
home from the lovely games at Nemea,
a boy contestant; and steering this destiny from God
he shows now
as one not ill-starred in his quest of prizes for wrestling,

laying his feet in the steps that are his by blood
of his grandfather, Praxidamas.
He was Olympionician and first
brought home to the Aiakidai from Alpheus the olive
    branches,
and went five times garlanded at the Isthmos,
thrice at Nemea, to abate forgetfulness

fallen upon Sokleidas, mightiest
of the sons of Hagesimachos.

For these three
have come home, bearing prizes; their achievement
    reached the uttermost;
and it was these who knew the struggle also. By God's
    grace,
boxing has brought forth no one house to possess
more garlands in any corner of all Hellas. I hope,
high though my speech be, it strikes the mark squarely,
as from a bow drawn true. My Muse, steer me the flight
of these my words
straight and glorious. For men pass,

but the songs
and the stories bring back the splendor of their deeds.
And the Bassidai have no dearth, their race is bespoken
    of old,
as on long voyages they have come with a freight of
    praise, for the gardeners of the Muses
giving occasion to hymns for the sake of high deeds.
Kallias also, of the blood of this same stock,
at sacred Pytho, his hands bound in the thongs,
won victory
and pleased the children of Lato of the gold hair,

and beside Kastalia at nightfall
was brightened in acclamation of the Graces.
The tireless bridge of the sea, at the two-year games
of the dwellers-about, where an ox is slaughtered,
glorified him in Poseidon's precinct.
And on a time the Lion's parsley
shaded his victor's brows in the dark glen
of Phleious under the primeval mountains.

Wide are the ways
from all sides, for the tellers of tales
to glorify this splendid island; for the Aiakidai
have made mighty its destiny, showing forth great things
     done in valor,
and over the earth and across the seas afar wings
the name of them; as far as the Aithiopians
it went suddenly when Memnon came not home. Heavy
was the assault of Achilles
when he came down from his chariot

and with the
edge of the angry sword struck down the child
of the shining Dawn. All this is a way the men
before me discovered long ago, but I follow it also, care-
     fully.
When the ship is laboring, always the wave that rolls
     nearest her forefoot,
they say, brings terror beyond aught else to all men's
hearts. But I gladly have taken on my back a twofold
     burden
and come a messenger,
heralding this twenty-fifth

triumph won from games that are called sacred.
Alkimidas, you have been true
to the splendor of your race. Twice, my child, at the
     precinct
of Kronian Zeus, only a random draw
despoiled you and Polytimidas of Olympian garlands.
Melesias I would liken
to a dolphin in his speed through the sea's water,
a man to guide the strength in a boy's hands.

                      Translated by Richmond Lattimore.

o

THE TRAGIC HERO

o

A TRILOGY: THE ORESTEIA

AESCHYLUS

o

AGAMEMNON

*(The entrance to the palace of the Atreidae at Argos.
Before the door stand sacred images. A* WATCHMAN *is
stationed on the roof)*

WATCHMAN. I've prayed God to deliver me from evil
    Throughout a long year's vigil, couched like a dog
    On the roof of the House of Atreus, where I scan
    The pageant of Night's starry populace,
    And in their midst, illustrious potentates,
    The shining constellations that bring men
    Summer and winter, as they rise and set.
    And still I keep watch for the beacon-sign,
    That radiant flame that shall flash out of Troy
    The message of her capture. So strong in hope
    A woman's heart, whose purpose is a man's.
    Night after night, tossed on this restless bed,
    With dew bedrenched, by no dreams visited,
    Not mine—no sleep, but at my pillow fear
    That keeps these eyes from slumber all too sound;
    And when I start to sing or hum a tune,
    And out of music cull sleep's antidote,
    I always weep the state of this great house,
    Not in high fettle as it used to be.

But now at last may good news in a flash
Scatter the darkness and deliver us!

(The beacon flashes)

Hail, lamp of joy, whose gleam turns night to day,
Hail, radiant sign of dances numberless
In Argos for our happy state! Ho there!
I summon Agamemnon's sleeping queen,
To leave her couch and lift the ringing voice
Of gracious alleluias through the house
To celebrate the beacon, if it be true
That Troy is taken, as this blaze portends.
And I will dance the overture myself.   *(Dances)*
My master's dice have fallen well, and I
For this night's work shall score a treble six.
Well, come what may, let it be mine to grasp
In this right hand my master's, home again!
The rest is secret: a heavy ox has trod
Across my tongue. These walls, if they had mouths,
Might tell tales all too plainly. I speak to those
Who know, to others—purposely forget.

*(He disappears into the palace. A woman's cry of joy
is heard within. Enter* CHORUS OF OLD MEN*)*

Parodos

Ten years is it since that plaintiff-at-arms
In the suit against Priam,
Menelaus, with lord Agamemnon his peer,
Twin-sceptred in sovranty ordered of Zeus,
Children of Atreus, strong brace of command,
Did embark with the fleet of a thousand ships
In a battle-array
And set out from the land of the Argives,
With a cry from the heart, with a clamour of war,
Like eagles bereft of their nestlings embowered

On a mountainous height, with a wheel and a whir
As of winged oars beating the waves of the wind,
Wasted the long watch
At the cradle and lost is their labour.
Yet aloft some God, maybe Apollo
Or Pan, or Zeus, giveth ear to the cry
Of the birds that have made
Their abode in the heavens, and lo, he doth send
On the head of the sinner a Fury!

(CLYTEMNESTRA *comes out of the palace and sacrifices
before the sacred images*)

Yea, so are the twin children of Atreus
By the mightier Zeus Hospitable sent
Unto Paris, to fight for a woman who knew
Many lovers, with many a knee bowed low
In the dust, spears bent, limbs locked in the sweat
Of the close-knit bridals of battle,
Bringing death to the Greek and the Trojan.
And howe'er it doth fare with them now, ordained
Is the end, unavailing the flesh and the wine
To appease God's fixed indignation.

As for us, in the frailty of age, unenrolled
In the martial array that is gathered and gone,
We are left, with the strength
Of a babe, no more, that doth lean on a staff.
For the youth of the marrow enthroned in the
        breast
Is at one with its age—
In neither the War-god stands at his post.
Old men, what are they? Fast fading the leaf,
Three-footed they walk, yet frail as a child,
As a dream set afloat in the daylight.

(They see CLYTEMNESTRA*)*

O Queen, O daughter of Tyndareus,
Clytemnestra, declare
What news, what tidings have come to thine ears,
What message hath moved
Thee to offer these prayers at the altars?
O see, at the shrines of our guardian gods,
Of the sky, of the earth,
Of the threshold and market alike—yea, all
Are ablaze with thy gifts of entreaty.
One lamp from another is kindled and soars
High as the heavens,
All charmed into flame by the innocent spell,
Soft-spoken enchantment of incense drawn
From the inmost stores of the palace.
Speak, make known what is lawful to tell;
So heal these cares consuming the heart,
Which now sometimes frown heavy and dark,
Sometimes bright hope from an altar aflame
Gleams forth with a message of comfort.

(CLYTEMNESTRA *goes out to tend the other altars
of the city*)

First Stasimon

Str. 1

Strong am I yet to declare that sign which sped
from the palace
Men in the fulness of power; for yet God-given
Prowess of song doth abide in the breast of the
aged:
To sing of two kings
United in spirit and sovranty, marshals of Hellas,

Sped with avenging sword by the warlike
Eagle in ships to the land of the Trojans,
Monarch of birds to the monarchs of men, black-
    plumed was the first, white-tailed was his fel-
    low—
Before the King's house
They appeared on the side of the spear-hand
Plainly for all to behold them,
Battening both on a hare still big with the burden
    of offspring,
Cut off before her course was run.
Ailinon, ailinon cry, but may well yet conquer!

Ant. 1
Then did the priest as he marked them, two and
    twain in their temper,
Feasting on hare's flesh, know them, the children
    of Atreus,
Lords of the host, and he spake in a prophecy say-
    ing:
"In time the great quest
Shall plunder the fortress of Priam and the herds of
    the people,
Teeming flocks at the gates, with a sudden
Judgment of Fate in the dust of destruction.
Only let no jealous eye from above fall blackening,
    blasting the host as it bridles
The mouth of high Troy. For the merciful Artemis
    hateth
Those twin hounds of the Father,
Slaying the cowering hare with her young unborn
    in the belly;
She loathes the eagles' feast of blood."
Ailinon, ailinon cry, but may well yet conquer!

Ep.

"O Goddess, gentle to the weak and helpless suck-
          ling of the raging lion,

Gentle to all young life that is nursed by the beasts
          of the wild, so now we beseech thee

Bring what is fair in the sign to a happy

End, what is faulty amend and set upright.

And lo, I cry unto Apollo, Healer,

Let her not visit the fleet

With a contrary wind, with an idle, helpless, storm-
          bound stay,

Driving them on to a feast unlike to the other, un-
          holy,

Builder of inborn strife that doth fear no man. It
          abides yet,

Terrible wrath that departs not,

Treachery keeping the house, long-memoried, chil-
          dren-avenging!"

Thus did the prophet declare great blessings
          mingled with sorrows

Destined to be, as he saw that sign at the great
          king's going.

So in the same strain:

Ailinon, ailinon cry, but may well yet conquer!

Str. 2

Zeus, whoe'er he be, if so it best

Pleaseth him to be addressed,

So shall he be named by me.

All things have I measured, yet

Naught have found save him alone,

Zeus, if a man from a heart heavy-laden with sor-
          row

Care would truly cast aside.

Ant. 2

Long since lived a master of the world,
Puffed with martial pride, of whom
None shall tell, his day is done;
Yea, and he who followed him
Met his master and is gone.
Zeus the victorious, praise him and gladly acclaim
    him;
Perfect wisdom shalt thou find.

Str. 3

He to wisdom leadeth man,
He hath stablished firm the law,
Man shall learn by suffering.
When deep slumber falls, remembered sins
Chafe the sore heart with fresh pain, and no
Welcome wisdom meets within.
Harsh the grace dispensed by powers immortal
On the awful bench enthroned.

Ant. 3

Even so the elder prince,
Marshal of the ships of Greece,
Never thought to doubt a priest;
Nay, his heart with swaying fortune swayed.
Harbour-locked, hunger-pinched, hard-oppressed,
Still the host of Hellas lay
Facing Chalcis, where the never-tiring
Tides of Aulis ebb and flow.

Str. 4

And still the storm blew from out the cold north,
With moorings wind-swept and hungry crews pent
In idle ships,

With tackling unspared and rotting timbers,
Till Time's insistent, slow erosion
Had all but stripped bare the bloom of Greek man-
    hood.
And then was found but one
Charm to allay the tempest—never a blast so bit-
    ter—
Cried in a loud voice by the priest, "Artemis!"
    whereat the Atreidae were afraid, each with
    his staff smiting the earth and weeping.

Ant. 4
And then the King spake, the elder, saying:
"A bitter thing surely not to hearken,
And bitter too
To slay my own child, my royal jewel,
With unclean hands before the altar
Myself, her father, | to spill a girl's pure blood.
Whate'er the choice, 'tis ill.
How shall I fail my thousand ships and desert my
    comrades?
So shall the storm cease, and the host eager for war
    crieth for that virginal blood righteously! So
    pray for a happy issue!"

Str. 5
And when he bowed down beneath the harness
Of dire compulsion, his spirit veering
With sudden sacrilegious change,
Regardless, reckless, he turned to foul sin.
For man is made bold with base-contriving
Impetuous madness, prime seed of much grief.
And so then he slew his own child
For a war to win a woman

And to speed the storm-bound ships from the shore
    to battle.

Ant. 5

She cried aloud "Father!" yet they heard not;
A maiden scarce flowered, yet they cared not,
The lords who gave the word for war.
Her father prayed, then he bade his servants
To seize her, where wrapt in robe and drooping
She lay, and lift her up, like a young kid,
With bold heart above the altar,
And her lovely lips to bridle
That they might not cry out, cursing the House of
    Atreus,

Str. 6

With gags, her mouth sealed in mute violence.
And then she let fall her cloak of saffron,
And glanced at each face around her
With eyes that dumbly craved compassion;
And like a picture | she would but could not speak;
For oft aforetime at home
Her father's guests, after they had feasted,
Their cups replenished, had sat while with sweet
    voice she sang
The hymn of thanksgiving, pure and spotless,
Standing beside her father.

Ant. 6

The end I saw not. It shall not be told.
The arts of Calchas were well accomplished.
But Justice leads man to wisdom
By suffering. Until the morrow
Appeareth, vex not thy heart; for vain it were

To weep before sorrow come.
It shall be soon known as clear as daybreak.
And so may all this at last end in good news, for
    which
The Queen doth pray, next of kin and single
Stay of the land of Argos.

(CLYTEMNESTRA *appears at the door of the palace*)

All honour, Clytemnestra, unto thee!
For meet it is, while our great master's throne
Stands empty, to pay homage to his queen.
What means this glad expectant sacrifice?
Is it good news? Pray speak! I long to hear.

CL. Good news! So charged, as the old proverb says,
May Morning rise out of the womb of Night!
'Tis yours to hear of joy surpassing hope.
My news is this: the Greeks have taken Troy.

CH. What? No! I cannot grasp it, incredible!

CL. The Greeks hold Troy. Is that not plain enough?

CH. Joy steals upon me, such joy as calls forth tears.

CL. Indeed your looks betray your loyalty.

CH. What is the proof? Have you no evidence?

CL. Of course I have—unless the Gods have cheated.

CH. You have given ear to some beguiling dream?

CL. I would not scream the fancies of my sleep.

CH. Rumours have wings—on these your heart has fed.

CL. You mock my wits as though I were a girl.

CH. But when? How long is it since the city fell?

CL. The night that gave birth to this dawning day.

CH. What messenger could bring the news so fast?

CL. The God of Fire from Ida sent forth light,
And beacon from beacon brought the trail of flame
To me. From Ida first to Hermes' cliff
On Lemnos, and from thence a third great lamp

Was flashed to Athos, lofty mount of Zeus;
Up, up it soared, and lured the dancing shoals
To skim the waves in rapture at the light;
A golden courier, like the sun, it sped
Post-haste its message to Macistus' rock,
Which vigilant and impatient bore it on
Across Euripus, till the flaming sign
Was marked by watchers on Messapium,
Who swift to answer kindled high the blaze
Of withered heath, whence with new strength the
    light
Undarkened yet rose like the radiant moon
Across the valley of Asopus, still
Relayed in glory, to Cithaeron's heights.
Onward it sped, not slow the sentinels
But burning more than was commanded them,
Till at one leap across Gorgopis' lake
To the peak of Aegiplanctus it passed the word
To burn and burn, and they unsparing flung
A flaming comet to the cape that looks
Over the gulf Saronian. Suddenly
It swooped, and pounced upon the Spider's Crag,
Next neighbour of this city, whence at last
It found its mark upon the roof of Atreus,
That beacon fathered by the fires of Ida.
Such were the stages of this torch-relay,
One from another snatching up the light,
And the last to run is victor in the race.
That is my evidence, the token which
My lord has signalled out of Troy to me.

CH. Lady, I will address the Gods anon,
But now with all my heart I long to hear
That tale again and take my fill of wonder.

CL. Today the Greeks hold Troy; and I divine

That city rings with ill-assorted cries.
If oil and vinegar were to be poured
Into one vessel, you would not call them friends.
Even so the conquered and their conquerors,
Two voices have they for their fortunes twain.
For those, prostrate over their fallen kin,
Brother by brother, old men beside their sons,
Lament with lips no longer free the fate
Of those they loved most dearly; while again
These others, spent after the restless night
Of battle-rout, troop hungry to what meal
The town affords, undrilled, unbilleted,
But seizing each what luck apportions them.
Already in those captive Trojan homes
They take their lodging, free from the frosty sky,
From heaven's dew delivered—O how blest
Their sleep shall be, off guard the whole night long!
And if they honour the presiding Gods
And altars of the plundered territory,
Then those despoilers shall not be despoiled.
Only let no desire afflict the host
To lay rapacious hands on sanctities.
The homeward journey lies before them yet,
The last lap of the race is still to run.
And if they came guiltless before the Gods,
The grievance of the dead might then become
Fair-spoken—barring sudden accident.
Such is the message brought you by a woman.
May good prevail, inclined decisively!
Blessings abound, and I would reap their fruit.

CH. Woman, your gracious words are like a man's,
Most wise in judgment. I accept the sign
And now once more turn to address the Gods.
Long labour has been well repaid in joy.

(CLYTEMNESTRA *retires into the palace*)

Second Stasimon

O Zeus Almighty, O bountiful Night,
Housekeeper of heaven's embroidery, thou
Hast entangled the towers of the city of Troy
In a fine-spun net, which none could escape,
Not a man nor a child, nay all are entrapped
In the far-flung coils of destruction.
Great Zeus the Hospitable, him do I praise,
Who hath punished at last the transgressor; for long
Was his bow outstretched with unerring intent,
That the shaft might not fall short nor escape
Far out in the starry expanses.

Str. 1

By Zeus struck down. 'Tis truly spoken,
With each step clear and plain to track out.
He willed, his will was done. It was declared once
That God regards not the man who hath trod
Beneath his feet holy sanctities. An unrighteous
        thought;
For lo, swift ruin worketh sure judgment on hearts
With pride puffed up and high presumption,
On all stored wealth that overpasseth
The bound of due measure. Far best to live
Free of want and griefless, rich in the gift of wis-
        dom.
    Help is there none for him who,
    Glutted with gold, in wanton
    Pride from his sight has kicked the great
    Altar of watchful Justice.

Ant. 1

As fell Temptation drives him onward,
The dread fore-scheming child of Ruin,

What cure avails to heal? Behold, not darkly
His curse doth shine forth, a bright, baleful light.
And like to false bronze betrayed by touch of sure-
    testing stone,
His hue turns black and shows the truth time-tried;
    he seems
A fond child chasing birds that take wing;
And one crime brands a mighty city.
He prays to deaf heaven, none hears his cry;
Justice drags him down to death for his wicked con-
    verse.
 Thus did the sinner Paris
 Come to the House of Atreus,
 Leaving the table spread for him
 Shamed with theft of a woman.

Str. 2
She left her own people shields massed for war,
And densely-thronged spears, a fleet manned and
    launched for battle;
She brought to Troy in lieu of dowry death.
On light foot through the gates she tripped—
A sin of sins! And long did they lament,
The seers, the King's prophets, saying darkly:
"Alas, the sad house and they that rule therein,
Alas, the bed tracked with print of love that fled!
Behold, in silence, | unhonoured, | without re-
    proach,
They sit upon the ground and weep.
Beyond the sea lies their love,
Here a wraith seems to rule the palace."
 Shapely the grace of statues,
 Yet doth her lord abhor them;
 Love is there none in lifeless eyes,
 Aphrodite has vanished.

Ant. 2

Delusive dream-shapes that float through the night
Beguile and bring him | delight sweet but unsub-
       stantial;
For idly, even while he seems to see,
The arms clasp empty air, and soon
The passing vision turns and glides away
On silent wing down the paths of slumber.
At home the hearth lies in sorrow such as this,
And more; in each house throughout the land of
       Greece
That sent its dearest to make war beyond the sea,
The brave heart is called to school itself
In slow endurance | against
Griefs that strike deep into the bosom:
    Those that were sent away they
    Knew, but now they receive back
    Not the faces they longed to see,
    Only a heap of ashes.

Str. 3

The God of War holds the twin scales of strife,
Cruel gold-changer merchandising men,
Embarking homeward from Troy a heap of dustfire-
       refined,
Making up its weight in grief,
Shapely vessels laden each
With the ashes of a friend.
They mourn and praise them, saying, "*He*
Was practised well in feats of war,
And *he,* who died a noble death—
All to avenge another man's wife."
It is muttered in a whisper,
And it spreads with growling envy of the sons of
       Atreus.

They lie still, the possessors
Each of a strip of Trojan
Soil, but the land that hides their fair
Limbs is a foe and foreign.

Ant. 3
A people's wrath voiced abroad bringeth grave
Danger, no less than public curse pronounced.
It still abideth for me, | a hidden fear wrapped in
    night.
Watchful are the Gods of all
Hands with slaughter stained. The black
Furies wait, and when a man
Has grown by luck, not justice, great,
With sudden overturn of chance
They wear him to a shade, and, cast
Down to perdition, who shall save him?
In excess of fame is danger.
With a jealous eye the Lord Zeus in a flash shall
    smite him.
    Mine be the life unenvied,
    Neither to plunder cities
    Nor myself a prisoner bow
    Down to the will of others.

—The tale of glad news afire
Throughout the town spreads its fleet
Rumour; yet if this be true,
Who knows? It is perhaps a trick played by God.
—Who is so childish or so maimed of wit
To let a mere fiery word
Inflame the heart, then with swiftly-changed import
Flicker out and fade to nought?
—A woman's heart ever thus
Accepteth joy ere the joy is brought to light.

—Too credulous a woman's longing flies
And spreading swiftly, swiftly dies,
An idle word noised abroad on woman's lips.

Soon shall we know what means this fleet exchange
Of lights relayed and beacon-messages—
Whether 'tis true, or like a dream it dawns,
This joyful daybreak, to beguile the mind.
Here is a herald running from the shore.
He wears a garland, and the thirsty dust,
Mire's brother and companion, testifies
That he shall not be dumb nor speak his news
With mountain pinewood flashing smoke and flame,
But either he shall bid us greater joy,
Or else—no, I abjure the contrary.
Glad shone the light, and gladly be it crowned!
Whoever prays that it be otherwise,
His be the harvest of his own offence!

(*Enter a* HERALD)

HERALD. Joy, land of Argos, joy to my father's soil!
After ten years this dawn has brought me home.
Many the broken hopes, but this has held.
Little I thought here in this Argive earth
To die and in dear hands be laid to rest.
O Land, I bid thee joy, and thee, O Sun,
And Zeus the Highest, and the Pythian King,
Bending no more at us his bitter shafts—
Thy wrath beside Scamander was enough,
And now defend us, Saviour, Healer too,
Our Lord Apollo! All the public Gods
I greet, and most that messenger beloved,
My patron Hermes, to all heralds dear;
And those heroic dead who sent us forth,
Prepare to welcome those whom war has spared!

Hail, royal palace, roof most dear to me,
And holy shrines, whose faces catch the sun,
Now, as of old, with radiance in your eyes
Greet worthily your lord who comes at last
Bringing at night a lamp to lighten you
And all here present, Agamemnon, King.
O welcome gladly, for it is right and meet,
Him who with mattock of just-dealing Zeus
Has levelled Troy and laid her valleys waste
And all her seed uprooted from the earth.
Such is the yoke he set on her proud neck,
Great son of Atreus, master, sovran, blest,
Most worthy to be honoured over all
Men of his day. For Paris and his Troy
No longer boast to have suffered less than done.
Of rape convicted and of brigandage,
He lost his booty and in utter ruin
Brought down the ancient mansion of his sires.
The sons of Priam paid double for their sin.

CH. Hail, Herald from the host, I bid you joy!
HE. 'Tis mine. Come, death! O God, I am content!
CH. Love for your fatherland has worn you out.
HE. So much that joy has filled my eyes with tears.
CH. Then bitterness was not unmixed with sweet.
HE. Sweetness? How so? Your wit eludes me there.
CH. You loved in absence those who loved again.
HE. The country yearned for us, who yearned for her?
CH. Even so, with many a groan of dark surmise.
HE. Whence came this sullen misgiving for our sake?
CH. Let silence heal—I learnt that long ago.
HE. How? In our absence had you cause to fear?
CH. As you have said, now it were joy to die.
HE. Yes, for the end is well. Our enterprise
      At last is well concluded, though in part

The issue be found wanting. Who but a God
Might live unscathed by sorrow all his days?
If I should tell those labours, the rough lodging,
The hard thwart's scant repose, the weary groans
That were our lot through watches of the day;
And then ashore ills more insufferable,
In camp beneath the beetling walls of Troy,
The rains from heaven and the dews that dripped
From sodden soils with cruel insistence, breeding
A host of vermin in our woollen cloaks;
If I should tell those winters, when the birds
Dropped dead and Ida heaped on us her snows,
Those summers, when unstirred by wind or wave
The sea lay pillowed in the sleep of noon—
But why lament that now? The toil is past—
Yes, for the dead so past that, where they lie,
No care shall trouble them to rise again.
Ah, those are spent: why count our losses then
And vex the quick with grievance of the dead?
So to adversity I bid farewell:
For us, survivors of the Argive arms,
Misfortune sinks, our vantage turns the scale.
And hence 'tis meet before yon rising sun
To cry o'er land and sea on wings of fame,
"Long since the Argive host which plundered Troy
Set up these spoils, a time-worn ornament,
Before this palace to the Gods of Greece."
Whereto in answer should this land be praised
With those who led her, and to Zeus the giver
Shall thanks be given. That is all my news.
Сн. Well said! Your say, I grant you, masters mine.
Old age is ever young enough to learn.
This news, although it shall enrich me too,
Concerns the palace, and most of all the Queen.

(CLYTEMNESTRA *appears at the door of the palace*)

CLYTEMNESTRA. Long since I raised my joyful alleluias
　　　When the first messenger flashed out of night
　　　The tidings of the fall of Ilium,
　　　And one rebuked me saying, "Has a beacon
　　　Persuaded you that Troy has now been taken?
　　　Truly a woman's heart is light as air."
　　　Such was their gossip, and they called me mad;
　　　But I still sacrificed, and through the town
　　　The women's alleluia taken up
　　　Was chanted gladly at the holy shrines,
　　　Lulling to sleep the sacramental flame.
　　　And now what need of further news from you?
　　　I shall soon hear all from the King himself,
　　　My honoured lord, for whom I shall prepare
　　　A welcome home as fair as may be. What
　　　Light could be sweeter in a woman's eyes
　　　Than to fling wide the gates for her beloved
　　　Whom God has saved from war? Go and command
　　　　　him
　　　To hasten back, the darling of his people,
　　　Where he shall find within his house a wife
　　　As loyal as he left her, a faithful hound
　　　Guarding his substance, to enemies unkind,
　　　And in all else the same, his treasuries
　　　Sealed all these years and still inviolate.
　　　Delight from other men and ill-report
　　　Are strange to me, as strange as tempered steel.
　　　　　　　　　　　(*She retires into the palace*)
HE. Such is her boast, and though 'tis big with truth,
　　　Is it not unseemly on a lady's lips?
CH. Such is her message, as you understand,
　　　To the instructed fair—in outward show.
　　　But tell me, messenger, what of Menelaus,

      Co-regent of this kingdom? Has he too
      Returned in safety to his fatherland?

HE. I cannot tell a falsehood fair to bring
      Enduring comfort to the friends I love.

CH. Can you not make your tale both fair and true?
      It is vain to hide disunion of the pair.

HE. The man has vanished from the Grecian host,
      Himself and ship together. 'Tis the truth.

CH. Did he embark from Troy before your eyes,
      Or was it a storm that struck the fleet at sea?

HE. A skilful archer, you have hit the mark
      And told a long disaster in a word.

CH. But what report did rumour spread of him
      Among the other seamen—alive or dead?

HE. We know not; none has certain news of him
      Unless the Sun, from whom this earth draws life.

CH. But tell us of that tempest that came down
      So suddenly, a bolt from angry heaven.

HE. It is not meet to mar a day of praise
      With voice of evil tidings: such offices
      Are not for Gods of Heaven. When a man
      Drags sadly home defeat long prayed-against,
      With twofold wound, one of the commonwealth,
      And one of each man driven from his home
      Beneath that double scourge, the curse of War,
      Armed with twin spears and double-braced for
         blood,
      Such dire event were fit to celebrate
      With some fell hymn to the infernal Furies;
      But when he brings deliverance and finds
      A land rejoicing in prosperity—
      How should I mingle foul with fair, and tell
      Of tempest stirred out of an angry sky?
      Water and Fire, old enemies before,
      Conspired together and made covenant

To overwhelm the fated ships of Greece.
When night had fallen, with a rising swell,
The fleet was battered by the winds of Thrace,
Hull against hull, till, gorged and buffeted
With blasts of hail and blinding hurricane,
An evil shepherd swept them out of sight.
And when at last the sun's pale light arose,
We saw the Aegean in blossom with the strewn
Flotsam of drowning men and shattered spars.
Our own ship went unscathed; it must have been
Some deity that touched the helm and snatched
Or begged us off, and then the saving spirit
Of Fortune took the wheel, our pilot, till
We passed between the rugged mountain-cliffs
And anchored where we shipped the foam no more;
And there, delivered from that watery hell,
We nursed in brooding hearts the sudden stroke
That had laid our great armada in the dust.
And now, if any of those others live,
Why, they must deem that we are dead and gone.
As they of us, so we surmise of them.
But pray still for the best. And Menelaus,
Though likeliest far that he is in distress,
Still, if some ray of sunlight from above
Marks him among the living, rescued by Zeus
Reluctant that his seed should wholly perish,
Then there is hope yet for his safe return.
In this, believe me, you have heard the truth.

(*The* HERALD *returns to the army*)

Third Stasimon

Str. 1
Who was he who named her name,
Justly called with perfect truth?
Surely one whom mortal eye may not see,

Prescient of her destiny,
Naming her with fatal chance
Bride of the lance and long dissension,
Helen—hell indeed she carried
Unto men and ships and a proud city, stealing
From the silk veils of her chamber, sailing seaward
With the Zephyr's breath behind her;
And the armed legions of men set out to hunt her
On the path that leaves no imprint
Till they beached on a leafy shore
Washed by Simois, bringing
War and the waste of bloodshed.

Ant. 1
Truly too for Ilium,
Turning into keeners kin,
Wrath, the instrument of God's will; at last
Claimed his payment for the spurned
Board of Zeus Hospitable,
Even from those who graced her nuptials
With the happy chant of Hymen
And acclaimed her coming with songs that soon
    were turned into weeping.
They have learned another music
In the length of time, and cry out
In a loud voice for the sin of Paris, naming
Him the groom of black betrothal,
Mourning the guilt that laid them low in the dust
    of battle,
Stricken and steeped in bloodshed.

Str. 2
Of old, so it is said, an oxherd did rear at the
    hearth a young
Lion-cub, as a fosterling, in his infancy bringing

Smiles to the face of the aged,
Innocent sport of the children,
Often pampered and caressed,
Fondled like a babe with hands
Licked by the fawning tongue that craved
Meat from the master's table.

Ant. 2
But Time brought to the light his true nature, after
    his kind, and then
Years of care were repaid in slaughter of pasturing
    cattle,
Tearing the hand that had tended,
Blood in the house, and the inmates
Bowed in helpless anguish, struck
Down beneath the heaven-sent
Carnage which they had nursed, a fell
Priest of avenging bloodshed.

Str. 3
And so it seemed once there came to Ilium
A sweet-smiling calm, without cloud, serene, be-
    guiling,
A rare gem set in crown of riches,
Shaft of a softly-glancing eye,
Bloom of love that doth prick the bosom.
But a change carried her bridals
To a bitter consummation.
To the proud children of Priam,
With the guidance | of the stern wrath
Of Zeus, she came as a fierce
Bridal-bewailing Fury.

(CLYTEMNESTRA *appears at the door of the palace*)

Ant. 3

A tale of old time is told on mortal lips,
That when man hath brought to full growth abun-
dant riches,
It dies not childless, nay it breedeth;
Whence from a happy life is reaped
Fruit of plenteous lamentation.
With a lone voice I deny it.
It is only deeds unholy
That increase, fruitful in offspring
Of the same breed as its fathers.
Where justice rules in the house,
Blest of God is the issue.

Str. 4

But ancient pride loves to put forth a fresh bloom
of sin out of human evil, soon or late.
Behold, whenever the time appointed come,
A cloud of deep night, spirit of vengeance irresisti-
ble,
Horror of dark disaster hung
Brooding within the palace,
True to the dam that bore it.

Ant. 4

But where is Justice? She lights up the smoke-
darkened hut, yea she loves humility.
From gilded pinnacles of polluted hands
She turns her eyes back unto the dwelling of the
pure in heart;
So, regarding not the false
Stamp on the face of wealth, leads
All to the end appointed.

(*Enter* AGAMEMNON *riding in a chariot and followed by another which carries* CASSANDRA *and other spoils of war*)

All hail, son of Atreus, captor of Troy,
All hail to thee, King!
How shall I greet thee, how tune my address
So as neither to fall too short nor surpass
Due measure of joy?
   Full many are they who unjustly respect
Mere semblance of truth, and all men are quick
With a tear to the eye for a neighbour's distress,
But with hearts untouched by his trouble.
Just so they rejoice with him, forcing a smile
Like his on their laughterless faces.
Yet he that can read in the book of the eyes
Man's nature, will not be deluded by looks
Which fawn with dissembled fidelity, false
Like wine that is mingled with water.
So surely, I will not deny it, when thou
Didst marshal the host to recover
Helen, willingly wanton, with thousands of lives,
I accounted thee like to a picture deformed
Or a helm ill-turned by the pilot.
   But now from the depth of the heart it is mine
To salute thee with love:
Toil happily crowned
Brings sweetness at last to the toiler.
And in time thou shalt learn to distinguish apart
The unjust and the just housekeeper among
Those who are set over thy people.

AGAMEMNON. First, it is just to greet this land of Argos
   With her presiding Gods, my partners in
   This homecoming, as in the just revenge

I brought to Priam's city. When the Gods
Heard that appeal unvoiced by mortal tongue,
They cast their votes decisive in the urn
Of blood with doom of death for Ilium
And uttermost destruction; and in the other
Hope hesitant still hovered on the brink.
The smoke of pillage marks that city yet,
The rites of ruin live. Her ashes breathe
Their last, with riches redolent, and die.
Wherefore 'tis right to render memorable
Thanks to the Gods. For that bold piracy
We have exacted payment; for a woman
That city lies in dust, struck by the fierce
Brood of the Horse, the Argive host in arms,
Which at the setting of the Pleiades
Leapt like a hungry lion across her towers
And slaked its thirst in streaming blood of kings
Such is my measured preface to the Gods.
I have marked well your loyal sentiments
At one with mine, and sealed with my assent.
Too few are they whose nature is to honour
A friend's good fortune without jealousy.
Malignant venom seated at the heart
Doubles the sick man's burden, as he groans
For his own case and grieves no less to see
His neighbour walking in prosperity.
Devotion seeming-full—an empty shadow
I call it, speaking from sure knowledge tried
In the true mirror of companionship.
Odysseus only, who sailed against his will,
Once harnessed, proved a trusty outrigger—
Alive or dead, I know not. What concerns
The city and the Gods we shall dispose
In public congress, and deliberate
How what is well may be continued so,

And where some sickness calls for remedy,
We shall with cautery or kindly knife
Of surgery essay to heal the sore.

But now, returning to my royal hearth,
My first act shall be to salute the Gods
Who led me hence and lead me home again;
Victory attends me: may she rest secure!

CL. People of Argos, elders assembled here,
I shall declare before you unashamed
My way with him I love; for diffidence
Dies in us all with time. I tell a tale
From my own heart of the unhappy life
I led while he fought under Ilium.
First, none can say how much a wife must bear,
Who sits at home, with no man's company,
And waits upon the train of evil news,
One messenger, then another with a tale
Of worse disaster shouted through the house;
And as for wounds, if he had met as many
As constant rumour poured into his home,
His limbs were like a net, pierced through and
        through.
If he had died, the prevalent report,
He was a second Geryon, with bodies three
And triple cloak of earth draped over them,
Three outstretched corpses and one death for each.
Beset with malignant rumours such as these,
Often the halter pressed my eager throat,
Released by others with no thanks from me.

And hence it is our child is not here present,
As it were meet, pledge of our plighted vows,
Orestes. Marvel not at this. He lives
Safe in the charge of an old friend at arms,
Strophius the Phocian, who admonished me
Of various dangers—your life in jeopardy,

A restive populace, and that fault of nature,
When man has been cast down, to trample on him.
In this excuse, believe me, lies the truth.

    As for myself, the fountains of my tears
Are drained away till not a drop is left.
The late night-vigils have outworn my eyes,
Weeping the light that was to burn for you,
With tears that went unheeded. Even in dreams
I would start up, roused by the tenuous beat
Of a gnat's wing from visions all of you,
Imagining more ills than credible
In the slow hours that kept me company.

    But now, all griefs endured with patient heart,
I name this man the watchdog of the fold,
Forestay that saves the ship, upsoaring oak
That holds the roof, a longed-for only child,
A shore unhoped-for spied by sailors' eyes!
This is my greeting, this my homage to him,
And may no envy follow it! Enough
Our sorrows heretofore; and now, beloved,
Step from the chariot, but do not set
Upon the ground those feet that trampled Troy.
Make haste, my handmaids who have been ap-
    pointed
To strew his path with outspread tapestry.
Prepare a road of purple coverlets
Where Justice leads to an unhoped-for home;
And there the rest our sleep-unvanquished care
Shall order justly, as the Gods ordain.

AG. Daughter of Leda, guardian of my home,
    Your greeting was prolonged, proportionate
    To my long absence; but tributes of due praise
    Should come from other lips; and furthermore
    Seek not to unman me with effeminate

       Graces and barbarous salaams agape
       In grovelling obeisance at my feet,
       Nor with invidious purple pave my way.
       Such honours are an appanage of God,
       And I, being mortal, cannot but fear to tread
       On this embroidered beauty, rich and rare.
       Honour me as a man, not as a God.
       Foot-mats and fine robes ring differently
       In Rumour's ill-tongued music, and of all
       God's gifts the chief is wisdom. Count him blest
       Whose life has ended in felicity.
       I shall act as I have told you, conscience-clear.
CL. Yet tell me frankly, according to your judgment—
AG. My judgment stands, make no mistake of that.
CL. Would you in danger have vowed to God this act?
AG. Yes, if the priesthood had commanded it.
CL. And what, if Priam had conquered, would *he* have
       done?
AG. He would have trod the purple, I do not doubt.
CL. Then give no thought to mortal tongues that wag.
AG. The clamour of a populace counts for much.
CL. Whom no man envies, no man shall admire.
AG. It is not for a woman to take part in strife.
CL. Well may the victor yield a victory!
AG. Do *you* set store by such a victory?
CL. Be tempted, freely vanquished, victor still!

AG. Well, if it be your will, let someone loose
       The sandals bound in service to my feet;
       And as they tread this ocean-purple, may
       No far-off God cast on me envious eyes!
       Deep shame there lies in prodigality
       Which tramples robes woven of silver worth.
       But be it so. And see this stranger here
       Is treated gently. Kingship kindly used

Wins favour in the sight of God above;
For no man willingly endures the yoke
Of servitude, and she, the army's gift,
Is a blossom culled out of uncounted wealth.
And now, constrained to accept these honours from
    you,
Treading the purple I pass into my home.

CL. There is still the sea, it shall not be dried up,
Renewing fresh from infinite abundance
Rich merchandise of purple-stained attire;
Wherein the Gods, my lord, have well endowed
A royal house that knows no penury.
How many robes would I have vowed to tread,
Had prophecy instructed, if thereby
I had contrived the ransom of one soul!
While the root lives, the foliage shall raise
Its shady arch against the burning Dog-star;
And, as your coming to your hearth and home
Signifies warmth that comes in wintry cold,
So, when Zeus from the bitter virgin-grape
Draws wine, then coolness fills the house at last,
As man made perfect moves about his home.

(AGAMEMNON *has gone into the palace*)

Zeus, Zeus the Perfecter, perfect thou my prayer,
And perfect also that which is thy care!

(CLYTEMNESTRA *goes into the palace*)

Fourth Stasimon

Str. 1

What is this insistent fear
Which in my prophetic heart
Set and steady beats with evil omen,
Chanting unbidden a brooding, oracular music?
Why can I not cast it out

Like a dream of dark import,
Setting good courage firm
On my spirit's empty throne?
In time the day came
When the Greeks, with anchors plunged
Deep in that shingle strand,
Moored the sloops of war, and men
Thronged the beach of Ilium;

Ant. 1
So today my eyes have seen
Safe at last their homecoming.
Still I hear a strain of stringless music,
Dissonant dirge of the Furies, a chant uninstructed
Quired in this uneasy breast,
Desolate of hope and cheer.
Not for naught beats the heart
Stirred with ebb and flow of fate
In righteous men: soon
What is feared shall come to pass.
Yet against hope I pray,
May it prove of no import,
Unfulfilled and falsified!

Str. 2
If a man's health be advanced over the due mean,
It will trespass soon upon sickness who stands
Close neighbour, between them a thin wall.
So doth the passage of life
Sped with a favouring breeze
Suddenly founder on reefs of destruction.
Caution seated at the helm
Casts a portion of the load
Overboard with measured throw.

So the ship shall come to shore;
So the house shall stand, if not
Overcharged with store of woe.
Plenty from Zeus and abundance that yieldeth a
    yearly return from the harvested furrows
Driveth hunger from the door.

Ant. 2

But if the red blood of a man ever be spilled on the
    ground, dripping and deadly, then who
Shall recall it again with his magic?
Even the healer who knew
Charms to recover the dead,
Zeus put an end to his wrongful powers.
Portions are there preordained,
Each supreme within its own
Bounds decreed eternally;
Else would heart outstripping tongue
Cast misgiving to the winds.
Now in darkness deep it groans,
Brooding in sickly despair, and no longer it hopes
    to resolve in an orderly web these
Mazes of a fevered mind.

(CLYTEMNESTRA *appears at the door of the palace*)

CLYTEMNESTRA. You too, Cassandra, come within; for
    Zeus
Of his great mercy grants to you a part
In our domestic sacrifice, to stand
Among the slaves before his altar there.
Step from the chariot, put by your pride.
Even great Heracles submitted once
To toil and eat the bread of slavery;
And should compulsion bring a man to this,

Much comfort lies in service to a house
Of immemorial riches. Those who have reaped
A harvest never hoped-for out of hand
Are strict upon the rule and show no mercy.
What is customary shall here be yours.

CH. To you she spoke, and made her meaning plain.
Caught in the casting-net of destiny,
'Twere best to yield; and yet perchance you will
not.

CL. Nay, if she speak not, like the babbling swallow,
Some barbarous tongue which none can under-
stand,
With mystic words I'll win the mind within.

CH. Go with her. Your plight affords no better choice.
Step from the chariot and do her will.

CL. I have no time to idle at the door.
The victims stand upon the palace hearth
Before the altar, ready for the knife
To render thanks for these unhoped-for joys.
If you too will take part, do not delay;
But, if you lack the wit to understand me,
Do *you* address her with barbarian hand.

CH. She needs, it seems, a clear interpreter.
Like some wild creature is she, newly-trapped.

CL. Nay, she is mad, and gives her ears to folly.
Her city newly-captured, hither brought
A slave, she knows not how to take the bit
Until her pride is foamed away in blood.
I'll waste no more words to demean myself.

(CLYTEMNESTRA *goes into the palace*)

CH. *I* feel no anger, for I pity you.
Unhappy girl, dismount and follow her,
Yield to your fate and take its yoke upon you.

Kommos

Str. 1

CA. Oh! Alas, Earth! Apollo, Apollo!
CH. What is this cry in the name of Loxias?
    He is not one to greet with lamentation.

Ant. 1

CA. Oh! Alas, Earth! Apollo, Apollo!
CH. Again she calls with blasphemous utterance
    The God who stands aloof from mourning cries.

Str. 2

CA. Apollo, Apollo, the Wayfarer! Destroyed by thee!
    Once more hast thou destroyed me wantonly!
CH. Her own sad fate, it seems, she will prophesy.
    She is now a slave, and yet God's gift abides.

Ant. 2

CA. Apollo, Apollo, the Wayfarer! Destroyed by thee!
    Ah, whither hast thou led me? What house is this?
CH. The House of the Atreidae. Nay, if that
    Thou knowest not, then hear the truth from me.

Str. 3

CA. Palace abhorred of God, conscious of hidden crime,
    Sanguinary, sullied with slaughtered kin,
    A charnel-house that streams with children's blood!
CH. Keen as a hound upon the scent she seems,
    This stranger, tracking down a murderous trail.

Ant. 3

CA. I can declare a testimony plain to read.
    Listen to them as they lament the foul
    Repast of roasted flesh for father's mouth!

Ch. We know of thy prophetic fame already,
    And have no need of an interpreter.

Str. 4

Ca. Out, out, alas! What is it plotted now?
    Horror unspeakable
    Is plotted in this house, insufferable,
    A hard cross for kinsfolk,
    Without cure. The hoped-for succour is far away.
Ch. This prophecy escapes me. Yet the first
    I recognised—the country cries of it.

Ant. 4

Ca. Alas, O wicked! Is thy purpose *that?*
    He who hath shared thy bed,
    To bathe his limbs, to smile—how speak the end?
    The end comes, and quickly:
    A hand reaching out, followed by a hand again!
Ch. Still at a loss am I; riddles before,
    Now sightless oracles obscure my way.

Str. 5

Ca. Ah, ah! O horrible!
    What is appearing now? Some net of mesh infernal.
    Mate of his bed and board, she is a snare
    Of slaughter! Oh, murderous ministers,
    Cry alleluia, cry,
    Fat with blood, dance and sing!

Str. 6

Ch. What is this Fury thou hast called to cry
    In exultation? It brings no cheer to me.
    Oh, to the heart it falls, saffron of hue, the drop
    Of blood which doth sink with life's setting sun,
    Smitten with edge of steel.
    Nearer, yet nearer draws the swift judgment-stroke.

Ant. 5

CA. Ah, ah! Beware, beware!
    Let not the cow come near! See how the bull is
        captured!
    She wraps him in the robe, the hornèd trap,
    Then strikes. He falls into the bath, the foul
    Treacherous bowl of blood. Such her skilled art-
        istry.

Ant. 6

CH. No gift I boast in reading prophecy,
    But this must signify calamity.
    When did a prophet's voice issue in happiness?
    Amidst mortal stress his word-woven art,
    Ever divining ill,
    Teacheth mankind before the hour chants of fear.

Str. 7

CA. Alas, alas, unhappy, pitiful destiny!
    Now I lament my own passion to fill the bowl.
    Oh whither hast thou led me? O my grief,
    Whither, unless that I with him must die?

Str. 8

CH. Spirit of frenzy borne on by the breath of God,
    Thy own mournful dirge
    Singest thou, like the red-brown bird
    Who never-weary pours out her full heart in song,
    Itys, Itys! she cries, sorrow hath filled her days,
    The sad nightingale.

Ant. 7

CA. Alas, alas, the sweet music of the nightingale!
    Body of wings the Gods fashioned to cover her,

And gave her, free of weeping, happy days.
For me there waits the stroke of two-edged steel.

Ant. 8

CH. Whence is this passionate madness inspired of God
That still streameth on?
Tales of fear told in uncouth cries,
Set to a strain of high-pitched and harsh har-
monies?
Whither the path of wild prophecy evil-tongued?
O where must it end?

Str. 9

CA. O fatal bridal-day, Paris the curse of all his kin!
O swift Scamander, streaming past my home,
Once on the banks of those waters I dwelt, and they
Nourished me as a child.
But now, it seems, my cries shall soon resound
Beside Cocytus and sad Acheron.

Str. 10

CH. What is it now? A cry simple for all to read.
Even a child may understand.
With sharp anguish cleft, as though red with blood,
My heart breaks, as these pitiful plaintive cries
Shatter the listening soul.

Ant. 9

CA. Alas the pain, the pain, agony of a plundered town!
Alas, the King's rich offerings at the gates,
Lavished from flocks and herds, little availed to
bring
Help to the city, so
That she might not have been what she is now.
And I distraught shall dash into the snare.

Ant. 10

CH. Like to the rest is this pitiful utterance.
What evil spirit hath possessed
Thy soul, cruelly bending those fevered lips
To give voice to such dolorous tunes of death?
Who shall divine the end?

CA. Listen! No more my prophecy shall glance
As through a veil, like a new-wedded maid.
Nay, bright and fresh, I tell thee, it shall flow
Against the sunrise, and like a wave engulf
The daybreak in disaster greater far
Than this. No riddles now; I shall instruct,
And you shall bear me witness step by step,
As I track down the scent of crimes of old.
On yonder housetop ever abides a choir
Of minstrels unmelodious, singing of ill;
And deeply-drunk, to fortify their spirit,
In human blood, those revellers yet abide,
Whom none can banish, Furies congenital,
And settled on the roof they chant the tune
Of old primordial Ruin, each in turn
Spewing with horror at a brother's outraged bed.
Say, have I missed, or marked my quarry down?
Am I a false prophet babbling at the gates?
Bear me on oath your witness that I know
The story of this household's ancient crimes.

CH. What could an oath, however truly sworn,
Avail to heal? Indeed I marvel at you,
Born far beyond the sea, speaking of this,
An alien country, as though you had been present.
CA. The seer Apollo bestowed that gift upon me.
CH. Was he smitten with the shaft of love, a God?

CA. Time was, shame would not let me speak of this.

CH. Prosperity makes man fastidious.

CA. Oh, but he wrestled strenuously for my love.

CH. Did he bring you to the act of getting child?

CA. First I consented, then I cheated him.

CH. Already captive to his craft divine?

CA. Already I foretold my people's fate.

CH. How did you find refuge from his displeasure?

CA. The price I paid was that none gave me heed.

CH. Your prophecies have earned belief from us.

CA. Oh misery!
Again the travail of true prophecy
With prelude wild makes tumult in my soul!
Do you not see them, seated on the roof,
Those children, like the ghastly shapes of dreams,
Murdered, it seems, by their own kith and kin,
Meat in their hands from some familiar meal,
The inward parts and bowels, of which their father
Ate—what a pitiable load is theirs!
That is the sin for which is planned revenge
By the faint-hearted lion, stretched in the bed,
Who keeps house for my master—being his slave,
I must needs name him so—now home again.
Little he knows what that foul bitch, with ears
Laid back and lolling tongue, will bring to pass
With vicious snap of treacherous destruction.
So dead to shame! woman to murder man!
What beast abominable is her name?
Double-faced amphisbene, or skulking Scylla
Among the cliffs, waylaying mariners,
A hellish dam raging against her own,
In strife that gives no quarter! How loud she sang
Her alleluias over the routed foe,
While feigning gladness at his safe return!

Believe me not, what matter? 'Tis all one.
The future comes, and when your eyes have seen,
You shall cry out in pity, "She spoke true."

CH. Thyestes' banquet of the flesh of babes
I understood, and shuddered, terrified
To hear that tale told with unerring truth;
But for the rest I wander far astray.

CA. I say you shall see Agamemnon's death.

CH. Unhappy girl, hush those ill-omened lips!

CA. No healing god is here—there is no cure.

CH. None, if it be so; and yet may it not be!

CA. While you are praying, others prepare to kill.

CH. What man would plot so foul a villainy?

CA. Ah, you have missed my meaning utterly.

CH. But who shall do it? That escapes me still.

CA. And yet I know too well the speech of Greece.

CH. So does the Delphian, yet are his sayings dark.

CA. Ah, how it burns, the fire! It sweeps upon me!
Oh, oh! Apollo! Oh alas, my sorrow!
That lioness two-footed, lying with
The wolf in absence of the noble lion,
Shall kill me, O unhappy, and as though
Mixing a potion pours in the cup of wrath
My wages too, and while she sets an edge
Upon the steel for him, she vows to make
Murder the price of my conveyance hither.

Why do I wear these tawdry mockeries,
This staff, this mantic wreath about my neck?
If I must die, then you shall perish first.
Down to perdition! Now you have your pay.
Bestow your fatal riches on another!
Behold Apollo stripping me himself
Of my prophetic raiment, regarding me,
Clad in his robes, a public laughing-stock

Of friend and enemy, one who has endured
The name of witch, waif, beggar, castaway.
So now the seer who made these eyes to see
Has led his servant to this mortal end.
No altar of my fathers waits for me,
But a block that drips blood at a dead man's grave.
    And yet we die not unavenged of heaven.
Another shall come to avenge us both,
Who for his father's sake shall kill his mother,
A wandering outcast, an exile far away,
He shall come back and set for his kin a crown
On this long tale of ruin. The Gods above
Have sworn a solemn covenant that his
Dead father's outstretched corpse shall call him
    home.
    Why do I weep for this so piteously?
Have I not seen the fall of Ilium?
And those who laid that city waste are thus
Discharged at last by heaven's arbitrament.
This door I name the gate of Hades: now
I will go and knock, I will endure to die.
My only prayer is that the blow be mortal,
To close these eyes in sleep without a struggle,
While my life's blood ebbs peacefully away.

CH. O woman in whose wisdom is much grief,
    Long have you spoken; and yet, if you know
    The end, why like the consecrated ox
    Walk with such patient step into the slaughter?
CA. Should the end linger, that is no escape.
CH. And yet the latest moment is the best.
CA. What should I gain by flight? My hour has come.
CH. You have the endurance of a valiant heart.
CA. Such words are common for those whom life has
    crossed.

CH. Yet there is comfort in honourable death.

CA. O father, father, and thy noble sons!

(CASSANDRA *approaches the door, then recoils*)

CH. What is it? What terror has turned you back?

CA. Faugh!

CH. What means that cry? Some sickening at the heart?

CA. The palace reeks with fumes of dripping blood.

CH. No, 'tis the smell of fireside sacrifice.

CA. A vapour such as issues from a tomb.

CH. No scent of Araby have you marked in it.

CA. Nay, I will go to weep inside the house
Agamemnon's fate and mine. Enough of life!
O hear me, friends!
I am not scared like a bird once limed that takes
Fright at a bush. Witness, when I am dead,
The day when woman for this woman dies
And man mismarried for a man lies low.
I beg this of you at the point of death.

CH. Poor soul, foredoomed to death, I pity you.

CA. Yet one word more I have to speak, my own
Dirge for myself. I pray the Sun in heaven,
On whom I look my last, that he may grant
To him who shall come to avenge my master
From those who hate me payment of the price
For this dead slave-girl slain with so light a stroke.
Alas, mortality! when fortunate,
A painted image; in adversity,
The sponge's moist touch wipes it all away.

CH. And this to me is far more pitiable.

(CASSANDRA *goes into the palace*)

Good fortune among mankind is a thing
Insatiable. Mansions of kings are marked

By the fingers of all, none warns her away,
None cries, O enter not hither!
Unto him the Immortals accorded the fall
Of the city of Troy,
And with honours divine he returns to his home.
But now, if the debt of the blood of the past
Is on him, if his death must crown it and pay
To the dead their price for the slaughtered of old,
Then who, when he hears these things, is assured
Of a life unwounded of sorrow?

AGAMEMNON. Oh me, I am struck down!
CH. Hark, did you not hear that cry? The stroke of
    death!
AG. Oh me, again!
CH. Ah, his voice it is, our King! The deed is done.
    Come, take counsel how to meet this perilous hour.
 1. I say, raise hue and cry—rally the people!
 2. Break in at once upon their dripping blade.
 3. Yes, let us act—no time for faltering now.
 4. This bloody deed spells tyranny to come.
 5. *They* spurn delay—*their* hands are not asleep.
 6. What can we do, old men whose strength is gone?
 7. No words of ours can raise the dead to life.
 8. Must we wear out our age in slavery?
 9. No, death is gentler than the tyrant's lash.
10. We heard his cries, but his death is still unproved.
11. Yes, we are only guessing—we must know.
12. Agreed, to find how is it with the King.

(*As the old men are about to enter the palace, the doors
are thrown open:* CLYTEMNESTRA *is seen standing over
the bodies of* AGAMEMNON *and* CASSANDRA, *which are
laid out on a purple robe*)

CLYTEMNESTRA. Now I shall feel no shame to contradict
    All that was said before to bide my time.
    How else should one who pondered on revenge
    Against a covert enemy, have strung the snare
    Of death so high as to outsoar his leaping?
    This duel, nurtured in my thoughts so long,
    Is crowned at last with perfect victory.
    I stand here, where I struck, over my work.
    And it was so contrived, I'll not deny,
    To leave no fissure, no escape from death.
    With this vast net, as might be cast for fish,
    I sieged him round in the fatal wealth of purple,
    And twice I struck him, and with two cries of pain
    He stretched his legs; then on his fallen body
    I gave the third blow, my drink-offering
    To the Zeus of Hell, Deliverer of the dead.
    There he lay prostrate, gasping out his soul,
    And pouring forth a sudden spurt of blood
    Rained thick these drops of deathly dew upon me,
    While I rejoiced like cornfields at the flow
    Of heavenly moisture in birth-pangs of the bud.
    So stands the case, elders of Argos, so
    Rejoice, if so it please you—I glory in it.
    For if due offerings were his to drink,
    Then those were justly his, and more than just.
    With bitter tears he filled the household bowl,
    Now he himself has drained it and is gone.
CH. I marvel at your tongue so brazen-bold
    That dares to speak so of your murdered king.
CL. You trifle with me as with a foolish woman,
    While, nothing daunted, to such as understand
    I say—commend or censure, as you will,
    It is no matter—here is Agamemnon,
    My husband, dead, the work of this right hand,
    A just artificer. That is the truth.

Str. 1

Cн. Woman, what evil charm bred out of earth or flow-
　　　　ing sea,
　　　Poison to eat or drink, hast thou devoured to take
　　　On thee a crime that cries out for a public curse?
　　　'Twas thine, the stroke, the blow—banishment shall
　　　　be thine,
　　　Hissed and hated of all men.

Cl. Your sentence now is banishment for me,
　　　Abhorred of all, cursed and abominated;
　　　But you did nothing then to contravene
　　　His purpose, when, to exorcise the storms,
　　　As though it were a ewe picked from his flocks
　　　Whose wealth of snowy fleeces never fails
　　　To multiply, unmoved, he killed his own
　　　Child, born to me in pain, my well-beloved.
　　　Why did you not drive *him* from hearth and home
　　　For that foul crime, reserving your stern judgment
　　　Until *I* acted? I bid you cast at me
　　　Such menaces as will make for mastery
　　　In combat match for match with one who stands
　　　Prepared to meet them; and if with the help of God
　　　The issue goes against you, suffering
　　　Shall school those gray hairs in humility.

Ant. 1

Cн. Spirit of wickedness and haughty utterance! As
　　　　now
　　　Over the drops of red murder the mind doth rave,
　　　So doth a fleck of red blood in the eyes appear.
　　　Dishonoured and deserted of thy friends, for this
　　　Stroke soon shalt thou be stricken.

Cl. Hark to the sanction of my solemn oath.

By perfect Justice who avenged my child,
By Ruin and the Fury unto whom
I slew this sacramental offering,
No thought of fear shall walk beneath this roof,
While on my hearth the fire is kindled by
Aegisthus, faithful to me from of old,
A shield and buckler strong in my defence.
Low lies the man that shamed his wedded wife,
Sweet solace of the Trojan Chryseids,
And stretched beside him this prisoner of war,
His paramour, this visionary seer,
His faithful bedfellow, who fondled him
On the ship's benches. Both have their deserts—
He as you see him; she like a swan has sung
Her last sad roundelay, and, lying there,
His leman, a side-dish for his nuptial bed,
She brings to me the spice that crowns my joy.

Str. 2

Ch. Oh for the gift of death, speedy and free of pain,
Free from watch at the sick-bed,
To bring the long sleep that knows no waking,
Now that my lord and loyal protector
Lieth slain. For woman's sake
Long he warred far away while he lived,
Now at home dies beneath a woman's hand.
O Helen, oh folly-beguiled,
One woman to take those thousands of lives
That were lost in the land of the Trojans,
Now thou hast set on the curse of the household
A crown of blood beyond ablution.
Such the world has never known,
Spirit of strife strong in man's destruction!

Cl. Pray not for the portion of death, though sore

Distressed is thy heart,
Nor turn upon Helen the edge of thy wrath,
Saying that she slew men without number,
One woman, a wound that shall close not.

Ant. 2

CH. Demon of blood and tears, swooping upon the two
Tribes of Tantalus' children,
Enthroned in two women single-hearted,
Victor art thou, and my soul is stricken.
See on the palace-roof he stands,
Like the foul raven, evil-tongued,
Hear him croak, jubilant, his chant of joy!

CL. Ah, now is a true thought framed on thy lips,
Naming this demon
Thrice fed on the race, who, glutted with blood,
With the old wound smarting, is craving to lap
Fresh blood, still young in his hunger.

Str. 3

CH. Demon of sudden destruction,
Laying the house in the dust for ever!
Oh me, 'tis an evil tale of ruin that never resteth.
Alas, I weep the will of Zeus
Who causeth all and worketh all;
For what without his will befalleth mortals,
And what here was not sent from heaven?
Oh me, I weep for my master and king.
How shall I mourn thee?
What words shall a fond heart speak thee?
In the coils of the spider, the web of a death
Ungodly, entangled thou diest.
Oh me, I lament thy unkingly bed,
With a sudden stroke of sharp
Two-edged treachery felled and slaughtered.

CL. Why dost thou declare that the murder was mine?
 Name it not so, nor
 Call me Agamemnon's wife. 'Tis not I
 But a ghost in the likeness of woman, the vengeful
 Shade of the banqueter whom Atreus fed,
 Now crowneth his own
 First-fruits with a perfect oblation.

 Ant. 3

CH. How art thou guiltless of murder?
 None is there, none that shall bear thee witness.
 No, no, but perchance some ancient shade of wrath
   was abettor.
 'Tis onward driven, stream on stream
 Of slaughter sprung from common seed,
 Murder red, that soon shall move to ransom
 The dried gore of the flesh of children.
  Oh me, I weep for my master and king.
  How shall I mourn thee?
  What words shall a fond heart speak thee?
  In the coils of the spider, the web of a death
  Ungodly, entangled thou diest.
  Oh me, I lament thy unkingly bed,
  With a sudden stroke of sharp
  Two-edged treachery felled and slaughtered.

CL. What of *him*? Did he not set ruin afoot
 In the house when he slew
 Iphigeneia, the child that I bore him?
 And with long bitter tears have I mourned her.
 So has he done, so is he done by.
 Let him not speak proudly in darkness below.
 With the death of the sword
 For the sin of the sword he has perished.

Str. 4

Cн. Alas, the mind strays disarmed, resourceless;
     Weakly it drifts, and whither
     To turn it knows not. The house is falling.
     I fear the sharp beat of blood will soon have laid
     The roof in ruins. The storm is growing.
     Another mortal stroke for Justice' hand
     Is now made sharp on other whetstones.
       Alas, Earth, Earth, would thou hadst taken
       This body before I had looked on my lord
       Laid low in the vessel of silver.
       Oh me, who shall bury him, who shall lament?
       Or wilt thou have the heart, having murdered
         thy own
       Master, to mourn at his tomb and to offer
       To his spirit a gift unacceptable, such
       Unholy return for his great deeds?
       Who shall intone at the tomb of a blessed spirit
       Tearful psalms of salutation,
       A tribute pure in heart and truthful?

Cʟ. That office is nothing to you—it is mine.
     I struck him and killed him, I'll bury him too,
     But not with mourners from home in his train,
     No, Iphigeneia, his daughter shall come,
     As is meet, to receive him, her father, beside
     Those waters of wailing, and throwing her arms
     On his neck with a kiss she shall greet him.

Ant. 4

Cн. The charge is answered with counter-charges.
     Who shall be judge between them?
     The spoiler spoiled, slaughtered he who slaughtered.
     The law abides yet beside the throne of Zeus,
     The sinner must suffer. So 'tis ordered.

The seed accurst, O who shall drive it out?
The whole house falleth, nailed to ruin.

CL. So naming the law, truth hast thou spoken.
As for me, I consent
On my oath to the demon that haunteth the house
To endure ills present, though heavy to bear;
Let him now go hence
And inflict upon others the burden of blood
Outpoured by the hand of a kinsman.
Then would a scanty
Pittance content me better than plenty,
As the house is absolved
From the madness of murder for murder.

(*Enter* AEGISTHUS *with a bodyguard*)

AE. O kindly light, O day of just reward,
Now have I proof there are avenging Gods
Who look down from above on human sin,
As I regard these purple snares of hell
Wherein to my delight this man doth lie,
Distrained by death for a father's treachery.
His father, Atreus, monarch of this realm,
Challenged in right of sovranty by mine,
Thyestes, his own brother, banished him
From hearth and home. A suppliant, he returned,
And found such safety for himself as not
To stain his native soil with his own blood;
But wicked Atreus, courteous more than kind,
Regaled him at a festive holiday
To a banquet of his children's flesh. The toes
And fingers set aside, the rest was laid
Disguised before him, where he sat apart.
My father unsuspecting took and ate—
A banquet prodigal in calamity

For this whole house. As soon as he divined
The monstrous crime, with a loud cry he fell
Back, spewing out the slaughtered flesh,
And cursed the House of Pelops—with a kick
That threw the table to the floor he cried,
"So perish all the seed of Pleisthenes!"
That is the sin for which this man lies here.
And that the plot should have been spun by me
Is also just; for, when I was a child
In swaddling-clothes, my father's third last hope,
I was condemned with him to banishment,
Till Justice reared me up and brought me home.
And so, though absent, still the blow was mine,
Mine were the threads of the conspiracy.
And now to die were sweet, since I have seen
My enemy caught by Justice in her snares.

CH. Aegisthus, insult in an evil hour
Wins no respect from me. If it be true
You killed with full intent, if you alone
Contrived this deed of bloodshed from afar,
Then be assured, your head shall not escape
The stones of an indignant people's curse.

AE. Such talk from lower benches to the helm
Of high command! 'Tis hard, as you shall find,
For age to learn, and yet you shall be taught.
Even in dotage, dungeons and the pangs
Of hunger make an excellent physician
To school the spirit. Have you not eyes to see?
Kick not against the pricks, or smart for it!

CH. Woman! A man returned from feats of war,
While you kept house at home and fouled his bed,
A great commander—*you* contrived his death!

AE. More talk that shall yet prove the seed of tears!
The tongue of Orpheus, contrary to yours,
Led all in listening rapture after him;

But you, a nuisance with your senseless bark,
Chains shall instruct you in docility.

CH. What? *you* my master, *you* tyrant of the land,
Who, though the plot was yours, yet lacked the
        courage
To raise a hand to execute the plot!

AE. Plainly, temptation was the woman's part;
I, as his ancient enemy, was suspect.
But now, with his possessions, I shall try
My hand at monarchy. Who disobeys
Shall groan beneath the yoke—no trace-horse he
Pampered with corn; no, slow starvation walled
In noisome darkness shall see him humbled yet.

CH. O craven spirit, who had no heart to kill
But left it to a woman, who defiles
Her Gods and country! Oh, does Orestes yet
Behold the light of life, that he may come
Favoured of fortune home, and prove himself
The sovran executioner of both?

AE. So? If you are bent on folly, you shall soon be
        taught.
Ho, my trusty guards, come forward, here is work
        to do.

CAPTAIN OF THE GUARD. Ho, let each man draw and
        hold his sword in readiness!

CH. Be it so, we too are ready, unafraid to die.

AE. Die! Well-spoken, we shall gladly take you at your
        word.

CL. Peace! my lord, forbear, and let no further ill be
        done.
Rich already is the harvest of calamity.
Grief is ours in plenty—draw no blood to make it
        more.
Go your ways, old men, and bow to destiny in due

Season, lest you suffer. What has been, it had to be.
Should this penance prove sufficient, though we
    bear the scars
Of an evil spirit's talons, we shall rest content.
Such the counsel of a woman; pray, be ruled by me.

AE. Must I listen to their wanton threats of violence,
    Flowers of insolence wherewith they trifle with
      their fate,
    So bereft of sense they know not who is master
      here?

CH. Men of Argos are not used to cringe before a knave.

AE. I shall overtake you yet—the reckoning is nigh.

CH. Not if saving fortune guide Orestes home again.

AE. Yes, I know the only food of castaways is hope.

CH. Gloat and grow fat, brag and blacken Justice while
    you dare!

AE. Soon the hour shall come when foolish talk shall
    cost you dear.

CH. Flaunt your feathers, fluster like a cock beside his
    hen!

CL. Do not heed their idle clamour. You and I, the new
    Masters of the house, henceforward shall direct it
    well.

O

CHOEPHOROE

(The scene as before. Enter ORESTES *and* PYLADES*)*

ORESTES. Hermes, whose home is in the earth, whose
    eyes
    Look down on my paternal heritage,
    Deliver me, do battle by my side!
    Unto my country I return, restored.

. . . . .

And now beside my father's tomb I call
On him to hear and hearken.

. . . . .

A lock to Inachus who nurtured me,
And now another in token of my grief.

. . . . .

I was not present, father, to lament
Thy death nor raise a hand in sorrow, when
They brought thy body from the house.

. . . . .

(*A cry is heard within.* ELECTRA *and the* CHORUS *of
serving-women come out of the palace*)

What do I see? What gathering is this
Of women clad in robes of sombre hue?
What sad occasion calls them? Can it be
A new affliction laid upon the house,
Or for my father, shall I say, they bring
Drink-offerings to propitiate the dead?
So it must be; for now I think I see
Electra too, my sister, walking bowed
In heavy grief. O Zeus, may I avenge
My father's death! Defend and fight for me!
Pylades, let us stand aside, until
We know the meaning of this act of prayer.

Parodos

Str. 1

I issue from the house to bring
Oblations forth with blow of beating hand.
Behold, my streaming cheek is freshly furrowed
Red and rent with cruel nail.
On grief's shrill cries my sick heart doth feed con-
tinually.

The sundered linen shrieketh loud in tune with
    lamentation; so
Raiment torn lays bare
Twin breasts to the beating palm for this occasion
    sad.

Ant. 1

A cry was heard, it pierced the night,
Prophetic terror breathing wrath to come;
Hair-raising panic swiftly scattered slumber,
Heavy, haunting shriek of fear;
It rang out loud and shrill, where the women's
    chambers are.
And then the prophets taught of God, after they
    had read the dream,
Cried out their message:
Dead men in the earth are wroth with those who
    murdered them.

Str. 2

Now to placate such ills implacable—
O hear, Earth, Mother!—fearful she hath sent me,
Godless woman! Nay, I dread e'en to utter such a
    name.
When blood is spilt, atonement is there none.
Alas, O sorrow-smitten home!
Alas, O roof in ruin laid,
Engulfed in these accursèd shades
Of sunless night, which have been drawn
Down by death of thy master!

Ant. 2

Respect for power unmatched in battle once,
In all ears and hearts public and pervasive,

Now hath drawn aside, and men fear; for happy
    fortune is
A God in mortal eyes and more than God.
And yet the scale of Justice stands
And watches, swift to visit some
In life, for others pain abides
In twilit realms, while on the rest
Night descends everlasting.

Str. 3

When blood is shed and drunk by mother Earth,
The vengeful gore congeals immovable.
Slow-paced judgment beareth the offender on, till
    grief
Glut his greedy appetite.

Ant. 3

As he who treads the virgin bower can find
No cure, so too, though stream on stream should
    pour
Their swift-cleansing waters on the hand of blood,
    the old
Stain shall not be wiped away.

Ep.

For me, the Gods drove the engines of fate
Against my city, from home they led me
A captive slave to dwell in bondage.
And so I must needs endure my masters'
Commandments, righteous or no, and hide
My bitter hatred; yet beneath my cloak I weep
With heart chilled in secret grief
To see the wanton state of those set over me.

ELECTRA. Bondswomen, ministrants to the royal house,

Since you are my companions in this act
Of intercession, what do you advise?
What shall I say to dedicate these gifts,
What prayer contrive to please a father's ear?
That I have brought them from a loving wife
To lord beloved, an offering from my mother?
No, that would be too shameless—then what else,
While on the tomb these holy oils are laid?
Or shall I speak the words appointed, saying,
"Bless those who send these garlands in thy honour
And give for good gifts goodly recompense"?
Or pour in silence without ceremony,
Even as he died, a draught for earth to drink,
As though to cast out scourings, then turn and fling
The vessel from me with averted eyes?
Such is the matter in which I ask of you
To share with me your counsel, as we share
Within these doors a common enemy.
Therefore, fear not nor hide your thoughts from me;
For Destiny as sure awaits the free
As those who serve perforce another's will.

CH. Since you desire it, as one to whom this tomb
Is as an altar, I will speak my mind.

EL. Yes, speak as a worshipper at my father's grave.

CH. Bless in the act all those who wish him well.

EL. Whom of my kinsfolk can I so entitle?

CH. Yourself, and then Aegisthus' enemies.

EL. The prayer must be made then for you and me?

CH. You understand; take thought accordingly.

EL. Who else can be joined to our company?

CH. Orestes far away; forget him not.

EL. Well said: oh, that indeed is good advice.

CH. Remember too those guilty of his blood.

EL. What shall I say? Instruct me in your meaning.

Ch. Ask him to grant that God or man shall come—

El. Shall come to judge them, or to execute?

Ch. Yes, say quite plainly, to take life for life.

El. Is that a righteous prayer to ask of heaven?

Ch. Why not?—to pray ill for your enemies.

El. O messenger between the quick and dead,
Hermes, whose home is underground, convey
My prayers to the infernal Gods who watch
Over my father's house, to Earth who brings
All creatures forth, and having nurtured them
Is quickened by them and conceives again,
While I pour out this lustral offering
And call upon my father to have mercy
On me and lead Orestes back to shine
A light unto the house; who both are now
As outcasts, sold and bartered by our mother
For her new lord, Aegisthus, who with her
Stands guilty of thy murder—I a slave,
Orestes banished, disinherited,
And they the proud usurpers of thy labours.
Oh, I beseech thee, speed Orestes home—
That is my prayer—O hear it, father, hear,
And grant to me in heart more chastity,
In hand more cleanness, than my mother had.
So much for us, and for thy enemies
Vouchsafe to come with judgment on their sins,
From those who took life justly taking life.
This evil supplication, made for *them,*
I set amid my own petitions fair.
To us be giver of good gifts, by grace
Of Heaven and Earth and of triumphant Right!
So having prayed, I pour these offerings.
Your part it is to crown them with lament
And with loud voice make music for the dead.

CH. Come and weep, let fall the plashing tear,
    Fall for our fallen lord,
    Before a tomb that shields the good
    And holds pollution hence, with these
    Propitiations paid. Hearken to us, O King;
    O lord, stir thy ghostly sense, wake and hear!
    Otototoi!
    Ah me, might he come, a warrior,
    One who shall free the House, one with a Scythian
        bow
    To bend afar off, and armed too with that
    Bludgeon of wood to wield in close fight as well!

EL. Our gifts the Earth has drunk, my father taken.
    And now I have strange news to share with you.

CH. What is it? My heart throbs in the dance of fear.

EL. I found this shorn lock resting on the tomb.

CH. Whose can it be? What man or maid has left it?

EL. So much is plain for all to understand.

CH. I understand not. Teach your elders truth.

EL. None would have laid it there save only me.

CH. True, those who should have mourned are enemies.

EL. And yet to look on it is very like.

CH. To whose? Tell me; I miss your meaning still.

EL. My own; in semblance it is close to mine.

CH. Orestes—can it be? A secret tribute?

EL. His hair was of this very quality.

CH. But how could he have dared to bring it hither?

EL. He sent it maybe to grace his father's grave.

CH. Why then, this news is greater cause for tears,
    If in the land he never shall set foot.

EL. I too am stricken to the heart. The waves
    Of sorrow swell and beat against my breast,
    While from these thirsty eyes falls drop by drop
    Unstaunched the surging tide, as I behold

These curls; for whom of all my countrymen
Can I account their owner, if not his?
Hers they could never be, the murderess,
My mother too, though how unmotherly
In spirit to her children, impious!
I know not how I can accept it thus,
A certain gift from him, my best-beloved,
Orestes; yet the hope still smiles on me.
Alas!
If only it could have spoken, a messenger
To calm my spirit tossed from doubt to doubt,
That I might know whether to cast it out
With loathing, shorn from some unloving head,
Or that being kin we might lament together
And grace this tomb with homage to our father!
The Gods whom I implore already know
The storm on which my helpless spirit drifts.
Yet, if it be ours to win deliverance,
From a small seed shall spring a mighty stem.
But look! Footprints—another testimony—
His own, and with them some companion's—
Two outlines are there here, two tracks of feet.
And see, the heels of these are like my own!
The impress of the instep measured out
Accords with mine and makes a perfect match.
What agony is here, what shattered wit!

(ORESTES *comes forward*)

OR. Thank God for the fulfillment of your prayer
   And ask a blessing for what is yet to come.
EL. For what am I indebted to him now?
OR. Behold the sight you have prayed so long to see.
EL. How do you know whom I have called upon?
OR. I know Orestes is your idol still.
EL. And how have I been favoured in my prayer?

Or. Here am I, and none dearer shall you find.

El. Ah, stranger, 'tis a trick you play on me.

Or. If so, I have conspired against myself.

El. You wish to make a mock of my distress.

Or. If I mock yours, I also mock my own.

El. As being Orestes then, I say to you—

Or. You see me here, and now you know me not.
Yet when you found that token of my tears,
And likewise when you followed up my tracks,
Your heart leapt at the fancied sight of me.
Compare that lock with those from whence 'twas
    cut,
Your brother's, of like measure to your own.
Look at this cloth—it is your handiwork:
See where your batten struck, and see the beasts
Which you designed in the embroidery.
Ah, calm yourself, restrain this burst of joy.
Our bitterest enemies are those most near.

El. O happy presence, in this heart endowed
With fourfold portion: father art thou to me,
To thee is turned a mother's love, for she
Is hated utterly, and a sister's, whom
They killed without pity; and last for thee,
My own true brother, thine is all my love.

Ch. O darling of thy father's house, O hope
Watered with tears, seed of deliverance,
Trust in thy courage, and thou shalt repossess
Thy father's heritage, if only Might
And Right stand by thy side, and with them third,
Of all the greatest, Zeus Deliverer!

Or. Zeus, Zeus, look down upon our state, regard
The eagle's offspring orphaned of their sire,
Whom the fell serpent folded in her coils
And crushed to death; for his bereaved are sore
Oppressed with hunger, lacking yet the strength

To bring the father's quarry to the nest.
And so we stand, my sister here and I,
Before thy face, a brood both robbed of sire,
Both fugitives from home. Our father, once
Thy priest, held thee in highest honour: so,
If thou destroy his nestlings, from what hand
So liberal shalt thou receive the gifts
Of festive sacrifice? If thou destroy
The eagle's brood, no more shalt thou have signs
To send from heaven, no more this royal stem,
This withered stump of greatness, will avail
To grace thy altar on the days appointed.
Oh, cherish it, restore it! Then this house,
That now seems fallen, shall once more be great.

CH. O children, saviours of your father's house,
Hush, lest some eavesdropper with idle tongue
Make all known to our masters, whom may I
See burnt alive in pools of spluttering pitch!
OR. Apollo will not break his faith, by whose
Almighty oracles I am commanded
To take on me this hazard. Loud and long
His prophetess predicted chilly blasts
Of pestilence to turn the heart's blood cold,
If I should fail to seek those murderers out
And put them to the death my father died,
Their lives for his, goaded to fury by
The heavy lash of disinheritance;
Or else the penalty, he said, would fall
On my own soul—a host of horrors, some
Sent up from earth by the resentful dead,
Which he named thus, ulcers to mount the flesh
With ravenous jaws and eat the substance up,
And out of them a crop of hoary hairs;
And worse, he told me of the fierce assault

Of Furies, sprung out of a father's blood.
Roused by petitionings of fallen kin,
The dusky weapon of infernal powers,
Madness and sudden panic in the night,
Doth haunt and harass, so he said, and scourge
The bruised and bleeding, execrated body
Out of the land; for such there is no part
In mixing of the wine, he may not pour
Drink-offerings at grace, his father's wrath
Unseen shall bar him from the altar, none
Shall give him welcome, none shall with him
    lodge—
Unhonoured, unbefriended, he shall waste
Lonely away to everlasting death.
Such were his oracles—shall I trust them not?
And, though I trust not, still it must be done.
Many desires all gather to one end—
The God's command, a son's grief for a father,
The pinch of hunger for my lost estate,
And anger that my glorious countrymen,
Whose valiant spirit captured Ilium,
Should be the subjects of two women; for
He has a woman's heart, as he shall see!

Kommos

Cɴ. O Fate Almighty, with favour of Zeus
Ordain that the end shall be set in the path
Where Righteousness walks into battle!
"For the tongue which hateth, let hatred of tongue
Be rendered!"—with these words Justice doth cry
In a loud voice claiming her payment:
"For a murderous blow let a murderous blow
Be struck." Let the doer be done by!—so
In a saying of old it is ordered.

Str. 1

Or. Teach me, O father, O father dread,
How by word or action
To waft upward thy soul from where
Earth in her bosom keeps it.
As day is reversed in night, so doth a dirge of
      praises
Appear unto the slain of old
Pleasing and full of comfort.

Str. 2

Ch. My son, the flames devour the flesh but not the
      spirit.
The soul of the dead in time shows to the quick
      his anger;
For a dirge to those departed is a lamp to light
      the sinner,
And the just lament of children for the father who
      begot them
From full hearts shall be sent a-hunting.

Ant. 1

El. Father, incline thine ear to this
Dirge of mournful numbers,
As each child doth address his own
Tribute of lamentation.
As suppliant I implore sanctuary, he as outcast.
We stand doomed to destruction—naught,
Naught is there here but evil.

Ch. And yet in his season shall God if he will
Set the voice to a happier tune: instead
Of a dirge at the tomb of the dead he shall raise

In the house of the king blithe music to greet
Good cheer in the flagon of friendship.

Str. 3

Or. Would that in Ilium, father, felled by a Trojan lance,
In fight laid low, thy life had ended,
To leave a fair name at home behind thee,
To leave these thy children | to walk eyed of all
men,
To rest in a sepulchre far, far away, and to sleep,
a peaceful
Load for the House of Atreus!

Ant. 2

Ch. Then loving, dearly loved of all who fell in battle,
A regent among the dead, now wouldst thou reign
in glory,
In attendance on the greatest of the lords who rule
the darkness
(For in life thou wast a great king), and dispense
the fate of mortals
With dread sceptre of lasting judgment.

Ant. 3

El. Ah, not a tomb in Troy, laid in dust with the rest
of those
That War struck down beneath her towers,
Beside the waters | of swift Scamander!
I wish rather those who destroyed him | had per-
ished,
Destroyed by their own, and their downfall been
told from afar, before we
Tasted of tribulation!

Ch. Ah, that were a bliss more precious than gold,
My daughter, beyond

All price; but thy prayer is vain, for
With the beat of a scourge double-dealt is the blow
Struck home, one blow for the champion at rest
Long since in the earth, and another for those
Who have unclean hands, our masters—what crime
So abhorrent to son and to daughter?

Str. 4

OR. That is a shot to the heart
Straight as a shaft from the bow.
Zeus, Zeus, from under the earth speed
Fatal revenge to follow
The foul hand of the mortal sinner,
Even a son that is like his mother!

Str. 5

CH. May these lips soon be moved in song
To chant gladly the alleluia
Over a man and woman
Stricken to death! for why still
Hide the hope that is beating
Within me? The heart's front is battered
Down by the fierce gust of a long-rankling rage and
        bitter spite.

Ant. 4

EL. When will he strike with his hand,
Zeus, in the fulness of power,
Oh, when shall the head be sundered?
Grant that a sign be given!
A just payment I seek from sinners.
Hear me, O Earth and ye shades majestic!

CH. Truly 'tis written that blood once shed
On the ground is athirst for the shedding of yet
More blood; foul murder is crying abroad

For a Fury to spring from the slaughtered and
crown
One violent end with another.

Str. 6

OR. Oh fie, Earth; shame, infernal sovranties!
Look on us, O ye mighty curses of the dead,
The seed of Atreus, a lonely remnant here,
Astray and lost, dispossessed
And homeless—O Zeus, shall naught avail us?

Ant. 5

CH. And yet fear shakes my fainting heart
At these ominous cries of anguish.
Hopeless awhile, it groweth
Black to the core in darkest
Fear for the words they utter.
But when soon with strength armed for action
Courage returns, then is despair banished, joy again
prevails.

Ant. 6

EL. With what words might | our purpose best be
won?
Is it the wrongs I bore at those motherly hands?
The tongue shall speak soft, but those are unas-
suaged;
For like the fierce wolf my heart
Is true to hers, deaf to all beguilement.

Str. 7

CH. I beat my breast and danced an eastern dirge,
And like a Cissian mourner mad
With clutching hands, with rending nails,
On breast and cheek I mingled tears with blood.

And up and down again the rapid rain of blows
Did beat on these brows in tune with loud lament.

EL. Oh me, hateful heart,
Oh wicked mother! hateful was his bearing-out,
A king, without followers,
With none to mourn over him,
Thou laidst him unwept in earth unhallowed.

Str. 8

OR. Ah, can it be? So dishonoured! Ah me,
For those dishonours she shall repay him,
With help of almighty powers,
With stroke of these hands of mine.
Let her but die, then let me be taken!

Ant. 8

CH. His limbs were lopped first—thou shalt be told
all—
Cut off by those hands that thus entombed him.
She sought by such means to load
Thy days with grief past compare.
And so he lies, buried in dishonour.

Ant. 7

EL. Such was my father's death, and I was kept
Dishonoured, deemed of no account,
Within my chamber kennelled like a dog,
With tears outstripping laughter in my eyes
In secret streams of solitary grief.
Remember all this, and write it in thy heart.

CH. Through unsealèd ear
Let sink the truth to still and steady sense.
For so the case standeth now,
But more the heart yearns to hear.
With calm resolve must | the lists be entered.

Str. 9

Or. I call on thee, father, fight beside thine own!

El. And I to his join a sorrowful complaint.

Ch. And all with one voice together cry aloud,
O hear us, rise from darkness, wake,
Stand by our side for battle!

Ant. 9

Or. With Strife shall Strife join in battle, Right with
Right.

El. O heaven, hear, grant our task a just event!

Ch. A shudder steals through my soul to hear them
pray.
The fatal end has long been fixed,
Now it is near fulfilment.

Str. 10

Evil inborn and bred,
Terrible stroke of bloodshed
Chanted to tunes of ruin!
O grief, grief that defies endurance,
O pain, pain that is past appeasement!

Ant. 10

Cure for the House is none
Save of itself; its own true
Kindred alone can heal it
In fell strife of avenging bloodshed.
We sing this to the powers of darkness.
Blest lords of the dead, lend ear unto this
Intercession, and graciously send unto these
Two children the strength that shall conquer!

Or. Father, who died a most unkingly death,
    Bequeath to us the sovranty of thy house!

El. And I entreat thee, father, make me free,
    Who now am sold in slavery to Aegisthus.

Or. And so thou shalt receive the solemn feasts
    By ancient custom ordered: else the rich
    Meats of the buried dead shall be denied thee.

El. Out of my dowry I shall bring thee gifts
    Upon my wedding-day, and in my heart
    Thy tomb shall ever hold the place of honour.

Or. Earth, send my father to look upon the battle!

El. Persephone, release his shining might!

Or. Father, remember the bath that was thy death!

El. Remember the strange net they spread for thee!

Or. And snared thy limbs in fetters of fine thread!

El. Ignobly trapped in cunning coverlets!

Or. Father, do these reproaches stir thee not?

El. Lift up to us that countenance beloved!

Or. Send Justice to do battle for thine own,
    Or grant that we get the like grip of them,
    If thou wouldst vanquish those who vanquished
        thee!

El. Give ear to one last cry: regard us here,
    Thy son and daughter, nestlings clustered round
    Thy tomb, and have compassion on our tears!

Or. Let not the seed of Pelops wholly perish:
    For so, in spite of death, thou art not dead!

El. Children are saving voices of remembrance
    Which tie the dead to life, as floats that draw
    The drag-net safe out of the vasty deep.

Or. Hear us; for thy sake have we cried to thee.
    Grant our entreaty and so save thyself!

Ch. These orisons have been commensurate

To recompense a long-neglected grave.
Now, since thy spirit is resolved to act,
'Tis time to put thy fortune to the proof.

OR. So shall it be; but first 'tis not amiss
To ask what prompted her to dedicate
These offerings at the tomb, what afterthought
Of tardy penance for a sin past cure?—
Not goodwill to the dead; for such a gift
Could earn no thanks nor cancel the offence.
A world of offerings bestowed on blood
Once shed were labour wasted, so 'tis said.
Can you instruct me in what she intended?

CH. I can, for I was with her. The wicked woman
Has sent these gifts because her heart was tossed
In dreams and rambling terrors of the night.

OR. Did she declare the nature of her vision?

CH. She said she dreamed to her was born a snake.

OR. What followed then? how did her story end?

CH. She nursed it like a child in swaddling-clothes.

OR. What nurture did it crave—a new-born serpent?

CH. She dreamed she gave it breast and suckled it.

OR. With paps unwounded by so vile a thing?

CH. Amidst her milk it drew a curd of blood.

OR. Ah, this should be no idle apparition.

CH. Then with a shriek of terror she awoke;
The lamps whose eyes were closed throughout the
house
At her command flared up, and then she sent
These offerings in hope of surgery
To heal the deep affliction of her spirit.

OR. I pray this Earth, I pray my father's tomb,
That this vision may prove oracular.
As I interpret it, it tallies well.
Since, issuing from whence I saw the light,
The serpent-child was wrapt in swaddling-clothes,

And since it mouthed the breast that nourished me,
With kindly milk mingling a curd of blood,
Whereat she cried in terror, it must be
That, even as she gave that monster life,
So she must die a violent death, and I,
The dragon of her dream, shall murder her.

Сн. Your reading of the portent I accept:
So be it. Now instruct your followers
What they must do and what forbear to do.

Or. 'Tis simply told. First, *she* must go within
And keep our convenant from all concealed,
That they whose cunning caught and killed a king
Be caught themselves by cunning in the trap
They laid for him, as Loxias commands,
The Lord Apollo, prophet ever true.
Then I, apparelled as a stranger, girt
With gear of travel, shall approach the door
With Pylades, my true confederate,
Affecting speech Parnassian, mimicking
The Phocian voice and accent; then, if no
Doorkeeper come to bid us welcome, since
It is a house bewitched with sin, we'll wait
Till passers-by take stock of us and say,
"Where is Aegisthus? is he not at home?
If he has been informed, why does he keep
The palace closed against petitioners?"
And, once across the threshold, if I find
That miscreant seated on my father's throne,
Or if he come to greet me and uplift
Those eyes, which soon, I swear, shall be cast down,
Before he ask, "Where is the stranger from?"
My steel shall strike and make a corpse of him,
And so a Fury never starved of slaughter
Shall drain her third draught of unmingled blood.

Meanwhile, to *you* I say, keep watch within
That all may fall out true to our design.
To *you* a tongue well-guarded I commend,
Silence in season and timeliness in speech.
The rest is for my comrade's eyes alone,
To guide me in this contest of the sword.

(ORESTES *and* PYLADES *withdraw;* ELECTRA *goes into
the palace*)

First Stasimon

Str. 1

Fearful beasts numberless,
Strange and hurtful, breed on earth;
Monsters foul swim the deep; teeming seas
Clasp them close; and baleful lights sweeping
    through the vaulted skies
Hang disastrous over all
Creatures that fly and that creep on the ground;
    and remember
How they rage, the stormy blasts.

Ant. 1

Yet the works dared by man's
Froward spirit who shall tell?
Woman too, whose perverse loves devise
Crimes of blood, provoking bloodstained revenges,
    sin for sin;
Once a woman's lawless lust
Gains the supremacy, swiftly it leads to destruction
Wedded ties in beast and man.

Str. 2

Those who be not fully fledged of wit,
Thus shall learn: let them
Take thought touching that

Flash of torch-lit treachery,
Which the hard heart of Althaea plotted,
By whose hand the firebrand was burnt which
Dated back to the day her son
Cried as he issued from her
Womb, and measured his span of life
On to the death appointed.

Ant. 2
No less hateful too was Scylla, that
Wicked daughter, whose
False heart foe-beguiled
Dared the death of dearest kin,
All for one necklace rare, wrought of fine gold,
A gift out of Crete: hence in secret,
While in slumber her Nisus lay,
Ah, she shore his immortal
Locks—a pitiless heart was hers!
Hermes led him to darkness.

Str. 3
And since I call back to mind the wicked crimes
Of old. . .—To no purpose! *This* unhallowed, vile
Union, which the house abhors,
A wife's deceit framed against a warrior,
Against her true-wedded lord—
Do you with disloyal heart approve of that?
I praise the hearth where no fires of passion burn,
A meek heart such as graces woman.

Ant. 3
—Of all the crimes told in tales the Lemnian
Is chief, a sin cried throughout the world with such
Horror that, if men relate
Some monstrous outrage, they call it Lemnian.

Abhorred of man, scorned of God,
Their seed is cast out, uprooted evermore;
For none respects what the Gods abominate.
Is *this* not well and justly spoken?

Str. 4
A sword of piercing steel is poised
To strike well home, which unerring Justice
Shall thrust to cleave the hearts of all
Those who trample underfoot
The sanctities
Of Zeus, to ungodly deeds inclining.

Ant. 4
The stem of Justice standeth firm,
And Fate's strong hand forgeth steel to arm her.
There comes to wipe away with fresh
Blood the blood of old a son,
Obeying some
Inscrutable | Fury's deadly purpose.

(*Enter* ORESTES *and* PYLADES. *They go up to the door*)

OR. Ho there, ho! Hear me, open to my knocking!
Ho, who is there? Ho, who is at home?
I call a third time for some answering step,
If Aegisthus permits the house to grant
Strangers their due of hospitality.

(*A* SERVANT *comes to the door*)

SE. All right, I hear you! Where is the stranger from?
OR. Announce me to the masters of the house.
My mission is to them—I bring them news.
Go quickly, for Night's dusky chariot
Draws on apace the time for travellers
To moor beneath some hospitable roof.

Let someone in authority come forth,
A woman, or more fittingly a man;
For then our converse need not wear the veil
Of modesty—man freely speaks with man
And in a sentence makes his purpose plain.

(CLYTEMNESTRA *appears at the door, attended by*
ELECTRA)

CL. Strangers, declare your wishes. You shall have
Such entertainment as befits this house—
Warm baths, a bed to ease limbs travel-tired,
And presence of an honest company;
But if you have in hand some graver matter,
That is man's work, to whom we shall impart it.

OR. I am a stranger out of Phocis, come
To Argos on an errand of my own.
Scarce had I set my feet upon the road,
When, meeting with a man unknown to me—
Strophius the Phocian was his name, he said—
"Stranger," said he to me, "if you are bound
For Argos, please convey from me this message:
Inform his parents that their son, Orestes,
Is dead, and bring me answer back again,
Whether his people wish to take him home
Or leave him buried in a foreign land,
For evermore an exile. Meanwhile the round
Ribs of a brazen urn enclose the dust
Of one whose death has had its meed of tears."
That is the message, though whether I address
One in authority and near to him,
I know not, but his parents should be told.

EL. Oh, all is gone, all pitilessly despoiled!
O Curse of this sad House, unconquerable,
How wide thy vision! Even that which seemed
Well-ordered, safe beyond the reach of harm,

Thou hast brought down with arrows from afar,
And left me desolate, stripped of all I loved.
And now Orestes—he who wisely thought
To keep his foot outside the miry clay,
Now that one hope prophetic which might yet
Have healed at last the wicked masquerade
Within this palace, mark it not as present.

OR. I could have wished, on coming to a house
So blest of heaven, that happy news had made
Me known to you and welcome; for what can be
So kindly as the sweet communion
Of host and stranger? Yet my judgment would
Have counted it a sin not to perform
So grave an office for those dear to me
According to my word and plighted vow.

CL. Nay, all that you deserve you shall be given.
Your news still leaves you welcome, for, if you
Had not conveyed it, others would have come.
And now it is the hour for travellers
To be attended after the long day's road.

(*To* ELECTRA) Escort him into the men's chambers,
        with
His follower and companion of the way,
And let their persons there be duly tended.
Do this, I say, as you shall answer for it.
We shall inform the master of the house,
And then, with friends in plenty, we shall take
Counsel together touching this event.

(CLYTEMNESTRA, ELECTRA, ORESTES *and* PYLADES *go
        into the palace*)

CH. Handmaids of the house all faithful and true,
        O when shall we lift
Our voices in praise of Orestes?
O hear, mother Earth, O tomb of the dead,

Who hidest the dust of a monarch-at-arms,
Answer us now, now send us thy power;
For the hour is at hand for Temptation to bring
Her deceits to the fray, for the God of the dead,
Hermes, to appear from the darkness and watch
This duel of sword and of slaughter.

(*The* Nurse *comes out of the palace*)

This stranger, it would seem, is making mischief.
Here is Orestes' old nurse, bathed in tears.
What brings you here, Cilissa, to the gates
With grief for your unchartered company?

Nu. My mistress has commanded me to bring
Aegisthus to the strangers instantly,
That he may hear their message man from man.
Before the servants she assumes a set
And sorrowful aspect, but in her eyes
There lurks a smile for what has come to pass
For her so happily, though for this house
The strangers' news means misery evermore.
And sure *his* heart will be uplifted too
To hear that message. Oh my heavy grief,
How many bitter agonies of old
And all confused this breast of mine has borne
Within these walls of Atreus, and yet none,
No sorrow so insufferable as this!
All else I bore with patiently, but now
My dear Orestes, my life's long loving care,
Entrusted from his mother's arms to mine,
Breaking my sleep with many a summons shrill,
With daily troubles multiplied in vain:
For sure, a witless babe, like a dumb beast,
Must needs have nurse's wit to nourish it.
A child in swaddling-clothes cannot declare

His wants, that he would eat, or drink, or make
Water, and childish bellies will not wait
Upon attendance. Of all this prophetess,
And often falsified—a laundress then
To wash the linen shining-white again,
Fuller and nurse set on a common task—
Such was the double trade I plied, as I
Nursed young Orestes, his father's son and heir.
And now, alas, they tell me he is dead,
And I must take to him whose wickedness
Infects the house news that will make him glad.

CH. With what equipment does she bid him come?
NU. Equipment? why? I do not understand.
CH. Attended by his retinue, or alone?
NU. She bids him bring his royal bodyguard.
CH. Then, since you hate him, not a word of that.
    Tell him to come alone, and quickly too,
    With naught to fear, and hear with gladdened
        heart.
NU. What, are you friendly to this present news?
CH. Who knows but Zeus may turn an ill-wind yet?
NU. How, if Orestes, our last hope, is gone?
CH. Not so would a good prophet read it yet.
NU. Ah, have you heard some contrary report?
CH. Go, take your message, do as you are bid.
    The Gods will care for that which is their care.
NU. I go and will obey you. May the Gods
    Grant that all this shall end in what is best!

                                  (*Exit*)

Second Stasimon

Str. 1

Now, I pray, lend us ear, Father Zeus,
Lord of high Olympus, vouch-

Safe success unto all those that seek
The rule of chaste wisdom enthroned again!
Naught have I asked of thee
But what is just: Zeus, I pray, defend us!
    Ah, let the champion
    Who hath gone in be upheld, Zeus,
    In the fray. Thou, who hast made him
    Great, shalt take at will
    A twofold recompense and threefold.

Ant. 1

Think of that sire beloved whose bereft
Colt is yoked to sorrow's car.
He who keeps measured pace most is like
To see sustained steady and even step
On till the long race is run,
Sped with feet surely striding forward.
    Ah, let the champion
    Who hath gone in be upheld, Zeus,
    In the fray. Thou, who hast made him
    Great, shalt take at will
    A twofold recompense and threefold.

Str. 2

Deities who dwell within,
Glad of heart, arbiters of royal wealth,
Hearken kindly to our prayer,
So with vengeance new redeem
The full debt of bloody deeds of yore.
No more let old murder breed and multiply.
    God of the great cavern in glory established,
    Let us rejoice, and set a crown on the palace;
    Oh, let it swiftly appear,
    Gleaming and friendly and free
    Out of the veil of encircling darkness!

Ant. 2
Justly may he join with us,
Maia's son, named the keen and cunning one;
Much at will he can reveal,
Night he draws dim and dark before the eye,
With voice veiled that none may understand,
Nor yet by day plainer doth his form appear.
    God of the great cavern in glory established,
    Let us rejoice, and set a crown on the palace;
    Oh, let it swiftly appear,
    Gleaming and friendly and free
    Out of the veil of encircling darkness!

Str. 3
Thus at last, after this
House hath found deliverance,
Music set to breezes fair,
Women's shrill songs of joy
Shall be heard, the wizard's chant:
"Well she sails!
Mine the gain, mine, as trouble draws aside,
Bringing peace to those I love."
    And with stout heart as the time comes
    For the act, cry to her, "Father!" as thy answer
    Unto her cry of "Child!"
    And so slay in blameless bloodshed.

Ant. 3
Keep within thy breast a heart
Strong as Perseus', bring to all
Those that love thee, some that lie
Under earth, some above,
Joy of glad deliverance.
Make the end

Bloody, and wipe out at last the guilty seed,
Wipe it out for evermore!
  And with stout heart as the time comes
  For the act, cry to her, "Father!" as thy answer
  Unto her cry of "Child!"
  And so slay in blameless bloodshed.

(*Enter* AEGISTHUS)

AE. I come in answer to the summoner.
They tell me of some news that has been brought
By strangers, tidings most unwelcome to us,
Orestes' death, another stroke of grief
To open ancient sores in this sad house,
Already maimed and stricken to the core.
How shall I judge whether it be the truth
Or woman's idle talk, by terror set
Aflame and soaring, and no death at all?
What proof have you of this to reason plain?

CH. We heard the news; but go within and ask
The strangers. Mere report is little worth
When a man can make inquiry on the spot.

AE. I want to see that messenger and ask
If he was present at the death himself
Or from faint rumour heard an empty tale.
I'll not be hoodwinked: my wits are not asleep.

(AEGISTHUS *goes into the palace*)

CH. Zeus, what shall I say, where rightly begin
With a prayer and a cry to thy name, and in true
Loyalty make this
My address to befit the occasion?
Yes, now the essay of the murderous blade
Is about to set over the house of the lord
Agamemnon destruction for ever;
Or if not, with the splendour of torches ablaze

For his freedom regained shall the son be enthroned
In the land of his sires
And recover the wealth of his fathers.
So much is at issue, and single he goes,
The heroic Orestes, and twain are his foes;
O grant that he goeth to conquer!

(*A cry from* AEGISTHUS *within*)

Oh!
How is this? How does all go within?
The work's afoot. Let us stand apart awhile,
That we be counted innocent of harm.
The issue of the battle has been sealed.

(*The* SERVANT *comes to the door*)

SE. Grief, utter grief! My master is struck down.
Oh heavy grief—a third cry for the dead!
Aegisthus is no more. Come, open quick!
Unbolt the women's chambers! A strong hand too
It needs—though not indeed to help the dead.
Ho!
Ah, they are deaf or sleeping, and my cries
Are wasted. What is Clytemnestra doing?
Where is she? Now at last, it seems, her neck
Shall touch the block beneath the axe of Justice.

(CLYTEMNESTRA *comes to the door*)

CL. What is it? What is the meaning of that shout?
SE. It means the living are being killed by the dead.
CL. Ah me, a riddle! yet I read its meaning.
We killed by cunning and by cunning die.
Quick, let me have a man-axe! let us see
Who wins, who loses! It has come to this.

(ORESTES *and* PYLADES *come out of the palace*)

OR. I want you. As for him, it is well enough.

CL. Aegisthus, dearest lord! Oh, he is dead!

OR. You love him? Well then, you shall share his grave,
In all things faithful, even unto death.

CL. O stay, my son! Dear child, have pity on
This bosom where in slumber long ago
Your toothless gums drew in the milk of life.

OR. Pylades, what shall I do? shall I have mercy?

PY. What then hereafter of the oracles
And solemn covenants of Loxias?
Let all men hate thee rather than the Gods.

OR. That is good counsel—your word shall prevail.
Come with me—I mean to kill you by his side.
While he lived, you preferred him to my father;
So sleep in death beside him, since you loved
Him, and hated whom you should have loved.

CL. I brought you up—with you I would grow old.

OR. What, dwell with me, my father's murderess?

CL. Fate was a partner to his death, my child.

OR. And that same fate has now decreed your own.

CL. Have you no dread, my child, of a mother's curse?

OR. Your child indeed, until you cast me out.

CL. No, not cast out—I sent you away to friends.

OR. Yes, the son of a royal father, foully sold.

CL. What was the payment that I took for you?

OR. I cannot answer that—for very shame.

CL. No, no—remember too *his* wantonness!

OR. Accuse him not—for you he toiled abroad.

CL. It is hard for a woman parted from her man.

OR. What but his labour keeps her safe at home?

CL. So then, my son, you mean to kill your mother?

OR. It is not I, it is you who kill yourself.

CL. Beware the hell-hounds of a mother's curse!

OR. And how, if I spared you, escape from his?
CL. My pleas are vain—warm tears on a cold tomb.
OR. My father's destiny has determined yours.
CL. Ah me, I bore a serpent, not a son.
OR. That fearful vision was indeed prophetic.
    Wrong shall be done you for the wrong you did.

(They go into the palace)

CH. I weep for both and for their double pain.
    Yet, since the tale of plenteous blood is crowned
    In brave Orestes, I choose to have it so,
    In order that the eye of this great house
    May rise again, not perish utterly.

Third Stasimon

Str. 1
Unto the sons of Priam Justice did come in time,
Heavy and harsh judgment;
To Agamemnon too and to his house it came,
A double lion, double strife.
Unto the uttermost he held his course heaven-sped,
Following well the Lord Apollo's command.
    Cry alleluia, lift up in the house a song,
    Deliverance from ill and from the waste of wealth
    By the unholy sinners twain,
    From rough thorny ways.

Ant. 1
And he hath come, the God who with a sly assault
Waiteth to work judgment;
Yea, and his hand was guided in the battle by
The child of Zeus begotten-true,
Whom it is right and meet that mortals name Right-
    eousness.
Deadly the blast she breathes on all evildoers!

Cry alleluia, lift up in the house a song,
Deliverance from ill and from the waste of wealth
By the unholy sinners twain,
From rough thorny ways.

Str. 2

Even as Loxias on Parnassus cried
Out of his holy shrine, so doth his will advance
Never at fault against
The ingrown disease which in the house is lodged.
For Godhead doth e'er prevail over sin
With sure surgery.
Worthy of praise the all-supreme power divine.
   On us the light hath shined, now is the bridle-bit
   Lifted from out the house.
   Gladly, O House, arise! for it was long enough
   The curb of sin did hold thee down.

Ant. 2

Soon shall the feet of Time Perfecter enter in,
In at the royal gates, when he hath cleansed the
      hearth
Of the defiling sin.
With clean flow of bloodshed he shall purify.
With kind fortune couched and fair-eyed to see
For all who have wept
Shall aliens within be laid low again.
   On us the light hath shined, now is the bridle-bit
   Lifted from out the house.
   Gladly, O House, arise! for it was long enough
   The curb of sin did hold thee down.

(*The doors are opened and torches are alight within,
      revealing the bodies of* AEGISTHUS *and* CLYTEM-
      NESTRA *wrapped in purple robes and laid
      upon a couch,* ORESTES *standing over them*)

OR. Behold our country's double tyranny,
The murderous pillagers of my father's house,
How stately once they sat upon their thrones,
And now how loving, as their condition shows,
They lie, still faithful to their plighted vows,
Both pledged to slay my father, likewise pledged
To die themselves together—they kept their word.
And you who hear of these calamities,
Behold the snare which they contrived to knot
About my hapless father's hands and feet.
What name becomes it, though I choose the best?
A pit for beasts, a winding-sheet to catch
A dead man's legs? or would you rather say
A net, or sweeping cloak that trips the heels,
Trick of some crafty highwayman who lives
On silver plundered from the traveller?
With such an equipage how many lives
He would waylay, how it would warm his heart!
Come, spread it out, stand round it in a ring,
This cunning coverlet, that he who is
Of all created father and looks down
On the whole world, the Sun, having beheld
My mother's wicked handiwork, may stand
My witness in the judgment yet to come,
And certify that I have sought her death
Justly—as for Aegisthus, he has paid
The price prescribed for all adulterous lechers;
But she, who planned this horror for her own
Master, to whom within the womb she once
Bore offspring, then a load of love, but now,
As shown by its sharp fangs, of deadly hate,
What do you think of her? If she had been
Some scorpion or sea-serpent, her very touch,
For sheer iniquity and wicked spirit,
Would breed corruption in the unbitten hand.

May such as she not share my house, but rather
May heaven destroy me and my seed for ever!

CH. Ah me, how dread was the work of thy hands,
How fearful the death that befell thee!
In the fulness of time
Retribution bursts into blossom.

OR. Was the deed hers or not? I have a witness,
This robe, that here she plunged Aegisthus' sword;
For bloodstains have conspired with time to wear
Much of the dye out of the threaded pattern.
Now I am here to speak my father's praises,
Now, only now, to make my lamentations.
And as I greet this web that wove his death,
I weep for all things done and suffered here,
For the whole race, and weep for my own fate,
Marked with the stains of this sad victory.

CH. No man upon earth shall be brought to the end
Of his days unwounded by sorrow.
Distress is for some
Here present, for others abides yet.

OR. So then, to tell you plainly—I know not what
My end will be—my wits are out of hand,
Like horses that with victory in sight
Stampede out of the course, and in my heart,
As fear strikes up her tune, the dance begins—
But, while I have my senses, I declare
To all my friends that I have killed my mother
In a just cause, my father's murderess,
A thing unclean, an execrable pest;
And to that desperate act my heart was lured
By homage to Apollo, who proclaimed
That, if I did this thing, I should be clear

Of guilt; if not—I will not name the price,
Horrors beyond the furthest shaft of wit.
And now behold me as I turn my steps,
With boughs of supplication garlanded,
Unto the midmost shrine of Loxias
And glorious light of his undying fire,
An exile stained with kindred blood; for he
Commanded me to seek no hearth but his.
And all my countrymen I call to give
In time to come their witness, how these things
Were brought to pass—meanwhile, a wanderer,
An outcast from my country, I commend
Into their charge, in life and death, my name.

CH. Thou hast done well, bend not thy lips to such
Ill-omened sayings and wild talk of woe.
Thou art deliverer of the land of Argos,
With one light stroke lopping two dragons' heads.
OR. Ah!
What are those women? See them, Gorgon-like,
All clad in sable and entwined with coils
Of writhing snakes! Oh away, away!
CH. What are these fancies, father's dearest son,
That fright thee? Stay and fear not. Thou hast won.
OR. To me they are no fancies—only too clear—
Can you not see them?—hounds of a mother's
         curse!
CH. Fresh is the bloodshed yet upon thy hands:
That is what brings confusion on thy wits.
OR. O Lord Apollo, see how thick they come,
And from their eyes are dripping gouts of blood!
CH. Thou shalt be purified! Apollo's touch
From these disasters shall deliver thee!
OR. You cannot see them—look, how clear they are!
They come to hunt me down! Away, away!

(Exit ORESTES*)*

CH. Fortune attend thee, may God graciously
Watch over thee and guide thee to the end!

On the house of the king with a turbulent blast
Has the third storm broke
And expended hath swept to its ending.
First came the unmerciful slaughter of babes
And the feast on their flesh;
Next followed the fall of a king, in the bath
Struck down, the Achaean commander who led
All Greece into war;
And the third now present is saviour—or else
Is destruction his name?
O when shall the end come, where shall the rage
Of calamity sink into slumber?

O

EUMENIDES

(Before the temple of Apollo at Delphi. Enter the
PRIESTESS*)*

PR. Chief of the Gods in prayer I venerate,
The first of prophets, Earth; and next to her
Themis, who from her mother, it is said,
Received the seat oracular; and the third,
Another child of Earth, the Titan maid
Phoebe, with free consent here found a home;
And she bestowed it as a birthday gift
On Phoebus, with it lending him her name.
The lakes and rocks of Delos he forsook,
And setting foot on Pallas' harboured shores

Came hither to Parnassus, on his way
Attended with all honour by the Sons
Of Hephaestus, who built a road for him
And tamed the wilderness before his feet.
And when he came, the people worshipped him
Under king Delphus, their lord and governor;
And Zeus, having inspired him with his art,
Set him, the fourth of prophets, on this throne,
Whence he is called Interpreter of Zeus,
Whose son he is, prophetic Loxias.
These Gods then are the preface to my prayers,
And with them I render the homage due
To Pallas of the Precinct, and likewise
The nymphs whose dwelling is the cavernous cliff
Corycian, home of birds and haunt beloved
Of spirits, the region held by Bromius
(This have I not forgotten) when he led
His Bacchants into battle and devised
The death of Pentheus like a hunted hare.
So, calling also on Poseidon's power,
Upon the springs of Pleistus, and last of all
On Zeus the Highest, Zeus the Perfecter,
I take my seat on the throne of prophecy.
And may this entry be more blest of them
Than any heretofore! Let Greeks approach
In the accustomed order of the lot;
As the God dictates, so shall I prophesy.

(*She enters the temple, utters a loud cry, and returns*)

Oh horror, horror to utter and behold,
Has driven me back from the house of Loxias;
Strengthless, with dragging step, upon my hands
I run. An aged woman terror-struck
Is nothing, or at most a child again.
I made my way into the laurelled shrine

And at the navel-stone I saw a man,
Defiled with murder, in suppliant posture, red
Blood dripping from the hands that grasped a
        sword
Fresh from the scabbard and a topmost branch
Of olive humbly garlanded with wool,
A fleece all silver-white. So much was plain;
But all around, asleep upon the thrones,
Lay a strange company of women—yet
Not women, Gorgons rather; nor again
To Gorgons can I liken them, for those
I saw once in a picture, plundering
The feast of Phineus; but no wings have these,
Yet black and utterly abominable,
Snoring in blasts that none may venture near,
With eyes that run with drops of loathsome rheum,
In raiment clad which it were a sin to bring
Near images of the Gods or roofs of men.
The tribe to which these visitants belong
I never saw, nor know what land could boast
Of such a brood and not repent her pangs.
As for the rest, let him take thought for it
Who owns the house, almighty Loxias,
Prophet and Healer, Interpreter of signs,
Himself of other houses Purifier.

(*The interior of the temple is revealed, as described;
with* APOLLO *and* HERMES *standing behind* ORESTES)

AP. I will keep faith, at watch continually,
    Close at thy side and vigilant from afar,
    And never gentle to thy enemies.
    And now thou seest them here in slumber seized,
    These ravenous monsters, stretched upon the
        ground,
    Maidens abominable, children gray with years,

With whom no God consorts, nor man nor beast,
Abhorred alike in heaven and on earth,
For evil born, even as the darkness where
They dwell is evil, the abyss of Tartarus.
Yet thou must fly and grow not faint of heart.
They will track down thy steps from shore to shore,
For ever travelling the wide ways of earth
Past island cities, over distant seas,
And nurse thy tribulation patiently
Until thou comest to the citadel
Of Pallas, where in supplication clasp
Her antique image in thine arms; for there,
With judgment of thy suit and gentle charms
Of speech, we shall find out at last a way
From all these evils to deliver thee,
Being moved by me even to kill thy mother.

OR. O Lord Apollo, thou knowest what is just,
And since thou knowest, O neglect it not!
Thy strength to do good lacks no warranty.

AP. Remember, let thy heart not yield to fear.
And thou, my brother begotten of one sire,
True to thy name, go with him, guide the feet
Of this my suppliant; for the sanctity
Of outcasts from mankind, who take the road
With guidance fair, is sacred unto Zeus.

(HERMES *and* ORESTES *go. Enter the* GHOST *of*
CLYTEMNESTRA)

CL. Oho! asleep! What good are you asleep?
And I, whom you dishonour, am reproached
Among the other dead unceasingly,
Hissed and cast out, homeless, a murderess!
I tell you they malign me shamefully,
While I, so cruelly treated by my own,

Slaughtered myself with matricidal hands,
No deity is indignant for my sake.
O let your conscience look upon these scars!
Remember all those sober blandishments,
Those wineless offerings which you have drunk,
Those sacrificial suppers on the hearth
At many a solemn midnight, which you shared
With none of heaven's deities: and now
All that is rudely trampled in the dust.
And *he* is gone: light as a fawn he sped
Out of the inmost meshes of your snare
And leapt away, and now he scoffs at you.
O hear as I plead with you for my soul!
O Goddesses of the underworld, awake!
I, Clytemnestra, call you now in dreams!

Ch. Mu, mu!

Cl. Ah, you may mew, but he is fled and gone;
　　For he has friends far different from mine.

Ch. Mu, mu!

Cl. Still slumbering and still compassionless!
　　The matricide, Orestes, has escaped!

Ch. Oh, oh!

Cl. Still whining in your drowsiness! Arise!
　　To do evil is your appointed task.

Ch. Oh, oh!

Cl. How sleep and weariness, strong confederates,
　　Have disenvenomed the fell dragon's rage!

Ch. Oh, oh! Find the scent, mark him down!

Cl. Though you give tongue like an unerring hound,
　　You chase the quarry only through your dreams.—
　　What are you doing? Rise, cast off fatigue!
　　Let not sleep soothe remembrance of your hurt!—
　　Let your heart ache with pangs of just reproach,
　　Which harry a good conscience like a scourge!—

Come, blow about his head your bloody breath,
Consume his flesh with blasts of bellied fire!
On, on, renew the hunt and wear him down!

(*Exit*)

Parodos

CH. Awake, awake her there as I wake thee!
Still sleeping? Rise, cast slumber underfoot!
Let us see whether our enchantment works.

Str. 1
Alas, alas, for shame! What have we suffered,
    friends!
Ah, suffered bitterly, and all in vain!
Suffered a fearful hurt, horrible! Oh the pain
Beyond strength to bear!
The game has leapt out of the snare and gone.
In slumber laid low, I let slip the prey.

Ant. 1
Aha, son of Zeus, pilferer, pillager!
A youth to trample ancient deities,
Honouring such a suppliant abhorred of God,
An unfilial son!
A God, to steal away the matricide!
O who denies this was unjustly done?

Str. 2
In dream there came to me a dread reproach,
A blow such as might descend from some
Charioteer's stout hand,
Under the ribs, under the flank.
It rankles yet, red and sore,
Chill as frost, like the fell
Assault of public scourger's lash.

Ant. 2

This is the doing of the younger Gods,
Who transgress the powers appointed them.
Dripping with death, red drops
Cover the heel, cover the head.
Behold the Earth's central stone
Black with big stains of blood,
Possessed of vast pollution vile.

Str. 3

A prophet he, his own prophetic cell
He has himself profaned.
His was the act, the asking,
Honouring mortal things, reckless of laws divine
And dealing death to Fates born of old.

Ant. 3

He injures me, yet *him* he shall not free,
Not in the depths of hell,
Ne'er shall he be delivered.
Suppliant unabsolved, soon shall he find his brow
Defiled again with guilt thrice as great.

Ap. Out, out, I say, begone! I bid you leave
This mantic cell of your vile presence free;
Or soon a silver scorpion taking wing
From golden bow shall lay you such smart
That from your swollen bellies you shall retch
The clotted blood from human bodies sucked.
No house is this to be approached by you,
But rather go where heads fall from the block,
Where eyes are gouged, throats slit, and boyhood's
        bloom
Blasted by gelding knife, where men are stoned,

And limbs lopped, and a piteous whimper heard
From spines impaled in dust. Such festivals
Are your delight and fill heaven with loathing.
So your whole shape and semblance testifies.
A den of lions lapping gore were fit
To entertain you, not this opulent seat
Of prophecy to bear so vile a taint.
Hence, loathsome creatures, hence unshepherded,
A herd for whom there is no love in heaven!

CH. O Lord Apollo, hear us in our turn.
Thou art not an abettor in this work;
Thou art the doer, on thee lies the whole guilt.

AP. How might that be? Prolong thy speech so far.

CH. He slew his mother obedient to thy word.

AP. My word commanded vengeance for his father.

CH. So promising acceptance of fresh blood.

AP. And for it absolution at this house.

CH. Would you insult the band which drove him hither?

AP. My mansion is not fit for such as you.

CH. And yet this is the task appointed us.

AP. What is this power and boasted privilege?

CH. We drive the mother-murderer from home.

AP. What of the woman then who slew her man?

CH. That is not death by kin and common blood.

AP. Dishonoured then and set at naught by thee
The marriage-bond which Zeus and Hera seal,
Dishonoured too the Cyprian, from whom
Mankind receive their nearest, dearest joys.
What bond is stronger than the bed of man
And wife, which Fate conjoins and Justice guards?
If then on those who slay their dearest thou
Dost not look down in wrath nor punish them,
Then I declare it is unjust in thee
To persecute Orestes—here I see
Anger, there quietness. But in this suit

The goddess Pallas shall regard and judge.

Cн. Him will I never leave nor let him go.

Ap. Pursue him then, pile up more labour lost.

Cн. No words of thine shall circumscribe my powers.

Ap. I would disdain such powers at a gift.

Cн. Ay, *thou* art called great at the throne of Zeus.
But I—a mother's blood is calling me
To seek revenge and follow up the hunt.

Ap. And I will help and guard my suppliant.
A fearful thing in heaven and on earth
Would be the wrath of such, if I broke faith.

*(Interval of one year. Before a shrine of Athena in
Athens: enter* ORESTES)

Or. O Queen Athena, at Loxias' command
I come to thee; receive me mercifully;
An outcast, yet no more with sullied hands,
The edge of my pollution worn away
At distant homes of men, on weary paths
By land and sea alike, obedient
To the prophetic word of Loxias,
Present before thy image, entering
Thy house, O Goddess, here with constant heart
I wait the consummation of my cause.

(Enter the CHORUS)

Cн. Aha! here are his traces plain to see.
Step where our dumb informer points the way;
For as the hound pursues the wounded fawn,
So follow I the smell of dripping blood.
With toil and sweat of many a weary day
My bosom pants; all the wide earth I roamed,
And traversing the sea in wingless flight,
Close in his vessel's wake, I follow still.

He must be crouching somewhere here—I feel
My senses wooed with smell of human blood.

—Beware, again beware!
Look on all sides, for fear
He find some escape, foul mother-murderer.
—Ah, here he is, craving help,
As in a close embrace he clasps that divine
Image, awaiting trial for his handiwork.
—It cannot be! The mother's blood he shed
Can ne'er be raised up again.
Low on the ground it lies, scattered away and lost.
—Soon from thy living flesh shalt thou repay
Offerings rich and red; and on an evil draught
From thee my lips shall feed in fat pasturage.
—Alive and wasted, I shall drag thee down
To pay the full price of that terrible act of blood,
—And others shalt thou see in hell who did
Evil to strangers, Gods,
Or unto those dearest that gave them life,
Each well requited with his just reward.
—For Hades is a stern inquisitor
Of mankind below;
All things are written down in that watchful heart.

Or. Taught in the school of suffering, I have learnt
The times and seasons when it is right to keep
Silence and when to break it; and in this matter
A wise instructor has charged me to speak.
The blood upon my hands has sunk to sleep,
The matricidal stain is washed away.
Still fresh it was when at the hearth divine
Of Phoebus it was purged by sacrifice.
Too many to recount the men who have
Received since then my presence without hurt;

And now with lips made pure and reverent
I call to my defence this country's Queen,
Athena, who with bloodless victory
Shall win me and my people to her side
In true alliance for all time to come.
So, whether on far shores of Libya,
By Trito's waters, where she came to birth,
Her foot be planted, covered or erect,
Defending those that love her, or her eyes,
Like some brave captain's, watch on Phlegra's
    heights,
O may she come—far off, she still can hear—
And from these miseries deliver me!

Ch. Neither Apollo nor Athena's power
Shall save thee from perdition, when, by all
Abandoned and forsaken, knowing not
Where in the bosom joy resides, shalt thou,
A bloodless shadow, make a feast for fiends.
Has thou no answer, dost thou spurn me so,
Fattened for me, my consecrated host?
Not slain upon the altar, nay alive
Thou shalt feed me, and now shalt hear a chant
Which binds thee fast unto my purposes.

First Stasimon

O come, let us dance in a ring and declare,
As our purpose is fixed,
To the tune of this terrible music
Those laws whereby
We determine the fortune of mortals.
Just, we avow, are our judgments and righteous.
All those who can show hands cleanly and pure,
Unharmed shall they live for the length of their
    days,

No anger of ours shall afflict them;
But the man, like him, who hath sinned and con-
  ceals
Hands dripping with blood shall be summoned
To attest for the slaughtered the truth of their
  cause
And to pay for their blood retribution.

Str. 1

Mother Night, thy children cry, hear, black Night,
As we deal to man in dark and day fell judgment!
The son born of Leto hath plundered my powers,
Stealing that trembling hare, held a due sacrifice
Mother's blood to expiate.
    Over the blood now to be shed madness and
      moil,
    Wither and waste, melody dismal and deathly.
    Hymn of hell to harp untuned,
    Chant to bind the soul in chains,
    Spell to parch the flesh to dust.

Ant. 1

This the Fates who move the whole world through,
  charged
Unto us to be our task for all time hence,
Watch to keep over all hands that drip red with
  kindred
Blood, to wait till the Earth open—then down in
  hell
Freedom hardly shall they find.
    Over the blood now to be shed madness and
      moil,
    Wither and waste, melody dismal and deathly.
    Hymn of hell to harp untuned,

Chant to bind the soul in chains,
Spell to parch the flesh to dust.

Str. 2

Such were the powers decreed as we came into
    being,
Only to touch not immortals, and none of Olympus
Seeketh a share in our banquets.
Part have we none in the raiment of white, for in
    such we delight not;
Other pleasures are our choice—
    Wreck of the house, when at the hearth
    Blood of its own drippeth in strife.
    Hard on his heels ever we run, and tho' his
        strength be great,
    Lured by fresh blood we waste and wear him
        out.

Ant. 2

Yet, as we seek to relieve other Gods of this office
And by our own intent endeavour exempt them
So that none call them to question,
Zeus doth debar this brood, bloodstained and ab-
    horrent, from converse,
Yea, disdains our company.
    Wreck of the house, when at the hearth
    Blood of its own drippeth in strife.
    Hard on his heels ever we run, and tho' his
        strength be great,
    Lured by fresh blood we waste and wear him
        out.

Str. 3

Glories of men, how great in the day is their gran-
    deur!

Yet shall they fade in the darkness of hell in dis-
    honour,
Faced with our raiment of sable and dancing
Feet well-tuned to melodies malign.
   Nimbly my feet leap and descend,
   High in the air, down to the earth,
   Heavy the tread of my tiptoe,
   Fugitive steps suddenly tripped up in fatal con-
       fusion.

Ant. 3

Caught unawares doth he stumble, his wickedness
    blinds him,
Such is the cloud of pollution that hovers around
    him.
Thick on the house is the darkness, a story
Which mankind shall tell with mournful tongue.
   Nimbly my feet leap and descend,
   High in the air, down to the earth,
   Heavy the tread of my tiptoe,
   Fugitive steps suddenly tripped up in fatal con-
       fusion.

Str. 4

Our task is such. Armed with quick
Resource and keen memories,
We keep with hard hearts unmoved constant watch
    on human sin.
What all dishonour honour we,
From whence the Gods are barred
By dark corruption foul, region of rugged ways
Both for the quick and dead, for blind and seeing
    too.

Ant. 4
What mortal then boweth not

In fear and dread, while he hears
The ordinance which Fate made ours, the gift of
    heaven too,
A perfect power and privilege
Of ancient ages? We
Are not unhonoured, tho' deep in the earth the
    clime
Set for us, sunk in sunless, everlasting gloom.

(*Enter* ATHENA)

AT. I heard a cry far off, calling to me,
    Where by Scamander's waters I received
    Possession of the lands which have been given
    By the Achaean princes for my own
    To have and hold for ever, a chosen gift
    To grace the sons of Theseus. Thence I came
    In fleet pursuit of never-wearied foot,
    With wingless beat of this deep-bosomed aegis—
    To such a car my lusty steeds were yoked.
    And now, regarding this strange company,
    I have no fear, yet wonder fills my eyes.
    Who can you be? To all I speak in common,
    Both to this stranger seated at my image,
    And you, resembling no begotten seed,
    Neither like goddesses beheld in heaven
    Nor fashioned in the figure of mankind.
    But to speak harm of others without cause
    Would ill accord with justice and with right.
CH. Daughter of Zeus, in brief thou shalt learn all.
    We are the dismal daughters of dark Night,
    Called Curses in the palaces of hell.
AT. Your names I know then and your origin.
CH. And now we will acquaint you with our powers.
AT. Teach me those also; I am fain to learn.
CH. We drive the homicide from hearth and home.

At. And tell me where his persecution ends.

Ch. Where to be joyful is a thing unknown.

At. Is that your hue and cry against this man?

Ch. It is; for he thought fit to kill his mother.

At. He feared, perhaps, some other grave displeasure?

Ch. What could have driven him to matricide?

At. Two parties are there and but half the cause.

Ch. Our oath he will not take, nor give his own.

At. You seek the name of justice, not the act.

Ch. How so? Instruct, since thou hast wealth of wit.

At. Seek not by oaths to make the wrong prevail.

Ch. Then try the case and give us a straight judgment.

At. Will you commit the verdict to my charge?

Ch. I will, since thou art worthy, and thy sire.

At. Stranger, what is thy answer? Let us know
Thy fatherland and family, and what
Misfortune overtook thee, and then meet
The charge they bring against thee. If with trust
In justice thou art stationed at my image,
A holy suppliant, as Ixion was,
Then render on each count a clear reply.

Or. O Queen Athena, those last words of thine
Shall be my preface to relieve thy care.
No suppliant I that would be purified.
With hands already spotless I embraced
Thy image and took session at thy shrine;
And I can give thee evidence. The law
Commands the manslayer to hold his peace
Till he has been anointed with the blood
Of new-born beast by purifying hands.
Long since at other houses and on paths
Of land and sea have I been thus absolved.
So, having cast this scruple from thy mind,
I will inform thee of my origin.
I am from Argos, and my father's name—

For asking that I thank thee—Agamemnon,
Marshal of men in ships, with whom of late
The city of Ilium thou hast made to be
No more a city. He died an evil death.
When he returned home, my black-hearted mother
Killed him, entrapped in cunningly contrived
Nets that bore witness to a bath of blood.
Therefore, when I returned from banishment,
I killed my mother—that I do confess—
In retribution for my father's death:
An act not wholly mine, for Loxias
Must answer for it too, who spoke to me
Of bitter anguish to afflict my spirit
If I should fail in vengeance on the guilty.
Whether 'twas just or no, be thou my judge.
I will accept thy ordering of my doom.

AT. Too grave a suit is this for mortal minds
To judge, nor is it right that such as I
Should pass my verdict on a suit of blood
Shed with such bitter wrath attending it;
And all the more since thou hast come to me
A suppliant pure and humbled; and also I
Respect thee, being innocent of wrong
Against my city. But no such gentleness
Has been appointed *these,* and if their plea
Fall short of victory, the poison which
Drips from their angry bosoms to the ground
Will lay this country waste with pestilence.
So stands the matter—let them stay or be
Dismissed, the issue is fraught with injury.
But be it so; since it is come to this,
Judges I will appoint for homicide,
A court set up in perpetuity.
Meanwhile do you call proofs and witnesses
As sworn supports of justice; then, having chosen

The best of all my people, I shall come
To pass true judgment on the present cause.

(*Exit* ATHENA)

Second Stasimon

Str. 1

Now shall ancient ordinance
Fall to naught, should the unjust appeal of that
    accurst
Matricide win the day.
Now shall all men be reconciled by that
Crime to acts of violence;
Many, many a pain awaiteth
Parents in the time to come,
Struck by true-begotten child.

Ant. 1

We who watch the works of men
Shall not send wrath to haunt evildoers, rather lend
Rein to all deeds of blood.
Then shall one, making known his neighbour's
    plight,
From another seek to learn
End or easement of his trouble—
Wretch, what shifting remedies
Shall he recommend in vain!

Str. 2

Then let none, if e'er he fall
Smitten by disaster, cry
Out in lamentation, "Oh
Justice, O Furies, hearken to my prayer!"—
Thus shall fathers groan and thus
Stricken mothers weep in vain;

Since the house of Righteousness
Falls in ruins to the ground.

Ant. 2

Times there be when fear is well;
Yea, it must continually
Watch within the soul enthroned.
Needful too straits to teach humility.
Who of those that never nursed
Healthy dread within the heart,
Be they men or peoples, shall
Show to Justice reverence?

Str. 3

Choose a life despot-free,
Yet restrained by rule of law. Thus and thus
God doth administer, yet he appointeth the mean
 as the master in all things.
Hear my word proportionate:
Wickedness breedeth, and pride is the name of her
 child,
While from the spirit
Of health is born blessedness
Prayed for and prized of all men.

Ant. 3

So in brief this I say,
Bow before the shrine of Right, neither be
Tempted by profit to spurn it with insolent feet;
 retribution shall follow.
Yet abides the end decreed.
See that thy father and mother are rightly es-
 teemed;
Grant to the stranger

Within thy gates all the due
Honours of entertainment.

Str. 4

The man who seeks what is right
Of choice and free will, shall not be unblest;
The seed of just men shall never perish.
Not so the froward | and foolish heart that bears
A motley cargo of iniquity.
His outspread sail shall soon be hauled down;
Caught in the growing storm his stout
Mast shall be rent and shattered.

Ant. 4

To ears that hear not he cries,
To angry seas which he cannot master;
His guardian spirit | doth laugh to see him,
Who rashly boasted | his ship would come to port,
So weak and faint he cannot breast the wave
And sinks unseen with all his riches,
Dashed on the reef of Justice, un-
Looked-on and unlamented.

(*Enter* ATHENA *with the* JUDGES, *followed by citizens
of Athens*)

AT. Herald, proclaim, hold back the multitude,
     Then let the trump Tyrrhenian, filled with breath
     Of human lips, raise its resounding cry!
     For while this great tribunal is enrolled,
     Silence is meet and study of my laws
     For this whole city now and evermore,
     And likewise for these litigants, and so
     Just judgment shall be given on their cause.

(Enter APOLLO*)*

CH. O Lord Apollo, rule where power is thine.
    What business is there that concerns thee here?

AP. I come both as a witness, the accused
    Being a suppliant at my sanctuary
    And purified of bloodshed at my hands,
    And also to be tried with him, for I
    Must answer for his mother's death. Do thou
    Open the case and judge as thou knowest how.

AT. The case is open. Yours it is to speak.
    The prosecutor shall take precedence
    And so instruct us truly what befell.

CH. Many in number, we shall be brief in speech.
    Give answer to our questions one by one.
    First, is it true that thou didst kill thy mother?

OR. I killed her. That is true, and not denied.

CH. So then the first of the three rounds is ours.

OR. You need not boast that you have thrown me yet.

CH. But, having killed her, thou must tell us how.

OR. I will. With drawn sword levelled at the throat.

CH. Who moved, who counselled thee to such an act?

OR. The oracle of the God who is my witness.

CH. The Prophet taught thee to do matricide!

OR. And I have not repented to this day.

CH. Condemned anon, thou shalt tell another tale.

OR. My father shall defend me from the grave.

CH. Ah, having slain thy mother, trust the dead!

OR. She was polluted with a double crime.

CH. How so? Expound thy meaning to the court.

OR. She slew her husband, and she slew my father.

CH. Well, she died guiltless, thou art still alive.

OR. Why, when she lived, did you not harass *her?*

CH. She was not bound by blood to him she slew.

OR. And am I then in blood bound to my mother?

CH. How did she nourish thee, abandoned wretch,
    Within the womb? Dost thou abjure the tie,
    Nearest and dearest, of a mother's blood?

OR. Do *thou* declare thy witness now; pronounce,
    Apollo, whether I was justified.
    I killed as I have said; that is confessed;
    But in thy judgment was it justly done?

AP. Athena's great tribunal, I will say,
    Justly; and I, as prophet, cannot lie.
    Never upon my throne of prophecy
    Have I spoke aught of people, man or woman
    But what my father Zeus commanded me.
    How strong that justice is instruct yourselves
    And do according to my father's will,
    Whose sovranty no oath shall override.

CH. Zeus, as thou sayest, gave thee this command,
    To charge Orestes to avenge his father
    Regardless of dishonouring his mother?

AP. 'Tis not the same, to kill a noble man
    Invested with all majesty from heaven,
    A woman too to kill him, and not with far
    Shafts of a valiant Amazon's archery,
    But in such manner as you shall be told,
    Thou, Pallas, and this bench of justicers
    Appointed to give judgment on this cause.
    When he returned from battle, bringing home
    A balance for the greater part of good,
    At first she welcomed him with gentle words,
    And then, attending while he bathed, at last,
    His head pavilioned in a trailing robe,
    She struck him, fettered in those opulent folds.
    Such was his end—a man, a king whom all
    The world had honoured, a mighty admiral,
    And such the woman who contrived his death
    As I have told, seeking to move the hearts

Of all who are assembled here to judge.

Cн. Then Zeus gives precedence to the father's death
According to thy plea. Yet Zeus it was
Who bound in chains his aged father Kronos.
How shall thy plea be reconciled with that?
Judges, I call upon you to take note.

Ap. Abominable monsters loathed of heaven,
Chains may be loosened, there are cures for that
And many a means to bring deliverance;
But once the dust has drunk a dead man's blood,
He shall not rise again—for that no charm
My father has appointed, though all else
He turns and overturns and sets in place
Without the endeavour of a laboured breath.

Cн. See what this plea for the acquittal means.
He spilt upon the ground his mother's blood,
And shall he still dwell in his father's house?
What altars of the people shall he use,
What holy water grant him fellowship?

Ap. That too will I declare, and mark the truth.
The mother is not the parent of the child,
Only the nurse of what she has conceived.
The parent is the father, who commits
His seed to her, a stranger, to be held
With God's help in safe keeping. In proof of this,
Father there might be and no mother: see
A witness here, child of Olympian Zeus,
Begotten not in wedlock neither bred
In darkness of the womb, a goddess whom
No other goddess could have brought to birth.
And therefore, Pallas, since in all things I
Shall strive to make thy land and people great,
I sent this man to be thy suppliant,
A faithful friend to thee eternally,
That thou, Goddess, might find a staunch ally

      In him and his hereafter, a covenant
      For this thy people to uphold for ever.

AT. Enough has now been spoken. Therefore shall I
      Command the judges to record their votes
      In righteous judgment according to their minds?

AP. Empty our quiver, every arrow spent.
      We wait to hear the issue of the trial.

AT. How shall my ruling be approved by you?

CH. Sirs, you have heard, and vote accordingly
      With hearty reverence for your solemn oath.

AT. People of Athens, hear my ordinance
      At this first trial for bloodshed. Evermore
      This great tribunal shall abide in power
      Among the sons of Aegeus; and this hill
      Whereon of old the Amazons encamped,
      When hate of Theseus rallied them to arms,
      And here a city newly-fortified
      Upraised against his own, and sacrificed
      To Ares, whereupon this rock was named
      The Areopagus—here Reverence
      And inbred Fear enthroned among my people
      Shall hold their hands from evil night and day,
      Only let them not tamper with their laws;
      For, should a stream of mire pollute the pure
      Fountain, the lips shall never find it sweet.
      I bid my people honour and uphold
      The mean between the despot and the slave,
      And not to banish terror utterly,
      For what man shall be upright without fear?
      And if you honour this high ordinance,
      Then shall you have for land and commonweal
      A stronghold of salvation, such as none
      Hath elsewhere in the world, in Scythia
      Nor in the isle of Pelops. I establish
      This great tribunal to protect my people,

Grave, quick to anger, incorruptible,
And ever vigilant over those that sleep.
Such is my exhortation unto all
My people for all generations. Now
Arise, take each his ballot, and upon
Your solemn oath give judgment. I have spoken.

Cʜ. Remember us, I charge you, visitants
Grave in displeasure, and respect our powers.

Aᴘ. I charge you to respect the oracles
Ordained of Zeus and see that they bear fruit.

Cʜ. Bloodshed is not thy office, and henceforth
The shrines which voice thy utterance are unholy.

Aᴘ. Then did my Father err when he resolved
To cleanse Ixion, the first murderer?

Cʜ. Prate on; but, if my cause should fail, I shall
Afflict this people with a heavy hand.

Aᴘ. Thou art unhonoured of all deities
Both young and old, and victory shall be mine.

Cʜ. In the house of Pheres once thou didst the like,
Tempting the Fates to make a man immortal.

Aᴘ. Is it not just at all times to befriend
A worshipper, and most in time of need?

Cʜ. Thou didst destroy the ancient dispensations,
Beguiling antique deities with wine.

Aᴘ. Thou, failing of the verdict presently,
Shalt spew thy poisons, but they shall do no harm.

Cʜ. Thy youth has trampled on my honoured age.
Therefore I wait the verdict, whether or no
Upon this city to let loose my rage.

Aᴛ. The final judgment is a task for me;
So for Orestes shall this vote be cast.
No mother gave me birth, and in all things
Save marriage I, my father's child indeed,
With all my heart commend the masculine.

Wherefore I shall not hold of higher worth
A woman who was killed because she killed
Her wedded lord and master of her home.
Upon an equal vote Orestes wins.
Let the appointed judges now proceed
To count the ballots from the emptied urn.

Or. O bright Apollo, how shall the judgment go?
Ch. O mother mine, black Night, dost thou behold?
Or. My hour has come—the halter or the light.
Ch. And mine—to keep my ancient powers, or perish.
Ap. Sirs, count the issue of the votes aright;
Divide them as you honour what is just.
If judgment fail, great harm shall come of it;
And oft one vote hath raised a fallen house.
At. He stands acquitted on the charge of blood.
The number of the counted votes is equal.
Or. O Pallas, O deliverer of my house,
I was an outcast from my country, thou
Hast brought me home again; and men shall say,
Once more he is an Argive and he dwells
In his paternal heritage by the grace
Of Pallas, and of Loxias, and third
Of him who orders all, Deliverer,
Who had regard unto my father's death
And has delivered me. Before I go
I pledge my honour to this land of thine
And to thy people for all plenitude
Of after generations that no prince
Of Argos shall lead forth his serried arms
In war against this city. We ourselves
Out of the grave which then shall cover us
Shall so afflict all those who would transgress
The pledge that I have given, with desperate
Obstructions, wanderings disconsolate

And adverse omens frowning on their march,
That they shall soon repent; but if they keep
Our covenant, continuing to honour
Athena's city with arms confederate,
With blessings rather shall we visit them.
And so farewell. May thou and those who rule
Thy populace stand firm in such a stance
As shall prevail against all enemies,
A strong salvation and victory at arms!   (*Exit*)

Kommos

Cн. Oho ye younger Gods, since ye have trod under
    foot
The laws of old and ancient powers purloined,
Then we, dishonoured, deadly in displeasure,
Shall spread poison foul
Through the land, with damp contagion
Of rage malignant, bleak and barren, blasting,
    withering up the earth,
Mildews on bud and birth abortive. Oh!
Venomous pestilence
Shall sweep this country with infectious death.
To weep?—nay, to work; yea, to work ill, to lay
    low the people!
Oh me, many the wrongs of these maids of Night
Mourning their plundered honours!

Aт. Let me persuade you from this passionate grief.
You are not vanquished; the issue of the trial
Has been determined by an equal vote.
Nay, Zeus it was who plainly testified,
Himself pronouncing his own evidence,
That for this deed Orestes should not suffer.
And therefore be not angry, let no dread

Displeasures fall upon this country, nor
Corrupt her fruits with drops of rank decay
And keen-edged cankers in the early bud.
Rather accept my honourable word
That ye shall have a cave wherein to dwell
Among this righteous people, and, enthroned
In honour at your altars, shall receive
The adoration of my citizens.

CH. Oho ye younger Gods, since ye have trod under
        foot
    The laws of old and ancient powers purloined,
    Then we, dishonoured, deadly in displeasure,
    Shall spread poison foul
    Through the land, with damp contagion
    Of rage malignant, bleak and barren, blasting,
        withering up the earth,
    Mildews on bud and birth abortive. Oh!
    Venomous pestilence
    Shall sweep this country with infectious death.
    To weep?—nay, to work; yea, to work ill, to lay
        low the people!
    Oh me, many the wrongs of these maids of Night
    Mourning their plundered honours!

AT. Nay, *not* dishonoured; neither let divine
    Displeasures plague this mortal populace.
    I too confide in Zeus—why speak of that?
    And I alone of all divinities
    Know of the keys which guard the treasury
    Of heaven's thunder. Of that there is no need:
    Be moved by my persuasion not to bring
    From angry tongues to birth a fruit accursed
    Nor sweep this country with calamities.
    Calm the black humours of embittered rage,
    Reside with me, and share my majesty;

And when from these wide acres you enjoy
Year after year the harvest offerings
That wedlock may be blest with issue, then
You will commend me for my intercession.

Ch. Me to be treated so!
Me with the sage wisdom of years to dwell here, oh
Ever debased, oh defiled!
Spirit of spleen and unyielding spite!
Give ear, O Earth!
Ah, the insufferable pangs sink deep.
Hear my passion, hear, black Night!
For the powers once mine, sealed long, long ago,
Have by the younger Gods been snatched all away.

At. My elder art thou, therefore I indulge
Thy passion; yet, though not so wise as thou,
To me also hath Zeus vouchsafed the gift
Of no mean understanding. I declare,
If you depart from this to other lands,
This country yet shall prove your heart's desire;
For with the tide of years shall flow increase
Of honour to my people; wherefore thou,
Honoured among them and enthroned hard by
The temple of Erechtheus, shalt receive
Such homage from the congregated throngs
Of men and women as shall ne'er be yours
Elsewhere in all the world. And so, I pray,
Lay not upon my territories the spur
Of internecine strife to prick the breast
Of manhood flown with passion as with wine;
Implant not in my sons the bravery
Of fighting-cocks, embroiled against their own.
Abroad let battle rage for every heart
Possessed by love of glory—that shall be theirs
In plenty. This then is my offer to you—

To give and take rich benefits and share
My honours in a land beloved of heaven.

CH. Me to be treated so!
Me with the sage wisdom of years to dwell here, oh
Ever debased, oh defiled!
Spirit of spleen and unyielding spite!
Give ear, O Earth!
Ah, the insufferable pangs sink deep.
Hear my passion, hear, black Night!
For the powers once mine, sealed long, long ago,
Have by the younger Gods been snatched all away.

AT. I will not weary of my benedictions,
Lest it be ever said that thou, so old
A deity, wast driven from the land
By me and by my mortal citizens,
Rejected without welcome and despised.
Nay, if Persuasion's holy majesty,
The sweet enchantment of these lips divine,
Is aught to thee, why then, reside with me;
But if thou wilt not, surely it were wrong
To lay upon my citizens a load
Of indignation and pernicious rage,
Since it is in thy power to own the soil
Justly attended with the highest honours.

CH. O Queen Athena, what dost thou promise me?
AT. A dwelling free of sorrow. Pray, accept.
CH. Say I accept, what honours shall be mine?
AT. No house shall prosper save by grace from thee.
CH. Wilt thou ensure me this prerogative?
AT. I will, and bless all those who worship thee.
CH. And pledge a warrant for all time to come?
AT. I need not promise what I would not do.

Cн. Thy charms are working, and my rage subsides.

Aт. Here make thy dwelling where thou shalt win
    friends.

Cн. What song then shall I chant over the land?

Aт. A song of faultless victory: from earth and sea,
From skies above may gentle breezes blow,
And, breathing sunshine, float from shore to shore;
That corn and cattle may continually
Increase and multiply, and that no harm
Befall the offspring of humanity;
And prosper too the fruit of righteous hearts;
For I, as one who tends flowers in a garden,
Delight in those, the seeds that bring no sorrow.
Such is thy part; and in the glorious
Arrays of battle I shall strive until
This city, over all victorious,
Enjoy an honoured name throughout the world.

Third Stasimon

Str. 1

Cн. I accept. Here with Pallas I will dwell,
Honouring the city which
Zeus Almighty with the aid of Ares
Holds a fortress for the Gods,
Jewelled crown of Greece and guardian of her
    sanctuaries.
So for her I pray with all
Graciousness of utterance
That smiling sun and bounteous earth unite to yield
Lifelong joys, fortunes fair,
Light and Darkness reconciled.

Aт. As a favour to all of my people have I
Given homes in the land unto these, whose power

Is so great and their anger so hard to appease—
All that concerneth mankind they dispense.
Yet whenever a man falls foul of their wrath,
He knoweth not whence his afflictions approach;
Apprehended to answer the sins of his sires,
He is led unto these to be judged, and the still
Stroke of perdition
In the dust shall stifle his proud boast.

Ant. 1

CH. Ne'er may foul winds be stirred to touch with blight
Budding tree—a grace from me;
Ne'er may parching droughts that blind the newly
Parted blossom trespass here;
Ne'er may blasts of noisome plague advance across
the fields;
Rather, Pan in season due
Grant that flocks and herds may yield
A twin increase of yearly wealth, and from the rich
Store which these Gods vouchsafe
May the Earth repay them well.

AT. O listen, ye guards of my city, and hear
What blessings they bring you! For great is the
power
Of the Furies in heaven and hell, and on earth
Unto some glad music, to others again
They dispense days darkened with weeping.

Str. 2

CH. Sudden death cutting short
Manhood's prime I bid away;
To all her comely daughters grant
Husband and home, O heavenly wardens of wed-
lock,

And ye too, dread Fates, born of the same mother's
    womb,
Spirits of justice divine, dwelling in every house-
    hold,
Present at every season, weighty in your majesty,
Praised and magnified in every place.

AT. Fair blessings are these they bestow on the land,
    And my heart is rejoiced.
To the eye of Persuasion I give all praise,
That with favour she looked on the breath of my
    lips
As I strove to appease these powers that once
Were averted in anger; but Zeus who is Lord
Of the eloquent word hath prevailed, and at last
In contention for blessings we conquer.

Ant. 2
CH. Ne'er, I pray, ne'er may that
    Root of evil, civil strife,
    Rage within her boundaries;
Ne'er may the earth's dust drink of the blood of her
    children,
And wroth thereat thirst greedily after revenge,
    Blood in requital of blood;
    Rather in friendly communion
    Gladness be rendered for gladness,
    All at one in love and hate.
Therein lies a cure for human ills.

AT. How quick is their sense to discover the paths
Of a tongue fair-spoken! From these dread shapes
Great gain do I see for my people: if ye
Pay homage to these and with favour regard
Their favour to you, then surely the fame

Of a city in justice and equity ruled
Shall be spread as a light unto all men.

(*Enter Escort of Women, carrying crimson robes and torches*)

Str. 3

Ch. Joy to you, joy of your justly appointed riches,
Joy to all the people, blest
With the Virgin's love, who sits
Next beside her Father's throne.
Wisdom ye have learned at last.
Folded under Pallas' wing,
Yours at last the grace of Zeus.

At. Joy to you likewise! Walking before you,
To the chambers appointed I show you the way,
Led by the sacred lights of the escort.
Come with me, come, and let solemn oblations
Speed you in joy to your homes in the earth,
Where all that is hurtful imprison, we pray,
And release what shall guide them to glory.
Lead them, O daughters of Cranaus, lead them,
And let all of you bear
Good will for the good that is given.

Ant. 3

Ch. Joy to you, joy—yet again we pronounce our bless-
ing—
Joy to all the citizens,
Mortals, deities alike.
While you hold this land and pay
Homage to our residence,
Ne'er shall you have cause to blame
Change and chance in human life.

AT. I thank you for these words of benison,
      And now with flames of torchlit splendour bright
      Escort you to your subterranean home,
      Attended by the wardens of my shrine,
      And justly so; for meet it is that all
      The eye of Theseus' people should come forth,
      This noble company of maidens fair,
      And women wed and venerable in years.
      Adorn them well in robes of crimson dye,
      And let these blazing torches lead the way,
      So that the good will of these residents
      Be proved in manly prowess of your sons.

(The CHORUS *has put on the crimson robes; and a procession is drawn up, led by twenty-four young men,
who are followed by the* CHORUS *and their escort, and
the main body of the citizens. The rest is sung as the
procession moves away)*

CHORUS *of the* ESCORT

Str. 1
Pass on your way, O ye powers majestic,
Daughters of darkness, in happy procession.
    Hush, O people, and speak all fair!

Ant. 1
Pass to the caverns of earth immemorial
There to be worshipped in honour and glory.
    Hush, O people, and speak all fair!

Str. 2
Gracious and kindly of heart to our people,
Hither, O holy ones, hither in gladness,
Follow the lamps that illumine the way.
    O sing at the end Alleluia!

Ant. 2
Peace to you, peace of a happy communion,
People of Pallas. Zeus who beholdeth
All with the Fates is at last reconciled.
    O sing at the end Alleluia!

Translated 1932 by George Thomson.

O

THE GREAT MAN

ARISTOTLE

3. Pride seems even from its name to be concerned with great things; what sort of great things, is the first question we must try to answer. It makes no difference whether we consider the state of character or the man characterized by it. Now the man is thought to be proud who thinks himself worthy of great things, being worthy of them; for he who does so beyond his deserts is a fool, but no virtuous man is foolish or silly. The proud man, then, is the man we have described. For he who is worthy of little and thinks himself worthy of little is temperate, but not proud; for pride implies greatness, as beauty implies a good-sized body, and little people may be neat and well-proportioned but cannot be beautiful. On the other hand, he who thinks himself worthy of great things, being unworthy of them, is vain; though not every one who thinks himself worthy of more than he really is worthy of is vain. The man who thinks himself worthy of less than he is really worthy of is unduly humble, whether his deserts be great or moderate, or his deserts be small but his claims yet smaller. And the man whose deserts are great would

seem *most* unduly humble; for what would he have done if they had been less? The proud man, then, is an extreme in respect of the greatness of his claims, but a mean in respect of the rightness of them; for he claims what is in accordance with his merits, while the others go to excess or fall short.

If, then, he deserves and claims great things, and above all the greatest things, he will be concerned with one thing in particular. Desert is relative to external goods; and the greatest of these, we should say, is that which we render to the gods, and which people of position most aim at, and which is the prize appointed for the noblest deeds; and this is honour; that is surely the greatest of external goods. Honours and dishonours, therefore, are the objects with respect to which the proud man is as he should be. And even apart from argument it is with honour that proud men appear to be concerned; for it is honour that they chiefly claim, but in accordance with their deserts. The unduly humble man falls short both in comparison with his own merits and in comparison with the proud man's claims. The vain man goes to excess in comparison with his own merits, but does not exceed the proud man's claims.

Now the proud man, since he deserves most, must be good in the highest degree; for the better man always deserves more, and the best man most. Therefore the truly proud man must be good. And greatness in every virtue would seem to be characteristic of a proud man. And it would be most unbecoming for a proud man to fly from danger, swinging his arms by his sides, or to wrong another; for to what end should he do disgraceful acts, he to whom nothing is great? If we consider him point by point, we shall see the utter absurdity of a proud man who is not good. Nor, again, would he be worthy of honour if he were bad; for honour is the prize of virtue, and it is to the good that it is rendered. Pride, then, seems to be a sort of crown of the virtues; for it makes them greater, and it is not found without them. Therefore it is hard to be truly proud; for it is impossible without nobility and goodness of character. It is chiefly with honours and dishonours, then, that the proud man is concerned; and at honours that are great and conferred by good men he will be moderately pleased, thinking that he is coming by his own or even less than his own; for there can be no honour that is worthy of perfect virtue, yet he will at any rate accept it since they have nothing greater to bestow on him; but honour from casual people and on trifling grounds he will utterly despise, since it is not this that he deserves, and dishonour too, since in his case it cannot be just. In the first place, then, as has been said, the proud man is concerned with honours; yet he will also bear himself with moderation towards wealth and power and all good or evil fortune, whatever may befall him, and will be neither over-joyed by good fortune nor over-pained by evil. For not even towards honour does he bear himself as if it were a very great thing. Power and wealth are desirable for the sake of honour (at least those who have them wish to get honour by means of them); and for him to whom even honour is a little thing the others must be so too. Hence proud men are thought to be disdainful.

The goods of fortune also are thought to contribute towards pride. For men who are well-born are thought worthy of honour, and so are those who enjoy power or wealth; for they are in a superior position, and everything that has a superiority in something good is held in greater honour. Hence even such things make men prouder; for they are honoured by some for having them; but in truth the good man alone is to be honoured;

he, however, who has both advantages is thought the more worthy of honour. But those who without virtue have such goods are neither justified in making great claims nor entitled to the name of "proud"; for these things imply perfect virtue. Disdainful and insolent, however, even those who have such goods become. For without virtue it is not easy to bear gracefully the goods of fortune; and, being unable to bear them, and thinking themselves superior to others, they despise others and themselves do what they please. They imitate the proud man without being like him, and this they do where they can; so they do not act virtuously, but they do despise others. For the proud man despises justly (since he thinks truly), but the many do so at random.

He does not run into trifling dangers, nor is he fond of danger, because he honours few things; but he will face great dangers, and when he is in danger he is unsparing of his life, knowing that there are conditions on which life is not worth having. And he is the sort of man to confer benefits, but he is ashamed of receiving them; for the one is the mark of a superior, the other of an inferior. And he is apt to confer greater benefits in return; for thus the original benefactor besides being paid will incur a debt to him, and will be the gainer by the transaction. They seem also to remember any service they have done, but not those they have received (for he who receives a service is inferior to him who has done it, but the proud man wishes to be superior), and to hear of the former with pleasure, of the latter with displeasure; this, it seems, is why Thetis did not mention to Zeus the services she had done him, and why the Spartans did not recount their services to the Athenians, but those they had received. It is a mark of the proud man also

to ask for nothing or scarcely anything, but to give help
readily, and to be dignified towards people who enjoy
high position and good fortune, but unassuming towards
those of the middle class; for it is a difficult and lofty
thing to be superior to the former, but easy to be so to
the latter, and a lofty bearing over the former is no mark
of ill-breeding, but among humble people it is as vulgar
as a display of strength against the weak. Again, it is
characteristic of the proud man not to aim at the things
commonly held in honour, or the things in which others
excel; to be sluggish and to hold back except where
great honour or a great work is at stake, and to be a man
of few deeds, but of great and notable ones. He must
also be open in his hate and in his love (for to conceal
one's feelings, i. e. to care less for truth than for what
people will think, is a coward's part), and must speak
and act openly; for he is free of speech because he is
contemptuous, and he is given to telling the truth, except when he speaks in irony to the vulgar. He must be
unable to make his life revolve round another, unless it
be a friend; for this is slavish, and for this reason all
flatterers are servile and people lacking in self-respect
are flatterers. Nor is he given to admiration; for nothing
to him is great. Nor is he mindful of wrongs; for it is not
the part of a proud man to have a long memory, especially for wrongs, but rather to overlook them. Nor is
he a gossip; for he will speak neither about himself nor
about another, since he cares not to be praised nor for
others to be blamed; nor again is he given to praise; and
for the same reason he is not an evil-speaker, even about
his enemies, except from haughtiness. With regard to
necessary or small matters he is least of all men given to
lamentation or the asking of favours; for it is the part
of one who takes such matters seriously to behave so

with respect to them. He is one who will possess beautiful and profitless things rather than profitable and useful ones; for this is more proper to a character that suffices to itself.

Further, a slow step is thought proper to the proud man, a deep voice, and a level utterance; for the man who takes few things seriously is not likely to be hurried, nor the man who thinks nothing great to be excited, while a shrill voice and a rapid gait are the results of hurry and excitement.

Such, then, is the proud man; the man who falls short of him is unduly humble, and the man who goes beyond him is vain. Now even these are not thought to be bad (for they are not malicious), but only mistaken. For the unduly humble man, being worthy of good things, robs himself of what he deserves, and seems to have something bad about him from the fact that he does not think himself worthy of good things, and seems also not to know himself; else he would have desired the things he was worthy of, since these were good. Yet such people are not thought to be fools, but rather unduly retiring. Such a reputation, however, seems actually to make them worse; for each class of people aims at what corresponds to its worth, and these people stand back even from noble actions and undertakings, deeming themselves unworthy, and from external goods no less. Vain people, on the other hand, are fools and ignorant of themselves, and that manifestly; for, not being worthy of them, they attempt honourable undertakings, and then are found out; and they adorn themselves with clothing and outward show and such things, and wish their strokes of good fortune to be made public, and speak about them as if they would be honoured for them. But undue humility is more opposed to pride than vanity is; for it is both commoner and worse.

Pride, then, is concerned with honour on the grand scale, as has been said.

From <i>Nicomachean Ethics</i>, Book IV, chap. 3.
Translated by W. D. Ross.

O

THE HAPPY MAN

ARISTOTLE

6. Now that we have spoken of the virtues, the forms of friendship, and the varieties of pleasure, what remains is to discuss in outline the nature of happiness, since this is what we state the end of human nature to be. Our discussion will be the more concise if we first sum up what we have said already. We said, then, that it is not a disposition; for if it were it might belong to some one who was asleep throughout his life, living the life of a plant, or, again, to some one who was suffering the greatest misfortunes. If these implications are unacceptable, and we must rather class happiness as an activity, as we have said before, and if some activities are necessary, and desirable for the sake of something else, while others are so in themselves, evidently happiness must be placed among those desirable in themselves, not among those desirable for the sake of something else; for happiness does not lack anything, but is self-sufficient. Now those activities are desirable in themselves from which nothing is sought beyond the activity. And of this nature virtuous actions are thought to be; for to do noble and good deeds is a thing desirable for its own sake.

Pleasant amusements also are thought to be of this nature; we choose them not for the sake of other things; for we are injured rather than benefited by them, since we are led to neglect our bodies and our property. But most of the people who are deemed happy take refuge in such pastimes, which is the reason why those who are ready-witted at them are highly esteemed at the courts of tyrants; they make themselves pleasant companions in the tyrants' favourite pursuits, and that is the sort of man they want. Now these things are thought to be of the nature of happiness because people in despotic positions spend their leisure in them, but perhaps such people prove nothing; for virtue and reason, from which good activities flow, do not depend on despotic position; nor, if these people, who have never tasted pure and generous pleasure, take refuge in the bodily pleasures, should these for that reason be thought more desirable; for boys, too, think the things that are valued among themselves are the best. It is to be expected, then, that, as different things seem valuable to boys and to men, so they should to bad men and to good. Now, as we have often maintained, those things are both valuable and pleasant which are such to the good man; and to each man the activity in accordance with his own disposition is most desirable, and, therefore, to the good man that which is in accordance with virtue. Happiness, therefore, does not lie in amusement; it would, indeed, be strange if the end were amusement, and one were to take trouble and suffer hardship all one's life in order to amuse oneself. For, in a word, everything that we choose we choose for the sake of something else—except happiness, which is an end. Now to exert oneself and work for the sake of amusement seems silly and utterly childish. But to amuse oneself in order that one may exert oneself, as Anacharsis puts it, seems right; for amusement is a sort of relaxation, and we need relaxation because we cannot work continuously. Relaxation, then, is not an end; for it is taken for the sake of activity.

The happy life is thought to be virtuous; now a virtuous life requires exertion, and does not consist in amusement. And we say that serious things are better than laughable things and those connected with amusement, and that the activity of the better of any two things—whether it be two elements of our being or two men—is the more serious; but the activity of the better is *ipso facto* superior and more of the nature of happiness. And any chance person—even a slave—can enjoy the bodily pleasures no less than the best man; but no one assigns to a slave a share in happiness—unless he assigns to him also a share in human life. For happiness does not lie in such occupations, but, as we have said before, in virtuous activities.

7. If happiness is activity in accordance with virtue, it is reasonable that it should be in accordance with the highest virtue; and this will be that of the best thing in us. Whether it be reason or something else that is this element which is thought to be our natural ruler and guide and to take thought of things noble and divine, whether it be itself also divine or only the most divine element in us, the activity of this in accordance with its proper virtue will be perfect happiness. That this activity is contemplative we have already said.

Now this would seem to be in agreement both with what we said before and with the truth. For, firstly, this activity is the best (since not only is reason the best thing in us, but the objects of reason are the best of knowable objects); and, secondly, it is the most continuous, since we can contemplate truth more continuously than we can *do* anything. And we think happiness has pleasure mingled with it, but the activity of philosophic wisdom is admittedly the pleasantest of virtuous activities; at all events the pursuit of it is thought to offer pleasures marvellous for their purity and their enduringness, and it is to be expected that those who know will pass their time more pleasantly than those who inquire. And the self-sufficiency that is spoken of must belong most to the contemplative activity. For while a philosopher, as well as a just man or one possessing any other virtue, needs the necessaries of life, when they are sufficiently equipped with things of that sort the just man needs people towards whom and with whom he shall act justly, and the temperate man, the brave man, and each of the others is in the same case, but the philosopher, even when by himself, can contemplate truth, and the better the wiser he is; he can perhaps do so better if he has fellow-workers, but still he is the most self-sufficient. And this activity alone would seem to be loved for its own sake; for nothing arises from it apart from the contemplating, while from practical activities we gain more or less apart from the action. And happiness is thought to depend on leisure; for we are busy that we may have leisure, and make war that we may live in peace. Now the activity of the practical virtues is exhibited in political or military affairs, but the actions concerned with these seem to be unleisurely. Warlike actions are completely so (for no one chooses to be at war, or provokes war, for the sake of being at war; any one would seem absolutely murderous if he were to make enemies of his friends in order to bring about battle and slaughter); but the action of the statesman is also unleisurely, and—apart from the political action itself—aims at despotic power and honours, or at all events happiness, for him and his fellow citizens—a happiness different from political action, and evidently sought as being different. So if among virtuous actions political and military actions are distinguished by nobility and greatness, and these are unleisurely and aim at an end and are not desirable for their own sake, but the activity of reason, which is contemplative, seems both to be superior in serious worth and to aim at no end beyond itself, and to have its pleasure proper to itself (and this augments the activity), and the self-sufficiency, leisureliness, unweariedness (so far as this is possible for man), and all the other attributes ascribed to the supremely happy man are evidently those connected with this activity, it follows that this will be the complete happiness of man, if it be allowed a complete term of life (for none of the attributes of happiness is *in*complete).

But such a life would be too high for man; for it is not in so far as he is man that he will live so, but in so far as something divine is present in him; and by so much as this is superior to our composite nature is its activity superior to that which is the exercise of the other kind of virtue. If reason is divine, then, in comparison with man, the life according to it is divine in comparison with human life. But we must not follow those who advise us, being men, to think of human things, and, being mortal, of mortal things, but must, so far as we can, make ourselves immortal, and strain every nerve to live in accordance with the best thing in us; for even if it be small in bulk, much more does it in power and worth surpass everything. This would seem, too, to be each man himself, since it is the authoritative and better part of him. It would be strange, then, if he were to choose not the life of his self but that of something else. And what we said before will apply now; that which is proper to each thing is by nature best and most pleasant for each thing; for man, therefore, the life according to reason is best and pleasantest, since reason more than anything else *is* man. This life therefore is also the happiest.

8. But in a secondary degree the life in accordance with the other kind of virtue is happy; for the activities in accordance with this befit our human estate. Just and brave acts, and other virtuous acts, we do in relation to each other, observing our respective duties with regard to contracts and services and all manner of actions and with regard to passions; and all of these seem to be typically human. Some of them seem even to arise from the body, and virtue of character to be in many ways bound up with the passions. Practical wisdom, too, is linked to virtue of character, and this to practical wisdom, since the principles of practical wisdom are in accordance with the moral virtues and rightness in morals as in accordance with practical wisdom. Being connected with the passions also, the moral virtues must belong to our composite nature; and the virtues of our composite nature are human; so, therefore, are the life and the happiness which correspond to these. The excellence of the reason is a thing apart; we must be content to say this much about it, for to describe it precisely is a task greater than our purpose requires. It would seem, however, also to need external equipment but little, or less than moral virtue does. Grant that both need the necessaries, and do so equally, even if the statesman's work is the more concerned with the body and things of that sort; for there will be little difference there; but in what they need for the exercise of their activities there will be much difference. The liberal man will need money for the doing of his liberal deeds, and the just man too will need it for the returning of services (for wishes are hard to discern, and even people who are not just pretend to wish to act justly); and the brave man will need power if he is to accomplish any of the acts that correspond to his virtue, and the temperate man will

need opportunity; for how else is either he or any of the others to be recognized? It is debated, too, whether the will or the deed is more essential to virtue, which is assumed to involve both; it is surely clear that its perfection involves both; but for deeds many things are needed, and more, the greater and nobler the deeds are. But the man who is contemplating the truth needs no such thing, at least with a view to the exercise of his activity; indeed they are, one may say, even hindrances, at all events to his contemplation; but in so far as he is a man and lives with a number of people, he chooses to do virtuous acts; he will therefore need such aids to living a human life.

But that perfect happiness is a contemplative activity will appear from the following consideration as well. We assume the gods to be above all other beings blessed and happy; but what sort of actions must we assign to them? Acts of justice? Will not the gods seem absurd if they make contracts and return deposits, and so on? Acts of a brave man, then, confronting dangers and running risks because it is noble to do so? Or liberal acts? To whom will they give? It will be strange if they are really to have money or anything of the kind. And what would their temperate acts be? Is not such praise tasteless, since they have no bad appetites? If we were to run through them all, the circumstances of action would be found trivial and unworthy of gods. Still, every one supposes that they *live* and therefore that they are active; we cannot suppose them to sleep like Endymion. Now if you take away from a living being action, and still more production, what is left but contemplation? Therefore the activity of God, which surpasses all others in blessedness, must be contemplative; and of human activities, therefore, that which is most akin to this must be most of the nature of happiness.

This is indicated, too, by the fact that the other animals have no share in happiness, being completely deprived of such activity. For while the whole life of the gods is blessed, and that of men too in so far as some likeness of such activity belongs to them, none of the other animals is happy, since they in no way share in contemplation. Happiness extends, then, just so far as contemplation does, and those to whom contemplation more fully belongs are more truly happy, not as a mere concomitant but in virtue of the contemplation; for this is in itself precious. Happiness, therefore, must be some form of contemplation.

But, being a man, one will also need external prosperity; for our nature is not self-sufficient for the purpose of contemplation, but our body also must be healthy and must have food and other attention. Still, we must not think that the man who is to be happy will need many things or great things, merely because he cannot be supremely happy without external goods; for self-sufficiency and action do not involve excess, and we can do noble acts without ruling earth and sea; for even with moderate advantages one can act virtuously (this is manifest enough; for private persons are thought to do worthy acts no less than despots—indeed even more); and it is enough that we should have so much as that; for the life of the man who is active in accordance with virtue will be happy. Solon, too, was perhaps sketching well the happy man when he described him as moderately furnished with externals but as having done (as Solon thought) the noblest acts, and lived temperately; for one can with but moderate possessions do what one ought. Anaxagoras also seems to have supposed the happy man not to be rich nor a despot, when he said that he would not be surprised if the happy man were to seem to most people a strange person; for they judge by externals, since these are all they perceive. The opinions of the wise seem, then, to harmonize with our arguments. But while even such things carry some conviction, the truth in practical matters is discerned from the facts of life; for these are the decisive factor. We must therefore survey what we have already said, bringing it to the test of the facts of life, and if it harmonizes with the facts we must accept it, but if it clashes with them we must suppose it to be mere theory. Now he who exercises his reason and cultivates it seems to be both in the best state of mind and most dear to the gods. For if the gods have any care for human affairs, as they are thought to have, it would be reasonable both that they should delight in that which was best and most akin to them (i. e. reason) and that they should reward those who love and honour this most, as caring for the things that are dear to them and acting both rightly and nobly. And that all these attributes belong most of all to the philosopher is manifest. He, therefore, is the dearest to the gods. And he who is that will presumably be also the happiest; so that in this way too the philosopher will more than any other be happy.

From *Nicomachean Ethics*, Book X, chaps. 6–8.
Translated by W. D. Ross.

O

THE PHILOSOPHIC HERO

PLATO

A MAN of sense ought not to say, nor will I be very confident, that the description which I have given of the soul and her mansions is exactly true. But I do say that, inasmuch as the soul is shown to be immortal, he may venture to think, not improperly or unworthily, that something of the kind is true. The venture is a glorious one, and he ought to comfort himself with words like these, which is the reason why I lengthen out the tale. Wherefore, I say, let a man be of good cheer about his soul, who having cast away the pleasures and ornaments of the body as alien to him and working harm rather than good, has sought after the pleasures of knowledge; and has arrayed the soul, not in some foreign attire, but in her own proper jewels, temperance, and justice, and courage, and nobility, and truth—in these adorned she is ready to go on her journey to the world below, when her hour comes. You, Simmias and Cebes, and all other men, will depart at some time or other. Me already, as a tragic poet would say, the voice of fate calls. Soon I must drink the poison; and I think that I had better repair to the bath first, in order that the women may not have the trouble of washing my body after I am dead.

When he had done speaking, Crito said: And have you any commands for us, Socrates—anything to say about your children, or any other matter in which we can serve you?

Nothing particular, Crito, he replied: only, as I have always told you, take care of yourselves; that is a service which you may be ever rendering to me and mine and to all of us, whether you promise to do so or not. But if you have no thought for yourselves, and care not to walk according to the rule which I have prescribed for you, not now for the first time, however much you may profess or promise at the moment, it will be of no avail.

We will do our best, said Crito: And in what way shall we bury you?

In any way that you like; but you must get hold of

me, and take care that I do not run away from you. Then he turned to us, and added with a smile:—I cannot make Crito believe that I am the same Socrates who have been talking and conducting the argument; he fancies that I am the other Socrates whom he will soon see, a dead body—and he asks, How shall he bury me? And though I have spoken many words in the endeavour to show that when I have drunk the poison I shall leave you and go to the joys of the blessed—these words of mine, with which I was comforting you and myself, have had, as I perceive, no effect upon Crito. And therefore I want you to be surety for me to him now, as at the trial he was surety to the judges for me: but let the promise be of another sort; for he was surety for me to the judges that I would remain, and you must be my surety to him that I shall not remain, but go away and depart; and then he will suffer less at my death, and not be grieved when he sees my body being burned or buried. I would not have him sorrow at my hard lot, or say at the burial, Thus we lay out Socrates, or, Thus we follow him to the grave or bury him; for false words are not only evil in themselves, but they infect the soul with evil. Be of good cheer then, my dear Crito, and say that you are burying my body only, and do with that whatever is usual, and what you think best.

When he had spoken these words, he arose and went into a chamber to bathe; Crito followed him and told us to wait. So we remained behind, talking and thinking of the subject of discourse, and also of the greatness of our sorrow; he was like a father of whom we were being bereaved, and we were about to pass the rest of our lives as orphans. When he had taken the bath his children were brought to him—(he had two young sons and an elder one); and the women of his family also came, and he talked to them and gave them a few directions in the presence of Crito; then he dismissed them and returned to us.

Now the hour of sunset was near, for a good deal of time had passed while he was within. When he came out, he sat down with us again after his bath, but not much was said. Soon the jailer, who was the servant of the Eleven, entered and stood by him, saying:—To you, Socrates, whom I know to be the noblest and gentlest and best of all who ever came to this place, I will not impute the angry feelings of other men, who rage and swear at me, when, in obedience to the authorities, I bid them drink the poison—indeed, I am sure that you will not be angry with me; for others, as you are aware, and not I, are to blame. And so fare you well, and try to bear lightly what must needs be—you know my errand. Then bursting into tears he turned away and went out.

Socrates looked at him and said: I return your good wishes, and will do as you bid. Then turning to us, he said, How charming the man is: since I have been in prison he has always been coming to see me, and at times he would talk to me, and was as good to me as could be, and now see how generously he sorrows on my account. We must do as he says, Crito; and therefore let the cup be brought, if the poison is prepared: if not, let the attendant prepare some.

Yet, said Crito, the sun is still upon the hill-tops, and I know that many a one has taken the draught late, and after the announcement has been made to him, he has eaten and drunk, and enjoyed the society of his beloved; do not hurry—there is time enough.

Socrates said: Yes, Crito, and they of whom you speak are right in so acting, for they think that they will be gainers by the delay; but I am right in not following their example, for I do not think that I should gain anything by drinking the poison a little later; I should only be ridiculous in my own eyes for sparing and saving a life which is already forfeit. Please then to do as I say, and not to refuse me.

Crito made a sign to the servant, who was standing by; and he went out, and having been absent for some time, returned with the jailer carrying the cup of poison. Socrates said: You, my good friend, who are experienced in these matters, shall give me directions how I am to proceed. The man answered: You have only to walk about until your legs are heavy, and then to lie down, and the poison will act. At the same time he handed the cup to Socrates, who in the easiest and gentlest manner, without the least fear or change of colour or feature, looking at the man with all his eyes, Echecrates, as his manner was, took the cup and said: What do you say about making a libation out of this cup to any god? May I, or not? The man answered: We only prepare, Socrates, just so much as we deem enough. I understand, he said: but I may and must ask the gods to prosper my journey from this to the other world—even so—and so be it according to my prayer. Then raising the cup to his lips, quite readily and cheerfully he drank off the poison. And hitherto most of us had been able to control our sorrow; but now when we saw him drinking, and saw too that he had finished the draught, we could no longer forbear, and in spite of myself my own tears were flowing fast; so that I covered my face and wept, not for him, but at the thought of my own calamity in having to part from such a friend. Nor was I the first; for Crito, when he found himself unable to restrain his tears, had got up, and I followed; and at that moment, Apollodorus, who had been weeping all the time, broke out in a loud and passionate cry which made cowards of us all. Socrates alone retained his calmness: What is this strange out-

cry? he said. I sent away the women mainly in order
that they might not misbehave in this way, for I have
been told that a man should die in peace. Be quiet then,
and have patience. When we heard his words we were
ashamed, and refrained our tears; and he walked about
until, as he said, his legs began to fail, and then he lay
on his back, according to the directions, and the man
who gave him the poison now and then looked at his
feet and legs; and after a while he pressed his foot hard,
and asked him if he could feel; and he said, No; and
then his leg, and so upwards and upwards, and showed
us that he was cold and stiff. And he felt them himself,
and said: When the poison reaches the heart, that will
be the end. He was beginning to grow cold about the
groin, when he uncovered his face, for he had covered
himself up, and said—they were his last words—he said:
Crito, I owe a cock to Asclepius; will you remember to
pay the debt? The debt shall be paid, said Crito; is there
anything else? There was no answer to this question; but
in a minute or two a movement was heard, and the attendants uncovered him; his eyes were set, and Crito
closed his eyes and mouth.

Such was the end, Echecrates, of our friend; concerning whom I may truly say, that of all the men of his time
whom I have known, he was the wisest and justest and
best.

From *Phaedo*. Translated by Benjamin Jowett.

o

THE ENGINEER

o

ARCHIMEDES

TZETZES

ARCHIMEDES the wise, the famous maker of engines, was a Syracusan by race, and worked at geometry till old age, surviving five-and-seventy-years; he reduced to his service many mechanical powers, and with his triple-pulley device, using only his left hand, he drew a vessel of fifty thousand medimni burden. Once, when Marcellus, the Roman general, was assaulting Syracuse by land and sea, first by his engines he drew up some merchant-vessels, lifted them up against the wall of Syracuse, and sent them in a heap again to the bottom, crews and all. When Marcellus had withdrawn his ships a little distance, the old man gave all the Syracusans power to lift stones large enough to load a wagon and, hurling them one after the other, to sink the ships. When Marcellus withdrew them a bow-shot, the old man constructed a kind of hexagonal mirror, and at an interval proportionate to the size of the mirror he set similar small mirrors with four edges, moved by links and by a form of hinge, and made it the centre of the sun's beams—its noon-tide beam, whether in summer or in mid-winter. Afterwards, when the beams were reflected in the mirror, a fearful kindling of fire was raised in the ships, and at the distance of a bow-shot he turned them into ashes. In this way did the old man prevail over Marcellus with his weapons. In his Doric dialect, and in its Syracusan variant, he declared: "If I have somewhere to stand, I will move the whole earth with my *charistion.*" Whether, as Diodorus asserts, Syracuse was betrayed and the citizens went in a body to Marcellus, or, as Dion tells, it was plundered by the Romans, while the citizens were keeping a night festival to Artemis, he died in this fashion at the hands of one of the Romans. He was stooping down, drawing some diagram in mechanics, when a Roman came up and began to drag him away to take him prisoner. But he, being wholly intent at the time on the diagram, and not perceiving who was tugging at him, said to the man: "Stand away, fellow, from my diagram." As the man continued pulling, he turned round and, realizing that he was a Roman, he cried, "Somebody give me one of my engines." But the Roman, scared, straightway slew him, a feeble old man but wonderful in his works.

From *Book of Histories.* Translated by Ivor Thomas.

PART THREE

NATURE

PHYSICS

○

THE FIRST SCIENCE

ARISTOTLE

BOOK IV

1. There is a science which investigates being as being
and the attributes which belong to this in virtue of its
own nature. Now this is not the same as any of the so-
called special sciences; for none of these others treats universally of being as being. They cut off a part of being
and investigate the attribute of this part; this is what the
mathematical sciences for instance do. Now since we
are seeking the first principles and the highest causes,
clearly there must be something to which these belong
in virtue of its own nature. If then those who sought the
elements of existing things were seeking these same principles, it is necessary that the elements must be elements
of being not by accident but just because it *is* being.
Therefore it is of being as being that we also must grasp
the first causes.

2. There are many senses in which a thing may be said
to "be," but all that "is" is related to one central point,
one definite kind of thing, and is not said to "be" by a
mere ambiguity. Everything which is healthy is related
to health, one thing in the sense that it preserves health,
another in the sense that it produces it, another in the
sense that it is a symptom of health, another because it is
capable of it. And that which is medical is relative to the

medical art, one thing being called medical because it possesses it, another because it is naturally adapted to it, another because it is a function of the medical art. And we shall find other words used similarly to these. So, too, there are many senses in which a thing is said to be, but all refer to one starting-point; some things are said to be because they are substances, others because they are affections of substance, others because they are a process towards substance, or destructions or privations or qualities of substance, or productive or generative of substance, or of things which are relative to substance, or negations of one of these things or of substance itself. It is for this reason that we say even of non-being that it *is* non-being. As, then, there is one science which deals with all healthy things, the same applies in the other cases also. For not only in the case of things which have one common notion does the investigation belong to one science, but also in the case of things which are related to one common nature; for even these in a sense have one common notion. It is clear then that it is the work of one science also to study the things that are, *qua* being.—But everywhere science deals chiefly with that which is primary, and on which the other things depend, and in virtue of which they get their names. If, then, this is substance, it will be of substances that the philosopher must grasp the principles and the causes.

Now for each one class of things, as there is one perception, so there is one science, as for instance grammar, being one science, investigates all articulate sounds. Hence to investigate all the species of being *qua* being is the work of a science which is generically one, and to investigate the several species is the work of the specific parts of the science.

If, now, being and unity are the same and are one thing in the sense that they are implied in one another as principle and cause are, not in the sense that they are explained by the same definition (though it makes no difference even if we suppose them to be like that—in fact this would even strengthen our case); for "one man" and "man" are the same thing, and so are "existent man" and "man," and the doubling of the words in "one man and one *existent* man" does not express anything different (it is clear that the two things are not separated either in coming to be or in ceasing to be); and similarly "*one* existent man" adds nothing to "existent man," so that it is obvious that the addition in these cases means the same thing, and unity is nothing apart from being; and if, further, the substance of each thing is one in no merely accidental way, and similarly is from its very nature something that *is:*—all this being so, there must be exactly as many species of being as of unity. And to investigate the essence of these is the work of a science which is generically one—I mean, for instance, the discussion of the same and the similar and the other concepts of this sort; and nearly all contraries may be referred to this origin; let us take them as having been investigated in the "Selection of Contraries."

And there are as many parts of philosophy as there are kinds of substance, so that there must necessarily be among them a first philosophy and one which follows this. For being falls immediately into genera; for which reason the sciences too will correspond to these genera. For the philosopher is like the mathematician, as that word is used; for mathematics also has parts, and there is a first and a second science and other successive ones within the sphere of mathematics.

Now since it is the work of one science to investigate opposites, and plurality is opposed to unity—and it belongs to one science to investigate the negation and the privation because in both cases we are really investigating the one thing of which the negation or the privation is a negation or privation (for we either say simply that that thing is not present, or that it is not present in some particular class; in the latter case difference is present over and above what is implied in negation; for negation means just the absence of the thing in question, while in privation there is also employed an underlying nature of which the privation is asserted):—in view of all these facts, the contraries of the concepts we named above, the other and the dissimilar and the unequal, and everything else which is derived either from these or from plurality and unity, must fall within the province of the science above named. And contrariety is one of these concepts; for contrariety is a kind of difference, and difference is a kind of otherness. Therefore, since there are many senses in which a thing is said to be one, these terms also will have many senses, but yet it belongs to one science to know them all; for a term belongs to different sciences not if it has different senses, but if it has not one meaning *and* its definitions cannot be referred to one central meaning. And since all things are referred to that which is primary, as for instance all things which are called one are referred to the primary one, we must say that this holds good also of the same and the other and of contraries in general; so that after distinguishing the various senses of each, we must then explain by reference to what is primary in the case of each of the predicates in question, saying how they are related to it; for some will be called what they are called because they possess it, others because they produce it, and others in other such ways.

It is evident, then, that it belongs to one science to be able to give an account of these concepts as well as of substance (this was one of the questions in our book of problems), and that it is the function of the philosopher to be able to investigate all things. For if it is not the function of the philosopher, who is it who will inquire whether Socrates and Socrates seated are the same thing, or whether one thing has one contrary, or what contrariety is, or how many meanings it has? And similarly with all other such questions. Since, then, these are essential modifications of unity *qua* unity and of being *qua* being, not *qua* numbers or lines or fire, it is clear that it belongs to this science to investigate both the essence of these concepts and their properties. And those who study these properties err not by leaving the sphere of philosophy, but by forgetting that substance, of which they have no correct idea, is prior to these other things. For number *qua* number has peculiar attributes, such as oddness and evenness, commensurability and equality, excess and defect, and these belong to numbers either in themselves or in relation to one another. And similarly the solid and the motionless and that which is in motion and the weightless and that which has weight have other peculiar properties. So too there are certain properties peculiar to being as such, and it is about these that the philosopher has to investigate the truth.—An indication of this may be mentioned:—dialecticians and sophists assume the same guise as the philosopher, for sophistic is Wisdom which exists only in semblance, and dialecticians embrace all things in their dialectic, and being is common to all things; but evidently their dialectic embraces these subjects because these are proper to philosophy.—For sophistic and dialectic turn on the same class of things as philosophy, but this differs from dialectic in the nature of the faculty required and from sophistic in respect of the purpose of the philosophic life. Dialectic is merely critical where philosophy claims to know, and sophistic is what appears to be philosophy but is not.

Again, in the list of contraries one of the two columns is privative, and all contraries are reducible to being and non-being, and to unity and plurality, as for instance rest belongs to unity and movement to plurality. And nearly all thinkers agree that being and substance are composed of contraries; at least all name contraries as their first principles—some name odd and even, some hot and cold, some limit and the unlimited, some love and strife. And all the others as well are evidently reducible to unity and plurality (this reduction we must take for granted), and the principles stated by other thinkers fall entirely under these as their genera. It is obvious then from these considerations too that it belongs to one science to examine being *qua* being. For all things are either contraries or composed of contraries, and unity and plurality are the starting-points of all contraries. And these belong to one science, whether they have or have not one single meaning. Probably the truth is that they have not; yet even if "one" has several meanings, the other meanings will be related to the primary meaning (and similarly in the case of the contraries), even if being or unity is not a universal and the same in every instance or is not separable from the particular instances (as in fact it probably is not; the unity is in some cases that of common reference, in some cases that of serial succession). And for this reason it does not belong to the geometer to inquire what is contrariety or completeness or unity or being or the same or the other, but only to presuppose these concepts and reason from this starting-point.—Obviously then it is the work of one science to examine being *qua* being, and the attributes which belong to it *qua* being, and the same science will examine not only substances but also their attributes, both those above named and the concepts "prior" and "posterior," "genus" and "species," "whole" and "part," and the others of this sort.

3. We must state whether it belongs to one or to different sciences to inquire into the truths which are in mathematics called axioms, and into substance. Evidently, the inquiry into these also belongs to one science, and that the science of the philosopher; for these truths hold good for everything that is, and not for some special genus apart from others. And all men use them, because they are true of being *qua* being and each genus has being. But men use them just so far as to satisfy their purposes; that is, as far as the genus to which their demonstrations refer extends. Therefore since these truths clearly hold good for all things *qua* being (for this is what is common to them), to him who studies being *qua* being belongs the inquiry into these as well. And for this reason no one who is conducting a special inquiry tries to say anything about their truth or falsity— neither the geometer nor the arithmetician. Some natural philosophers indeed have done so, and their procedure was intelligible enough; for they thought that they alone were inquiring about the whole of nature and about being. But since there is one kind of thinker who is above even the natural philosopher (for nature is only one particular genus of being), the discussion of these truths also will belong to him whose inquiry is universal and deals with primary substance. Physics also is a kind of Wisdom, but it is not the first kind.—And the attempts of some of those who discuss the terms on which truth should be accepted, are due to a want of training in logic; for they should know these things already when they come to a special study, and not be inquiring into them while they are listening to lectures on it.

Evidently then it belongs to the philosopher, i. e. to him who is studying the nature of all substance, to inquire also into the principles of syllogism. But he who knows best about each genus must be able to state the most certain principles of his subject, so that he whose subject is existing things *qua* existing must be able to state the most certain principles of all things. This is the philosopher, and the most certain principle of all is that regarding which it is impossible to be mistaken; for such a principle must be both the best known (for all men may be mistaken about things which they do not know), and non-hypothetical. For a principle which every one must have who understands anything that is, is not a hypothesis; and that which every one must know who knows anything, he must already have when he comes to a special study. Evidently then such a principle is the most certain of all; which principle this is, let us proceed to say. It is, that the same attribute cannot at the same time belong and not belong to the same subject and in the same respect; we must presuppose, to guard against dialectical objections, any further qualifications which might be added. This, then, is the most certain of all principles, since it answers to the definition given above. For it is impossible for any one to believe the same thing to be and not to be, as some think Heraclitus says. For what a man says, he does not necessarily believe; and if it is impossible that contrary attributes should belong at the same time to the same subject (the usual qualifications must be presupposed in this premiss too), and if an opinion which contradicts another is contrary to it, obviously it is impossible for the same man at the same time to believe the same thing to be and not to be; for if a man were mistaken on this point he would have contrary opinions at the same time. It is for this reason that all who are carrying out a demonstration reduce it to this as an ultimate belief; for this is naturally the starting-point even for all the other axioms.

BOOK VI

1. We are seeking the principles and the causes of the things that are, and obviously of them *qua* being. For, while there is a cause of health and of good condition, and the objects of mathematics have first principles and elements and causes, and in general every science which is ratiocinative or at all involves reasoning deals with causes and principles, more or less precise, all these sciences mark off some particular being—some genus, and inquire into this, but not into being simply nor *qua* being, nor do they offer any discussion of the essence of the things of which they treat; but starting from the essence—some making it plain to the senses, others assuming it as a hypothesis—they then demonstrate, more or less cogently, the essential attributes of the genus with which they deal. It is obvious, therefore, that such an induction yields no demonstration of substance or of the essence, but some other way of exhibiting it. And similarly the sciences omit the question whether the genus with which they deal exists or does not exist, because it belongs to the same kind of thinking to show what it is and that it is.

And since natural science, like other sciences, is in fact about one class of being, i. e. to that sort of substance which has the principle of its movement and rest present in itself, evidently it is neither practical nor productive. For in the case of things made the principle is in the maker—it is either reason or art or some faculty, while in the case of things done it is in the doer—viz. will, for that which is done and that which is willed are the same. Therefore, if all thought is either practical or productive or theoretical, physics must be a theoretical science, but it will theorize about such being as admits of being moved, and about substance-as-defined for the most part only as not separable from matter. Now, we must not fail to notice the mode of being of the essence and of its definition, for, without this, inquiry is but idle. Of things defined, i. e. of "whats," some are like "snub," and some like "concave." And these differ because "snub" is bound up with matter (for what is snub is a concave *nose*), while concavity is independent of perceptible matter. If then all natural things are analogous to the snub in their nature—e. g. nose, eye, face, flesh, bone, and, in general, animal; leaf, root, bark, and, in general, plant (for none of these can be defined without reference to movement—they always have matter), it is clear how we must seek and define the "what" in the case of natural objects, and also that it belongs to the student of nature to study even soul in a certain sense, i. e. so much of it as is not independent of matter.

That physics, then, is a theoretical science, is plain from these considerations. Mathematics also, however, is theoretical; but whether its objects are immovable and separable from matter, is not at present clear; still, it is clear that *some* mathematical theorems *consider* them *qua* immovable and *qua* separable from matter. But if there is something which is eternal and immovable and separable, clearly the knowledge of it belongs to a theoretical science—not, however, to physics (for physics deals with certain movable things) nor to mathematics, but to a science prior to both. For physics deals with things which exist separately but are not immovable, and some parts of mathematics deal with things which are immovable but presumably do not exist separately, but as embodied in matter; while the first science deals with things which both exist separately and are immovable. Now all causes must be eternal, but especially these; for they are the causes that operate on so much of the divine as appears to us. There must, then, be three theoretical philosophies, mathematics, physics, and what we may call theology, since it is obvious that if the divine is present anywhere, it is present in things of this sort. And the highest science must deal with the highest genus. Thus, while the theoretical sciences are more to be desired than the other sciences, this is more to be desired than the other theoretical sciences. For one might raise the question whether first philosophy is universal, or deals with one genus, i. e. some one kind of being; for not even the mathematical sciences are all alike in this respect—geometry and astronomy deal with a certain particular kind of thing, while universal mathematics applies alike to all. We answer that if there is no substance other than those which are formed by nature, natural science will be the first science; but if there is an immovable substance, the science of this must be prior and must be first philosophy, and universal in this way, because it is first. And it will belong to this to consider being *qua* being—both what it is and the attributes which belong to it *qua* being.

From *Metaphysics*, Book IV, chaps. 1–3; Book VI, chap. 1.
Translated by W. D. Ross.

O

NATURE

ARISTOTLE

BOOK II

1. Of things that exist, some exist by nature, some from other causes.

"By nature" the animals and their parts exist, and the

plants and the simple bodies (earth, fire, air, water)—
for we say that these and the like exist "by nature."

All the things mentioned present a feature in which
they differ from things which are *not* constituted by nature. Each of them has *within itself* a principle of motion and of stationariness (in respect of place, or of
growth and decrease, or by way of alteration). On the
other hand, a bed and a coat and anything else of that
sort, *qua* receiving these designations—i. e. in so far as
they are products of art—have no innate impulse to
change. But in so far as they happen to be composed of
stone or of earth or of a mixture of the two, they *do* have
such an impulse, and just to that extent—which seems
to indicate that *nature is a source or cause of being
moved and of being at rest in that to which it belongs
primarily,* in virtue of itself and not in virtue of a concomitant attribute.

I say "not in virtue of a concomitant attribute," because (for instance) a man who is a doctor might cure
himself. Nevertheless it is not in so far as he is a patient
that he possesses the art of medicine: it merely has happened that the same man is doctor and patient—and
that is why these attributes are not always found together. So it is with all other artificial products. None of
them has in itself the source of its own production. But
while in some cases (for instance houses and the other
products of manual labour) that principle is in something else external to the thing, in others—those which
may cause a change in themselves in virtue of a concomitant attribute—it lies in the things themselves (but not
in virtue of what they are).

"Nature" then is what has been stated. Things "have a
nature" which have a principle of this kind. Each of
them is a substance; for it is a subject, and nature always
implies a subject in which it inheres.

The term "according to nature" is applied to all these things and also to the attributes which belong to them in virtue of what they are, for instance the property of fire to be carried upwards—which is not a "nature" nor "has a nature" but is "by nature" or "according to nature."

What nature is, then, and the meaning of the terms "by nature" and "according to nature," has been stated. *That* nature exists, it would be absurd to try to prove; for it is obvious that there are many things of this kind, and to prove what is obvious by what is not is the mark of a man who is unable to distinguish what is self-evident from what is not. (This state of mind is clearly possible. A man blind from birth might reason about colours. Presumably therefore such persons must be talking about words without any thought to correspond.)

Some identify the nature or substance of a natural object with that immediate constituent of it which taken by itself is without arrangement, e. g. the wood is the "nature" of the bed, and the bronze the "nature" of the statue.

As an indication of this Antiphon points out that if you planted a bed and the rotting wood acquired the power of sending up a shoot, it would not be a bed that would come up, but *wood*—which shows that the arrangement in accordance with the rules of the art is merely an incidental attribute, whereas the real nature is the other, which, further, persists continuously through the process of making.

But if the material of each of these objects has itself the same relation to something else, say bronze (or gold) to water, bones (or wood) to earth and so on, *that* (they say) would be their nature and essence. Consequently some assert earth, others fire or air or water or some or all of these, to be the nature of the things that are. For whatever any one of them supposed to have this character—whether one thing or more than one thing—this or these he declared to be the whole of substance, all else being its affections, states, or dispositions. Every such thing they held to be eternal (for it could not pass into anything else), but other things to come into being and cease to be times without number.

This then is one account of "nature," namely that it is the immediate material substratum of things which have in themselves a principle of motion or change.

Another account is that "nature" is the shape or form which is specified in the definition of the thing.

For the word "nature" is applied to what is according to nature and the natural in the same way as "art" is applied to what is artistic or a work of art. We should not say in the latter case that there is anything artistic about a thing, if it is a bed only potentially, not yet having the form of a bed; nor should we call it a work of art. The same is true of natural compounds. What is potentially flesh or bone has not yet its own "nature," and does not exist "by nature," until it receives the form specified in the definition, which we name in defining what flesh or bone is. Thus in the second sense of "nature" it would be the shape or form (not separable except in statement) of things which have in themselves a source of motion. (The combination of the two, e. g. man, is not "nature" but "by nature" or "natural.")

The form indeed is "nature" rather than the matter; for a thing is more properly said to be what it is when it has attained to fulfilment than when it exists potentially. Again man is born from man, but not bed from bed. That is why people say that the figure is not the nature of a bed, but the wood is—if the bed sprouted not a bed but wood would come up. But even if the figure *is* art, then on the same principle the shape of man is his nature. For man is born from man.

We also speak of a thing's nature as being exhibited in the process of growth by which its nature is attained. The "nature" in this sense is not like "doctoring," which leads not to the art of doctoring but to health. Doctoring must start from the art, not lead to it. But it is not in this way that nature (in the one sense) is related to nature (in the other). What grows *qua* growing grows from something into something. Into what then does it grow? Not into that form which it arose but into that to which it tends. The shape then is nature.

"Shape" and "nature," it should be added, are used in two senses. For the privation too is in a way form. But whether in unqualified coming to be there is privation, i. e. a contrary to what comes to be, we must consider later.

2. We have distinguished, then, the different ways in which the term "nature" is used.

The next point to consider is how the mathematician differs from the physicist. Obviously physical bodies contain surfaces and volumes, lines and points, and these are the subject-matter of mathematics.

Further, is astronomy different from physics or a department of it? It seems absurd that the physicist should be supposed to know the nature of sun or moon, but not to know any of their essential attributes, particularly as the writers on physics obviously do discuss their shape also and whether the earth and the world are spherical or not.

Now the mathematician, though he too treats of these things, nevertheless does not treat of them as the limits of a physical body; nor does he consider the attributes indicated as the attributes of such bodies. That is why he separates them; for in thought they are separable from motion, and it makes no difference, nor does any falsity result, if they are separated. The holders of the theory of Forms do the same, though they are not aware of it; for they separate the objects of physics, which are less separable than those of mathematics. This becomes plain if one tries to state in each of the two cases the definitions of the things and of their attributes. "Odd" and "even," "straight" and "curved," and likewise "number," "line," and "figure," do not involve motion; not so "flesh" and "bone" and "man"—*these* are defined like "snub nose," not like "curved."

Similar evidence is supplied by the more physical of the branches of mathematics, such as optics, harmonics, and astronomy. These are in a way the converse of geometry. While geometry investigates physical lines but not *qua* physical, optics investigates mathematical lines, but *qua* physical, not *qua* mathematical.

Since "nature" has two senses, the form and the matter, we must investigate its objects as we would the essence of snubness. That is, such things are neither independent of matter nor can be defined in terms of matter only. Here too indeed one might raise a difficulty. Since there are two natures, with which is the physicist concerned? Or should he investigate the combination of the two? But if the combination of the two, then also each severally. Does it belong then to the same or to different sciences to know each severally?

If we look at the ancients, physics would seem to be concerned with the *matter*. (It was only very slightly that Empedocles and Democritus touched on the forms and the essence.)

But if on the other hand art imitates nature, and it is the part of the same discipline to know the form and the matter up to a point (e. g. the doctor has a knowledge of health and also of bile and phlegm, in which health is realized, and the builder both of the form of the house and of the matter, namely that it is bricks and beams, and so forth): if this is so, it would be the part of physics also to know nature in both its senses.

Again, "that for the sake of which," or the end, belongs to the same department of knowledge as the means. But the nature is the end or "that for the sake of which." For if a thing undergoes a continuous change and there is a stage which is last, this stage is the end or "that for the sake of which." (That is why the poet was carried away into making an absurd statement when he said "he has the end for the sake of which he was born." For not every stage that is last claims to be an end, but only that which is best.)

For the arts make their material (some simply "make" it, others make it serviceable), and we use everything as if it was there for our sake. (We also are in a sense an end. "That for the sake of which" has two senses: the distinction is made in our work *On Philosophy*.) The arts, therefore, which govern the matter and have knowledge are two, namely the art which uses the product and the art which directs the production of it. That is why the using art also is in a sense directive; but it differs in that it knows the form, whereas the art which is directive as being concerned with production knows the matter. For the helmsman knows and prescribes what sort of form a helm should have, the other from what wood it should be made and by means of what operations. In the products of art, however, we make the material with a view to the function, whereas in the products of nature the matter is there all along.

Again, matter is a relative term: to each form there corresponds a special matter. How far then must the physicist know the form or essence? Up to a point, perhaps, as the doctor must know sinew or the smith bronze (i. e. until he understands the purpose of each): and the physicist is concerned only with things whose forms are separable indeed, but do not exist apart from matter. Man is begotten by man and by the sun as well. The mode of existence and essence of the separable it is the business of the primary type of philosophy to define.

3. Now that we have established these distinctions, we must proceed to consider causes, their character and number. Knowledge is the object of our inquiry, and men do not think they know a thing till they have grasped the "why" of it (which is to grasp its primary cause). So clearly we too must do this as regards both coming to be and passing away and every kind of physical change, in order that, knowing their principles, we may try to refer to these principles each of our problems.

In one sense, then, (1) that out of which a thing comes to be and which persists, is called "cause," e. g. the bronze of the statue, the silver of the bowl, and the genera of which the bronze and the silver are species.

In another sense (2) the form or the archetype, i. e. the statement of the essence, and its genera, are called "causes" (e. g. of the octave the relation of 2 : 1, and generally number), and the parts in the definition.

Again (3) the primary source of the change or coming to rest; e. g. the man who gave advice is a cause, the father is cause of the child, and generally what makes of what is made and what causes change of what is changed.

Again (4) in the sense of end or "that for the sake of which" a thing is done, e. g. health is the cause of walking about. ("Why is he walking about?" we say. "To be healthy," and, having said that, we think we have assigned the cause.) The same is true also of all the intermediate steps which are brought about through the action of something else as means towards the end, e. g. reduction of flesh, purging, drugs, or surgical instruments are means towards health. All these things are "for the sake of" the end, though they differ from one another in that some are activities, others instruments.

This then perhaps exhausts the number of ways in which the term "cause" is used.

As the word has several senses, it follows that there are several causes of the same thing (not merely in virtue of a concomitant attribute), e. g. both the art of the sculptor and the bronze are causes of the statue. These are causes of the statue *qua* statue, not in virtue of anything else that it may be—only not in the same way, the one being the material cause, the other the cause whence the motion comes. Some things cause each other reciprocally, e. g. hard work causes fitness and *vice versa,* but again not in the same way, but the one as end, the other as the origin of change. Further the same thing is the cause of contrary results. For that which by its presence brings about one result is sometimes blamed for bringing about the contrary by its absence. Thus we ascribe the wreck of a ship to the absence of the pilot whose presence was the cause of its safety.

All the causes now mentioned fall into four familiar divisions. The letters are the causes of syllables, the material of artificial products, fire, &c., of bodies, the parts of the whole, and the premisses of the conclusion, in the sense of "that from which." Of these pairs the one set are causes in the sense of substratum, e. g. the parts, the other set in the sense of essence—the whole and the combination and the form. But the seed and the doctor and the adviser, and generally the maker, are all sources whence the change or stationariness originates, while the others are causes in the sense of the end or the good of the rest; for "that for the sake of which" means what is best and the end of the things that lead up to it. (Whether we say the "good itself" or the "apparent good" makes no difference.)

Such then is the number and nature of the kinds of cause.

Now the modes of causation are many, though when brought under heads they too can be reduced in number. For "cause" is used in many senses and even within the same kind one may be prior to another (e. g. the doctor and the expert are causes of health, the relation 2 : 1 and number of the octave), and always what is inclusive to what is particular. Another mode of causation is the incidental and its genera, e. g. in one way "Polyclitus," in another "sculptor" is the cause of a statue, because "being Polyclitus" and "sculptor" are incidentally conjoined. Also the classes in which the incidental attribute is included; thus "a man" could be said to be the cause of a statue or, generally, "a living creature." An incidental attribute too may be more or less remote, e. g. suppose that "a pale man" or "a musical man" were said to be the cause of the statue.

All causes, both proper and incidental, may be spoken of either as potential or as actual; e. g. the cause of a house being built is either "house-builder" or "house-builder building."

Similar distinctions can be made in the things of which the causes are causes, e. g. of "this statue" or of "statue" or of "image" generally, of "this bronze" or of "bronze" or of "material" generally. So too with the incidental attributes. Again we may use a complex expression for either and say, e. g., neither "Polyclitus" nor "sculptor" but "Polyclitus, sculptor."

All these various uses, however, come to six in number, under each of which again the usage is twofold. Cause means either what is particular or a genus, or an incidental attribute or a genus of that, and these either as a complex or each by itself; and all six either as actual or as potential. The difference is this much, that causes which are actually at work and particular exist and cease to exist simultaneously with their effect, e. g. this healing person with this being-healed person and that house-building man with that being-built house; but this is not always true of potential causes—the house and the house-builder do not pass away simultaneously.

In investigating the cause of each thing it is always necessary to seek what is most precise (as also in other things): thus man builds because he is a builder, and a builder builds in virtue of his art of building. This last cause then is prior: and so generally.

Further, generic effects should be assigned to generic causes, particular effects to particular causes, e. g. statue to sculptor, this statue to this sculptor; and powers are relative to possible effects, actually operating causes to things which are actually being effected.

This must suffice for our account of the number of causes and the modes of causation.

4. But chance also and spontaneity are reckoned among causes: many things are said both to be and to come to be as a result of chance and spontaneity. We must inquire therefore in what manner chance and spontaneity are present among the causes enumerated, and whether they are the same or different, and generally what chance and spontaneity are.

Some people[1] even question whether they are real or not. They say that nothing happens by chance, but that everything which we ascribe to chance or spontaneity has some definite cause, e. g. coming "by chance" into the market and finding there a man whom one wanted but did not expect to meet is due to one's wish to go and buy in the market. Similarly in other cases of chance it is always possible, they maintain, to find something which is the cause; but not chance, for if chance were real, it would seem strange indeed, and the question might be raised, why on earth none of the wise men of old in speaking of the causes of generation and decay took account of chance; whence it would seem that they too did not believe that anything is by chance. But there is a further circumstance that is surprising. Many things both come to be and are by chance and spontaneity, and although all know that each of them can be ascribed to some cause (as the old argument said which denied chance), nevertheless they speak of some of these things as happening by chance and others not. For this reason also they ought to have at least referred to the matter in some way or other.

Certainly the early physicists found no place for chance among the causes which they recognized—love, strife, mind, fire, or the like. This is strange, whether they supposed that there is no such thing as chance or whether they thought there is but omitted to mention it—and that too when they sometimes used it, as Empedocles does when he says that the air is not always separated into the highest region, but "as it may chance." At any rate he says in his cosmogony that "it happened to run that way at that time, but it often ran otherwise." He tells us also that most of the parts of animals came to be by chance.

---

[1] *Apparently Democritus is meant.*

There are some too who ascribe this heavenly sphere and all the worlds to spontaneity. They say that the vortex arose spontaneously, i. e. the motion that separated and arranged in its present order all that exists. This statement might well cause surprise. For they are asserting that chance is not responsible for the existence or generation of animals and plants, nature or mind or something of the kind being the cause of them (for it is not any chance thing that comes from a given seed but an olive from one kind and a man from another); and yet at the same time they assert that the heavenly sphere and the divinest of visible things arose spontaneously, having no such cause as is assigned to animals and plants. Yet if this is so, it is a fact which deserves to be dwelt upon, and something might well have been said about it. For besides the other absurdities of the statement, it is the more absurd that people should make it when they see nothing coming to be spontaneously in the heavens, but much happening by chance among the things which as they say are not due to chance; whereas we should have expected exactly the opposite.

Others[1] there are who, indeed, believe that chance is a cause, but that it is inscrutable to human intelligence, as being a divine thing and full of mystery.

Thus we must inquire what chance and spontaneity are, whether they are the same or different, and how they fit into our division of causes.

5. First then we observe that some things always come to pass in the same way, and others for the most part. It is clearly of neither of these that chance is said to be the cause, nor can the "effect of chance" be identified with any of the things that come to pass by necessity

[1] Democritus.

and always, or for the most part. But as there is a third class of events besides these two—events which all say are "by chance"—it is plain that there is such a thing as chance and spontaneity; for we know that things of this kind are due to chance and that things due to chance are of this kind.

But, secondly, some events are for the sake of something, others not. Again, some of the former class are in accordance with deliberate intention, others not, but both are in the class of things which are for the sake of something. Hence it is clear that even among the things which are outside the necessary and the normal, there are some in connexion with which the phrase "for the sake of something" is applicable. (Events that are for the sake of something include whatever may be done as a result of thought or of nature.) Things of this kind, then, when they come to pass incidentally are said to be "by chance." For just as a thing is something either in virtue of itself or incidentally, so may it be a cause. For instance, the housebuilding faculty is in virtue of itself the cause of a house, whereas the pale or the musical [1] is the incidental cause. That which is *per se* cause of the effect is determinate, but the incidental cause is indeterminable, for the possible attributes of an individual are innumerable. To resume then; when a thing of this kind comes to pass among events which are for the sake of something, it is said to be spontaneous or by chance. (The distinction between the two must be made later—for the present it is sufficient if it is plain that both are in the sphere of things done for the sake of something.)

Example: A man is engaged in collecting subscriptions for a feast. He would have gone to such and such a place for the purpose of getting the money, if he had

---

[1] *Incidental attributes of the housebuilder.*

known. He actually went there for another purpose, and it was only incidentally that he got his money by going there; and this was not due to the fact that he went there as a rule or necessarily, nor is the end effected (getting the money) a cause present in himself—it belongs to the class of things that are intentional and the result of intelligent deliberation. It is when these conditions are satisfied that the man is said to have gone "by chance." If he had gone of deliberate purpose and for the sake of this—if he always or normally went there when he was collecting payments—he would not be said to have gone "by chance."

It is clear then that chance is an incidental cause in the sphere of those actions for the sake of something which involve purpose. Intelligent reflection, then, and chance are in the same sphere, for purpose implies intelligent reflection.

It is necessary, no doubt, that the causes of what comes to pass by chance be indefinite; and that is why chance is supposed to belong to the class of the indefinite and to be inscrutable to man, and why it might be thought that, in a way, nothing occurs by chance. For all these statements are correct, because they are well grounded. Things *do*, in a way, occur by chance, for they occur incidentally and chance is an *incidental cause*. But strictly it is not the *cause*—without qualification—of anything; for instance, a housebuilder is the cause of a house; incidentally, a flute-player may be so.

And the causes of the man's coming and getting the money (when he did not come for the sake of that) are innumerable. He may have wished to see somebody or been following somebody or avoiding somebody, or may have gone to see a spectacle. Thus to say that chance is a thing contrary to rule is correct. For "rule" applies to what is always true or true for the most part, whereas chance belongs to a third type of event. Hence, to conclude, since causes of this kind are indefinite, chance too is indefinite. (Yet in some cases one might raise the question whether *any* incidental fact might be the cause of the chance occurrence, e. g. of health the fresh air or the sun's heat may be the cause, but having had one's hair cut *cannot;* for some incidental causes are more relevant to the effect than others.)

Chance or fortune is called "good" when the result is good, "evil" when it is evil. The terms "good fortune" and "ill fortune" are used when either result is of considerable magnitude. Thus one who comes within an ace of some great evil or great good is said to be fortunate or unfortunate. The mind affirms the presence of the attribute, ignoring the hair's breadth of difference. Further, it is with reason that good fortune is regarded as unstable; for chance is unstable, as none of the things which result from it can be invariable or normal.

Both are then, as I have said, incidental causes—both chance and spontaneity—in the sphere of things which are capable of coming to pass not necessarily, nor normally, and with reference to such of these as might come to pass for the sake of something.

6. They differ in that "spontaneity" is the wider term. Every result of chance is from what is spontaneous, but not everything that is from what is spontaneous is from chance.

Chance and what results from chance are appropriate to agents that are capable of good fortune and of moral action generally. Therefore necessarily chance is in the sphere of moral actions. This is indicated by the fact that good fortune is thought to be the same, or nearly the same, as happiness, and happiness to be a kind of moral action, since it is well-doing. Hence what is not capable of moral action cannot do anything by chance. Thus an inanimate thing or a lower animal or a child cannot do anything by chance, because it is incapable of deliberate intention; nor can "good fortune" or "ill fortune" be ascribed to them, except metaphorically, as Protarchus, for example, said that the stones of which altars are made are fortunate because they are held in honour, while their fellows are trodden under foot. Even these things, however, can in a way be affected by chance, when one who is dealing with them does something to them by chance, but not otherwise.

The spontaneous on the other hand is found both in the lower animals and in many inanimate objects. We say, for example, that the horse came "spontaneously," because, though his coming saved him, he did not come for the sake of safety. Again, the tripod fell "of itself," because, though when it fell it stood on its feet so as to serve for a seat, it did not fall for the sake of that.

Hence it is clear that events which (1) belong to the general class of things that may come to pass for the sake of something, (2) do not come to pass for the sake of what actually results, and (3) have an external cause, may be described by the phrase "from spontaneity." These "spontaneous" events are said to be "from chance" if they have the further characteristics of being the objects of deliberate intention and due to agents capable of that mode of action. This is indicated by the phrase "in vain," which is used when A, which is for the sake of B, does not result in B. For instance, taking a walk is for the sake of evacuation of the bowels; if this does not follow after walking, we say that we have walked "in vain" and that the walking was "vain." This implies that what is naturally the means to an end is "in vain," when it does not effect the end towards which it was the natural means—for it would be absurd for a man to say that he had bathed in vain because the sun was not eclipsed, since the one was not done with a view to the other. Thus the spontaneous is even according to its derivation the case in which the thing itself happens in vain. The stone that struck the man did not fall for the purpose of striking him; therefore it fell spontaneously, because it might have fallen by the action of an agent and for the purpose of striking. The difference between spontaneity and what results by chance is greatest in things that come to be by nature; for when anything comes to be contrary to nature, we do not say that it came to be by chance, but by spontaneity. Yet strictly this too is different from the spontaneous proper; for the cause of the latter is external, that of the former internal.

We have now explained what chance is and what spontaneity is, and in what they differ from each other. Both belong to the mode of causation "source of change," for either some natural or some intelligent agent is always the cause; but in this sort of causation the number of possible causes is infinite.

Spontaneity and chance are causes of effects which, though they might result from intelligence or nature, have in fact been caused by something *incidentally*. Now since nothing which is incidental is prior to what is *per se*, it is clear that no incidental cause can be prior to a cause *per se*. Spontaneity and chance, therefore, are posterior to intelligence and nature. Hence, however true it may be that the heavens are due to spontaneity, it will still be true that intelligence and nature will be prior causes of this All and of many things in it besides.

7. It is clear then that there are causes, and that the number of them is what we have stated. The number is the same as that of the things comprehended under the

question "why." The "why" is referred ultimately either (1), in things which do not involve motion, e. g. in mathematics, to the "what" (to the definition of "straight line" or "commensurable," &c.), or (2) to what initiated a motion, e. g. "why did they go to war?—because there had been a raid"; or (3) we are inquiring "for the sake of what?"—"that they may rule"; or (4), in the case of things that come into being, we are looking for the matter. The causes, therefore, are these and so many in number.

Now, the causes being four, it is the business of the physicist to know about them all, and if he refers his problems back to all of them, he will assign the "why" in the way proper to his science—the matter, the form, the mover, "that for the sake of which." The last three often coincide; for the "what" and "that for the sake of which" are one, while the primary source of motion is the same in species as these (for man generates man), and so too, in general, are all things which cause movement by being themselves moved; and such as are not of this kind are no longer inside the province of physics, for they cause motion not by possessing motion or a source of motion in themselves, but being themselves incapable of motion. Hence there are three branches of study, one of things which are incapable of motion, the second of things in motion, but indestructible, the third of destructible things.

The question "why," then, is answered by reference to the matter, to the form, and to the primary moving cause. For in respect of coming to be it is mostly in this last way that causes are investigated—"what comes to be after what? what was the primary agent or patient?" and so at each step of the series.

Now the principles which cause motion in a physical way are two, of which one is not physical, as it has no principle of motion in itself. Of this kind is whatever causes movement, not being itself moved, such as (1) that which is completely unchangeable, the primary reality, and (2) the essence of that which is coming to be, i. e. the form; for this is the end or "that for the sake of which." Hence since nature is for the sake of something, we must know this cause also. We must explain the "why" in all the senses of the term, namely, (1) that from this that will necessarily result ("from this" either without qualification or in most cases); (2) that "this must be so if that is to be so" (as the conclusion presupposes the premises); (3) that this was the essence of the thing; and (4) because it is better thus (not without qualification, but with reference to the essential nature in each case).

8. We must explain then (1) that Nature belongs to the class of causes which act for the sake of something; (2) about the necessary and its place in physical problems, for all writers ascribe things to this cause, arguing that since the hot and the cold, &c., are of such and such a kind, therefore certain things *necessarily* are and come to be—and if they mention any other cause (one[1] his "friendship and strife," another[2] his "mind"), it is only to touch on it, and then good-bye to it.

A difficulty presents itself: why should not nature work, not for the sake of something, nor because it is better so, but just as the sky rains, not in order to make the corn grow, but of necessity? What is drawn up must cool, and what has been cooled must become water and descend, the result of this being that the corn grows. Similarly if a man's crop is spoiled on the threshing-floor, the rain did not fall for the sake of this—in order

---

[1] *Empedocles.*
[2] *Anaxagoras.*

that the crop might be spoiled—but that result just followed. Why then should it not be the same with the parts in nature, e. g. that our teeth should come up *of necessity*—the front teeth sharp, fitted for tearing, the molars broad and useful for grinding down the food—since they did not arise for this end, but it was merely a coincident result; and so with all other parts in which we suppose that there is purpose? Wherever then all the parts came about just what they would have been if they had come to be for an end, such things survived, being organized spontaneously in a fitting way; whereas those which grew otherwise perished and continue to perish, as Empedocles says his "man-faced ox-progeny" did.

Such are the arguments (and others of the kind) which may cause difficulty on this point. Yet it is impossible that this should be the true view. For teeth and all other natural things either invariably or normally come about in a given way; but of not one of the results of chance or spontaneity is this true. We do not ascribe to chance or mere coincidence the frequency of rain in winter, but frequent rain in summer we do; nor heat in the dog-days, but only if we have it in winter. If then, it is agreed that things are either the result of coincidence or for an end, and these cannot be the result of coincidence or spontaneity, it follows that they must be for an end; and that such things are all due to nature even the champions of the theory which is before us would agree. Therefore action for an end is present in things which come to be and are by nature.

Further, where a series has a completion, all the preceding steps are for the sake of that. Now surely as in intelligent action, so in nature; and as in nature, so it is in each action, if nothing interferes. Now intelligent action is for the sake of an end; therefore the nature of things also is so. Thus if a house, e. g., had been a thing made by nature, it would have been made in the same way as it is now by art; and if things made by nature were made also by art, they would come to be in the same way as by nature. Each step then in the series is for the sake of the next; and generally art partly completes what nature cannot bring to a finish, and partly imitates her. If, therefore, artificial products are for the sake of an end, so clearly also are natural products. The relation of the later to the earlier terms of the series is the same in both.

This is most obvious in the animals other than man: they make things neither by art nor after inquiry or deliberation. Wherefore people discuss whether it is by intelligence or by some other faculty that these creatures work—spiders, ants, and the like. By gradual advance in this direction we come to see clearly that in plants too that is produced which is conducive to the end—leaves, e. g. grow to provide shade for the fruit. If then it is both by nature and for an end that the swallow makes its nest and the spider its web, and plants grow leaves for the sake of the fruit and send their roots down (not up) for the sake of nourishment, it is plain that this kind of cause is operative in things which come to be and are by nature. And since "nature" means two things, the matter and the form, of which the latter is the end, and since all the rest is for the sake of the end, the form must be the cause in the sense of "that for the sake of which."

Now mistakes come to pass even in the operations of art: the grammarian makes a mistake in writing and the doctor pours out the wrong dose. Hence clearly mistakes are possible in the operations of nature also. If then in art there are cases in which what is rightly produced serves a purpose, and if where mistakes occur there was a purpose in what was attempted, only it was not attained, so must it be also in natural products, and monstrosities will be failures in the purposive effort. Thus in the original combinations the "ox-progeny" if they failed to reach a determinate end must have arisen through the corruption of some principle corresponding to what is now the seed.

Further, seed must have come into being first, and not straightway the animals: the words "whole-natured first . . ." [1] must have meant seed.

Again, in plants too we find the relation of means to end, though the degree of organization is less. Were there then in plants also "olive-headed vine-progeny," like the "man-headed ox-progeny," or not? An absurd suggestion; yet there must have been, if there were such things among animals.

Moreover, among the seeds anything must have come to be at random. But the person who asserts this entirely does away with "nature" and what exists "by nature." For those things are natural which, by a continuous movement originated from an internal principle, arrive at some completion: the same completion is not reached from every principle; nor any chance completion, but always the tendency in each is towards the same end, if there is no impediment.

The end and the means towards it may come about by chance. We say, for instance, that a stranger has come by chance, paid the ransom, and gone away, when he does so as if he had come for that purpose, though it was not for that that he came. This is incidental, for chance is an incidental cause, as I remarked before. But when an event takes place always or for the most part, it is not incidental or by chance. In natural products the sequence is invariable, if there is no impediment.

It is absurd to suppose that purpose is not present

---

[1] *Empedocles*, Fr. 62. 4.

because we do not observe the agent deliberating. Art does not deliberate. If the ship-building art were in the wood, it would produce the same results *by nature*. If, therefore, purpose is present in art, it is present also in nature. The best illustration is a doctor doctoring himself: nature is like that.

It is plain then that nature is a cause, a cause that operates for a purpose.

9. As regards what is "of necessity," we must ask whether the necessity is "hypothetical," or "simple" as well. The current view places what is of necessity in the process of production, just as if one were to suppose that the wall of a house necessarily comes to be because what is heavy is naturally carried downwards and what is light to the top, wherefore the stones and foundations take the lowest place, with earth above because it is lighter, and wood at the top of all as being the lightest. Whereas, though the wall does not come to be *without* these, it is not *due* to these, except as its material cause: it comes to be for the sake of sheltering and guarding certain things. Similarly in all other things which involve production for an end; the product cannot come to be without things which have a necessary nature, but it is not due to these (except as its material); it comes to be for an end. For instance, why is a saw such as it is? To effect so-and-so and for the sake of so-and-so. This end, however, cannot be realized unless the saw is made of iron. It is, therefore, necessary for it to be of iron, *if* we are to have a saw and perform the operation of sawing. What is necessary then, is necessary *on a hypothesis;* it is not a result necessarily determined by antecedents. Necessity is in the matter, while "that for the sake of which" is in the definition.

Necessity in mathematics is in a way similar to necessity in things which come to be through the operation of nature. Since a straight line is what it is, it is necessary that the angles of a triangle should equal two right angles. But not conversely; though if the angles are *not* equal to two right angles, then the straight line is not what it is either. But in things which come to be for an end, the reverse is true. If the end is to exist or does exist, that also which precedes it will exist or does exist; otherwise just as there, if the conclusion is not true, the premiss will not be true, so here the end or "that for the sake of which" will not exist. For this too is itself a starting-point, but of the reasoning, not of the action; while in mathematics the starting-point is the starting-point of the reasoning only, as there is no action. If then there is to be a house, such-and-such things must be made or be there already or exist, or generally the matter relative to the end, bricks and stones if it is a house. But the end is not due to these except as the matter, nor will it come to exist because of them. Yet if they do not exist at all, neither will the house, or the saw—the former in the absence of stones, the latter in the absence of iron—just as in the other case the premisses will not be true, if the angles of the triangle are not equal to two right angles.

The necessary in nature, then, is plainly what we call by the name of matter, and the changes in it. Both causes must be stated by the physicist, but especially the end; for that is the cause of the matter, not *vice versa;* and the end is "that for the sake of which," and the beginning starts from the definition or essence; as in artificial products, since a house is of such-and-such a kind, certain things must *necessarily* come to be or be there already, or since health is this, these things must necessarily come to be or be there already. Similarly if man is this, then these; if these, then those. Perhaps the necessary is present also in the definition. For if one defines the operation of sawing as being a certain kind of dividing, then this cannot come about unless the saw has teeth of a certain kind; and these cannot be unless it is of iron. For in the definition too there are some parts that are, as it were, its matter.

From *Physics*, Book II, chaps. 1–9.
Translated by R. P. Hardie and R. K. Gaye.

o

MATHEMATICS

o

NUMBER AND PROPORTION

EUCLID

FIRST PRINCIPLES

Definitions

1. A *unit* is that in virtue of which each of the things that exist is called one.

2. A *number* is a multitude composed of units.

3. A number is a *part* of a number, the less of the greater, when it measures the greater.

4. But *parts*, when it does not measure it.

5. The greater number is a *multiple* of the less when it is measured by the less.

6. An *even number* is one that is divisible into two equal parts.

7. An *odd number* is one that is not divisible into two equal parts, or that differs from an even number by a unit.

8. An *even-times even number* is one that is measured by an even number according to an even number.

9. An *even-times-odd number* is one that is measured by an even number according to an odd number.

[10. An *odd-times even number* is one that is measured by an odd number according to an even number.]

11. An *odd-times odd number* is one that is measured by an odd number according to an odd number.

12. A *prime number* is one that is measured by the unit alone.

13. Numbers *prime to one another* are those which are measured by a unit alone as a common measure.

14. A *composite number* is one that is measured by some number.

15. Numbers *composite to one another* are those which are measured by some number as a common measure.

16. A number is said to *multiply* a number when that which is multiplied is added to itself as many times as there are units in the other, and so some number is produced.

17. And when two numbers have multiplied each other so as to make some number, the resulting number is called *plane*, and its sides are the numbers which have multiplied each other.

18. And when three numbers have multiplied each other so as to make some number, the resulting number is *solid*, and its sides are the numbers which have multiplied each other.

19. A *square number* is equal multiplied by equal, or one that is contained by two equal numbers.

20. And a *cube* is equal multiplied by equal and again by equal, or a number that is contained by three equal numbers.

21. Numbers are *proportional* when the first is the

same multiple, or the same part, or the same parts, of the second as the third is of the fourth.

22. *Similar plane* and *solid* numbers are those which have their sides proportional.

23. A *perfect number* is one that is equal to [the sum of] its own parts.

Common Notions

1. Things which are equal to the same thing are equal one to another.

2. If equals are added to equals, the wholes are equal.

3. If equals are substracted from equals, the remainders are equal.

7. Things which coincide with one another are equal one to another.

8. The whole is greater than the part.

THEORY OF PROPORTION

Definitions

1. A magnitude is a *part* of a magnitude, the less of the greater, when it measures the greater.

2. The greater is a multiple of the less when it is measured by the less.

3. A *ratio* is a sort of relation in respect of size between two magnitudes of the same kind.

4. Magnitudes are said to have a ratio one to another which are capable, when multiplied, of exceeding one another.

5. Magnitudes are said to be in the same ratio, the first to the second and the third to the fourth, when, if any equimultiples whatever be taken of the first and third, and any equimultiples whatever of the second and fourth. the former equimultiples alike exceed, are alike

equal to, or alike fall short of, the latter equimultiples respectively taken in corresponding order.

6. Let magnitudes which have the same ratio be called *proportional*.

7. When, of the equimultiples, the multiple of the first magnitude exceeds the multiple of the second, but the multiple of the third does not exceed the multiple of the fourth, then the first is said *to have a greater ratio* to the second than the third has to the fourth.

8. A proportion in three terms is the least possible.

9. When three magnitudes are proportional, the first is said to have to the third the *duplicate ratio* of that which it has to the second.

10. When four magnitudes are proportional the first is said to have to the fourth the *triplicate* ratio of that which it has to the second, and so on continually, whatever the proportion.

11. The term *corresponding magnitudes* is used of antecedents in relation to antecedents and of consequents in relation to consequents.

12. *Alternate ratio* means taking the antecedent in relation to the antecedent, and the consequent in relation to the consequent.

13. *Inverse ratio* means taking the consequent as antecedent in relation to the antecedent as consequent.

14. *Composition of a ratio* means taking the antecedent together with the consequent as one in relation to the consequent by itself.

15. *Separation of a ratio* means taking the excess by which the antecedent exceeds the consequent in relation to the consequent by itself.

16. *Conversion of a ratio* means taking the antecedent in relation to the excess by which the antecedent exceeds the consequent.

17. A ratio *ex aequali* arises when, there being several

magnitudes and another set equal to them in multitude which taken two by two are in the same proportion, as the first is to the last in the first set of magnitudes, so is the first to the last in the second set of magnitudes; in other words, a taking of the extremes by removal of the intermediate terms.

18. A *perturbed proportion* arises when, there being three magnitudes and another set equal to them in multitude, as antecedent is to consequent in the first magnitudes, so is antecedent to consequent in the second magnitudes, while as the consequent is to the other term in the first magnitudes, so is the other term to the antecedent in the second magnitudes.

From Elements. Translated 1941 by Ivor Thomas.

O

MEASUREMENT OF THE EARTH

CLEOMEDES

ERATOSTHENES' method of investigating the size of the earth depends on a geometrical argument, and gives the impression of being more obscure. What he says will, however, become clear if the following assumptions are made. Let us suppose, in this case also, first that Syene and Alexandria lie under the same meridian circle; secondly, that the distance between the two cities is 5000 stades; and thirdly, that the rays sent down from different parts of the sun upon different parts of the earth are parallel; for the geometers proceed on this assumption. Fourthly, let us assume that, as is proved by the geometers, straight lines falling on parallel straight lines make the alternate angles equal, and fifthly, that the arcs subtended by equal angles are similar, that is, have the same proportion and the same ratio to their proper circles—this also being proved by the geometers. For whenever arcs of circles are subtended by equal angles, if any one of these is (say) one-tenth of its proper circle, all the remaining arcs will be tenth parts of their proper circles.

Anyone who has mastered these facts will have no difficulty in understanding the method of Eratosthenes, which is as follows. Syene and Alexandria, he asserts, are under the same meridian. Since meridian circles are great circles in the universe, the circles on the earth which lie under them are necessarily great circles also. Therefore, of whatever size this method shows the circle on the earth through Syene and Alexandria to be, this will be the size of the great circle on the earth. He then asserts, as is indeed the case, that Syene lies under the summer tropic. Therefore, whenever the sun, being in the Crab at the summer solstice, is exactly in the middle of the heavens, the pointers of the sundials necessarily throw no shadows, the sun being in the exact vertical line above them; and this is said to be true over a space 300 stades in diameter. But in Alexandria at the same hour the pointers of the sundials throw shadows, because this city lies farther to the north than Syene. As the two cities lie under the same meridian great circle, if we draw an arc from the extremity of the shadow of the pointer to the base of the pointer of the sundial in Alexandria, the arc will be a segment of a great circle in the bowl of the sundial, since the bowl lies under the great circle. If then we conceive straight lines produced in order from each of the pointers through the earth, they will meet at the centre of the earth. Now since the sundial at Syene is vertically under the sun, if we conceive a straight line drawn from the sun to the top of the pointer of the sundial, the line stretching from the sun to the centre of the earth will be one straight line. If now we conceive another straight line drawn upwards from the extremity of the shadow of the pointer of the sundial in Alexandria, through the top of the pointer to the sun, this straight line and the aforesaid straight line will be parallel, being straight lines drawn through from different parts of the sun to different parts of the earth. Now on these parallel straight lines there falls the straight line drawn from the centre of the earth to the pointer at Alexandria, so that it makes the alternate angles equal; one of these is formed at the centre of the earth by the intersection of the straight lines drawn from the sundials to the centre of the earth; the other is at the intersection of the top of the pointer in Alexandria and the straight line drawn from the extremity of its shadow to the sun through the point where it meets the pointer. Now this latter angle subtends the arc carried round from the extremity of the shadow of the pointer to its base, while the angle at the centre of the earth subtends the arc stretching from Syene to Alexandria. But the arcs are similar since they are subtended by equal angles. Whatever ratio, therefore, the arc in the bowl of the sundial has to its proper circle, the arc reaching from Syene to Alexandria has the same ratio. But the arc in the bowl is found to be the fiftieth part of its proper circle. Therefore the distance from Syene to Alexandria must necessarily be a fiftieth part of the great circle of the earth. And this distance is 5000 stades. Therefore the whole great circle is 250,000 stades. Such is the method of Eratosthenes.

From *On the Circular Motion of the Heavenly Bodies.*
Translated 1941 by Ivor Thomas.

o

MEDICINE

o

ON AIRS, WATERS, AND PLACES

HIPPOCRATES

WHOEVER wishes to investigate medicine properly, should proceed thus: in the first place to consider the seasons of the year, and what effects each of them produces (for they are not at all alike, but differ much from themselves in regard to their changes). Then the winds, the hot and the cold, especially such as are common to all countries, and then such as are peculiar to each locality. We must also consider the qualities of the waters, for as they differ from one another in taste and weight, so also do they differ much in their qualities. In the same manner, when one comes into a city to which he is a stranger, he ought to consider its situation, how it lies as to the winds and the rising of the sun; for its influence is not the same whether it lies to the north or the south, to the rising or to the setting sun. These things one ought to consider most attentively, and concerning the waters which the inhabitants use, whether they be marshy and soft, or hard, and running from elevated and rocky situations, and then if saltish and unfit for cooking; and the ground, whether it be naked and deficient in water, or wooded and well watered, and whether it lies in a hollow, confined situation, or is elevated and cold; and the mode in which the inhabitants live, and what are their pursuits, whether they are fond of drinking and eating to excess, and given to indolence, or are fond of exercise and labor, and not given to excess in eating and drinking.

2. From these things he must proceed to investigate everything else. For if one knows all these things well, or at least the greater part of them, he cannot miss knowing, when he comes into a strange city, either the diseases peculiar to the place, or the particular nature of common diseases, so that he will not be in doubt as to the treatment of the diseases, or commit mistakes, as is likely to be the case provided one had not previously considered these matters. And in particular, as the season and the year advances, he can tell what epidemic diseases will attack the city, either in summer or in winter, and what each individual will be in danger of experiencing from the change of regimen. For knowing the changes of the seasons, the risings and settings of the stars, how each of them takes place, he will be able to know beforehand what sort of a year is going to ensue. Having made these investigations, and knowing beforehand the seasons, such a one must be acquainted with each particular, and must succeed in the preservation of health, and be by no means unsuccessful in the practice of his art. And if it shall be thought that these things belong rather to meteorology, it will be admitted, on second thoughts, that astronomy contributes not a little, but a very great deal, indeed, to medicine. For with the seasons the digestive organs of men undergo a change.

3. But how each of the aforementioned things should be investigated and explained, I will now declare in a clear manner. A city that is exposed to hot winds (these are between the wintry rising, and the wintry setting of the sun), and to which these are peculiar, but which is sheltered from the north winds; in such a city the waters will be plenteous and saltish, and as they run

from an elevated source, they are necessarily hot in summer, and cold in winter; the heads of the inhabitants are of a humid and pituitous constitution, and their bellies subject to frequent disorders, owing to the phlegm running down from the head; the forms of their bodies, for the most part, are rather flabby; they do not eat nor drink much; drinking wine in particular, and more especially if carried to intoxication, is oppressive to them; and the following diseases are peculiar to the district: in the first place, the women are sickly and subject to excessive menstruation; then many are unfruitful from disease, and not from nature, and they have frequent miscarriages; infants are subject to attacks of convulsions and asthma, which they consider to be connected with infancy, and hold to be a sacred disease (epilepsy). The men are subject to attacks of dysentery, diarrhoea, hepialus,[1] chronic fevers in winter, of epinyctis,[2] frequently, and of hemorrhoids about the anus. Pleurisies, peripneumonies, ardent fevers, and whatever diseases are reckoned acute, do not often occur, for such diseases are not apt to prevail where the bowels are loose. Ophthalmies occur of a humid character, but not of a serious nature, and of short duration, unless they attack epidemically from the change of the seasons. And when they pass their fiftieth year, defluxions supervening from the brain, render them paralytic when exposed suddenly to strokes of the sun, or to cold. These diseases are endemic to them, and, moreover, if any epidemic disease connected with the change of the seasons, prevail, they are also liable to it.

4. But the following is the condition of cities which

---

[1] The Hepialus is a species of intermittent fever, very common in warm climates. It would appear to be a variety of the quotidian. See PAULUS ÆGINETA, Vol. I., 252, Syd. Soc. edition.

[2] Frequent mention of this disease of the skin occurs in the works of the ancient writers on medicine.

have the opposite exposure, namely, to cold winds, between the summer settings and the summer risings of the sun, and to which these winds are peculiar, and which are sheltered from the south and the hot breezes. In the first place the waters are, for the most part, hard and cold. The men must necessarily be well braced and slender, and they must have the discharges downwards of the alimentary canal hard, and of difficult evacuation, while those upwards are more fluid, and rather bilious than pituitous. Their heads are sound and hard, and they are liable to burstings (of vessels?) for the most part. The diseases which prevail epidemically with them, are pleurisies, and those which are called acute diseases. This must be the case when the bowels are bound; and from any causes, many become affected with suppurations in the lungs, the cause of which is the tension of the body, and hardness of the bowels; for their dryness and the coldness of the water dispose them to ruptures (of vessels?). Such constitutions must be given to excess of eating, but not of drinking; for it is not possible to be gourmands and drunkards at the same time. Ophthalmies, too, at length supervene; these being of a hard and violent nature, and soon ending in rupture of the eyes; persons under thirty years of age are liable to severe bleedings at the nose in summer; attacks of epilepsy are rare but severe. Such people are likely to be rather long-lived; their ulcers are not attended with serious discharges, nor of a malignant character; in disposition they are rather ferocious than gentle. The diseases I have mentioned are peculiar to the men, and besides they are liable to any common complaint which may be prevailing from the changes of the seasons. But the women, in the first place, are of a hard constitution, from the waters being hard, indigestible, and cold; and their menstrual discharges are not regular, but in small quantity, and painful. Then they have difficult parturition, but are not very subject to abortions. And when they do bring forth children, they are unable to nurse them; for the hardness and indigestible nature of the water puts away their milk. Phthisis frequently supervenes after childbirth, for the efforts of it frequently bring on ruptures and strains. Children while still little are subject to dropsies in the testicle, which disappear as they grow older; in such a town they are late in attaining manhood. It is, as I have now stated, with regard to hot and cold winds and cities thus exposed.

5. Cities that are exposed to winds between the summer and the winter risings of the sun, and those the opposite to them, have the following characters:—Those which lie to the rising of the sun are all likely to be more healthy than such as are turned to the North, or those exposed to the hot winds, even if there should not be a furlong between them. In the first place, both the heat and cold are more moderate. Then such waters as flow to the rising sun, must necessarily be clear, fragrant, soft, and delightful to drink, in such a city. For the sun in rising and shining upon them purifies them, by dispelling the vapors which generally prevail in the morning. The persons of the inhabitants are, for the most part, well colored and blooming, unless some disease counteract. The inhabitants have clear voices, and in temper and intellect are superior to those which are exposed to the north, and all the productions of the country in like manner are better. A city so situated resembles the spring as to moderation between heat and cold, and the diseases are few in number, and of a feeble kind, and bear a resemblance to the diseases which prevail in regions exposed to hot winds. The women there are very prolific, and have easy deliveries. Thus it is with regard to them.

6. But such cities as lie to the west, and which are sheltered from winds blowing from the east, and which the hot winds and the cold winds of the north scarcely touch, must necessarily be in a very unhealthy situation: in the first place the waters are not clear, the cause of which is, because the mist prevails commonly in the morning, and it is mixed up with the water and destroys its clearness, for the sun does not shine upon the water until he be considerably raised above the horizon. And in summer, cold breezes from the east blow and dews fall; and in the latter part of the day the setting sun particularly scorches the inhabitants, and therefore they are pale and enfeebled, and are partly subject to all the foresaid diseases, but no one is peculiar to them. Their voices are rough and hoarse owing to the state of the air, which in such a situation is generally impure and unwholesome, for they have not the northern winds to purify it; and these winds they have are of a very humid character, such being the nature of the evening breezes. Such a situation of a city bears a great resemblance to autumn as regards the changes of the day, inasmuch as the difference between morning and evening is great. So it is with regard to the winds that are conducive to health, or the contrary.

7. And I wish to give an account of the other kinds of waters, namely, of such as are wholesome and such as are unwholesome, and what bad and what good effects may be derived from water; for water contributes much towards health. Such waters then as are marshy, stagnant, and belong to lakes, are necessarily hot in summer, thick, and have a strong smell, since they have no current; but being constantly supplied by rain-water, and the sun heating them, they necessarily want their proper color, are unwholesome and form bile; in winter, they become congealed, cold, and muddy with the snow and ice,

so that they are most apt to engender phlegm, and bring on hoarseness; those who drink them have large and obstructed spleens, their bellies are hard, emaciated, and hot; and their shoulders, collar-bones, and faces are emaciated; for their flesh is melted down and taken up by the spleen, and hence they are slender; such persons then are voracious and thirsty; their bellies are very dry both above and below, so that they require the strongest medicines.[1] This disease is habitual to them both in summer and in winter, and in addition they are very subject to dropsies of the most fatal character; and in summer dysenteries, diarrhoeas, and protracted quartan fevers frequently seize them, and these diseases when prolonged dispose such constitutions to dropsies, and thus prove fatal. These are the diseases which attack them in summer; but in winter younger persons are liable to pneumonia, and maniacal affections; and older persons to ardent fevers, from hardness of the belly. Women are subject to œdema and leucophlegmasiae;[2] when pregnant they have difficult deliveries; their infants are large and swelled, and then during nursing they become wasted and sickly, and the lochial discharge after parturition does not proceed properly with the women. The children are particularly subject to hernia, and adults to varices and ulcers on their legs, so that persons with such constitutions cannot be long-lived, but before the usual period they fall into a state of premature old age. And further, the women appear to be with child, and when the time of parturition arrives, the fulness of the belly disappears, and this happens from dropsy of the uterus. Such waters then I reckon bad for

[1] It can scarcely admit of a doubt that our author here alludes to scurvy.

[2] The leucophlegmasia is treated of in different parts of the Hippocratic treatises, as Aphor. vii., 29; de Morb. ii. By it he evidently meant a species of dropsy.

every purpose. The next to them in badness are those which have their fountains in rocks, so that they must necessarily be hard, or come from a soil which produces thermal waters, such as those having iron, copper, silver, gold, sulphur, alum, bitumen, or nitre (soda) in them; for all these are formed by the force of heat. Good waters cannot proceed from such a soil, but those that are hard and of a heating nature, difficult to pass by urine, and of difficult evacuation by the bowels. The best are those which flow from elevated grounds, and hills of earth; these are sweet, clear, and can bear a little wine; they are hot in summer and cold in winter, for such necessarily must be the waters from deep wells. But those are most to be commended which run to the rising of the sun, and especially to the summer sun; for such are necessarily more clear, fragrant, and light. But all such as are saltish, crude, and hard, are not good for drink, but there are certain constitutions and diseases with which such waters agree when drunk, as I will explain presently. These characters are as follows: the best are such as have their fountains to the east; the next, those between the summer risings; and third, those between the summer and winter settings; but the worst are those to the south, and the parts between the winter rising and setting, and those to the south are very bad, but those to the north are better. They are to be used as follows: whoever is in good health and strength need not mind, but may always drink whatever is at hand. But whoever wishes to drink the most suitable for any disease, may accomplish his purpose by attending to the following directions: To persons whose bellies are hard and easily burnt up, the sweetest, the lightest, and the most limpid waters will be proper; but those persons whose bellies are soft, loose, and pituitous, should choose the hardest, those kinds that are most crude, and the saltest, for thus will they be most readily dried up; for such waters as are adapted for boiling, and are of a very solvent nature, naturally loosen readily and melt down the bowels; but such as are intractable, hard, and by no means proper for boiling, these rather bind and dry up the bowels. People have deceived themselves with regard to salt waters, from inexperience, for they think these waters purgative, whereas they are the very reverse; for such waters are crude, and ill adapted for boiling, so that the belly is more likely to be bound up than loosened by them. And thus it is with regard to the waters of springs.

8. I will now tell how it is with respect to rain water, and water from snow. Rain waters, then, are the lightest, the sweetest, the thinnest, and the clearest; for originally the sun raises and attracts the thinnest and lightest part of the water, as is obvious from the nature of salts; for the saltish part is left behind owing to its thickness and weight, and forms salts; but the sun attracts the thinnest part, owing to its lightness, and he abstracts this not only from the lakes, but also from the sea, and from all things which contain humidity, and there is humidity in everything; and from man himself the sun draws off the thinnest and lightest part of the juices. As a strong proof of this, when a man walks in the sun, or sits down having a garment on, whatever parts of the body the sun shines upon do not sweat, for the sun carries off whatever sweat makes its appearance; but those parts which are covered by the garment, or anything else, sweat, for the particles of sweat are drawn and forced out by the sun, and are preserved by the cover so as not to be dissipated by the sun; but when the person comes into the shade the whole body equally perspires, because the sun no longer shines upon it. Wherefore, of all kinds of water, these spoil the soonest; and rain water has a bad smell, because its particles are

collected and mixed together from most objects, so as to spoil the soonest. And in addition to this, when attracted and raised up, being carried about and mixed with the air, whatever part of it is turbid and darkish is separated and removed from the other, and becomes cloud and mist, but the most attenuated and lightest part is left, and becomes sweet, being heated and concocted by the sun, for all other things when concocted become sweet. While dissipated then and not in a state of consistence it is carried aloft. But when collected and condensed by contrary winds, it falls down wherever it happens to be most condensed. For this is likely to happen when the clouds being carried along and moving with a wind which does not allow them to rest, suddenly encounters another wind and other clouds from the opposite direction: there it is first condensed, and what is behind is carried up to the spot, and thus it thickens, blackens, and is conglomerated, and by its weight it falls down and becomes rain. Such, to all appearance, are the best of waters, but they require to be boiled and strained; for otherwise they have a bad smell, and occasion hoarseness and thickness of the voice to those who drink them. Those from snow and ice are all bad, for when once congealed, they never again recover their former nature; for whatever is clear, light, and sweet in them, is separated and disappears; but the most turbid and weightiest part is left behind. You may ascertain this in the following manner: If in winter you will pour water by measure into a vessel and expose it to the open air until it is all frozen, and then on the following day bring it into a warm situation where the ice will thaw, if you will measure the water again when dissolved you will find it much less in quantity. This is a proof that the lightest and thinnest part is dissipated and dried up by the congelation, and not the heaviest and thickest, for that is impossible:

wherefore I hold that waters from snow and ice, and those allied to them, are the worst of any for all purposes whatever. Such are the characters of rain water, and those from ice and snow.

9. Men become affected with the stone, and are seized with diseases of the kidneys, strangury, sciatica, and become ruptured, when they drink all sorts of waters, and those from great rivers into which other rivulets run, or from a lake into which many streams of all sorts flow, and such as are brought from a considerable distance. For it is impossible that such waters can resemble one another, but one kind is sweet, another saltish and aluminous, and some flow from thermal springs; and these being all mixed up together disagree, and the strongest part always prevails; but the same kind is not always the strongest, but sometimes one and sometimes another, according to the winds, for the north wind imparts strength to this water, and the south to that, and so also with regard to the others. There must be deposits of mud and sand in the vessels from such waters, and the aforesaid diseases must be engendered by them when drunk, but why not to all I will now explain. When the bowels are loose and in a healthy state, and when the bladder is not hot, nor the neck of the bladder very contracted, all such persons pass water freely, and no concretion forms in the bladder; but those in whom the belly is hot, the bladder must be in the same condition; and when preternaturally heated, its neck becomes inflamed; and when these things happen, the bladder does not expel the urine, but raises its heat excessively. And the thinnest part of it is secreted, and the purest part is passed off in the form of urine, but the thickest and most turbid part is condensed and concreted, at first in small quantity, but afterwards in greater; for being rolled about in the urine, whatever is

of a thick consistence it assimilates to itself, and thus it increases and becomes indurated. And when such persons make water, the stone forced down by the urine falls into the neck of the bladder and stops the urine, and occasions intense pain; so that calculous children rub their privy parts and tear at them, as supposing that the obstruction to the urine is situated here. As a proof that it is as I say, persons affected with calculus have very limpid urine, because the thickest and foulest part remains and is concreted. Thus it generally is in cases of calculus. It forms also in children from milk, when it is not wholesome, but very hot and bilious, for it heats the bowels and bladder, so that the urine being also heated undergoes the same change. And I hold that it is better to give children only the most diluted wine, for such will least burn up and dry the veins. Calculi do not form so readily in women, for in them the urethra is short and wide, so that in them the urine is easily expelled; neither do they rub the pudendum with their hands, nor handle the passage like males; for the urethra in women opens direct into the pudendum, which is not the case with men, neither in them is the urethra so wide, and they drink more than children do. Thus, or nearly so, is it with reward to them.

10. And respecting the seasons, one may judge whether the year will prove sickly or healthy from the following observations:—If the appearances connected with the rising and setting stars be as they should be; if there be rains in autumn; if the winter be mild, neither very tepid nor unseasonably cold, and if in spring the rains be seasonable, and so also in summer, the year is likely to prove healthy. But if the winter be dry and northerly, and the spring showery and southerly, the summer will necessarily be of a febrile character, and give rise to ophthalmies and dysenteries. For when suf-

focating heat sets in all of a sudden, while the earth is moistened by the vernal showers, and by the south wind, the heat is necessarily doubled from the earth, which is thus soaked by rain and heated by a burning sun, while, at the same time, men's bellies are not in an orderly state, nor the brain properly dried; for it is impossible, after such a spring, but that the body and its flesh must be loaded with humors, so that very acute fevers will attack all, but especially those of a phlegmatic constitution. Dysenteries are also likely to occur to women and those of a very humid temperament. And if at the rising of the Dogstar rain and wintry storms supervene, and if the etesian winds blow, there is reason to hope that these diseases will cease, and that the autumn will be healthy; but if not, it is likely to be a fatal season to children and women, but least of all to old men; and that convalescents will pass into quartans, and from quartans into dropsies; but if the winter be southerly, showery and mild, but the spring northerly, dry, and of a wintry character, in the first place women who happen to be with child, and whose accouchement should take place in spring, are apt to miscarry; and such as bring forth, have feeble and sickly children, so that they either die presently or are tender, feeble, and sickly, if they live. Such is the case with the women. The others are subject to dysenteries and dry opthalmies, and some have catarrhs beginning in the head and descending to the lungs. Men of a phlegmatic temperament are likely to have dysenteries; and women, also, from the humidity of their nature, the phlegm descending downwards from the brain; those who are bilious, too, have dry ophthalmies from the heat and dryness of their flesh; the aged, too, have catarrhs from their flabbiness and melting of the veins, so that some of them die suddenly and some become paralytic on the right side or the left.

For when, the winter being southerly and the body hot, the blood and veins are not properly constringed; a spring that is northerly, dry, and cold, having come on, the brain when it should have been expanded and purged, by the coryza and hoarseness is then constringed and contracted, so that the summer and the heat occurring suddenly, and a change supervening, these diseases fall out. And such cities as lie well to the sun and winds, and use good waters, feel these changes less, but such as use marshy and pooly waters, and lie well both as regards the winds and the sun, these all feel it more. And if the summer be dry, those diseases soon cease, but if rainy, they are protracted; and there is danger of any sore that there is becoming phagedenic from any cause; and lienteries and dropsies supervene at the conclusion of diseases; for the bowels are not readily dried up. And if the summer be rainy and southerly, and next the autumn, the winter must, of necessity, be sickly, and ardent fevers are likely to attack those that are phlegmatic, and more elderly than forty years, and pleurisies and peripneumonies those that are bilious. But if the summer is parched and northerly, but the autumn rainy and southerly, headache and sphacelus of the brain are likely to occur; and in addition hoarseness, coryza, coughs, and in some cases, consumption. But if the season is northerly and without water, there being no rain, neither after the Dogstar nor Arcturus; this state agrees best with those who are naturally phlegmatic, with those who are of a humid temperament, and with women; but it is most inimical to the bilious; for they become much parched up, and ophthalmies of a dry nature supervene, fevers both acute and chronic, and in some cases melancholy; for the most humid and watery part of the bile being consumed, the thickest and most acrid portion is left, and of the blood likewise, when these diseases come upon them. But all these are beneficial to the phlegmatic, for they are thereby dried up, and reach winter not oppressed with humors, but with them dried up.

11. Whoever studies and observes these things may be able to foresee most of the effects which will result from the changes of the seasons; and one ought to be particularly guarded during the greatest changes of the seasons, and neither willingly give medicines, nor apply the cautery to the belly, nor make incisions there until ten or more days be past. Now, the greatest and most dangerous are the two solstices, and especially the summer, and also the two equinoxes, but especially the autumnal. One ought also to be guarded about the rising of the stars, especially of the Dogstar, then of Arcturus, and then the setting of the Pleiades; for diseases are especially apt to prove critical in those days, and some prove fatal, some pass off, and all others change to another form and another constitution. So it is with regard to them.

12. I wish to show, respecting Asia and Europe, how, in all respects, they differ from one another, and concerning the figure of the inhabitants, for they are different, and do not at all resemble one another. To treat of all would be a long story, but I will tell you how I think it is with regard to the greatest and most marked differences. I say, then, that Asia differs very much from Europe as to the nature of all things, both with regard to the productions of the earth and the inhabitants, for everything is produced much more beautiful and large in Asia; the country is milder, and the dispositions of the inhabitants also are more gentle and affectionate. The cause of this is the temperature of the seasons, because it lies in the middle of the risings of the sun towards the east, and removed from the cold (and heat), for nothing

tends to growth and mildness so much as when the climate has no predominant quality, but a general equality of temperature prevails. It is not everywhere the same with regard to Asia, but such parts of the country as lie intermediate between the heat and the cold, are the best supplied with fruits and trees, and have the most genial climate, and enjoy the purest waters, both celestial and terrestrial. For neither are they much burnt up by the heat, nor dried up by the drought and want of rain, nor do they suffer from the cold; since they are well watered from abundant showers and snow, and the fruits of the season, as might be supposed, grow in abundance, both such as are raised from seed that has been sown, and such plants as the earth produces of its own accord, the fruits of which the inhabitants make use of, training them from their wild state and transplanting them to a suitable soil; the cattle also which are reared there are vigorous, particularly prolific, and bring up young of the fairest description; the inhabitants too, are well fed, most beautiful in shape, of large stature, and differ little from one another either as to figure or size; and the country itself, both as regards its constitution and mildness of the seasons, may be said to bear a close resemblance to the spring. Manly courage, endurance of suffering, laborious enterprise, and high spirit, could not be produced in such a state of things either among the native inhabitants or those of a different country, for there pleasure necessarily reigns. For this reason, also, the forms of wild beasts there are much varied. Thus it is, as I think, with the Egyptians and Libyans.

13. But concerning those on the right hand of the summer risings of the sun as far as the Palus Mæotis (for this is the boundary of Europe and Asia), it is with them as follows: the inhabitants there differ far more from one another than those I have treated of above, owing

to the differences of the seasons and the nature of the soil. But with regard to the country itself, matters are the same there as among all other men; for where the seasons undergo the greatest and most rapid changes, there the country is the wildest and most unequal; and you will find the greatest variety of mountains, forests, plains, and meadows; but where the seasons do not change much there the country is the most even; and, if one will consider it, so is it also with regard to the inhabitants; for the nature of some is like to a country covered with trees and well watered; of some, to a thin soil deficient in water; of others, to fenny and marshy places; and of some again, to a plain of bare and parched land. For the seasons which modify their natural frame of body are varied, and the greater the varieties of them the greater also will be the differences of their shapes.

14. I will pass over the smaller differences among the nations, but will now treat of such as are great either from nature, or custom; and, first, concerning the Macrocephali. There is no other race of men which have heads in the least resembling theirs. At first, usage was the principal cause of the length of their head, but now nature cooperates with usage. They think those the most noble who have the longest heads. It is thus with regard to the usage: immediately after the child is born, and while its head is still tender, they fashion it with their hands, and constrain it to assume a lengthened shape by applying bandages and other suitable contrivances whereby the spherical form of the head is destroyed, and it is made to increase in length. Thus, at first, usage operated, so that this constitution was the result of force: but, in the course of time, it was formed naturally; so that usage had nothing to do with it; for the semen comes from all parts of the body, sound from the sound parts, and unhealthy from the unhealthy parts. If, then,

children with bald heads are born to parents with bald
heads; and children with blue eyes to parents who have
blue eyes; and if the children of parents having distorted
eyes squint also for the most part; and if the same may
be said of other forms of the body, what is to prevent it
from happening that a child with a long head should be
produced by a parent having a long head? But now these
things do not happen as they did formerly, for the custom no longer prevails owing to their intercourse with
other men. Thus it appears to me to be with regard to
them.

15. As to the inhabitants of Phasis, their country is
fenny, warm, humid, and wooded; copious and severe
rains occur there at all seasons; and the life of the inhabitants is spent among the fens; for their dwellings are
constructed of wood and reeds, and are erected amidst
the waters; they seldom practice walking either to the
city or the market, but sail about, up and down, in
canoes constructed out of single trees, for there are many
canals there. They drink the hot and stagnant waters,
both when rendered putrid by the sun, and when swollen with rains. The Phasis itself is the most stagnant of
all rivers, and runs the smoothest; all the fruits which
spring there are unwholesome, of feeble and imperfect
growth, owing to the redundance of water, and on this
account they do not ripen, for much vapor from the
waters overspreads the country. For these reasons the
Phasians have shapes different from those of all other
men; for they are large in stature, and of a very gross
habit of body, so that not a joint nor vein is visible; in
color they are sallow, as if affected with jaundice. Of all
men they have the roughest voices, from their breathing
an atmosphere which is not clear, but misty and humid;
they are naturally rather languid in supporting bodily
fatigue. The seasons undergo but little change either as

to heat or cold; their winds for the most part are southerly, with the exception of one peculiar to the country, which sometimes blows strong, is violent and hot, and is called by them the wind *cenchron*. The north wind scarcely reaches them, and when it does blow it is weak and gentle. Thus it is with regard to the different nature and shape of the inhabitants of Asia and Europe.

16. And with regard to the pusillanimity and cowardice of the inhabitants, the principal reason why the Asiatics are more unwarlike and of more gentle disposition than the Europeans is, the nature of the seasons, which do not undergo any great changes either to heat or cold, or the like; for there is neither excitement of the understanding nor any strong change of the body by which the temper might be ruffled, and they be roused to inconsiderate emotion and passion, rather than living as they do always in the same state. It is changes of all kinds which arouse the understanding of mankind, and do not allow them to get into a torpid condition. For these reasons, it appears to me, the Asiatic race is feeble, and further, owing to their laws; for monarchy prevails in the greater part of Asia, and where men are not their own masters nor independent, but are the slaves of others, it is not a matter of consideration with them how they may acquire military discipline, but how they may seem not to be warlike, for the dangers are not equally shared, since they must serve as soldiers, perhaps endure fatigue, and die for their masters, far from their children, their wives, and other friends; and whatever noble and manly actions they may perform lead only to the aggrandizement of their masters, whilst the fruits which they reap are dangers and death; and, in addition to all this, the lands of such persons must be laid waste by the enemy and want of culture. Thus, then, if any one be naturally warlike and courageous, his disposition will be changed by

the institutions. As a strong proof of all this, such Greeks or barbarians in Asia as are not under a despotic form of government, but are independent, and enjoy the fruits of their own labors, are of all others the most warlike; for these encounter dangers on their own account, bear the prizes of their own valor, and in like manner endure the punishment of their own cowardice. And you will find the Asiatics differing from one another, for some are better and others more dastardly; of these differences, as I stated before, the changes of the seasons are the cause. Thus it is with Asia.

17. In Europe there is a Scythian race, called Sauromatæ, which inhabits the confines of the Palus Mæotis, and is different from all other races. Their women mount on horseback, use the bow, and throw the javelin from their horses, and fight with their enemies as long as they are virgins; and they do not lay aside their virginity until they kill three of their enemies, nor have any connection with men until they perform the sacrifices according to law. Whoever takes to herself a husband, gives up riding on horseback unless the necessity of a general expedition obliges her. They have no right breast; for while still of a tender age their mothers heat strongly a copper instrument constructed for this very purpose, and apply it to the right breast, which is burnt up, and its development being arrested, all the strength and fullness are determined to the right shoulder and arm.

18. As the other Scythians have a peculiarity of shape, and do not resemble any other, the same observation applies to the Egyptians, only that the latter are oppressed by heat and the former by cold. What is called the Scythian desert is a prairie, abound in meadows, high-lying, and well watered; for the rivers which carry off the water from the plains are large. There live those Scythians which are called Nomades, because they have

no houses, but live in wagons. The smallest of these wagons have four wheels, but some have six; they are covered in with felt, and they are constructed in the manner of houses, some having but a single apartment, and some three; they are proof against rain, snow, and winds. The wagons are drawn by yokes of oxen, some of two and others of three, and all without horns, for they have no horns, owing to the cold. In these wagons the women live, but the men are carried about on horses, and the sheep, oxen, and horses accompany them; and they remain on any spot as long as there is provender for their cattle, and when that fails they migrate to some other place. They eat boiled meat, and drink the milk of mares, and also eat *hippace*, which is cheese prepared from the milk of the mare. Such is their mode of life and their customs.

19. In respect of the seasons and figure of body, the Scythian race, like the Egyptian, have a uniformity of resemblance, different from all other nations; they are by no means prolific, and the wild beasts which are indigenous there are small in size and few in number, for the country lies under the Northern Bears, and the Rhiphæan mountains, whence the north wind blows; the sun comes very near to them only when in the summer solstice, and warms them but for a short period, and not strongly; and the winds blowing from the hot regions of the earth do not reach them, or but seldom, and with little force; but the winds from the north always blow, congealed, as they are, by the snow, the ice, and much water, for these never leave the mountains, which are thereby rendered uninhabitable. A thick fog covers the plains during the day, and amidst it they live, so that winter may be said to be always present with them; or, if they have summer, it is only for a few days, and the heat is not very strong. Their plains are high-lying and

naked, not crowned with mountains, but extending upwards under the Northern Bears. The wild beasts there are not large, but such as can be sheltered underground; for the cold of winter and the barrenness of the country prevent their growth, and because they have no covert nor shelter. The changes of the seasons, too, are not great nor violent, for, in fact, they change gradually; and therefore their figures resemble one another, as they all equally use the same food, and the same clothing summer and winter, respiring a humid and dense atmosphere, and drinking water from snow and ice; neither do they make any laborious exertions, for neither body nor mind is capable of enduring fatigue when the changes of the seasons are not great. For these reasons their shapes are gross and fleshy, with ill-marked joints, of a humid temperament, and deficient in tone: the internal cavities, and especially those of the intestines, are full of humors; for the belly cannot possibly be dry in such a country, with such a constitution and in such a climate; but owing to their fat, and the absence of hairs from their bodies, their shapes resemble one another, the males being all alike, and so also with the women; for the seasons being of a uniform temperature, no corruption or deterioration takes place in the concretion of the semen, unless from some violent cause, or from disease.

20. I will give you a strong proof of the humidity (laxity?) of their constitutions. You will find the greater part of the Scythians, and all the Nomades, with marks of the cautery on their shoulders, arms, wrists, breasts, hip-joints, and loins, and that for no other reason but the humidity and flabbiness of their constitution, for they can neither strain with their bows, nor launch the javelin from their shoulder owing to their humidity and atony: but when they are burnt, much of the humidity in their joints is dried up, and they become better braced, better

fed, and their joints get into a more suitable condition. They are flabby and squat at first, because, as in Egypt, they are not swathed (?); and then they pay no attention to horsemanship, so that they may be adepts at it; and because of their sedentary mode of life; for the males, when they cannot be carried about on horseback, sit the most of their time in the wagon, and rarely practise walking, because of their frequent migrations and shiftings of situation; and as to the women, it is amazing how flabby and sluggish they are. The Scythian race are tawny from the cold, and not from the intense heat of the sun, for the whiteness of the skin is parched by the cold, and becomes tawny.

21. It is impossible that persons of such a constitution could be prolific, for, with the man, the sexual desires are not strong, owing to the laxity of his constitution, the softness and coldness of his belly, from all which causes it is little likely that a man should be given to venery; and besides, from being jaded by exercise on horseback, the men become weak in their desires. On the part of the men these are the causes; but on that of the women, they are embonpoint and humidity; for the womb cannot take in the semen, nor is the menstrual discharge such as it should be, but scanty and at too long intervals; and the mouth of the womb is shut up by fat and does not admit the semen; and, moreover, they themselves are indolent and fat, and their bellies cold and soft. From these causes the Scythian race is not prolific. Their female servants furnish a strong proof of this; for they no sooner have connection with a man than they prove with child, owing to their active course of life and the slenderness of body.

22. And, in addition to these, there are many eunuchs among the Scythians, who perform female work, and speak like women. Such persons are called effeminates.

The inhabitants of the country attribute the cause of their impotence to a god, and venerate and worship such persons, every one dreading that the like might befall himself; but to me it appears that such affections are just as much divine as all others are, and that no one disease is either more divine or more human than another, but that all are alike divine, for that each has its own nature, and that no one arises without a natural cause. But I will explain how I think that the affection takes its rise. From continued exercise on horseback they are seized with chronic defluxions in their joints owing to their legs always hanging down below their horses; they afterwards become lame and stiff at the hip-joint, such of them, at least, as are severely attacked with it. They treat themselves in this way: when the disease is commencing, they open the vein behind either ear, and when the blood flows, sleep, from feebleness, seizes them, and afterwards they awaken, some in good health and others not. To me it appears that the semen is altered by this treatment, for there are veins behind the ears which, if cut, induce impotence; now, these veins would appear to me to be cut. Such persons afterwards, when they go in to women and cannot have connection with them, at first do not think much about it, but remain quiet; but when, after making the attempt two, three, or more times, they succeed no better, fancying they have committed some offence against the god whom they blame for the affection, they put on female attire, reproach themselves for effeminacy, play the part of women, and perform the same work as women do. This the rich among the Scythians endure, not the basest, but the most noble and powerful, owing to their riding on horseback; for the poor are less affected, as they do not ride on horses. And yet, if this disease had been more divine than the others, it ought not to have befallen the most noble and the richest of the Scythians alone, but all alike, or rather those who have little, as not being able to pay honors to the gods, if, indeed, they delight in being thus rewarded by men, and grant favors in return; for it is likely that the rich sacrifice more to the gods, and dedicate more votive offerings, inasmuch as they have wealth, and worship the gods; whereas the poor, from want, do less in this way, and, moreover, upbraid the gods for not giving them wealth, so that those who have few possessions were more likely to bear the punishments of these offences than the rich. But, as I formerly said, these affections are divine just as much as others, for each springs from a natural cause, and this disease arises among the Scythians from such a cause as I have stated. But it attacks other men in like manner, for whenever men ride much and very frequently on horseback, then many are affected with rheums in the joints, sciatica, and gout, and they are inept at venery. But these complaints befall the Scythians, and they are the most impotent of men for the aforesaid causes, and because they always wear breeches, and spend the most of their time on horseback, so as not to touch their privy parts with the hands, and from the cold and fatigue they forget the sexual desire, and do not make the attempt until after they have lost their virility. Thus it is with the race of the Scythians.

23. The other races in Europe differ from one another, both as to stature and shape, owing to the changes of the seasons, which are very great and frequent, and because the heat is strong, the winters severe, and there are frequent rains, and again protracted droughts, and winds, from which many and diversified changes are induced. These changes are likely to have an effect upon generation in the coagulation of the semen, as this process cannot be the same in summer as in winter, nor in

rainy as in dry weather; wherefore, I think, that the
figures of Europeans differ more than those of Asiatics;
and they differ very much from one another as to stature
in the same city; for vitiations of the semen occur in its
coagulation more frequently during frequent changes of
the seasons, than where they are alike and equable. And
the same may be said of their dispositions, for the wild,
and unsociable, and the passionate occur in such a constitution; for frequent excitement of the mind induces wild-
ness, and extinguishes sociableness and mildness of disposition, and therefore I think the inhabitants of Europe
more courageous than those of Asia; for a climate which
is always the same induces indolence, but a changeable
climate, laborious exertions both of body and mind; and
from rest and indolence cowardice is engendered, and
from laborious exertions and pains, courage. On this account the inhabitants of Europe are more warlike than
the Asiatics, and also owing to their institutions, because
they are not governed by kings like the latter, for where
men are governed by kings there they must be very
cowardly, as I have stated before; for their souls are enslaved, and they will not willingly, or readily undergo
dangers in order to promote the power of another; but
those that are free undertake dangers on their own account, and not for the sake of others; they court hazard
and go out to meet it, for they themselves bear off the
rewards of victory, and thus their institutions contribute
not a little to their courage.

Such is the general character of Europe and Asia.

24. And there are in Europe other tribes, differing
from one another in stature, shape, and courage: the differences are those I formerly mentioned, and will now
explain more clearly. Such as inhabit a country which is
mountainous, rugged, elevated, and well watered, and
where the changes of the seasons are very great, are

likely to have great variety of shapes among them, and to be naturally of an enterprising and warlike disposition; and such persons are apt to have no little of the savage and ferocious in their nature; but such as dwell in places which are low-lying, abounding in meadows and ill ventilated, and who have a larger proportion of hot than of cold winds, and who make use of warm waters—these are not likely to be of large stature nor well proportioned, but are of a broad make, fleshy, and have black hair; and they are rather of a dark than of a light complexion, and are less likely to be phlegmatic than bilious; courage and laborious enterprise are not naturally in them, but may be engendered in them by means of their institutions. And if there be rivers in the country which carry off the stagnant and rain water from it, these may be wholesome and clear; but if there be no rivers, but the inhabitants drink the waters of fountains, and such as are stagnant and marshy, they must necessarily have prominent bellies and enlarged spleens. But such as inhabit a high country, and one that is level, windy, and well-watered, will be large of stature, and like to one another; but their minds will be rather unmanly and gentle. Those who live on thin, ill-watered, and bare soils, and not well attempered in the changes of the seasons, in such a country they are likely to be in their persons rather hard and well braced, rather of a blond than a dark complexion, and in disposition and passions haughty and self-willed. For, where the changes of the seasons are most frequent, and where they differ most from one another, there you will find their forms, dispositions, and nature the most varied. These are the strongest of the natural causes of difference, and next the country in which one lives, and the waters; for, in general, you will find the forms and dispositions of mankind to correspond with the nature of the country; for where the land is fertile, soft, and well-watered, and supplied with waters from very elevated situations, so as to be hot in summer and cold in winter, and where the seasons are fine, there the men are fleshy, have ill-formed joints, and are of a humid temperament; they are not disposed to endure labor, and, for the most part, are base in spirit; indolence and sluggishness are visible in them, and to the arts they are dull, and not clever nor acute. When the country is bare, not fenced, and rugged, blasted by the winter and scorched by the sun, there you may see the men hardy, slender, with well-shaped joints, well-braced, and shaggy; sharp industry and vigilance accompany such a constitution; in morals and passions they are haughty and opinionative, inclining rather to the fierce than to the mild; and you will find them acute and ingenious as regards the arts, and excelling in military affairs; and likewise all the other productions of the earth corresponding to the earth itself. Thus it is with regard to the most opposite natures and shapes; drawing conclusions from them, you may judge of the rest without any risk of error.

From *Works of Hippocrates*. Translated by Francis Adams.

O

GROWTH

GALEN

THIS Nature which shapes and gradually adds to the parts is most certainly extended throughout their whole substance. Yes indeed, she shapes and nourishes and increases them through and through, not on the outside only. For Praxiteles and Phidias and all the other statuaries used merely to decorate their material on the outside, in so far as they were able to touch it; but its inner parts they left unembellished, unwrought, unaffected by art or forethought, since they were unable to penetrate therein and to reach and handle all portions of the material. It is not so, however, with Nature. Every part of a bone she makes bone, every part of the flesh she makes flesh, and so with fat and all the rest; there is no part which she has not touched, elaborated, and embellished. Phidias, on the other hand, could not turn wax into ivory and gold, nor yet gold into wax: for each of these remains as it was at the commencement, and becomes a perfect statue simply by being clothed externally in a form and artificial shape. But Nature does not preserve the original character of any kind of matter; if she did so, then all parts of the animal would be blood —that blood, namely, which flows to the semen from the impregnated female and which is, so to speak, like the statuary's wax, a single uniform matter, subjected to the artificer. From this blood there arises no part of the animal which is as red and moist [as blood is], for bone, artery, vein, nerve, cartilage, fat, gland, membrane, and marrow are not blood, though they arise from it. . . .

Imagine the heart to be, at the beginning, so small as to differ in no respect from a millet-seed, or, if you will, a bean; and consider how otherwise it is to become large than by being extended in all directions and acquiring nourishment throughout its whole substance, in the way that, as I showed a short while ago, the semen is nourished. But even this was unknown to Erasistratus— the man who sings the artistic skill of Nature! He imagines that animals grow like webs, ropes, sacks, or baskets, each of which has, woven on to its end or margin, other material similar to that of which it was originally composed.

But this, most sapient sir, is not growth, but genesis! For a bag, sack, garment, house, ship, or the like is said to be still coming into existence [undergoing genesis] so long as the appropriate form for the sake of which it is being constructed by the artificer is still incomplete. Then, when does it grow? Only when the basket, being complete, with a bottom, a mouth, and a belly, as it were, as well as the intermediate parts, now becomes larger in all these respects. "And how can this happen?" someone will ask. Only by our basket suddenly becoming an animal or a plant; for growth belongs to living things alone. Possibly you imagine that a house *grows* when it is being built, or a basket when being plaited, or a garment when being woven? It is not so, however. Growth belongs to that which has already been completed in respect to its form, whereas the process by which that which is still *becoming* attains its form is termed not growth but genesis. That which *is,* grows, while that which *is not,* becomes.

From *On the Natural Faculties,* Book II, chaps. 3–4.
Translated by Arthur John Brock.

PART FOUR

MAN

○

ETHICS

○

MAN

SOPHOCLES

Numberless are the world's wonders, but none
More wonderful than man; the stormgrey sea
Yields to his prows, the huge crests bear him high;
Earth, holy and inexhaustible, is graven
With shining furrows where his plows have gone
Year after year, the timeless labour of stallions.

The lightboned birds and beasts that cling to cover,
The lithe fish lighting their reaches of dim water,
All are taken, tamed in the net of his mind;
The lion on the hill, the wild horse windy-maned,
Resign to him; and his blunt yoke has broken
The sultry shoulders of the mountain bull.

Words also, and thought as rapid as air,
He fashions to his good use; statecraft is his,
And his the skill that deflects the arrows of snow,
The spears of winter rain: from every wind
He has made himself secure—from all but one:
In the late wind of death he cannot stand.

O clear intelligence, force beyond all measure!
O fate of man, working both good and evil!
When the laws are kept, how proudly his city stands!
When the laws are broken, what of his city then?

Never may the anarchic man find rest at my hearth,
Never be it said that my thoughts are his thoughts.

From *Antigone*. Translated by Dudley Fitts and Robert Fitzgerald.

O

HUMAN IMPERFECTION

SIMONIDES

Hard it is wholly to win worthy manhood,
with hand and foot and heart alike to be foursquare,
an ashlar cut without a flaw.
Who is not bad, not all a niddering, who knows
the right that makes the city stand—
a sound man he: not I indeed
will ever fault him, for of fools
the generation's endless. All, all is fair
that is not mingled with the base.

Harmony sings not in Pittacus' proverb,
nay, not for me, although a wight of wisdom spake
the word, that *to excel is hard.*
A god alone could have such privilege: a man
undone by a resistless fate
must needs be bad. Yes: every man
is worthy if his luck is good,
and bad if it goes badly. They most excel
who are belovèd by the gods.

Therefore I seek no impossible being,
I squander not my life's allotted term, in vain,
on an impracticable hope—
faultless humanity—beyond their power who win
the bread of life from spacious earth;

when 'tis discovered, I shall tell.
Honour and love to every man
who wills to do no baseness; but not the gods
themselves oppose necessity.

Translated by Gilbert Highet.

O

SELF-LOVE

ARISTOTLE

8. The question is also debated, whether a man should love himself most, or some one else. People criticize those who love themselves most, and call them self-lovers, using this as an epithet of disgrace, and a bad man seems to do everything for his own sake, and the more so the more wicked he is—and so men reproach him, for instance, with doing nothing of his own accord —while the good man acts for honour's sake, and the more so the better he is, and acts for his friend's sake, and sacrifices his own interest.

But the facts clash with these arguments, and this is not surprising. For men say that one ought to love best one's best friend, and a man's best friend is one who wishes well to the object of his wish for his sake, even if no one is to know of it; and these attributes are found most of all in a man's attitude towards himself, and so are all the other attributes by which a friend is defined; for, as we have said, it is from this relation that all the characteristics of friendship have extended to our neighbours. All the proverbs, too, agree with this, e.g. "a single soul," and "what friends have is common property," and "friendship is equality," and "charity begins at home"; for all these marks will be found most in a

man's relation to himself; he is his own best friend and
therefore ought to love himself best. It is therefore a
reasonable question, which of the two views we should
follow; for both are plausible.

Perhaps we ought to mark off such arguments from
each other and determine how far and in what respects
each view is right. Now if we grasp the sense in which
each school uses the phrase "lover of self," the truth may
become evident. Those who use the term as one of reproach ascribe self-love to people who assign to themselves the greater share of wealth, honours, and bodily
pleasures; for these are what most people desire, and
busy themselves about as though they were the best of
all things, which is the reason, too, why they become objects of competition. So those who are grasping with
regard to these things gratify their appetites and in general their feelings and the irrational element of the soul;
and most men are of this nature (which is the reason
why the epithet has come to be used as it is—it takes its
meaning from the prevailing type of self-love, which is
a bad one); it is just, therefore, that men who are lovers
of self in this way are reproached for being so. That it
is those who give themselves the preference in regard to
objects of this sort that most people usually call lovers
of self is plain; for if a man were always anxious that he
himself, above all things, should act justly, temperately,
or in accordance with any other of the virtues, and in
general were always to try to secure for himself the honourable course, no one will call such a man a lover of
self or blame him.

But such a man would seem more than the other a
lover of self; at all events he assigns to himself the things
that are noblest and best, and gratifies the most authoritative element in himself and in all things obeys this;
and just as a city or any other systematic whole is most

properly identified with the most authoritative element in it, so is a man; and therefore the man who loves this and gratifies it is most of all a lover of self. Besides, a man is said to have or not to have self-control according as his reason has or has not the control, on the assumption that this is the man himself; and the things men have done on a rational principle are thought most properly their own acts and voluntary acts. That this is the man himself, then, or is so more than anything else, is plain, and also that the good man loves most this part of him. Whence it follows that he is most truly a lover of self, of another type than that which is a matter of reproach, and as different from that as living according to a rational principle is from living as passion dictates, and desiring what is noble from desiring what seems advantageous. Those, then, who busy themselves in an exceptional degree with noble actions all men approve and praise; and if *all* were to strive towards what is noble and strain every nerve to do the noblest deeds, everything would be as it should be for the common weal, and every one would secure for himself the goods that are greatest, since virtue is the greatest of goods.

Therefore the good man should be a lover of self (for he will both himself profit by doing noble acts, and will benefit his fellows), but the wicked man should not; for he will hurt both himself and his neighbours, following as he does evil passions. For the wicked man, what he does clashes with what he ought to do, but what the good man ought to do he does; for reason in each of its possessors chooses what is best for itself, and the good man obeys his reason. It is true of the good man too that he does many acts for the sake of his friends and his country, and if necessary dies for them; for he will throw away both wealth and honours and in general the goods that are objects of competition, gaining for himself no-

ARISTOTLE   475

bility; since he would prefer a short period of intense
pleasure to a long one of mild enjoyment, a twelve-
month of noble life to many years of humdrum existence,
and one great and noble action to many trivial ones.
Now those who die for others doubtless attain this result;
it is therefore a great prize that they choose for themselves. They will throw away wealth too on condition
that their friends will gain more; for while a man's
friend gains wealth he himself achieves nobility; he is
therefore assigning the greater good to himself. The
same too is true of honour and office; all these things he
will sacrifice to his friend; for this is noble and laudable
for himself. Rightly then is he thought to be good, since
he chooses nobility before all else. But he may even give
up actions to his friend; it may be nobler to become the
cause of his friend's acting than to act himself. In all the
actions, therefore, that men are praised for, the good
man is seen to assign to himself the greater share in what
is noble. In this sense, then, as has been said, a man
should be a lover of self; but in the sense in which most
men are so, he ought not.

9. It is also disputed whether the happy man will need
friends or not. It is said that those who are supremely
happy and self-sufficient have no need of friends; for
they have the things that are good, and therefore being
self-sufficient they need nothing further, while a friend,
being another self, furnishes what a man cannot provide
by his own effort; whence the saying "when fortune is
kind, what need of friends?" But it seems strange, when
one assigns all good things to the happy man, not to assign friends, who are thought the greatest of external
goods. And if it is more characteristic of a friend to do
well by another than to be well done by, and to confer
benefits is characteristic of the good man and of virtue,

and it is nobler to do well by friends than by strangers, the good man will need people to do well by. This is why the question is asked whether we need friends more in prosperity or in adversity, on the assumption that not only does a man in adversity need people to confer benefits on him, but also those who are prospering need people to do well by. Surely it is strange, too, to make the supremely happy man a solitary; for no one would choose the whole world on condition of being alone, since man is a political creature and one whose nature is to live with others. Therefore even the happy man lives with others; for he has the things that are by nature good. And plainly it is better to spend his days with friends and good men than with strangers or any chance persons. Therefore the happy man needs friends.

From *Nicomachean Ethics*, Book IX, chaps. 8–9.
Translated by W. D. Ross.

○

NATURE AND CULTURE

ANTIPHON

THE commands of law (nomos) are artificial, those of nature (physis) necessary. The commands of law are the result of agreement, not of growth; the commands of nature are the result of growth, not of agreement. Therefore the transgressor of the law, if he escapes the notice of those who made the agreement, is free of dishonor or punishment, but not if he is seen. But suppose a man goes against possibility and does violence to something that has grown up in nature, if he escapes the notice of all men, the harm is no less; if all see him, the harm is no greater. For the damage is not a matter of opinion but of reality. The point of this inquiry is that the majority of the rights laid down by law are at enmity with nature.

Translated by R. Webster.

O

SELF-CONTROL

EPICTETUS

OF ALL existing things some are in our power, and others are not in our power. In our power are thought, impulse, will to get and will to avoid, and, in a word, everything which is our own doing. Things not in our power include the body, property, reputation, office, and, in a word, everything which is not our own doing. Things in our power are by nature free, unhindered, untrammelled; things not in our power are weak, servile, subject to hindrance, dependent on others. Remember then that if you imagine that what is naturally slavish is free and what is naturally another's is your own, you will be hampered, you will mourn, you will be put to confusion, you will blame gods and men; but if you think that only your own belongs to you, and that what is another's is indeed another's, no one will ever put compulsion or hindrance on you, you will blame none, you will accuse none, you will do nothing against your will, no one will harm you, you will have no enemy, for no harm can touch you.

1. Aiming then at these high matters, you must remember that to attain them requires more than ordinary effort; you will have to give up some things entirely, and put off others for the moment. And if you would have these also—office and wealth—it may be that you will

fail to get them, just because your desire is set on the former, and you will certainly fail to attain those things which alone bring freedom and happiness.

Make it your study then to confront every harsh impression with the words, "You are but an impression, and not at all what you seem to be." Then test it by those rules that you possess; and first by this—the chief test of all—"Is it concerned with what is in our power or with what is not in our power?" And if it is concerned with what is not in our power, be ready with the answer that it is nothing to you.

2. Remember that the will to get promises attainment of what you will, and the will to avoid promises escape from what you avoid; and he who fails to get what he wills is unfortunate, and he who does not escape what he wills to avoid is miserable. If then you try to avoid only what is unnatural in the region within your control, you will escape from all that you avoid; but if you try to avoid disease or death or poverty you will be miserable.

Therefore let your will to avoid have no concern with what is not in man's power; direct it only to things in man's power that are contrary to nature. But for the moment you must utterly remove the will to get; for if you will to get something not in man's power you are bound to be unfortunate; while none of the things in man's power that you could honourably will to get is yet within your reach. Impulse to act and not to act, these are your concern; yet exercise them gently and without strain, and provisionally.

3. When anything, from the meanest thing upwards, is attractive or serviceable or an object of affection, remember always to say to yourself, "What is its nature?" If you are fond of a jug, say you are fond of a jug; then you will not be disturbed if it be broken. If you kiss your

child or your wife, say to yourself that you are kissing a human being, for then if death strikes it you will not be disturbed.

4. When you are about to take something in hand, remind yourself what manner of thing it is. If you are going to bathe put before your mind what happens in the bath—water pouring over some, others being jostled, some reviling, others stealing; and you will set to work more securely if you say to yourself at once: "I want to bathe, and I want to keep my will in harmony with nature," and so in each thing you do; for in this way, if anything turns up to hinder you in your bathing, you will be ready to say, "I did not want only to bathe, but to keep my will in harmony with nature, and I shall not so keep it, if I lose my temper at what happens."

5. What disturbs men's minds is not events but their judgments on events. For instance, death is nothing dreadful, or else Socrates would have thought it so. No, the only dreadful thing about it is men's judgment that it is dreadful. And so when we are hindered, or disturbed, or distressed, let us never lay the blame on others, but on ourselves, that is, on our own judgments. To accuse others for one's own misfortunes is a sign of want of education; to accuse oneself shows that one's education has begun; to accuse neither oneself nor others shows that one's education is complete.

6. Be not elated at an excellence which is not your own. If the horse in his pride were to say, "I am handsome," we could bear with it. But when you say with pride, "I have a handsome horse," know that the good horse is the ground of your pride. You ask then what you can call your own. The answer is—the way you deal with your impressions. Therefore when you deal with your impressions in accord with nature, then you may be proud in-

deed, for your pride will be in a good which is your own.

7. When you are on a voyage, and your ship is at anchorage, and you disembark to get fresh water, you may pick up a small shellfish or a truffle by the way, but you must keep your attention fixed on the ship, and keep looking towards it constantly, to see if the Helmsman calls you; and if he does, you have to leave everything, or be bundled on board with your legs tied like a sheep. So it is in life. If you have a dear wife or child given you, they are like the shellfish or the truffle, they are very well in their way. Only, if the Helmsman call, run back to your ship, leave all else, and do not look behind you. And if you are old, never go far from the ship, so that when you are called you may not fail to appear.

8. Ask not that events should happen as you will, but let your will be that events should happen as they do, and you shall have peace.

9. Sickness is a hindrance to the body, but not to the will, unless the will consent. Lameness is a hindrance to the leg, but not to the will. Say this to yourself at each event that happens, for you shall find that though it hinders something else it will not hinder you.

10. When anything happens to you, always remember to turn to yourself and ask what faculty you have to deal with it. If you see a beautiful boy or a beautiful woman, you will find continence the faculty to exercise there; if trouble is laid on you, you will find endurance; if ribaldry, you will find patience. And if you train yourself in this habit your impressions will not carry you away.

11. Never say of anything, "I lost it," but say, "I gave it back." Has your child died? It was given back. Has your wife died? She was given back. Has your estate been taken from you? Was not this also given back? But you say, "He who took it from me is wicked." What does it matter to you through whom the Giver asked it back?

As long as He gives it you, take care of it, but not as your own; treat it as passers-by treat an inn.

12. If you wish to make progress, abandon reasonings of this sort: "If I neglect my affairs I shall have nothing to live on"; "If I do not punish my son, he will be wicked." For it is better to die of hunger, so that you be free from pain and free from fear, than to live in plenty and be troubled in mind. It is better for your son to be wicked than for you to be miserable. Wherefore begin with little things. Is your drop of oil spilt? Is your sup of wine stolen? Say to yourself, "This is the price paid for freedom from passion, this is the price of a quiet mind." Nothing can be had without a price. When you call your slave-boy, reflect that he may not be able to hear you, and if he hears you, he may not be able to do anything you want. But he is not so well off that it rests with him to give you peace of mind.

13. If you wish to make progress, you must be content in external matters to seem a fool and a simpleton; do not wish men to think you know anything, and if any should think you to be somebody, distrust yourself. For know that it is not easy to keep your will in accord with nature and at the same time keep outward things; if you attend to one you must needs neglect the other.

14. It is silly to want your children and your wife and your friends to live for ever, for that means that you want what is not in your control to be in your control, and what is not your own to be yours. In the same way if you want your servant to make no mistakes, you are a fool, for you want vice not to be vice but something different. But if you want not to be disappointed in your will to get, you can attain to that.

Exercise yourself then in what lies in your power. Each man's master is the man who has authority over what he wishes or does not wish, to secure the one or to take away the other. Let him then who wishes to be free not wish for anything or avoid anything that depends on others; or else he is bound to be a slave.

15. Remember that you must behave in life as you would at a banquet. A dish is handed round and comes to you; put out your hand and take it politely. It passes you; do not stop it. It has not reached you; do not be impatient to get it, but wait till your turn comes. Bear yourself thus towards children, wife, office, wealth, and one day you will be worthy to banquet with the gods. But if when they are set before you, you do not take them but despise them, then you shall not only share the gods' banquet, but shall share their rule. For by so doing Diogenes and Heraclitus and men like them were called divine and deserved the name.

16. When you see a man shedding tears in sorrow for a child abroad or dead, or for loss of property, beware that you are not carried away by the impression that it is outward ills that make him miserable. Keep this thought by you: "What distresses him is not the event, for that does not distress another, but his judgment on the event." Therefore do not hesitate to sympathize with him so far as words go, and if it so chance, even to groan with him; but take heed that you do not also groan in your inner being.

17. Remember that you are an actor in a play, and the Playwright chooses the manner of it: if he wants it short, it is short; if long, it is long. If he wants you to act a poor man you must act the part with all your powers; and so if your part be a cripple or a magistrate or a plain man. For your business is to act the character that is given you and act it well; the choice of the cast is Another's.

18. When a raven croaks with evil omen, let not the impression carry you away, but straightway distinguish

in your own mind and say, "These portents mean nothing to me; but only to my bit of a body or my bit of property or name, or my children or my wife. But for me all omens are favourable if I will, for, whatever the issue may be, it is in my power to get benefit therefrom."

19. You can be invincible, if you never enter on a contest where victory is not in your power. Beware then that when you see a man raised to honour or great power or high repute you do not let your impression carry you away. For if the reality of good lies in what is in our power, there is no room for envy or jealousy. And you will not wish to be praetor, or prefect or consul, but to be free; and there is but one way to freedom—to despise what is not in our power.

20. Remember that foul words or blows in themselves are no outrage, but your judgment that they are so. So when any one makes you angry, know that it is your own thought that has angered you. Wherefore make it your first endeavour not to let your impressions carry you away. For if once you gain time and delay, you will find it easier to control yourself.

21. Keep before your eyes from day to day death and exile and all things that seem terrible, but death most of all, and then you will never set your thoughts on what is low and will never desire anything beyond measure.

22. If you set your desire on philosophy you must at once prepare to meet with ridicule and the jeers of many who will say, "Here he is again, turned philosopher. Where has he got these proud looks?" Nay, put on no proud looks, but hold fast to what seems best to you, in confidence that God has set you at this post. And remember that if you abide where you are, those who first laugh at you will one day admire you, and that if you give way to them, you will get doubly laughed at.

23. If it ever happen to you to be diverted to things

outside, so that you desire to please another, know that you have lost your life's plan. Be content then always to be a philosopher; if you wish to be regarded as one too, show yourself that you are one and you will be able to achieve it.

24. Let not reflections such as these afflict you: "I shall live without honour, and never be of any account"; for if lack of honour is an evil, no one but yourself can involve you in evil any more than in shame. Is it your business to get office or to be invited to an entertainment?

Certainly not.

Where then is the dishonour you talk of? How can you be "of no account anywhere," when you ought to count for something in those matters only which are in your power, where you may achieve the highest worth?

"But my friends," you say, "will lack assistance."

What do you mean by "lack assistance"? They will not have cash from you and you will not make them Roman citizens. Who told you that to do these things is in our power, and not dependent upon others? Who can give to another what is not his to give?

"Get them then," says he, "that we may have them."

If I can get them and keep my self-respect, honour, magnanimity, show the way and I will get them. But if you call on me to lose the good things that are mine, in order that you may win things that are not good, look how unfair and thoughtless you are. And which do you really prefer? Money, or a faithful, modest friend? Therefore help me rather to keep these qualities, and do not expect from me actions which will make me lose them.

"But my country," says he, "will lack assistance, so far as lies in me."

Once more I ask, What assistance do you mean? It will not owe colonnades or baths to you. What of that?

It does not owe shoes to the blacksmith or arms to the shoemaker; it is sufficient if each man fulfils his own function. Would you do it no good if you secured to it another faithful and modest citizen?

"Yes."

Well, then, you would not be useless to it.

"What place then shall I have in the city?"

Whatever place you can hold while you keep your character for honour and self-respect. But if you are going to lose these qualities in trying to benefit your city, what benefit, I ask, would you have done her when you attain to the perfection of being lost to shame and honour?

25. Has some one had precedence of you at an entertainment or a levée or been called in before you to give advice? If these things are good you ought to be glad that he got them; if they are evil, do not be angry that you did not get them yourself. Remember that if you want to get what is not in your power, you cannot earn the same reward as others unless you act as they do. How is it possible for one who does not haunt the great man's door to have equal shares with one who does, or one who does not go in his train equality with one who does; or one who does not praise him with one who does? You will be unjust then and insatiable if you wish to get these privileges for nothing, without paying their price. What is the price of a lettuce? An obol perhaps. If then a man pays his obol and gets his lettuces, and you do not pay and do not get them, do not think you are defrauded. For as he has the lettuces so you have the obol you did not give. The same principle holds good too in conduct. You were not invited to some one's entertainment? Because you did not give the host the price for which he sells his dinner. He sells it for compliments, he sells it for attentions. Pay him the price then, if it is to your profit.

But if you wish to get the one and yet not give up the other, nothing can satisfy you in your folly.

What! you say, you have nothing instead of the dinner?

Nay, you have this, you have not praised the man you did not want to praise, you have not had to bear with the insults of his doorstep.

26. It is in our power to discover the will of Nature from those matters on which we have no difference of opinion. For instance, when another man's slave has broken the wine-cup we are very ready to say at once, "Such things must happen." Know then that when your own cup is broken, you ought to behave in the same way as when your neighbour's was broken. Apply the same principle to higher matters. Is another's child or wife dead? Not one of us but would say, "Such is the lot of man"; but when one's own dies, straightway one cries, "Alas! miserable am I." But we ought to remember what our feelings are when we hear it of another.

27. As a mark is not set up for men to miss it, so there is nothing intrinsically evil in the world.

From *The Manual*, sections 1–27.
Translated 1916 by P. E. Matheson.

O

LOVE

SOPHOCLES

Love, unconquerable
Waster of rich men, keeper
Of warm lights and all-night vigil
In the soft face of a girl:
Sea-wanderer, forest-visitor!

Even the pure Immortals cannot escape you,
And mortal man, in his one day's dusk,
Trembles before your glory.

Surely you swerve upon ruin
The just man's consenting heart,
As here you have made bright anger
Strike between father and son—
And none has conquered but Love!
A girl's glance working the will of heaven:
Pleasure to her alone who mocks us,
Merciless Aphrodite.

From *Antigone*.
Translated by Dudley Fitts and Robert Fitzgerald.

O

EROS

PLATO

"WHAT then is Love?" I asked; "Is he mortal?"
"No." "What then?" "As in the former instance,
he is neither mortal nor immortal, but in a mean between
the two." "What is he, Diotima?" "He is a great spirit
(δαίμων), and like all spirits he is intermediate between
the divine and the mortal." "And what," I said, "is his
power?" "He interprets," she replied, "between gods and
men, conveying and taking across to the gods the prayers
and sacrifices of men, and to men the commands and replies of the gods; he is the mediator who spans the chasm
which divides them, and therefore in him all is bound
together, and through him the arts of the prophet and
the priest, their sacrifices and mysteries and charms, and
all prophecy and incantation, find their way. For God
mingles not with man; but through Love all the inter-

course and converse of god with man, whether awake or asleep, is carried on. The wisdom which understands this is spiritual; all other wisdom, such as that of arts and handicrafts, is mean and vulgar. Now these spirits or intermediate powers are many and diverse, and one of them is Love." "And who," I said, "was his father, and who his mother?" "The tale," she said, "will take time; nevertheless I will tell you. On the birthday of Aphrodite there was a feast of the gods, at which the god Poros or Plenty, who is the son of Metis or Discretion, was one of the guests. When the feast was over, Penia or Poverty, as the manner is on such occasions, came about the doors to beg. Now Plenty, who was the worse for nectar (there was no wine in those days), went into the garden of Zeus and fell into a heavy sleep; and Poverty considering her own straitened circumstances, plotted to have a child by him, and accordingly she lay down at his side and conceived Love, who partly because he is naturally a lover of the beautiful, and because Aphrodite is herself beautiful, and also because he was born on her birthday, is her follower and attendant. And as his parentage is, so also are his fortunes. In the first place he is always poor, and anything but tender and fair, as the many imagine him; and he is rough and squalid, and has no shoes, nor a house to dwell in; on the bare earth exposed he lies under the open heaven, in the streets, or at the doors of houses, taking his rest; and like his mother he is always in distress. Like his father too, whom he also partly resembles, he is always plotting against the fair and good; he is bold, enterprising, strong, a mighty hunter, always weaving some intrigue or other, keen in the pursuit of wisdom, fertile in resources; a philosopher at all times, terrible as an enchanter, sorcerer, sophist. He is by nature neither mortal nor immortal, but alive and flourishing at one moment when he is in plenty, and dead at another moment, and again alive by reason of his father's nature. But that which is always flowing in is always flowing out, and so he is never in want and never in wealth; and, further, he is in a mean between ignorance and knowledge. The truth of the matter is this: No god is a philosopher or seeker after wisdom, for he is wise already; nor does any man who is wise seek after wisdom. Neither do the ignorant seek after wisdom. For herein is the evil of ignorance, that he who is neither good nor wise is nevertheless satisfied with himself: he has no desire for that of which he feels no want." "But who then, Diotima," I said, "are the lovers of wisdom, if they are neither the wise nor the foolish?" "A child may answer that question," she replied; "they are those who are in a mean between the two; Love is one of them. For wisdom is a most beautiful thing, and Love is of the beautiful; and therefore Love is also a philosopher or lover of wisdom, and being a lover of wisdom is in a mean between the wise and the ignorant. And of this too his birth is the cause; for his father is wealthy and wise, and his mother poor and foolish. Such, my dear Socrates, is the nature of the spirit Love. The error in your conception of him was very natural, and as I imagine from what you say, has arisen out of a confusion of love and the beloved, which made you think that love was all beautiful. For the beloved is the truly beautiful, and delicate, and perfect, and blessed; but the principle of love is of another nature, and is such as I have described."

I said: "O thou stranger woman, thou sayest well; but, assuming Love to be such as you say, what is the use of him to men?" "That, Socrates," she replied, "I will attempt to unfold: of his nature and birth I have already spoken; and you acknowledge that love is of the beautiful. But some one will say: Of the beautiful in what, Socrates and Diotima?—or rather let me put the question more clearly, and ask: When a man loves the beautiful, what does he desire?" I answered her "That the beautiful may be his." "Still," she said, "the answer suggests a further question: What is given by the possession of beauty?" "To what you have asked," I replied, "I have no answer ready." "Then," she said, "let me put the word 'good' in the place of the beautiful, and repeat the question once more: If he who loves loves the good, what is it then that he loves?" "The possession of the good," I said. "And what does he gain who possesses the good?" "Happiness," I replied; "there is less difficulty in answering that question." "Yes," she said, "the happy are made happy by the acquisition of good things. Nor is there any need to ask why a man desires happiness; the answer is already final." "You are right," I said. "And is this wish and this desire common to all? and do all men always desire their own good, or only some men? —what say you?" "All men," I replied; "the desire is common to all." "Why, then," she rejoined, "are not all men, Socrates, said to love, but only some of them? whereas you say that all men are always loving the same things." "I myself wonder," I said, "why this is." "There is nothing to wonder at," she replied; "the reason is that one part of love is separated off and receives the name of the whole, but the other parts have other names." "Give an illustration," I said. She answered me as follows: "There is poetry, which, as you know, is complex and manifold. All creation or passage of non-being into being is poetry or making, and the processes of all art are creative; and the masters of arts are all poets or makers." "Very true." "Still," she said, "you know that they are not called poets, but have other names; only that portion of the art which is separated off from the rest, and is concerned with music and metre, is termed poetry, and they who possess poetry in this sense of the word are called poets." "Very true," I said. "And the same holds of love. For you may say generally that all desire of good and happiness is only the great and subtle power of love; but they who are drawn towards him by any other path, whether the path of money-making or gymnastics or philosophy, are not called lovers—the name of the whole is appropriated to those whose affection takes one form only—they alone are said to love, or to be lovers." "I dare say," I replied, "that you are right." "Yes," she added, "and you hear people say that lovers are seeking for their other half; but I say that they are seeking neither for the half of themselves, nor for the whole, unless the half or the whole be also a good. And they will cut off their own hands and feet and cast them away, if they are evil; for they love not what is their own, unless perchance there be some one who calls what belongs to him the good, and what belongs to another the evil. For there is nothing which men love but the good. Is there anything?" "Certainly, I should say, that there is nothing." "Then," she said, "the simple truth is, that men love the good." "Yes," I said. "To which must be added that they love the possession of the good?" "Yes, that must be added." "And not only the possession, but the everlasting possession of the good?" "That must be added too." "Then love," she said, "may be described generally as the love of the everlasting possession of the good?" "That is most true."

"Then if this be the nature of love, can you tell me further," she said, "what is the manner of the pursuit? what are they doing who show all this eagerness and heat which is called love? and what is the object which they have in view? Answer me." "Nay, Diotima," I replied, "if I had known, I should not have wondered at your wisdom, neither should I have come to learn from you about this very matter." "Well," she said, "I will teach you:—The object which they have in view is birth in beauty, whether of body or soul." "I do not understand you," I said; "the oracle requires an explanation." "I will make my meaning clearer," she replied. "I mean to say, that all men are bringing to the birth in their bodies and in their souls. There is a certain age at which human nature is desirous of procreation—procreation which must be in beauty and not in deformity; and this procreation is the union of man and woman, and is a divine thing; for conception and generation are an immortal principle in the mortal creature, and in the inharmonious they can never be. But the deformed is always inharmonious with the divine, and the beautiful harmonious. Beauty, then, is the destiny or goddess of parturition who presides at birth, and therefore, when approaching beauty, the conceiving power is propitious, and diffusive, and benign, and begets and bears fruit: at the sight of ugliness she frowns and contracts and has a sense of pain, and turns away, and shrivels up, and not without a pang refrains from conception. And this is the reason why, when the hour of conception arrives, and the teeming nature is full, there is such a flutter and ecstasy about beauty whose approach is the alleviation of the pain of travail. For love, Socrates, is not, as you imagine, the love of the beautiful only." "What then?" "The love of generation and of birth in beauty." "Yes," I said. "Yes, indeed," she replied. "But why of generation?" "Because to the mortal creature, generation is a sort of eternity and immortality," she replied; "and if, as has been already admitted, love is of the everlasting possession of the good, all men will necessarily desire im-

mortality together with good: Wherefore love is of immortality."

All this she taught me at various times when she spoke
of love. And I remember her once saying to me, "What
is the cause, Socrates, of love, and the attendant desire?
See you not how all animals, birds, as well as beasts, in
their desire of procreation, are in agony when they take
the infection of love, which begins with the desire of
union; whereto is added the care of offspring, on whose
behalf the weakest are ready to battle against the strongest even to the uttermost, and to die for them, and will
let themselves be tormented with hunger or suffer anything in order to maintain their young. Man may be supposed to act thus from reason; but why should animals
have these passionate feelings? Can you tell me why?"
Again I replied that I did not know. She said to me:
"And do you expect ever to become a master in the
art of love, if you do not know this?" "But I have told
you already, Diotima, that my ignorance is the reason
why I come to you; for I am conscious that I want a
teacher; tell me then the cause of this and of the other
mysteries of love." "Marvel not," she said, "if you believe that love is of the immortal, as we have several
times acknowledged; for here again, and on the same
principle too, the mortal nature is seeking as far as is
possible to be everlasting and immortal: and this is only
to be attained by generation, because generation always
leaves behind a new existence in the place of the old.
Nay even in the life of the same individual there is succession and not absolute unity: a man is called the same,
and yet in the short interval which elapses between
youth and age, and in which every animal is said to
have life and identity, he is undergoing a perpetual
process of loss and reparation—hair, flesh, bones, blood,

and the whole body are always changing. Which is true not only of the body, but also of the soul, whose habits, tempers, opinions, desires, pleasures, pains, fears, never remain the same in any one of us, but are always coming and going; and equally true of knowledge, and what is still more surprising to us mortals, not only do the sciences in general spring up and decay, so that in respect of them we are never the same; but each of them individually experiences a like change. For what is implied in the word 'recollection,' but the departure of knowledge, which is ever being forgotten, and is renewed and preserved by recollection, and appears to be the same although in reality new, according to that law of succession by which all mortal things are preserved, not absolutely the same, but by substitution, the old worn-out mortality leaving another new and similar existence behind—unlike the divine, which is always the same and not another? And in this way, Socrates, the mortal body, or mortal anything, partakes of immortality; but the immortal in another way. Marvel not then at the love which all men have of their offspring; for that universal love and interest is for the sake of immortality."

I was astonished at her words, and said: "Is this really true, O thou wise Diotima?" And she answered with all the authority of an accomplished sophist: "Of that, Socrates, you may be assured—think only of the ambition of men, and you will wonder at the senselessness of their ways, unless you consider how they are stirred by the love of an immortality of fame. They are ready to run all risks greater far than they would have run for their children, and to spend money and undergo any sort of toil, and even to die, for the sake of leaving behind them a name which shall be eternal. Do you imagine that Alcestis would have died to save Admetus, or Achilles to avenge Patroclus, or your own Codrus in order to

preserve the kingdom for his sons, if they had not imagined that the memory of their virtues, which still
survives among us, would be immortal? Nay," she said,
"I am persuaded that all men do all things, and the
better they are the more they do them, in hope of the
glorious fame of immortal virtue; for they desire the immortal.

"Those who are pregnant in the body only, betake
themselves to women and beget children—this is the
character of their love; their offspring, as they hope, will
preserve their memory and give them the blessedness
and immortality which they desire in the future. But
souls which are pregnant—for there certainly are men
who are more creative in their souls than in their bodies
—conceive that which is proper for the soul to conceive
or contain. And what are these conceptions?—wisdom
and virtue in general. And such creators are poets and
all artists who are deserving of the name inventor. But
the greatest and fairest sort of wisdom by far is that
which is concerned with the ordering of states and families, and which is called temperance and justice. And
he who in youth has the seed of these implanted in him
and is himself inspired, when he comes to maturity desires to beget and generate. He wanders about seeking
beauty that he may beget offspring—for in deformity he
will beget nothing—and naturally embraces the beautiful rather than the deformed body; above all when he
finds a fair and noble and well-nurtured soul, he embraces the two in one person, and to such an one he is
full of speech about virtue and the nature and pursuits
of a good man; and he tries to educate him; and at the
touch of the beautiful which is ever present to his memory, even when absent, he brings forth that which he
had conceived long before, and in company with him
tends that which he brings forth; and they are married

by a far nearer tie and have a closer friendship than those who beget mortal children, for the children who are their common offspring are fairer and more immortal. Who, when he thinks of Homer and Hesiod and other great poets, would not rather have their children than ordinary human ones? Who would not emulate them in the creation of children such as theirs, which have preserved their memory and given them everlasting glory? Or who would not have such children as Lycurgus left behind him to be the saviours, not only of Lacedaemon, but of Hellas, as one may say? There is Solon, too, who is the revered father of Athenian laws; and many others there are in many other places, both among Hellenes and barbarians, who have given to the world many noble works, and have been the parents of virtue of every kind; and many temples have been raised in their honour for the sake of children such as theirs; which were never raised in honour of any one, for the sake of his mortal children.

"These are the lesser mysteries of love, into which even you, Socrates, may enter; to the greater and more hidden ones which are the crown of these, and to which, if you pursue them in a right spirit, they will lead, I know not whether you will be able to attain. But I will do my utmost to inform you, and do you follow if you can. For he who would proceed aright in this matter should begin in youth to visit beautiful forms; and first, if he be guided by his instructor aright, to love one such form only—out of that he should create fair thoughts; and soon he will of himself perceive that the beauty of one form is akin to the beauty of another; and then if beauty of form in general is his pursuit, how foolish would he be not to recognize that the beauty in every form is one and the same! And when he perceives this he will abate his violent love of the one, which he will

despise and deem a small thing, and will become a lover
of all beautiful forms; in the next stage he will consider
that the beauty of the mind is more honourable than the
beauty of the outward form. So that if a virtuous soul
have but a little comeliness, he will be content to love
and tend him, and will search out and bring to the birth
thoughts which may improve the young, until he is
compelled to contemplate and see the beauty of institutions and laws, and to understand that the beauty of
them all is of one family, and that personal beauty is a
trifle; and after laws and institutions he will go on to the
sciences, that he may see their beauty, being not like
a servant in love with the beauty of one youth or man or
institution, himself a slave mean and narrow-minded,
but drawing towards and contemplating the vast sea of
beauty, he will create many fair and noble thoughts
and notions in boundless love of wisdom; until on that
shore he grows and waxes strong, and at last the vision
is revealed to him of a single science, which is the science of beauty everywhere. To this I will proceed;
please to give me your very best attention:

"He who has been instructed thus far in the things
of love, and who has learned to see the beautiful in due
order and succession, when he comes toward the end
will suddenly perceive a nature of wondrous beauty
(and this, Socrates, is the final cause of all our former
toils)—a nature which in the first place is everlasting,
not growing and decaying, or waxing and waning; secondly, not fair in one point of view and foul in another,
or at one time or in one relation or at one place fair, at
another time or in another relation or at another place
foul, as if fair to some and foul to others, or in the likeness of a face or hands or any other part of the bodily
frame, or in any form of speech or knowledge, or existing in any other being, as for example, in an animal, or

in heaven, or in earth, or in any other place; but beauty absolute, separate, simple, and everlasting, which without diminution and without increase, or any change, is imparted to the ever-growing and perishing beauties of all other things. He who from these ascending under the influence of true love, begins to perceive that beauty, is not far from the end. And the true order of going, or being led by another, to the things of love, is to begin from the beauties of earth and mount upwards for the sake of that other beauty, using these as steps only, and from one going on to two, and from two to all fair forms, and from fair forms to fair practices, and from fair practices to fair notions, until from fair notions he arrives at the notion of absolute beauty, and at last knows what the essence of beauty is. This, my dear Socrates," said the stranger of Mantineia, "is that life above all others which man should live, in the contemplation of beauty absolute; a beauty which if you once beheld, you would see not to be after the measure of gold, and garments, and fair boys and youths, whose presence now entrances you; and you and many a one would be content to live seeing them only and conversing with them without meat or drink, if that were possible—you only want to look at them and to be with them. But what if man had eyes to see the true beauty—the divine beauty, I mean, pure and clear and unalloyed, not clogged with the pollutions of mortality and all the colours and vanities of human life—thither looking, and holding converse with the true beauty simple and divine? Remember how in that communion only, beholding beauty with the eye of the mind, he will be enabled to bring forth, not images of beauty, but realities (for he has hold not of an image but of a reality), and bringing forth and nourishing true virtue to become the friend of God and be immortal, if mortal man may. Would that be an ignoble life?"

Such, Phaedrus—and I speak not only to you, but to all of you—were the words of Diotima; and I am persuaded of their truth. And being persuaded of them, I try to persuade others, that in the attainment of this end human nature will not easily find a helper better than love. And therefore, also, I say that every man ought to honour him as I myself honour him, and walk in his ways, and exhort others to do the same, and praise the power and spirit of love according to the measure of my ability now and ever.

The words which I have spoken, you, Phaedrus, may call an encomium of love, or anything else which you please.

From *Symposium*. Translated by Benjamin Jowett.

○

LITERARY FORMS

○

LYRIC

I

ALCAEUS

Drink, Melanippus, and be drunk with me.
How can you think that you will ever see,

Once over Ácheron, the pure bright day
Again? Come, throw such proud desires away.

Sîsyphus, wisest of men, thought he could find
An artifice that should leave death behind,

But fate decreed his wisdom should not save
Him from twice crossing Ácheron's rough wave,

And Cronus' son gave him great sufferings
Below the dark earth. Hope not for such things,

While we are young. Now is the moment, now,
To take what happiness the gods allow.

Translated by C. M. Bowra.

II

ANACREON

Roving god, whose playfellows
Over the mountains' airy brows
    In happy chase are led;
Where Love, who breaks the heart of pride,
Or Nymphs amuse thee, violet-eyed,
Or Aphrodîtê keeps thy side,
    The goddess rosy-red—
Lord Dionyse, I kneel to thee;
Stoop to me of thy charity
    And this my prayer receive:
Dear Lord, thy best persuasion use,
Bid Cleobûlus not refuse
    The gift of love I give.

Translated by T. F. Higham.

III

MELEAGER

Still in his mother's lap, a child playing with dice in the morning, Love played my life away.

Translated by J. W. Mackail.

IV

SAPPHO

Blest beyond earth's bliss, with heaven I deem him
  Blest, the man that in thy presence near thee
Face to face may sit, and while thou speakest,
  Listening may hear thee,

And thy sweet-voiced laughter—In my bosom
  The rapt heart so troubleth, wildly stirred:
Let me see thee, but a glimpse—and straightway
  Utterance of word

Fails me; no voice comes; my tongue is palsied;
  Thrilling fire through all my flesh hath run;
Mine eyes cannot see, mine ears make dinning
  Noises that stun;

The sweat streameth down—my whole frame seized with
  Shivering—and wan paleness o'er me spread,
Greener than the grass; I seem with faintness
  Almost as dead.

Translated by Walter Headlam.

V

SAPPHO

The moon has set and the Pleiades; it is midnight, the time is going by and I lie alone.

Translated by Edwin Marion Cox.

VI

SAPPHO

Some say that the fairest thing upon the dark earth is a host of foot-soldiers, and others again a fleet of ships, but for me it is my beloved. And it is easy to make anyone understand this.

When Helen saw the most beautiful of mortals, she chose for best that one, the destroyer of all the house of Troy, and thought not much of children or dear parent, but was led astray by love to bestow her heart far off, for woman is ever easy to lead astray when she thinks of no account what is near and dear.

Even so, Anactoria, you do not remember, it seems, when she is with you, one the gentle sound of whose footfall I would rather hear and the brightness of whose shining face I would rather see than all the chariots and mail-clad footmen of Lydia.

I know that in this world man cannot have the best; yet to pray for a part of what was once shared is better than to forget it.

Translated by Edwin Marion Cox.

O

EPITAPH

I

SIMONIDES

Strange dust covers thy body, and the lot of death took thee, O Cleisthenes, wandering in the Euxine sea; and thou didst fail of sweet and dear homecoming, nor ever didst reach sea-girt Chios.

II

CALLIMACHUS

Philip the father laid here the twelve-years-old child, his high hope, Nicoteles.

III

ANON.

I Homonoea, who was far clearer-voiced than the Sirens, I who was more golden than the Cyprian herself at revellings and feasts, I the chattering bright swallow lie here, leaving tears to Atimetus, to whom I was dear from girlhood; but unforeseen fate scattered all that great affection.

IV

ANON.

Naiads and chill cattle-pastures, tell to the bees when they come on their springtide way, that old Leucippus perished on a winter's night, setting snares for scamper-

ing hares, and no longer is the tending of the hives dear
to him; but the pastoral dells mourn sore for him who
dwelt with the mountain peak for neighbour.

v

PALLADAS

Breathing thin air in our nostrils we live and look on
the torch of the sun, all we who live what is called life;
and are as organs, receiving our spirits from quickening
airs. If one then chokes that little breath with his hand,
he robs us of life, and brings us down to Hades. Thus
being nothing we wax high in hardihood, feeding on air
from a little breath.

Translated by J. W. Mackail.

O

PASTORAL

THEOCRITUS

IDYLL II: THE SORCERESS

Simaitha, forsaken by her lover, the young athlete Delphis,
endeavours by various magic rites to draw him back to her
house, invoking the Moon by her three names of Selene,
Hekate and Artemis. Afterwards she tells the Goddess the
tale of her love, and of her desertion by her lover, and finally
vows to poison him, if her charms should fail.

It is uncertain whether the scene of this Idyll is the island
of Kos, or of Rhodes, or some town on the Karian coast. The
subject, and to some extent the form, are said by the Greek
commentator, or Scholiast, to have been suggested to Theocritus by one of the lost prose mimes of Sophron, who, however,

had given Simaitha's attendant, Thestylis, a share in the dialogue. Virgil's imitation in his eighth Eclogue is a frigid academic exercise, with none of the passion, the realism and the poetic beauty, which make this Idyll perhaps the greatest love-poem in the whole of classical and modern literature.

WHERE are those laurels? Bring them, Thestylis
——and the love-charms too.
Wreath the cauldron with a crimson fillet of fine wool;
That I may cast a fire-spell on the unkind man I love,
Who now for twelve whole days, the wretch, has never
    come this way,
Nor even knows whether I be alive or dead, nor once
Has he knocked at my doors, ah cruel! Can it be that
    Love
And Aphrodite have borne off his roving heart else-
    whither?
To Timagētos' wrestling school tomorrow will I go,
And find him and reproach him with the wrong he is
    doing me.
But now by fire-magic will I bind him. Thou, O Moon,
Shine fair; for to thee softly, dread Goddess, will I chant,
And to infernal Hekate, at whom the very whelps
Shudder, as she goes between the dead men's tombs
    and the dark blood.
Hail, awful Hekate! and be thou my helper to the end,
Making these charms prove no less potent than the spells
    of Circe,
Or of Medea, or the gold-haired sorceress Perimede.
    O magic wheel, draw hither to my house the man I
    love.
First in the fire barley grains must burn. Come, throw
    them on,
Thestylis. Miserable girl, whither now are flown thy
    wits?

Even to thee am I, vile wretch, become a thing to scorn?
Cast them on, and say thus, "the bones of Delphis I am
    casting."
    O magic wheel, draw hither to my house the man I
    love.

Delphis has wrought me anguish, so against Delphis do
    I burn
This laurel shoot: and as it catches fire and crackles
    loud,
And is burnt up so suddenly, we see not even the ash,
So may the flesh of Delphis be wasted in the flames.
    O magic wheel, draw hither to my house the man I
    love.

Even as now I melt this wax by the aid of Hekate,
So speedily may Myndian Delphis melt away through
    love.
And even as turns this brazen wheel by Aphrodite's
    power,
So restlessly may he too turn and turn around my doors.
    O magic wheel, draw hither to my house the man I
    love.

Now will I burn the bran. Yea thou, Artemis, thou hast
    power
To move Hell's adamantine gates, and all else that is
    stubborn.
Thestylis, hark, the dogs are baying now throughout the
    town:
At the cross-roads is the Goddess. Quick, beat the brazen
    gong.
    O magic wheel, draw hither to my house the man I
    love.

Behold, the sea is silent, and silent are the winds;
But never silent is the anguish here within my breast,
Since I am all on fire for him who has made me, un-
    happy me,

Not a wife, but a worthless woman, a maiden now no
 more.

O magic wheel, draw hither to my house the man I
 love.

Thrice do I pour libation, Goddess, and thrice speak this
 prayer:

Whether it be a woman lies beside him, or a man,

Let such oblivion seize him, as on Dia[1] once, they tell,

Seized Theseus, when he quite forgot the fair-tressed
 Ariadne.

O magic wheel, draw hither to my house the man I
 love.

Horse-madness is a herb that grows in Arcady, and
 maddens

All the colts that range the hills, and the fleet-footed
 mares.

Even so frenzied may I now see Delphis: to this house

May he speed like a madman from the oily wrestling
 school.

O magic wheel, draw hither to my house the man I
 love.

This fringe from his mantle did Delphis lose, which now

I pluck to shreds and cast it into the ravenous fire.

Woe's me, remorseless Love, why clinging like a fen-
 born leech

Hast thou sucked from my body the dark blood every
 drop?

O magic wheel, draw hither to my house the man I
 love.

A lizard will I bray, and bring him a deadly draught
 tomorrow.

But now, Thestylis, take these magic herbs, and secretly

Smear them upon his upper lintel, while it is night still,

---

[1] Dia is another name for the island of Naxos, one of the Cyclades.

Then spit, and say, "It is the bones of Delphis that I
    smear."
   O magic wheel, draw hither to my house the man I
    love.

Now that I am alone, whence am I to bewail my love?
Wherefrom begin my tale? Who was it brought this woe
    upon me?
   Anaxo, daughter of Euboulos, bearing the mystic
    basket,
Passed this way in procession to the grove of Artemis,
Many a wild beast thronging round her, among them a
    lioness.
   Bethink thee of my love and whence it came, O holy
    Moon.
So Theucharidas' Thracian nurse, who since has gone to
    bliss,
But then was living at our doors, besought and entreated
    me
To come and see the pageant; and I, poor luckless fool,
Went with her in a linen gown, a lovely trailing robe,
Over which I had thrown a cloak that Klearista lent me.
   Bethink thee of my love and whence it came, O holy
    Moon.
And now, half way along the road, as we passed Lykon's
    house,
I saw Delphis and Eudamippos walking side by side.
Their beards were more golden than flower of heli-
    chryse,
And far more brightly shone their breasts than thou thy-
    self, O Moon;
For from the wrestling school they came, fresh from their
    noble toil.
   Bethink thee of my love and whence it came, O holy
    Moon.

O then I saw, and fell mad straight, and my whole heart
 was fired,
(Woe is me!) and my comely cheeks grew pale; nor did
 I heed
That pageant any longer. And how I came back home
I know not; but a parching fever seized me and con-
 sumed me,
So that I lay pining in bed for ten days and ten nights.
 Bethink thee of my love and whence it came, O holy
 Moon.

And often pale as boxwood grew the colour of my flesh,
And the hairs kept falling from my head, till what was
 left of me
Was naught but skin and bones. To whom did I not now
 resort?
What old crone's house did I not visit, who was skilled in
 spells?
But that way remedy was none; and time fled swiftly by.
 Bethink thee of my love and whence it came, O holy
 Moon.

So at last I told the whole truth to my serving-maid, and
 said:
"Go, Thestylis; find me some cure for my sore malady.
Wholly am I become (woe's me!) the Myndian's slave.
 But go,
Go now and lie in wait for him at the school of Tima-
 gētos;
For there it is he most resorts, there that he loves to
 lounge.
 Bethink thee of my love and whence it came, O holy
 Moon.

And when you are sure no one is near, nod to him
 silently,
And say, 'Simaitha calls you,' and bring him hither
 straight."

So did I speak; and she went hence, and brought back to
    my house
Delphis, the sleek-limbed youth. But I, no sooner was I
    ware
Of his light footfall, as he crossed the threshold of my
    door—
    Bethink thee of my love and whence it came, O holy
      Moon.
—In every limb I froze more cold than snow, and from
    my brow
The sweat came streaming forth and trickling down like
    drops of dew.
Nor had I strength to speak one word, not so much as
    a child's
Whimpering murmur, when it calls to its mother dear in
    sleep;
But all my lovely body turned as stiff as any doll.
    Bethink thee of my love and whence it came, O holy
      Moon.
Then, seeing me, that heartless man, with eyes fixed on
    the ground,
Seated himself upon my bed, and sitting there spoke
    thus:
"Truly, Simaitha, your command by just so much out-
    stripped
My coming, when you called me hither to your house,
    as I
Outstripped charming Philinos not long since in the race.
    Bethink thee of my love and whence it came, O holy
      Moon.
For of myself I should have come, yes, by sweet Love,
    I should,
With comrades two or three besides, as soon as it was
    night,
Carrying in my tunic-folds apples of Dionysus,

A wreath of poplar garlanding my brows, the holy tree
Of Herakles, with twining purple ribbons all enlaced.

   Bethink thee of my love and whence it came, O holy
     Moon.

And had you welcomed me, why then, it had been joy;
     for famed
Am I among my comrades for beauty and speed of
     foot.
Had I but kissed your lovely mouth, I would have slept
     content.
But if you had repulsed me, and bolted fast the door,
With axes and with torches you would then have been
     besieged.

   Bethink thee of my love and whence it came, O holy
     Moon.

And now to the Cyprian in truth first do I owe my
     thanks;
But after Cypris, it is you, Lady, who from the flames
Have rescued me, when thus you sent to invite me to
     your house,
Half-consumed as I am. Yea Love enkindles oft a blaze
More fiery than Hephaistos' self, the God of Lipara:—

   Bethink thee of my love and whence it came, O holy
     Moon.

—And he drives with evil frenzy both the maiden from
     her bower,
And the bride from her lord's embrace, leaving the bed
     yet warm."
So did he speak: and I, that was so easy to be won,
Took him by the hand and drew him down to the soft
     couch.
And soon limbs at the touch of limbs grew love-ripe, and
     our faces
Glowed warmer still and yet more warm, and we whis-
     pered sweet words.

So, not to lengthen out my tale and weary thee, dear
    Moon,
The greatest deeds of love were done, and we both
    reached our desire.

Since then so long as yesterday no fault had he to find
In me, nor I in him. But now today there came to me
The mother of our flute-player Philista, and of Melixo,
Just when the horses of the Sun were climbing up the
    sky,
Bearing forth from the Ocean the Dawn with rosy arms.
After much other gossip she said Delphis was in love;
But what desire has mastered him, for a woman or a
    man,
She was not sure, but knew this only, that he was ever
    pledging
His love in cups of unmixed wine, and at last rushed
    away
Swearing he'ld crown with garlands the threshold of
    his dear.

Such is the tale the woman told me; and it is the truth.
For he was wont to visit me three or four times each day,
And often would he leave his Dorian oil-flask with me
    here.
But now 'tis twelve whole days since I so much as looked
    on him.
Can he have found some other solace, and forgotten me?
    Now with these philtres will I strive to enchant him.
    But if still
He should grieve me, at Hell's gate soon, by the Fates,
    he shall knock:
Such evil drugs to work his bane here in a chest I store,
Whose use, dear Mistress, an Assyrian stranger taught
    me once.
But thou, Goddess, farewell, and turn thy steeds to the
    Ocean stream,

And I will endure my misery still, even as I have borne it.
Farewell, bright-faced Selene; and farewell too, ye stars,
That follow the slow-moving chariot of the tranquil
 Night.

From *The Idylls of Theocritus*. Translated by R. C. Trevelyan.

O

FABLE

AESOP

THE OWL AND THE BIRDS

AN OWL, in her wisdom, counseled the Birds, when the acorn first began to sprout, to pull it up by all means out of the ground, and not to allow it to grow because it would produce the mistletoe, from which an irremediable poison, the bird-lime, would be extracted, by which they would be captured. The Owl next advised them to pluck up the seed of the flax, which men had sown, as it was a plant which boded no good to them. And, lastly, the Owl, seeing an archer approach, predicted that this man, being on foot, would contrive darts armed with feathers, which should fly faster than the wings of the Birds themselves. The Birds gave no credence to these warning words, but considered the Owl to be beside herself, and said that she was mad. But afterwards, finding her words were true, they wondered at her knowledge, and deemed her to be the wisest of birds. Hence it is that when she appears they resort to her as knowing all things; while she no longer gives them advice, but in solitude laments their past folly.

THE MAN AND THE SATYR

A MAN and a Satyr once poured out libations together in token of a bond of alliance being formed between them. One very cold wintry day, as they talked together, the Man put his fingers to his mouth and blew on them. On the Satyr inquiring the reason of this, he told him that he did it to warm his hands, they were so cold. Later on in the day they sat down to eat, the food prepared being quite scalding. The Man raised one of the dishes a little towards his mouth and blew in it. On the Satyr again inquiring the reason of this, he said that he did it to cool the meat, it was so hot. "I can no longer consider you as a friend," said the Satyr, "a fellow who with the same breath blows hot and cold."

THE GOODS AND THE ILLS

A LL the *Goods* were once driven out by the *Ills* from that common share which they each had in the affairs of mankind; for the *Ills* by reason of their numbers had prevailed to possess the earth. The *Goods* wafted themselves to heaven, and asked for a righteous vengeance on their persecutors. They entreated Zeus that they might no longer be associated with the *Ills,* as they had nothing in common and could not live together, but were engaged in unceasing warfare, and that an indissoluble law might be laid down for their future protection. Zeus granted their request, and decreed that henceforth the *Ills* should visit the earth in company with each other, but that the *Goods* should one by one enter the habitations of men. Hence it arises that *Ills* abound, for they come not one by one, but in troops, and by no means singly: while the *Goods* proceed from

Zeus, and are given not alike to all, but singly, and separately; and one by one to those who are able to discern them.

O

CHARACTER STUDIES

THEOPHRASTUS

TACTLESSNESS

NOW Tactlessness is a pain-giving failure to hit upon the right moment; and your Tactless man he that will acost a busy friend and ask his advice, or serenade his sweetheart when she is sick of a fever. He will go up to one that has gone bail and lost it, and pray him be his surety; and will come to bear witness after the verdict is given. Should you bid him to a wedding, he will inveigh against womankind. Should you be but now returned from a long journey, he will invite you to a walk. He is given to bringing you one that will pay more when your bargain is struck; and to rising from his seat to tell a tale all afresh to such as have heard it before and know it well. He is forward to undertake for you what you would not have done but cannot well decline. If you are sacrificing and put to great expense, that is the day he chooses to come and demand his usury. At the flogging of your servant he will stand by and tell how a boy of his hanged himself after just such a flogging as this; at an arbitration he will set the parties by the ears when both wish to be reconciled; and when he would dance, lay hold of another who is not yet drunk.

SUPERSTITIOUSNESS

SUPERSTITIOUSNESS, I need hardly say, would
seem to be a sort of Cowardice with respect to the
divine;[1] and your Superstitious man such as will not sally
forth for the day till he have washed his hands and sprinkled himself at the Nine Springs,[2] and put a bit of bay-
leaf from a temple in his mouth. And if a cat cross
his path he will not proceed on his way till someone
else be gone by, or he have cast three stones across
the street. Should he espy a snake in his house, if it
be one of the red sort he will call upon Sabazius, if of
the sacred, build a shrine then and there. When he
passes one of the smooth stones set up at crossroads he
anoints it with oil from his flask, and will not go his ways
till he have knelt down and worshipped it. If a mouse
gnaw a bag of his meal, he will off to the wizard's and
ask what he must do, and if the answer be "send it
to the cobbler's to be patched," he neglects the advice
and frees himself of the ill by rites of aversion. He is
for ever purifying his house on the plea that Hecate has
been drawn thither. Should owls hoot when he is abroad,
he is much put about, and will not on his way till he
have cried "Athena forfend!" Set foot on a tomb he will
not, nor come nigh a dead body nor a woman in child-
bed; he must keep himself unpolluted. On the fourth
and seventh days of every month he has wine mulled
for his household, and goes out to buy myrtle-boughs,
frankincense, and a holy picture, and then returning
spends the livelong day doing sacrifice to the Her-
maphrodites and putting garlands about them. He never
has a dream but he flies to a diviner, or a soothsayer,

---

[1] Or *spiritual*.
[2] Or *at three springs*.

or an interpreter of visions, to ask what God or Goddess he should appease; and when he is about to be initiated into the holy orders of Orpheus, he visits the priests every month and his wife with him, or if she have not the time, the nurse and children. He would seem to be one of those who are for ever going to the seaside to besprinkle themselves; and if ever he see one of the figures of Hecate at the crossroads wreathed with garlic, he is off home to wash his head and summon priestesses whom he bids purify him with the carrying around him of a squill or a puppy-dog. If he catch sight of a madman or an epilept, he shudders and spits in his bosom.

From *Characters*. Translated 1927 by J. M. Edmonds.

O

BIOGRAPHY

PHILOSTRATUS

POLEMO

POLEMO the sophist was neither a native of Smyrna, as is commonly supposed, nor from Phrygia as some say, but he was born at Laodicea in Caria, a city which lies on the river Lycus and, though far inland, is more important than those on the seacoast. Polemo's family has produced many men of consular rank, and still does, and many cities were in love with him, but especially Smyrna. For the people having from his boyhood observed in him a certain greatness, heaped on the head of Polemo all the wreaths of honour that were theirs to give, decreeing for himself and his family the distinctions most sought after in Smyrna; for they bestowed on him and his descendants the right to pre-

side over the Olympic games founded by Hadrian, and
to go on board the sacred trireme. For in the month
Anthesterion a trireme in full sail is brought in procession to the agora, and the priest of Dionysus, like a pilot,
steers it as it comes from the sea, loosing its cables.

By opening his school at Smyrna he benefited the city
in the following ways. In the first place he made her
appear far more populous than before, since the youth
flowed into her from both continents and the islands;
nor were they a dissolute and promiscuous rabble, but
select and genuinely Hellenic. Secondly, he brought
about a harmonious government free from faction. For,
before that, Smyrna was rent by factions, and the inhabitants of the higher district were at variance with
those on the seashore. Also he proved to be of great
value to the city by going on embassies to the Emperors
and defending the community. Hadrian, at any rate, had
hitherto favoured Ephesus, but Polemo so entirely con-
verted him to the cause of Smyrna that in one day he
lavished a million drachmae on the city, and with this
the corn-market was built, a gymnasium which was the
most magnificent of all those in Asia, and a temple that
can be seen from afar, the one on the promontory that
seems to challenge Mimas. Moreover, when they made
mistakes in their public policy, Polemo would rebuke
them, and often gave them wise advice; thus he was
of great use to them, and at the same time he cured
them of arrogance and every kind of insolence, an
achievement that was all the greater because it was not
like the Ionian to reform his ancient customs. He helped
them also in the following manner. The suits which they
brought against one another he did not allow to be carried anywhere abroad, but he would settle them at home.
I mean the suits about money, for those against adulter-
ers, sacrilegious persons and murderers, the neglect of

which breeds pollution, he not only urged them to carry them out of Smyrna but even to drive them out. For he said that they needed a judge with a sword in his hand.

Though he excited the disapproval of many, because when he travelled he was followed by a long train of baggage-animals and many horses, many slaves and many different breeds of dogs for various kinds of hunting, while he himself would ride in a chariot from Phrygia or Gaul, with silver-mounted bridles, by all this he acquired glory for Smyrna. For just as its market-place and a splendid array of buildings reflect lustre on a city, so does an opulent establishment; for not only does a city give a man renown, but itself acquires it from a man. Polemo administered the affairs of Laodicea as well, for he often visited his relatives there, and gave what assistance he could in public affairs.

The following privileges were bestowed on him by the Emperors. By the Emperor Trajan the right to travel free of expense by land and sea, and Hadrian extended this to all his descendants, and also enrolled him in the circle of the Museum, with the Egyptian right of free meals. And when he was in Rome and demanded 250,-000 drachmae,[1] he gave him that sum and more, though Polemo had not said that he needed it, nor had the Emperor said beforehand that he would give it. When the people of Smyrna accused him of having expended on his own pleasures a great part of the money that had been given by the Emperor for them, the Emperor sent a letter to the following effect: "Polemo has rendered me an account of the money given to you by me." And though one may say that this was an act of clemency, nevertheless it would not have been possible for him to win clemency in the affair of the money, had he not won pre-eminence for virtue of another kind. The temple

---

[1] The drachma was worth about ninepence.

of Olympian Zeus at Athens had been completed at last after an interval of five hundred and sixty years, and when the Emperor consecrated it as a marvellous triumph of time, he invited Polemo also to make an oration at the sacrifice. He fixed his gaze, as was his custom, on the thoughts that were already taking their place in his mind, and then flung himself into his speech, and delivered a long and admirable discourse from the base of the temple. As the prooemium of his speech he declared that not without a divine impulse was he inspired to speak on that theme.

Moreover, the Emperor reconciled his own son Antoninus with Polemo, at the time when he handed over his sceptre and became a god instead of a mortal. I must relate how this happened. Antoninus was proconsul of the whole of Asia without exception, and once he took up his lodging in Polemo's house because it was the best in Smyrna and belonged to the most notable citizen. However, Polemo arrived home at night from a journey and raised an outcry at the door that he was outrageously treated in being shut out of his own house, and next he compelled Antoninus to move to another house. The Emperor was informed of this, but he held no inquiry into the affair, lest he should reopen the wound. But in considering what would happen after his death, and that even mild natures are often provoked by persons who are too aggressive and irritating, he became anxious about Polemo. Accordingly in his last testament on the affairs of the Empire, he wrote: "And Polemo, the sophist, advised me to make this arrangement." By this means he opened the way for him to win favour as a benefactor, and forgiveness enough and to spare. And in fact Antoninus used to jest with Polemo about what had happened in Smyrna, thus showing that he had by no means forgotten it, though by the honours with which he exalted him on every occasion he seemed to pledge himself not to bear it in mind. This is the sort of jest he would make. When Polemo came to Rome, Antoninus embraced him, and then said: "Give Polemo a lodging and do not let anyone turn him out of it." And once when a tragic actor who had performed at the Olympic games in Asia, over which Polemo presided, declared that he would prosecute him, because Polemo had expelled him at the beginning of the play, the Emperor asked the actor what time it was when he was expelled from the theatre, and when he replied that it happened to be at noon, the Emperor made this witty comment: "But it was midnight when he expelled *me* from his house, and I did not prosecute him."

Let this suffice to show how mild an Emperor could be, and how arrogant a mere man. For in truth Polemo was so arrogant that he conversed with cities as his inferiors, Emperors as not his superiors, and the gods as his equals. For instance, when he gave a display to the Athenians of extempore speeches on first coming to Athens, he did not condescend to utter an encomium on the city, though there were so many things that one might say in honour of the Athenians; nor did he make a long oration about his own renown, although this style of speech is likely to win favour for sophists in their public declamations. But since he well knew that the natural disposition of the Athenians needs to be held in check rather than encouraged to greater pride, this was his introductory speech: "Men say, Athenians, that as an audience you are accomplished judges of oratory. I shall soon find out." And once when the ruler of the Bosporus, a man who had been trained in all the culture of Greece, came to Smyrna in order to learn about Ionia, Polemo not only did not take his place among those who went to salute him, but even when the other begged him to visit him he postponed it again and again, until he compelled the king to come to his door with a fee of ten talents. Again, when he came to Pergamon suffering from a disease of the joints, he slept in the temple, and when Asclepius appeared to him and told him to abstain from drinking anything cold, "My good sir," said Polemo, "but what if you were doctoring a cow?"

This proud and haughty temper he contracted from Timocrates the philosopher, with whom he associated for four years when he came to Ionia. It would do no harm to describe Timocrates also. This man came from the Pontus and his birthplace was Heraclea whose citizens admire Greek culture. At first he devoted himself to the study of writings on medicine and was well versed in the theories of Hippocrates and Democritus. But when he had once heard Euphrates[1] of Tyre, he set full sail for his kind of philosophy. He was irascible beyond measure, so much so that while he was arguing his beard and the hair on his head stood up like a lion's when it springs to the attack. His language was fluent, vigorous and ready, and it was on this account that Polemo, who loved this headlong style of oratory, valued him so highly. At any rate, when a quarrel arose between Timocrates and Scopelian, because the latter had become addicted to the use of pitch-plasters and professional "hair-removers," the youths who were then residing in Smyrna took different sides, but Polemo, who was the pupil of both men, became one of the faction of Timocrates and called him "the father of my eloquence." And when he was defending himself before Timocrates for his speeches against Favorinus, he cowered before him in awe and submission, like boys who fear blows from their teachers when they have been disobedient.

This same humility Polemo showed also towards Sco-

---

[1] Euphrates had much influence with Vespasian.

pelian somewhat later, when he was elected to go on
an embassy on behalf of Smyrna, and begged for Scopelian's power of persuasion as though it were the arms of
Achilles. His behaviour to Herodes the Athenian was in
one way submissive and in another arrogant. I wish to
relate how this came about, for it is a good story and
worth remembering. Herodes, you must know, felt a
keener desire to succeed in extempore speaking than to
be called a consul and the descendant of consuls, and
so, before he was acquainted with Polemo, he came to
Smyrna in order to study with him. It was at the time
when Herodes alone was regulating the status of the free
cities. When he had embraced Polemo and saluted him
very affectionately by kissing him on the mouth, he
asked: "Father, when shall I hear you declaim?" Now
Herodes thought that he would put off the declamation
and would say that he hesitated to run any risks in the
presence of so great a man, but Polemo, without any
such pretext, replied: "Hear me declaim today, and let
us be going." Herodes says that when he heard this, he
was struck with admiration of the man and the ready
facility both of his tongue and brain. This incident illus-
trates Polemo's pride and, by Zeus, the cleverness with
which he was wont to dazzle his hearers, but the following shows equally his modesty and sense of propriety.
For when the other arrived to hear him declaim, he received him with a long and appropriate panegyric on the
words and deeds of Herodes.

The scenic effects which he employed in his declamations we may learn from Herodes, since they are described in one of the letters that he wrote to Varus, and
I will relate them from that source. He would come forward to declaim with a countenance serene and full of
confidence, and he always arrived in a litter, because his
joints were already diseased. When a theme had been

proposed, he did not meditate on it in public but would withdraw from the crowd for a short time. His utterance was clear and incisive, and there was a fine ringing sound in the tones of his voice. Herodes says also that he used to rise to such a pitch of excitement that he would jump up from his chair when he came to the most striking conclusions in his argument, and whenever he rounded off a period he would utter the final clause with a smile, as though to show clearly that he could deliver it without effort, and at certain places in the argument he would stamp the ground just like the horse in Homer. Herodes adds that he listened to his first declamation like an impartial judge, to the second like one who longs for more, to the third as one who can but admire; and that he attended his lectures for three days. Moreover, Herodes has recorded the themes of the declamations at which he was present. The first was: "Demosthenes swears that he did not take the bribe of fifty talents," the charge which Demades brought against him, on the ground that Alexander had communicated this fact to the Athenians, having learned it from the account-books of Darius. In the second, on the conclusion of peace after the Peloponnesian war, he urged: "That the trophies erected by the Greeks should be taken down." The third argument was to persuade the Athenians to return to their demes after the battle of Aegos Potami. Herodes says that in payment for this he sent him 150,000 drachmae, and called this the fee for his lectures. But since he did not accept it, Herodes thought that he had been treated with contempt, but Munatius the critic, when drinking with him (this man came from Tralles), remarked: "Herodes, I think that Polemo dreamed of 250,-000 drachmae, and so thinks that he is being stinted because you did not send so large a sum." Herodes says that he added the 100,000 drachmae, and that Polemo took the money without the least hesitation, as though he were receiving only what was his due. Herodes gave Polemo leave not to appear after him to give an exhibition of his oratory, and not to have to maintain a theme after him, and allowed him to depart from Smyrna by night, lest he should be compelled to do this, since Polemo thought it outrageous to be compelled to do anything. And from that time forward he never failed to commend Polemo, and to think him beyond praise. For instance, in Athens, when Herodes had brilliantly maintained the argument about the war trophies, and was being complimented on the fluency and vigour of his speech, he said: "Read Polemo's declamation, and then you will know a great man." And at the Olympic games when all Greece acclaimed him, crying: "You are the equal of Demosthenes!" he replied: "I wish I were the equal of the Phrygian," applying this name to Polemo because in those days Laodicea counted as part of Phrygia. When the Emperor Marcus asked him: "What is your opinion of Polemo?" Herodes gazed fixedly before him and said:

"The sound of swift-footed horses strikes upon mine ears;"

thus indicating how resonant and far-echoing was his eloquence. And when Varus the consul asked him what teachers he had had, he replied: "This man and that, while I was being taught, but Polemo, when I was teaching others."

Polemo says that he studied also with Dio, and that in order to do so he paid a visit to the people of Bithynia. He used to say that the works of prose writers needed to be brought out by armfuls, but the works of poets by the wagon-load. Among the honours that he received were also the following. Smyrna was contending on behalf of her temples and their rights, and when he had already reached the last stage of his life, appointed Polemo as one of her advocates. But since he died at the very outset of the journey to defend those rights, the city was entrusted to other advocates. Before the imperial tribunal they presented their case very badly, whereupon the Emperor looked towards the counsel from Smyrna and said: "Had not Polemo been appointed as your public advocate in this suit?" "Yes," they replied, "if you mean the sophist." "Then, perhaps," said the Emperor, "he wrote down some speech in defence of your rights, inasmuch as he was to speak for the defence in my presence and on behalf of such great issues." "Perhaps, O Emperor," they replied, "but not as far as we know." Whereupon the Emperor adjourned the case until the speech could be brought, and when it had been read aloud in court the Emperor gave his decision in accordance with it; and so Smyrna carried off the victory, and the citizens departed declaring that Polemo had come to life to help them.

Now inasmuch as, when men have become illustrious, not only what they said in earnest but also what they said in jest is worthy of record, I will write down Polemo's witticisms also, so that I may not seem to have neglected even them. There was an Ionian youth who was indulging in a life of dissipation at Smyrna to a degree not customary with the Ionians, and was being ruined by his great wealth, which is a vicious teacher of ill-regulated natures. Now the youth's name was Varus, and he had been so spoiled by parasites that he had convinced himself that he was the fairest of the fair, the tallest of the tall, and the noblest and most expert of the youths at the wrestling-ground, and that not even the Muses could strike up a prelude more sweetly than he, whenever he had a mind to sing. He had the same notions about the sophists; that is to say, that he could outstrip even their tongues whenever he declaimed—and he actually used to declaim—and those who borrowed money from him used to reckon their attendance at his declamations as part of the interest. Even Polemo, when he was still a young man and not yet an invalid, was induced to pay this tribute, for he had borrowed money from him, and when he did not pay court to him or attend his lectures, the youth resented it and threatened him with a summons to recover the debt. This summons is a writ issued by the law court proclaiming judgement by default against the debtor who fails to pay. Thereupon his friends reproached Polemo with being morose and discourteous, seeing that when he could avoid being sued and could profit by the young man's money by merely giving him an amiable nod of approval, he would not do this, but provoked and irritated him. Hearing this sort of thing said, he did indeed come to the lecture, but when, late in the evening, the youth's declamation was still going on, and no place of anchorage for his speech was in sight, and everything he said was full of solecisms, barbarisms, and inconsistencies, Polemo jumped up, and stretching out his hands, cried: "Varus, bring your summons." On another occasion, when the consul was putting to the torture a bandit who had been convicted on several charges, and declared that he could not think of any penalty for him that would match his crimes, Polemo who was present said: "Order him to learn by heart some antiquated stuff." For though this sophist had learned by heart a great number of passages, he nevertheless considered that this is the most wearisome of all exercises. Again, on seeing a gladiator dripping with sweat out of sheer terror of the life-and-death struggle before him, he remarked: "You are in as great an agony as though you were going to declaim." Again, when he met a sophist who was buying sausages, sprats, and other cheap dainties of that sort, he said: "My good sir, it is impossible for one who lives on this diet to act convincingly the arrogance of Darius and Xerxes." When Timocrates the philosopher remarked to him that Favorinus had become a chatterbox, Polemo said wittily: "And so is every old woman," thus making fun of him for being like a eunuch. Again, when a tragic actor at the Olympic games in Smyrna pointed to the ground as he uttered the words, "O Zeus!" then raised his hands to heaven at the words, "and Earth!" Polemo, who was presiding at the Olympic games, expelled him from the contest, saying: "The fellow has committed a solecism with his hand." I will say no more on this subject, for this is enough to illustrate the charming wit of the man.

Polemo's style of eloquence is passionate, combative, and ringing to the echo, like the trumpet at the Olympic games. The Demosthenic cast of his thought lends it distinction and a gravity which is not dull or inert but brilliant and inspired, as though delivered from the tripod. But they fail to understand the man who says that he handles invective more skilfully than any other sophist, but is less skilful in making a defence. Such a criticism is proved to be untrue by this and that declamation in which he speaks for the defence, but especially by the speech in which Demosthenes swears that he did not accept the fifty talents. For in establishing a defence so difficult to make, his ornate rhetoric and technical skill were fully equal to the argument. I observe the same error in the case of those who hold that he was not qualified to sustain simulated arguments, but was forced off the course like a horse for whom the ground is too rough, and that he deprecated the use of these themes when he quoted the maxim of Homer:

"For hateful to me even as the gates of hell is he that hideth one thing in his heart and uttereth another."

Perhaps he used to say this with a double meaning, and to illustrate by this allusion how intractable are such themes; nevertheless, these too he sustained with great skill, as is evident from his *Adulterer Unmasked* or his *Xenophon refuses to survive Socrates;* or his *Solon demands that his laws be rescinded after Peisistratus has obtained a bodyguard.* Then there are the three on Demosthenes, the first where he denounced himself after Chaeronea, the second in which he pretends that he ought to be punished with death for the affair of Harpalus, lastly that in which he advises the Athenians to flee on their triremes at the approach of Philip, though Aeschines had carried a law that anyone who mentioned the war should be put to death. For in these more than any other of the simulated themes that he produced, he has given free reins to the argument, and yet the ideas preserve the effect of presenting both sides.

When the doctors were regularly attending him for hardening of the joints, he exhorted them to "dig and carve in the stone-quarries of Polemo." And in writing to Herodes about this disease he sent this bulletin: "I must eat, but I have no hands; I must walk, but I have no feet; I must endure pain, and then I find I have both feet and hands."

When he died he was about fifty-six years old, but this age-limit, though for the other learned professions it is the beginning of senility, for a sophist still counts as youthfulness, since in this profession a man's knowledge grows more adaptable with advancing age.

He has no tomb in Smyrna, though several there are said to be his. For some say that he was buried in the garden of the temple of Virtue; others, not far from that place near the sea, and there is a small temple thereabouts with a statue of Polemo in it, arrayed as he was when he performed the sacred rites on the trireme, and beneath his statue they say that the man himself lies; while others say that he was buried in the courtyard of his house under the bronze statues. But none of these accounts is true, for if he had died in Smyrna there is not one of the marvellous temples in that city in which he would have been deemed unworthy to lie. But yet another version is nearer the truth, namely that he lies at Laodicea near the Syrian gate, where, in fact, are the sepulchres of his ancestors; that he was buried while still alive, for so he had enjoined on his nearest and dearest; and that, as he lay in the tomb, he thus exhorted those who were shutting up the sepulchre: "Make haste, make haste! Never shall the sun behold me reduced to silence!" And when his friends wailed over him, he cried with a loud voice: "Give me a body and I will declaim!"

With Polemo ended the house of Polemo, for his descendants, though they were his kindred, were not the sort of men who could be compared with his surpassing merit.

HERMOGENES

HERMOGENES, who was born at Tarsus, by the time he was fifteen had attained such a reputation as a sophist that even the Emperor Marcus became eager to hear him. At any rate Marcus made the journey to hear him declaim, and was delighted with his formal discourse, but marvelled at him when he declaimed extempore, and gave him splendid presents. But when Hermogenes arrived at manhood his powers suddenly deserted him, though this was not due to any apparent disease, and this provided the envious with an occasion for their wit. For they declared that his words were in very truth "winged," as Homer says, and that Hermogenes had moulted them, like wing-feathers. And once

Antiochus the sophist, jesting at his expense, said: "Lo, here is that fellow Hermogenes, who among boys was an old man, but among the old is a boy." The following will show the kind of eloquence that he affected. In a speech that he was delivering before Marcus, he said, "You see before you, Emperor, an orator who still needs an attendant to take him to school, an orator who still looks to come of age." He said much more of this sort and in the same facetious vein. He died at a ripe old age, but accounted as one of the rank and file, for he became despised when his skill in his art deserted him.

From *Lives of the Sophists*.
Translated 1922 by Wilmer Cave Wright.

PART FIVE

SOCIETY

O

TYPES OF STATES

ARISTOTLE

7. There are still two forms besides democracy and oligarchy; one of them is universally recognized and included among the four principal forms of government, which are said to be (1) monarchy, (2) oligarchy, (3) democracy, and (4) the so-called aristocracy or government of the best. But there is also a fifth, which retains the generic name of polity or constitutional government; this is not common, and therefore has not been noticed by writers who attempt to enumerate the different kinds of government; like Plato, in their books about the state, they recognize four only. The term "aristocracy" is rightly applied to the form of government which is described in the first part of our treatise; for that only can be rightly called aristocracy which is a government formed of the best men absolutely, and not merely of men who are good when tried by any given standard. In the perfect state the good man is absolutely the same as the good citizen; whereas in other states the good citizen is only good relatively to his own form of government. But there are some states differing from oligarchies and also differing from the so-called polity or constitutional government; these are termed aristocracies, and in them magistrates are certainly chosen, both according to their wealth and according to their merit. Such a form of government differs from each of the two just now mentioned, and is termed an aristocracy. For indeed in states which do not make virtue the aim of the community, men of merit and reputation for virtue may be found. And so where a government has regard to wealth, virtue,

534

and numbers, as at Carthage, that is aristocracy; and also where it has regard only to two out of the three, as at Lacedaemon, to virtue and numbers, and the two principles of democracy and virtue temper each other. There are these two forms of aristocracy in addition to the first and perfect state, and there is a third form, viz. the constitutions which incline more than the so-called polity towards oligarchy.

8. I have yet to speak of the so-called polity and of tyranny. I put them in this order, not because a polity or constitutional government is to be regarded as a perversion any more than the above-mentioned aristocracies. The truth is, that they all fall short of the most perfect form of government, and so they are reckoned among perversions, and the really perverted forms are perversions of these, as I said in the original discussion. Last of all I will speak of tyranny, which I place last in the series because I am inquiring into the constitutions of states, and this is the very reverse of a constitution.

Having explained why I have adopted this order, I will proceed to consider constitutional government; of which the nature will be clearer now that oligarchy and democracy have been defined. For polity or constitutional government may be described generally as a fusion of oligarchy and democracy; but the term is usually applied to those forms of government which incline towards democracy, and the term aristocracy to those which incline towards oligarchy, because birth and education are commonly the accompaniments of wealth. Moreover, the rich already possess the external advantages the want of which is a temptation to crime, and hence they are called noblemen and gentlemen. And inasmuch as aristocracy seeks to give predominance to the best of the citizens, people say also of oligarchies that they are composed of noblemen and gentlemen. Now it appears to be an impossible thing that the state which is governed not by the best citizens but by the worst should be well-governed, and equally impossible that the state which is ill-governed should be governed by the best. But we must remember that good laws, if they are not obeyed, do not constitute good government. Hence there are two parts of good government; one is the actual obedience of citizens to the laws, the other part is the goodness of the laws which they obey; they may obey bad laws as well as good. And there may be a further subdivision; they may obey either the best laws which are attainable to them, or the best absolutely.

The distribution of offices according to merit is a special characteristic of aristocracy, for the principle of an aristocracy is virtue, as wealth is of an oligarchy, and freedom of a democracy. In all of them there of course exists the right of the majority, and whatever seems good to the majority of those who share in the government has authority. Now in most states the form called polity exists, for the fusion goes no further than the attempt to unite the freedom of the poor and the wealth of the rich, who commonly take the place of the noble. But as there are three grounds on which men claim an equal share in the government, freedom, wealth, and virtue (for the fourth or good birth is the result of the two last, being only ancient wealth and virtue), it is clear that the admixture of the two elements, that is to say, of the rich and poor, is to be called a polity or constitutional government; and the union of the three is to be called aristocracy or the government of the best, and more than any other form of government, except the true and ideal, has a right to this name.

Thus far I have shown the existence of forms of states other than monarchy, democracy, and oligarchy, and what they are, and in what aristocracies differ from one another, and polities from aristocracies—that the two latter are not very unlike is obvious.

9. Next we have to consider how by the side of oligarchy and democracy the so-called polity or constitutional government springs up, and how it should be organized. The nature of it will be at once understood from a comparison of oligarchy and democracy; we must ascertain their different characteristics, and taking a portion from each, put the two together, like the parts of an indenture. Now there are three modes in which fusions of government may be effected. In the first mode we must combine the laws made by both governments, say concerning the administration of justice. In oligarchies they impose a fine on the rich if they do not serve as judges, and to the poor they give no pay; but in democracies they give pay to the poor and do not fine the rich. Now (1) the union of these two modes is a common or middle term between them, and is therefore characteristic of a constitutional government, for it is a combination of both. This is one mode of uniting the two elements. Or (2) a mean may be taken between the enactments of the two: thus democracies require no property qualification, or only a small one, from members of the assembly, oligarchies a high one; here neither of these is the common term, but a mean between them. (3) There is a third mode, in which something is borrowed from the oligarchical and something from the democratical principle. For example, the appointment of magistrates by lot is thought to be democratical, and the election of them oligarchical; democratical again when there is no property qualification, oligarchical when there is. In the aristocratical or constitutional state, one element will be taken from each—from oligarchy the principle of electing to offices, from

democracy the disregard of qualification. Such are the various modes of combination.

There is a true union of oligarchy and democracy when the same state may be termed either a democracy or an oligarchy; those who use both names evidently feel that the fusion is complete. Such a fusion there is also in the mean; for both extremes appear in it. The Lacedaemonian constitution, for example, is often described as a democracy, because it has many democratical features. In the first place the youth receive a democratical education. For the sons of the poor are brought up with the sons of the rich, who are educated in such a manner as to make it possible for the sons of the poor to be educated like them. A similar equality prevails in the following period of life, and when the citizens are grown up to manhood the same rule is observed; there is no distinction between the rich and poor. In like manner they all have the same food at their public tables, and the rich wear only such clothing as any poor man can afford. Again, the people elect to one of the two greatest offices of state, and in the other they share; for they elect the Senators and share in the Ephoralty. By others the Spartan constitution is said to be an oligarchy, because it has many oligarchical elements. That all offices are filled by election and none by lot, is one of these oligarchical characteristics; that the power of inflicting death or banishment rests with a few persons is another; and there are others. In a well attempered polity there should appear to be both elements and yet neither; also the government should rely on itself, and not on foreign aid, and on itself not through the good will of a majority —they might be equally well-disposed when there is a vicious form of government—but through the general willingness of all classes in the state to maintain the constitution

Enough of the manner in which a constitutional government, and in which the so-called aristocracies ought to be framed.

10. Of the nature of tyranny I have still to speak, in order that it may have its place in our inquiry (since even tyranny is reckoned by us to be a form of government), although there is not much to be said about it. I have already in the former part of this treatise discussed royalty or kingship according to the most usual meaning of the term, and considered whether it is or is not advantageous to states, and what kind of royalty should be established, and from what source, and how.

When speaking of royalty we also spoke of two forms of tyranny, which are both according to law, and therefore easily pass into royalty. Among Barbarians there are elected monarchs who exercise a despotic power; despotic rulers were also elected in ancient Hellas, called Aesymnetes or dictators. These monarchies, when compared with one another, exhibit certain differences. And they are, as I said before, royal, in so far as the monarch rules according to law over willing subjects; but they are tyrannical in so far as he is despotic and rules according to his own fancy. There is also a third kind of tyranny, which is the most typical form, and is the counterpart of the perfect monarchy. This tyranny is just that arbitrary power of an individual which is responsible to no one, and governs all alike, whether equals or better, with a view to its own advantage, not to that of its subjects, and therefore against their will. No freeman, if he can escape from it, will endure such a government.

The kinds of tyranny are such and so many, and for the reasons which I have given.

11. We have now to inquire what is the best constitution for most states, and the best life for most men, neither assuming a standard of virtue which is above ordinary persons, nor an education which is exceptionally favoured by nature and circumstances, nor yet an ideal state which is an aspiration only, but having regard to the life in which the majority are able to share, and to the form of government which states in general can attain. As to those aristocracies, as they are called, of which we were just now speaking, they either lie beyond the possibilities of the greater number of states, or they approximate to the so-called constitutional government, and therefore need no separate discussion. And in fact the conclusion at which we arrive respecting all these forms rests upon the same grounds. For if what was said in the *Ethics* is true, that the happy life is the life according to virtue lived without impediment, and that virtue is a mean, then the life which is in a mean, and in a mean attainable by every one, must be the best. And the same principles of virtue and vice are characteristic of cities and of constitutions; for the constitution is in a figure the life of the city.

Now in all states there are three elements: one class is very rich, another very poor, and a third in a mean. It is admitted that moderation and the mean are best, and therefore it will clearly be best to possess the gifts of fortune in moderation; for in that condition of life men are most ready to follow rational principle. But he who greatly excels in beauty, strength, birth, or wealth, or on the other hand who is very poor, or very weak, or very much disgraced, finds it difficult to follow rational principle. Of these two the one sort grow into violent and great criminals, the others into rogues and petty rascals. And two sorts of offences correspond to them, the one committed from violence, the other from roguery. Again, the middle class is least likely to shrink from rule, or to be over-ambitious for it; both of which are injuries to the state. Again, those who have too much of the goods of fortune, strength, wealth, friends, and the like, are neither willing nor able to submit to authority. The evil begins at home; for when they are boys, by reason of the luxury in which they are brought up, they never learn, even at school, the habit of obedience. On the other hand, the very poor, who are in the opposite extreme, are too degraded. So that the one class cannot obey, and can only rule despotically; the other knows not how to command and must be ruled like slaves. Thus arises a city, not of freemen, but of masters and slaves, the one despising, the other envying; and nothing can be more fatal to friendship and good fellowship in states than this: for good fellowship springs from friendship; when men are at enmity with one another, they would rather not even share the same path. But a city ought to be composed, as far as possible, of equals and similars; and these are generally the middle classes. Wherefore the city which is composed of middle-class citizens is necessarily best constituted in respect of the elements of which we say the fabric of the state naturally consists. And this is the class of citizens which is most secure in a state, for they do not, like the poor, covet their neighbours' goods; nor do others covet theirs, as the poor covet the goods of the rich; and as they neither plot against others, nor are themselves plotted against, they pass through life safely. Wisely then did Phocylides pray—"Many things are best in the mean; I desire to be of a middle condition in my city."

Thus it is manifest that the best political community is formed by citizens of the middle class, and that those states are likely to be well-administered, in which the middle class is large, and stronger if possible than both the other classes, or at any rate than either singly; for the addition of the middle class turns the scale, and prevents either of the extremes from being dominant. Great then is the good fortune of a state in which the citizens have a moderate and sufficient property; for where some possess much, and the others nothing, there may arise an extreme democracy, or a pure oligarchy; or a tyranny may grow out of either extreme—either out of the most rampant democracy, or out of an oligarchy; but it is not so likely to arise out of the middle constitutions and those akin to them. I will explain the reason of this hereafter, when I speak of the revolutions of states. The mean condition of states is clearly best, for no other is free from faction; and where the middle class is large, there are least likely to be factions and dissensions. For a similar reason large states are less liable to faction than small ones, because in them the middle class is large; whereas in small states it is easy to divide all the citizens into two classes who are either rich or poor, and to leave nothing in the middle. And democracies are safer and more permanent than oligarchies, because they have a middle class which is more numerous and has a greater share in the government; for when there is no middle class, and the poor greatly exceed in number, troubles arise, and the state soon comes to an end. A proof of the superiority of the middle class is that the best legislators have been of a middle condition; for example, Solon, as his own verses testify; and Lycurgus, for he was not a king; and Charondas, and almost all legislators.

These considerations will help us to understand why most governments are either democratical or oligarchical. The reason is that the middle class is seldom numerous in them, and whichever party, whether the rich or the common people, transgresses the mean and predominates, draws the constitution its own way, and thus arises either oligarchy or democracy. There is another reason —the poor and the rich quarrel with one another, and whichever side gets the better, instead of establishing a just or popular government, regards political supremacy as the prize of victory, and the one party sets up a democracy and the other an oligarchy. Further, both the parties which had the supremacy in Hellas looked only to the interest of their own form of government, and established in states, the one, democracies, and the other, oligarchies; they thought of their own advantage, of the public not at all. For these reasons the middle form of government has rarely, if ever, existed, and among a very few only. One man alone of all who ever ruled in Hellas was induced to give this middle constitution to states. But it has now become a habit among the citizens of states, not even to care about equality; all men are seeking for dominion, or, if conquered, are willing to submit.

What then is the best form of government, and what makes it the best, is evident; and of other constitutions, since we say that there are many kinds of democracy and many of oligarchy, it is not difficult to see which has the first and which the second or any other place in the order of excellence, now that we have determined which is the best. For that which is nearest to the best must of necessity be better, and that which is furthest from it worse, if we are judging absolutely and not relatively to given conditions: I say "relatively to given conditions," since a particular government may be preferable, but another form may be better for some people.

12. We have now to consider what and what kind of government is suitable to what and what kind of men. I may begin by assuming, as a general principle common to all governments, that the portion of the state which

desires the permanence of the constitution ought to be stronger than that which desires the reverse. Now every city is composed of quality and quantity. By quality I mean freedom, wealth, education, good birth, and by quantity, superiority of numbers. Quality may exist in one of the classes which make up the state, and quantity in the other. For example, the meanly-born may be more in number than the well-born, or the poor than the rich, yet they may not so much exceed in quantity as they fall short in quality; and therefore there must be a comparison of quantity and quality. Where the number of the poor is more than proportioned to the wealth of the rich, there will naturally be a democracy, varying in form with the sort of people who compose it in each case. If, for example, the husbandmen exceed in number, the first form of democracy will then arise; if the artisans and labouring class, the last; and so with the intermediate forms. But where the rich and the notables exceed in quality more than they fall short in quantity, there oligarchy arises, similarly assuming various forms according to the kind of superiority possessed by the oligarchs.

The legislator should always include the middle class in his government; if he makes his laws oligarchical, to the middle class let him look; if he makes them democratical, he should equally by his laws try to attach this class to the state. There only can the government ever be stable where the middle class exceeds one or both of the others, and in that case there will be no fear that the rich will unite with the poor against the rulers. For neither of them will ever be willing to serve the other, and if they look for some form of government more suitable to both, they will find none better than this, for the rich and the poor will never consent to rule in turn, because they mistrust one another. The arbiter is always the one trusted, and he who is in the middle is an arbiter. The more perfect the admixture of the political elements, the more lasting will be the constitution. Many even of those who desire to form aristocratical governments make a mistake, not only in giving too much power to the rich, but in attempting to overreach the people. There comes a time when out of a false good there arises a true evil, since the encroachments of the rich are more destructive to the constitution than those of the people.

From *Politics*, Book IV, chaps. 7-12. Translated by W. D. Ross.

O

THE JUST SOCIETY

PLATO

HOW then can we rightly order the distribution of the land? In the first place, the number of the citizens has to be determined, and also the number and size of the divisions into which they will have to be formed; and the land and the houses will then have to be apportioned by us as fairly as we can. The number of citizens can only be estimated satisfactorily in relation to the territory and the neighbouring states. The territory must be sufficient to maintain a certain number of inhabitants in a moderate way of life—more than this is not required; and the number of citizens should be sufficient to defend themselves against the injustice of their neighbours, and also to give them the power of rendering efficient aid to their neighbours when they are wronged. After having taken a survey of theirs and their neighbours' territory, we will determine the limits of them in fact as well as in theory. And now, let us proceed to legislate with a view to perfecting the form and outline of our state. The number of our citizens shall be 5040—this will be a convenient number; and these shall be owners of the land and protectors of the allotment. The houses and the land will be divided in the same way, so that every man may correspond to a lot. Let the whole number be first divided into two parts, and then into three; and the number is further capable of being divided into four or five parts, or any number of parts up to ten. Every legislator ought to know so much arithmetic as to be able to tell what number is most likely to be useful to all cities; and we are going to take that number which contains the greatest and most regular and unbroken series of divisions. The whole of number has every possible division, and the number 5040 can be divided by exactly fifty-nine divisors, and ten of these proceed without interval from one to ten: this will furnish numbers for war and peace, and for all contracts and dealings, including taxes and divisions of the land. These properties of number should be ascertained at leisure by those who are bound by law to know them; for they are true, and should be proclaimed at the foundation of the city, with a view to use. Whether the legislator is establishing a new state or restoring an old and decayed one, in respect of Gods and temples—the temples which are to be built in each city, and the Gods or demigods after whom they are to be called—if he be a man of sense, he will make no change in anything which the oracle of Delphi, or Dodona, or the God Ammon, or any ancient tradition has sanctioned in whatever manner, whether by apparitions or reputed inspiration of Heaven, in obedience to which mankind have established sacrifices in connection with mystic rites, either originating on the spot, or derived from Tyrrhenia or Cyprus or some other place, and on the strength of which traditions they have consecrated oracles and images, and altars and temples, and portioned out a sacred domain for each of them. The least part of all these ought not to be disturbed by the legislator; but he should assign to the several districts some God, or demi-god, or hero, and, in the distribution of the soil, should give to these first their chosen domain and all things fitting, that the inhabitants of the several districts may meet at fixed times, and that they may readily supply their various wants, and entertain one another with sacrifices, and become friends and acquaintances; for there is no greater good in a state than that the citizens should be known to one another. When not light but darkness and ignorance of each other's characters prevails among them, no one will receive the honour of which he is deserving, or the power or the justice to which he is fairly entitled: wherefore, in every state, above all things, every man should take heed that he have no deceit in him, but that he be always true and simple; and that no deceitful person take any advantage of him.

The next move in our pastime of legislation, like the withdrawal of the stone from the holy line in the game of draughts, being an unusual one, will probably excite wonder when mentioned for the first time. And yet, if a man will only reflect and weigh the matter with care, he will see that our city is ordered in a manner which, if not the best, is the second best. Perhaps also some one may not approve this form, because he thinks that such a constitution is ill adapted to a legislator who has not despotic power. The truth is, that there are three forms of government, the best, the second and the third best, which we may just mention, and then leave the selection to the ruler of the settlement. Following this method in the present instance, let us speak of the states which are respectively first, second, and third in excellence, and then we will leave the choice to Cleinias now, or to any one else who may hereafter have to make a similar choice among constitutions, and may desire to give to his state some feature which is congenial to him and which he approves in his own country.

The first and highest form of the state and of the government and of the law is that in which there prevails most widely the ancient saying, that "Friends have all things in common." Whether there is anywhere now, or will ever be, this communion of women and children and of property, in which the private and individual is altogether banished from life, and things which are by nature private, such as eyes and ears and hands, have become common, and in some way see and hear and act in common, and all men express praise and blame and feel joy and sorrow on the same occasions, and whatever laws there are unite the city to the utmost—whether all this is possible or not, I say that no man, acting upon any other principle, will ever constitute a state which will be truer or better or more exalted in virtue. Whether such a state is governed by Gods or sons of Gods, one, or more than one, happy are the men who, living after this manner, dwell there; and therefore to this we are to look for the pattern of the state, and to cling to this, and to seek with all our might for one which is like this. The state which we have now in hand, when created, will be nearest to immortality and the only one which takes the second place; and after that, by the grace of God, we will complete the third one. And we will begin by speaking of the nature and origin of the second.

Let the citizens at once distribute their land and houses, and not till the land in common, since a community of goods goes beyond their proposed origin, and nurture, and education. But in making the distribution, let the several possessors feel that their particular lots also belong to the whole city; and seeing that the earth is their parent, let them tend her more carefully than children do their mother. For she is a goddess and their queen, and they are her mortal subjects. Such also are the feelings which they ought to entertain to the Gods and demi-gods of the country. And in order that the distribution may always remain, they ought to consider further that the present number of families should be always retained, and neither increased nor diminished. This may be secured for the whole city in the following manner:—Let the possessor of a lot leave the one of his children who is his best beloved, and one only, to be the heir of his dwelling, and his successor in the duty of ministering to the Gods, the state and the family, as well the living members of it as those who are departed when he comes into the inheritance; but of his other children, if he have more than one, he shall give the females in marriage according to the law to be hereafter enacted, and the males he shall distribute as sons to those citizens who have no children, and are disposed to receive them; or if there should be none such, and particular individuals have too many children, male or female, or too few, as in the case of barrenness—in all these cases let the highest and most honourable magistracy created by us judge and determine what is to be done with the redundant or deficient, and devise a means that the number of 5040 houses shall always remain the same. There are many ways of regulating numbers; for they in whom generation is affluent may be made to refrain, and, on the other hand, special care may be taken to increase the number of births by rewards and stigmas, or we may meet the evil by the elder men giving advice and administering rebuke to the younger—in this way the object may be attained. And if after all there be very great difficulty about the equal preservation of the 5040 houses, and there be an excess of citizens, owing to the too great love of those who live together, and we are at our wits' end, there is still the old device often mentioned by us of sending out a colony, which will part friends with us, and be composed of suitable persons. If, on the other hand, there come a wave bearing a deluge of disease, or a plague of war, and the inhabitants become much fewer than the appointed number by reason of bereavement, we ought not to introduce citizens of spurious birth and education, if this can be avoided; but even God is said not to be able to fight against necessity.

Wherefore let us suppose this "high argument" of ours to address us in the following terms:—Best of men, cease not to honour according to nature similarity and equality and sameness and agreement, as regards number and every good and noble quality. And, above all, observe the aforesaid number 5040 throughout life; in the second place, do not disparage the small and modest proportions of the inheritances which you received in the distribution, by buying and selling them to one another. For then neither will the God who gave you the lot be your friend, nor will the legislator; and indeed the law declares to the disobedient that these are the terms upon which he may or may not take the lot. In the first place, the earth as he is informed is sacred to the Gods; and in the next place, priests and priestesses will offer up prayers over a first, and second, and even a third sacrifice, that he who buys or sells the houses or lands which he has received, may suffer the punishment which he deserves; and these their prayers they shall write down in the temples, on tablets of cypress-wood, for the instruction of posterity. Moreover they will set a watch over all these things, that they may be observed—the magistracy which has the sharpest eyes shall keep watch that any infringement of these commands may be discovered and punished as offences both against the law and the

God. How great is the benefit of such an ordinance to all those cities, which obey and are administered accordingly, no bad man can ever know, as the old proverb says; but only a man of experience and good habits. For in such an order of things there will not be much opportunity for making money; no man either ought, or indeed will be allowed, to exercise any ignoble occupation, of which the vulgarity is a matter of reproach to a freeman, and should never want to acquire riches by any such means.

Further, the law enjoins that no private man shall be allowed to possess gold and silver, but only coin for daily use, which is almost necessary in dealing with artisans, and for payment of hirelings, whether slaves or immigrants, by all those persons who require the use of them. Wherefore our citizens, as we say, should have a coin passing current among themselves, but not accepted among the rest of mankind; with a view, however, to expeditions and journeys to other lands—for embassies, or for any other occasion which may arise of sending out a herald, the state must also possess a common Hellenic currency. If a private person is ever obliged to go abroad, let him have the consent of the magistrates and go; and if when he returns he has any foreign money remaining, let him give the surplus back to the treasury, and receive a corresponding sum in the local currency. And if he is discovered to appropriate it, let it be confiscated, and let him who knows and does not inform be subject to curse and dishonour equally with him who brought the money, and also to a fine not less in amount than the foreign money which has been brought back. In marrying and giving in marriage, no one shall give or receive any dowry at all; and no one shall deposit money with another whom he does not trust as a friend, nor shall he lend money upon interest; and the borrower should be under no obligation to repay either capital or interest. That these principles are best, any one may see who compares them with the first principle and intention of a state. The intention, as we affirm, of a reasonable statesman, is not what the many declare to be the object of a good legislator, namely, that the state for the true interests of which he is advising should be as great and as rich as possible, and should possess gold and silver, and have the greatest empire by sea and land—this they imagine to be the real object of legislation, at the same time adding, inconsistently, that the true legislator desires to have the city the best and happiest possible. But they do not see that some of these things are possible, and some of them are impossible; and he who orders the state will desire what is possible, and will not indulge in vain wishes or attempts to accomplish that which is impossible. The citizen must indeed be happy and good, and the legislator will seek to make him so; but very rich and very good at the same time he cannot be, not, at least, in the sense in which the many speak of riches. For they mean by "the rich" the few who have the most valuable possessions, although the owner of them may quite well be a rogue. And if this is true, I can never assent to the doctrine that the rich man will be happy— he must be good as well as rich. And good in a high degree, and rich in a high degree at the same time, he cannot be. Some one will ask, why not? And we shall answer, Because acquisitions which come from sources which are just and unjust indifferently, are more than double those which come from just sources only; and the sums which are expended neither honourably nor disgracefully, are only half as great as those which are expended honourably and on honourable purposes. Thus, if the one acquires double and spends half, the other who is in the opposite case and is a good man cannot possibly be wealthier than he. The first—I am speaking of the saver and not of the spender—is not always bad; he may indeed in some cases be utterly bad, but, as I was saying, a good man he never is. For he who receives money unjustly as well as justly, and spends neither justly nor unjustly, will be a rich man if he be also thrifty. On the other hand, the utterly bad is in general profligate, and therefore very poor; while he who spends on noble objects, and acquires wealth by just means only, can hardly be remarkable for riches, any more than he can be very poor. Our statement, then, is true, that the very rich are not good, and, if they are not good, they are not happy. But the intention of our laws was, that the citizens should be as happy as may be, and as friendly as possible to one another. And men who are always at law with one another, and amongst whom there are many wrongs done, can never be friends to one another, but only those among whom crimes and lawsuits are few and slight. Therefore we say that gold and silver ought not to be allowed in the city, nor much of the vulgar sort of trade which is carried on by lending money, or rearing the meaner kinds of live stock; but only the produce of agriculture, and only so much of this as will not compel us in pursuing it to neglect that for the sake of which riches exist—I mean, soul and body, which without gymnastics, and without education, will never be worth anything; and therefore, as we have said not once but many times, the care of riches should have the last place in our thoughts. For there are in all three things about which every man has an interest; and the interest about money, when rightly regarded, is the third and lowest of them: midway comes the interest of the body; and, first of all, that of the soul; and the state which we are describing will have been rightly constituted if it ordains honours according to this scale. But

if, in any of the laws which have been ordained, health
has been preferred to temperance, or wealth to health
and temperate habits, that law must clearly be wrong.
Wherefore, also, the legislator ought often to impress
upon himself the question—"What do I want?" and "Do
I attain my aim, or do I miss the mark?" In this way, and
in this way only, he may acquit himself and free others
from the work of legislation.

Let the allottee then hold his lot upon the conditions
which we have mentioned.

It would be well that every man should come to the
colony having all things equal; but seeing that this is not
possible, and one man will have greater possessions than
another, for many reasons and in particular in order to
preserve equality in special crises of the state, qualifications of property must be unequal, in order that offices
and contributions and distributions may be proportioned
to the value of each person's wealth, and not solely to
the virtue of his ancestors or himself, nor yet to the
strength and beauty of his person, but also to the measure of his wealth or poverty; and so by a law of inequality, which will be in proportion to his wealth, he
will receive honours and offices as equally as possible,
and there will be no quarrels and disputes. To which end
there should be four different standards appointed according to the amount of property: there should be a
first and a second and a third and a fourth class, in which
the citizens will be placed, and they will be called by
these or similar names: they may continue in the same
rank, or pass into another in any individual case, on becoming richer from being poorer, or poorer from being
richer. The form of law which I should propose as the
natural sequel would be as follows:—In a state which
is desirous of being saved from the greatest of all plagues
—not faction, but rather distraction—there should exist

among the citizens neither extreme poverty, nor, again, excess of wealth, for both are productive of both these evils. Now the legislator should determine what is to be the limit of poverty or wealth. Let the limit of poverty be the value of the lot; this ought to be preserved, and no ruler, nor any one else who aspires after a reputation for virtue, will allow the lot to be impaired in any case. This the legislator gives as a measure, and he will permit a man to acquire double or triple, or as much as four times the amount of this. But if a person have yet greater riches, whether he has found them, or they have been given to him, or he has made them in business, or has acquired by any stroke of fortune that which is in excess of the measure, if he give back the surplus to the state, and to the Gods who are the patrons of the state, he shall suffer no penalty or loss of reputation; but if he disobeys this our law, any one who likes may inform against him and receive half the value of the excess, and the delinquent shall pay a sum equal to the excess out of his own property, and the other half of the excess shall belong to the Gods. And let every possession of every man, with the exception of the lot, be publicly registered before the magistrates whom the law appoints, so that all suits about money may be easy and quite simple.

The next thing to be noted is, that the city should be placed as nearly as possible in the centre of the country; we should choose a place which possesses what is suitable for a city, and this may easily be imagined and described. Then we will divide the city into twelve portions, first founding temples to Hestia, to Zeus and to Athene, in a spot which we will call the Acropolis, and surround with a circular wall, making the division of the entire city and country radiate from this point. The twelve portions shall be equalized by the provision that those which are of good land shall be smaller, while those of inferior quality shall be larger. The number of the lots shall be 5040, and each of them shall be divided into two, and every allotment shall be composed of two such sections; one of land near the city, the other of land which is at a distance. This arrangement shall be carried out in the following manner: The section which is near the city shall be added to that which is on the borders, and form one lot, and the portion which is next nearest shall be added to the portion which is next farthest; and so of the rest. Moreover, in the two sections of the lots the same principle of equalization of the soil ought to be maintained; the badness and goodness shall be compensated by more and less. And the legislator shall divide the citizens into twelve parts, and arrange the rest of their property, as far as possible, so as to form twelve equal parts; and there shall be a registration of all. After this they shall assign twelve lots to twelve Gods, and call them by their names, and dedicate to each God their several portions, and call the tribes after them. And they shall distribute the twelve divisions of the city in the same way in which they divided the country; and every man shall have two habitations, one in the centre of the country, and the other at the extremity. Enough of the manner of settlement.

Now we ought by all means to consider that there can never be such a happy concurrence of circumstances as we have described; neither can all things coincide as they are wanted. Men who will not take offence at such a mode of living together, and will endure all their life long to have their property fixed at a moderate limit, and to beget children in accordance with our ordinances, and will allow themselves to be deprived of gold and other things which the legislator, as is evident from these enactments, will certainly forbid them; and will endure, further, the situation of the land with the city in the middle and dwellings round about—all this is as if the legislator were telling his dreams, or making a city and citizens of wax. There is truth in these objections, and therefore every one should take to heart what I am going to say. Once more, then, the legislator shall appear and address us:—"O my friends," he will say to us, "do not suppose me ignorant that there is a certain degree of truth in your words; but I am of opinion that, in matters which are not present but future, he who exhibits a pattern of that at which he aims, should in nothing fall short of the fairest and truest; and that if he finds any part of this work impossible of execution he should avoid and not execute it, but he should contrive to carry out that which is nearest and most akin to it; you must allow the legislator to perfect his design, and when it is perfected, you should join with him in considering what part of his legislation is expedient and what will arouse opposition; for surely the artist who is to be deemed worthy of any regard at all, ought always to make his work self-consistent."

Having determined that there is to be a distribution into twelve parts, let us now see in what way this may be accomplished. There is no difficulty in perceiving that the twelve parts admit of the greatest number of divisions of that which they include, or in seeing the other numbers which are consequent upon them, and are produced out of them up to 5040; wherefore the law ought to order phratries and demes and villages, and also military ranks and movements, as well as coins and measures, dry and liquid, and weights, so as to be commensurable and agreeable to one another. Nor should we fear the appearance of minuteness, if the law commands that all the vessels which a man possesses should have a common measure, when we consider generally that the divisions and variations of numbers have a use

in respect of all the variations of which they are suscepti-
ble, both in themselves and as measures of height and
depth, and in all sounds, and in motions, as well those
which proceed in a straight direction, upwards or downwards, as in those which go round and round. The legislator is to consider all these things and to bid the citizens,
as far as possible, not to lose sight of numerical order;
for no single instrument of youthful education has such
mighty power, both as regards domestic economy and
politics, and in the arts, as the study of arithmetic. Above
all, arithmetic stirs up him who is by nature sleepy and
dull, and makes him quick to learn, retentive, shrewd,
and aided by art divine he makes progress quite beyond
his natural powers. All such things, if only the legislator,
by other laws and institutions, can banish meanness and
covetousness from the souls of men, so that they can use
them properly and to their own good, will be excellent
and suitable instruments of education. But if he cannot,
he will unintentionally create in them, instead of wisdom, the habit of craft, which evil tendency may be
observed in the Egyptians and Phoenicians, and many
other races, through the general vulgarity of their pursuits and acquisitions, whether some unworthy legislator
of theirs has been the cause, or some impediment of
chance or nature. For we must not fail to observe, O
Megillus and Cleinias, that there is a difference in places,
and that some beget better men and others worse; and
we must legislate accordingly. Some places are subject
to strange and fatal influences by reason of diverse winds
and violent heats, some by reason of waters; or, again,
from the character of the food given by the earth, which
not only affects the bodies of men for good or evil, but
produces similar results in their souls. And in all such
qualities those spots excel in which there is a divine inspiration, and in which the demigods have their ap-

pointed lots, and are propitious, not adverse, to the settlers in them. To all these matters the legislator, if he have any sense in him, will attend as far as man can, and frame his laws accordingly.

From Laws, Book V. Translated by Benjamin Jowett.

O

PUBLIC EDUCATION

PLATO

Persons of the Dialogue

AN ATHENIAN STRANGER   CLEINIAS, *A Cretan*
MEGILLUS, *a Lacedaemonian*

ATHENIAN: Any change whatever except from evil is the most dangerous of all things; this is true in the case of the seasons and of the winds, in the management of our bodies and the habits of our minds—true of all things except, as I said before, of the bad. He who looks at the constitution of individuals accustomed to eat any sort of meat, or drink any drink, or to do any work which they can get, may see that they are at first disordered by them, but afterwards, as time goes on, their bodies grow adapted to them, and they learn to know and like variety, and have good health and enjoyment of life; and if ever afterwards they are confined again to a superior diet, at first they are troubled with disorders, and with difficulty become habituated to their new food. A similar principle we may imagine to hold good about the minds of men and the natures of their souls. For when they have been brought up in certain laws, which by some Divine Providence have remained unchanged during long ages, so that no one has any memory or tradition of their ever having been otherwise than they are, then every one is afraid and ashamed to change that which is established. The legislator must somehow find a way of implanting this reverence for antiquity, and I would propose the following way:—People are apt to fancy, as I was saying before, that when the plays of children are altered they are merely plays, not seeing that the most serious and detrimental consequences arise out of the change; and they readily comply with the child's wishes instead of deterring him, not considering that these children who make innovations in their games, when they grow up to be men, will be different from the last generation of children, and, being different, will desire a different sort of life, and under the influence of this desire will want other institutions and laws; and no one of them reflects that there will follow what I just now called the greatest of evils to states. Changes in bodily fashions are no such serious evils, but frequent changes in the praise and censure of manners are the greatest of evils, and require the utmost prevision.

CLE. To be sure.

ATH. And now do we still hold to our former assertion, that rhythms and music in general are imitations of good and evil characters in men? What say you?

CLE. That is the only doctrine which we can admit.

ATH. Must we not, then, try in every possible way to prevent our youth from even desiring to imitate new modes either in dance or song? nor must any one be allowed to offer them varieties of pleasures.

CLE. Most true.

ATH. Can any of us imagine a better mode of effecting this object than that of the Egyptians?

CLE. What is their method?

ATH. To consecrate every sort of dance or melody. First

we should ordain festivals—calculating for the year what they ought to be, and at what time, and in honour of what Gods, sons of Gods, and heroes they ought to be celebrated; and, in the next place, what hymns ought to be sung at the several sacrifices, and with what dances the particular festival is to be honoured. This has to be arranged at first by certain persons, and, when arranged, the whole assembly of the citizens are to offer sacrifices and libations to the Fates and all the other Gods, and to consecrate the several odes to Gods and heroes: and if any one offers any other hymns or dances to any one of the Gods, the priests and priestesses, acting in concert with the guardians of the law, shall, with the sanction of religion and the law, exclude him, and he who is excluded, if he do not submit, shall be liable all his life long to have a suit of impiety brought against him by any one who likes.

CLE. Very good.

ATH. In the consideration of this subject, let us remember what is due to ourselves.

CLE. To what are you referring?

ATH. I mean that any young man, and much more any old one, when he sees or hears anything strange or unaccustomed, does not at once run to embrace the paradox, but he stands considering, like a person who is at a place where three paths meet, and does not very well know his way—he may be alone or he may be walking with others, and he will say to himself and them, "Which is the way?" and will not move forward until he is satisfied that he is going right. And this is what we must do in the present instance:—A strange discussion on the subject of law has arisen, which requires the utmost consideration, and we should not at our age be too ready to speak about such great matters, or be confident that we can say anything certain all in a moment.

CLE. Most true.

ATH. Then we will allow time for reflection, and decide when we have given the subject sufficient consideration. But that we may not be hindered from completing the natural arrangement of our laws, let us proceed to the conclusion of them in due order; for very possibly, if God will, the exposition of them, when completed, may throw light on our present perplexity.

CLE. Excellent, Stranger; let us do as you propose.

ATH. Let us then affirm the paradox that strains of music are our laws (νόμοι), and this latter being the name which the ancients gave to lyric songs, they probably would not have very much objected to our proposed application of the word. Some one, either asleep or awake, must have had a dreamy suspicion of their nature. And let our decree be as follows:—No one in singing or dancing shall offend against public and consecrated models, and the general fashion among the youth, any more than he would offend against any other law. And he who observes this law shall be blameless; but he who is disobedient, as I was saying, shall be punished by the guardians of the laws, and by the priests and priestesses. Suppose that we imagine this to be our law.

CLE. Very good.

ATH. Can any one who makes such laws escape ridicule? Let us see. I think that our only safety will be in first framing certain models for composers. One of these models shall be as follows:—If when a sacrifice is going on, and the victims are being burnt according to law— if, I say, any one who may be a son or brother, standing by another at the altar and over the victims, horribly blasphemes, will not his words inspire despondency and evil omens and forebodings in the mind of his father and of his other kinsmen?

CLE. Of course.

ATH. And this is just what takes place in almost all our cities. A magistrate offers a public sacrifice, and there come in not one but many choruses, who take up a position a little way from the altar, and from time to time pour forth all sorts of horrible blasphemies on the sacred rites, exciting the souls of the audience with words and rhythms and melodies most sorrowful to hear; and he who at the moment when the city is offering sacrifice makes the citizens weep most, carries away the palm of victory. Now, ought we not to forbid such strains as these? And if ever our citizens must hear such lamentations, then on some unblest and inauspicious day let there be choruses of foreign and hired minstrels, like those hirelings who accompany the departed at funerals with barbarous Carian chants. That is the sort of thing which will be appropriate if we have such strains at all; and let the apparel of the singers be, not circlets and ornaments of gold, but the reverse. Enough of all this. I will simply ask once more whether we shall lay down as one of our principles of song——

CLE. What?

ATH. That we should avoid every word of evil omen; let that kind of song which is of good omen be heard everywhere and always in our state. I need hardly ask again, but shall assume that you agree with me.

CLE. By all means; that law is approved by the suffrages of us all.

ATH. But what shall be our next musical law or type? Ought not prayers to be offered up to the Gods when we sacrifice?

CLE. Certainly.

ATH. And our third law, if I am not mistaken, will be to the effect that our poets, understanding prayers to be requests which we make to the Gods, will take especial heed that they do not by mistake ask for evil instead of good. To make such a prayer would surely be too ridiculous.

CLE. Very true.

ATH. Were we not a little while ago quite convinced that no silver or golden Plutus should dwell in our state?

CLE. To be sure.

ATH. And what has it been the object of our argument to show? Did we not imply that the poets are not always quite capable of knowing what is good or evil? And if one of them utters a mistaken prayer in song or words, he will make our citizens pray for the opposite of what is good in matters of the highest import; than which, as I was saying, there can be few greater mistakes. Shall we then propose as one of our laws and models relating to the Muses——

CLE. What?—will you explain the law more precisely?

ATH. Shall we make a law that the poet shall compose nothing contrary to the ideas of the lawful, or just, or beautiful, or good, which are allowed in the state? nor shall he be permitted to communicate his compositions to any private individuals, until he shall have shown them to the appointed judges and the guardians of the law, and they are satisfied with them. As to the persons whom we appoint to be our legislators about music and as to the director of education, these have been already indicated. Once more then, as I have asked more than once, shall this be our third law, and type, and model— What do you say?

CLE. Let it be so, by all means.

ATH. Then it will be proper to have hymns and praises of the Gods, intermingled with prayers; and after the Gods prayers and praises should be offered in like manner to demigods and heroes, suitable to their several characters.

CLE. Certainly.

ATH. In the next place there will be no objection to a law, that citizens who are departed and have done good and energetic deeds, either with their souls or with their bodies, and have been obedient to the laws, should receive eulogies; this will be very fitting.

CLE. Quite true.

ATH. But to honour with hymns and panegyrics those who are still alive is not safe; a man should run his course, and make a fair ending, and then we will praise him; and let praise be given equally to women as well as men who have been distinguished in virtue. The order of songs and dances shall be as follows:—There are many ancient musical compositions and dances which are excellent, and from these the newly-founded city may freely select what is proper and suitable; and they shall choose judges of not less than fifty years of age, who shall make the selection, and any of the old poems which they deem sufficient they shall include; any that are deficient or altogether unsuitable, they shall either utterly throw aside, or examine and amend, taking into their counsel poets and musicians, and making use of their poetical genius; but explaining to them the wishes of the legislator in order that they may regulate dancing, music, and all choral strains, according to the mind of the judges; and not allowing them to indulge, except in some few matters, their individual pleasures and fancies. Now the irregular strain of music is always made ten thousand times better by attaining to law and order, and rejecting the honeyed Muse—not however that we mean wholly to exclude pleasure, which is the characteristic of all music. And if a man be brought up from childhood to the age of discretion and maturity in the use of the orderly and severe music, when he hears the opposite he detests it, and calls it illiberal; but if trained in the sweet and vulgar music, he deems the severer kind cold and displeasing. So that, as I was saying before, while he who hears them gains no more pleasure from the one than from the other, the one has the advantage of making those who are trained in it better men, whereas the other makes them worse.

CLE. Very true.

ATH. Again, we must distinguish and determine on some general principle what songs are suitable to women, and what to men, and must assign to them their proper melodies and rhythms. It is shocking for a whole harmony to be inharmonical, or for a rhythm to be unrhythmical, and this will happen when the melody is inappropriate to them. And therefore the legislator must assign to these also their forms. Now both sexes have melodies and rhythms which of necessity belong to them; and those of women are clearly enough indicated by their natural difference. The grand, and that which tends to courage, may be fairly called manly; but that which inclines to moderation and temperance, may be declared both in law and in ordinary speech to be the more womanly quality.

. . .

ATH. A fair time for a boy of ten years old to spend in letters is three years; the age of thirteen is the proper time for him to begin to handle the lyre, and he may continue at this for another three years, neither more nor less, and whether his father or himself like or dislike the study, he is not to be allowed to spend more or less time in learning music than the law allows. And let him who disobeys the law be deprived of those youthful honours of which we shall hereafter speak. Hear, however, first of all, what the young ought to learn in the early years of life, and what their instructors ought to teach them. They ought to be occupied with their letters until they are able to read and write; but the acquisition of perfect beauty or quickness in writing, if nature has not stimulated them to acquire these accomplishments in the given number of years, they should let alone. And as to the learning of compositions committed to writing which are not set to the lyre, whether metrical or without rhythmical divisions, compositions in prose, as they are termed, having no rhythm or harmony—seeing how dangerous are the writings handed down to us by many writers of this class—what will you do with them, O most excellent guardians of the law? or how can the lawgiver rightly direct you about them? I believe that he will be in great difficulty.

CLE. What troubles you, Stranger? and why are you so perplexed in your mind?

ATH. You naturally ask, Cleinias, and to you and Megillus, who are my partners in the work of legislation, I must state the more difficult as well as the easier parts of the task.

CLE. To what do you refer in this instance?

ATH. I will tell you. There is a difficulty in opposing many myriads of mouths.

CLE. Well, and have we not already opposed the popular voice in many important enactments?

ATH. That is quite true; and you mean to imply that the road which we are taking may be disagreeable to some but is agreeable to as many others, or if not to as many, at any rate to persons not inferior to the others, and in company with them you bid me, at whatever risk, to proceed along the path of legislation which has opened out of our present discourse, and to be of good cheer, and not to faint.

CLE. Certainly.

ATH. And I do not faint; I say, indeed, that we have a great many poets writing in hexameter, trimeter, and all sorts of measures—some who are serious, others who aim only at raising a laugh—and all mankind declare that the youth who are rightly educated should be brought up in them and saturated with them; some insist that they should be constantly hearing them read aloud, and always learning them, so as to get by heart entire poets; while others select choice passages and long speeches, and make compendiums of them, saying that these ought to be committed to memory, if a man is to be made good and wise by experience and learning of many things. And you want me now to tell them plainly in what they are right and in what they are wrong.

CLE. Yes, I do.

ATH. But how can I in one word rightly comprehend all of them? I am of opinion, and, if I am not mistaken, there is a general agreement, that every one of these poets has said many things well and many things the reverse of well; and if this be true, then I do affirm that much learning is dangerous to youth.

CLE. How would you advise the guardian of the law to act?

ATH. In what respect?

CLE. I mean to what pattern should he look as his guide in permitting the young to learn some things and forbidding them to learn others. Do not shrink from answering.

ATH. My good Cleinias, I rather think that I am fortunate.

CLE. How so?

ATH. I think that I am not wholly in want of a pattern, for when I consider the words which we have spoken from early dawn until now, and which, as I believe, have been inspired by Heaven, they appear to me to be quite like a poem. When I reflected upon all these words of ours, I naturally felt pleasure, for of all the discourses which I have ever learnt or heard, either in poetry or prose, this seemed to me to be the justest, and most suitable for young men to hear; I cannot imagine any better pattern than this which the guardian of the law who is also the director of education can have. He cannot do better than advise the teachers to teach the young these words and any which are of a like nature, if he should happen to find them, either in poetry or prose, or if he come across unwritten discourses akin to ours, he should certainly preserve them, and commit them to writing. And, first of all, he shall constrain the teachers themselves to learn and approve them, and any of them who will not, shall not be employed by him, but those whom he finds agreeing in his judgment, he shall make use of and shall commit to them the instruction and education of youth. And here and on this wise let my fanciful tale about letters and teachers of letters come to an end.

CLE. I do not think, Stranger, that we have wandered out of the proposed limits of the argument; but whether we are right or not in our whole conception, I cannot be very certain.

ATH. The truth, Cleinias, may be expected to become clearer when, as we have often said, we arrive at the end of the whole discussion about laws.

CLE. Yes.

ATH. And now that we have done with the teacher of letters, the teacher of the lyre has to receive orders from us.

CLE. Certainly.

ATH. I think that we have only to recollect our previous discussions, and we shall be able to give suitable regulations touching all this part of instruction and education to the teachers of the lyre.

CLE. To what do you refer?

ATH. We were saying, if I remember rightly, that the

sixty-year-old choristers of Dionysus were to be specially quick in their perceptions of rhythm and musical composition, that they might be able to distinguish good and bad imitation, that is to say, the imitation of the good or bad soul when under the influence of passion, rejecting the one and displaying the other in hymns and songs, charming the souls of youth, and inviting them to follow and attain virtue by the way of imitation.

CLE. Very true.

ATH. And with this view the teacher and the learner ought to use the sounds of the lyre, because its notes are pure, the player who teaches and his pupil rendering note for note in unison; but complexity, and variation of notes, when the strings give one sound and the poet or composer of the melody gives another—also when they make concords and harmonies in which lesser and greater intervals, slow and quick, or high and low notes, are combined—or, again, when they make complex variations of rhythms, which they adapt to the notes of the lyre—all that sort of thing is not suited to those who have to acquire a speedy and useful knowledge of music in three years; for opposite principles are confusing, and create a difficulty in learning, and our young men should learn quickly, and their mere necessary acquirements are not few or trifling, as will be shown in due course. Let the director of education attend to the principles concerning music which we are laying down. As to the songs and words themselves which the masters of choruses are to teach and the character of them, they have been already described by us, and are the same which, when consecrated and adapted to the different festivals, we said were to benefit cities by affording them an innocent amusement.

CLE. That, again, is true.

ATH. Then let him who has been elected a director of

music receive these rules from us as containing the very truth; and may he prosper in his office! Let us now proceed to lay down other rules in addition to the preceding about dancing and gymnastic exercise in general. Having said what remained to be said about the teaching of music, let us speak in like manner about gymnastic. For boys and girls ought to learn to dance and practise gymnastic exercises—ought they not?

CLE. Yes.

ATH. Then the boys ought to have dancing masters, and the girls dancing mistresses to exercise them.

CLE. Very good.

ATH. Then once more let us summon him who has the chief concern in the business, the superintendent of youth [i. e. the director of education]; he will have plenty to do, if he is to have the charge of music and gymnastic.

CLE. But how will an old man be able to attend to such great charges?

ATH. O my friend, there will be no difficulty, for the law has already given and will give him permission to select as his assistants in this charge any citizens, male or female, whom he desires; and he will know whom he ought to choose, and will be anxious not to make a mistake, from a due sense of responsibility, and from a consciousness of the importance of his office, and also because he will consider that if young men have been and are well brought up, then all things go swimmingly, but if not, it is not meet to say, nor do we say, what will follow, lest the regarders of omens should take alarm about our infant state. Many things have been said by us about dancing and about gymnastic movements in general; for we include under gymnastics all military exercises, such as archery, and all hurling of weapons, and the use of the light shield, and all fighting with heavy arms, and military evolutions, and movements of armies, and encampings, and all that relates to horsemanship. Of all these things there ought to be public teachers, receiving pay from the state, and their pupils should be the men and boys in the state, and also the girls and women, who are to know all these things. While they are yet girls they should have practised dancing in arms and the whole art of fighting—when grown-up women, they should apply themselves to evolutions and tactics, and the mode of grounding and taking up arms; if for no other reason, yet in case the whole military force should have to leave the city and carry on operations of war outside, that those who will have to guard the young and the rest of the city may be equal to the task; and, on the other hand, when enemies, whether barbarian or Hellenic, come from without with mighty force and make a violent assault upon them, and thus compel them to fight for the possession of the city, which is far from being an impossibility, great would be the disgrace to the state, if the women had been so miserably trained that they could not fight for their young, as birds will, against any creature however strong, and die or undergo any danger, but must instantly rush to the temples and crowd at the altars and shrines, and bring upon human nature the reproach, that of all animals man is the most cowardly!

CLE. Such a want of education, Stranger, is certainly an unseemly thing to happen in a state, as well as a great misfortune.

ATH. Suppose that we carry our law to the extent of saying that women ought not to neglect military matters, but that all citizens, male and female alike, shall attend to them?

CLE. I quite agree.

ATH. Of wrestling we have spoken in part, but of what

I should call the most important part we have not spoken, and cannot easily speak without showing at the same time by gesture as well as in word what we mean; when word and action combine, and not till then, we shall explain clearly what has been said, pointing out that of all movements wrestling is most akin to the military art, and is to be pursued for the sake of this, and not this for the sake of wrestling.

CLE. Excellent.

ATH. Enough of wrestling; we will now proceed to speak of other movements of the body. Such motion may be in general called dancing, and is of two kinds: one of nobler figures, imitating the honourable, the other of the more ignoble figures, imitating the mean; and of both these there are two further subdivisions. Of the serious, one kind is of those engaged in war and vehement action, and is the exercise of a noble person and a manly heart; the other exhibits a temperate soul in the enjoyment of prosperity and modest pleasures, and may be truly called and is the dance of peace. The warrior dance is different from the peaceful one, and may be rightly termed Pyrrhic; this imitates the modes of avoiding blows and missiles by dropping or giving way, or springing aside, or rising up or falling down; also the opposite postures which are those of action, as, for example, the imitation of archery and the hurling of javelins, and of all sorts of blows. And when the imitation is of brave bodies and souls, and the action is direct and muscular, giving for the most part a straight movement to the limbs of the body—that, I say, is the true sort; but the opposite is not right. In the dance of peace what we have to consider is whether a man bears himself naturally and gracefully, and after the manner of men who duly conform to the law. But before proceeding I must distinguish the dancing about which there is any doubt, from that about which there is no doubt. Which is the doubtful kind, and how are the two to be distinguished? There are dances of the Bacchic sort, both those in which, as they say, they imitate drunken men, and which are named after the Nymphs, and Pan, and Silenuses, and Satyrs; and also those in which purifications are made or mysteries celebrated—all this sort of dancing cannot be rightly defined as having either a peaceful or a warlike character, or indeed as having any meaning whatever, and may, I think, be most truly described as distinct from the warlike dance, and distinct from the peaceful, and not suited for a city at all. There let it lie; and so leaving it to lie, we will proceed to the dances of war and peace, for with these we are undoubtedly concerned. Now the unwarlike muse, which honours in dance the Gods and the sons of the Gods, is entirely associated with the consciousness of prosperity; this class may be subdivided into two lesser classes, of which one is expressive of an escape from some labour or danger into good, and has greater pleasures, the other expressive of preservation and increase of former good, in which the pleasure is less exciting—in all these cases, every man when the pleasure is greater, moves his body more, and less when the pleasure is less; and, again, if he be more orderly and has learned courage from discipline he moves less, but if he be a coward, and has no training or self-control, he makes greater and more violent movements, and in general when he is speaking or singing he is not altogether able to keep his body still; and so out of the imitation of words in gestures the whole art of dancing has arisen. And in these various kinds of imitation one man moves in an orderly, another in a disorderly manner; and as the ancients may be observed to have given many names which are according to nature and deserving of praise, so there is an excellent one which they have given to the dances of men who in their times of prosperity are moderate in their pleasures —the giver of names, whoever he was, assigned to them a very true, and poetical, and rational name, when he called them Emmeleiai, or dances of order, thus establishing two kinds of dances of the nobler sort, the dance of war which he called the Pyrrhic, and the dance of peace which he called Emmeleia, or the dance of order; giving to each their appropriate and becoming name. These things the legislator should indicate in general outline, and the guardian of the law should enquire into them and search them out, combining dancing with music, and assigning to the several sacrificial feasts that which is suitable to them; and when he has consecrated all of them in due order, he shall for the future change nothing, whether of dance or song. Thenceforward the city and the citizens shall continue to have the same pleasures, themselves being as far as possible alike, and shall live well and happily.

I have described the dances which are appropriate to noble bodies and generous souls. But it is necessary also to consider and know uncomely persons and thoughts, and those which are intended to produce laughter in comedy, and have a comic character in respect of style, song, and dance, and of the imitations which these afford. For serious things cannot be understood without laughable things, nor opposites at all without opposites, if a man is really to have intelligence of either; but he cannot carry out both in action, if he is to have any degree of virtue. And for this very reason he should learn them both, in order that he may not in ignorance do or say anything which is ridiculous and out of place—he should command slaves and hired strangers to imitate such things, but he should never take any serious interest in them himself, nor should any freeman or freewoman be discovered taking pains to learn them; and there should always be some element of novelty in the imitation. Let these then be laid down, both in law and in our discourse, as the regulations of laughable amusements which are generally called comedy. And, if any of the serious poets, as they are termed, who write tragedy, come to us and say—"O strangers, may we go to your city and country or may we not, and shall we bring with us our poetry—what is your will about these matters?" —how shall we answer the divine men? I think that our answer should be as follows:—Best of strangers, we will say to them, we also according to our ability are tragic poets, and our tragedy is the best and noblest; for our whole state is an imitation of the best and noblest life, which we affirm to be indeed the very truth of tragedy. You are poets and we are poets, both makers of the same strains, rivals and antagonists in the noblest of dramas, which true law can alone perfect, as our hope is. Do not then suppose that we shall all in a moment allow you to erect your stage in the agora, or introduce the fair voices of your actors, speaking above our own, and permit you to harangue our women and children, and the common people, about our institutions, in language other than our own, and very often the opposite of our own. For a state would be mad which gave you this licence, until the magistrates had determined whether your poetry might be recited, and was fit for publication or not. Wherefore, O ye sons and scions of the softer Muses, first of all show your songs to the magistrates, and let them compare them with our own, and if they are the same or better we will give you a chorus; but if not, then, my friends, we cannot. Let these, then, be the customs ordained by law about all dances and the teaching of them, and let matters relating to slaves be separated from those relating to masters, if you do not object.

CLE. We can have no hesitation in assenting when you put the matter thus.

ATH. There still remain three studies suitable for freemen. Arithmetic is one of them; the measurement of length, surface, and depth is the second; and the third has to do with the revolutions of the stars in relation to one another. Not every one has need to toil through all these things in a strictly scientific manner, but only a few, and who they are to be we will hereafter indicate at the end, which will be the proper place; not to know what is necessary for mankind in general, and what is the truth, is disgraceful to every one: and yet to enter into these matters minutely is neither easy, nor at all possible for every one; but there is something in them which is necessary and cannot be set aside, and probably he who made the proverb about God originally had this in view when he said, that "not even God himself can fight against necessity"—he meant, if I am not mistaken, divine necessity; for as to the human necessities of which the many speak, when they talk in this manner, nothing can be more ridiculous than such an application of the words.

CLE. And what necessities of knowledge are there, Stranger, which are divine and not human?

ATH. I conceive them to be those of which he who has no use nor any knowledge at all cannot be a God, or demi-god, or hero to mankind, or able to take any serious thought or charge of them. And very unlike a divine man would he be, who is unable to count one, two, three, or to distinguish odd and even numbers, or is unable to count at all, or reckon night and day, and who is totally unacquainted with the revolution of the sun and moon, and the other stars. There would be great folly in supposing that all these are not necessary parts of knowledge to him who intends to know anything about the highest kinds of knowledge; but which these are, and how many there are of them, and when they are to be learned, and what is to be learned together and what apart, and the whole correlation of them, must be rightly apprehended first; and these leading the way we may proceed to the other parts of knowledge. For so necessity grounded in nature constrains us, against which we say that no God contends, or ever will contend.

From *Laws*, Book VII. Translated by Benjamin Jowett.

O

UTOPIA

O

THE BIRDS

ARISTOPHANES

(SCENE:—*A wild and desolate region; only thickets, rocks, and a single tree are seen.* EUELPIDES *and* PITHE-TAERUS *enter, each with a bird in his hand.*)

EUELPIDES, *to his jay:* Do you think I should walk straight for yon tree?

PITHETAERUS, *to his crow:* Cursed beast, what are you croaking to me? . . . to retrace my steps?

EUELPIDES: Why, you wretch, we are wandering at random, we are exerting ourselves only to return to the same spot; we're wasting our time.

PITHETAERUS: To think that I should trust to this crow, which has made me cover more than a thousand furlongs!

EUELPIDES: And that I, in obedience to this jay, should have worn my toes down to the nails!

PITHETAERUS: If only I knew where we were. . . .

EUELPIDES: Could you find your country again from here?

PITHETAERUS: No, I feel quite sure I could not, any more than could Execestides find his.

EUELPIDES: Alas!

PITHETAERUS: Aye, aye, my friend, it's surely the road of "alases" we are following.

EUELPIDES: That Philocrates, the bird-seller, played us a scurvy trick, when he pretended these two guides could help us to find Tereus, the Epops, who is a bird, without being born of one. He has indeed sold us this jay, a true son of Tharrhelides, for an obolus, and this crow for three, but what can they do? Why, nothing whatever but bite and scratch! *To his jay:* What's the matter with you then, that you keep opening your beak? Do you want us to fling ourselves headlong down these rocks? There is no road that way.

PITHETAERUS: Not even the vestige of a trail in any direction

EUELPIDES: And what does the crow say about the road to follow?

PITHETAERUS: By Zeus, it no longer croaks the same thing it did.

EUELPIDES: And which way does it tell us to go now?

PITHETAERUS: It says that, by dint of gnawing, it will devour my fingers.

EUELPIDES: What misfortune is ours! we strain every nerve to get to the crows, do everything we can to that end, and we cannot find our way! Yes, spectators, our madness is quite different from that of Sacas. He is not a citizen, and would fain be one at any cost; we, on the contrary, born of an honourable tribe and family and living in the midst of our fellow-citizens, we have fled from our country as hard as ever we could go. It's not that we hate it; we recognize it to be great and rich,

likewise that everyone has the right to ruin himself paying taxes; but the crickets only chirrup among the fig-
trees for a month or two, whereas the Athenians spend
their whole lives in chanting forth judgments from their
law-courts. That is why we started off with a basket, a
stew-pot and some myrtle boughs and have come to
seek a quiet country in which to settle. We are going to
Tereus, the Epops, to learn from him, whether, in his
aerial flights, he has noticed some town of this kind.

PITHETAERUS: Here! look!

EUELPIDES: What's the matter?

PITHETAERUS: Why, the crow has been directing me
to something up there for some time now.

EUELPIDES: And the jay is also opening its beak and
craning its neck to show me I know not what. Clearly,
there are some birds about here. We shall soon know,
if we kick up a noise to start them.

PITHETAERUS: Do you know what to do? Knock your
leg against this rock.

EUELPIDES: And you your head to double the noise.

PITHETAERUS: Well then use a stone instead; take one
and hammer with it.

EUELPIDES: Good idea! *He does so.* Ho there, within!
Slave! slave!

PITHETAERUS: What's that, friend! You say, "slave,"
to summon Epops? It would be much better to shout,
"Epops, Epops!"

EUELPIDES: Well then, Epops! Must I knock again?
Epops!

TROCHILUS, *rushing out of a thicket:* Who's there?
Who calls my master?

PITHETAERUS, *in terror:* Apollo the Deliverer! what
an enormous beak! *He defecates. In the confusion both
the jay and the crow fly away.*

TROCHILUS, *equally frightened:* Good god! they are bird-catchers.

EUELPIDES, *reassuring himself:* But is it so terrible? Wouldn't it be better to explain things?

TROCHILUS, *also reassuring himself:* You're done for.

EUELPIDES: But we are not men.

TROCHILUS: What are you, then?

EUELPIDES, *defecating also:* I am the Fearling, an African bird.

TROCHILUS: You talk nonsense.

EUELPIDES: Well, then, just ask it of my feet.

TROCHILUS: And this other one, what bird is it? *To* PITHETAERUS: Speak up!

PITHETAERUS, *weakly:* I? I am a Crapple, from the land of the pheasants.

EUELPIDES: But you yourself, in the name of the gods! what animal are you?

TROCHILUS: Why, I am a slave-bird.

EUELPIDES: Why, have you been conquered by a cock?

TROCHILUS: No, but when my master was turned into a hoopoe, he begged me to become a bird also, to follow and to serve him.

EUELPIDES: Does a bird need a servant, then?

TROCHILUS: That's no doubt because he was once a man. At times he wants to eat a dish of sardines from Phalerum; I seize my dish and fly to fetch him some. Again he wants some pea-soup; I seize a ladle and a pot and run to get it.

EUELPIDES: This is, then, truly a running-bird. Come, Trochilus, do us the kindness to call your master.

TROCHILUS: Why, he has just fallen asleep after a feed of myrtle-berries and a few grubs.

EUELPIDES: Never mind; wake him up.

TROCHILUS: I am certain he will be angry. However, I will wake him to please you. *He goes back into the thicket.*

PITHETAERUS, *as soon as* TROCHILUS *is out of sight:* You cursed brute! why, I am almost dead with terror!

EUELPIDES: Oh! my god! it was sheer fear that made me lose my jay.

PITHETAERUS: Ah! you big coward! were you so frightened that you let go your jay?

EUELPIDES: And did you not lose your crow, when you fell sprawling on the ground? Tell me that.

PITHETAERUS: Not at all.

EUELPIDES: Where is it, then?

PITHETAERUS: It flew away.

EUELPIDES: And you did not let it go? Oh! you brave fellow!

EPOPS, *from within:* Open the thicket, that I may go out! *He comes out of the thicket.*

EUELPIDES: By Heracles! what a creature! what plumage! What means this triple crest?

EPOPS: Who wants me?

EUELPIDES, *banteringly:* The twelve great gods have used you ill, it seems.

EPOPS: Are you twitting me about my feathers? I have been a man, strangers.

EUELPIDES: It's not you we are jeering at.

EPOPS: At what, then?

EUELPIDES: Why, it's your beak that looks so ridiculous to us.

EPOPS: This is how Sophocles outrages me in his tragedies. Know, I once was Tereus.

EUELPIDES: You were Tereus, and what are you now? a bird or a peacock?

EPOPS: I am a bird.

EUELPIDES: Then where are your feathers? I don't see any.

EPOPS: They have fallen off.

EUELPIDES: Through illness?

EPOPS: No. All birds moult their feathers, you know, every winter, and others grow in their place. But tell me, who are you?

EUELPIDES: We? We are mortals.

EPOPS: From what country?

EUELPIDES: From the land of the beautiful galleys.

EPOPS: Are you dicasts?

EUELPIDES: No, if anything, we are anti-dicasts.

EPOPS: Is that kind of seed sown among you?

EUELPIDES: You have to look hard to find even a little in our fields.

EPOPS: What brings you here?

EUELPIDES: We wish to pay you a visit.

EPOPS: What for?

EUELPIDES: Because you formerly were a man, like we are, formerly you had debts, as we have, formerly you did not want to pay them, like ourselves; furthermore, being turned into a bird, you have when flying seen all lands and seas. Thus you have all human knowledge as well as that of birds. And hence we have come to you to beg you to direct us to some cosy town, in which one can repose as if on thick coverlets.

EPOPS: And are you looking for a greater city than Athens?

EUELPIDES: No, not a greater, but one more pleasant to live in.

EPOPS: Then you are looking for an aristocratic country.

EUELPIDES: I? Not at all! I hold the son of Scellias in horror.

EPOPS: But, after all, what sort of city *would* please you best?

EUELPIDES: A place where the following would be the most important business transacted.—Some friend would come knocking at the door quite early in the morning saying, "By Olympian Zeus, be at my house early, as soon as you have bathed, and bring your children too. I am giving a nuptial feast, so don't fail, or else don't cross my threshold when I am in distress."

EPOPS: Ah! that's what may be called being fond of hardships! *To* PITHETAERUS: And what say you?

PITHETAERUS: My tastes are similar.

EPOPS: And they are?

PITHETAERUS: I want a town where the father of a handsome lad will stop in the street and say to me reproachfully as if I had failed him, "Ah! Is this well done, Stilbonides? You met my son coming from the bath after the gymnasium and you neither spoke to him, nor kissed him, nor took him with you, nor ever once felt his balls. Would anyone call you an old friend of mine?"

EPOPS: Ah! wag, I see you are fond of suffering. But there is a city of delights such as you want. It's on the Red Sea.

EUELPIDES: Oh, no. Not a sea-port, where some fine morning the Salaminian galley can appear, bringing a process-server along. Have you no Greek town you can propose to us?

EPOPS: Why not choose Lepreum in Elis for your settlement?

EUELPIDES: By Zeus! I could not look at Lepreum without disgust, because of Melanthius.

EPOPS: Then, again, there is the Opuntian Locris, where you could live.

EUELPIDES: I would not be Opuntian for a talent. But

come, what is it like to live with the birds? You should know pretty well.

EPOPS: Why, it's not a disagreeable life. In the first place, one has no purse.

EUELPIDES: That does away with a lot of roguery.

EPOPS: For food the gardens yield us white sesame, myrtle-berries, poppies and mint.

EUELPIDES: Why, 'tis the life of the newly-wed indeed.

PITHETAERUS: Ha! I am beginning to see a great plan, which will transfer the supreme power to the birds, if you will but take my advice.

EPOPS: Take your advice? In what way?

PITHETAERUS: In what way? Well, firstly, do not fly in all directions with open beak; it is not dignified. Among us, when we see a thoughtless man, we ask, "What sort of bird is this?" and Teleas answers, "It's a man who has no brain, a bird that has lost his head, a creature you cannot catch, for it never remains in any one place."

EPOPS: By Zeus himself! your jest hits the mark. What then is to be done?

PITHETAERUS: Found a city.

EPOPS: We birds? But what sort of city should we build?

PITHETAERUS: Oh, really, really! you talk like such a fool! Look down.

EPOPS: I am looking.

PITHETAERUS: Now look up.

EPOPS: I am looking.

PITHETAERUS: Turn your head round.

EPOPS: Ah! it will be pleasant for me if I end in twisting my neck off!

PITHETAERUS: What have you seen?

EPOPS: The clouds and the sky.

PITHETAERUS: Very well! is not this the pole of the birds then?

EPOPS: How their pole?

PITHETAERUS: Or, if you like it, their place. And since it turns and passes through the whole universe, it is called "pole." If you build and fortify it, you will turn your pole into a city. In this way you will reign over mankind as you do over the grasshoppers and you will cause the gods to die of rabid hunger.

EPOPS: How so?

PITHETAERUS: The air is between earth and heaven. When we want to go to Delphi, we ask the Boeotians for leave of passage; in the same way, when men sacrifice to the gods, unless the latter pay you tribute, you exercise the right of every nation towards strangers and don't allow the smoke of the sacrifices to pass through your city and territory.

EPOPS: By earth! by snares! by network! by cages! I never heard of anything more cleverly conceived; and, if the other birds approve, I am going to build the city along with you.

PITHETAERUS: Who will explain the matter to them?

EPOPS: You must yourself. Before I came they were quite ignorant, but since I have lived with them I have taught them to speak.

PITHETAERUS: But how can they be gathered?

EPOPS: Easily, I will hasten down to the thicket to waken my dear Procné and as soon as they hear our voices, they will come to us hot wing.

PITHETAERUS: My dear bird, lose no time, please! Fly at once into the thicket and awaken Procné. EPOPS *rushes into the thicket.*

EPOPS, *from within; singing:* Chase off drowsy sleep, dear companion. Let the sacred hymn gush from thy divine throat in melodious strains; roll forth in soft cadence your refreshing melodies to bewail the fate of Itys, which has been the cause of so many tears to us both. Your pure notes rise through the thick leaves of the yew-tree right up to the throne of Zeus, where Phoebus listens to you, Phoebus with his golden hair. And his ivory lyre responds to your plaintive accents; he gathers the choir of the gods and from their immortal lips pours forth a sacred chant of blessed voices. *The flute is played behind the scene, imitating the song of the nightingale.*

PITHETAERUS: Oh! by Zeus! what a throat that little bird possesses. He has filled the whole thicket with honey-sweet melody!

EUELPIDES: Hush!

PITHETAERUS: What's the matter?

EUELPIDES: Be still!

PITHETAERUS: What for?

EUELPIDES: Epops is going to sing again.

EPOPS, *in the thicket, singing: Epopopoi popoi popopopoi popoi,* here, here, quick, quick, quick, my comrades in the air; all you who pillage the fertile lands of the husbandmen, the numberless tribes who gather and devour the barley seeds, the swift flying race that sings so sweetly. And you whose gentle twitter resounds through the fields with the little cry of *tiotiotiotiotiotiotiotio;* and you who hop about the branches of the ivy in the gardens; the mountain birds, who feed on the wild olive-berries or the arbutus, hurry to come at my call, *trioto, trioto, totobrix;* you also, who snap up the sharp-stinging gnats in the marshy vales, and you who dwell in the fine plain of Marathon, all damp with dew, and you, the francolin with speckled wings; you too, the halcyons, who flit over the swelling waves of the sea, come hither to hear the tidings; let all the tribes of long-necked birds assemble here; know that a clever old man has come to us, bringing an entirely new idea and proposing great reforms. Let all come to the debate here, here, here, here. *Torotorotorotorotix, kikkabau, kikkabau, torotorotorolililix.*

PITHETAERUS: Can you see any bird?

EUELPIDES: By Phoebus, no! and yet I am straining my eyesight to scan the sky.

PITHETAERUS: It was hardly worth Epops' while to go and bury himself in the thicket like a hatching plover.

A BIRD, *entering: Torotix, torotix.*

PITHETAERUS: Wait, friend, there's a bird.

EUELPIDES: By Zeus, it *is* a bird, but what kind? Isn't it a peacock?

PITHETAERUS, *as* EPOPS *comes out of the thicket:* Epops will tell us. What is this bird?

EPOPS: It's not one of those you are used to seeing; it's a bird from the marshes.

EUELPIDES: Oh! oh! but he is very handsome with his wings as crimson as flame.

EPOPS: Undoubtedly; indeed he is called flamingo.

EUELPIDES, *excitedly:* Hi! I say! You!

PITHETAERUS: What are you shouting for?

EUELPIDES: Why, here's another bird.

PITHETAERUS: Aye, indeed; this one's a foreign bird too. *To* EPOPS: What is this bird from beyond the mountains with a look as solemn as it is stupid?

EPOPS: He is called the Mede.

EUELPIDES: The Mede! But, by Heracles, how, if a Mede, has he flown here without a camel?

PITHETAERUS: Here's another bird with a crest. *From here on, the numerous birds that make up the* CHORUS *keep rushing in.*

EUELPIDES: Ah! that's curious. I say, Epops, you are not the only one of your kind then?

EPOPS: This bird is the son of Philocles, who is the

son of Epops; so that, you see, I am his grandfather; just as one might say, Hipponicus, the son of Callias, who is the son of Hipponicus.

EUELPIDES: Then this bird is Callias! Why, what a lot of his feathers he has lost!

EPOPS: That's because he is honest; so the informers set upon him and the women too pluck out his feathers.

EUELPIDES: By Posidon, do you see that many-coloured bird? What is his name?

EPOPS: This one? That's the glutton.

EUELPIDES: Is there another glutton besides Cleonymus? But why, if he is Cleonymus, has he not thrown away his crest? But what is the meaning of all these crests? Have these birds come to contend for the double stadium prize?

EPOPS: They are like the Carians, who cling to the crests of their mountains for greater safety.

PITHETAERUS: Oh, Posidon! look what awful swarms of birds are gathering here!

EUELPIDES: By Phoebus! what a cloud! The entrance to the stage is no longer visible so closely do they fly together.

PITHETAERUS: Here is the partridge.

EUELPIDES: Why, there is the francolin.

PITHETAERUS: There is the poachard.

EUELPIDES: Here is the kingfisher. *To* EPOPS: What's that bird behind the kingfisher?

EPOPS: That's the barber.

EUELPIDES: What? a bird a barber?

PITHETAERUS: Why, Sporgilus is one.

EPOPS: Here comes the owl.

EUELPIDES: And who is it brings an owl to Athens?

EPOPS, *pointing to the various species:* Here is the magpie, the turtle-dove, the swallow, the horned-owl, the buzzard, the pigeon, the falcon, the ring-dove, the cuckoo, the red-foot, the red-cap, the purple-cap, the kestrel, the diver, the ousel, the osprey, the woodpecker . . .

PITHETAERUS: Oh! what a lot of birds!

EUELPIDES: Oh! what a lot of blackbirds!

PITHETAERUS: How they scold, how they come rushing up! What a noise! what a noise!

EUELPIDES: Can they be bearing us ill-will?

PITHETAERUS: Oh! there! there! they are opening their beaks and staring at us.

EUELPIDES: Why, so they are.

LEADER OF THE CHORUS: *Popopopopopo.* Where is he who called me? Where am I to find him?

EPOPS: I have been waiting for you a long while! I never fail in my word to my friends.

LEADER OF THE CHORUS: *Tititititititi.* What good news have you for me?

EPOPS: Something that concerns our common safety, and that is just as pleasant as it is to the point. Two men, who are subtle reasoners, have come here to seek me.

LEADER OF THE CHORUS: Where? How? What are you saying?

EPOPS: I say, two old men have come from the abode of humans to propose a vast and splendid scheme to us.

LEADER OF THE CHORUS: Oh! it's a horrible, unheard-of crime! What are you saying?

EPOPS: Never let my words scare you.

LEADER OF THE CHORUS: What have you done to me?

EPOPS: I have welcomed two men, who wish to live with us.

LEADER OF THE CHORUS: And you have dared to do that!

EPOPS: Yes, and I am delighted at having done so.

LEADER OF THE CHORUS: And are they already with us?

EPOPS: Just as much as I am.

CHORUS, *singing:* Ah! ah! we are betrayed; 'tis sacrilege! Our friend, he who picked up corn-seeds in the same plains as ourselves, has violated our ancient laws; he has broken the oaths that bind all birds; he has laid a snare for me, he has handed us over to the attacks of that impious race which throughout all time, has never ceased to war against us.

LEADER OF THE CHORUS: As for this traitorous bird, we will decide his case later, but the two old men shall be punished forthwith; we are going to tear them to pieces.

PITHETAERUS: It's all over with us.

EUELPIDES: You are the sole cause of all our trouble. Why did you bring me from down yonder?

PITHETAERUS: To have you with me.

EUELPIDES: Say rather to have me melt into tears.

PITHETAERUS: Go on! you are talking nonsense. How will you weep with your eyes pecked out?

CHORUS, *singing:* Io! io! forward to the attack, throw yourselves upon the foe, spill his blood; take to your wings and surround them on all sides. Woe to them! let us get to work with our beaks, let us devour them. Nothing can save them from our wrath, neither the mountain forests, nor the clouds that float in the sky, nor the foaming deep.

LEADER OF THE CHORUS: Come, peck, tear to ribbons. Where is the chief of the cohort? Let him engage the right wing. *They rush at the two Athenians.*

EUELPIDES: This is the fatal moment. Where shall I fly to, unfortunate wretch that I am?

PITHETAERUS: Wait! Stay here!

EUELPIDES: That they may tear me to pieces?

PITHETAERUS: And how do you think to escape them?

EUELPIDES: I don't know at all.

PITHETAERUS: Come, I will tell you. We must stop and fight them. Let us arm ourselves with these stew-pots.

EUELPIDES: Why with the stew-pots?

PITHETAERUS: The owl will not attack us then.

EUELPIDES: But do you see all those hooked claws?

PITHETAERUS: Take the spit and pierce the foe on your side.

EUELPIDES: And how about my eyes?

PITHETAERUS: Protect them with this dish or this vinegar-pot.

EUELPIDES: Oh! what cleverness! what inventive genius! You are a great general, even greater than Nicias, where stratagem is concerned.

LEADER OF THE CHORUS: Forward, forward, charge with your beaks! Come, no delay. Tear, pluck, strike, flay them, and first of all smash the stew-pot.

EPOPS, *stepping in front of the* CHORUS: Oh, most cruel of all animals, why tear these two men to pieces, why kill them? What have they done to you? They belong to the same tribe, to the same family as my wife.

LEADER OF THE CHORUS: Are wolves to be spared? Are they not our most mortal foes? So let us punish them.

EPOPS: If they are your foes by nature, they are your friends in heart, and they come here to give you useful advice.

LEADER OF THE CHORUS: Advice or a useful word from their lips, from them, the enemies of my forebears?

EPOPS: The wise can often profit by the lessons of a foe, for caution is the mother of safety. It is just such a thing as one will not learn from a friend and which an enemy compels you to know. To begin with, it's the foe and not the friend that taught cities to build high walls, to equip long vessels of war; and it's this knowledge that protects our children, our slaves and our wealth.

LEADER OF THE CHORUS: Well then, I agree, let us

first hear them, for that is best; one can even learn something in an enemy's school.

PITHETAERUS, *to* EUELPIDES: Their wrath seems to cool. Draw back a little.

EPOPS: It's only justice, and you will thank me later.

LEADER OF THE CHORUS: Never have we opposed your advice up to now.

PITHETAERUS: They are in a more peaceful mood; put down your stew-pot and your two dishes; spit in hand, doing duty for a spear, let us mount guard inside the camp close to the pot and watch in our arsenal closely; for we must not fly.

EUELPIDES: You are right. But where shall we be buried, if we die?

PITHETAERUS: In the Ceramicus; for, to get a public funeral, we shall tell the Strategi that we fell at Orneae, fighting the country's foes.

LEADER OF THE CHORUS: Return to your ranks and lay down your courage beside your wrath as the hoplites do. Then let us ask these men who they are, whence they come, and with what intent. Here, Epops, answer me.

EPOPS: Are you calling me? What do you want of me?

LEADER OF THE CHORUS: Who are they? From what country?

EPOPS: Strangers, who have come from Greece, the land of the wise.

LEADER OF THE CHORUS: And what fate has led them hither to the land of the birds?

EPOPS: Their love for you and their wish to share your kind of life; to dwell and remain with you always.

LEADER OF THE CHORUS: Indeed, and what are their plans?

EPOPS: They are wonderful, incredible, unheard of.

LEADER OF THE CHORUS: Why, do they think to see some advantage that determines them to settle here? Are they hoping with our help to triumph over their foes or to be useful to their friends?

EPOPS: They speak of benefits so great it is impossible either to describe or conceive them; all shall be yours, all that we see here, there, above and below us; this they vouch for.

LEADER OF THE CHORUS: Are they mad?

EPOPS: They are the sanest people in the world.

LEADER OF THE CHORUS: Clever men?

EPOPS: The sylest of foxes, cleverness its very self, men of the world, cunning, the cream of knowing folk.

LEADER OF THE CHORUS: Tell them to speak and speak quickly; why, as I listen to you, I am beside myself with delight.

EPOPS, *to two attendants:* Here, you there, take all these weapons and hang them up inside close to the fire, near the figure of the god who presides there and under his protection; *to* PITHETAERUS: as for you, address the birds, tell them why I have gathered them together.

PITHETAERUS: Not I, by Apollo, unless they agree with me as the little ape of an armourer agreed with his wife, not to bite me, nor pull me by the balls, nor shove things into my . . .

EUELPIDES, *bending over and pointing his finger at his anus:* Do you mean this?

PITHETAERUS: No, I mean my eyes.

LEADER OF THE CHORUS: Agreed.

PITHETAERUS: Swear it.

LEADER OF THE CHORUS: I swear it and, if I keep my promise, let judges and spectators give me the victory unanimously.

PITHETAERUS: It is a bargain.

LEADER OF THE CHORUS: And if I break my word, may I succeed by one vote only.

EPOPS, *as* HERALD: Hearken, ye people! Hoplites, pick

up your weapons and return to your firesides; do not
fail to read the decrees of dismissal we have posted.

CHORUS, *singing:* Man is a truly cunning creature, but
nevertheless explain. Perhaps you are going to show me
some good way to extend my power, some way that I
have not had the wit to find out and which you have discovered. Speak! 'tis to your own interest as well as to
mine, for if you secure me some advantage, I will surely
share it with you.

LEADER OF THE CHORUS: But what object can have
induced you to come among us? Speak boldly, for I shall
not break the truce—until you have told us all.

PITHETAERUS: I am bursting with desire to speak; I
have already mixed the dough of my address and nothing prevents me from kneading it. . . . Slave! bring the
chaplet and water, which you must pour over my hands.
Be quick!

EUELPIDES: Is it a question of feasting? What does it
all mean?

PITHETAERUS: By Zeus, no! but I am hunting for fine,
tasty words to break down the hardness of their hearts.
To the CHORUS: I grieve so much for you, who at one
time were kings . . .

LEADER OF THE CHORUS: We kings? Over whom?

PITHETAERUS: . . . of all that exists, firstly of me and
of this man, even of Zeus himself. Your race is older than
Saturn, the Titans and the Earth.

LEADER OF THE CHORUS: What, older than the Earth!

PITHETAERUS: By Phoebus, yes.

LEADER OF THE CHORUS: By Zeus, but I never knew
that before!

PITHETAERUS: That's because you are ignorant and
heedless, and have never read your Aesop. He is the one
who tells us that the lark was born before all other creatures, indeed before the Earth; his father died of sick-

ness, but the Earth did not exist then; he remained unburied for five days, when the bird in its dilemma decided, for want of a better place, to entomb its father in its own head.

EUELPIDES: So that the lark's father is buried at Cephalae.

PITHETAERUS: Hence, if they existed before the Earth, before the gods, the kingship belongs to them by right of priority.

EUELPIDES: Undoubtedly, but sharpen your beak well; Zeus won't be in a hurry to hand over his sceptre to the woodpecker.

PITHETAERUS: It was not the gods, but the birds, who were formerly the masters and kings over men; of this I have a thousand proofs. First of all, I will point you to the cock, who governed the Persians before all other monarchs, before Darius and Megabazus. It's in memory of his reign that he is called the Persian bird.

EUELPIDES: For this reason also, even today, he alone of all the birds wears his tiara straight on his head, like the Great King.

PITHETAERUS: He was so strong, so great, so feared, that even now, on account of his ancient power, everyone jumps out of bed as soon as ever he crows at daybreak. Blacksmiths, potters, tanners, shoemakers, bathmen, corn-dealers, lyre-makers and armourers, all put on their shoes and go to work before it is daylight.

EUELPIDES: I can tell you something about that. It was the cock's fault that I lost a splendid tunic of Phrygian wool. I was at a feast in town, given to celebrate the birth of a child; I had drunk pretty freely and had just fallen asleep, when a cock, I suppose in a greater hurry than the rest, began to crow. I thought it was drawn and set out for Halimus. I had hardly got beyond the walls, when a footpad struck me in the back with his bludgeon;

down I went and wanted to shout, but he had already made off with my mantle.

Pithetaerus: Formerly also the kite was ruler and king over the Greeks.

Leader of the Chorus: The Greeks?

Pithetaerus: And when he was king, he was the one who first taught them to fall on their knees before the kites.

Euelpides: By Zeus! that's what I did myself one day on seeing a kite; but at the moment I was on my knees, and leaning backwards with mouth agape, I bolted an obolus and was forced to carry my meal-sack home empty.

Pithetaerus: The cuckoo was king of Egypt and of the whole of Phoenicia. When he called out "cuckoo," all the Phoenicians hurried to the fields to reap their wheat and their barley.

Euelpides: Hence no doubt the proverb, "Cuckoo! cuckoo! go to the fields, ye circumcised."

Pithetaerus: So powerful were the birds that the kings of Grecian cities, Agamemnon, Menelaus, for instance, carried a bird on the tip of their sceptres, who had his share of all presents.

Euelpides: That I didn't know and was much astonished when I saw Priam come upon the stage in the tragedies with a bird, which kept watching Lysicrates to see if he got any present.

Pithetaerus: But the strongest proof of all is that Zeus, who now reigns, is represented as standing with an eagle on his head as a symbol of his royalty; his daughter has an owl, and Phoebus, as his servant, has a hawk.

Euelpides: By Demeter, the point is well taken. But what are all these birds doing in heaven?

Pithetaerus: When anyone sacrifices and, according

to the rite, offers the entrails to the gods, these birds take their share before Zeus. Formerly men always swore by the birds and never by the gods.

EUELPIDES: And even now Lampon swears by the goose whenever he wishes to deceive someone.

PITHETAERUS: Thus it is clear that you were once great and sacred, but now you are looked upon as slaves, as fools, as Maneses; stones are thrown at you as at raving madmen, even in holy places. A crowd of bird-catchers sets snares, traps, limed twigs and nets of all sorts for you; you are caught, you are sold in heaps and the buyers finger you over to be certain you are fat. Again, if they would but serve you up simply roasted; but they rasp cheese into a mixture of oil, vinegar and laserwort, to which another sweet and greasy sauce is added, and the whole is poured scalding hot over your back, for all the world as if you were diseased meat.

CHORUS, *singing:* Man, your words have made my heart bleed; I have groaned over the treachery of our fathers, who knew not how to transmit to us the high rank they held from their forefathers. But 'tis a benevolent Genius, a happy Fate, that sends you to us; you shall be our deliverer and I place the destiny of my little ones and my own in your hands with every confidence.

LEADER OF THE CHORUS: But hasten to tell me what must be done; we should not be worthy to live, if we did not seek to regain our royalty by every possible means.

PITHETAERUS: First I advise that the birds gather together in one city and that they build a wall of great bricks, like that at Babylon, round the plains of the air and the whole region of space that divides earth from heaven.

EPOPS: Oh, Cebriones! oh, Porphyrion! what a terribly strong place!

PITHETAERUS: Then, when this has been well done and completed, you demand back the empire from Zeus; if he will not agree, if he refuses and does not at once confess himself beaten, you declare a sacred war against him and forbid the gods henceforward to pass through your country with their tools up, as hitherto, for the purpose of laying their Alcmenas, their Alopés, or their Semelés! if they try to pass through, you put rings on their tools so that they can't make love any longer. You send another messenger to mankind, who will proclaim to them that the birds are kings, that for the future they must first of all sacrifice to them, and only afterwards to the gods; that it is fitting to appoint to each deity the bird that has most in common with it. For instance, are they sacrificing to Aphrodité, let them at the same time offer barley to the coot; are they immolating a sheep to Posidon, let them consecrate wheat in honour of the duck; if a steer is being offered to Heracles, let honey-cakes be dedicated to the gull; if a goat is being slain for King Zeus, there is a King-Bird, the wren, to whom the sacrifice of a male gnat is due before Zeus himself even.

EUELPIDES: This notion of an immolated gnat delights me! And now let the great Zeus thunder!

LEADER OF THE CHORUS: But how will mankind recognize us as gods and not as jays? Us, who have wings and fly?

PITHETAERUS: You talk rubbish! Hermes is a god and has wings and flies, and so do many other gods. First of all, Victory flies with golden wings, Eros is undoubtedly winged too, and Iris is compared by Homer to a timorous dove.

EUELPIDES: But will not Zeus thunder and send his wingéd bolts against us?

LEADER OF THE CHORUS: If men in their blindness **do** not recognize us as gods and so continue to worship **the** dwellers in Olympus?

PITHETAERUS: Then a cloud of sparrows greedy for corn must descend upon their fields and eat up all their seeds; we shall see them if Demeter will mete them out any wheat.

EUELPIDES: By Zeus, she'll take good care she does not, and you will see her inventing a thousand excuses.

PITHETAERUS: The crows too will prove your divinity to them by pecking out the eyes of their flocks and of their draught-oxen; and then let Apollo cure them, since he is a physician and is paid for the purpose.

EUELPIDES: Oh! don't do that! Wait first until I have sold my two young bullocks.

PITHETAERUS: If on the other hand they recognize that you are God, the principle of life, that you are Earth, Saturn, Posidon, they shall be loaded with benefits.

LEADER OF THE CHORUS: Name me one of these then.

PITHETAERUS: Firstly, the locusts shall not eat up their vine-blossoms; a legion of owls and kestrels will devour them. Moreover, the gnats and the gallbugs shall no longer ravage the figs; a flock of thrushes shall swallow the whole host down to the very last.

LEADER OF THE CHORUS: And how shall we give wealth to mankind? This is their strongest passion.

PITHETAERUS: When they consult the omens, you will point them to the richest mines, you will reveal the paying ventures to the diviner, and not another shipwreck will happen or sailor perish.

LEADER OF THE CHORUS: No more shall perish? How is that?

PITHETAERUS: When the auguries are examined before starting on a voyage, some bird will not fail to say,

"Don't start! there will be a storm," or else, "Go! you will make a most profitable venture."

EUELPIDES: I shall buy a trading-vessel and go to sea. I will not stay with you.

PITHETAERUS: You will discover treasures to them, which were buried in former times, for you know them. Do not all men say, "None knows where my treasure lies, unless perchance it be some bird."

EUELPIDES: I shall sell my boat and buy a spade to unearth the vessels.

LEADER OF THE CHORUS: And how are we to give them health, which belongs to the gods?

PITHETAERUS: If they are happy, is not that the chief thing towards health? The miserable man is never well.

LEADER OF THE CHORUS: Old Age also dwells in Olympus. How will they get at it? Must they die in early youth?

PITHETAERUS: Why, the birds, by Zeus, will add three hundred years to their life.

LEADER OF THE CHORUS: From whom will they take them?

PITHETAERUS: From whom? Why, from themselves. Don't you know the cawing crow lives five times as long as a man?

EUELPIDES: Ah! ah! these are far better kings for us than Zeus!

PITHETAERUS, *solemnly:* Far better, are they not? And firstly, we shall not have to build them temples of hewn stone, closed with gates of gold; they will dwell amongst the bushes and in the thickets of green oak; the most venerated of birds will have no other temple than the foliage of the olive tree; we shall not go to Delphi or to Ammon to sacrifice; but standing erect in the midst of arbutus and wild olives and holding forth our hands filled with wheat and barley, we shall pray them to admit us to a share of the blessings they enjoy and shall at once obtain them for a few grains of wheat.

LEADER OF THE CHORUS: Old man, whom I detested, you are now to me the dearest of all; never shall I, if I can help it, fail to follow your advice.

CHORUS, *singing:* Inspirited by your words, I threaten my rivals the gods, and I swear that if you march in alliance with me against the gods and are faithful to our just, loyal and sacred bond, we shall soon have shattered their sceptre.

LEADER OF THE CHORUS: We shall charge ourselves with the performance of everything that requires force; that which demands thought and deliberation shall be yours to supply.

EPOPS: By Zeus! it's no longer the time to delay and loiter like Nicias; let us act as promptly as possible. . . . In the first place, come, enter my nest built of brushwood and blades of straw, and tell me your names.

PITHETAERUS: That is soon done; my name is Pithetaerus, and his, Euelpides, of the deme Crioa.

EPOPS: Good! and good luck to you.

PITHETAERUS: We accept the omen.

EPOPS: Come in here.

PITHETAERUS: Very well, you are the one who must lead us and introduce us.

EPOPS: Come then. *He starts to fly away.*

PITHETAERUS, *stopping himself:* Oh! my god! do come back here. Hi! tell us how we are to follow you. You can fly, but we cannot.

EPOPS: Well, well.

PITHETAERUS: Remember Aesop's fables. It is told there that the fox fared very badly, because he had made an alliance with the eagle.

EPOPS: Be at ease. You shall eat a certain root and wings will grow on your shoulders.

PITHETAERUS: Then let us enter. Xanthias and Manodorus, pick up our baggage.

LEADER OF THE CHORUS: Hi! Epops! do you hear me?

EPOPS: What's the matter?

LEADER OF THE CHORUS: Take them off to dine well and call your mate, the melodious Procné, whose songs are worthy of the Muses; she will delight our leisure moments.

PITHETAERUS: Oh! I conjure you, accede to their wish; for this delightful bird will leave her rushes at the sound of your voice; for the sake of the gods, let her come here, so that we may contemplate the nightingale.

EPOPS: Let it be as you desire. Come forth, Procné, show yourself to these strangers. PROCNÉ *appears; she resembles a young flute-girl.*

PITHETAERUS: Oh! great Zeus! what a beautiful little bird! what a dainty form! what brilliant plumage! Do you know how dearly I should like to get between her thighs?

EUELPIDES: She is dazzling all over with gold, like a young girl. Oh! how I should like to kiss her!

PITHETAERUS: Why, wretched man, she has two little sharp points on her beak!

EUELPIDES: I would treat her like an egg, the shell of which we remove before eating it; I would take off her mask and then kiss her pretty face.

EPOPS: Let us go in.

PITHETAERUS: Lead the way, and may success attend us. EPOPS *goes into the thicket, followed by* PITHETAERUS *and* EUELPIDES.

CHORUS, *singing:* Lovable golden bird, whom I cherish above all others, you, whom I associate with all my songs, nightingale, you have come, you have come, to show yourself to me and to charm me with your notes. Come, you, who play spring melodies upon the harmonious flute, lead off our anapests. *The* CHORUS *turns and faces the audience.*

LEADER OF THE CHORUS: Weak mortals, chained to the earth, creatures of clay as frail as the foliage of the woods, you unfortunate race, whose life is but darkness, as unreal as a shadow, the illusion of a dream, hearken to us, who are immortal beings, ethereal, ever young and occupied with eternal thoughts, for we shall teach you about all celestial matters; you shall know thoroughly what is the nature of the birds, what the origin of the gods, of the rivers, of Erebus, and Chaos; thanks to us, even Prodicus will envy you your knowledge.

At the beginning there was only Chaos, Night, dark Erebus, and deep Tartarus. Earth, the air and heaven had no existence. Firstly, black-winged Night laid a germless egg in the bosom of the infinite deeps of Erebus, and from this, after the revolution of long ages, sprang the graceful Eros with his glittering golden wings, swift as the whirlwinds of the tempest. He mated in deep Tartarus with dark Chaos, winged like himself, and thus hatched forth our race, which was the first to see the light. That of the Immortals did not exist until Eros had brought together all the ingredients of the world, and from their marriage Heaven, Ocean, Earth and the imperishable race of blessed gods sprang into being. Thus our origin is very much older than that of the dwellers in Olympus. We are the offspring of Eros; there are a thousand proofs to show it. We have wings and we lend assistance to lovers. How many handsome youths, who had sworn to remain insensible, have opened their thighs because of our power and have yielded themselves to their lovers when almost at the end of their youth, being led away by the gift of a quail, a waterfowl, a goose, or a cock.

And what important services do not the birds render to mortals! First of all, they mark the seasons for them, springtime, winter, and autumn. Does the screaming crane migrate to Libya—it warns the husbandman to sow, the pilot to take his ease beside his tiller hung up in his dwelling, and Orestes to weave a tunic, so that the rigorous cold may not drive him any more to strip other folk. When the kite reappears, he tells of the return of spring and of the period when the fleece of the sheep must be clipped. Is the swallow in sight? All hasten to sell their warm tunic and to buy some light clothing. We are your Ammon, Delphi, Dodona, your Phoebus Apollo. Before undertaking anything, whether a business transaction, a marriage, or the purchase of food, you consult the birds by reading the omens, and you give this name of omen to all signs that tell of the future. With you a word is an omen, you call a sneeze an omen, a meeting an omen, an unknown sound an omen, a slave or an ass an omen. Is it not clear that we are a prophetic Apollo to you? *More and more rapidly from here on.* If you recognize us as gods, we shall be your divining Muses, through us you will know the winds and the seasons, summer, winter, and the temperate months. We shall not withdraw ourselves to the highest clouds like Zeus, but shall be among you and shall give to you and to your children and the children of your children, health and wealth, long life, peace, youth, laughter, songs and feasts; in short, you will all be so well off, that you will be weary and cloyed with enjoyment.

FIRST SEMI-CHORUS, *singing:* Oh, rustic Muse of such varied note, *tiotiotiotiotiotinx,* I sing with you in the groves and on the mountain tops, *tiotiotiotinx.* I poured forth sacred strains from my golden throat in honour of the god Pan, *tiotiotiotinx,* from the top of the thickly leaved ash, and my voice mingles with the mighty choirs who extol Cybelé on the mountain tops, *totototototototototinx.* 'Tis to our concerts that Phrynichus comes to pillage like a bee the ambrosia of his songs, the sweetness of which so charms the ear, *tiotiotiotinx.*

LEADER OF FIRST SEMI-CHORUS: If there is one of you spectators who wishes to spend the rest of his life quietly among the birds, let him come to us. All that is disgraceful and forbidden by law on earth is on the contrary honourable among us, the birds. For instance, among you it's a crime to beat your father, but with us it's an estimable deed; it's considered fine to run straight at your father and hit him, saying, "Come, lift your spur if you want to fight." The runaway slave, whom you brand, is only a spotted francolin with us. Are you Phrygian like Spintharus? Among us you would be the Phrygian bird, the goldfinch, of the race of Philemon. Are you a slave and a Carian like Execestides? Among us you can create yourself forefathers; you can always find relations. Does the son of Pisias want to betray the gates of the city to the foe? Let him become a partridge, the fitting offspring of his father; among us there is no shame in escaping as cleverly as a partridge.

SECOND SEMI-CHORUS, *singing:* So the swans on the banks of the Hebrus, *tiotiotiotiotiotinx,* mingle their voices to serenade Apollo, *tiotiotiotinx,* flapping their wings the while, *tiotiotiotinx;* their notes reach beyond the clouds of heaven; they startle the various tribes of the beasts; a windless sky calms the waves, *totototototototototinx;* all Olympus resounds, and astonishment seizes its rulers; the Olympian graces and Muses cry aloud the strain, *tiotiotiotinx.*

LEADER OF SECOND SEMI-CHORUS: There is nothing more useful nor more pleasant than to have wings. To begin with, just let us suppose a spectator to be dying with hunger and to be weary of the choruses of the tragic poets; if he were winged, he would fly off, go home to dine and come back with his stomach filled. Some Patroclides, needing to take a crap, would not have to spill it out on his cloak, but could fly off, satisfy his requirements, let a few farts and, having recovered his breath, return. If one of you, it matters not who, had adulterous relations and saw the husband of his mistress in the seats of the senators, he might stretch his wings, fly to her, and, having laid her, resume his place. Is it not the most priceless gift of all, to be winged? Look at Diitrephes! His wings were only wicker-work ones, and yet he got himself chosen Phylarch and then Hipparch; from being nobody, he has risen to be famous; he's now the finest gilded cock of his tribe. PITHETAERUS *and* EUELPIDES *return; they now have wings.*

PITHETAERUS: Halloa! What's this? By Zeus! I never saw anything so funny in all my life.

EUELPIDES: What makes you laugh?

PITHETAERUS: Your little wings. D'you know what you look like? Like a goose painted by some dauber.

EUELPIDES: And you look like a close-shaven blackbird.

PITHETAERUS: We ourselves asked for this transformation, and, as Aeschylus has it, "These are no borrowed feathers, but truly our own."

EPOPS: Come now, what must be done?

PITHETAERUS: First give our city a great and famous name, then sacrifice to the gods.

EUELPIDES: I think so too.

LEADER OF THE CHORUS: Let's see. What shall our city be called?

PITHETAERUS: Will you have a high-sounding Laconian name? Shall we call it Sparta?

EUELPIDES: What! call my town Sparta? Why, I would not use *esparto* for my bed, even though I had nothing but bands of rushes.

PITHETAERUS: Well then, what name can you suggest?

EUELPIDES: Some name borrowed from the clouds, from these lofty regions in which we dwell—in short, some well-known name.

PITHETAERUS: Do you like Nephelococcygia?

LEADER OF THE CHORUS: Oh! capital! truly that's a brilliant thought!

EUELPIDES: Is it in Nephelococcygia that all the wealth of Theogenes and most of Aeschines' is?

PITHETAERUS: No, it's rather the plain of Phlegra, where the gods withered the pride of the sons of the Earth with their shafts.

LEADER OF THE CHORUS: Oh! what a splendid city! But what god shall be its patron? for whom shall we weave the peplus?

EUELPIDES: Why not choose Athené Polias?

PITHETAERUS: Oh! what a well-ordered town it would be to have a female deity armed from head to foot, while Clisthenes was spinning!

LEADER OF THE CHORUS: Who then shall guard the Pelargicon?

PITHETAERUS: A bird.

LEADER OF THE CHORUS: One of us? What kind of bird?

PITHETAERUS: A bird of Persian strain, who is everywhere proclaimed to be the bravest of all, a true chick of Ares.

EUELPIDES: Oh! noble chick!

PITHETAERUS: Because he is a god well suited to live on the rocks. Come! into the air with you to help the workers who are building the wall; carry up rubble, strip

yourself to mix the mortar, take up the hod, tumble down
the ladder, if you like, post sentinels, keep the fire smoul-
dering beneath the ashes, go round the walls, bell in
hand, and go to sleep up there yourself; then despatch
two heralds, one to the gods above, the other to mankind on earth and come back here.

EUELPIDES: As for yourself, remain here, and may the
plague take you for a troublesome fellow! *He departs.*

PITHETAERUS: Go, friend, go where I send you, for
without you my orders cannot be obeyed. For myself, I
want to sacrifice to the new god, and I am going to summon the priest who must preside at the ceremony.
Slaves! slaves! bring forward the basket and the lustral
water.

CHORUS, *singing:* I do as you do, and I wish as you
wish and I implore you to address powerful and solemn
prayers to the gods, and in addition to immolate a sheep
as a token of our gratitude. Let us sing the Pythian chant
in honour of the god, and let Chaeris accompany our
voices.

PITHETAERUS, *to the flute-player:* Enough! but, by
Heracles! what is this? Great gods! I have seen many
prodigious things, but I never saw a muzzled raven. *The*
PRIEST *arrives.* Priest! it's high time! Sacrifice to the new
gods.

PRIEST: I begin, but where is the man with the basket? Pray to the Hestia of the birds, to the kite, who presides over the hearth, and to all the god and goddess-
birds who dwell in Olympus . . .

PITHETAERUS: Oh! Hawk, the sacred guardian of
Sunium, oh, god of the storks!

PRIEST: . . . to the swan of Delos, to Leto the mother
of the quails, and to Artemis, the goldfinch . . .

PITHETAERUS: It's no longer Artemis Colaenis, but
Artemis the goldfinch.

PRIEST: . . . to Bacchus, the finch and Cybelé, the ostrich and mother of the gods and mankind . . .

PITHETAERUS: Oh! sovereign ostrich Cybelé, mother of Cleocritus!

PRIEST: . . . to grant health and safety to the Nephelococcygians as well as to the dwellers in Chios . . .

PITHETAERUS: The dwellers in Chios! Ah! I am delighted they should be thus mentioned on all occasions.

PRIEST: . . . to the heroes, the birds, to the sons of heroes, to the porphyrion, the pelican, the spoon-bill, the redbreast, the grouse, the peacock, the horned-owl, the teal, the bittern, the heron, the stormy petrel, the fig-pecker, the titmouse . . .

PITHETAERUS: Stop! stop! you drive me crazy with your endless list. Why, wretch, to what sacred feast are you inviting the vultures and the sea-eagles? Don't you see that a single kite could easily carry off the lot at once? Begone, you and your fillets and all; I shall know how to complete the sacrifice by myself. *The* PRIEST *departs.*

CHORUS, *singing:* It is imperative that I sing another sacred chant for the rite of the lustral water, and that I invoke the immortals, or at least one of them, provided always that you have some suitable food to offer him; from what I see here, in the shape of gifts, there is naught whatever but horn and hair.

PITHETAERUS: Let us address our sacrifices and our prayers to the winged gods. *A* POET *enters.*

POET: Oh, Muse! celebrate happy Nephelococcygia in your hymns.

PITHETAERUS: What have we here? Where did you come from, tell me? Who are you?

POET: I am he whose language is sweeter than honey, the zealous slave of the Muses, as Homer has it.

PITHETAERUS: You a slave! and yet you wear your hair long?

POET: No, but the fact is all we poets are the assiduous slaves of the Muses, according to Homer.

PITHETAERUS: In truth your little cloak is quite holy too through zeal! But, poet, what ill wind drove you here?

POET: I have composed verses in honour of your Nephelococcygia, a host of splendid dithyrambs and parthenia worthy of Simonides himself.

PITHETAERUS: And when did you compose them? How long since?

POET: Oh! 'tis long, aye, very long, that I have sung in honour of this city.

PITHETAERUS: But I am only celebrating its foundation with this sacrifice; I have only just named it, as is done with little babies.

POET: "Just as the chargers fly with the speed of the wind, so does the voice of the Muses take its flight. Oh! thou noble founder of the town of Aetna, thou, whose name recalls the holy sacrifices, make us such gift as thy generous heart shall suggest." *He puts out his hand.*

PITHETAERUS: He will drive us silly if we do not get rid of him by some present. *To the* PRIEST'S *acolyte:* Here! you, who have a fur as well as your tunic, take it off and give it to this clever poet. Come, take this fur; you look to me to be shivering with cold.

POET: My Muse will gladly accept this gift; but engrave these verses of Pindar's on your mind.

PITHETAERUS: Oh! what a pest! It's impossible then to get rid of him!

POET: "Straton wanders among the Scythian nomads, but has no linen garment. He is sad at only wearing an animal's pelt and no tunic." Do you get what I mean?

PITHETAERUS: I understand that you want me to offer you a tunic. Hi! you (*to the acolyte*), take off yours; we must help the poet. . . . Come, you, take it and get out.

POET: I am going, and these are the verses that I address to this city: "Phoebus of the golden throne, celebrate this shivery, freezing city; I have travelled through fruitful and snow-covered plains. Tralalá! Tralalá!" *He departs.*

PITHETAERUS: What are you chanting us about frosts? Thanks to the tunic, you no longer fear them. Ah! by Zeus! I could not have believed this cursed fellow could so soon have learnt the way to our city. *To a slave:* Come, take the lustral water and circle the altar. Let all keep silence! *An* ORACLE-MONGER *enters.*

ORACLE-MONGER: Let not the goat be sacrificed.

PITHETAERUS: Who are you?

ORACLE-MONGER: Who am I? An oracle-monger.

PITHETAERUS: Get out!

ORACLE-MONGER: Wretched man, insult not sacred things. For there is an oracle of Bacis, which exactly applies to Nephelococcygia.

PITHETAERUS: Why did you not reveal it to me before I founded my city?

ORACLE-MONGER: The divine spirit was against it.

PITHETAERUS: Well, I suppose there's nothing to do but hear the terms of the oracle.

ORACLE-MONGER: "But when the wolves and the white crows shall dwell together between Corinth and Sicyon . . ."

PITHETAERUS: But how do the Corinthians concern me?

ORACLE-MONGER: It is the regions of the air that Bacis indicates in this manner. "They must first sacrifice a white-fleeced goat to Pandora, and give the prophet who first reveals my words a good cloak and new sandals."

PITHETAERUS: Does it say sandals there?

ORACLE-MONGER: Look at the book. "And besides this a goblet of wine and a good share of the entrails of the victim."

PITHETAERUS: Of the entrails—does it say that?

ORACLE-MONGER: Look at the book. "If you do as I command, divine youth, you shall be an eagle among the clouds; if not, you shall be neither turtle-dove, nor eagle, nor woodpecker."

PITHETAERUS: Does it say all that?

ORACLE-MONGER: Look at the book.

PITHETAERUS: This oracle in no sort of way resembles the one Apollo dictated to me: "If an impostor comes without invitation to annoy you during the sacrifice and to demand a share of the victim, apply a stout stick to his ribs."

ORACLE-MONGER: You are drivelling.

PITHETAERUS: Look at the book. "And don't spare him, were he an eagle from out of the clouds, were it Lampon himself or the great Diopithes."

ORACLE-MONGER: Does it say that?

PITHETAERUS: Look at the book and go and hang yourself.

ORACLE-MONGER: Oh! unfortunate wretch that I am. *He departs.*

PITHETAERUS: Away with you, and take your prophecies elsewhere. *Enter* METON, *with surveying instruments.*

METON: I have come to you . . .

PITHETAERUS, *interrupting:* Yet another pest! What have you come to do? What's your plan? What's the purpose of your journey? Why these splendid buskins?

METON: I want to survey the plains of the air for you and to parcel them into lots.

PITHETAERUS: In the name of the gods, who are you?

METON: Who am I? Meton, known throughout Greece and at Colonus.

PITHETAERUS: What are these things?

METON: Tools for measuring the air. In truth, the spaces in the air have precisely the form of a furnace. With this bent ruler I draw a line from top to bottom; from one of its points I describe a circle with the compass. Do you understand?

PITHETAERUS: Not in the least.

METON: With the straight ruler I set to work to inscribe a square within this circle; in its centre will be the market-place, into which all the straight streets will lead, converging to this centre like a star, which, although only orbicular, sends forth its rays in a straight line from all sides.

PITHETAERUS: A regular Thales! Meton . . .

METON: What d'you want with me?

PITHETAERUS: I want to give you a proof of my friendship. Use your legs.

METON: Why, what have I to fear?

PITHETAERUS: It's the same here as in Sparta. Strangers are driven away, and blows rain down as thick as hail.

METON: Is there sedition in your city?

PITHETAERUS: No, certainly not.

METON: What's wrong then?

PITHETAERUS: We are agreed to sweep all quacks and impostors far from our borders.

METON: Then I'll be going.

PITHETAERUS: I'm afraid it's too late. The thunder growls already. *He beats him.*

METON: Oh, woe! oh, woe!

PITHETAERUS: I warned you. Now, be off, and do your surveying somewhere else.

METON *takes to his heels. He is no sooner gone than an* INSPECTOR *arrives.*

INSPECTOR: Where are the Proxeni?

PITHETAERUS: Who is this Sardanapalus?

INSPECTOR: I have been appointed by lot to come to Nephelococcygia as inspector.

PITHETAERUS: An inspector! and who sends you here, you rascal?

INSPECTOR: A decree of Teleas.

PITHETAERUS: Will you just pocket your salary, do nothing, and get out?

INSPECTOR: Indeed I will; I am urgently needed to be at Athens to attend the Assembly; for I am charged with the interests of Pharnaces.

PITHETAERUS: Take it then, and get on your way. This is your salary. *He beats him.*

INSPECTOR: What does this mean?

PITHETAERUS: This is the assembly where you have to defend Pharnaces.

INSPECTOR: You shall testify that they dare to strike me, the inspector.

PITHETAERUS: Are you not going to get out with your urns? It's not to be believed, they send us inspectors before we have so much as paid sacrifice to the gods.

The INSPECTOR *goes into hiding. A* DEALER IN DECREES *arrives.*

DEALER IN DECREES, *reading:* "If the Nephelococcygian does wrong to the Athenian . . ."

PITHETAERUS: What trouble now? What book is that?

DEALER IN DECREES: I am a dealer in decrees, and I have come here to sell you the new laws.

PITHETAERUS: Which?

DEALER IN DECREES: "The Nephelococcygians shall

adopt the same weights, measures and decrees as the Olophyxians."

PITHETAERUS: And you shall soon be imitating the Ototyxians. *He beats him.*

DEALER IN DECREES: Ow! what are you doing?

PITHETAERUS: Now will you get out of here with your decrees? For I am going to let *you* see some severe ones.

The DEALER IN DECREES *departs; the* INSPECTOR *comes out of hiding.*

INSPECTOR, *returning:* I summon Pithetaerus for outrage for the month of Munychion.

PITHETAERUS: Ha! my friend! are you still here?

The DEALER IN DECREES *also returns.*

DEALER IN DECREES: "Should anyone drive away the magistrates and not receive them, according to the decree duly posted . . ."

PITHETAERUS: What! rascal! you are back too? *He rushes at him.*

INSPECTOR: Woe to you! I'll have you condemned to a fine of ten thousand drachmae.

PITHETAERUS: And I'll smash your urns.

INSPECTOR: Do you recall that evening when you crapped on the column where the decrees are posted?

PITHETAERUS: Here! here! let him be seized. *The* INSPECTOR *runs off.* Why, don't you want to stay any longer? But let us get indoors as quick as possible; we will sacrifice the goat inside.

FIRST SEMI-CHORUS, *singing:* Henceforth it is to me that mortals must address their sacrifices and their prayers. Nothing escapes my sight nor my might. My glance embraces the universe, I preserve the fruit in the flower by destroying the thousand kinds of voracious insects the soil produces, which attack the trees and feed on the germ when it has scarcely formed in the calyx; I destroy those who ravage the balmy terrace gardens like a deadly plague; all these gnawing crawling creatures perish beneath the lash of my wing.

LEADER OF FIRST SEMI-CHORUS: I hear it proclaimed everywhere: "A talent for him who shall kill Diagoras of Melos, and a talent for him who destroys one of the dead tyrants." We likewise wish to make our proclamation: "A talent to him among you who shall kill Philocrates, the Struthian; four, if he brings him to us alive. For this Philocrates skewers the finches together and sells them at the rate of an obolus for seven. He tortures the thrushes by blowing them out, so that they may look bigger, sticks their own feathers into the nostrils of blackbirds, and collects pigeons, which he shuts up and forces them, fastened in a net, to decoy others." That is what we wish to proclaim. And if anyone is keeping birds shut up in his yard, let him hasten to let them loose; those who disobey shall be seized by the birds and we shall put them in chains, so that in their turn they may decoy other men.

SECOND SEMI-CHORUS, *singing:* Happy indeed is the race of winged birds who need no cloak in winter! Neither do I fear the relentless rays of the fiery dog-days; when the divine grasshopper, intoxicated with the sunlight, as noon is burning the ground, is breaking out into shrill melody; my home is beneath the foliage in the flowery meadows. I winter in deep caverns, where I frolic with the mountain nymphs, while in spring I despoil the gardens of the Graces and gather the white, virgin berry on the myrtle bushes.

LEADER OF SECOND SEMI-CHORUS: I want now to speak to the judges about the prize they are going to award; if they are favourable to us, we will load them with benefits far greater than those Paris received. Firstly, the owls of Laurium, which every judge desires above all things, shall never be wanting to you; you shall see them homing with you, building their nests in your money-bags and laying coins. Besides, you shall be housed like the gods, for we shall erect gables over your dwellings; if you hold some public post and want to do a little pilfering, we will give you the sharp claws of a hawk. Are you dining in town, we will provide you with stomachs as capacious as a bird's crop. But, if your award is against us, don't fail to have metal covers fashioned for yourselves, like those they place over statues; else, look out! for the day you wear a white tunic all the birds will soil it with their droppings.

PITHETAERUS: Birds! the sacrifice is propitious. But I see no messenger coming from the wall to tell us what is happening. Ah! here comes one running himself out of breath as though he were in the Olympic stadium.

MESSENGER, *running back and forth:* Where, where, where is he? Where, where, where is he? Where, where, where is he? Where is Pithetaerus, our leader?

PITHETAERUS: Here am I.

MESSENGER: The wall is finished.

PITHETAERUS: That's good news.

MESSENGER: It's a most beautiful, a most magnificent work of art. The wall is so broad that Proxenides, the Braggartian, and Theogenes could pass each other in their chariots, even if they were drawn by steeds as big as the Trojan horse.

PITHETAERUS: That's fine!

MESSENGER: Its length is one hundred stadia; I measured it myself.

PITHETAERUS: A decent length, by Posidon! And who built such a wall?

MESSENGER: Birds—birds only; they had neither Egyptian brickmaker, nor stonemason, nor carpenter; the birds did it all themselves; I could hardly believe my eyes. Thirty thousand cranes came from Libya with a supply of stones, intended for the foundations. The water-rails chiselled them with their beaks. Ten thousand storks were busy making bricks; plovers and other water fowl carried water into the air.

PITHETAERUS: And who carried the mortar?

MESSENGER: Herons, in hods.

PITHETAERUS: But how could they put the mortar into the hods?

MESSENGER: Oh! it was a truly clever invention; the geese used their feet like spades; they buried them in the pile of mortar and then emptied them into the hods.

PITHETAERUS: Ah! to what use cannot feet be put?

MESSENGER: You should have seen how eagerly the ducks carried bricks. To complete the tale, the swallows came flying to the work, their beaks full of mortar and their trowels on their backs, just the way little children are carried.

PITHETAERUS: Who would want paid servants after this? But tell me, who did the woodwork?

MESSENGER: Birds again, and clever carpenters too, the pelicans, for they squared up the gates with their beaks in such a fashion that one would have thought they were using axes; the noise was just like a dockyard. Now the whole wall is tight everywhere, securely bolted and well guarded; it is patrolled, bell in hand; the sentinels stand everywhere and beacons burn on the towers. But I must run off to clean myself; the rest is your business. *He departs.*

LEADER OF THE CHORUS, *to* PITHETAERUS: Well! what do you say to it? Are you not astonished at the wall being completed so quickly?

PITHETAERUS: By the gods, yes, and with good reason. It's really not to be believed. But here comes another messenger from the wall to bring us some further news! What a fighting look he has!

SECOND MESSENGER, *rushing in:* Alas! alas! alas! alas! alas! alas!

PITHETAERUS: What's the matter?

SECOND MESSENGER: A horrible outrage has occurred; a god sent by Zeus has passed through our gates and has penetrated the realms of the air without the knowledge of the jays, who are on guard in the daytime.

PITHETAERUS: It's a terrible and criminal deed. What god was it?

SECOND MESSENGER: We don't know that. All we know is, that he has got wings.

PITHETAERUS: Why were not patrolmen sent against him at once?

SECOND MESSENGER: We have despatched thirty thousand hawks of the legion of Mounted Archers. All the hook-clawed birds are moving against him, the kestrel, the buzzard, the vulture, the great-horned owl; they cleave the air so that it resounds with the flapping of their wings; they are looking everywhere for the god, who cannot be far away; indeed, if I mistake not, he is coming from yonder side.

PITHETAERUS: To arms, all, with slings and bows! This way, all our soldiers; shoot and strike! Some one give me a sling!

CHORUS, *singing:* War, a terrible war is breaking out between us and the gods! Come, let each one guard Air, the son of Erebus, in which the clouds float. Take care no immortal enters it without your knowledge.

LEADER OF THE CHORUS: Scan all sides with your glance. Hark! methinks I can hear the rustle of the swift wings of a god from heaven. *The Machine brings in* IRIS, *in the form of a young girl.*

PITHETAERUS: Hi! you woman! where, where, where are you flying to? Halt, don't stir! keep motionless! not a beat of your wing! *She pauses in her flight.* Who are you and from what country? You must say whence you come.

IRIS: I come from the abode of the Olympian gods.

PITHETAERUS: What's your name, ship or head-dress?

IRIS: I am swift Iris.

PITHETAERUS: Paralus or Salaminia?

IRIS: What do you mean?

PITHETAERUS: Let a buzzard rush at her and seize her.

IRIS: Seize me? But what do all these insults mean?

PITHETAERUS: Woe to you!

IRIS: I do not understand it.

PITHETAERUS: By which gate did you pass through the wall, wretched woman?

IRIS: By which *gate*? Why, great gods, I don't know.

PITHETAERUS: You hear how she holds us in derision. Did you present yourself to the officers in command of the jays? You don't answer. Have you a permit, bearing the seal of the storks?

IRIS: Am I dreaming?

PITHETAERUS: Did you get one?

IRIS: Are you mad?

PITHETAERUS: No head-bird gave you a safe-conduct?

IRIS: A safe-conduct to *me*. You poor fool!

PITHETAERUS: Ah! and so you slipped into this city on the sly and into these realms of air-land that don't belong to you.

IRIS: And what other roads can the gods travel?

PITHETAERUS: By Zeus! I know nothing about that, not I. But they won't pass this way. And you still dare to complain? Why, if you were treated according to your deserts, no Iris would ever have more justly suffered death.

IRIS: I am immortal.

PITHETAERUS: You would have died nevertheless.—
Oh! that would be truly intolerable! What! should the
universe obey us and the gods alone continue their insolence and not understand that they must submit to
the law of the strongest in their due turn? But tell me,
where are you flying to?

IRIS: I? The messenger of Zeus to mankind, I am going to tell them to sacrifice sheep and oxen on the altars
and to fill their streets with the rich smoke of burning
fat.

PITHETAERUS: Of which gods are you speaking?

IRIS: Of which? Why, of ourselves, the gods of heaven.

PITHETAERUS: You, gods?

IRIS: Are there others then?

PITHETAERUS: Men now adore the birds as gods, and
it's to them, by Zeus, that they must offer sacrifices, and
not to Zeus at all!

IRIS, *in tragic style:* Oh! fool! fool! Rouse not the
wrath of the gods, for it is terrible indeed. Armed with
the brand of Zeus, Justice would annihilate your race;
the lightning would strike you as it did Licymnius and
consume both your body and the porticos of your palace.

PITHETAERUS: Here! that's enough tall talk. Just you
listen and keep quiet! Do you take me for a Lydian or
a Phrygian and think to frighten me with your big
words? Know, that if Zeus worries me again, I shall go
at the head of my eagles, who are armed with lightning,
and reduce his dwelling and that of Amphion to cinders.
I shall send more than six hundred porphyrions clothed
in leopards' skins up to heaven against him; and formerly a single Porphyrion gave him enough to do. As
for you, his messenger, if you annoy me, I shall begin
by getting between your thighs, and even though you
are Iris, you will be surprised at the erection the old

man can produce; it's three times as good as the ram
on a ship's prow!

IRIS: May you perish, you wretch, you and your infamous words!

PITHETAERUS: Won't you get out of here quickly?
Come, stretch your wings or look out for squalls!

IRIS: If my father does not punish you for your insults
. . . *The Machine takes* IRIS *away.*

PITHETAERUS: Ha! . . . but just you be off elsewhere
to roast younger folk than us with your lightning.

CHORUS, *singing:* We forbid the gods, the sons of
Zeus, to pass through our city and the mortals to send
them the smoke of their sacrifices by this road.

PITHETAERUS: It's odd that the messenger we sent to
the mortals has never returned. *The* HERALD *enters,
wearing a golden garland on his head.*

HERALD: Oh! blessed Pithetaerus, very wise, very illustrious, very gracious, thrice happy, very . . . Come,
prompt me, somebody, do—

PITHETAERUS: Get to your story!

HERALD: All peoples are filled with admiration for
your wisdom, and they award you this golden crown.

PITHETAERUS: I accept it. But tell me, why do the
people admire me?

HERALD: Oh you, who have founded so illustrious a
city in the air, you know not in what esteem men hold
you and how many there are who burn with desire to
dwell in it. Before your city was built, all men had a
mania for Sparta; long hair and fasting were held in
honour, men went dirty like Socrates and carried staves.
Now all is changed. Firstly, as soon as it's dawn, they all
spring out of bed together to go and seek their food, the
same as you do; then they fly off towards the notices
and finally devour the decrees. The bird-madness is so
clear that many actually bear the names of birds. There

is a halting victualler, who styles himself the partridge; Menippus calls himself the swallow; Opuntius the one-eyed crow; Philocles the lark; Theogenes the fox-goose; Lycurgus the ibis; Chaerephon the bat; Syracosius the magpie; Midias the quail; indeed he looks like a quail that has been hit hard on the head. Out of love for the birds they repeat all the songs which concern the swallow, the teal, the goose or the pigeon; in each verse you see wings, or at all events a few feathers. This is what is happening down there. Finally, there are more than ten thousand folk who are coming here from earth to ask you for feathers and hooked claws; so, mind you supply yourself with wings for the immigrants.

PITHETAERUS: Ah! by Zeus, there's no time for idling. *To some slaves:* Go as quick as possible and fill every hamper, every basket you can find with wings. Manes will bring them to me outside the walls, where I will welcome those who present themselves.

CHORUS, *singing:* This town will soon be inhabited by a crowd of men. Fortune favours us alone and thus they have fallen in love with our city.

PITHETAERUS, *to the slave* MANES, *who brings in a basket full of wings:* Come, hurry up and bring them along.

CHORUS, *singing:* Will not man find here everything that can please him—wisdom, love, the divine Graces, the sweet face of gentle peace?

PITHETAERUS, *as* MANES *comes in with another basket:* Oh! you lazy servant! won't you hurry yourself?

CHORUS, *singing:* Let a basket of wings be brought speedily. Come, beat him as I do, and put some life into him; he is as lazy as an ass.

PITHETAERUS: Aye, Manes is a great craven.

CHORUS, *singing:* Begin by putting this heap of wings in order; divide them in three parts according to the birds from whom they came; the singing, the prophetic and the aquatic birds; then you must take care to distribute them to the men according to their character.

PITHETAERUS, *to* MANES, *who is bringing in another basket:* Oh! by the kestrels! I can keep my hands off you no longer; you are too slow and lazy altogether. *He hits* MANES, *who runs away. A young* PARRICIDE *enters.*

PARRICIDE, *singing:* Oh! might I but become an eagle, who soars in the skies! Oh! might I fly above the azure waves of the barren sea!

PITHETAERUS: Ha! it would seem the news was true; I hear someone coming who talks of wings.

PARRICIDE: Nothing is more charming than to fly; I am bird-mad and fly towards you, for I want to live with you and to obey your laws.

PITHETAERUS: Which laws? The birds have many laws.

PARRICIDE: All of them; but the one that pleases me most is that among the birds it is considered a fine thing to peck and strangle one's father.

PITHETAERUS: Yes, by Zeus! according to us, he who dares to strike his father, while still a chick, is a brave fellow.

PARRICIDE: And therefore I want to dwell here, for I want to strangle my father and inherit his wealth.

PITHETAERUS: But we have also an ancient law written in the code of the storks, which runs thus, "When the stork father has reared his young and has taught them to fly, the young must in their turn support the father."

PARRICIDE, *petulantly:* It's hardly worth while coming all this distance to be compelled to keep my father!

PITHETAERUS: No, no, young friend, since you have come to us with such willingness, I am going to give you these black wings, as though you were an orphan bird;

furthermore, some good advice, that I received myself in infancy. Don't strike your father, but take these wings in one hand and these spurs in the other; imagine you have a cock's crest on your head and go and mount guard and fight; live on your pay and respect your father's life. You're a gallant fellow! Very well, then! Fly to Thrace and fight.

PARRICIDE: By Bacchus! You're right; I will follow your counsel.

PITHETAERUS: It's acting wisely, by Zeus. *The* PARRICIDE *departs, and the dithyrambic poet* CINESIAS *arrives.*

CINESIAS, *singing:* "On my light pinions I soar off to Olympus; in its capricious flight my Muse flutters along the thousand paths of poetry in turn . . ."

PITHETAERUS: This is a fellow will need a whole shipload of wings.

CINESIAS, *singing:* ". . . and being fearless and vigorous, it is seeking fresh outlet."

PITHETAERUS: Welcome, Cinesias, you lime-wood man! Why have you come here twisting your game leg in circles?

CINESIAS, *singing:* "I want to become a bird, a tuneful nightingale."

PITHETAERUS: Enough of that sort of ditty. Tell me what you want.

CINESIAS: Give me wings and I will fly into the topmost airs to gather fresh songs in the clouds, in the midst of the vapours and the fleecy snow.

PITHETAERUS: Gather songs in the clouds?

CINESIAS: 'Tis on them the whole of our latter-day art depends. The most brilliant dithyrambs are those that flap their wings in empty space and are clothed in mist and dense obscurity. To appreciate this, just listen.

PITHETAERUS: Oh! no, no, no!

CINESIAS: By Hermes! but indeed you shall. *He*

sings. "I shall travel through thine ethereal empire like a winged bird, who cleaveth space with his long neck . . ."

PITHETAERUS: Stop! Way enough!

CINESIAS: ". . . as I soar over the seas, carried by the breath of the winds . . ."

PITHETAERUS: By Zeus! I'll cut your breath short. *He picks up a pair of wings and begins trying to stop* CINESIAS' *mouth with them.*

CINESIAS, *running away:* ". . . now rushing along the tracks of Notus, now nearing Boreas across the infinite wastes of the ether." Ah! old man, that's a pretty and clever idea truly!

PITHETAERUS: What! are you not delighted to be cleaving the air?

CINESIAS: To treat a dithyrambic poet, for whom the tribes dispute with each other, in this style!

PITHETAERUS: Will you stay with us and form a chorus of winged birds as slender as Leotrophides for the Cecropid tribe?

CINESIAS: You are making game of me, that's clear; but know that I shall never leave you in peace if I do not have wings wherewith to traverse the air. CINESIAS *departs and an* INFORMER *arrives.*

INFORMER: What are these birds with downy feathers, who look so pitiable to me? Tell me, oh swallow with the long dappled wings.

PITHETAERUS: Oh! it's a regular invasion that threatens us. Here comes another one, humming along.

INFORMER: Swallow with the long dappled wings, once more I summon you.

PITHETAERUS: It's his cloak I believe he's addressing; it stands in great need of the swallows' return.

INFORMER: Where is he who gives out wings to all comers?

PITHETAERUS: Here I am, but you must tell me for what purpose you want them.

INFORMER: Ask no questions. I want wings, and wings I must have.

PITHETAERUS: Do you want to fly straight to Pellené?

INFORMER: I? Why, I am an accuser of the islands, an informer . . .

PITHETAERUS: A fine trade, truly!

INFORMER: . . . a hatcher of lawsuits. Hence I have great need of wings to prowl round the cities and drag them before justice.

PITHETAERUS: Would you do this better if you had wings?

INFORMER: No, but I should no longer fear the pirates; I should return with the cranes, loaded with a supply of lawsuits by way of ballast.

PITHETAERUS: So it seems, despite all your youthful vigour, you make it your trade to denounce strangers?

INFORMER: Well, and why not? I don't know how to dig.

PITHETAERUS: But, by Zeus! there are honest ways of gaining a living at your age without all this infamous trickery.

INFORMER: My friend, I am asking you for wings, not for words.

PITHETAERUS: It's just my words that gives you wings.

INFORMER: And how can you give a man wings with your words?

PITHETAERUS: They all start this way.

INFORMER: How?

PITHETAERUS: Have you not often heard the father say to young men in the barbers' shops, "It's astonishing how Diitrephes' advice has made my son fly to horse-riding."—"Mine," says another, "has flown towards tragic poetry on the wings of his imagination."

INFORMER: So that words give wings?

PITHETAERUS: Undoubtedly; words give wings to the mind and make a man soar to heaven. Thus I hope that my wise words will give you wings to fly to some less degrading trade.

INFORMER: But I do not want to.

PITHETAERUS: What do you reckon on doing then?

INFORMER: I won't belie my breeding; from generation to generation we have lived by informing. Quick, therefore, give me quickly some light, swift hawk or kestrel wings, so that I may summon the islanders, sustain the accusation here, and haste back there again on flying pinions.

PITHETAERUS: I see. In this way the stranger will be condemned even before he appears.

INFORMER: That's just it.

PITHETAERUS: And while he is on his way here by sea, you will be flying to the islands to despoil him of his property.

INFORMER: You've hit it, precisely; I must whirl hither and thither like a perfect humming-top.

PITHETAERUS: I catch the idea. Wait, I've got some fine Corcyraean wings. How do you like them?

INFORMER: Oh! woe is me! Why, it's a whip!

PITHETAERUS: No, no; these are the wings, I tell you, that make the top spin.

INFORMER, *as* PITHETAERUS *lashes him:* Oh! oh! oh!

PITHETAERUS: Take your flight, clear off, you miserable cur, or you will soon see what comes of quibbling and lying. *The* INFORMER *flees. To his slaves:* Come, let us gather up our wings and withdraw. *The baskets are taken away.*

CHORUS, *singing:* In my ethereal flights I have seen many things new and strange and wondrous beyond belief. There is a tree called Cleonymus belonging to an unknown species; it has no heart, is good for nothing and is as tall as it is cowardly. In springtime it shoots forth calumnies instead of buds and in autumn it strews the ground with bucklers in place of leaves.

Far away in the regions of darkness, where no ray of light ever enters, there is a country, where men sit at the table of the heroes and dwell with them always—except in the evening. Should any mortal meet the hero Orestes at night, he would soon be stripped and covered with blows from head to foot. PROMETHEUS *enters, masked to conceal his identity.*

PROMETHEUS: Ah! by the gods! if only Zeus does not espy me! Where is Pithetaerus?

PITHETAERUS: Ha! what is this? A masked man!

PROMETHEUS: Can you see any god behind me?

PITHETAERUS: No, none. But who are you, pray?

PROMETHEUS: What's the time, please?

PITHETAERUS: The time? Why, it's past noon. Who are you?

PROMETHEUS: Is it the fall of day? Is it no later than that?

PITHETAERUS: This is getting dull!

PROMETHEUS: What is Zeus doing? Is he dispersing the clouds or gathering them?

PITHETAERUS: Watch out for yourself!

PROMETHEUS: Come, I will raise my mask.

PITHETAERUS: Ah! my dear Prometheus!

PROMETHEUS: Sh! Sh! speak lower!

PITHETAERUS: Why, what's the matter, Prometheus?

PROMETHEUS: Sh! sh! Don't call me by my name; you will be my ruin, if Zeus should see me here. But, if you want me to tell you how things are going in heaven, take this umbrella and shield me, so that the gods don't see me.

PITHETAERUS: I can recognize Prometheus in this cunning trick. Come, quick then, and fear nothing; speak on.

PROMETHEUS: Then listen.

PITHETAERUS: I am listening, proceed!

PROMETHEUS: Zeus is done for.

PITHETAERUS: Ah! and since when, pray?

PROMETHEUS: Since you founded this city in the air. There is not a man who now sacrifices to the gods; the smoke of the victims no longer reaches us. Not the smallest offering comes! We fast as though it were the festival of Demeter. The barbarian gods, who are dying of hunger, are bawling like Illyrians and threaten to make an armed descent upon Zeus, if he does not open markets where joints of the victims are sold.

PITHETAERUS: What! there are other gods besides you, barbarian gods who dwell above Olympus?

PROMETHEUS: If there were no barbarian gods, who would be the patron of Execestides?

PITHETAERUS: And what is the name of these gods?

PROMETHEUS: Their name? Why, the Triballi.

PITHETAERUS: Ah, indeed! 'tis from that no doubt that we derive the word "tribulation."

PROMETHEUS: Most likely. But one thing I can tell you for certain, namely, that Zeus and the celestial Triballi are going to send deputies here to sue for peace. Now don't you treat with them, unless Zeus restores the sceptre to the birds and gives you Basileia in marriage.

PITHETAERUS: Who is this Basileia?

PROMETHEUS: A very fine young damsel, who makes the lightning for Zeus; all things come from her, wisdom, good laws, virtue, the fleet, calumnies, the public pay-master and the triobolus.

PITHETAERUS: Ah! then she is a sort of general man-ageress to the god.

PROMETHEUS: Yes, precisely. If he gives you her for your wife, yours will be the almighty power. That is

what I have come to tell you; for you know my constant
and habitual goodwill towards men.

PITHETAERUS: Oh, yes! it's thanks to you that we roast
our meat.

PROMETHEUS: I hate the gods, as you know.

PITHETAERUS: Aye, by Zeus, you have always detested
them.

PROMETHEUS: Towards them I am a veritable Timon;
but I must return in all haste, so give me the umbrella;
if Zeus should see me from up there, he would think I
was escorting one of the Canephori.

PITHETAERUS: Wait, take this stool as well. PROME-
THEUS *leaves.* PITHETAERUS *goes into the thicket.*

CHORUS, *singing:* Near by the land of the Sciapodes
there is a marsh, from the borders whereof the unwashed
Socrates evokes the souls of men. Pisander came one
day to see his soul, which he had left there when still
alive. He offered a little victim, a camel, slit his throat
and, following the example of Odysseus, stepped one
pace backwards. Then that bat of a Chaerephon came
up from hell to drink the camel's blood. POSIDON *enters,*
accompanied by HERACLES *and* TRIBALLUS.

POSIDON: This is the city of Nephelococcygia, to which
we come as ambassadors. *To* TRIBALLUS. Hi! what are
you up to? you are throwing your cloak over the left
shoulder. Come, fling it quick over the right! And why,
pray, does it draggle in this fashion? Have you ulcers to
hide like Laespodias? Oh! democracy! whither, oh!
whither are you leading us? Is it possible that the gods
have chosen such an envoy? You are undisturbed? Ugh!
you cursed savage! you are by far the most barbarous of
all the gods.—Tell me, Heracles, what are we going to
do?

HERACLES: I have already told you that I want to
strangle the fellow who dared to wall us out.

POSIDON: But, my friend, we are envoys of peace.

HERACLES: All the more reason why I wish to strangle him.

PITHETAERUS *comes out of the thicket, followed by slaves, who are carrying various kitchen utensils; one of them sets up a table on which he places poultry dressed for roasting.*

PITHETAERUS: Hand me the cheese-grater; bring me the silphium for sauce; pass me the cheese and watch the coals.

HERACLES: Mortal! we who greet you are three gods.

PITHETAERUS: Wait a bit till I have prepared my silphium pickle.

HERACLES: What are these meats?

PITHETAERUS: These are birds that have been punished with death for attacking the people's friends.

HERACLES: And you are going to season them before answering us?

PITHETAERUS, *looking up from his work for the first time:* Ah! Heracles! welcome, welcome! What's the matter?

POSIDON: The gods have sent us here as ambassadors to treat for peace.

PITHETAERUS, *ignoring this:* There's no more oil in the flask.

HERACLES: And yet the birds must be thoroughly basted with it.

POSIDON: We have no interest to serve in fighting you; as for you, be friends and we promise that you shall always have rain-water in your pools and the warmest of warm weather. So far as these points go we are plenipotentiaries.

PITHETAERUS: We have never been the aggressors, and even now we are as well disposed for peace as yourselves, provided you agree to one equitable condition, namely, that Zeus yield his sceptre to the birds. If only this is agreed to, I invite the ambassadors to dinner.

HERACLES: That's good enough for me. I vote for peace.

POSIDON: You wretch! you are nothing but a fool and a glutton. Do you want to dethrone your own father?

PITHETAERUS: What an error. Why, the gods will be much more powerful if the birds govern the earth. At present the mortals are hidden beneath the clouds, escape your observation, and commit perjury in your name; but if you had the birds for your allies, and a man, after having sworn by the crow and Zeus, should fail to keep his oath, the crow would dive down upon him unawares and pluck out his eye.

POSIDON: Well thought of, by Posidon!

HERACLES: My notion too.

PITHETAERUS, *to* TRIBALLUS: And you, what's your opinion?

TRIBALLUS: *Nabaísatreu.*

PITHETAERUS: D'you see? he also approves. But listen, here is another thing in which we can serve you. If a man vows to offer a sacrifice to some god, and then procrastinates, pretending that the gods can wait, and thus does not keep his word, we shall punish his stinginess.

POSIDON: Ah! and how?

PITHETAERUS: While he is counting his money or is in the bath, a kite will relieve him, before he knows it, either in coin or in clothes, of the value of a couple of sheep, and carry it to the god.

HERACLES: I vote for restoring them the sceptre.

POSIDON: Ask Triballus.

HERACLES: Hi! Triballus, do you want a thrashing?

TRIBALLUS: Sure, bashum head withum stick.

HERACLES: He says, "Right willingly."

POSIDON: If that be the opinion of both of you, why, I consent too.

HERACLES: Very well! we accord you the sceptre.

PITHETAERUS: Ah! I was nearly forgetting another condition. I will leave Heré to Zeus, but only if the young Basileia is given me in marriage.

POSIDON: Then you don't want peace. Let us withdraw.

PITHETAERUS: It matters mighty little to me. Cook, look to the gravy.

HERACLES: What an odd fellow this Posidon is! Where are you off to? Are we going to war about a woman?

POSIDON: What else is there to do?

HERACLES: What else? Why, conclude peace.

POSIDON: Oh! you blockhead! do you always want to be fooled? Why, you are seeking your own downfall. If Zeus were to die, after having yielded them the sovereignty, you would be ruined, for you are the heir of all the wealth he will leave behind.

PITHETAERUS: Oh! by the gods! how he is cajoling you. Step aside, that I may have a word with you. Your uncle is getting the better of you, my poor friend. The law will not allow you an obolus of the paternal property, for you are a bastard and not a legitimate child.

HERACLES: I a bastard! What's that you tell me?

PITHETAERUS: Why, certainly; are you not born of a stranger woman? Besides, is not Athené recognized as Zeus' sole heiress? And no daughter would be that, if she had a legitimate brother.

HERACLES: But what if my father wished to give me his property on his death-bed, even though I be a bastard?

PITHETAERUS: The law forbids it, and this same Posidon would be the first to lay claim to his wealth, in virtue of being his legitimate brother. Listen; thus runs

Solon's law: "A bastard shall not inherit, if there are legitimate children; and if there are no legitimate children, the property shall pass to the nearest kin."

HERACLES: And I get nothing whatever of the paternal property?

PITHETAERUS: Absolutely nothing. But tell me, has your father had you entered on the registers of his phratry?

HERACLES: No, and I have long been surprised at the omission.

PITHETAERUS: Why do you shake your fist at heaven? Do you want to fight? Why, be on my side, I will make you a king and will feed you on bird's milk and honey.

HERACLES: Your further condition seems fair to me. I cede you the young damsel.

POSIDON: But I, I vote against this opinion.

PITHETAERUS: Then it all depends on the Triballus. *To the* TRIBALLUS: What do you say?

TRIBALLUS: Givum bird pretty gel bigum queen.

HERACLES: He says give her.

POSIDON: Why no, he does not say anything of the sort, or else, like the swallows he does not know how to walk.

PITHETAERUS: Exactly so. Does he not say she must be given to the swallows?

POSIDON, *resignedly:* All right, you two arrange the matter; make peace, since you wish it so; I'll hold my tongue.

HERACLES: We are of a mind to grant you all that you ask. But come up there with us to receive Basileia and the celestial bounty.

PITHETAERUS: Here are birds already dressed, and very suitable for a nuptial feast.

HERACLES: You go and, if you like, I will stay here to roast them.

PITHETAERUS: You to roast them? you are too much the glutton; come along with us.

HERACLES: Ah! how well I would have treated myself!

PITHETAERUS: Let some one bring me a beautiful and magnificent tunic for the wedding.

The tunic is brought. PITHETAERUS *and the three gods depart.*

CHORUS, *singing:* At Phanae, near the Clepsydra, there dwells a people who have neither faith nor law, the Englottogastors, who reap, sow, pluck the vines and the figs with their tongues; they belong to a barbaric race, and among them the Philippi and the Gorgiases are to be found; 'tis these Englottogastorian Philippi who introduced the custom all over Attica of cutting out the tongue separately at sacrifices.

A MESSENGER *enters.*

MESSENGER, *in tragic style:* Oh, you, whose unbounded happiness I cannot express in words, thrice happy race of airy birds, receive your king in your fortunate dwellings. More brilliant than the brightest star that illumes the earth, he is approaching his glittering golden palace; the sun itself does not shine with more dazzling glory. He is entering with his bride at his side, whose beauty no human tongue can express; in his hand he brandishes the lightning, the winged shaft of Zeus; perfumes of unspeakable sweetness pervade the ethereal realms. 'Tis a glorious spectacle to see the clouds of incense wafting in light whirlwinds before the breath of the zephyr! But here he is himself. Divine Muse! let thy sacred lips begin with songs of happy omen.

PITHETAERUS *enters, with a crown on his head; he is accompanied by* BASILEIA.

CHORUS, *singing:* Fall back! to the right! to the left! advance! Fly around this happy mortal, whom Fortune loads with her blessings. Oh! oh! what grace! what beauty! Oh, marriage so auspicious for our city! All honour to this man! 'tis through him that the birds are called to such glorious destinies. Let your nuptial hymns, your nuptial songs, greet him and his Basileia! 'Twas in the midst of such festivities that the Fates formerly united Olympian Heré to the King who governs the gods from the summit of his inaccessible throne. Oh! Hymen! oh! Hymenaeus! Rosy Eros with the golden wings held the reins and guided the chariot; 'twas he, who presided over the union of Zeus and the fortunate Heré. Oh! Hymen! oh! Hymenaeus!

PITHETAERUS: I am delighted with your songs, I applaud your verses. Now celebrate the thunder that shakes the earth, the flaming lightning of Zeus and the terrible flashing thunderbolt.

CHORUS, *singing:* Oh, thou golden flash of the lightning! oh, ye divine shafts of flame, that Zeus has hitherto shot forth! Oh, ye rolling thunders, that bring down the rain! 'Tis by the order of *our* king that ye shall now stagger the earth! Oh, Hymen! 'tis through thee that he commands the universe and that he makes Basileia, whom he has robbed from Zeus, take her seat at his side. Oh! Hymen! oh! Hymeanaeus!

PITHETAERUS, *singing:* Let all the winged tribes of our fellow-citizens follow the bridal couple to the palace of Zeus and to the nuptial couch! Stretch forth your hands, my dear wife! Take hold of me by my wings and let us dance; I am going to lift you up and carry you through the air.

PITHETAERUS *and* BASILEIA *leave dancing; the* CHORUS *follows them.*

CHORUS, *singing:* Alalaí! Ië Paión! Tenélla kálliníke! Loftiest art thou of gods!

O

PLATO IN SICILY

Plato to the kindred and friends of Dion—Prosperity

Ye have written to me, that I ought to think your
sentiments are the same as those which Dion held;
and, moreover, you exhort me to make a common cause,
as far as I can, in word and deed. If ye have the same
opinion and desires with him I agree to unite with you;
but if not, to take frequent counsel with myself. Now
what his sentiments and desires were, I can tell pretty
nearly, not by conjecture, but by having known them
clearly.

For when I came originally to Syracuse, being then
nearly forty years old, Dion was of the age that Hip-
parinus is now; and the opinion he then held, he has
still continued to hold, namely, that the Syracusans
ought to be free and live according to the best laws. So
that it is by no means wonderful, if some god has caused
the latter to agree in the same opinion with the former
on the subject of a polity. But what was the method of
producing this, is a thing not unworthy for the young
and not young to hear; and I will endeavour to relate
it to you from the beginning; for the present events offer
the opportunity.

When I was a young man, I was affected as the many
are. I thought, if I became quickly my own master, to
betake myself immediately to the public affairs of the
state. Now some such circumstances as these fell out
relating to state affairs. Of the polity existing at that
time, when it was abused by many, a change took place:
and over the change one and fifty men presided as gov-

ernors, eleven in the city and ten in the Piraeus; and each of these had a jurisdiction about the Agora, and whatever else it was necessary to regulate in the cities, while thirty of them were invested with supreme authority. Some of these happened to be my relatives and acquaintances; and they forthwith invited me (to attend) to state-affairs, as being a suitable pursuit. And how I was affected is, on account of my youth, not at all wonderful. For I thought that they would, by leading the city from an unjust mode of living to a just one, administer it in the way it was meet; so that I diligently gave my mind to what they did. But when I saw these men proving in a short time that the previous form of government had been (as it were) gold, and that they committed other acts (unjustly), and sent my friend Socrates, advanced in years, whom I am not ashamed to say was nearly the most righteous man of those then living, together with certain others, against one of the citizens, and to bring him by force, in order that he might be executed, so that he (Socrates) might have a share in their deeds, whether he wished it or not, and that he did not comply, but ran the risk of suffering every thing, rather than take any part in their impious acts—all this when I saw, and other similar acts of no trifling kind, I felt indignant, and withdrew myself from the evil men of that period.

Not long after this, the power of the thirty fell by a revolution, together with the whole of the then existing form of government. Again, therefore, but somewhat more slowly, did a desire still drag me on to engage in public and political affairs. Now in these, as being in a troubled state, many things took place, at which any one might be indignant; nor was it wonderful, that in revolutions the punishment of hostile factions should have been rather severe in the case of some; although they who returned acted with considerable clemency. But by some chance some of those in power brought before a court of justice our friend Socrates, laying upon him an accusation the most unholy, and belonging the least of all to Socrates. For some brought him to trial, and others gave their vote against him, and destroyed the man, who had been unwilling to share in the unholy act of a removal relating to one of his then exiled friends, when the exiles themselves were unfortunate. On reflecting then upon these matters, and on the persons who managed political affairs, and on the laws and customs, the more I considered them, and I advanced in years, by so much the more difficult did it appear to me to administer correctly state affairs. For it is not possible to do so without friends and faithful associates; whom, existing at that time, it was not easy to find—for our city was then no longer administered according to the manners and institutions of our fathers—and it was impossible to acquire new ones with any facility; while the written laws and customs were corrupted, and (unholiness) was increasing to a degree how wonderful!

So that I, who had been at first full of ardour towards engaging in affairs of state, did, upon looking at these things and seeing them carried along in every way and on every side, become giddy; but not so as to withdraw from considering how at any time something better might take place respecting these very matters, and likewise the whole form of government, but to be wisely waiting continually for opportunities of acting. At last I perceived that all states existing at present were badly governed. For what relates to their laws is nearly in an incurable state, without some wonderful arrangement in conjunction with fortune. I was therefore compelled to say, in praise of true philosophy, that through it we are enabled to perceive all that is just as regards the state and individuals; and hence that the human race will never cease from ills, until the race of those, who philosophize correctly and truthfully, shall come to political power, or persons of power in states shall, by a certain divine allotment, philosophize really.

Holding these sentiments I arrived in Italy and Sicily, when I first came there. But on my arrival, the life, which is there called happy, pleased me at no time or manner; (a life) full of the tables prepared by Italiotes and Syracusans; and where one is filled twice a day; and never lies alone by night, and (has) such other pursuits as follow a life of this kind. For from these habits, no man under heaven, having such pursuits from his youth, would ever become prudent, not even if he were mixed up with a wondrous nature by some god; but to become temperate it will never be his care. And the same thing may be said respecting the remaining portion of virtue. Nor will any state rest quietly according to any laws whatever, while men conceive that it is proper to waste every thing on excesses, and deem that they ought to be idle in every thing except good living and drinking, and the laboured exertions made for sexual intercourse. But it is necessary for such states never to cease changing their tyrannies, oligarchies, and democracies, and for the powerful in them not to endure even the name of a polity just and with equal laws.

With these and the above-mentioned sentiments I passed over to Syracuse; perhaps through an accident of fortune; at least it seems that by the planning of some superior being a beginning was laid of the doings, that have lately taken place relating to Dion and of those too relating to Syracuse, and there is a fear, to still more persons, if you do not yield to me, when giving advice a second time. How then do I assert that my journey to Sicily was the beginning of all the then doings? For while associating with Dion, then a young man, and pointing out to him by words that, what seemed good to me would be the best for mankind, and counselling him so to act, I was nearly ignorant that I was unconsciously planning in some manner the dissolution of a tyranny. For Dion being very docile, both with respect to other things, and the reasons urged by me, he heard so quickly and attentively, as not one ever did of the young men whom I had fallen in with; and he was desirous of passing the remainder of his life in a manner superior to the majority of the Italiotes and Siceliotes, by loving virtue rather than pleasure and the rest of luxuries; and hence he lived rather odious to those, who passed their lives according to tyrannical institutions, until the death of Dionysius occurred. Subsequently, however, he perceived that the sentiments, which he held under the influence of correct reasoning, did not exist in him alone, but in some others; not numerous indeed, but amongst some, one of whom he thought would be probably Dionysius (the younger), if the gods assisted; and should this take place, that both his own life, and that of the other Syracusans, would turn out to be beyond all measure happy. He thought, moreover, that I ought by all means to come as quickly as possible to Syracuse, to take part in these doings; for he remembered how our mutual intercourse had easily worked him up to the desire of a life the most beautiful and best; which if he could but accomplish, as he was attempting to do, in the case of Dionysius, he had great hopes that he could, without slaughter and death, and the evils which have now taken place, make, in the whole of the country, life to be happy and rational.

With these correct sentiments Dion persuaded Dionysius to send for me; and he himself requested me by all means to come as quickly as possible, before certain other persons, associating with Dionysius, should turn him aside to a life different from the best. But it is necessary to relate what he requested, although it is a rather long story. What opportunity, said he, shall we wait for, greater than that through a certain divine fortune? and giving a statement of their command over Italy and Sicily, and of his own power in it, and of the youth of Dionysius, and of the desire he felt so vehemently for philosophy and instruction, and saying how his cousins and kindred were to be easily exhorted to the reasoning and mode of life ever laid down by myself, and that they were most competent to exhort Dionysius, so that now, if ever, all the hope would be fulfilled of the same persons becoming philosophers and rulers of mighty states. Such then and many others of a like kind were his exhortations. But a fear still possessed my mind, as to how, perchance, the conduct of the young men would turn out; for the passions of such persons are hasty, and are often borne along in a direction contrary to themselves. I knew, however, that Dion was naturally of a steady disposition and of a moderate age. Hence, while I was considering and doubting whether I ought to go, or how, the balance inclined that I ought (to go). For if perchance any one should attempt to give effect to my ideas upon laws and a form of government, I ought to attempt it now. For by persuading only one person, I should work out every good. With these ideas and confidence, and not from what some imagined, I set sail from home; feeling for myself the greatest shame, lest I should seem to myself to be altogether mere talk, and never willing to lay hold of any thing to be done; and run the risk of betraying first the hospitality and friendship of Dion, exposed in reality to no small dangers; and should he suffer aught, or, being driven out by Dionysius and his other enemies, fly to us, and making an inquiry, say—"I am come to you, Plato, an exile; but I am neither in want of cavalry nor of heavy-armed soldiers to ward off my enemies, but of words and persuasion; by which I know you are especially able to turn young persons to what is good and just, and to place them on each occasion on terms of friendship and fellowship with each other; through the want of which on your part I have now left Syracuse, and am present here. What relates to myself indeed will bring upon you less disgrace; but the philosophy, which you are always praising, and which you say is held in dishonour by the rest of mankind, how is it not now betrayed by you together with myself, as far as depends upon you? If, indeed, we had been inhabitants of Megara, you would surely have come to me as an assistant for what I had called you, or I should have considered you the meanest of men. But now, excusing yourself by the length of the journey, and the danger of the voyage, and the greatness of the trouble, think you that you shall avoid perchance the charge of cowardice? It will be far from this."

To language like this, what would have been a becoming answer? There is none. But I came with reason and justice, as much as it is possible for a man, having left my own pursuits, which were not unbecoming, under a tyranny, which was neither suited to my discourses nor myself. But by my coming I liberated myself (from any charge), and exhibited myself to be unreproved by Zeus, who presides over hospitality and the allotment of philosophy, which would have been exposed to reproach, had I acted an effeminate part, and through cowardice shared in disgrace and shame. On my arrival then—for there is no need to be prolix—I found all the affairs of Dionysius full of sedition and calumnies on the part of a tyranny respecting Dion. I defended Dion, therefore, to the utmost of my power; but I was able to do but little. But nearly in the fourth month after my arrival, Dionysius accused Dion of plotting against his power, and putting him on board a small vessel, sent him out with dishonour. Whereupon all of us, who were the friends of Dion, were fearful lest he should accuse and punish some one of us as an accomplice in the plot of Dion. And a report went abroad at Syracuse, that I had been put to death by Dionysius, as being forsooth the cause of all that happened at that time. But on perceiving that we were all thus disposed, and dreading lest something of greater consequence should arise from our fear, he received all of us most kindly into his favour, consoled me, and exhorted me to be of good cheer, and requested me by all means to stay; for there would be an advantage to him from my not flying away, but from my remaining; and on this account he pretended to make an urgent request. We know however that the requests of tyrants are mingled with necessity. By a contrivance, therefore, he prevented my sailing away. For taking me to the Acropolis, he made me reside there; from whence no ship-master could carry me off, not through Dionysius forbidding it merely, but unless Dionysius himself sent a person with an order, commanding him to lead me out. Nor was there any foreign trader, nor even one of those having jurisdiction over the departures from the country, who would have overlooked my going away alone; but he would immediately have laid hold of me and brought me back again to Dionysius; especially since it had been already bruited abroad contrary to what had been done before, that Dionysius was again holding Plato to his arms in a wonderful manner. And indeed this was the case, for it is necessary to speak the truth. He did indeed hold me to his arms, ever as time went on, more (and more) in respect to the intercourse of my manner and habits. But he wished me to praise him more than Dion, and to hold him as a friend in a far greater degree than the other; and for such an end he made wonderful efforts. But the way by which this might have taken place in the best manner, if it took place at all, he omitted; for he shrunk to become familiar and to associate with me, by hearing and learning discourses on philosophy, through the fear lest, (according) to the language of calumniators, he should be shackled, and Dion administer all affairs. However I endured every thing, keeping to the original sentiments, with which I arrived, if by any means he should come to the desire of a philosophic life. But he, by his pulling in a contrary direction, obtained the victory. In this way then happened to turn out the first period of my sojourning and pursuits in Sicily. After this I went away and came back again, through Dionysius having sent for me with all earnestness. But on what account (I came), and what I did, as being reasonable and just, I will, having first advised you what you ought to do, after what has just now taken place, subsequently relate in detail, for the sake of those who are inquiring with what view I came a second time to Sicily; and that deeds of no moment may not happen to be mentioned as deeds of moment.

I say then something that I ought to say. For the party, who gives advice to a sick man and to one who uses a diet improper for good health, it is especially necessary in the first place to change the mode of living, and to recommend to the patient, willing to comply, the other things that are proper; but if he is unwilling, I consider that he, who retires from advising such a person, acts like a man and a physician; but that he, who stays, like a person unmanly and devoid of art. The same is the case of a state, whether its master be one or many.

If, while the government is proceeding in a right road according to the constitution, it takes counsel about what is conducive to its interest, it is the part of a man with mind to give to such parties advice; but in the case of those, who are proceeding entirely out of a straight-forward polity, and not at all willing to walk in its steps, and who proclaim to the adviser to leave alone the form of government, and not to disturb it—since, if he does disturb it, he shall suffer death—and at the same time exhort him to minister to their wishes and passions, and to advise in what way these may for all time to come be gratified, I should consider the person, who endures to give such advice, unmanly; but him, who does not endure, a man.

Holding then such sentiments, whenever any one consults with myself about any thing of the greatest moment relating to his life, such as the acquisition of wealth, or the care of his body or soul, I readily advise with him, if he appears to me to live day by day in an orderly manner, or is willing to be persuaded by me when giving advice, nor do I desist, as if I have gone through merely a formal rite. But if either he does not consult me at all, or is evidently not about to follow my advice, I do not go self-called to such a person to counsel him, nor would I do so by compulsion, even if he were my son. But I would give advice to a slave, and force him, even unwilling, (to follow it). I should however think it not holy to force my father or mother, unless they were, through disease, afflicted with silliness. But if persons are living an established mode of life, pleasing to themselves, but not to me, I should not, when admonishing them in vain, dislike them, nor yet by flattering, minister to them, and afford them the means of gratifying their desires, which if I were to embrace, I should not wish to live. With the same sentiments respecting a state a prudent man ought to live, and speak out, if it appears to him not to have a good form of government, (and) if he is about not to speak in vain, nor to lose his life by speaking; but never to apply violence to his country on account of a change in the form of government, unless it cannot become the best without the banishment and slaughter of persons; but leading a quiet life, to pray for the good both of himself and of the state.

In this very manner I would advise you (to act); and so did I together with Dion advise Dionysius to live day by day, so that in the first place he might be about to become the master of himself, and acquire faithful friends and associates, in order that he might not suffer what his father did; who, after he had got possession of many and great cities in Sicily, which had been laid waste by the Barbarians, was not able to establish and preserve in each of them forms of government, faithful under his associates, or strangers coming from any part whatever, or brothers, whom he himself had brought up as being younger, and had made them rulers, after being merely private persons, and remarkably rich, after being (very) poor. For among these he could not attach to himself a single one as sharer of his dominion, although working upon them by persuasion, and teaching, and kindnesses, and alliances; and he was sevenfold worse off than Darius; who, placing a trust in persons not his brothers, nor brought up by him, but in those alone associated with himself in their mastery over the eunuch, divided amongst them seven parts of his dominions, each larger than the whole of Sicily, and made use of them as faithful associates, and attacking neither himself, nor each other; and gave likewise an example of what a lawgiver and a king ought to be. For he established laws, by which he has preserved even now the

Persian power; and besides this the Athenians, although they had not colonized themselves many Grecian cities, which had been overturned by the Barbarians, but merely got hold of them, when already inhabited, preserved their empire over them for seventy years, through having persons friendly to them in each of the towns. But Dionysius having through his wisdom brought together the whole of Sicily into one state, yet, through confiding in no one, was with difficulty saved. For he was poor in persons friendly and faithful; than which there is no greater sign as regards virtue and vice, than in being destitute or not of men of that kind. I therefore and Dion advised Dionysius, since what he had received from his father had come to him unacquainted with instruction, and unacquainted too with befitting associates, in the first place to proceed in that direction, to procure for himself friends, different from his relations, but both his equals in age and in accordance with him respecting virtue. But we particularly advised him to be in accord with himself; for that he was wonderfully deficient in this we asserted, not indeed in such clear terms—for this was not safe—but in hints and contending in our discourses, that in this way every man will preserve both himself and those over whom he is the ruler; but that by not turning himself in this direction he will bring to pass every thing the very reverse. But if, after going on, as we said, and rendering himself prudent and temperate, he peopled the cities of Sicily, that had been made desolate, and bound them together with laws and forms of government, so as to be of one family with himself and an assistance to each other against the Barbarians, he would not only double his ancestral dominion, but make it in reality much larger. For if this were done, it would be much more easy to enslave the Carthaginians, than was the slavery effected by them during the reign of Gelon; but not as now on the contrary, his father fixed the tribute he was to carry to the Barbarians.

This is what was said and the advice given to Dionysius by us, who were plotting against him, as the reports were circulated on many sides. Such, that after prevailing with Dionysius, they caused him to drive out Dion, and threw myself into a state of terror. But, that I may bring to a close not a few events which occurred in a short time, Dion, departing from Peloponnesus and Athens, admonished Dionysius indeed. Since then (Dion) had liberated and twice restored the town to the citizens, the Syracusans were affected in the same manner towards him, as Dionysius had been, when he endeavoured by educating and bringing him up to make him thus a worthy partner of his power through the whole of life. But (he gave his ear) to those that were calumniating Dion, and saying that he was doing all that he did at that time, while plotting against the absolute power of Dionysius, in order that the one, being lulled in his mind by his attention to instruction, might neglect his kingdom, and commit it to Dion, and the other make it his own by fraud, and cast out Dionysius from his dominions.

These reports being then bruited a second time among the Syracusans prevailed by a victory very absurd and disgraceful to those who were the causes of it. For how it happened it is proper for those to hear, who are calling upon me on the subject of the present affairs.

Being an Athenian, and the associate of Dion, and one who had battled with him against the tyrant, I arrived, that I might produce a peace instead of a war; but while battling against the calumniators I was overcome. But Dionysius, attempting to bribe me by honours and riches, to become on his side a witness and a friend, touching the propriety of his casting out Dion, failed in all of these things happening to him. And Dion afterwards, on returning home from exile, brought with him two Athenian brothers, who had become his friends, not through philosophy, but through that acquaintance, which runs through the generality of friends, and which they formed from paying the rites of hospitality, and from being Mystae and Epoptae. Moreover these two, by having brought Dion back, had become friends, and, from such causes, and the assisting him in his return from exile, his companions. But when, on their arrival in Sicily, they understood that Dion had been exposed by those Siceliotes, who had become free through him, to the calumny of plotting to become a tyrant, they not only betrayed their associate and guest, but became, as it were, the perpetrators of a murder, in that, with weapons in their hands, they stood by to assist the murderers. However, I neither pass by this base and unholy deed, nor do I detail it; for to many others it (has been) a care to hymn it, and it will be so at some future time.

But the charge, which has been alleged respecting the Athenians, how that it was they, who bound this disgrace around the city, I will take away. For I say that he too was an Athenian, who did not betray this very person, when it was in his power to obtain wealth and many other honours. For he did not become a friend through a shipmate friendship, but through the communion of a liberal education; to which alone he, who is endued with mind, ought to trust, rather than to the alliance of souls and bodies; so that those were not fit to bring disgrace on the city through having murdered Dion, as being persons of no account at any time. All this has been said for the sake of the advice given to the friends and kindred of Dion.

I give you besides the same counsel, and for the third time address you three in the same words. Do not place

Sicily, or any other city, as a slave under persons with despotic power, but under laws; such at least is my dictum. For this is not the better either for the enslaving or the enslaved, or for their children or their children's descendants; but the experiment is altogether a destructive one. For souls, whose habits are little and illiberal, love to seize upon gain of this kind, as knowing nothing of what is good and just for the future and present time, nor of things human and divine. Of this I endeavoured to persuade Dion first, and secondly Dionysius, and now I do you the third. Be persuaded then by me, for the sake of Zeus the third saviour. In the next place look to the case of Dionysius and Dion; the former of whom by not being persuaded is now living not honourably; whereas the latter, by being persuaded, died honourably. For it is a thing altogether correct and honourable for him, who aspires after things the most honourable both for himself and his country, to suffer whatever he may suffer; for not one of us is naturally immortal; nor, if this should happen to any one, would he become happy, as it seems he would to the multitude. For in things inanimate there is nothing either good or evil worthy of mention; but good or ill will happen to each soul, either existing with the body or separated from it. But it is ever requisite to trust really to the sacred accounts of the olden time, which inform us that the soul is immortal, and has judges of its conduct, and suffers the greatest punishments, when it is liberated from the body. Hence it is requisite to think it is a lesser evil to suffer, than to do, the greatest sins and injuries. This, indeed, the man who is fond of money and poor in soul does not hear; and should he hear, he laughs it down, as he imagines, and impudently snatches from all sides whatever he thinks he can, like a wild beast, eat or drink, or can contribute (aught) to the miscalled pleasure of sexual intercourse, at once servile and graceless. (For) being blind, he is not able to see how great an evil, ever united to each act of wrong, follows the never being satisfied with the unholy perpetration of such snatchings; which it is necessary for him, who has acted unjustly, to drag along with himself, both while he is moving about upon the earth, and when he takes under the earth a journey without honour, and thoroughly miserable in every way.

By detailing these and other reasons of the like kind, I was enabled to persuade Dion. And I should have felt most justly against those, who murdered him, an anger, in a certain manner, almost as great as against Dionysius; for both had injured myself and all the rest, so to say, in the highest degree. For the former had destroyed a man, who was willing to make use of justice; while the latter (was) unwilling to make use of it through the whole of his dominions, although possessing the greatest power. In which (dominions) had philosophy and power existed really, as it were in the same (dwelling), they would have set up amongst all men, both Greeks and Barbarians, an opinion not vainly shining, (and) in every respect the true one, that neither a state nor a man can ever be happy, unless by leading a life with prudence in subjection to justice, whether possessing those things themselves, or by being brought up in the habits of holy persons their rulers, or instructed in justice.

This injury did Dionysius inflict. But the rest would have been a trifling wrong, as compared to these. But he, who murdered Dion, did not know that he had done the same deed as Dionysius. For I clearly know, as far as it is possible for one man to speak confidently of another, that if Dion had retained his power, he would never have changed it to any other form of government than to that, by which he first (caused) Syracuse, his own country, after he had delivered it from slavery, to look joyous, and had put it into the garb of freedom; and after this, he would by every contrivance have adorned the citizens with laws both befitting and the best; and he would have been ready to do what followed in due order after this; and have colonized the whole of Sicily, and have freed it from the Barbarians, by expelling some and subduing others, more easily than Hiero did. But if these things had taken place, through a man just, and brave, and temperate, and who was a philosopher, the same opinion of virtue would have been produced amongst the multitude, as would have been amongst all men, so to say; and have saved Dionysius, had he been persuaded by me. But now some daemon surely, or some evil spirit, falling upon with iniquity and impiety, and, what is the greatest matter, with the audacity of ignorance, in which all evils are rooted, and from which they spring up, and afterwards produce fruit the most bitter to those, who have begotten it, this has a second time subverted and destroyed every thing. However, let us, for the sake of a good augury, keep for the third time a well-omened silence.

I advise therefore you, my friends, to imitate Dion, in the good-will he felt for his country, and in his temperate mode of living, but for the better. But under what auspices you ought to endeavour to fulfil his wishes, and what they are, you have clearly heard from me. But upon the person, who is among you unable to live according to his country's customs in a Dorian fashion, but adopts the life of the murderers of Dion, and what is followed in Sicily, do not call; nor believe that he will in any thing ever act faithfully and sincerely. But call upon the rest to form a settlement of the whole of Sicily, and introduce both from Sicily itself and all Pelopon-

nesus an equality of laws, and do not fear the Athenians;
for men are there, who surpass all others in virtue, and
who hate the daring of guest-murderers.

From *Epistle* VII.

O

THE SICILIAN EXPEDITION

THUCYDIDES

THE Athenians next made an expedition against the
island of Melos with thirty ships of their own, six
Chian, and two Lesbian, 1,200 hoplites and 300 archers
besides twenty mounted archers of their own, and about
1,500 hoplites furnished by their allies in the islands.
The Melians are colonists of the Lacedaemonians who
would not submit to Athens like the other islanders. At
first they were neutral and took no part. But when the
Athenians tried to coerce them by ravaging their lands,
they were driven into open hostilities. The generals,
Cleomedes the son of Lycomedes and Tisias the son of
Tisimachus, encamped with the Athenian forces on the
island. But before they did the country any harm they
sent envoys to negotiate with the Melians. Instead of
bringing these envoys before the people, the Melians
desired them to explain their errand to the magistrates
and to the chief men. They spoke as follows:

85. "Since we are not allowed to speak to the people,
lest, forsooth, they should be deceived by seductive and
unanswerable arguments which they would hear set
forth in a single uninterrupted oration (for we are perfectly aware that this is what you mean in bringing us
before a select few), you who are sitting here may as
well make assurance yet surer. Let us have no set

speeches at all, but do you reply to each several statement of which you disapprove, and criticise it at once.
Say first of all how you like this mode of proceeding."

86. The Melian representatives answered: "The quiet
interchange of explanations is a reasonable thing, and
we do not object to that. But your warlike movements,
which are present not only to our fears but to our eyes,
seem to belie your words. We see that, although you
may reason with us, you mean to be our judges; and that
at the end of the discussion, if the justice of our cause
prevail and we therefore refuse to yield, we may expect
war; if we are convinced by you, slavery."

87. *Athenians:* Nay, but if you are only going to argue
from fancies about the future, or if you meet us with
any other purpose than that of looking your circumstances in the face and saving your city, we have done;
but if this is your intention we will proceed.

88. *Melians:* It is an excusable and natural thing that
men in our position should have much to say and should
indulge in many fancies. But we admit that this conference has met to consider the question of our preservation; and therefore let the argument proceed in the
manner which you propose.

89. *Athenians:* Well, then, we Athenians will use no
fine words; we will not go out of our way to prove at
length that we have a right to rule, because we over-
threw the Persians; or that we attack you now because
we are suffering any injury at your hands. We should
not convince you if we did; nor must you expect to convince us by arguing that, although a colony of the Lacedaemonians, you have taken no part in their expeditions,
or that you have never done us any wrong. But you and
we should say what we really think, and aim only at
what is possible, for we both alike know that into the
discussion of human affairs the question of justice only

enters where the pressure of necessity is equal, and that the powerful exact what they can, and the weak grant what they must.

90. *Melians:* Well, then, since you set aside justice and invite us to speak of expediency, in our judgment it is certainly expedient that you should respect a principle which is for the common good; and that to every man when in peril a reasonable claim should be accounted a claim of right, and any plea which he is disposed to urge, even if failing of the point a little, should help his cause. Your interest in this principle is quite as great as ours, inasmuch as you, if you fall, will incur the heaviest vengeance, and will be the most terrible example to mankind.

91. *Athenians:* The fall of our empire, if it should fall, is not an event to which we look forward with dismay; for ruling states such as Lacedaemon are not cruel to their vanquished enemies. And we are fighting not so much against the Lacedaemonians, as against our own subjects who may some day rise up and overcome their former masters. But this is a danger which you may leave to us. And we will now endeavour to show that we have come in the interests of our empire, and that in what we are about to say we are only seeking the preservation of your city. For we want to make you ours with the least trouble to ourselves, and it is for the interest of us both that you should not be destroyed.

92. *Melians:* It may be your interest to be our masters, but how can it be ours to be your slaves?

93. *Athenians:* To you the gain will be that by submission you will avert the worst; and we shall be all the richer for your preservation.

94. *Melians:* But must we be your enemies? Will you not receive us as friends if we are neutral and remain at peace with you?

95. *Athenians:* No, your enmity is not half so mischievous to us as your friendship; for the one is in the eyes of our subjects an argument of our power, the other of our weakness.

96. *Melians:* But are your subjects really unable to distinguish between states in which you have no concern, and those which are chiefly your own colonies, and in some cases have revolted and been subdued by you?

97. *Athenians:* Why, they do not doubt that both of them have a good deal to say for themselves on the score of justice, but they think that states like yours are left free because they are able to defend themselves, and that we do not attack them because we dare not. So that your subjection will give us an increase of security, as well as an extension of empire. For we are masters of the sea, and you who are islanders, and insignificant islanders too, must not be allowed to escape us.

98. *Melians:* But do you not recognise another danger? For, once more, since you drive us from the plea of justice and press upon us your doctrine of expediency, we must show you what is for our interest, and, if it be for yours also, may hope to convince you: Will you not be making enemies of all who are now neutrals? When they see how you are treating us they will expect you some day to turn against them; and if so, are you not strengthening the enemies whom you already have, and bringing upon you others who, if they could help, would never dream of being your enemies at all?

99. *Athenians:* We do not consider our really dangerous enemies to be any of the peoples inhabiting the mainland who, secure in their freedom, may defer indefinitely any measures of precaution which they take against us, but islanders who, like you, happen to be under no control, and all who may be already irritated by the necessity of submission to our empire—these are

our real enemies, for they are the most reckless and most likely to bring themselves as well as us into a danger which they cannot but foresee.

100. *Melians:* Surely then, if you and your subjects will brave all this risk, you to preserve your empire and they to be quit of it, how base and cowardly would it be in us, who retain our freedom, not to do and suffer anything rather than be your slaves.

101. *Athenians:* Not so, if you calmly reflect: for you are not fighting against equals to whom you cannot yield without disgrace, but you are taking counsel whether or no you shall resist an overwhelming force. The question is not one of honour but of prudence.

102. *Melians:* But we know that the fortune of war is sometimes impartial, and not always on the side of numbers. If we yield now, all is over; but if we fight, there is yet hope that we may stand upright.

103. *Athenians:* Hope is a good comforter in the hour of danger, and when men have something else to depend upon, although hurtful, she is not ruinous. But when her spendthrift nature has induced them to stake their all, they see her as she is in the moment of their fall, and not till then. While the knowledge of her might enable them to beware of her, she never fails. You are weak and a single turn of the scale might be your ruin. Do not you be thus deluded; avoid the error of which so many are guilty, who, although they might still be saved if they would take the natural means, when visible grounds of confidence forsake them, have recourse to the invisible, to prophecies and oracles and the like, which ruin men by the hopes which they inspire in them.

104. *Melians:* We know only too well how hard the struggle must be against your power, and against fortune, if she does not mean to be impartial. Nevertheless we do not despair of fortune; for we hope to stand as

high as you in the favour of heaven, because we are righteous, and you against whom we contend are unrighteous; and we are satisfied that our deficiency in power will be compensated by the aid of our allies the Lacedaemonians; they cannot refuse to help us, if only because we are their kinsmen, and for the sake of their own honour. And therefore our confidence is not so utterly blind as you suppose.

105. *Athenians:* As for the gods, we expect to have quite as much of their favour as you: for we are not doing or claiming anything which goes beyond common opinion about divine or men's desires about human things. Of the gods we believe, and of men we know, that by a law of their nature wherever they can rule they will. This law was not made by us, and we are not the first who have acted upon it; we did but inherit it, and shall bequeath it to all time, and we know that you and all mankind, if you were as strong as we are, would do as we do. So much for the gods; we have told you why we expect to stand as high in their good opinion as you. And then as to the Lacedaemonians—when you imagine that out of very shame they will assist you, we admire the simplicity of your idea, but we do not envy you the folly of it. The Lacedaemonians are exceedingly virtuous among themselves, and according to their national standard of morality. But, in respect of their dealings with others, although many things might be said, a word is enough to describe them, of all men whom we know they are the most notorious for identifying what is pleasant with what is honourable, and what is expedient with what is just. But how inconsistent is such a character with your present blind hope of deliverance!

106. *Melians:* That is the very reason why we trust them; they will look to their interest, and therefore will not be willing to betray the Melians, who are their own

colonists, lest they should be distrusted by their friends in Hellas and play into the hands of their enemies.

107. *Athenians:* But do you not see that the path of expediency is safe, whereas justice and honour involve danger in practice, and such dangers the Lacedaemonians seldom care to face?

108. *Melians:* On the other hand, we think that whatever perils there may be, they will be ready to face them for our sakes, and will consider danger less dangerous where we are concerned. For if they need to act we are close at hand, and they can better trust our loyal feeling because we are their kinsmen.

109. *Athenians:* Yes, but what encourages men who are invited to join in a conflict is clearly not the good-will of those who summon them to their side, but a decided superiority in real power. To this no men look more keenly than the Lacedaemonians; so little confidence have they in their own resources, that they only attack their neighbours when they have numerous allies, and therefore they are not likely to find their way by themselves to an island, when we are masters of the sea.

110. *Melians:* But they may send their allies: the Cretan sea is a large place; and the masters of the sea will have more difficulty in overtaking vessels which want to escape than the pursued in escaping. If the attempt should fail they may invade Attica itself, and find their way to allies of yours whom Brasidas did not reach: and then you will have to fight, not for the conquest of a land in which you have no concern, but nearer home, for the preservation of your confederacy and of your own territory.

111. *Athenians:* Help may come from Lacedaemon to you as it has come to others, and should you ever have actual experience of it, then you will know that never once have the Athenians retired from a siege

through fear of a foe elsewhere. You told us that the safety of your city would be your first care, but we remark that, in this long discussion, not a word has been uttered by you which would give a reasonable man expectation of deliverance. Your strongest grounds are hopes deferred, and what power you have is not to be compared with that which is already arrayed against you. Unless after we have withdrawn you mean to come, as even now you may, to a wiser conclusion, you are showing a great want of sense. For surely you cannot dream of flying to that false sense of honour which has been the ruin of so many when danger and dishonour were staring them in the face. Many men with their eyes still open to the consequences have found the word honour too much for them, and have suffered a mere name to lure them on, until it has drawn down upon them real and irretrievable calamities; through their own folly they have incurred a worse dishonour than fortune would have inflicted upon them. If you are wise you will not run this risk; you ought to see that there can be no disgrace in yielding to a great city which invites you to become her ally on reasonable terms, keeping your own land, and merely paying tribute; and that you will certainly gain no honour if, having to choose between two alternatives, safety and war, you obstinately prefer the worse. To maintain our rights against equals, to be politic with superiors, and to be moderate towards inferiors is the path of safety. Reflect once more when we have withdrawn, and say to yourselves over and over again that you are deliberating about your one and only country, which may be saved or may be destroyed by a single decision.

112. The Athenians left the conference: the Melians, after consulting among themselves, resolved to persevere in their refusal, and answered as follows, "Men of Ath-

ens, our resolution is unchanged; and we will not in a moment surrender that liberty which our city, founded 700 years ago, still enjoys; we will trust to the good-fortune which, by the favour of the gods, has hitherto preserved us, and for human help to the Lacedaemonians, and endeavour to save ourselves. We are ready however to be your friends, and the enemies neither of you nor of the Lacedaemonians, and we ask you to leave our country when you have made such a peace as may appear to be in the interest of both parties."

113. Such was the answer of the Melians; the Athenians, as they quitted the conference, spoke as follows, "Well, we must say, judging from the decision at which you have arrived, that you are the only men who deem the future to be more certain than the present, and regard things unseen as already realised in your fond anticipation, and that the more you cast yourselves upon the Lacedaemonians and fortune, and hope, and trust them, the more complete will be your ruin."

114. The Athenian envoys returned to the army; and the generals, when they found that the Melians would not yield, immediately commenced hostilities. They surrounded the town of Melos with a wall, dividing the work among the several contingents. They then left troops of their own and of their allies to keep guard both by land and by sea, and retired with the greater part of their army; the remainder carried on the blockade.

115. About the same time the Argives made an inroad into Phliasia, and lost nearly eighty men, who were caught in an ambuscade by the Phliasians and the Argive exiles. The Athenian garrison in Pylos took much spoil from the Lacedaemonians; nevertheless the latter did not renounce the peace and go to war, but only notified by a proclamation that if any one of their own peo-

ple had a mind to make reprisals on the Athenians he might. The Corinthians next declared war upon the Athenians on some private grounds, but the rest of the Peloponnesians did not join them. The Melians took that part of the Athenian wall which looked towards the agora by a night assault, killed a few men, and brought in as much corn and other necessaries as they could; they then retreated and remained inactive. After this the Athenians set a better watch. So the summer ended.

116. In the following winter the Lacedaemonians had intended to make an expedition into the Argive territory, but finding that the sacrifices which they offered at the frontier were unfavourable they returned home. The Argives, suspecting that the threatened invasion was instigated by citizens of their own, apprehended some of them; others however escaped.

About the same time the Melians took another part of the Athenian wall; for the fortifications were insufficiently guarded. Whereupon the Athenians sent fresh troops, under the command of Philocrates the son of Demeas. The place was now closely invested, and there was treachery among the citizens themselves. So the Melians were induced to surrender at discretion. The Athenians thereupon put to death all who were of military age, and made slaves of the women and children. They then colonised the island, sending thither 500 settlers of their own.

II

1. During the same winter the Athenians conceived a desire of sending another expedition to Sicily, larger than that commanded by Laches and Eurymedon. They hoped to conquer the island. Of its great size and numerous population, barbarian as well as Hellenic, most

of them knew nothing, and they never reflected that they were entering on a struggle almost as arduous as the Peloponnesian War. . . .

They virtuously professed that they were going to assist their own kinsmen and their newly acquired allies,[1] but the simple truth was that they aspired to the empire of Sicily. They were principally instigated by an embassy which had come from Egesta and was urgent in requesting aid. The Egestaeans had gone to war with the neighbouring city of Selinus about certain questions of marriage and about a disputed piece of land. The Selinuntians summoned the Syracusans to their assistance, and their united forces reduced the Egestaeans to great straits both by sea and land. The Egestaean envoys reminded the Athenians of the alliance which they had made with the Leontines under Laches in the former war, and begged them to send ships to their relief. Their chief argument was, that if the Syracusans were not punished for the expulsion of the Leontines, but were allowed to destroy the remaining allies of the Athenians, and to get the whole of Sicily into their own hands, they would one day come with a great army, Dorians assisting Dorians, who were their kinsmen, and colonists assisting their Peloponnesian founders, and would unite in overthrowing Athens herself. Such being the danger, the Athenians would be wise in combining with the allies who were still left to them in Sicily against the Syracusans, especially since the Egestaeans would themselves provide money sufficient for the war. These arguments were constantly repeated in the ears of the Athenian assembly by the Egestaeans and their partisans; at length the people passed a vote that they would at all events send envoys to ascertain on the spot whether the Egestaeans really had the money which they professed

---

[1] The Camarinaeans, Agrigentines, and some of the Sicels.

to have in their treasury and in their temples, and to report on the state of the war with Selinus. So the Athenian envoys were despatched to Sicily.

7. During the same winter the Lacedaemonians and their allies, all but the Corinthians, made an expedition into the Argive territory, of which they devastated a small part, and, having brought with them waggons, carried away a few loads of corn. They settled the Argive exiles at Orneae, where they left a small garrison, and having made an agreement that the inhabitants of Orneae and the Argives should not injure one another's land for a given time, returned home with the rest of their army. Soon afterwards the Athenians arrived with thirty ships and 600 hoplites. They and the people of Argos with their whole power went out and blockaded Orneae for a day, but at night the Argive exiles within the walls got away unobserved by the besiegers, who were encamped at some distance. On the following day the Argives, perceiving what had happened, razed Orneae to the ground and returned. Soon afterwards the Athenian fleet returned likewise.

The Athenians also conveyed by sea cavalry of their own, and some Macedonian exiles who had taken refuge with them, to Methone on the borders of Macedonia, and ravaged the territory of Perdiccas. Whereupon the Lacedaemonians sent to the Thracian Chalcidians, who were maintaining an armistice terminable at ten days' notice with the Athenians, and commanded them to assist Perdiccas, but they refused. So the winter ended, and with it the sixteenth year in the Peloponnesian War of which Thucydides wrote the history.

8. Early in the next spring the Athenian envoys returned from Sicily. They were accompanied by Egestaeans who brought sixty talents of uncoined silver, being a month's pay for sixty vessels which they hoped

to obtain from Athens. The Athenians called an assembly, and when they heard both from their own and from the Egestaean envoys, amongst other inviting but untrue statements, that there was abundance of money lying ready in the temples and in the treasury of Egesta, they passed a vote that sixty ships should be sent to Sicily; Alcibiades the son of Cleinias, Nicias the son of Niceratus, and Lamachus the son of Xenophanes were appointed commanders. They were told to assist Egesta against Selinus; if this did not demand all their military strength they were empowered to restore the Leontines, and generally to further in such manner as they deemed best the Athenian interest in Sicily. Five days afterwards another assembly was called to consider what steps should be taken for the immediate equipment of the expedition, and to vote any additional supplies which the generals might require. Nicias, who had been appointed general against his will, thought that the people had come to a wrong conclusion, and that upon slight and flimsy grounds they were aspiring to the conquest of Sicily, which was no easy task. So, being desirous of diverting the Athenians from their purpose, he came forward and admonished them in the following terms:

9. "I know that we are assembled here to discuss the preparations which are required for our expedition to Sicily, but in my judgment it is still a question whether we ought to go thither at all; we should not be hasty in determining a matter of so much importance, or allow ourselves to rush into an impolitic war at the instigation of foreigners. Yet to me personally war brings honour; and I am as careless as any man about my own life: not that I think the worse of a citizen who takes a little thought about his life or his property, for I believe that the sense of a man's own interest will quicken his interest in the prosperity of the state. But I have never been in-

duced by the love of reputation to say a single word contrary to what I thought; neither will I now: I will say simply what I believe to be best. If I told you to take care of what you have and not to throw away present advantages in order to gain an uncertain and distant good, my words would be powerless against a temper like yours. I would rather argue that this is not the time, and that your great aims will not be easily realised.

10. "I tell you that in going to Sicily you are leaving many enemies behind you, and seem to be bent on bringing new ones hither. You are perhaps relying upon the treaty recently made, which if you remain quiet may retain the name of a treaty; for to a mere name the intrigues of certain persons both here and at Lacedaemon have nearly succeeded in reducing it. But if you meet with any serious reverse, your enemies will be upon you in a moment, for the agreement was originally extracted from them by the pressure of misfortune, and the discredit of it fell to them and not to us. In the treaty itself there are many disputed points; and, unsatisfactory as it is, to this hour several cities, and very powerful cities too, persist in rejecting it. Some of these are at open war with us already; others may declare war at ten days' notice; and they only remain at peace because the Lacedaemonians are indisposed to move. And in all probability, if they find our power divided (and such a division is precisely what we are striving to create), they will eagerly join the Sicilians, whose alliance in the war they would long ago have given anything to obtain. These considerations should weigh with us. The state is far from the desired haven, and we should not run into danger and seek to gain a new empire before we have fully secured the old. The Chalcidians in Thrace have been rebels all these years and remain unsubdued, and there are other subjects of ours in various parts of the

mainland who are uncertain in their allegiance. And we forsooth cannot lose a moment in avenging the wrongs of our allies the Egestaeans, while we still defer the punishment of our revolted subjects, whose offences are of long standing.

11. "And yet if we subdue the Chalcidian rebels we may retain our hold on them; but Sicily is a populous and distant country, over which, even if we are victorious, we shall hardly be able to maintain our dominion. And how foolish is it to select for attack a land which no conquest can secure, while he who fails to conquer will not be where he was before!

"I should say that the Sicilians are not dangerous to you, certainly not in their present condition, and they would be even less so if they were to fall under the sway of the Syracusans (and this is the prospect with which the Egestaeans would fain scare you). At present individuals might cross the sea out of friendship for the Lacedaemonians; but if the states of Sicily were all united in one empire they would not be likely to make war upon another empire. For whatever chance they may have of overthrowing us if they unite with the Peloponnesians, there will be the same chance of their being overthrown themselves if the Peloponnesians and Athenians are ever united against them. The Hellenes in Sicily will dread us most if we never come; in a less degree if we display our strength and speedily depart; but if any disaster occur, they will despise us and be ready enough to join the enemies who are attacking us here. We all know that men have the greatest respect for that which is farthest off, and for that of which the reputation has been least tested; and this, Athenians, you may verify by your own experience. There was a time when you feared the Lacedaemonians and their allies, but now you have got the better of them, and because your first fears have not been realised you despise them, and even hope to conquer Sicily. But you ought not to be elated at the chance mishaps of your enemies; before you can be confident you should have gained the mastery over their minds. Remember that the Lacedaemonians are sensitive to their disgrace, and that their sole thought is how they may even yet find a way of inflicting a blow upon us which will retrieve their own character; the rather because they have laboured so earnestly and so long to win a name for valour. If we are wise we shall not trouble ourselves about the barbarous Egestaeans in Sicily; the real question is how we can make ourselves secure against the designs of an insidious oligarchy.

12. "We must remember also that we have only just recovered in some measure from a great plague and a great war, and are beginning to make up our losses in men and money. It is our duty to expend our new resources upon ourselves at home, and not upon begging exiles who have an interest in successful lies; who find it expedient only to contribute words, and let others fight their battles; and who, if saved, prove ungrateful; if they fail, as they very likely may, only involve their friends in a common ruin.

"I dare say there may be some young man here who is delighted at holding a command, and the more so because he is too young for his post; and he, regarding only his own interest, may recommend you to sail; he may be one who is much admired for his stud of horses, and wants to make something out of his command which will maintain him in his extravagance. But do not you give him the opportunity of indulging his own magnificent tastes at the expense of the state. Remember that men of this stamp impoverish themselves and defraud the public. An expedition to Sicily is a serious business, and not one which a mere youth can plan and carry into execution off-hand.

13. "The youth of whom I am speaking has summoned to his side young men like himself, whom, not without alarm, I see sitting by him in this assembly, and I appeal against them to you elder citizens. If any of you should be placed next one of his supporters, I would not have him ashamed, or afraid, of being thought a coward if he does not vote for war. Do not, like them, entertain a desperate craving for things out of your reach; you know that by prevision many successes are gained, but few or none by mere greed. On behalf of our country, now on the brink of the greatest danger which she has ever known, I entreat you to hold up your hands against them. Do not interfere with the boundaries which divide us from Sicily. I mean the Ionian gulf which parts us if we sail along the coast, the Sicilian sea if we sail through the open water; these are quite satisfactory. The Sicilians have their own country; let them manage their own concerns. And let the Egestaeans in particular be informed that, having originally gone to war with the Selinuntians on their own account, they must make peace on their own account. Let us have no more allies such as ours have too often been, whom we are expected to assist when they are in misfortune, but to whom we ourselves when in need may look in vain.

14. "And you, Prytanis, as you wish to be a good citizen, and believe that the welfare of the state is entrusted to you, put my proposal to the vote, and lay the question once more before the Athenians. If you hesitate, remember that in the presence of so many witnesses there can be no question of breaking the law, and that you will be the physician of the state at the critical moment. The first duty of the good magistrate is to do the very best

which he can for his country, or, at least, to do her no harm which he can avoid."

15. Such were the words of Nicias. Most of the Athenians who came forward to speak were in favour of war, and reluctant to rescind the vote which had been already passed, although a few took the other side. The most enthusiastic supporter of the expedition was Alcibiades the son of Cleinias; he was determined to oppose Nicias, who was always his political enemy and had just now spoken of him in disparaging terms; but the desire to command was even a stronger motive with him. He was hoping that he might be the conqueror of Sicily and Carthage; and that success would repair his private fortunes, and gain him money as well as glory. He had a great position among the citizens and was devoted to horse-racing and other pleasures which outran his means. And in the end his wild courses went far to ruin the Athenian state. For the people feared the extremes to which he carried his lawless self-indulgence, and the far-reaching purposes which animated him in all his actions. They thought that he was aiming at a tyranny and set themselves against him. And therefore, although his talents as a military commander were unrivalled, they entrusted the administration of the war to others, because they personally objected to his private life; and so they speedily shipwrecked the state. He now came forward and spoke as follows:

16. "I have a better right to command, men of Athens, than another; for as Nicias has attacked me, I must begin by praising myself; and I consider that I am worthy. Those doings of mine for which I am so much cried out against are an honour to myself and to my ancestors, and a solid advantage to my country. In consequence of the distinguished manner in which I represented the state

at Olympia, the other Hellenes formed an idea of our power which even exceeded the reality, although they had previously imagined that we were exhausted by war. I sent into the lists seven chariots, no other private man ever did the like; I was victor, and also won the second and fourth prize; and I ordered everything in a style worthy of my victory. The general sentiment honours such magnificence; and the energy which is shown by it creates an impression of power. At home, again, whenever I gain éclat by providing choruses or by the performance of some other public duty, although the citizens are naturally jealous of me, to strangers these acts of munificence are a new argument of our strength. There is some use in the folly of a man who at his own cost benefits not only himself, but the state. And where is the injustice, if I or any one who feels his own superiority to another refuses to be on a level with him? The unfortunate keep their misfortunes to themselves. We do not expect to be recognised by our acquaintance when we are down in the world; and on the same principle why should any one complain when treated with disdain by the more fortunate? He who would have proper respect shown to him should himself show it towards others. I know that men of this lofty spirit, and all who have been in any way illustrious, are hated while they are alive, by their equals especially, and in a lesser degree by others who have to do with them; but that they leave behind them to after-ages a reputation which leads even those who are not of their family to claim kindred with them, and that they are the glory of their country, which regards them, not as aliens or as evil-doers, but as her own children, of whose character she is proud. These are my own aspirations, and this is the reason why my private life is assailed; but let me ask you, whether in the management of public affairs any man surpasses me. Did I not, without involving you in any great danger or expense, combine the most powerful states of Peloponnesus against the Lacedaemonians, whom I compelled to stake at Mantinea all that they had upon the fortune of one day? And even to this hour, although they were victorious in the battle, they have hardly recovered courage.

17. "These were the achievements of my youth, and of what is supposed to be my monstrous folly; thus did I by winning words conciliate the Peloponnesian powers, and my heartiness made them believe in me and follow me. And now do not be afraid of me because I am young, but while I am in the flower of my days and Nicias enjoys the reputation of success, use the services of us both. Having determined to sail, do not change your minds under the impression that Sicily is a great power. For although the Sicilian cities are populous, their inhabitants are a mixed multitude, and they readily give up old forms of government and receive new ones from without. No one really feels that he has a city of his own; and so the individual is ill-provided with arms, and the country has no regular means of defence. A man looks only to what he can win from the common stock by arts of speech or by party violence; hoping, if he is overthrown, at any rate to carry off his prize and enjoy it elsewhere. They are a motley crew, who are never of one mind in counsel, and are incapable of any concert in action. Every man is for himself, and will readily come over to any one who makes an attractive offer; the more readily if, as report says, they are in a state of revolution. They boast of their hoplites, but, as has proved to be the case in all Hellenic states, the number of them is grossly exaggerated. Hellas has been singularly mistaken about her heavy infantry; and even in this war it was as much as she could do to collect enough of them. The obstacles

then which will meet us in Sicily, judging of them from the information which I have received, are not great; indeed, I have overrated them, for there will be many barbarians who, through fear of the Syracusans, will join us in attacking them. And at home there is nothing which, viewed rightly, need interfere with the expedition. Our forefathers had the same enemies whom we are now told that we are leaving behind us, and the Persian besides; but their strength lay in the greatness of their navy, and by that and that alone they gained their empire. Never were the Peloponnesians more hopeless of success than at the present moment; and let them be ever so confident, they can only invade us by land, which they will equally do whether we go to Sicily or not. But on the sea they cannot hurt us, for we shall leave behind us a navy equal to theirs.

18. "What reason can we give to ourselves for hesitation? What excuse can we make to our allies for denying them aid? We have sworn to them, and have no right to argue that they never assisted us. In seeking their alliance we did not intend that they should come and help us here, but that they should harass our enemies in Sicily, and prevent them from coming hither. Like all other imperial powers, we have acquired our dominion by our readiness to assist any one, whether barbarian or Hellene, who may have invoked our aid. If we are all to sit and do nothing, or to draw distinctions of race when our help is requested, we shall add little to our empire, and run a great risk of losing it altogether. For mankind do not await the attack of a superior power, they anticipate it. We cannot cut down an empire as we might a household; but having once gained our present position, we must keep a firm hold upon some, and contrive occasion against others; for if we are not rulers we shall be subjects. You cannot afford to regard inaction in

the same light as others might, unless you impose a corresponding restriction on your policy. Convinced then that we shall be most likely to increase our power here if we attack our enemies there, let us sail. We shall humble the pride of the Peloponnesians when they see that, scorning the delights of repose, we have attacked Sicily. By the help of our acquisitions there, we shall probably become masters of all Hellas; at any rate we shall injure the Syracusans, and at the same time benefit ourselves and our allies. Whether we succeed and remain or depart, in either case our navy will ensure our safety; for at sea we shall be more than a match for all Sicily. Nicias must not divert you from your purpose by preaching indolence, and by trying to set the young against the old; rather in your accustomed order, old and young taking counsel together, after the manner of your fathers who raised Athens to this height of greatness, strive to rise yet higher. Consider that youth and age have no power unless united; but that the lighter and the more exact and the middle sort of judgment, when duly tempered, are likely to be most efficient. The state, if at rest, like everything else will wear herself out by internal friction. Every pursuit which requires skill will bear the impress of decay, whereas by conflict fresh experience is always being gained, and the city learns to defend herself, not in theory, but in practice. My opinion in short is, that a state used to activity will quickly be ruined by the change to inaction; and that they of all men enjoy the greatest security who are truest to themselves and their institutions even when they are not the best."

19. Such were the words of Alcibiades. After hearing him and the Egestaeans and certain Leontine exiles who came forward and earnestly entreated assistance, reminding the Athenians of the oaths which they had sworn, the people were more than ever resolved upon

war. Nicias, seeing that his old argument would no longer deter them, but that he might possibly change their minds if he insisted on the magnitude of the force which would be required, came forward again and spoke as follows:

20. "Men of Athens, as I see that you are thoroughly determined to go to war, I accept the decision, and will advise you accordingly, trusting that the event will be such as we all wish. The cities which we are about to attack are, I am informed, powerful, and independent of one another; they are not inhabited by slaves, who would gladly pass out of a harder into an easier condition of life; and they are very unlikely to accept our rule in exchange for their present liberty. As regards numbers, although Sicily is but one island, it contains a great many Hellenic states. Not including Naxos and Catana (of which the inhabitants, as I hope, will be our allies because they are the kinsmen of the Leontines), there are seven other cities fully provided with means of warfare similar to our own, especially Selinus and Syracuse, the cities against which our expedition is particularly directed. For they have numerous hoplites, archers, and javelin-men, and they have many triremes which their large population will enable them to man; besides their private wealth, they have the treasures of the Selinuntian temples; and the Syracusans receive a tribute which has been paid them from time immemorial by certain barbarian tribes. Moreover, they have a numerous cavalry, and grow their own corn instead of importing it: in the two last respects they have a great advantage over us.

21. "Against such a power more is needed than an insignificant force of marines; if we mean to do justice to our design we must embark a multitude of infantry; neither must we allow ourselves to be kept within our lines by the numbers of their cavalry. For what if the

Sicilians in terror combine against us, and we make no friends except the Egestaeans who can furnish us with horsemen capable of opposing theirs? To be driven from the island or to send for reinforcements, because we were wanting in forethought at first, would be disgraceful. We must take a powerful armament with us from home, in the full knowledge that we are going to a distant land, and that the expedition will be of a kind very different from any which you have hitherto made among your subjects against some enemy in this part of the world, yourselves the allies of others. Here a friendly country is always near, and you can easily obtain supplies. There you will be dependent on a country which is entirely strange to you, and whence during the four winter months hardly even a message can be sent hither.

22. "I say, therefore, that we must take with us a large heavy-armed force both of Athenians and of allies, whether our own subjects or any Peloponnesians whom we can persuade or attract by pay to our service; also plenty of archers and javelin-men to act against the enemy's cavalry. Our naval superiority must be overwhelming, that we may not only be able to fight, but may have no difficulty in bringing in supplies. And there is the food carried from home, such as wheat and parched barley, which will have to be conveyed in merchant-vessels; we must also have bakers, drafted in a certain proportion from each mill, who will receive pay, but will be forced to serve, in order that, if we should be detained by a calm, the army may not want food; for it is not every city that will be able to receive so large a force as ours. We must make our preparations as complete as possible, and not be at the mercy of others; above all, we must take out with us as much money as we can; for as to the supplies of the Egestaeans which are said to be awaiting us, we had better assume that they are imaginary.

23. "Even supposing we leave Athens with a force of our own, not merely equal to that of the enemy, but in every way superior, except indeed as regards the number of hoplites which they can put into the field, for in that respect equality is impossible, still it will be no easy task to conquer Sicily, or indeed to preserve ourselves. You ought to consider that we are like men going to found a city in a land of strangers and enemies, who on the very day of their disembarkation must have command of the country; for if they meet with a disaster they will have no friends. And this is what I fear. We shall have much need of prudence; still more of good-fortune (and who can guarantee this to mortals?). Wherefore I would trust myself and the expedition as little as possible to accident, and would not sail until I had taken such precautions as will be likely to ensure our safety. This I conceive to be the course which is the most prudent for the whole state, and, for us who are sent upon the expedition, a security against danger. If any one thinks otherwise, to him I resign the command."

24. These were the words of Nicias. He meant either to deter the Athenians by bringing home to them the vastness of the undertaking, or to provide as far as he could for the safety of the expedition if he were compelled to proceed. The result disappointed him. Far from losing their enthusiasm at the disagreeable prospect, they were more determined than ever; they approved of his advice, and were confident that every chance of danger was now removed. All alike were seized with a passionate desire to sail, the elder among them convinced that they would achieve the conquest of Sicily, at any rate such an armament could suffer no disaster; the youth were longing to see with their own eyes the marvels of a distant land, and were confident of a safe return; the main body of the troops expected to receive

present pay, and to conquer a country which would be an inexhaustible mine of pay for the future. The enthusiasm of the majority was so overwhelming that, although some disapproved, they were afraid of being thought unpatriotic if they voted on the other side, and therefore held their peace. . . .

III

Meanwhile reports of the expedition were coming in to Syracuse from many quarters, but for a long time nobody gave credit to them. At length an assembly was held. Even then different opinions were expressed, some affirming and others denying that the expedition was coming. At last Hermocrates the son of Hermon, believing that he had certain information, came forward, and warned the Syracusans in the following words:

33. "I dare say that, like others, I shall not be believed when I tell you that the expedition is really coming; and I am well aware that those who are either the authors or reporters of tidings which seem incredible not only fail to convince others, but are thought fools for their pains. Yet, when the city is in danger, fear shall not stop my mouth; for I am convinced in my own mind that I have better information than anybody. The Athenians, wonder as you may, are coming against us with a great fleet and army; they profess to be assisting their Egestaean allies and to be restoring the Leontines. But the truth is that they covet Sicily, and especially our city. They think that, if they can conquer us, they will easily conquer the rest. They will soon be here, and you must consider how with your present resources you can make the most successful defence. You should not let them take you by surprise because you despise them, or neglect the whole matter because you will not believe that

they are coming at all. But to him who is not of this un-
believing temper I say: Do not be dismayed at their
audacity and power. They cannot do more harm to us
than we can do to them; the very greatness of their armament may be an advantage to us; it will have a good
effect on the other Sicilians, who will be alarmed, and
in their terror will be the more ready to assist us. Then,
again, if in the end we overpower them, or at any rate
drive them away baffled, for I have not the slightest fear
of their accomplishing their purpose, we shall have
achieved a noble triumph. And of this I have a good
hope. Rarely have great expeditions, whether Hellenic
or barbarian, when sent far from home, met with success.
They are not more numerous than the inhabitants and
their neighbours, who all combine through fear; and if
owing to scarcity of supplies in a foreign land they miscarry, although their ruin may be chiefly due to themselves, they confer glory on those whom they meant to
overthrow. The greatness of these very Athenians was
based on the utter and unexpected ruin of the Persians,
who were always supposed to have directed their expedition against Athens. And I think that such a destiny
may very likely be reserved for us.

34. "Let us take courage then, and put ourselves into
a state of defence; let us also send envoys to the Sicels,
and, while we make sure of our old allies, endeavour to
gain new ones. We will despatch envoys to the rest of
Sicily, and point out that the danger is common to all;
we will also send to the Italian cities in the hope that
they may either join us, or at any rate refuse to receive
the Athenians. And I think that we should send to the
Carthaginians; the idea of an Athenian attack is no novelty to them; they are always living in apprehension of
it. They will probably feel that if they leave us to our
fate, the trouble may reach themselves, and therefore

they may be inclined in some way or other, secretly, if not openly, to assist us. If willing to help, of all existing states they are the best able; for they have abundance of gold and silver, and these make war, like other things, go smoothly. Let us also send to the Lacedaemonians and Corinthians and entreat them to come to our aid speedily, and at the same time to revive the war in Hellas. I have a plan which in my judgment is the best suited to the present emergency, although it is the last which you in your habitual indolence will readily embrace. Let me tell you what it is. If all the Sicilian Greeks, or at least if we and as many as will join us, taking two months' provisions, would put out to sea with all our available ships and meet the Athenians at Tarentum and the promontory of Iapygia, thereby proving to them that before they fight for Sicily they must fight for the passage of the Ionian Sea, we should strike a panic into them. They would then reflect that at Tarentum (which receives us), we, the advanced guard of Sicily, are among friends, and go forth from a friendly country, and that the sea is a large place not easy to traverse with so great an armament as theirs. They would know that after a long voyage their ships will be unable to keep in line, and coming up slowly and few at a time will be at our mercy. On the other hand, if they lighten their vessels and meet us in a compact body with the swifter part of their fleet, they may have to use oars, and then we shall attack them when they are exhausted. Or if we prefer not to fight, we can retire again to Tarentum. Having come over with slender supplies and prepared for a naval engagement, they will not know what to do on these desolate coasts. If they remain we can blockade them; if they attempt to sail onwards they will cut themselves off from the rest of their armament, and will be discouraged; for they will be far from certain whether the cities of Italy and Sicily will receive them. In my opinion the anticipation of these difficulties will hamper them to such a degree, that they will never leave Corcyra. While they are holding consultations, and sending out spies to discover our number and exact position, they will find themselves driven into winter; or in dismay at the unexpected opposition, they may very likely break up the expedition; especially if, as I am informed, the most experienced of their generals has taken the command against his will, and would gladly make any considerable demonstration on our part an excuse for retreating. I am quite sure that rumour will exaggerate our strength. The minds of men are apt to be swayed by what they hear; and they are most afraid of those who commence an attack, or who at any rate show to the aggressor betimes that he will meet with resistance; for then they reflect that the risk is equally divided. And so it will be with the Athenians. They are now attacking us because they do not believe that we shall defend ourselves, and in this opinion they are justified by our refusal to join with the Lacedaemonians in putting them down. But, if they see us enterprising almost to rashness, they will be more dismayed at our unexpected resistance than at our real power. Take my advice; if possible, resolve on this bold step, but if not, adopt other measures of defence as quickly as possible. Remember each and all of you that the true contempt of an invader is shown by deeds of valour in the field, and that meanwhile the greatest service which you can render to the state is to act as if you were in the presence of danger, considering that safety depends on anxious preparation. The Athenians are coming; I am certain that they are already on the sea and will soon be here."

35. Thus spoke Hermocrates. Great was the contention which his words aroused among the Syracusan peo-

ple, some asserting that the Athenians would never come, and that he was not speaking truth, others asking, "And if they should come, what harm could they do to us nearly so great as we could do to them?" while others were quite contemptuous, and made a jest of the whole matter. A few only believed Hermocrates and realised the danger. At last Athenagoras, the popular leader, who had at that time the greatest influence with the multitude, came forward and spoke as follows:

36. "He is either a coward or a traitor who would not rejoice to hear that the Athenians are so mad as to come hither and deliver themselves into our hands. The audacity of the people who are spreading these alarms does not surprise me, but I do wonder at their folly if they cannot see that their motives are transparent. Having private reasons for being afraid, they want to strike terror into the whole city that they may hide themselves under the shadow of the common fear. And now, what is the meaning of these rumours? They do not grow of themselves; they have been got up by persons who are the troublers of our state. And you, if you are wise, will not measure probabilities by their reports, but by what we may assume to be the intentions of shrewd and experienced men such as I conceive the Athenians to be. They are not likely to leave behind them a power such as Peloponnesus. The war which they have already on their hands is far from settled, and will they go out of their way to bring upon themselves another as great? In my opinion they are only too glad that we are not attacking them, considering the number and power of our states.

37. "Even if the rumour of their coming should turn out to be true, I am sure that Sicily is more able than Peloponnesus to maintain a great war. The whole island is better supplied in every way, and our own city is herself far more than a match for the army which is said

to be threatening us; aye, and for another as great. I know that they will not bring cavalry with them, and will find none here, except the few horsemen which they may procure from Egesta. They cannot provide a force of hoplites equal to ours, for they have to cross the sea; and to come all this distance, if only with ships and with no troops or lading, would be work enough. I know too that an armament which is directed against so great a city as ours will require immense supplies. Nay, I venture to assert that if they come hither, having at their command another city close upon our border as large as Syracuse, and could there settle and carry on war against us from thence, they would still be destroyed to a man; how much more when the whole country will be their enemy (for Sicily will unite), and when they must pitch their camp the moment they are out of their ships, and will have nothing but their wretched huts and meagre supplies, being prevented by our cavalry from advancing far beyond their lines? Indeed I hardly think that they will effect a landing at all. So far superior, in my judgment, are our forces to theirs.

38. "The Athenians, I repeat, know all that I am telling you, and do not mean to throw away what they have got: I am pretty sure of that. But some of our people are fabricating reports which neither are, nor are ever likely to be, true. I know, and have always known, that by words like these, and yet more mischievous, if not by acts, they want to intimidate you, the Syracusan people, and make themselves chiefs of the state. And I am afraid that if they persevere they will succeed at last, and that we shall be delivered into their hands before we have had the sense to take precautions or to detect and punish them. This is the reason why our city is always in a state of unrest and disorganisation, fighting against herself

quite as much as against foreign enemies, and from time
to time subjected to tyrants and to narrow and wicked
oligarchies. If the people will only support me I shall
endeavour to prevent any such misfortunes happening
in our day. With you I shall use persuasion, but to these
conspirators I shall apply force; and I shall not wait
until they are detected in the act (for who can catch
them?), but I shall punish their intentions and the
mischief which they would do if they could. For the
thoughts of our enemies must be punished before they
have ripened into deeds. If a man does not strike first, he
will be the first struck. As to the rest of the oligarchical
party, I must expose them and have an eye on their designs; I must also instruct them; that, I think, will be the
way by which I can best deter them from their evil
courses. Come now, young men, and answer me a question which I have often asked myself. "What can you
want?" To hold office already? But the law forbids. And
the law was not intended to slight you had you been capable; it was passed because you were incapable. And
so you would rather not be on an equality with the
many? But when there is no real difference between
men, why should there be a privileged class?

39. "I shall be told that democracy is neither a wise
nor a just thing, and that those who have the money are
most likely to govern well. To which I answer, first of all,
that the people is the name of the whole, the oligarchy
of a part; secondly, that the rich are the best guardians
of the public purse, the wise the best counsellors, and
the many, when they have heard a matter discussed, the
best judges; and that each and all of these classes have
in a democracy equal privileges. Whereas an oligarchy,
while giving the people the full share of danger, not
merely takes too much of the good things, but absolutely

monopolises them. And this is what the powerful among you and the young would like to have, and what in a great city they will never obtain.

40. "O most senseless of men, for such you are indeed if you do not see the mischief of your own schemes; never in all my experience have I known such blindness among Hellenes, or such wickedness if you have your eyes open to what you are doing. Yet even now learn if you are stupid, repent if you are guilty; and let your aim be the welfare of the whole country. Remember that the good among you will have an equal or larger share in the government of it than the people; while if you want more you will most likely lose all. Away with these reports; we know all about them, and are determined to suppress them. Let the Athenians come, and Syracuse will repel her enemies in a manner worthy of herself; we have generals who will look to the matter. But if, as I suspect, none of your tales are true, the state is not going to be deceived, and will not in a moment of panic admit you to power, or impose upon her own neck the yoke of slavery. She will take the matter into her own hands, and when she gives judgment will reckon words to be equally criminal with actions. She will not be talked out of her liberty by you, but will do her utmost to preserve it; she will be on her guard, and will put you down with a strong hand."

41. Thus spoke Athenagoras. Whereupon one of the generals rose, and suffering no one else to come forward, closed the discussion himself in the following words, "There is little wisdom in exchanging abuse or in sitting by and listening to it; let us rather, in view of the reported danger, see how the whole city and every man in it may take measures for resisting the invaders worthily. Why should not the city be richly furnished with arms, horses, and all the pride and pomp of war; where

is the harm even if they should not be wanted? We, who are generals, will take in hand all these matters and examine into them ourselves; and we will send messengers to the neighbouring cities in order to obtain information, and for any other purpose which may be necessary. Some precautions we have taken already, and whatever occurs to us we will communicate to you." When the general had thus spoken, the assembly dispersed.

IV

Before he attacked Epipolae, Demosthenes wished to try what could be effected with engines against the counter-wall. But the engines which he brought up were burnt by the enemy, who fought from the wall, and, after making assaults at several points, the Athenian forces were repulsed. He now determined to delay no longer, and persuaded Nicias and his colleagues to carry out the plan of attacking Epipolae. To approach during the daytime and ascend the heights undetected appeared to be impossible; so he resolved to attack by night. He ordered provisions for five days, and took with him all the masons and carpenters in the army; also a supply of arrows and of the various implements which would be required for siege-works if he were victorious. About the first watch he, Eurymedon, and Menander led out the whole army and marched towards Epipolae. Nicias was left in the Athenian fortifications. Reaching Epipolae at the Euryelus, where their first army had originally ascended, and advancing undiscovered by the garrison to the fort which the Syracusans had there erected, they took it and killed some of the guards. But the greater number made good their escape and carried the news to the three fortified camps, one of the Syracusans, one of the other Sicilians, and one of the allies, which had been formed on Epipolae; they also gave the alarm to the 600 who were an advanced guard stationed on this part of Epipolae. They hastened to the rescue, but Demosthenes and the Athenians came upon them and, in spite of a vigorous resistance, drove them back. The Athenians immediately pressed forward; they were determined not to lose a moment or to slacken their onset until they had accomplished their purpose. Others took the first part of the Syracusan counter-wall and began to drag off the battlements; the guards ran away. Meanwhile the Syracusans, the allies, and Gylippus with his own troops, were hurrying from the outworks. The boldness of this night attack quite amazed them. They had not recovered from their terror when they met the Athenians, who were at first too strong for them and drove them back. But now the conquerors, in the confidence of victory, began to advance in less order; they wanted to force their way as quickly as they could through all that part of the enemy which had not yet fought, and they were afraid that if they relaxed their efforts the Syracusans might rally. The Boeotians were the first to make a stand: they attacked the Athenians, turned, and put them to flight.

44. The whole army now fell into utter disorder, and the perplexity was so great that from neither side could the particulars of the conflict be exactly ascertained. In the daytime the combatants see more clearly; though even then only what is going on immediately around them, and that imperfectly—nothing of the battle as a whole. But in a night engagement, like this in which two great armies fought—the only one of the kind which occurred during the war—who could be certain of anything? The moon was bright, and they saw before them, as men naturally would in the moonlight, the figures of one another, but were unable to distinguish with certainty who was friend or foe. Large bodies of heavy-

armed troops, both Athenian and Syracusan, were moving about in a narrow space; of the Athenians some were already worsted, while others, still unconquered, were carrying on the original movement. A great part of their army had not yet engaged, but either had just mounted the heights, or were making the ascent; and no one knew which way to go. For in front they were defeated already; there was nothing but confusion, and all distinction between the two armies was lost by reason of the noise. The victorious Syracusans and their allies, who had no other means of communication in the darkness, cheered on their comrades with loud cries as they received the onset of their assailants. The Athenians were looking about for each other; and every one who met them, though he might be a friend who had turned and fled, they imagined to be an enemy. They kept constantly asking the watchword (for there was no other mode of knowing one another), and thus they not only caused great confusion among themselves by all asking at once, but revealed the word to the enemy. The watchword of the Syracusans was not so liable to be discovered, because being victorious they kept together and were more easily recognised. So that when they were encountered by a superior number of the enemy they, knowing the Athenian watchword, escaped; but the Athenians in a like case, failing to answer the challenge, were killed. Most disastrous of all were the mistakes caused by the sound of the paean, which, the same being heard in both armies, was a great source of perplexity. For there were in the battle Argives, Corcyraeans, and other Dorian allies of the Athenians, and when they raised the paean they inspired as much alarm as the enemy themselves; so that in many parts of the army, when the confusion had once begun, not only did friends terrify friends and citizens their fellow-citizens, but they attacked one another, and were with difficulty disentangled. The greater number of those who were pursued and killed perished by throwing themselves from the cliffs; for the descent from Epipolae is by a narrow path. The fugitives who reached the level ground, especially those who had served in the former army and knew the neighbourhood, mostly escaped to the camp. But of the newly arrived many missed their way, and, wandering about until daybreak, were then cut off by the Syracusan cavalry who were scouring the country.

45. On the following day the Syracusans erected two trophies, one on Epipolae at the summit of the ascent, the other at the spot where the Boeotians made the first stand. The Athenians received their dead under a truce. A considerable number of them and of their allies had fallen; there were however more arms taken than there were bodies of the slain; for those who were compelled to leap from the heights, whether they perished or not, had thrown away their shields.

46. The confidence of the Syracusans was restored by their unexpected success, and they sent Sicanus with fifteen ships to Agrigentum, then in a state of revolution, that he might win over the place if he could. Gylippus had gone off again by land to collect a new army in the other parts of Sicily, hoping after the victory of Epipolae to carry the Athenian fortifications by storm.

47. Meanwhile the Athenian generals, troubled by their recent defeat and the utter discouragement which prevailed in the army, held a council of war. They saw that their attempts all failed, and that the soldiers were weary of remaining. For they were distressed by sickness, proceeding from two causes: the season of the year was that in which men are most liable to disease; and the place in which they were encamped was damp and unhealthy. And they felt that the situation was in every

way hopeless. Demosthenes gave his voice against remaining; he said that the decisive attack upon Epipolae had failed, and, in accordance with his original intention, he should vote for immediate departure, while the voyage was possible, and while with the help of the ships which had recently joined them they had the upper hand at any rate by sea. It was more expedient for the city that they should make war upon the Peloponnesians, who were raising a fort in Attica, than against the Syracusans, whom they could now scarcely hope to conquer; and there was no sense in carrying on the siege at a vast expense and with no result. This was the opinion of Demosthenes.

48. Nicias in his own mind took the same gloomy view of their affairs; but he did not wish openly to confess their weakness, or by a public vote given in a numerous assembly to let their intention reach the enemy's ears, and so to lose the advantage of departing secretly whenever they might choose to go. He had moreover still some reason to suppose that the Syracusans, of whose condition he was better informed than the other generals, were likely to be worse off than themselves if they would only persevere in the siege; they would be worn out by the exhaustion of their resources; and now the Athenians with their additional ships had much greater command of the sea. There was a party in Syracuse itself which wanted to surrender the city to the Athenians, and they kept sending messages to Nicias and advising him not to depart. Having this information he was still wavering and considering, and had not made up his mind. But in addressing the council he positively refused to withdraw the army; he knew, he said, that the Athenian people would not forgive their departure if they left without an order from home. The men upon whose votes their fate would depend would not, like

themselves, have seen with their own eyes the state of affairs; they would only have heard the criticisms of others, and would be convinced by any accusations which a clever speaker might bring forward. Indeed many or most of the very soldiers who were now crying out that their case was desperate would raise the opposite cry when they reached home, and would say that the generals were traitors, and had been bribed to depart; and therefore he, knowing the tempers of the Athenians, would for his own part rather take his chance and fall, if he must, alone by the hands of the enemy, than die unjustly on a dishonourable charge at the hands of the Athenians. And, after all, the Syracusans were in a condition worse than their own; for they had to maintain mercenary troops; they were spending money on garrisons, and had now kept up a large navy for a whole year; already in great difficulties, they would soon be in greater; they had expended 2,000 talents, and were heavily in debt; the whole of their large army had to be fed, and if there were any lack of provisions their affairs would be ruined. For they depended on mercenaries, who, unlike the Athenian allies, were under no compulsion to serve. Therefore he said they ought to persevere in the siege, and not go away disheartened by the greatness of the expense, for they were far richer than the enemy.

49. Nicias spoke thus decidedly because he knew exactly how matters stood in Syracuse; he was aware of their want of money, and of the secret existence of that party within the walls which wished well to the Athenians, and was continually sending word to him not to depart; and the confidence in his navy, if not in his army, which now possessed him was greater than ever. But Demosthenes would not hear for an instant of persisting in the siege; if, he said, the army must remain and ought

not to be removed without a vote of the assembly, then they should retire to Thapsus or Catana, whence they might overrun the whole country with their land-forces, maintaining themselves at the expense of the enemy and doing him great damage. They would thus fight their battles, not cooped up in the harbour, which gave an advantage to the enemy, but in the open sea, where their skill would be available and their charges and retreats would not be circumscribed by the narrow space which now hampered their movements whenever they had to put in or out. In a word, he wholly disapproved of the Athenians continuing in their present position; they should with all speed break up the siege and be gone. Eurymedon took the same side. Still Nicias resisted; there was delay and hesitation, and a suspicion that he might have some ground which they did not know for his unwillingess to yield. And so the Athenians stayed on where they were.

50. Meanwhile Gylippus and Sicanus returned to Syracuse. Sicanus had not succeeded in his design upon Agrigentum; for 'while he was at Gela on his way the party inclined to friendship with the Syracusans had been driven out. Gylippus brought back a large army, together with the hoplites who had been sent in merchant-vessels from Peloponnesus in the spring, and had come by way of Libya to Selinus. They had been driven to Libya by stress of weather, and the Cyrenaeans had given them two triremes and pilots. On their voyage they had made common cause with the Evesperitae, who were besieged by the Libyans. After defeating the Libyans they sailed on to Neapolis, a Carthaginian trading-port which is the nearest point to Sicily, the passage taking two days and a night only; thence they crossed and came to Selinus. On their arrival, the Syracusans immediately prepared to renew their attack upon the Athe-

nians, both by land and sea. And the Athenian generals, seeing that their enemy had been reinforced by a new army, and that their own affairs, instead of improving, were daily growing worse in every respect, and being especially troubled by the sickness of their troops, repented that they had not gone before. Even Nicias now no longer objected, but only made the condition that there should be no open voting. So, maintaining such secrecy as they could, they gave orders for the departure of the expedition; the men were to prepare themselves against a given signal. The preparations were made and they were on the point of sailing, when the moon, being just then at the full, was eclipsed.[1] The mass of the army was greatly moved, and called upon the generals to remain. Nicias himself, who was too much under the influence of divination and omens, refused even to discuss the question of their removal until they had remained thrice nine days, as the soothsayers prescribed. This was the reason why the departure of the Athenians was finally delayed.

51. And now the Syracusans, having heard what had happened, were more eager than ever to prosecute the war to the end; they saw in the intention of the Athenians to depart a confession that they were no longer superior to themselves, either by sea or land; and they did not want them to settle down in some other part of Sicily where they would be more difficult to manage, but sought to compel them forthwith to fight at sea under the disadvantages of their present position. So they manned their ships and exercised for as many days as they thought sufficient. When the time came they began by attacking the Athenian lines. A small number both of the hoplites and of the cavalry came out of some of the gates to meet them; they cut off however a portion of

[1] *August 27, 413 B.C.*

the hoplites, and, putting the whole body to flight, drove them within their walls. The entrance was narrow, and the Athenians lost seventy horses and a few infantry.

52. The Syracusan army then retired. On the next day their ships, in number seventy-six, sailed forth, and at the same time their land-forces marched against the walls. The Athenians on their side put out with eighty-six ships; and the two fleets met and fought. Eurymedon, who commanded the right wing of the Athenians, hoping to surround the enemy, extended his line too far towards the land, and was defeated by the Syracusans, who, after overcoming the Athenian centre, shut him up in the inner bay of the harbour. There he was slain, and the vessels which were under his command and had followed him were destroyed. The Syracusans now pursued and began to drive ashore the rest of the Athenian fleet.

53. Gylippus, observing the discomfiture of the enemy, who were being defeated and driven to land beyond their own palisade and the lines of their camp, hastened with a part of his army to the causeway which ran along the harbour, intending to kill all who landed, and to assist the Syracusans in capturing the ships, which could be more easily towed away if the shore was in the hands of their friends. The Tyrrhenians, who guarded this part of the Athenian lines, seeing Gylippus and his forces advance in disorder, rushed out, and attacking the foremost put them to flight, and drove them into the marsh called Lysimeleia. But soon the Syracusans and their allies came up in greater numbers. The Athenians in fear for their ships advanced to the support of the Tyrrhenians, and joined in the engagement; the Syracusans were overcome and pursued, and a few of their heavy-armed slain. Most of the Athenian ships were saved and brought back to the Athenian station. Still the Syra-

cusans and their allies took eighteen, and killed the whole of their crews. Then, hoping to burn the remainder of the fleet, they procured an old merchant-vessel, which they filled with faggots and brands; these they lighted, and as the wind blew right upon the enemy they let the ship go. The Athenians, alarmed for the safety of their fleet, contrived means by which they extinguished the flames, and succeeded in keeping the fire-ship at a distance. Thus the danger was averted.

54. The Syracusans now raised a trophy of their naval victory, and another marking their interception of the hoplites on the higher ground close to the wall at the place where they took the horses. The Athenians raised a trophy of the victory over the land-forces whom the Tyrrhenians drove into the marsh, and of that which they had themselves gained with the rest of the army.

55. The Syracusans, who up to this time had been afraid of the reinforcements of Demosthenes, had now gained a brilliant success by sea as well as by land; the Athenians were in utter despair. Great was their surprise at the result, and still greater their regret that they had ever come. The Sicilian were the only cities which they had encountered similar in character to their own, enjoying the same democratic institutions[1] and strong in ships, cavalry, and population. They were not able by holding out the prospect of a change of government to introduce an element of discord among them which might have gained them over, nor could they master them by a decided superiority of force. They had failed at almost every point, and were already in great straits, when the defeat at sea, which they could not have thought possible, reduced their fortunes to a still lower ebb.

[1] Athens usually tried to overthrow oligarchies and establish democracies in other cities.

56. The Syracusans at once sailed round the shore of the harbour without fear, and determined to close the mouth, that the Athenians might not be able, even if they wanted, to sail out by stealth. For they were now striving, no longer to achieve their own deliverance, but to cut off the escape of the Athenians; they considered their position already far superior, as indeed it was, and they hoped that if they could conquer the Athenians and their allies by sea and land, their success would be glorious in the eyes of all the Hellenes, who would at once be set free, some from slavery, others from fear. For the Athenians, having lost so much of their power, would never be able to face the enemies who would rise up against them. And the glory of the deliverance would be ascribed to the Syracusans, who would be honoured by all living men and all future ages. The conflict was still further ennobled by the thought that they were now conquering, not only the Athenians, but a host of their allies. And they themselves were not alone, but many had come to their support; they were the leaders of a war in which Corinth and Lacedaemon were their partners; they had offered their own city to bear the brunt of the encounter, and they had made an immense advance in naval power. More nations met at Syracuse than ever gathered around any single city, although not so many as the whole number of nations enrolled in this war under the Athenians and Lacedaemonians.

57. I will now enumerate the various peoples who came to Sicily as friends or enemies, to share either in the conquest or in the defence of the country, and who fought before Syracuse, choosing their side, not so much from a sense of right or from obligations of kinship, as from the accident of compulsion or their own interest.

The Athenians themselves, who were Ionians, went of their own free will against the Syracusans, who were

Dorians; they were followed by the Lemnians and Imbrians, and the then inhabitants of Aegina, and by the Hestiaeans dwelling at Hestiaea in Euboea: all these were their own colonists, speaking the same language with them, and retaining the same institutions.

Of the rest who joined in the expedition, some were subjects, others independent allies, some again mercenaries. Of the subjects and tributaries, the Eretrians, Chalcidians, Styreans, and Carystians came from Euboea; the Ceans, Andrians, and Tenians from the islands; the Milesians, Samians, and Chians from Ionia. Of these however the Chians were independent, and instead of paying tribute, provided ships. All or nearly all were Ionians and descendants of the Athenians, with the exception of the Carystians, who are Dryopes. They were subjects and constrained to follow, but still they were Ionians fighting against Dorians. There were also Aeolians, namely the Methymnaeans, who furnished ships but were not tributaries, and the Tenedians and Aenians, who paid tribute. These Aeolians were compelled to fight against their Aeolian founders, the Boeotians, who formed part of the Syracusan army. The Plataeans were the only Boeotians opposed to Boeotians; an antagonism which was natural, for they hated one another. The Rhodians and Cytherians were both Dorians; the Cytherians, although Lacedaemonian colonists, bore arms in the Athenian cause against the Lacedaemonians who came with Gylippus; and the Rhodians, though by descent Argive, were compelled to fight against the Syracusans, who were Dorians, and against the Geloans, who were actually their own colony, and were taking part with Syracuse. Of the islanders around Peloponnesus, the Cephallenians and Zacynthians were independent; still, being islanders, they followed under a certain degree of constraint; for the Athenians were masters of the sea. The Corcyraeans, who were not only Dorians but actually Corinthians, were serving against Corinthians and Syracusans, although they were the colonists of the one and the kinsmen of the other; they followed under a decent appearance of compulsion, but gladly, because they hated the Corinthians. The Messenians too, as the inhabitants of Naupactus were now called, including the garrison of Pylos, which was at that time held by the Athenians, were taken by them to the war. A few Megarians, having the misfortune to be exiles, were thus induced to fight against the Selinuntians, who were Megarians like themselves.

The service of the remaining allies was voluntary. The Argives, not so much because they were allies of Athens, as because they hated the Lacedaemonians, and individually for the sake of their own immediate advantage, followed the Athenians, who were Ionians, being themselves Dorians, to fight against Dorians. The Mantineans and other Arcadians were mercenaries accustomed to attack any enemy who from time to time might be pointed out to them, and were now ready, if they were paid, to regard the Arcadians, who were in the service of the Corinthians, as their enemies. The Cretans and Aetolians also served for hire; the Cretans, who had once joined with the Rhodians in the foundation of Gela, came with reluctance; nevertheless for pay they consented to fight against their own colonists. Some of the Acarnanians came to aid their Athenian allies, partly from motives of gain, but much more out of regard for Demosthenes and good-will to Athens. All these dwelt on the eastern side of the Ionian Gulf.

Of the Hellenes in Italy, the Thurians and Metapontians, compelled by the necessities of a revolutionary period, joined in the enterprise; of the Hellenes in Sicily, the Naxians and Catanaeans. Of barbarians, there were the Egestaeans, who invited the expedition, and the greater part of the Sicels, and, besides native Sicilians, certain Tyrrhenians who had a quarrel with the Syracusans; also Iapygians, who served for hire. These were the nations who followed the Athenians.

58. The Syracusans, on the other hand, were assisted by the Camarinaeans, who were their nearest neighbours, and by the Geloans, who dwelt next beyond them; and then (for the Agrigentines, who came next, were neutral) by the still more distant Selinuntians. All these inhabited the region of Sicily which lies towards Libya. On the side looking towards the Tyrrhenian Gulf the Himeraeans, the only Hellenic people in those parts, were also their only allies. These were the Hellenic peoples in Sicily who fought on the side of the Syracusans; they were Dorians and independent. As for the barbarians, they had only such of the Sicels as had not gone over to the Athenians.

Of Hellenes who were not inhabitants of Sicily, the Lacedaemonians provided a Spartan general; the Lacedaemonian forces were all Neodamodes and Helots. (The meaning of the word Neodamode is freedman.) The Corinthians were the only power which furnished both sea and land forces. Their Leucadian and Ambraciot kinsmen accompanied them; from Arcadia came mercenaries sent by Corinth; there were also Sicyonians who served under compulsion; and of the peoples beyond the Peloponnese, the Boeotians. This external aid however was small compared with the numerous troops of all kinds which the Sicilians themselves supplied; for they dwelt in great cities, and had collected many ships and horses and hoplites, besides a vast multitude of other troops. And again, the proportion furnished by the Syracusans themselves was greater than that of all the rest put together, on account of the size of the city and the magnitude of their own danger.

59. Such were the allies who were assembled on both sides. At that time they were all on the spot, and nothing whatever came afterwards to either army.

The Syracusans and the allies naturally thought that the struggle would be brought to a glorious end if, after having defeated the Athenian fleet, they took captive the whole of their great armament, and did not allow them to escape either by sea or land. So they at once began to close the mouth of the Great Harbour, which was about a mile wide, by means of triremes, merchant-vessels, and small boats, placed broadside, which they moored there. They also made every preparation for a naval engagement, should the Athenians be willing to hazard another; and all their thoughts were on a grand scale.

60. The Athenians, seeing the closing of the harbour and inferring the intentions of the enemy, proceeded to hold a council. The generals and officers met and considered the difficulties of their position. The most pressing was the want of food. For they had already sent to Catana, when they intended to depart, and stopped the supplies; and they could get no more unless they recovered the command of the sea. They resolved therefore to quit their lines on the higher ground and to cut off by a cross-wall a space close to their ships, no greater than was absolutely required for their baggage and for their sick; after leaving a guard there they meant to put on board every other man, and to launch all their ships, whether fit for service or not; they would then fight a decisive battle, and, if they conquered, go to Catana; but if not, they would burn their ships, and retreat by land in good order, taking the nearest way to some friendly country, barbarian or Hellenic. This design they

proceeded to execute, and withdrawing quietly from the upper walls, manned their whole fleet, compelling every man of any age at all suitable for service to embark. The entire number of the ships which they manned was about 110. They put on board numerous archers and javelin-men, Acarnanians, and other foreigners, and made such preparations for action as the nature of the plan imposed upon them by their necessities allowed. When all was nearly ready, Nicias, perceiving that the soldiers were depressed by their severe defeat at sea, which was so new an experience to them, while at the same time the want of provisions made them impatient to risk a battle with the least possible delay, called his men together, and before they engaged exhorted them as follows:

61. "Soldiers of Athens and of our allies, we have all the same interest in the coming struggle; every one of us as well as of our enemies will now have to fight for his life and for his country, and if only we can win in the impending sea-fight, every one may see his native city and his own home once more. But we must not be faint-hearted, nor behave as if we were mere novices in the art of war, who when defeated in their first battle are full of cowardly apprehensions and continually retain the impress of their disaster. You, Athenians, have had great military experience; and you, allies, are always fighting at our side. Remember the sudden turns of war; let your hope be that fortune herself may yet come over to us; and prepare to retrieve your defeat in a manner worthy of the greatness of your own army which you see before you.

62. "We have consulted the pilots about any improvements which seemed likely to avail against the crowding of ships in the narrow harbour, as well as against the troops on the enemy's decks, which in previous engage-

ments did us so much harm, and we have adopted them as far as we had the means. Many archers and javelin-men will embark, and a great number of other troops, whom if we were going to fight in the open sea we should not employ because they increase the weight of the ships, and therefore impede our skill; but here, where we are obliged to fight a land-battle on ship-board, they will be useful. We have thought of all the changes which are necessary in the construction of our ships, and in order to counteract the thickness of the beams on the enemy's prows, for this did us more mis-chief than anything else, we have provided iron grapnels, which will prevent the ship striking us from retreating if the marines are quick and do their duty. For, as I tell you, we are positively driven to fight a land-battle on ship-board, and our best plan is neither to back water ourselves nor to allow the enemy to back water after we have once closed with him. Recollect that the shore, ex-cept so far as our land-forces extend, is in their hands.

63. "Knowing all this, you must fight to the last with all your strength, and not be driven ashore. When ship strikes ship refuse to separate until you have swept the enemy's heavy-armed from their decks. I am speaking to the hoplites rather than to the sailors; for this is the special duty of the men on deck. We may still reckon on the superiority of our infantry. The sailors I would ex-hort, nay I would implore them, not to be paralysed by their disasters; for they will find the arrangements on deck improved, and the numbers of the fleet increased. Some among you have long been deemed Athenians, though they are not; and to them I say: Consider how precious is that privilege, and how worthy to be de-fended. You were admired in Hellas because you spoke our language and adopted our manners, and you shared equally with ourselves in the substantial advantages of

our empire, while you gained even more than we by the dread which you inspired in subject-states and in your security against injustice. You alone have been free partners in that empire; you ought not to betray it now. And so, despising the Corinthians whom you have beaten again and again, and the Sicilians who never dared to withstand us when our fleet was in its prime, repel your enemies, and show that your skill even amid weakness and disaster is superior to the strength of another in the hour of his success.

64. "Let me appeal once more to you who are Athenians, and remind you that there are no more ships like these in the dockyards of the Piraeus, and that you have no more recruits fit for service. In any event but victory your enemies here will instantly sail against Athens, while our countrymen at home, who are but a remnant, will be unable to defend themselves against the attacks of their former foes reinforced by the new invaders. You who are in Sicily will instantly fall into the hands of the Syracusans (and you know how you meant to deal with them), and your friends at Athens into the hands of the Lacedaemonians. In this one struggle you have to fight for yourselves and them. Stand firm therefore now, if ever, and remember one and all of you who are embarking that you are both the fleet and army of your country, and that on you hangs the whole state and the great name of Athens: for her sake if any man exceed another in skill or courage let him display them now; he will never have a better opportunity of doing good to himself and saving his country."

65. Nicias, as soon as he had done speaking, gave orders to man the ships. Gylippus and the Syracusans could see clearly enough from the preparations which the Athenians were making that they were going to fight. But they had also previous notice, and had been

told of the iron grapnels; and they took precautions against this as against all the other devices of the Athenians. They covered the prows of their vessels with hides, extending a good way along the upper part of their sides, so that the grapnels might slip and find no hold. When all was ready, Gylippus and the other generals exhorted their men in the following words:

66. "That our recent actions have been glorious, and that in the coming conflict we shall be fighting for a glorious prize, most of you, Syracusans and allies, seem to be aware: what else would have inspired you with so much energy? But if any one is not so quick in apprehending these things as he ought to be, he shall hear of them from me. The Athenians came hither intending to enslave first of all Sicily, and then, if they succeeded, Peloponnesus and the rest of Hellas, they having already the largest dominion of any Hellenic power, past or present. But you set mankind the example of withstanding that invincible navy; which you have now defeated in several engagements at sea, and which you will probably defeat in this. For when men are crippled in what they assume to be their strength, any vestige of self-respect is more completely lost than if they had never believed in themselves at all. When once their pride has had a fall they throw away the power of resistance which they might still exert. And this we may assume to be the condition of the Athenians.

67. "Far otherwise is it with us. The natural courage, which even in the days of our inexperience dared to risk all, is now better assured, and when we go on to reflect that he is the strongest who has overcome the strongest, the hopes of every one are redoubled. And in all enterprises the highest hopes infuse the greatest courage. Their imitation of our modes of fighting will be useless to them. To us they come naturally, and we shall readily

adapt ourselves to any arrangements of ours which they have borrowed. But to them the employment of troops on deck is a novelty; they will be encumbered with crowds of hoplites and of javelin-men, Acarnanians and others, who are mere awkward landsmen put into a ship, and will not even know how to discharge their darts when they are required to keep their places. Will they not imperil the ships? And their own movements will be so unnatural to them that they will all fall into utter confusion. The greater number of the enemy's ships will be the reverse of an advantage to him, should any of you fear your inequality in that respect; for a large fleet confined in a small space will be hampered in action and far more likely to suffer from our devices. And I would have you know what I believe on the best authority to be the simple truth. Their misfortunes paralyse them, and they are driven to despair at finding themselves helpless. They have grown reckless, and have no confidence in their own plans. They will take their chance as best they can, and either force a way out to sea, or in the last resort retreat by land; for they know that they cannot in any case be worse off than they are.

68. "Against such disorder, and against hateful enemies whose good-fortune has run away from them to us, let us advance with fury. We should remember in the first place that men are doing a most lawful act when they take vengeance upon an enemy and an aggressor, and that they have a right to satiate their heart's animosity; secondly, that this vengeance, which is proverbially the sweetest of all things, will soon be within our grasp. I need not tell you that they are our enemies, and our worst enemies. They came against our land that they might enslave us, and if they had succeeded they would have inflicted the greatest sufferings on our men, and the worst indignities upon our wives and children,

and would have stamped a name of dishonour upon our whole city. Wherefore let no one's heart be softened towards them. Do not congratulate yourselves at the mere prospect of getting safely rid of them. Even if they conquer they can only depart. But supposing that we obtain, as we most likely shall, the fulness of our desires, in the punishment of the Athenians and in the confirmation to Sicily of the liberties which she now enjoys, how glorious will be our prize! Seldom are men exposed to hazards in which they lose little if they fail, and win all if they succeed."

69. When Gylippus and the other Syracusan generals had, like Nicias, encouraged their troops, perceiving the Athenians to be manning their ships, they presently did the same. Nicias, overwhelmed by the situation, and seeing how great and how near the peril was (for the ships were on the very point of rowing out), feeling too, as men do on the eve of a great struggle, that all which he had done was nothing, and that he had not said half enough, again addressed the captains, and calling each of them by his father's name, and his own name, and the name of his tribe, he entreated those who had made any reputation for themselves not to be false to it, and those whose ancestors were eminent not to tarnish their hereditary fame. He reminded them that they were the inhabitants of the freest country in the world, and how in Athens there was no interference with the daily life of any man. He spoke to them of their wives and children and their fathers' Gods, as men will at such a time; for then they do not care whether their commonplace phrases seem to be out of date or not, but loudly reiterate the old appeals, believing that they may be of some service at the awful moment. When he thought that he had exhorted them, not enough, but as much as the scanty time allowed, he retired, and led the land-

forces to the shore, extending the line as far as he could, so that they might be of the greatest use in encouraging the combatants on board ship. Demosthenes, Menander, and Euthydemus, who had gone on board the Athenian fleet to take the command, now quitted their own station, and proceeded straight to the closed mouth of the harbour, intending to force their way to the open sea where a passage was still left.

70. The Syracusans and their allies had already put out with nearly the same number of ships as before. A detachment of them guarded the entrance of the harbour; the remainder were disposed all round it in such a manner that they might fall on the Athenians from every side at once, and that their land-forces might at the same time be able to co-operate wherever the ships retreated to the shore. Sicanus and Agatharchus commanded the Syracusan fleet, each of them a wing; Pythen and the Corinthians occupied the centre. When the Athenians approached the closed mouth of the harbour the violence of their onset overpowered the ships which were stationed there; they then attempted to loosen the fastenings. Whereupon from all sides the Syracusans and their allies came bearing down upon them, and the conflict was no longer confined to the entrance, but extended throughout the harbour. No previous engagement had been so fierce and obstinate. Great was the eagerness with which the rowers on both sides rushed upon their enemies whenever the word of command was given; and keen was the contest between the pilots as they manoeuvred one against another. The marines too were full of anxiety that, when ship struck ship, the service on deck should not fall short of the rest; every one in the place assigned to him was eager to be foremost among his fellows. Many vessels meeting—and never did so many fight in so small a space, for the two

fleets together amounted to nearly 200—they were seldom able to strike in the regular manner, because they had no opportunity of first retiring or breaking the line; they generally fouled one another as ship dashed against ship in the hurry of flight or pursuit. All the time that another vessel was bearing down, the men on deck poured showers of javelins and arrows and stones upon the enemy; and when the two closed, the marines fought hand to hand, and endeavoured to board. In many places, owing to the want of room, they who had struck another found that they were struck themselves; often two or even more vessels were unavoidably entangled about one, and the pilots had to make plans of attack and defence, not against one adversary only, but against several coming from different sides. The crash of so many ships dashing against one another took away the wits of the sailors, and made it impossible to hear the boatswains, whose voices in both fleets rose high, as they gave directions to the rowers, or cheered them on in the excitement of the struggle. On the Athenian side they were shouting to their men that they must force a passage and seize the opportunity now or never of returning in safety to their native land. To the Syracusans and their allies was represented the glory of preventing the escape of their enemies, and of a victory by which every man would exalt the honour of his own city. The commanders too, when they saw any ship backing water without necessity, would call the captain by his name, and ask, of the Athenians, whether they were retreating because they expected to be more at home upon the land of their bitterest foes than upon that sea which had been their own so long; on the Syracusan side, whether, when they knew perfectly well that the Athenians were only eager to find some means of flight, they would themselves fly from the fugitives.

71. While the naval engagement hung in the balance the two armies on shore had great trial and conflict of mind. The Sicilian soldier was animated by the hope of increasing the glory which he had already won, while the invader was tormented by the fear that his fortunes might sink lower still. The last chance of the Athenians lay in their ships, and their anxiety was dreadful. The fortune of the battle varied; and it was not possible that the spectators on the shore should all receive the same impression of it. Being quite close and having different points of view, they would some of them see their own ships victorious; their courage would then revive, and they would earnestly call upon the gods not to take from them their hope of deliverance. But others, who saw their ships worsted, cried and shrieked aloud, and were by the sight alone more utterly unnerved than the defeated combatants themselves. Others again, who had fixed their gaze on some part of the struggle which was undecided, were in a state of excitement still more terrible; they kept swaying their bodies to and fro in an agony of hope and fear as the stubborn conflict went on and on; for at every instant they were all but saved or all but lost. And while the strife hung in the balance you might hear in the Athenian army at once lamentation, shouting, cries of victory or defeat, and all the various sounds which are wrung from a great host in extremity of danger. Not less agonising were the feelings of those on board. At length the Syracusans and their allies, after a protracted struggle, put the Athenians to flight, and triumphantly bearing down upon them, and encouraging one another with loud cries and exhortations, drove them to land. Then that part of the navy which had not been taken in the deep water fell back in confusion to the shore, and the crews rushed out of the ships into the camp. And the land-forces, no longer now divided in

feeling, but uttering one universal groan of intolerable anguish, ran, some of them to save the ships, others to defend what remained of the wall; but the greater number began to look to themselves and to their own safety. Never had there been a greater panic in an Athenian army than at that moment. They now suffered what they had done to others at Pylos. For at Pylos the Lacedaemonians, when they saw their ships destroyed, knew that their friends who had crossed over into the island of Sphacteria were lost with them. And so now the Athenians, after the rout of their fleet, knew that they had no hope of saving themselves by land unless events took some extraordinary turn.

72. Thus, after a fierce battle and a great destruction of ships and men on both sides, the Syracusans and their allies gained the victory. They gathered up the wrecks and bodies of the dead, and sailing back to the city, erected a trophy. The Athenians, overwhelmed by their misery, never so much as thought of recovering their wrecks or of asking leave to collect their dead. Their intention was to retreat that very night. Demosthenes came to Nicias and proposed that they should once more man their remaining vessels and endeavour to force the passage at daybreak, saying that they had more ships fit for service than the enemy. For the Athenian fleet still numbered sixty, but the enemy had less than fifty. Nicias approved of his proposal, and they would have manned the ships, but the sailors refused to embark; for they were paralysed by their defeat, and had no longer any hope of succeeding. So the Athenians all made up their minds to escape by land.

73. Hermocrates the Syracusan suspected their intention, and dreading what might happen if their vast army, retreating by land and settling somewhere in Sicily, should choose to renew the war, he went to the

authorities, and represented to them that they ought not to allow the Athenians to withdraw by night (mentioning his own suspicion of their intentions), but that all the Syracusans and their allies should march out before them, wall up the roads, and occupy the passes with a guard. They thought very much as he did, and wanted to carry out his plan, but doubted whether their men, who were too glad to repose after a great battle, and in time of festival—for there happened on that very day to be a sacrifice to Heracles—could be induced to obey. Most of them, in the exultation of victory, were drinking and keeping holiday, and at such a time how could they ever be expected to take up arms and go forth at the order of the generals? On these grounds the authorities decided that the thing was impossible. Whereupon Hermocrates himself, fearing lest the Athenians should gain a start and quietly pass the most difficult places in the night, contrived the following plan: when it was growing dark he sent certain of his own acquaintances, accompanied by a few horsemen, to the Athenian camp. They rode up within earshot, and pretending to be friends (there were known to be men in the city who gave information to Nicias of what went on) called to some of the soldiers, and bade them tell him not to withdraw his army during the night, for the Syracusans were guarding the roads; he should make preparation at leisure and retire by day. Having delivered their message they departed, and those who had heard them informed the Athenian generals.

74. On receiving this message, which they supposed to be genuine, they remained during the night. And having once given up the intention of starting immediately, they decided to remain during the next day, that the soldiers might, as well as they could, put together their baggage in the most convenient form, and depart,

taking with them the bare necessaries of life, but nothing else.

Meanwhile the Syracusans and Gylippus, going forth before them with their land-forces, blocked the roads in the country by which the Athenians were likely to pass, guarded the fords of the rivers and streams, and posted themselves at the best points for receiving and stopping them. Their sailors rowed up to the beach and dragged away the Athenian ships. The Athenians themselves burnt a few of them, as they had intended, but the rest the Syracusans towed away, unmolested and at their leisure, from the places where they had severally run aground, and conveyed them to the city.

75. On the third day after the sea-fight, when Nicias and Demosthenes thought that their preparations were complete, the army began to move. They were in a dreadful condition; not only was there the great fact that they had lost their whole fleet, and instead of their expected triumph had brought the utmost peril upon Athens as well as upon themselves, but also the sights which presented themselves as they quitted the camp were painful to every eye and mind. The dead were unburied, and when any one saw the body of a friend lying on the ground he was smitten with sorrow and dread, while the sick or wounded who still survived but had to be left were even a greater trial to the living, and more to be pitied than those who were gone. Their prayers and lamentations drove their companions to distraction; they would beg that they might be taken with them, and call by name any friend or relation whom they saw passing; they would hang upon their departing comrades and follow as far as they could, and when their limbs and strength failed them and they dropped behind many were the imprecations and cries which they uttered. So that the whole army was in tears, and such was

their despair that they could hardly make up their minds to stir, although they were leaving an enemy's country, having suffered calamities too great for tears already, and dreading miseries yet greater in the unknown future. There was also a general feeling of shame and self-reproach—indeed they seemed, not like an army, but like the fugitive population of a city captured after a siege; and of a great city too. For the whole multitude who were marching together numbered not less than 40,000. Each of them took with him anything he could carry which was likely to be of use. Even the heavy-armed and cavalry, contrary to their practice when under arms, conveyed about their persons their own food, some because they had no attendants, others because they could not trust them; for they had long been deserting, and most of them had gone off all at once. Nor was the food which they carried sufficient; for the supplies of the camp had failed. Their disgrace and the universality of the misery, although there might be some consolation in the very community of suffering, was nevertheless at that moment hard to bear, especially when they remembered from what pomp and splendour they had fallen into their present low estate. Never had an Hellenic army experienced such a reverse. They had come intending to enslave others, and they were going away in fear that they would be themselves enslaved. Instead of the prayers and hymns with which they had put to sea, they were now departing amid appeals to heaven of another sort. They were no longer sailors but landsmen, depending, not upon their fleet, but upon their infantry. Yet in face of the great danger which still threatened them all these things appeared endurable.

76. Nicias, seeing the army disheartened at their terrible fall, went along the ranks and encouraged and consoled them as well as he could. In his fervour he

raised his voice as he passed from one to another and
spoke louder and louder, desiring that the benefit of his
words might reach as far as possible:

77. "Even now, Athenians and allies, we must hope:
men have been delivered out of worse straits than these,
and I would not have you judge yourselves too severely
on account either of the reverses which you have sustained or of your present undeserved miseries. I too am
as weak as any of you; for I am quite prostrated by my
disease, as you see. And although there was a time when
I might have been thought equal to the best of you in
the happiness of my private and public life, I am now
in as great danger, and as much at the mercy of fortune,
as the meanest. Yet my days have been passed in the
performance of many a religious duty, and of many a
just and blameless action. Therefore my hope of the future remains unshaken, and our calamities do not ap-
pall me as they might. Who knows that they may not
be lightened? For our enemies have had their full share
of success, and if our expedition provoked the jealousy
of any god, by this time we have been punished enough.
Others ere now have attacked their neighbours; they
have done as men will do, and suffered what men can
bear. We may therefore begin to hope that the gods
will be more merciful to us; for we now invite their pity
rather than their jealousy. And look at your own well-
armed ranks; see how many brave soldiers you are,
marching in solid array, and do not be dismayed; bear
in mind that wherever you plant yourselves you are a
city already, and that no city of Sicily will find it easy
to resist your attack, or can dislodge you if you choose
to settle. Provide for the safety and good order of your
own march, and remember every one of you that on
whatever spot a man is compelled to fight, there if he
conquer he may find a home and a fortress. We must

press forward day and night, for our supplies are but scanty. The Sicels through fear of the Syracusans still adhere to us, and if we can only reach any part of their territory we shall be among friends, and you may consider yourselves secure. We have sent to them, and they have been told to meet us and bring food. In a word, soldiers, let me tell you that you must be brave; there is no place near to which a coward can fly. And if you now escape your enemies, those of you who are not Athenians may see once more the home for which they long, while you Athenians will again rear aloft the fallen greatness of Athens. For men, and not walls or ships in which are no men, constitute a state."

78. Thus exhorting his troops Nicias passed through the army, and wherever he saw gaps in the ranks or the men dropping out of line, he brought them back to their proper place. Demosthenes did the same for the troops under his command, and gave them similar exhortations. The army marched disposed in a hollow oblong: the division of Nicias leading, and that of Demosthenes following; the hoplites enclosed within their ranks the baggage-bearers and the rest of the army. When they arrived at the ford of the river Anapus they found a force of the Syracusans and of their allies drawn up to meet them; these they put to flight, and getting command of the ford, proceeded on their march. The Syracusans continually harassed them, the cavalry riding along-side, and the light-armed troops hurling darts at them. On this day the Athenians proceeded about four and a half miles and encamped at a hill. On the next day they started early, and, having advanced more than two miles, descended into a level plain, and encamped. The country was inhabited, and they were desirous of obtaining food from the houses, and also water which they might carry with them, as there was little to be had for many miles

in the country which lay before them. Meanwhile the Syracusans had gone on before them, and at a point where the road ascends a steep hill called the Acraean height, and there is a precipitous ravine on either side, were blocking up the pass by a wall. On the next day the Athenians advanced, although again impeded by the numbers of the enemy's cavalry who rode along-side, and of their javelin-men who threw darts at them. For a long time the Athenians maintained the struggle, but at last retired to their own encampment. Their supplies were now cut off, because the horsemen circumscribed their movements.

79. In the morning they started early and resumed their march. They pressed onwards to the hill where the way was barred, and found in front of them the Syracusan infantry drawn up to defend the wall, in deep array, for the pass was narrow. Whereupon the Athenians advanced and assaulted the barrier, but the enemy, who were numerous and had the advantage of position, threw missiles upon them from the hill, which was steep, and so, not being able to force their way, they again retired and rested. During the conflict, as is often the case in the fall of the year, there came on a storm of rain and thunder, whereby the Athenians were yet more disheartened, for they thought that everything was conspiring to their destruction. While they were resting, Gylippus and the Syracusans despatched a division of their army to raise a wall behind them across the road by which they had come; but the Athenians sent some of their own troops and frustrated their intention. They then retired with their whole army in the direction of the plain and passed the night. On the following day they again advanced. The Syracusans now surrounded and attacked them on every side, and wounded many of them. If the Athenians advanced they retreated, but

charged them when they retired, falling especially upon
the hindermost of them, in the hope that, if they could
put to flight a few at a time, they might strike a panic
into the whole army. In this fashion the Athenians struggled on for a long time, and having advanced about
three-quarters of a mile rested in the plain. The Syracusans then left them and returned to their own encampment.

80. The army was now in a miserable plight, being in
want of every necessary; and by the continual assaults
of the enemy great numbers of the soldiers had been
wounded. Nicias and Demosthenes, perceiving their condition, resolved during the night to light as many watch-
fires as possible and to lead off their forces. They intended to take another route and march towards the sea
in the direction opposite to that from which the Syracusans were watching them. Now their whole line of
march lay, not towards Catana, but towards the other
side of Sicily, in the direction of Camarina and Gela,
and the cities, Hellenic or barbarian, of that region. So
they lighted numerous fires and departed in the night.
And then, as constantly happens in armies, especially in
very great ones, and as might be expected when they
were marching by night in an enemy's country, and with
the enemy from whom they were flying not far off, there
arose a panic among them, and they fell into confusion.
The army of Nicias, which led the way, kept together,
and was considerably in advance, but that of Demosthenes, which was the larger half, got severed from the
other division, and marched in less order. At daybreak
they succeeded in reaching the sea, and striking into the
Helorine road marched along it, intending as soon as
they arrived at the river Cacyparis to follow up the
stream through the interior of the island. They were ex-
pecting that the Sicels for whom they had sent would

meet them on this road. When they had reached the
river they found there also a guard of the Syracusans
cutting off the passage by a wall and palisade. They
forced their way through, and crossing the river, passed
on towards another river which is called the Erineus,
this being the direction in which their guides led them.

81. When daylight broke and the Syracusans and
their allies saw that the Athenians had departed, most
of them thought that Gylippus had let them go on purpose, and were very angry with him. They easily found
the line of their retreat, and quickly following, came up
with them about the time of the midday meal. The
troops of Demosthenes were last; they were marching
slowly and in disorder, not having recovered from the
panic of the previous night, when they were overtaken
by the Syracusans, who immediately fell upon them and
fought. Separated as they were from the others, they
were easily hemmed in by the Syracusan cavalry and
driven into a narrow space. The division of Nicias was
as much as six miles in advance, for he marched faster,
thinking that their safety depended at such a time, not
in remaining and fighting, if they could avoid it, but in
retreating as quickly as they could, and resisting only
when they were positively compelled. Demosthenes, on
the other hand, who had been more incessantly harassed
throughout the retreat, because marching last he was
first attacked by the enemy, now, when he saw the Syracusans pursuing him, instead of pressing onward, had
ranged his army in order of battle. Thus lingering he
was surrounded, and he and the Athenians under his
command were in the greatest danger and confusion.
For they were crushed into a walled enclosure, having
a road on both sides and planted thickly with olive-
trees, and missiles were hurled at them from all points.
The Syracusans naturally preferred this mode of attack

to a regular engagement. For to risk themselves against desperate men would have been only playing into the hands of the Athenians. Moreover, every one was sparing of his life; their good fortune was already assured, and they did not want to fall in the hour of victory. Even by this irregular mode of fighting they thought that they could overpower and capture the Athenians.

82. And so when they had gone on all day assailing them with missiles from every quarter, and saw that they were quite worn out with their wounds and all their other sufferings, Gylippus and the Syracusans made a proclamation, first of all to the islanders, that any of them who pleased might come over to them and have their freedom. But only a few cities accepted the offer. At length an agreement was made for the entire force under Demosthenes. Their arms were to be surrendered, but no one was to suffer death, either from violence or from imprisonment, or from want of the bare means of life. So they all surrendered, being in number 6,000, and gave up what money they had. This they threw into the hollows of shields and filled four. The captives were at once taken to the city. On the same day Nicias and his division reached the river Erineus, which he crossed, and halted his army on a rising ground.

83. On the following day he was overtaken by the Syracusans, who told him that Demosthenes had surrendered, and bade him do the same. He, not believing them, procured a truce while he sent a horseman to go and see. Upon the return of the horseman bringing assurance of the fact, he sent a herald to Gylippus and the Syracusans, saying that he would agree, on behalf of the Athenian state, to pay the expenses which the Syracusans had incurred in the war, on condition that they should let his army go; until the money was paid he would give Athenian citizens as hostages, a man for a

talent. Gylippus and the Syracusans would not accept
these proposals, but attacked and surrounded this division of the army as well as the other, and hurled missiles at them from every side until the evening. They too
were grievously in want of food and necessaries. Nevertheless they meant to wait for the dead of the night and
then to proceed. They were just resuming their arms,
when the Syracusans discovered them and raised the
paean. The Athenians, perceiving that they were detected, laid down their arms again, with the exception
of about 300 men who broke through the enemy's guard,
and made their escape in the darkness as best they could.

84. When the day dawned Nicias led forward his
army, and the Syracusans and the allies again assailed
them on every side, hurling javelins and other missiles
at them. The Athenians hurried on to the river Assinarus.
They hoped to gain a little relief if they forded the river,
for the mass of horsemen and other troops overwhelmed
and crushed them; and they were worn out by fatigue
and thirst. But no sooner did they reach the water than
they lost all order and rushed in; every man was trying
to cross first, and, the enemy pressing upon them at the
same time, the passage of the river became hopeless.
Being compelled to keep close together they fell one
upon another, and trampled each other under foot: some
at once perished, pierced by their own spears; others got
entangled in the baggage and were carried down the
stream. The Syracusans stood upon the further bank of
the river, which was steep, and hurled missiles from
above on the Athenians, who were huddled together in
the deep bed of the stream and for the most part were
drinking greedily. The Peloponnesians came down the
bank and slaughtered them, falling chiefly upon those
who were in the river. Whereupon the water at once
became foul, but was drunk all the same, although

muddy and dyed with blood, and the crowd fought for it.

85. At last, when the dead bodies were lying in heaps upon one another in the water and the army was utterly undone, some perishing in the river, and any who escaped being cut off by the cavalry, Nicias surrendered to Gylippus, in whom he had more confidence than in the Syracusans. He entreated him and the Lacedaemonians to do what they pleased with himself, but not to go on killing the men. So Gylippus gave the word to make prisoners. Thereupon the survivors, not including however a large number whom the soldiers concealed, were brought in alive. As for the 300 who had broken through the guard in the night, the Syracusans sent in pursuit and seized them. The total of the public prisoners when collected was not great; for many were appropriated by the soldiers, and the whole of Sicily was full of them, they not having capitulated like the troops under Demosthenes. A large number also perished; the slaughter at the river being very great, quite as great as any which took place in the Sicilian war; and not a few had fallen in the frequent attacks which were made upon the Athenians during their march. Still many escaped, some at the time, others ran away after an interval of slavery, and all these found refuge at Catana.

86. The Syracusans and their allies collected their forces and returned with the spoil, and as many prisoners as they could take with them, into the city. The captive Athenians and allies they deposited in the quarries, which they thought would be the safest place of confinement. Nicias and Demosthenes they put to the sword, although against the will of Gylippus. For Gylippus thought that to carry home with him to Lacedaemon the generals of the enemy, over and above all his other successes, would be a brilliant triumph. One of them,

Demosthenes, happened to be the greatest foe, and the other the greatest friend of the Lacedaemonians, both in the same matter of Pylos and Sphacteria. For Nicias had taken up their cause, and had persuaded the Athenians to make the peace which set at liberty the prisoners taken in the island. The Lacedaemonians were grateful to him for the service, and this was the main reason why he trusted Gylippus and surrendered himself to him. But certain Syracusans, who had been in communication with him, were afraid (such was the report) that on some suspicion of their guilt he might be put to the torture and bring trouble on them in the hour of their prosperity. Others, and especially the Corinthians, feared that, being rich, he might by bribery escape and do them further mischief. So the Syracusans gained the consent of the allies and had him executed. For these or the like reasons he suffered death. No one of the Hellenes in my time was less deserving of so miserable an end; for he lived in the practice of every customary virtue.

87. Those who were imprisoned in the quarries were at the beginning of their captivity harshly treated by the Syracusans. There were great numbers of them, and they were crowded in a deep and narrow place. At first the sun by day was still scorching and suffocating, for they had no roof over their heads, while the autumn nights were cold, and the extremes of temperature engendered violent disorders. Being cramped for room they had to do everything on the same spot. The corpses of those who died from their wounds, exposure to the weather, and the like, lay heaped one upon another. The smells were intolerable; and they were at the same time afflicted by hunger and thirst. During eight months they were allowed only about half a pint of water and a pint of food a day. Every kind of misery which could befall man in such a place befell them. This was the condition

of all the captives for about ten weeks. At length the Syracusans sold them, with the exception of the Athenians and of any Sicilian or Italian Greeks who had sided with them in the war. The whole number of the public prisoners is not accurately known, but they were not less than 7,000.

Of all the Hellenic actions which took place in this war, or indeed of all Hellenic actions which are on record, this was the greatest—the most glorious to the victors, the most ruinous to the vanquished; for they were utterly and at all points defeated, and their sufferings were prodigious. Fleet and army perished from the face of the earth; nothing was saved, and of the many who went forth few returned home.

Thus ended the Sicilian expedition.

From *Peloponnesian War*, Books V–VII.
Translated by Benjamin Jowett.

87196